CW01066518

INTERNATIONAL PEACEKEEPING

International Peacekeeping

The Yearbook of
International Peace Operations

edited by

HARVEY LANGHOLTZ
BORIS KONDOCH
ALAN WELLS

Volume 9

MARTINUS NIJHOFF PUBLISHERS
LEIDEN / BOSTON

A C.I.P. Catalogue record for this book is available from the Library of Congress.

ISBN 90-04-14315-7
ISSN 1380-748-X

Printed on acid-free paper.

Printed and bound in The Netherlands

International Peacekeeping:
The Yearbook of International Peace Operations

Table of Contents

XIII International Seminar on the "Challenges of Peace Operations: Into the 21st Century", organized by the Centre for Strategic Research of the Turkish Ministry of Foreign Affairs, Ankara, Turkey, 18-20 November 2003

Conference "Contemporary Legal Issues: The Rule of Law in Conflict and Post-Conflict Situations", held at the George C. Marshall European Center for Security Studies, Garmisch-Partenkirchen, 15-19 September 2003

Conference "Reflections on the War in Iraq", organized by the Institute for International Law of Peace and Armed Conflict (IFHV) of the Ruhr-University of Bochum in collaboration with the German Red Cross, The Hague, 27 June 2003

Conference "9th Annual Conference of the IAPTC", Wertheim, Germany, 19-23 October 2003

Book Reviews

Documents on CD-ROM

Introduction to the CD-ROM

UN Security Council Resolutions. 1 January – 31 December 2003 – Overview

Security Council Resolution 1455 on Threats to International Peace and Security
Caused by Terrorist Acts, S/RES/1455 of 17 January 2003
Security Council Resolution 1456 on High-level Meeting of the Security Council:
Combating Terrorism, S/RES/1456 of 20 January 2003
Security Council Resolution 1457 on the Situation Concerning the Democratic
Republic of the Congo, S/RES/1457 of 24 January 2003
Security Council Resolution 1458 on the Situation in Liberia, S/RES/1458 of 28
January 2003
Security Council Resolution 1459 on the Kimberley Process Certification Scheme,
S/RES/1459 of 28 January 2003
Security Council Resolution 1460 on Children and Armed Conflict, S/RES/1460 of
30 January 2003
Security Council Resolution 1461 on the Situation in the Middle East, S/RES/1461
of 30 January 2003
Security Council Resolution 1462 on the Situation in Georgia, S/RES/1462 of 30
January 2003
Security Council Resolution 1463 on the Situation Concerning Western Sahara,
S/RES/1463 of 30 January 2003
Security Council Resolution 1464 on the Situation in Côte d'Ivoire, S/RES/1464 of
4 February 2003
Security Council Resolution 1465 on Threats to International Peace and Security
Caused by Terrorist Acts, S/RES/1465 of 13 February 2003

UN Peacekeeping

Annual Report of the Secretary General on the Work of the Organization (A/58/1) of 28 August 2003

The War against Iraq

Preface

During 2003 the international community saw peacekeeping redefined, criticised, expanded, and challenged. While the Security Council debate over the conflict in Iraq and subsequent military operations occupied centre stage, the nature of peace operations around the world continued to expand and evolve.

At the beginning of 2003 there were 39,652 military personnel, military observers, and civilian police serving on 15 UN peacekeeping missions. With the closing of the United Nations Iraq-Kuwait Observer Mission (UNIKOM) in October 2003 and the establishment of the United Nations Mission in Liberia (UNMIL) in September 2003, by the end of 2003 the number of UN peacekeepers had grown to 45,815. There were 64 UN peacekeepers who gave their lives in the pursuit of peace during 2003 and among these were the Special Representative of the Secretary-General, Sergio Vieira de Meīlo, and 16 others who died when a suicide bomber drove a bomb-laden cement truck into UN Offices in Baghdad on 19 August 2003.

In addition to UN peacekeeping, 2003 also witnessed an increased role of the European Union (EU) and the African Union (AU) in maintaining international peace and security. The EU launched Operation Concordia in The Former Yugoslav Republic of Macedonia based on the Joined Action of the Council of the European Union of 18 March 2003. It conducted Operation Artemis in the Democratic Republic of Congo based on the Joined Action of the Council of the European Union adopted on 5 June 2003 and UN Security Council Resolution 1484 of 30 May 2003. In April 2003 the AU began deploying its first peacekeeping contingent ever, sending 100 South African soldiers (as the initial deployment of an AU force expected eventually to number 3,500) to Burundi to shore up an uncertain cease-fire in the country's decade-old civil war.

The steady increase of non-military personnel and non-UN personnel involved in peacekeeping also continued. By the end of 2003 there were over 3500 International Civilians, 7500 Local Civilians, and 3500 United Nations Volunteers (UNVs) serving on UN peacekeeping missions. There were four missions where UN civilians outnumbered UN military personnel. In addition to these UN peacekeeping missions, the situations in Iraq and Afghanistan and also in Sudan, Burundi, and the DRC created a growing demand for skilled and dedicated civilian personnel willing to serve on operations of relief and reconstruction sponsored by governments, non-government organisations (NGOs), and private for-profit corporations. This expansion of non-military actors is likely to continue. At the same time, military peacekeepers were being called upon to serve both in traditional soldiering roles, confronting insurgents and maintaining security, while also supporting the reconstruction of utilities, schools, and civil infrastructure.

It is not possible in a yearbook on peacekeeping to cover everything that happened, every issue that was debated, or every aspect of historical perspective. In the subsequent pages and the accompanying CD we have tried to document many of the high points and also represent some of the current issues. In the article by James Cockayne and David Malone, entitled *United Nations Peace Operations Then and Now*, we take an historical perspective and consider how peacekeeping has evolved since the days of Ralph Bunche and others influential in the early conceptualisation and definition of peacekeeping. Michael Schmitt and Charles Garraway's article offers the authors' view of International Law and the occupation of Iraq. Matthew Dunsmore and Harvey Langholtz examine the conflicting demands placed on soldiers serving as war fighters or peacekeepers. Clifford Bernath's article discusses the experience of Refugees International regarding MONUC. Thorsten Stodiek examines the role of international police forces in peace operations. Elizabeth Griffin's article outlines one peacekeeping teaching technique. And Ray Murphy presents the dilemma faced by Ireland as it withdrew from participation in the EU Peacekeeping Mission to Macedonia.

While the direction and definition of peacekeeping are shaped in the debate of the Security Council, the General Assembly, the Special Committee on Peacekeeping Operations, the Department of Peacekeeping Operations, and other bodies within the UN, scholarly and diplomatic debate continues in other fora around the world and we have summarised some of those discussions here. Michael Sahlin and Annika Hilding Norberg have provided a summary of the XII International Seminar in the Series: Challenges of Peace Operations: Into the 21st Century, *Peace Operations and Counter-Terrorism*, held at Krusenberg, Sweden, 23-25 May 2003, while Murat Bilhan has reported on the XIII International Seminar *The Nature of Peace Operations and the Continuing Need for Reform* organized by the Centre for Strategic Research of the Turkish Ministry of Foreign Affairs, Ankara, Turkey, 18-20 November 2003. Dieter Fleck has reported on and provided conclusions from the conference *Contemporary Legal Issues: The Rule of Law in Conflict and Post-Conflict Situations*, held at the George C. Marshall European Center for Security Studies, Garmisch-Partenkirchen, 15-19 September 2003. Included are papers by Torsten Stein, *Preemption and Terrorism*, Franklin Berman entitled *Preemption and Weapons of Mass Destruction*, Thomas McShane on *The State of the State: Redefining Sovereignty in the 21st Century*, Gregory Belanger on *Iraq Legal Issues: Perspectives from the Field*, David Hayden discusses *Targeting Issues in Afghanistan*, Justin McClelland on *Humanitarian Intervention and Preemption*, David Jividen examining *Targeting Norms and International Humanitarian Law*, and Lewis Bumgardner considering *The Rule of Law in Post-Conflict Situations: Conflict Termination, Legitimacy, and Peace Building*.

Noëlle Quénivet reports on the conference *Reflections on the War in Iraq*, organised by the Institute for International Law of Peace and Armed Conflict (IFHV) of the Ruhr-University of Bochum in collaboration with the German Red Cross, The

Hague, 27 June 2003. Victoria Firmo-Fontan summarises this year's meeting of the International Association of Peacekeeping Training Centers in *The 9th Annual Conference of the IAPTC*, Wertheim, Germany, 19-23 October 2003.

In the book review section Matt Densmore reviews Thomas Britt and Amy Adler's, *The Psychology of the Peacekeeper: Lessons from the Field.* In another book review, Dieter Fleck comments on *Humanitarian Intervention, Ethical, Legal and Political Dilemma*, edited by Holzgrefe and Keohane. In the Chronicle we report month-by-month on developments in specific conflicts and also on individual topical issues.

In the accompanying CD-ROM we have provided an introduction to and the actual text of the most important documents pertaining to peacekeeping during 2003. On this CD-ROM the reader will find 12 folders including *inter alia*, all UN Security Council Resolutions adopted in 2003, the annual report of the Secretary General and the Special Committee on Peacekeeping Operations, documents on UN Peacekeeping and peace operations of the AU and the EU as well as on the conflicts in Afghanistan, Côte d'Ivoire, the DRC, Liberia and the Middle East.

During 2003 diplomats, statesmen, and military leaders examined the limits, bounds, and definitions of peacekeeping, peace enforcement, self defence, sovereignty, and international law. At the same time, UN military peacekeepers, civilian police, and civilians served alongside humanitarian relief workers around the world to bring peace and relief to regions torn by strife. In this *Yearbook of International Peace Operations* we have attempted to chronicle and analyse the activities of 2003.

Harvey Langholtz, Boris Kondoch, and Alan Wells

United Nations Peace Operations Then and Now

James Cockayne and David Malone*

Introduction

August 7, 2003, marked the centennial of the birth of Ralph Bunche.[1] Scholar, civil rights activist and Nobel Peace Laureate, Bunche's most enduring legacy lies in the field of United Nations peacekeeping. The centennial of his birth served not only as an opportunity to celebrate that legacy, but also as a catalyst for all those interested in the role of the UN in world politics to reflect on the changes that have occurred in UN peacekeeping since Bunche's day.

In Bunche's day, "peacekeeping" – as a term and as an operational reality – was well-defined and clearly understood. Today, UN "peace operations" extend to cover a multiplicity of UN field activities in support of peace, ranging from essentially preventive deployments to long-term peace-building missions. The turning-point in the expansion of the Organization's approach came with the end of the Cold War, after which the UN Security Council was able to agree to tackle the wreckage of that ideological confrontation, the so-called "regional conflicts" in Central America, Southeast Asia and in various parts of Africa, and to address new, often internal conflicts in other regions.

---

*   James Cockayne is a Graduate Fellow of the Institute for International Law and Justice at New York University Law School. David Malone is President of the International Peace Academy (IPA), an independent research and policy development institution in New York. When a Canadian ambassador at the UN, he chaired the work of the UN's Special Committee on Peacekeeping Operations, 1992-94. The genesis of this essay was a speech by David Malone on 20 November 2003, one in a series organized by the Ralph Bunche Institute and others to celebrate Bunche's legacy. The founding President of IPA was Indian General Indar Jit Rhikye, previous Military Advisor to the UN Secretary-General, was also a close associate of Ralph Bunche, who he still remembers vividly.
1   Many sources cite 1904, rather than 1903, as Bunche's year of birth, and he, in fact, appears to have accepted 1904 as his own date of birth. For further explanation *see* Brian Urquhart, *Ralph Bunche: An American Life* (W.W. Norton & Company, New York, 1993), pp. 25-26, fn.

Harvey Langholtz, Boris Kondoch, Alan Wells (Eds.),
International Peacekeeping: The Yearbook of International Peace Operations, Volume 9, 2004, pp. 1-26.
© *Koninklijke Brill N.V. Printed in the Netherlands*

This essay aims to describe and analyse the major shifts in UN peace operations since Bunche's day. We begin by describing how peacekeeping operations looked then, in Bunche's era. Next, we describe how they look now, identifying both continuities and changes, before analyzing the reasons for these changes. We outline the consequences of these changes for the UN's involvement in world politics and reflect on the shape of UN peace operations tomorrow.

1.   Peacekeeping Then

Peacekeeping emerged not by design but out of necessity. The Founding Members of the UN had included in Chapter VII of the Charter an Article (Article 42) which allowed the UN to take "action by air, sea, or land forces as may be necessary to maintain or restore international peace and security". But the Founding Members' vision of a body of national military forces permanently available to the Security Council "on its call" (Article 43) and serving as the instrument of collective security did not materialize. Cold War antagonisms overtook this vision, making the commitment of forces in accordance with Article 43 politically unfeasible. To this day, no Member of the UN has concluded an agreement with the UN putting elements of its military force on UN call. Paradoxically, the same Cold War antagonisms which prevented the establishment of such a dedicated UN military capacity simultaneously served to increase the need for an independent and impartial actor on the world stage, ensuring that conflicts did not spiral out of control and further fuel the emerging confrontation between capitalist and communist camps.

Bunche – and a cast of other notables, including Secretaries-General Trygve Lie and Dag Hammarskjöld, members of the UN Secretariat such as Brian Urquhart and key players from the Member States, particularly Lester Pearson, Canadian Minister for External Affairs (and later Prime Minister) – stepped into that gap.[2] They generated an operational capacity for the UN where previously only a limited on-the-ground presence was imagined for the Organization. Bunche himself volunteered that the Secretariat staff "started from scratch", unaware of what peacekeeping would involve, improvising as they went along, and making mistakes.[3]

The system of peacekeeping they generated involved UN missions staffed by "blue helmets" (as they came to be known), operating with light arms – or none at

---

2   Brian Urquhart was Bunche's closest associate for much of his UN career, and we have been fortunate to be able to consult him on aspects of peacekeeping in recent years. We have also benefited greatly from personal contact with the late F.T. Liu and with George Sherry, two other key colleagues of Bunche at the UN.

3   Informal lecture by Ralph Bunche on Palestine delivered to the UN Secretariat, 16 June 1949, quoted in Urquhart, *supra* note 1, p. 187, at note 2.

all – under the strict instruction to use force only in self-defense. These were creatively crafted "Chapter VI and a half" peace operations, requiring, in principle, an invitation or consent on the part of the recipient state.[4] They operated under UN command, primarily undertaking activities agreed upon by belligerents, such as the cantonment and separation of warring parties, border monitoring, the withdrawal of foreign troops, and monitoring the cessation of aid to irregular or insurrectionist movements.

The guiding principle of this early peacekeeping was that peace operations must not give an advantage to either side involved in the conflict.[5] Bunche was particularly responsible for developing and implementing this principle through his direction of the first UN military-observer group, between Israel and Lebanon (UNTSO),[6] and the first classic UN peacekeeping operation, in the Sinai (UNEF),[7] and in later missions in Cyprus, Congo and elsewhere. Blue helmets sought to adopt an attitude of strict impartiality and objectivity, and to that end went largely unarmed.[8] This was considered necessary both to avoid provoking the parties to a conflict, and because in the early days, "observers were untried and could not be depended upon not to shoot at the wrong time at the wrong people."[9] Bunche and his peers also generated a UN aesthetic which helped reinforce the independent identity of the UN – the blue helmet, white vehicles with large black UN letters on the side and top, the non-display of national flags by contingents in UN forces.[10] The mechanics of peacekeeping were also laid down during this period, including the processes for solicitation and acceptance of national contingents into UN peacekeeping forces.[11]

The aims of peacekeeping in this earlier era were limited. UNTSO's primary mandate was to assist the United Nations Mediator and the Truce Commission in

---

4 George Sherry, who worked closely with Bunche during this period, and for many years afterwards, has recently revealed that Bunche "expressed interest in the possibility of invoking Article 40" of the UN Charter as a basis for peace operations. This would have established peace operations as a "provisional measure" taken by the Security Council under Chapter VII. This would have given those peace operations a greater independence of their hosts – since they would be obliged to cooperate with the peacekeeping forces, as a consequence of their Chapter VII mandate – but at the cost of those operations being more tightly controlled by the Security Council. By choosing not to go down this route, Bunche firmly imprinted Secretariat control over peace operations. Professor George Sherry, Interview with James Cockayne, New York, March 26, 2003.

5 *See* B. Urquhart, *supra* note 1, pp. 161, 169.

6 United Nations Truce Supervision Organization, established in 1948 in Palestine.

7 United Nations Emergency Force, ran 1956-1967, first to supervise withdrawal of forces following the Suez Crisis, then to act as a buffer between Egyptian and Israeli forces.

8 *Ibid.*, p. 161.

9 Brian Urquhart, "Ralph Bunche and the Development of UN Peace-keeping", in Benjamin Rivlin, ed., *Ralph Bunche. The Man and His Times* (Holmes & Meier, New York, 1990), p. 190.

10 *See, e.g.*, B. Urquhart, *supra* note 1, p. 161.

11 *Ibid.*, p. 267.

supervising the observance of the truce negotiated in Palestine in 1948, and later
to supervise the implementation of the General Armistice Agreements Bunche facil-
itated on Rhodes in 1949, for which he received the Nobel Peace Prize in 1950.
UNEF, established by the General Assembly in the wake of the Suez Crisis, was
mandated with supervision of the withdrawal of foreign troops, and later with acting as a buffer between Egypt and Israel. It managed this successfully until 1967,
when Egyptian President Nasser requested UNEF's withdrawal. Its departure from
the terrain, followed immediately by the Six Day War, reminded Member States of
the potential value at tense moments on the ground of even a limited peacekeeping
force with no military power, though U Thant's decision to acquiesce to Nasser's
demands is still hotly debated. The mandate of ONUC[12] in the Congo, which Bunche
directed, was more complex. It was established to ensure the withdrawal of Belgian
forces and assist in the immediate post-independence period, and was later charged
with ensuring Congolese territorial integrity and political independence, removing
foreign forces including mercenaries and preventing civil war. It was an exception
to the rule, with other peacekeeping operations, in Cyprus,[13] Kashmir,[14] Yemen[15]
and elsewhere playing a role largely confined to ceasefire, truce or armistice monitoring.

2.   Peacekeeping Now – What is the Same?

There is a great deal about peacekeeping now that is similar to the peacekeeping
operations of this earlier era. A small number of the operations which Bunche oversaw remain alive today, notably UNTSO in the Middle East, UNMOGIP in Kashmir,
and UNFICYP in Cyprus. In other areas, notably the Congo, the operations of
Bunche's day were completed, only to find themselves, in different forms, back on
the Security Council's agenda today. In part, that continuity is a product of the
approach adopted by Bunche and his colleagues, which they saw largely as a mechanism for buying time to allow political and diplomatic developments to identify a
solution where none had previously been apparent.[16] As Bunche stated to Abba
Eban, then Israel's Permanent Representative to the UN, in December 1956,

---

12   Opération des Nations Unies au Congo, ran 1960 to 1964.
13   UNFICYP, established 1964, mandated to use its best efforts to prevent a recurrence of fighting
     and, as necessary, to contribute to the maintenance and restoration of law and order and a return
     to normal conditions.
14   UNMOGIP, established 1949, monitoring the ceasefire in Jammu and Kashmir, and UNIPOM, ran
     September 1965 to March 1966, supervised the withdrawal of Indian and Pakistani troops in Jammu
     and Kashmir.
15   UNYOM, ran July 1963 to September 1964, mandated to observe and certify the implementation
     of the disengagement agreement between Saudi Arabia and the United Arab Republic.
16   Both much of the Israel-Arab and the inter-Congolese problems that existed during Bunche's tenure

the real importance of UNEF is that it does buy valuable time. It is not in itself a political instrument, but it does purchase time in which political developments can take place and progress on fundamental issues can be made.[17]

The danger is that long-term peacekeeping can help to ossify an unresolved situation, sometimes only deferring further conflict until a later date – a charge some lay at the UN's door for its mission to Cyprus since 1974 and in its role in the Middle East in 1967. The same danger may exist with the UN's involvement today in Kosovo.

Many of the operational challenges the UN's contemporary peace operations face are also the same challenges that faced these early missions. Weak command and control, inadequate communication and logistical equipment, little prior opportunity for detailed planning, under-equipped and ill-trained military personnel are all as much issues today as they were in Bunche's day, if not more so. In one area at least there has been a marked decline: the promptness with which the UN could deploy a peacekeeping force. In Bunche's day a mission might be on the ground within weeks – or on occasion even days – of the decision to deploy; today it takes months. A recent audit of recruitment practices in the UN's Department of Peacekeeping Operations (DPKO) establishes that it takes, on average, 347 days to fill DPKO positions – almost three times the UN target.[18]

Peacekeeping has grown within the UN, both in terms of its budget, and its staff. DPKO is an infinitely larger bureaucratic behemoth than the very few and trusty associates Bunche used to turn to in the Department of Special Political Affairs. The consequences of this growth were highlighted by the Brahimi Panel, appointed by Kofi Annan to make recommendations for changes in UN peacekeeping in a report that came to be known after its chair, Lakhdar Brahimi, a former Algerian diplomat and Secretary-General's Special Representative or Envoy to a number of countries, notably Haiti, Afghanistan and now Iraq.[19] The Brahimi Report placed the spotlight on the diffusion of responsibility resulting from DPKO's size and structure. This was less of a problem in Bunche's day, not especially because of the smaller number of missions or their size – ONUC reached almost 20,000 personnel,

---

are still with us today and, while Bunche would have liked to see them resolved, he was too much of a realist to have expected outright success for most UN efforts.

17 Record of meeting with Abba Eban, December 12, 1956, quoted in B. Urquhart, *supra* note 1, p. 273. The UN was again to deploy a peacekeeping operation in the Sinai, UNEF II, between 1973 and 1979, that made way for a multinational force, still on the ground today, monitoring implementation of the Israel-Egypt peace treaty of 1979.

18 *See Report of the Office of Internal Oversight Services on the audit of the policies and procedures for recruiting Department of Peace-keeping Operations staff. Note by the Secretary-General*, UN Doc. A/58/704, 6 February 2004.

19 *Report of the Panel on UN Peace Operations*, UN Doc. A/55/305 – S/2000/809, 21 August 2000.

at one point – but perhaps because of Bunche's undisputed and central role in peace-keeping affairs.

The challenge of financing peacekeeping remains constant. Bunche knew the problems of the "tin cup" approach to financing, as he called it, only too well.[20] His words of 1964 remain pertinent today:

> Serious people everywhere should cogitate on this, the indispensability of the United Nations in our present world, in situations where it alone affords the chance to avoid war, measured against its present meager resources of money and authority. It bears emphasis that, while most governments in the end give the United Nations their warm and loyal support in critical situations, the organization (and the world) sometimes finds itself on the very brink of disaster of incalculable dimensions before the essential support is forthcoming.[21]

So, too, the vulnerability of peace-keepers seems to be similar now to the situation in Bunche's day. A study published in the *Journal of the American Medical Association* suggests that the rate of fatalities in UN peace operations stayed largely static over the first fifty years, although the proportion of fatalities caused by hostile acts does appear to have risen in the 1990s.[22] This might be explained by the changes wrought to peacekeeping since the end of the Cold War, discussed further below, most notably the increased involvement of peacekeeping operations in essentially internal conflicts.[23] Nor is it clear how the Security Council's increased willingness, since the late 1990s, to give UN peace operations a robust mandate for the use of force in the defense of the mission and better technical self-defense capacity has affected fatality rates. The devastating attack on UN offices in Baghdad on August 19, 2003 which killed Sergio Vieira de Mello and 21 other UN staff makes one thing clear: terrorism remains as much of a threat to the Organization and its officials now as it did when Bunche's then-superior, Count Folke Bernadotte, UN Mediator in Palestine, was assassinated in September 1948.[24] It can be only a cold comfort that these attacks,

---

20   Ralph J. Bunche, "The UN Operation in the Congo, 1964", in Charles P. Henry, ed., *Ralph J. Bunche. Selected Speeches and Writings* (University of Michigan, 1995), p. 203.

21   *Ibid.*, p. 204.

22   Benjamin Seet and Gilbert Burnham, "Fatality Trends in United Nations Peacekeeping Operations, 1948-1998", *Journal of the American Medical Association*, August 2, 2000, vol. 284, no. 5, pp. 598-603.

23   In describing certain conflicts as internal or civil, we generally add the prior qualifier "essentially" because these conflicts rarely remain strictly internal for long. Great powers sometimes have an interest in them, and neighboring states frequently become involved. These conflicts can spill over, as the turmoil in Colombia does into Peru and Ecuador (as well as into the domestic politics of Venezuela), while in the Democratic Republic of the Congo, the armies of five neighboring states spilled in at one point, thoroughly internationalizing what, in many respects, remained a domestically-rooted conflict.

24   *See* B. Urquhart, *supra* note 1, pp. 178 *et seq.*

separated by more than half a century, stand as testament to the ongoing power of the UN as a symbol of effective change: the enemies of that change continue to attack it now as they attacked it in Bunche's day.

3. Peacekeeping Now – What Has Changed?

While there are many continuities between peacekeeping then and now, much has also changed. Today's peace missions involve operations which do not simply monitor cease-fires or supervise the implementation of a peace agreement between states, but more often aim to resolve internal conflicts characterized by inter-communal strife, crises of democracy, fighting marked by the struggle to control national resources and wealth, and a host of other precipitating causes of war. Peacekeeping tends increasingly to implement a preventive approach to the recurrence of conflict, creating an operational and political space in which international actors take on a host of peace building activities. In Bunche's day peacekeeping aimed to buttress essentially self-enforcing cease-fires during the Cold War; today it aims to build the foundations of a self-renewing peace.

These surface-level differences are the consequence of five deeper evolutions in peace operations: changes resulting from the removal of Cold War constraints; a deeper engagement with conflicts traditionally considered as "internal"; an increased role for regional organizations; the impact of North-South politics; and changing considerations in mandating peace operations.

3.1. *From Cold War to P-5 Concord*

The end of the Cold War brought a new complexion to Security Council discussions of peacekeeping. The end of that era, which partially paralyzed the Security Council, was signalled by Soviet President Gorbachev's famous *Pravda* and *Izvestia* article on 17 September 1987 calling for

> wider use of . . . the institution of UN military observers and UN peace-keeping forces in disengaging the troops of warring sides, observing ceasefires and armistice agreements.[25]

With the collapse of the Soviet Union, and the succession of the Russian Federation to its permanent seat on the Security Council, the five permanent members (P-5)

---

25   Mikhail S. Gorbachev, "Reality and the Guarantees of a Secure World", in FBIS *Daily Report: Soviet Union*, 17 September 1987, pp. 23-28.

adopted a more cooperative approach to peacekeeping. This P-5 concord underwrote almost a decade of unprecedented Security Council activism. Buoyed by the success of the UN-mandated enforcement operation against Iraq in 1990, the Council massively accelerated its pace of work. In the period between March 1991 and October 1993, it passed 185 resolutions (a rate about five times greater than that of previous decades) and launched 15 new peacekeeping and observer missions (as against 17 in the preceding 46 years).[26] P-5 cooperation largely continued throughout the 1990s, with Russian concerns over Yugoslavia and Chinese concerns over Taiwan mostly quarantined from other issues. Only six substantive vetoes were cast from May 1990 to June 1997, compared to 193 in the first 45 years – roughly one fifth of the frequency with which vetoes were cast in the earlier period.

There were, of course, exceptions to this concord. The P-5 is frequently divided over the appropriate approach to developments in the Israeli-Palestinian conflict, so the Security Council has remained largely unassertive on that issue. Divisions between the Europeans and the US on Bosnia characterized and caused Security Council inaction in the early 1990s, until finally consensus formed in support of the Dayton Agreements. Kosovo, too, caused deep divisions, this time between the Europeans and the US, on one side, and Russia, on the other. Since 1997, the Council has been divided on how best to handle the situation in Iraq.

In some ways these exceptions serve to prove the importance of the new rule, the P-5 concord. The concord has paved the way for peacekeeping missions in Iran and Iraq, Angola, Namibia, Central America, Western Sahara, Cambodia, Somalia, Bosnia, Mozambique, Rwanda, Uganda, Georgia, Liberia, Chad, Libya, Tajikistan, Haiti, Croatia, Macedonia, Eastern Slavonia, Guatemala, Central African Republic, Sierra Leone, Kosovo, East Timor, Democratic Republic of Congo, Ethiopia and Eritrea. Several of these missions have achieved remarkable successes – though some have produced spectacular failures. The broader point is that the removal of Cold War constraints has largely freed the Council to engage in peacekeeping in places and forms of which it could not even dream during the Cold War.

3.2. *From Inter-State to Internal Conflict*

A key characteristic of the Council's new approach has been its willingness to intervene more often in essentially internal conflicts. This involvement in internal conflicts and complex humanitarian situations – already signaled by the use of UN guards

---

26   *See* David Malone, "The UN Security Council in the Post-Cold War World: 1987-97", *Security Dialogue*, vol. 28, no. 4, December 1997, p. 394. At times this proliferation of resolutions has in fact served to undermine the legitimacy of the Council, because of the gap between its stated intentions and the resources made available to implement Resolutions.

in northern Iraq in 1991 as symbolic protection for Kurdish refugees – took UN peace operations down a new path.

Contemporary UN peace operations adopt a more multidisciplinary approach than their precursors,[27] emphasizing not simply the cessation of military hostilities, but the creation of conditions for a durable and self-renewing peace. Recent generations of peace operations have exercised complex mandates significantly more ambitious than in the past, with perhaps one significant exception in the ONUC case.[28]

Today's peace operations often center on objectives such as the provision of humanitarian assistance (in the short term), civil administration functions, police monitoring and training, human rights monitoring and training, economic reconstruction and other essentially civilian functions. While the military components of these missions often remain the largest, the mission objectives are not necessarily ones to which the military can or wish to contribute greatly. Sometimes, as in the Balkans and Afghanistan, the military components retain their own lines of command and control outside the UN structure. These essential changes in the structure and objectives of UN peace operations have occurred in slow motion, with practice in one mission often influencing the design of ensuing ones in the same country (e.g. Haiti) or elsewhere. The evolutionary nature of this change has robbed it of media coverage, although some acute observers in the academic community have advanced helpful analysis.[29] Some scholars, particularly Elizabeth Cousens and Karin Wermester have argued, rightly in our view, that the type of peace building in which the UN engages is much more a political activity than a mechanical developmental effort, but this view remains at least mildly controversial.[30]

The deeper engagement with essentially internal conflicts has also forced the UN to identify new tools for peace. The Security Council has looked increasingly

---

27 *Multidisciplinary Peace-keeping: Lessons from Recent Experience*, United Nations DPKO, April 1999.

28 For discussion of the evolution of peacekeeping mandates, *see in particular* Thomas G. Weiss, David P. Forsythe and Roger A Coate, *The United Nations in a Changing World*, 2nd Ed. (Boulder, CO: Westview Press, 1997); *see also* Michael C. Williams, *Civil-military relations and peace keeping* (London; New York: Oxford University Press, 1998).

29 *See esp.* Stephen John Stedman, Donald Rothchild and Elizabeth M. Cousens, eds., *Ending Civil Wars: The Success and Failure of Negotiated Settlements in Civil War* (Boulder, Lynne Rienner: 2002) and Chester A. Crocker, Fen Osler Hampson and Pamela R. Aall, eds., *Herding Cats: Multiparty Mediation in a Complex World* (USIP, 1999).

30 *See* Elizabeth M. Cousens, Chetan Kumar and Karin Wermester, *Peacebuilding as Politics: Cultivating Peace in Fragile Societies* (Boulder, Lynne Rienner: 2001). In part in order to test some of the ideas advanced by these authors and others and to chart progress on the ground, IPA in December 2003 launched a new program exploring the policy nexus between development and security. Findings should begin to become available in late 2005.

to sanctions regimes, as an alternative to – or a tool to be used alongside – the use of force. Sanctions were implemented only once in Bunche's era, against Southern Rhodesia in 1966 – and they were not particularly successful. Further sanctions followed, against South Africa, in 1977. Since 1990 the Security Council has imposed sanctions or embargoes on 15 different countries or groups. Sanctions, often accompanied by a naval blockade, became a key tool in the Security Council's enforcement apparatus. These regimes have become increasingly sophisticated, targeting specific individuals, groups and asset or goods types. Blanket economic sanctions have fallen out of vogue as their humanitarian costs have become apparent, first in Haiti, then in Iraq. The ability of government regimes in countries struck by sanctions to enrich themselves greatly by controlling black markets in prohibited products also took some time to sink in.[31]

The UN has also begun to explore the role that accountability mechanisms can play, both in removing the architects of violations of international peace from political power, and in regenerating the social fabric of war-torn societies. The Security Council's decision to use its Chapter VII powers to create *ad hoc* international criminal tribunals for, first, the former Yugoslavia, and then Rwanda, indicated a fundamental revision of the notion of what the Charter permitted the Council to do to maintain international peace and security. That development has been further cemented by the UN's involvement in the establishment of war crimes tribunals in Sierra Leone, Kosovo, East Timor and now Cambodia. The creation of the criminal tribunals for the former Yugoslavia and Rwanda by the Security Council fiat in turn produced significant pressure elsewhere for a more universal International Criminal Court that has now come into being and the statute of which envisages a complex relationship with the Council.[32] That relationship remains a flashpoint for diverging conceptions of the role of the Security Council and its relationship to international law.

The Secretary-General and the Security Council have also encouraged alternative approaches both to deterrence and to post-conflict national reconciliation, notably

---

31 *See generally* David Cortright and George A. Lopez, *Sanctions and the Search for Security: Challenges to UN Action* (Boulder, Lynne Rienner: 2002); David Cortright and George A. Lopez, *The Sanctions Decade: Assessing UN Strategies in the 1990s* (Boulder and London, Lynne Rienner Publishers: 2000), and *Making Targeted Sanctions Effective: Guidelines for the implementation of UN Policy Options*, Report of the Stockholm Process, February 14, 2003, available at <http://www.smart-sanctions.se>. *See also* David Cortright and George A. Lopez, "Reforming Sanctions", in David M. Malone, ed., *The UN Security Council from the Cold War to the 21st Century* (Boulder, Lynne Rienner: 2004), p. 167; Peter van Walsum, "The Iraq Sanctions Committee", in *ibid.*, p. 181; and David J.R. Angell, "The Angola Sanctions Committee", in *ibid.*, p. 195.

32 *See* Philippe Kirsch, John T. Holmes and Mora Johnson, "International Tribunals and Courts", in Malone, *supra* note 31, pp. 281-294.

through Truth Commissions, some of which have been considered generally successful, as in South Africa, El Salvador and Guatemala, although critics abound. (Other Truth Commissions, sometimes shamefully gerrymandered by sitting governments, have failed miserably, such as Haiti's sorry effort in 1995.)[33]

3.3. *The Rise of Regional Organizations*

The removal of Cold War constraints has, in turn, allowed regional organizations to step forward, taking a more active role in peacekeeping. The Security Council's exclusive role in authorizing the use of force internationally has been challenged, due to its own inaction, by the Economic Community of West African States (ECOWAS) in Liberia and Sierra Leone, by NATO in Kosovo and most recently by a US and UK-led coalition of the willing in Iraq. The UN increasingly relies on regional mechanisms to discharge peacekeeping responsibilities, mandating regional organizations to take on peacekeeping operations in the former Yugoslavia (NATO), Liberia and Sierra Leone (ECOMOG), Democratic Republic of Congo (European Union), and Afghanistan (NATO).[34]

There are many arguments in favour of the integration of regional arrangements into the UN peacekeeping system.[35] Regional institutions often enjoy a special legitimacy amongst local actors, and consequently enjoy levels of access and influence that UN actors cannot hope to emulate. Regional institutions may, in addition, be more familiar with local conditions than UN actors, particularly with the regional dimensions of conflict,[36] and may be able to mobilise political and other incentives amongst affected actors in ways that the UN cannot. Regional organizations also have an important role to play in establishing the horizontal peer networks that are so crucial to generating a culture of human rights, transparency, accountability and democracy. Moreover, the UN's attention and resource allocation is inevitably split between multiple conflicts worldwide; regional organizations have a greater incentive to stay the course and implement long-term conflict prevention and monitoring strategies.

---

33 *See esp.* Priscilla Hayner, *Unspeakable Truths: Confronting State Terror and Atrocity* (New York, Routledge: 2001).

34 ECOMOG is the Economic Community of West African States (ECOWAS) Military Observer Group. Operation Artemis (2003) in the Democratic Republic of Congo, was technically an EU operation though it was dominated by France. NATO assumed control of ISAF in Afghanistan in August 2003.

35 *For general discussion see* Michael Pugh and Waheguru Pal Singh Sidhu, eds., *The United Nations and Regional Security: Europe and Beyond* (Boulder, Lynne Rienner: 2003).

36 *See, e.g.,* Michael Pugh and Neil Cooper with Jonathan Goodhand, eds., *War Economies in a Regional Context* (Boulder, Lynne Rienner: 2004).

There are, however, also many arguments *against* an increased reliance on regional arrangements in peacekeeping. The key arguments focus on political opposition to regional peacekeeping and on the disparity between resources available to different regional arrangements, which could lead to a "de facto class system" of regional responses depending on the interest a particular crisis holds for the major powers.[37]

Integrated into the UN system in the right way, we argue regional arrangements could form an important bridge between the international system and local actors, improving the effectiveness of UN action. As we move forward, the UN should consider ways to make a virtue of this necessity of increased involvement of regional arrangements in peace operations. The Security Council cannot give up its monopoly over the authority to mandate the use of force (except in self defence); but it could build on Chapter VIII of the Charter to devolve greater monitoring and assessment powers to regional institutions, with the Security Council exercising a centralized standard-setting, monitoring and supervision role.[38]

3.4. *The Impact of North-South Politics*

The removal of Cold War constraints also signalled a shift away from East-West cleavages in world politics to North-South divides. These cleavages originally emerged in the heyday of decolonization, but several UN decision-making bodies, notably the General Assembly and the Economic and Social Council, have thus far failed to overcome them.[39] Decolonization led to a proliferation of states, many of them weak and poor, who collectively exercised a powerful voice at the UN. It has not, however, automatically translated into strengthened domestic capacity or prosperity within those states. In the context of globalization – which has only accelerated with the removal of Cold War political constraints on the expansion and deepening of the global market – the chasm between Northern state capacity and wealth and Southern incapacity and poverty has become even more stark. This has led to an increasing focus at the UN on the disparities of wealth and influence between countries in the North and countries in the South.

---

37 *See* Shepard Forman and Andrew Grene, "Collaboraitng with Regional Organizations", in D. Malone, *supra* note 31, p. 295 at pp. 302-304.

38 *For discussion of some of the building-blocks of such a system see, e.g.,* Frank Berman, "The Authorization Model: Resolution 678 and Its Effects" in Malone, *supra* note 31, p. 153.

39 *See* David M. Malone and Lotta Hagman, "The North-South Divide at the United Nations", *Security Dialogue*, Vol. 33, No. 4, December 2002, pp. 399-414; and David M. Malone, "L'affrontement Nord-Sud aux Nations unies: un anachronisme sur le déclin?", *Politique étrangère*, 1/2003, pp. 149-164.

North-South politics has emerged as a key feature of UN peace operations in the last decade, but those politics have often played out in complex ways. The Security Council's increased willingness after the end of the Cold War to authorize peacekeeping operations in essentially internal conflicts led to peacekeeping missions tackling the legacies of state failure in the global South. It did not take long for Northern states – most notably the United States, as a consequence of attacks on its troops in Somalia – to lose appetite for participating in such interventions. At the same time, though, the complexity of these internal emergencies often required UN missions to adopt a more assertive military strategy than they had become used to – as the disasters in Somalia, Rwanda and Srebrenica demonstrated. However this "peace enforcement" – usually mandated under Chapter VII of the UN Charter, rather than the Chapter VI or Chapter "VI and a half" operations of earlier peace operations – required the kind of high tech military punch that only Northern militaries could pack, and even then not always successfully (*viz.* Somalia).

UN Secretary-General Boutros Boutros-Ghali concluded by 1994 that the UN should not itself seek to conduct large-scale enforcement activities. Consequently, the Security Council increasingly resorted for enforcement of its decisions to "coalitions of the willing" such as that staffing Operation Uphold Democracy in Haiti in 1994-95; IFOR and then SFOR in Bosnia since 1995; MISAB in the Central African Republic, 1997; KFOR in Kosovo since 1999; INTERFET in East Timor in 1999-2000; ISAF in Afghanistan since early 2002; and now the Multinational Interim Force in Haiti since March 2004.[40] The result of this shift is that enforcement action now only occurs where there is an adequate coalition of countries who are "willing" – willing to make available the lift, troops, finance, political capital and military hardware necessary for the success of such a peace enforcement mission.

This has had profound results on the demography of UN peace operations around the world. Increasingly, with the exception of West Africa, enforcement actions are advocated, then carried out, by the global North, while traditional peacekeeping operations are executed by the global South.[41] The result is a three-tiered structure. Developing countries today make up over three-quarters of the troop contributors for peacekeeping operations under the command of the United Nations, notably in Africa. A number of industrialized countries (especially those in NATO) provide troops that operate under national command but with UN authorization, in operations

---

40   *See* UNSC Resolution 1529 (2004), 29 February 2004. For an excellent reference work covering UN peacekeeping operations from 1947 to 1999, *see* Oliver Ramsbotham and Tom Woodhouse, *Encyclopedia of international peace-keeping operations* (Santa Barbara, CA: ABC-CLIO, 1999).

41   David M. Malone and Ramesh Thakur, "Racism in Peace-keeping", *Globe and Mail* (Toronto), 30 October 2000.

such as SFOR, KFOR, and ISAF, in effect allowing the militaries of the industrialized world to operate with each other. And the United States, in addition to participating selectively in NATO activities, effectively operates as a free agent.

US hegemony – most pronounced in the military sphere, where Washington
spends as much on defense as the next dozen or so countries combined – exacer-
bates North-South politics further. Perhaps *the* key challenge for peacekeeping in
Bunche's day was bipolarity; many today would suggest that *the* key challenge for
peacekeeping is unipolarity. The approval of the Dayton Accords (on Bosnia), brokered by Washington, was apparently a turning point in UN affairs: according to
one Security Council Ambassador in early 1996, after Dayton, the U.S. was no
longer the sole remaining superpower, but simply "the supreme power".[42] The terrorist attacks of September 11, 2001 in the eastern U.S. instilled a new sense of
vulnerability in the U.S., epitomized in the 2002 *National Security Strategy*, which
further complicated the international management of U.S. unilateral impulses (in
themselves as old as the U.S. itself). Greater hostility in Washington towards attempts
at the UN and elsewhere to constrain U.S. power has been matched by growing
suspicions elsewhere of Washington's intentions and of the wisdom of some of its
actions, notably in attacking Iraq.

Unipolarity threatens to render UN peacekeeping either a handmaiden to US
power or a cast-off. The challenge for the Security Council is meaningfully to engage
the United States on the major security challenges without acquiescing in dangerous initiatives; to "have the courage to disagree with the USA when it is wrong and
the maturity to agree with it when it is right".[43] Michael Doyle, who served as
Assistant Secretary-General in Kofi Annan's office early in 2003, has summarized
this challenge nicely:

> The Council's performance on Iraq in March 2003, was both – and in about equal measure –
> a massive disappointment and a surprising relief. It disappointed all hopes that this essential
> international forum for multilateral policy could achieve a viable common policy. At the same
> time, it demonstrated to the surprise of many that it would not let itself be bullied or bribed
> by any power, permanent or even hyper. The so far unanswered question is: Can it meet the
> challenge of keeping intact its integrity while improving its effectiveness?[44]

---

42   Confidential interview with David Malone.
43   Confidential interview of an ambassador to the UN with David Malone, January 26, 2003. The
     reassignment in 2003 of Chile's admired ambassador at the UN, Juan Gabriel Valdés, after com-
     plaints from Washington to Santiago about his stance in the Council on Iraq, did little to foster a
     sense amongst UN diplomats that the US would perceive such objectivity as a sign of "maturity".
44   Interview with Michael W. Doyle, New York, May 16, 2003, cited in David M. Malone, "Conclusion",
     in Malone, *supra* note 31, p. 644.

U.S. military power today is so overwhelming relative to that of its principal partners that its patience with the tedium of multilateral bargaining will continue to
wear thin when crises appear to it to be acute. A clear risk for the Council is that
Washington will conceive this body's role mainly, at best, as one of long-term peace
building following short and sharp US-led military interventions (the latter whether
mandated by the Council or not). This was apparent in President Bush's address to
the UN General Assembly on September 22, 2003, when the US-led occupation of
Iraq was facing serious difficulties.[45] UN "peace operations" risk becoming "picking up the pieces operations" – as could again be the case in Haiti after Paris and
Washington in February 2004 worked together to force the democratically elected
if inept President Jean Bertrand Aristide out of office. Movement in that direction
would only serve to undermine the legitimacy – and consequently the effectiveness – of UN peace operations in the eyes of the global South.

3.5. *Changing Considerations in Mandating Peace Operations*

These developments in both the geopolitical landscape and the operational realities
of UN peacekeeping have also affected UN decisions to mount a peace operation.
In the contemporary climate, peace operations are often triggered by a mix of humanitarian and democratic imperatives which go far beyond the conditions which triggered peacekeeping operations in Bunche's era.

The UN system has long been concerned with the humanitarian plight of refugees
and other civilian victims of armed conflict. In the 1990s, however, the Security
Council increasingly invoked the plight of refugees and their implied destabilizing
effect on neighboring states as grounds for its own involvement in conflicts, as it
did in Yugoslavia, Somalia, Haiti and later in Kosovo. In addition, the globalization of civil society, particularly in the 1990s, created at least two pressures on the
Security Council to adopt a more interventionist approach to dealing with these
problems.[46] The first was the so-called "CNN effect" of selective but intensive media
coverage of humanitarian disasters, which brought the realities of war and state failure home to the democratic publics of the North, creating pressure on Northern governments to "do something". They, in turn, looked to the UN, with its specialized
expertise and "critical mass" in the areas of refugee protection and humanitarian
assistance, as a means of "doing something" while sharing the burden of doing it
with other UN Member States.

---

45   *See* <http://www.state.gov/p/io/rls/rm/2003/24321.htm>.
46   *For a more expansive discussion, see* Thomas G. Weiss, "The Humanitarian Impulse", in
      D. Malone, *supra* note 31, p. 37 and Joanna Wechsler, "Human Rights", in *ibid.*, p. 55.

The second pressure came from a combination of the mainstreaming of human rights discourse and the transnationalisation of non-governmental activist networks, which shared techniques and resources in an effort to mobilise public opinion in support of action to realize and protect human rights.[47] The "mainstreaming" of human rights in the UN system was assured with the appointment of a UN High Commissioner for Human Rights in 1994, and particularly with the appointment of Mary Robinson, a former president of Ireland, to that post. Kofi Annan, elected to the post of Secretary-General in late 1996, also – somewhat unexpectedly – staked out new ground in championing human rights and concern for civilians in war as key themes.

A third pressure on the Security Council came from the lessons it learned from the failures of UN peace operations in the 1990s, particularly in Bosnia and Rwanda. Then, it stood by while innocent civilians were massacred, sheltering behind the veil of sovereignty. Now, this is seen as a failure of the UN to discharge its responsibilities. As Kofi Annan recently put it at a conference to mark the tenth anniversary of the Rwanda genocide:

> The international community is guilty of sins of omission . . . This painful memory, along with that of Bosnia and Herzegovina, has influenced much of my thinking, and many of my actions, as Secretary-General.[48]

By the late 1990s, the pressures for a more pro-active approach to humanitarian crisis and serious human rights violations had lead some Northern states to break with the Security Council and undertake their own unauthorized "humanitarian interventions", as NATO did in Kosovo in 1999, when Western powers perceived that the Council would prevent them from "doing something" vital to protect lives and order in their backyard. Resistance to such an approach came from several quarters within the UN, including some Southern governments, but also from Russia (over Kosovo) and China, who saw it as incompatible with their own positions.[49] Other Southern governments saw benefits in supporting a more interventionist approach: the Constitutive Act of the African Union, for example, adopted in July 2000 to replace the Organization of African Unity and modelled largely after the European Union, explicitly authorised the Union to intervene in a Member State "in respect

---

47   *See* Margaret Keck and Kathryn Sikkink, *Activists beyond Borders: Advocacy Networks in International Politics* (Ithaca: Cornell University Press, 1998).

48   Secretary-General's remarks at Memorial Conference on the Rwanda Genocide, New York, 26 March 2004, available at <http://www.un.org/apps/sg/sgstats.asp?nid=840>.

49   Support of Muslim countries for the NATO strike did much to defeat criticism of the West at the UN over Kosovo.

of grave circumstances, namely: war crimes, genocide and crimes against humanity".[50]

Democratic principles also now play a more important role in mandating peace operations than they did in the past.[51] Since the end of the Cold War, UN peace operations have increasingly been taken in support of sustainable internal political arrangements, the organization of elections and the defense of democracy, for example in Haiti, Cambodia, El Salvador, Mozambique, Kosovo, East Timor, Afghanistan and perhaps in the near future Iraq.[52] Democracy has become both a reason for intervention and an exit strategy: the holding of national elections, perhaps after a longer democratic process of constitutional reform, marks one of the few clearly-agreed indicators of performance success in complex state-building peace operations. At the same time, the reliance on representative democracy carries risks for the Organization, including involvement in processes which do not lead to stable outcomes or, worse, as in East Timor in 1999, are not backed up by adequate measures to protect the civilian population.

4. Tomorrow's Peace Operations: Challenges for the Future

Today's peace operations are, it is clear, substantially different from the peace operations of Ralph Bunche's era. But where does that leave us? What can we expect of tomorrow's peace operations? It is difficult to predict long-term trends; but by reflecting on the current state and objectives of peace operations, and the changes we have just identified, we can offer some tentative speculations about the challenges of the immediate future: those of state-building, with all its operational and policy complexities; a longer-term shift in the UN's approach to both sovereignty and security; and the need for realism, which may mandate devolution of power to regional institutions and an increased focus on forward-planning.

4.1. *The Challenge of State-Building*

The transformation of the peacekeeping missions Bunche knew and directed – focused on the implementation of inter-state peace processes – into today's multidimensional peace operations – focused on dealing with state failure – is not likely

---

50   *See* Constitutive Act of the African Union, adopted in Lomé, July 11, 2000, Art 4(h), available at <http://www.africa-union.org/home/Welcome.htm>.

51   *See generally* Gregory H. Fox, "Democratization", in D. Malone, *supra* note 31, p. 69.

52   For the only clear-cut case in which the Security Council authorized the use of force to restore democracy, *see* David Malone, "Haiti and the International Community: A Case Study", *Survival*, vol. 39, no. 2, Summer 1997, pp. 126-146.

to reverse any time soon. The UN's involvement in state-building[53] is irreversible: if anything, the difficulties faced by the US-led coalition in post-war Iraq have only pressed home that the UN is, to adapt a phrase used by former US Secretary of State Madeline Albright, the "indispensable organization", if often an exasperating one. The complexities facing outsiders assisting a people to build a state are so many and so great – from the technical expertise required to the need for coordination of the political positions of contributing states – that perhaps only a multilateral organization with the universal legitimacy of the UN can hope to pull it off.[54] Perhaps we might say that if the UN did not exist we would have to invent it – for this purpose alone.

At the same time, those complexities are no less daunting for the UN than for any state that may attempt them. In some ways, the UN faces challenges those states do not: it has not traditionally been in the business of day-to-day government, so its learning curve as "virtual trustee" in Eastern Slavonia, East Timor and Kosovo has been steep. The move to virtual trusteeship,[55] like the increased involvement in state building more generally, has produced a civilianization of peace operations, particularly through the inclusion of civil administration, humanitarian assistance, policing, electoral, human rights monitoring, economic revival and development functions and personnel. While military components of peace operations continue often to be the largest components of these complex peace operations, they incorporate an increasing diversity of civilian components. This diversification creates significant problems of coordination, which increasingly falls to a civilian leadership. Peace operations today are generally directed by a civilian Special Representative of the Secretary-General (SRSG) rather than by a military force commander. Civilian leadership of recent large UN peacekeeping operations was initiated with great success in Namibia in 1989-90 by Martti Ahtisaari, later President of Finland.

The complexities of state-building extend beyond mere coordination questions. The policy objectives of specific exercises in trusteeship and state building often remain unclear. What kind of state should the UN attempt to build? What are the indicators of success? There is, as we saw earlier, a convergence around the paradigm of representative democracy, both as an extrapolation of the right to self-determination, and, on a more pragmatic level, as an identifiable endpoint triggering UN exit. But further reflection is required to ascertain what the UN expects to achieve through these interventions.

---

53   *See* Simon Chesterman, *You, The People: The United Nations, Transitional Administration, and State-Building* (Oxford: Oxford University Press, 2004).

54   *See* Simon Chesterman, "Bush, the United Nations and Nation-building", *Survival*, vol. 46, no. 1, Spring 2004, pp. 101-116.

55   *See* Simon Chesterman, "Virtual Trusteeship", in D. Malone, *supra* note 31, p. 219.

Too often, peace operations arise as an *ad hoc* response by the Security Council to a situation spiraling out of control. To be successful, state building demands something more than this fire-fighting. It requires taking seriously the connection between conflict prevention and development, between human rights and security.[56] It requires the involvement of members of the UN family whose mandate we have traditionally perceived as falling outside "peace operations": the World Bank, UNDP, even the World Health Organization. That may mean that complex peace operations require a more deliberate, whole-of-organization approach, with the Secretary-General and the Security Council acting as the coordinating focus for the broader UN family. The Council has a poor record on post-conflict peacebuilding strategies – witness the failure to generate stability in Haiti. The whole-of-organization approach might require it to delegate portions of that role elsewhere within the organization, as the UK, the Netherlands and Italy suggested in 2001 might occur through the Economic and Social Council.[57]

Setting policy objectives, performance benchmarks and exit strategies for, and coordinating the elements involved in, peace operations has proved difficult in peace operations to date: the challenge posed by ongoing engagement with state building is difficult to understate.

4.2. *Re-Evaluating Sovereignty and Security*

The convergence of peacekeeping and state-building points to a deeper trend at work in UN processes: a fundamental re-evaluation of sovereignty. Sovereignty is still the *lingua franca* of UN diplomatic discourse. But while this professional lip service continues to be paid to the absolute and equal sovereignty of UN Member States, the degree of intrusiveness the Security Council was prepared to mandate throughout the 1990s was striking, constituting a sharp redefinition in practice of what constitutes a threat to international peace and security justifying the piercing of the veil of sovereignty. The convergence of peacekeeping and state-building suggests that the sovereignty of most states is not equal, with the most powerful – particularly the P-5 – being more equal than the rest.

This gap between *de jure* and *de facto* sovereignty fuels perceptions of a North-South divide in world politics. The position of the Southern states is made more complex by their suspicion that the discourses of human rights and humanitarianism

---

56   *See, e.g.,* Chandra Lekha Sriram and Karin Wermester, *From Promise to Practice: Strengthening UN Capacities for the Prevention of Violence Conflict, Final Report,* International Peace Academy, New York, May 2003.

57   To date these efforts have resulted only in a modestly conceived Council-ECOSOC Working Group on Guinea-Bissau.

that the Secretariat has embraced – especially under the leadership of the current Secretary-General – serve as a kind of Trojan Horse for the political interests of the North. The emergence of the notion of "human security" is, for the South, a two-edged sword: on the one hand, it offers a basis for arguing that the North should focus its resources as much on dealing with the threats of poverty, deprivation and disease as on terrorism and the proliferation of weapons of mass destruction; on the other, it offers the North a platform to argue for a broader scope to pierce the veil of sovereignty around Southern states, because of their failure to guarantee their citizens' human security.[58]

These attitudes were particularly manifest in the approach taken to some of the reforms suggested by the Brahimi Report of 2000.[59] The Report is named for the chair – Lakhdar Brahimi, a former Algerian diplomat and Secretary-General's Special Representative or Envoy to a number of countries, notably Haiti, Afghanistan and now Iraq – of a Panel appointed by Kofi Annan to make recommendations for changes in UN peacekeeping. The Report recommended a number of administrative reforms, including vastly improved forward planning, the hiring of new staff in the Department of Peacekeeping Operations, the creation of a new information and strategic analysis unit to enhance conflict prevention activities, and the establishment of an interdepartmental task force for each mission. The recommendations met with a mixed response from Member States, not least because representatives of the South worried about the potential intrusiveness of improved UN information management. The North (no more admirably) was worried about financial, personnel, and materiel over-commitment in the peacekeeping field.

Ultimately, neither the UN, nor the Member States are likely soon to forget the difficult lessons of the 1990s on the cost of excessive respect for "sovereignty". Kofi Annan's focus on human rights advocacy and humanitarianism as core objectives of all UN activities have set the UN on a course that requires a careful re-evaluation of the notion of sovereignty. Increasingly, sovereignty is coming to be seen not just as a source of rights, but as a source of duties to provide human security, a "Responsibility to Protect". This idea was born from the Canadian-inspired International Commission on Intervention and State Sovereignty (ICISS) in December 2001.[60] The Commission's Report was discussed during a Security Council retreat

---

58   An interesting illustration of the difficulties changing notions of security pose for UN action emerged in 2000. The then-Permanent Representative of the US, Richard Holbrooke, strongly promoted a conception of AIDS as a critical security threat to Africa. Many delegations complained in the corridors that the Security Council was poaching the General Assembly's agenda. To his credit, Holbrooke persevered.

59   *See supra* note 19.

60   *See* <http://www.iciss.gc.ca/menu-e.asp>.

in early 2002, but has to date achieved more in the world of ideas than in the decisions of the Council. All the same, there may be growing support for the redistribution of rights and responsibilities captured by the phrase "Responsibility to Protect"; we should not be surprised if that support crystallises, at some point relatively soon, into action.

Taking the Responsibility to Protect seriously has consequences not only for states and what we expect of them, but also for the UN, and what we expect of it. We could not, for example, seriously claim to take the Responsibility to Protect seriously while we allowed UN interventions in failed states to be held hostage to the political interests of Northern states, as we have suggested above they risk becoming. If there is no coalition, nor even any state, able and willing to protect those at risk of serious human rights violations, the responsibility must somehow devolve to the international community itself. That means that we must find ways to allow the Member States of the UN to adopt a more cooperative approach to security governance, so that the UN can discharge this responsibility. Northern states must take the responsibility to deal with an absence of protection more seriously, and must learn to recognize their own long-term interest in preventing and dealing with state failure, not least to prevent collapsed states in the South becoming breeding grounds for diffuse, non-state military threats. At the same time, Southern states must acknowledge their own relatively weak capacity to provide the protection increasingly required of them, and adopt a more cooperative approach to working with Northern states to improve that capacity.[61]

The need for a cooperative approach has become only more self-evident since the tragic events of September 11, 2001 in the eastern United States, and, more recently, March 11, 2004 in Madrid. Terrorism poses enormous challenges for UN peacekeeping.[62] It makes UN peacekeepers targets, as the Organization was tragically reminded through the murder of Sergio Vieira de Mello and 21 other staff in Baghdad on 19 August 2003. It drives the North, in particular the United States, which feels newly vulnerable to terrorist attack, to pursue a more aggressively interventionist approach to security. That interventionism meets stiff resistance from the sovereign governments of the South, although many of those governments are themselves targets for terrorist attack. Transnational non-state terrorism seems simply to

---

61   One of the key means of securing this cooperative approach to security governance may be reform of the working procedures – if not the structure – of the Security Council. Already, the Council has made its deliberations more representative of the interests affected by a given crisis by working with "Groups of Friends": *see* Teresa Whitfield, "Groups of Friends", in D. Malone, *supra* note 31, p. 311.

62   *See generally* Edward C. Luck, "Tackling Terrorism", in Malone, *supra* note 31, p. 85 and Andrés Franco, "Armed Nonstate Actors", in *ibid.*, p. 117.

fall outside the capacities and paradigm of UN peace operations. As a result, Northern states are increasingly pushing to use the Chapter VII powers of the Security Council not as the basis for UN peace operations, but as the basis for legislation and regulation. This direct regulation approach emerged first in the 1990s with the establishment of the *ad hoc* criminal tribunals and the establishment of the Oil-For-Food program, but it has moved to center stage with the establishment and operation of the Counter-Terrorism Committee under Resolution 1373, and current moves to use the Security Council to criminalize activities resulting in the proliferation of weapons of mass destruction (WMD). These moves raise serious questions about the future of peace operations at the UN, suggesting in particular that they may have to compete for scarce UN resources with other forms of Security Council intervention, notably command-and-control regulatory monitoring, review and supervision.

4.3. *The Need for Realism*

The challenges of state-building and the re-evaluation of sovereignty and security have emerged as a long process of evolution from Bunche's day to the present. One challenge remains constant for the UN: to marry its idealistic, long-term objectives with realistic, short-term tactics. Today's peace operations already reflect a number of hard lessons that have been learned about that need for realism, whether in the changed approach to impartiality in peace operations or in changed approaches to the mandating of peace operations. Tomorrow's peace operations require us to be both bold and realistic about what we can achieve in the short term: pushing harder for a rapid response capacity, making a virtue of necessity in the move to greater regionalism, and accepting that Africa is likely to remain at the center of the peace-keeping agenda for many years to come.

Peace operations in Somalia taught the Security Council a hard lesson: that a UN force must, at the very least, be mandated, organized, equipped and trained to protect itself and its mission. The lessons of Bosnia[63] and Rwanda[64] taught these principles again and forced on the UN system an additional lesson: that peace-keepers must not only be empowered to defend themselves, but also, in many circumstances, civilian victims of war. The 1990s taught the UN system that impartial peacekeeping cannot be equated with moral equivalence among the parties to a conflict in extreme circumstances, nor with unwillingness to intervene to prevent atrocities.[65] The Brahimi Report strongly argued for the abandonment of any idea

---

63   *See Report on the Fall of Srebrenica*, UN Doc. A/54/549, 15 November 1999.

64   *See Report of the Independent Inquiry into the Actions of the United Nations During the 1994 Genocide in Rwanda*, UN Doc. S/1999/1257, 15 December 1999.

65   UNAMSIL in Sierra Leone was authorized, under Chapter VII of the Charter, and where resources

that the UN should not only be "impartial", but also "neutral".[66] The Report also emphasized the importance of a more realistic match between the mandates handed down by the Security Council and the troops and hardware offered by Member States to discharge those mandates. That has led to the introduction of a principle whereby the Security Council does not approve troop figures in a peacekeeping mandate until the Secretary-General has first received assurances from Member States that the requisite military capacity is available.

Looking more to the future, there are two main places we might focus our "realism". The first is in reducing deployment times. Two keys to improved performance on this front are reducing the time it takes to hire staff for peacekeeping missions and, on a parallel track, providing greater support to fledgling attempts to establish a rapid response capacity. Scandinavian countries have taken the lead in attempts to move this idea forward, notably through their cooperation, with other member states, in the SHIRBRIG (Standby High Readiness Brigade) project. UN cooperation with regional rapid reaction capacities is also an option. This brings us to our second focus for realistic advancement of the long-term peace operations agenda: a better defined relationship between the UN and regional organizations. Regional organizations and other, more flexible enforcement and sometimes peacekeeping arrangements involving several states will likely play more, and the UN less, of a role in international security in the future unless the UN can demonstrate greater capacity for effective collective decision-making. The UN could, however, make a virtue of a necessity, and use the threatened dilution of Security Council authority as an opportunity to devolve more power and greater roles more routinely to regional organizations, while maintaining mandating, oversight, monitoring and standard-setting capabilities itself.[67]

Realism also dictates that we accept that Africa will remain at the center of the peacekeeping agenda for many years to come. The Security Council spends the majority of its time on African issues, often without success. The regionalization of conflicts in West Africa and the Great Lakes (not to mention the many other conflicts in which the UN is currently represented by peace operations) has posed challenges to the UN's traditional model of peacekeeping with which it is strill struggling to deal. The severe under-development of most of Africa lies at the root of many of

---

and circumstances allowed, to use force to protect civilians – *see* UN Security Council resolution 1270, 22 February 2000. Other Chapter VII mandated forces have since received similar authorization.

66   In July 2001, the UN Special Committee on Peacekeeping operations (the so-called Committee of 34) concluded a lengthy debate on the Brahimi Report, endorsing many of the recommendations within the remit of member states. This positive outcome remains somewhat obscured by the bitter, often ill informed, discussions preceding it.

67   This schema would seem to be truer to the terms of the Charter's Chapter VIII than piecemeal recent practice has been.

the causes of the conflicts which continue to wrack the continent. UN peace operations can expect to continue to remain engaged with conflicts throughout the continent until that fundamental structural issue is addressed.

4.   Conclusion: Building on Ralph Bunche's Legacy

Contemporary peace operations occur in circumstances and ways that have changed
radically since Ralph Bunches' day.

The end of the Cold War led to heightened activism on the part of the Security
Council and a more cooperative approach amongst the P-5 to peacekeeping. The
Council remains split over the Israeli-Palestinian conflict, as it was split over Kosovo
and Iraq, but these are exceptions to the broader rule of an increased willingness
to mandate peacekeeping interventions. A key consequence has been an increased
engagement by the UN with essentially internal conflicts, with complex results,
including a movement to a multi-disciplinary approach in peacekeeping, a re-evaluation of impartiality, and experimentation with new tools for peace such as accountability mechanisms and sanctions.

The removal of Cold War constraints has also had important geopolitical
ramifications which have played out in peacekeeping. Regional organizations play
an increasingly important role in discharging peacekeeping and peace enforcement
mandates. At the same time, UN politics has shifted from an East-West axis to a
North-South axis. This has been reflected in peacekeeping in part by a *de facto* dif-
ferentiation of participation, with the North taking on peace enforcement activities
and the South more often performing more traditional peacekeeping roles. This risks
making peace enforcement a tool of Northern policy. The perception of this risk is
heightened by US military hegemony, which poses a significant challenge for the
Security Council, which must find ways to engage the US and constrain its unilateralist impulses without alienating it and rendering the Council irrelevant.

The considerations involved in mandating peace operations have also changed
significantly. The "CNN effect" and the transnationalisation of global civil society
have both led to increasing pressures on democratic governments in the North to
adopt a more pro-active approach to intervention in the face of humanitarian crisis
and massive violations of human rights. This has led some Northern states to undertake "humanitarian interventions", as NATO did in Kosovo in 1999, without Security
Council authorization, when they perceived that the Council would prevent them
from "doing something" vital to protect lives and order in their backyard. Democratic
principles have also come to play a more significant role in mandating peace operations, and as a basis for UN exit.

These changes point to three deeper imperatives in the evolution of UN peacekeeping operations. The first is the challenge of engagement with state-building.

The shift from the traditional focus of peacekeeping, buttressing a self-enforcing peace, to state-building, requiring the creation of conditions for the emergence of a self-renewing peace, is difficult to understate. It poses enormous operational challenges for the UN system, which may in the long-run require a move towards a more integrated whole-of-organization approach. Greater attention must be paid to clarification of the objectives of state-building, both in general and in specific cases, in particular the identification of indicators of success. Nevertheless, the UN remains essential to success in most state-building exercises; as the US is learning in Iraq, even the most powerful states struggle to muster the combination of resources, expertise and, crucially, legitimacy, that is needed to build a state. Only the UN offers that combination; if it did not exist, we might have to invent it, for that reason alone.

This points to a second imperative: the re-evaluation of sovereignty and security. The UN learnt hard lessons in the 1990s about the dangers of the "old" conceptions of sovereignty and security, and now stands on the brink of a fundamental re-positioning. A consensus may be emerging which aligns the concepts of sovereignty and human security around the notion of states' Responsibility to Protect, but much work remains to be done to secure and implement that consensus. That work is made all the more challenging by the scourge of terrorism, which throws the utility of peace operations into doubt and problematizes both Northern and Southern attitudes to military interventions in the name of "peace and security".

This, in turn, points us to the third imperative: the perennial need for realism. We must focus on concrete strategies for regenerating the UN's capacity to meet the peacekeeping needs of today's – and tomorrow's – world. These strategies should include finding ways to improve the responsiveness of UN peacekeeping operations and of integrating regional arrangements into the peacekeeping system. Unless we take these concrete strategies, we risk squandering Ralph Bunche's legacy. We risk failing to make that progress that Bunche hoped for, by which the United Nations would move "toward digging up the deeply imbedded roots of war".[68]

The responsibility of building on Bunche's legacy rests to a large degree with the blue-ribbon panel (the so-called "High Level Panel") assembled by the Secretary General in 2003 to consider a variety of threats to security and how the UN could address them more convincingly. This panel has been meeting regularly and will deliver its report in early December 2004, expected to make significant recommendations for reform within the Organization. The perceived urgency of such change and related institutional reforms is much greater outside the Organization

---

68   Ralph J. Bunche, "Man, Democracy and Peace – Foundations for Peace: Human Rights and Fundamental Freedoms, 1950", in C. Henry, *supra* note 20, p. 166.

than within it. While UN delegates tend to regard the UN as their preserve, rather than theirs in trust for humanity, to be changed by incremental reform and not radical overhauls, outsiders hope for fundamental change.

How can this impasse be overcome? Should a "second San Francisco" conference be considered in order to design renewed and reformed Charter-based structures? The danger with such an approach is the high risk of failure. Where the Second World War served to focus the minds of delegates at San Francisco on the need to prevent the "scourge of war", even the events of 9/11 do not serve to bind delegates to a common purpose today.

UN reform needs to be based on a meaningful compromise between the priorities of the North and the priorities of the South leading to forward motion on achievement of both. Bunche would have advocated and expected no less. Tinkering at the margins is not enough: the challenge for the Panel is to identify new and more convincing approaches for the UN to the challenges of terrorism, weapons of mass destruction, state failure and related economic and social phenomena.

We must not underestimate the challenge today's military and human security threats, and today's geopolitical circumstances, pose to the UN's ongoing ability to perform its customarily useful peacekeeping role. We must be both bold and realistic in our attempts at reform. When we face resistance, we might simply recall what Ralph Bunche said upon receiving his Nobel Peace Prize more than half a century ago:

> the United Nations exists not merely to preserve the peace but also to make change – even radical change – possible without violent upheaval. The United Nations has no vested interest in the status quo.[69]

Much has changed in United Nations peace operations since Bunche's day; this, it seems, will remain constant.

---

69   Ralph Bunche, *Some Reflections on Peace in Our Time*, Nobel Peace Prize Lecture, Oslo, Norway, 11 December 1950, reprinted as Appendix C in Benjamin Rivlin, ed., *Ralph Bunche. The Man and His Times* (Holmes & Meier, New York, 1990), p. 235.

Occupation Policy in Iraq and International Law*

Michael N. Schmitt** and Charles H.B. Garraway***

On 20 March 2003, a US and UK-led coalition attacked Iraq, formally basing its action on UN Security Council resolutions stretching back over a decade.[1] The operation, Iraqi Freedom, engendered widespread criticism by States, non-governmental organizations, and respected academics.[2] However, even as the debate continued, Coalition forces quickly defeated the Iraqi military and conquered the country. Less than two months after commencement of military action, US President Bush declared from the deck of the *USS Abraham Lincoln* that "major combat operations in Iraq have ended".[3]

---

*   Current as of 11 February 2004. The views expressed are those of the authors in their personal capacity. The authors wish to thank the British Institute of International and Comparative Law for its support of this project.

**   Professor Michael N. Schmitt, George C. Marshall European Center for Security Studies, Garmisch-Partenkirchen, Germany, email: schmittm@marschallcenter.org.

*** Colonel Charles H.B. Garraway, CBE, Senior Research Fellow, British Institute of International and Comparative Law, London, United Kingdom, e-mail: charlesgarraway@hotmail.com.

1   Letter dated 20 March 2003 from the Permanent Representative of the United States of America to the United Nations addressed to the President of the Security Council, UN Doc. S/2003/351 (March 21, 2003), <http://www.newsmax.com/archives/articles/2003/3/22/195522.shtml>; Letter dated 20 March 2003 from the Permanent Representative of the United Kingdom of Great Britain and Northern Ireland to the United Nations addressed to the President of the Security Council, UN Doc. S/2003/350 (Mar. 21, 2003), <http://www.newsmax.com/archives/articles/2003/3/22/195522.shtml>.

2   France and Germany, traditional US allies, openly opposed the operations. Secretary-General Kofi Annan also harbored doubts as to its legality. Patrick E. Tyler and Felicity Barringer, "Annan Says U.S. Will Violate Charter if it Acts Without Approval", *New York Times*, March 11, 2003, at A10. Many academics criticized the operation as illegal in the absence of UN sanction. *See, e.g.*, the letter from 16 law professors, *The Guardian*, March 7, 2003, at 29. At the time of the attack, 48 nations were publicly committed to the Coalition. Support ranged from contributions of troops to political actions. White House Press Release, Operation Iraqi Freedom: Coalition Members, March 21, 2003, <http:// www.whitehouse.gov/news/releases/2003/03/20030321-4.html>.

3   George W. Bush, Remarks from the USS Abraham Lincoln, May 1, 2003, <http://www.white-house.gov/news/releases/2003/05/iraq/2003501-15.html>.

Harvey Langholtz, Boris Kondoch, Alan Wells (Eds.),
International Peacekeeping: The Yearbook of International Peace Operations, Volume 9, 2004, pp. 27-61.
© *Koninklijke Brill N.V. Printed in the Netherlands*

This article explores, from a legal perspective, the published Coalition occupation policies implemented since the Iraqi defeat. Occupation authorities (the Coalition Provisional Authority-CPA) have promulgated most as regulations and orders.[4] For purposes of analysis, they are grouped into five categories: governance, security, relief, the economy, and legal system.

The 1907 Hague Convention IV (annexed Regulations) and the 1949 Fourth Geneva Convention contain the relevant occupation law. Although 1977 Protocol Additional I to the Geneva Conventions includes some occupation provisions, since neither the United States nor Iraq are Parties, it is inapplicable, except as it restates customary international law.[5] Acting under Chapter VII of the UN Charter, the Security Council has also adopted resolutions that both limit Coalition occupation activities, and expand them beyond the strict confines of international humanitarian law. These treaties and resolutions will serve as the normative standards against which Coalition policies will be evaluated.[6]

1.   Commencement of the Occupation

Hague Regulations Article 42 sets forth the accepted formula for commencement of occupation: "Territory is considered occupied when it is actually placed under the authority of the hostile army. The occupation extends only to the territory where such authority has been established and can be exercised". Thus, the date occupation law attaches is an issue of fact; territory is placed under enemy occupation

---

4   Regulations "define the institutions and authorities" of the CPA, whereas orders are "binding instructions or directives to the Iraqi people that create penal consequences or have a direct bearing on the way Iraqis are regulated, including changes to Iraqi law". The CPA also issues memoranda and public notices. The former "expand on Orders or Regulations by creating or adjudging procedures applicable to an Order or Regulation", while the latter "communicate the intention of the Administrator to the public and may require adherence to security measures that have no penal consequences or reinforces aspects of existing law that the CPA intends to enforce". All are available on the CPA website at <http://www.cpa-iraq.org/cpa_documents.html>. Unfortunately, the dates of the scanned actual regulations and orders which appear on the CPA website and those used in the Official Gazette of Iraq differ. In this article, the dates on the originals are used because most, by their own terms, enter into force on the date of signature.

5   Respectively, Convention (IV) respecting the Laws and Customs of War on Land, Annexed Regulations, Oct. 18, 1907, 36 Stat. 2277, 205 Consol. T.S. 277 [hereinafter Hague IV]; Geneva Convention Relative to the Protection of Civilian Persons in Time of War, Aug. 12, 1949, 6 U.S.T. 3516, 75 U.N.T.S. 287 [hereinafter Geneva Convention IV]; Protocol Additional to the Geneva Conventions Relating to the Protection of Victims of International Armed Conflicts, June 8, 1977, UN Doc. A/32/144, 16 I.L.M. 1391 [hereinafter Protocol Additional I].

6   For an excellent survey of occupation law, *see* Eyal Benvenisti, *The International Law of Occupation* (Princeton N.J.: Princeton University Press, 1993); *see also* Adam Roberts, "What is a Military Occupation?", 66 *British Yearbook of International Law* 249 (1984).

when the government thereof is incapable of exercising authority over it and the attacker is in a position to impose measures of control. This generally occurs once major hostilities end and the attacking force can turn its attention to occupation tasks.

No requirement exists for formal declaration of an occupation such as that proclaimed upon defeat of Germany in 1945.[7] Nor may a State avoid occupation responsibilities by simply choosing not to exercise authority, for occupation law both grants rights to occupiers and seeks to ensure the civilian population's well-being. That said, attackers need not unreasonably adjust combat operations to fulfill occupation duties; military necessity tempers occupation law, often expressly.[8]

Importantly, occupation rights and duties attach as territory, not the State itself, is seized. Thus, occupation status flows with the enemy advance.[9] Iraq offers an excellent example of this principle. In late March, Coalition forces overran territory in the south (with the exception of Basra), thereby assuming occupier status. However, even after the regime's collapse on 9 April 2003, some elements of Iraq's military continued resisting, most notably in Saddam Hussein's hometown of Tikrit, which fell on April 14.[10] Finally, on 16 April, Coalition Commander, General Franks, issued a Message of Freedom to the Iraqi People.[11] The CPA generally uses this date in its policy instruments as a reference point for countrywide occupation.

Coalition actions demonstrate a full understanding of its occupation responsibilities, and their immediacy. For instance, the US Office of Reconstruction and Humanitarian Aid (ORHA) began formal occupation planning some time before the war began.[12] Then, the day Tikrit fell, Prime Minister Blair acknowledged Coalition occupation responsibilities in a House of Commons address, stating that in the first phase of occupation, which would begin "shortly", the Coalition and ORHA would have "responsibility under the Geneva and Hague Conventions for ensuring that Iraq's immediate and security needs are met".[13] The next day, ORHA chief Jay

---

7 Declaration Regarding the Defeat of Germany and the Assumption of Supreme Authority by Allied Powers, June 5, 1945 (Generals Eisenhower, Zhukov, Montgomery, and Lattre de Tassiny), 3 *Treaties and Other International Agreements of the United States of America* (Multilateral 1931-1945), available at <http://www.yale.edu/lawweb/avalon/wwii/ger01>.

8 For example, rapidly advancing forces are not required to slow their pace nor leave forces behind to conduct occupation duties. Rather, elements thereof would either return when no longer essential to prosecuting the attack, or, more likely, follow-on forces would assume occupation duties.

9 Some resistance may still be present. However, if indigenous armed forces continue to operate in the area in an organized and significant way, occupation has not begun.

10 All dates are derived from the Iraq Chronology developed by the Royal United Services Institute (RUSI). <http://www.iraqcrisis.co.uk/events.php>.

11 Cited in CPA/ORD/23 May 2003/2, Dissolution of Entities, at pmbl.

12 January 2003.

13 According to the Prime Minister, this phase would yield to a second, during which an Interim Authority would be established. In the third, a fully representative Iraqi government would assume

Garner convened a meeting of Iraqi resistance groups, who agreed to a 13-point reconstruction program.[14] At that point, the CPA "disestablished" the Baath Party of Iraq.[15]

Events moved very quickly following the President's announcement of an end to major combat operations. On 8 May, the US and UK notified the Security Council that they had created the CPA, which included ORHA, to exercise temporarily governmental powers.[16] The entity issued its first order and regulation on the 16th.[17] In Regulation No. 1, newly appointed CPA Administrator, L. Paul Bremer, formally assumed governmental authority "in order to provide for the effective administration of Iraq during the period of transitional administration, to restore conditions of security and stability, to create conditions in which the Iraqi people can freely determine their own political future, including by advancing efforts to restore and establish national and local institutions for representative governance and facilitating economic recovery and sustainable reconstruction and development".[18] Bremer cited the "laws and usages of war" and "U.N. Security Council resolutions, including Resolution 1483 (2003)" as legal bases for the action. The latter recognized CPA authority to govern Iraq.[19]

The interplay between occupation law and UN law is critical. Occupation law applied from the time Coalition forces were in a position to exercise authority over territory within Iraq. It continues in effect today. Resolution 1483 acknowledges as much by calling upon "all concerned to comply fully with their obligations under international law including in particular the Geneva Conventions of 1949 and the Hague Regulations of 1907". In doing so, it specifically referred to the "occupying powers under unified command (the 'Authority')".

From 22 May, Resolution 1483's adoption date, UN law, as expressed in this and subsequent resolutions, also applied pursuant to the Security Council's Chapter VII authority.[20] Thus, two bodies of law coexist and compliment each other in Iraq.

---

control of the country. Prime Minister Tony Blair, Address to the House of Commons, April 14, 2003, <http://www.iraqcrisis.co.uk/resources.php?idtag=R3E9BC863DOE3C>.

14   Nasiriya Statement, The 13 Point Programme, April 15, 2003, <http://www.iraqcrisis.co.uk/resources.php?idtag+R3EAD40C8AA4EB>. On April 28, Garner again met with the Iraqi resistance to conduct further planning.

15   Acknowledged in CPA/ORD/16 May 2003/1, De-Baathification of Iraqi Society, and UNSC Res. 1483 (May 22, 2003).

16   Letter dated May 08, 2003 from the Permanent Representatives of the United Kingdom of Great Britain and Northern Ireland and the United States of America to the United Nations addressed to the President of the Security Council, UN Doc. S/2003/538.

17   CPA Order No. 1, *see supra* note 15; CPA/REG/16 May 2003/1, The Coalition Provisional Authority.

18   CPA Regulation No. 1, *see supra* note 17.

19   This was curious, for Resolution 1483 (*supra* note 15), while granting the CPA authority to govern Iraq, was not adopted by the Security Council until nearly a week after issuance of the regulation.

20   On several previous occasions, the Council had set the terms for de facto "foreign occupations",

To the extent that CPA activities exceed the rights granted in occupation law, a Security Council mandate must "authorize" them, at least implicitly. This is an important point because occupation law is typically conservative in nature; it seeks preservation of the *status quo*. However, Iraq desperately needs economic reconstruction and development, as well as political and legal reform, which far exceed the limits of occupation law. Security Council involvement permits this to occur as a matter of law.

Note that despite the existence of an occupation, humanitarian law related to the conduct of hostilities continues to govern actions with a direct nexus to the conflict. An example is a planned deliberate attack against occupation forces.[21] Additionally, captured combatants benefit from prisoner of war status, a point illustrated by Saddam Hussein's designation as such.

On the other hand, actions with no direct nexus to the hostilities are subject to human rights law, law imposed by the occupier, and any domestic penal law remaining in force. For instance, the European Court held in *Loizidou* that the European Convention on Human Rights applied to Turkish occupation of northern Cyprus.[22] In such cases, law enforcement guidelines such as minimal force apply to the occupier's duty to maintain security.[23] Of course, given the existence of an armed conflict,

---

most notably in Kosovo and East Timor. UNSC Res. 1244 (June 10, 1999), Kosovo; UNSC Res. 1264 (Sept. 15, 1999)/UNSC Res. 1272 (Oct. 25, 1999), East Timor. However, in neither case did the Council reference occupation law in the operative resolution. Moreover, in both, the adoption of an empowering resolution preceded the entry of foreign forces into the countries. For a discussion of the interplay of occupation and UN law, *see* David J. Scheffer, "Beyond Occupation Law", 97 *American Journal of International Law* 842 (2003).

21 Those attacking are either combatants (members of the military) or "directly participating" in hostilities. The former may be attacked wherever and whenever found, whereas the later may be targeted directly when "and for such time as they take a direct part in hostilities". Protocol Additional I, *see supra* note 5, art. 51.3.

22 Loizidou v. Turkey, Merits, No. 40/1993/435/514, Eur. Ct. H.R., Dec. 18, 1996. Most notably, Article 2 prohibits the deprivation of life "when it results from the use of force which is no more than absolutely necessary: in the defense of any person from unlawful violence; in order to effect a lawful arrest or prevent escape of a person lawfully detained; [or] in action lawfully taken for the purpose of quelling a riot or insurrection". Convention for the Protection of Human Rights and Fundamental Freedoms, Nov. 4, 1950, art. 2.1, E.T.S. No. 5, 213 U.N.T.S. 222.

One difference between the situation in Cyprus and that in Iraq is that the Cypriots already benefited from Convention rights, for Cyprus was a Party thereto. Reference should also be made to the Bankovic case, in which the Court, albeit dismissing on jurisdictional grounds, referred to situations of occupation. Bankovic & Others v. Belgium, the Czech Republic, Denmark, France, Germany, Greece, Hungary, Iceland, Italy, Luxembourg, the Netherlands, Norway, Poland, Portugal, Spain, Turkey and the United Kingdom, (Admissibility), Eur. Ct. H.R., App. No. 52207/99, Dec. 12, 2001.

23 Obviously, it will often be difficult for soldiers on the ground to distinguish between those about to attack them and those engaging in lawlessness unrelated to the hostilities. Thus, the rules of engagement for handling potential threats, and the resulting "soldier cards", are critical in

States Party to applicable human rights treaties could derogate from all but the non-derogable provisions thereof. In the case of Iraq, neither the United States nor the United Kingdom has done so.

Finally, it essential to understand the *jus ad bellum* has no relevance to occupation law, which is a component of the *jus in bello*. Thus, the legality, or lack thereof, of Operation Iraqi Freedom has no bearing on the occupation rights and duties of Coalition forces.[24]

2.   Governance

Traditional occupation law both presumes the continued existence of an indigenous government which functions in a manner compatible with the occupation regime, and seeks to return full authority to it. Indeed, because the occupier now possesses "the authority of the legitimate power", it must "take all the measures in his power to restore, and ensure, as far as possible, public order and safety, while respecting, unless absolutely prevented, the laws in force in the country".[25] Occupying authorities simply fill voids in the provision of the civilian population's basic needs until such duties can revert to the government.

Humanitarian law also envisages a situation whereby a State is only responsible for territory over which its forces exercise control. This approach sits uneasily with coalition operations. In post-war Germany, the matter was resolved through creation of four distinct zones of occupation. However, in Iraq there is but a single zone.

Following formal US and UK notification to the Security Council of their occupation of Iraq,[26] the Council recognized, in Resolution 1483, "the specific authorities, responsibilities and obligations under applicable international law of the States

---

operationalizing the different legal regimes. Some solace for the occupier is found in the well-accepted principle that a reasonable mistake of fact precludes criminal responsibility under the law of war. For instance, Article 32 of the International Criminal Court Statute provides that mistake of fact is a ground for excluding criminal responsibility if it negates the mental intent element of the offense. Rome Statute of the International Criminal Court, July 17, 1998, art. 32, UN Doc. A/CONF.183/9* (1998), 37 ILM 1999.

24   Somewhat paradoxically, the nature of the Baathist regime legitimately influenced, as will be explained, actions taken by occupation authorities.

25   Hague Regulations, *see supra* note 5, art. 43 Technically, a "military government" serves as the administrative entity, although, despite its title, the occupation government may be military, civilian, or mixed in composition, as it is in the case of the CPA. There is no restriction on forming an international military government, even if forces from different nations seized distinct pieces of territory.

26   Letter to the Security Council from US and UK Permanent Representative, *supra* note 1.

as occupying powers under unified command (the 'Authority')".[27] The result is an occupation regime in which the two States operate together with joint and several responsibility for compliance with all relevant legal provisions. This unusual set-up could create difficulties where the partners have differing legal obligations. For example, the UK is a party to Additional Protocol I and the European Convention on Human Rights, whereas the US is not. The question is the extent to which acts of one occupation power in its own area of responsibility create legal responsibility on the part of another.[28] No clear answer exists.

L. Paul Bremer promulgated Regulation No. 1, setting forth the powers of the CPA, on 16 May.[29] Because he issued the regulation before adoption of Resolution 1483, the sole basis for the powers it purported to assume was occupation law.[30] Significantly, the regulation directed that Iraqi laws in force on 16 April 2003 remain valid insofar as they do not "prevent the CPA from exercising its rights and fulfilling its obligations, or conflict with the present or any other Regulation or Order issued by the CPA". As to CPA regulations and orders, the regulation requires publication in the "relevant languages". It also provides that they take force "as specified therein"; many specify the date of signature. In the event of a conflict between Iraqi and CPA law, the latter takes precedence.

The CPA's first major step was disestablishment of the Baath Party on 16 April 2003.[31] In Order No. 1, which memorialized that action in writing, the CPA propounded two justifications for taking the measure.[32] First, it noted the "grave concern of Iraqi society regarding the threat posed by the continuation of Baath Party networks and personnel in the administration of Iraq, and the intimidation of the people of Iraq by Baath Party officials." Second, the order cited "the continuing threat to the security of the Coalition Forces posed by the Iraqi Baath Party". The underlying objective, apart from security, was ensuring "that representative government in Iraq is not threatened by Baathist elements returning to power and that those in positions of authority in the future are acceptable to the Iraqi people".[33]

---

27 In order to avoid occupant status on the part of those States contributing forces other than the United Kingdom and United States (such as Poland), the Resolution 1483 notes "other States that are not occupying powers are working now or in the future may work under the Authority".

28 Precisely this situation appeared in the case of Bankovic before the European Court of Human Rights. In that case, the petitioners sought relief against the European NATO States in relation to an action that was reportedly carried out by the United States, a State not subject to the European Convention, during a NATO operation. The issue remained unresolved as the case was dismissed on a technical point during preliminary proceedings. Bankovic, *supra* note 22.

29 CPA/REG/16 May 2003/1, Coalition Provisional Authority.

30 Curiously, and like the de-Baathification Order, it referenced the Resolution.

31 CPA/ORD/16 May 2003/1, De-Baathification of Iraqi Society.

32 *Id.*

33 Actual implementation of de-Baathification was provided for in CPA/MEMO/3 June 2003/1, Implementation of De-Baathification Order No. 1, and CPA/MEMO/4 November 2003/7, Delegation

Order No. 1 directed removal of "senior party members" and banned them from future public sector employment.[34] It also ordered investigation of the three top management layers in "every national government ministry, affiliated corporations and other government institutions (e.g., universities and hospitals)". Anyone determined to be a full member of the Baath Party, including junior members, was to be removed. In November 2003, responsibility for de-Baaathification was delegated to the Governing Council.[35]

Following adoption of Resolution 1483, the CPA employed its now enhanced authority more robustly. The next day, Bremer issued Order No. 2, dissolving certain Iraqi entities and seizing their assets "on behalf of and for the benefit of the Iraqi people" in the recovery of Iraq.[36] The order covered organizations used "to oppress the Iraqi people and as instruments of torture, repression and corruption". Included were the Ministries of Defense; Ministry of Information; Ministry of State for Military Affairs; Iraqi Intelligence Service; National Security Bureau; Directorate of National Security; Special Security Organization; Saddam Hussein's bodyguards; regular armed forces; paramilitaries; and such other organizations as the National Olympic Committee and revolutionary, special, and national security courts.[37] To preclude the rise of abusive governmental entities in the future, the CPA has since delegated the authority to establish a "Commission on Public Integrity" as a body "responsible for enforcing anti-corruption laws and public service standards" to the Governing Council.[38]

Over the ensuing months, the CPA established a number of entities to fill the governance void, meet the population's needs, and facilitate return of authority to Iraqis. After two months of consultations, composition of the "transitional administration run by Iraqis" referenced in Resolution 1483 was agreed upon. Although Bremer initially envisaged it as a consultative body, Iraqi dissatisfaction with this approach led to CPA acquiescence in the formation of an entity with meaningful power. On 13 July 2003, the Governing Council announced its formation as "the

---

of Authority Under De-Baathification Order No. 1. The Council (authorized in CPA/ORDER/25 May 2003/5, Establishment of the Iraqi De-Baathification Council) was never formed.

34 Senior Part Members included "[f]ull members of the Baath Party holding the ranks of 'Udw Qutriyya' (Regional Command Member), 'Udw Far' (Branch Member), 'Udw Shu'bah' (Section Member) and 'Udw Firqah' (Group Member)". *Id.*, sect. para 2. Those who lost their position in public service were subsequently denied pension benefits. CPA/ORD/8 September 2003/30, Reform of Salaries and Employment Conditions of State Employees.

35 CPA Memorandum 7, *see supra* note 33.

36 CPA Order No. 2, *see supra* note 11.

37 CPA/ORD/23 May 2003/2/ANNEX, Dissolution of Entities. The Annex was misnumbered as CPA Order 3.

38 CPA/ORD/28 January 2004/55, Delegation of Authority Regarding the Iraq Commission on Public Integrity.

principal body of the Iraqi interim administration".[39] The same day, the CPA recognized the Governing Council in a regulation requiring consultation and coordination between the Council and CPA "on all matters involving temporary governance of Iraq".[40] UN Special Representative, Sergio Vieira de Mello, blessed this action, stating that it brought the country "one step closer towards fulfilling the explicit wish of the Security Council which, in its Resolution 1483, resolved that the day when Iraqis govern themselves must come quickly".[41] The following month, the Security Council welcomed the "establishment of the broadly representative Governing Council of Iraq" in Resolution 1500.[42]

Over time, the CPA has established a number of government ministries, some in place of those dissolved pursuant to Order No. 2. For instance, it replaced the Ministry of Atomic Energy with a Ministry of Science and Technology.[43] Soon thereafter, the CPA created a Ministry of the Environment,[44] and, acting with the Governing Council, a Ministry of Displacement and Migration.[45] The CPA also established various security sector ministries and other agencies.[46]

On 1 September 2003, the Governing Council appointed the Iraqi Cabinet Ministers, a move hailed by Bremer as "an important step toward sovereign self-government".[47] The CPA formally recognized the appointments two days later.[48]

Interestingly, the CPA has also sought to enhance civil society by regulating the growing number of domestic and international NGOs active in Iraq. Registration is required and all are susceptible to audit by the NGO Assistance Office within the Ministry of Planning and Development Cooperation. Those failing to comply with CPA requirements risk dissolution by the Administrator.[49]

Efforts are presently underway to draft a new constitution and hold democratic

39   Event cited in CPA/REG/13 July 2003/6, Governing Council of Iraq.

40   *Id.*

41   Sergio Vieira de Mello, Statement on the Occasion of the Formation of the Governing Council of Iraq, July 13, 2003, <http://www.un.org/apps/news/infocusnewsiraq1.asp?NewsID=562&sID=12>.

42   UNSC Res. 1500 (Aug. 14, 2003).

43   CPA/ORD/24 August 2003/24, Ministry of Science and Technology.

44   CPA/ORD/24 November 2003/44, Establishment of the Ministry of Environment (establishment was retroactive to 7 August).

45   For instance, the Governing Council established the Ministry of Displacement and Migration in Governing Council Resolution No. 30, which was subsequently ratified by the CPA in CPA/ORD/11 January 2003 [sic]/50, Establishment of the Ministry of Environment. The misdate by Bremer is on the original. The actual year is 2004.

46   *See* discussion below.

47   L. Paul Bremer, CPA Update Briefing, Sept. 2, 2003, <http//:www.cpairaq.org/transcripts/20030903_TranscriptPC2Sep>. In some cases, interim Ministers were appointed pended establishment of their ministry.

48   CPA/MEM/3 September 2003/6, Implementation of Regulation on the Governing Council Number 6.

49   CPA/ORD/27 November 2003/45, Non-governmental Organizations.

elections. Unfortunately, disagreement has erupted over both the content of the constitution and the method of choosing the new government.[50] Nevertheless, the CPA has taken the firm position that its authority will devolve to a representative Iraqi government by 1 July 2004. Under the leadership of Lahkdar Brahimi, a UN team is assisting Iraqi interim officials for both purposes.[51] In the event, it is apparent that occupation authorities are intent on passing control of the country back to Iraqis as quickly as possible.

2.1. *Legal Assessment*

Most Coalition actions in the field of governance have been consistent with international law. Clearly, the CPA is pressing hard to return authority to the Iraqis, a core principle underlying occupation law.

Since de-Baathification began before Resolution 1483's adoption, its legality depends on occupation law. Hague Regulations, Article 43, requires the occupying power to take measures in its power to "restore, and ensure, as far as possible, public order and safety". Furthermore, Geneva Convention IV, Article 54, although emphasizing the need to preserve the status of public officials and judges, recognizes the occupier's right to remove public officials. The convention's Official Commentary, albeit less than clear on the subject, indicates legitimate bases for dismissal by suggesting that occupying forces be generous in retaining officials because those who later abuse their power or exercise it to the occupier's detriment can be removed.[52] As a matter of law, security concerns justified the de-Baathification program because the party had previously demonstrated its propensity for repression, violence, and other abuses.[53] It is worth noting, however, that regime change alone is not a basis for removal of government officials, even when the pre-existing government is unrepresentative.[54]

---

50   In Resolution 1511, the Security Council supported the Governing Council's appointment of a "cabinet of ministers and a preparatory constitutional committee to lead a process in which the Iraqi people will progressively take control of their own affairs". UNSC Res. 1511 (Oct. 16, 2003).

51   CPA Press Release, U.N. Election Team to Work in Iraq, Feb. 9, 2003, <http://www.cpairaq.org/press-releases/UB_back>.

52   International Committee of the Red Cross, IV Commentary: Geneva Convention Relative to the Protection of Civilian Persons 308 (Jean S. Pictet ed., 1958).

53   *See, e.g.*, Human Rights Watch, Forcible Expulsion of Ethnic Minorities (March 2003); Human Rights Watch, Iraq: The Death Penalty, Executions, and "Prison Cleansing" (March 2003); Human Rights Watch, The Iraqi Government Assault on the Marsh Arabs (January 2003); Amnesty International, Annual Country Reports (1995-2003), <http://www.amnestyusa.org/countries/iraq/index.do>; Reports of the Special Rapporteur of the UN Commission on Human Rights on the Situation of Human Rights in Iraq, <http://www.unhcr.ch/html/menu2/7/a/mirq.htm>.

54   Of course, democratization may certainly be a fortuitous by-product of valid security actions, as it is in this case.

The occupation law basis for disestablishment of government entities mirrors that under girding removal of Baathist officials. In that disestablishment was determined by the respective body's role in abusing the population, it had a direct nexus to the security situation. Resolution 1483 strengthens this position in its call upon "the Authority . . . to promote the welfare of the Iraqi people through the effective administration of the territory, including in particular working towards the restoration of conditions of security and stability and the creation of conditions in which the Iraqi people can freely determine their own political future".

Creation of the Governing Council and Iraqi ministries, together with appointment of ministers by the Governing Council, likewise comply with occupation law and relevant Security Council resolutions. As noted, the underlying premise of occupation law is that government authority will eventually revert to the occupied State.[55] In the same vein, Resolution 1483, which specifically backed formation of an Iraqi interim administration, labels free determination "of their own political future and control over their natural resources" a "right of the Iraqi people" and expresses "resolve that the day when Iraqis govern themselves must come quickly". It goes on to encourage "efforts by the people of Iraq to form a representative government".

The only question regarding creation of the Iraqi Governing Council was whether it was a mere CPA puppet or a valid interim, reasonably representative entity. World War II is replete with examples of occupiers imposing puppet governments; none were treated as legitimate by the international community.[56]

The Governing Council is hardly a puppet government. As noted, the Security Council removed any doubt when it "determined" in Resolution 1511 that "the Governing Council and its ministers are the principal bodies of the Iraqi interim administration, which, without prejudice to its further evolution, embodies the sovereignty of the State of Iraq during the transitional period until an internationally

---

55 A point best illustrated by the requirement that indigenous laws remain in place to the extent possible (Hague Regulations, *supra* note 5, art. 43; Geneva Convention IV, *supra* note 5, art. 64) and by limitations on treatment of public officials (Geneva Convention IV, *supra* note 5, art. 54).

56 For instance, the Japanese created the "State of Manchuko" in Manchuria in 1932. The League of Nations recommended that its members refuse recognition (League of Nations, Assembly Resolution, Feb. 24, 1933) after the Lytton Commission condemned the action and characterized the territory as occupied by the Japanese (Report of the Commission of Enquiry into the Sino-Japanese Dispute, 1932 Leaguie of Nations Publications, VII Political, 1932.VII.12, at 97). Indeed, the term "Quisling" derives from Vidkun Quisling, who served as Prime Minister of the puppet government emplaced by the Germans during their occupation of Norway. A notable recent example is the Kuwaiti puppet government established by the Iraqis following their 1990 invasion. Colonel Alaa Hussein served as Prime Minister, Defense Minister, and Interior Minister of "The Provisional Government of Free Kuwait" before annexation of the country by Iraq. Interestingly, Hussein fled to Norway after falling out with his mentor, Saddam Hussein. He later returned to Kuwait where, in 2000, he was sentenced to death.

recognized, representative government is established and assumes the responsibilities of the Authority".[57]

Finally, democratic elections are obviously consistent with both the Security Council's insistence on returning "governing responsibilities and authorities to the people of Iraq as soon as practicable" and the humanitarian law principle of retention of sovereignty.[58]

A possible problem is that the CPA's publication and translation policy for its orders and regulations appears to conflict with the Geneva Convention IV, Article 65, requirement that "the penal provisions enacted by the Occupying Power shall not come into force before they have been published and brought to the knowledge of the inhabitants in their own language". Regulations and orders are currently posted on the CPA website in English, but not Arabic. They appear in both languages in the Official Gazette of Iraq, *Al-waqai Al-Iraqiya*, which published laws before the conflict. However, logistical obstacles have made it difficult to publish and distribute the Gazette quickly in sufficient quantities; therefore, there is usually a delay between signature of the order or regulation and its publication in the Gazette.

Although it might appear that publishing documents in a specialist journal is insufficient to bring them "to the knowledge of the inhabitants", the official Commentary to Geneva Convention IV specifically refers to publication, *inter alia*, "in an 'Official Gazette',"[59] On the other hand, the purported entry into force of penal orders prior to publication appears contrary to Article 65.[60]

3.   Security

As occupation began, responsibility for maintaining law and order fell entirely on the Coalition forces, for the court system was inoperative and the police in disarray. A significant issue at the time, one that has continued to draw attention even as Iraqis assume security duties, was treatment of detainees. Three categories exist: prisoners of war (POW), including those captured during the occupation; security detainees; and common criminals. POWs are handled pursuant to the 1949 Geneva

---

57   UNSC Res. 1511, *see supra* note 50.
58   *Id.*
59   Commentary, *see supra* note 52, at 338.
60   While most are not, a few orders are penal in nature. For instance, Order No. 3 on Weapons Control creates offenses in relation to the possession of weapons and authorizes punishment that can include a year of imprisonment. A revised version of the Order authorizes imprisonment for up to life; in some cases, the mandatory *minimum* term is 30 years. CPA/ORD/31 December 2003/3 (revised & amended), Weapons Control. Signed on 23 May 2003 and purporting to "enter into force on the dated [sic] of signature", Order No. 2 was published in the Gazette on 17 June 2003.

Convention Relative to the Treatment of Prisoners of War, and therefore outside the scope of occupation law.[61] However, Geneva Convention IV addresses the latter categories.

In the case of criminal detainees, the CPA initially introduced a system whereby criminal suspects are brought before a "judicial officer" (judge advocate) as rapidly as possible, and provided the right to legal advice. Although lacking a right to legal advice, CPA Memorandum No. 3 entitles "security internees" to an initial appeal proceeding and the right to review of continued detention in six months. Moreover, the memorandum allows the International Committee of the Red Cross (ICRC) access to them.[62]

As of January 2004, Coalition forces had roughly 9,500 individuals in detention.[63] Within 72 hours of detention, Coalition forces categorize detainees into one of the three categories. Those assessed to be common criminals are now, given the existence of functioning Iraqi law enforcement and judicial systems, turned over to Iraqi authorities for trial. Detainees determined to have "committed a crime against US-led Coalition forces", other than those qualifying as POWs, are classified as security detainees.[64]

In January 2004, a review process began which led to the release of 506 detainees; individuals who had committed acts of violence against Coalition forces were

---

61 Geneva Convention Relative to the Treatment of Prisoners of War, Aug. 12, 1949, 6 U.S.T. 3316,75 U.N.T.S. 135. By Article 4, the following are entitled to POW status: members of the armed forces, including militias or volunteer forces forming part of the armed forces; members of other militias and volunteer corps, including resistance movements, who a commanded by a person responsible for his subordinates, display a fixed distinctive sign (uniform, patch, etc.) recognizable at a distance, openly carry their arms, and conduct operations in accordance with the laws of war; members of armed forces who profess allegiance to a government or authority not recognized by the detaining power; those who accompany the armed forces with authorization, such as civilian aircrew members; crews of merchant vessels or aircraft of the parties to the conflict, unless they benefit from more favorable treatment pursuant to international law; and inhabitants of a non-occupied territory who spontaneously take up arms to resist invading forces.

62 CPA/MEM/18 June 2003/3, Criminal Procedures. Article 136-138 of Geneva Convention IV requires information concerning protected persons to be passed to the Central Information Agency, normally run by the ICRC. This provision is extended under Article 33 of Additional Protocol I to all persons detained imprisoned or otherwise held in captivity for more than two weeks as a result of hostilities or occupation, whether or not they are Protected persons under the Fourth Convention. Memorandum No. 3 allows the ICRC to record information on detainees, thereby complying with the general requirement that detainees not be held incommunicado.

63 Coalition Provisional Authority Briefing, Jan. 8, 2004, <www.defenselink.mil/transcripts/2004/tr20040108-1121>. This excludes approximately 3,500 detainees of the Mujahedin-e Khalq, which acts as a umbrella organization for factions working for the liberation of Iran. Their status is being assessed as this article is being written.

64 UN Office for the Coordination of Humanitarian Affairs, Integrated Regional Information Network Report, Oct. 8, 2003, <http://www.cidi.org/humanitarian/hsr/iraq/ixl56>, quoting Brigadier General Janis Karpinsky.

ineligible. Judge advocates and military intelligence officers reviewed the remaining files and sent some 1200 to a three-member board (consisting of a judge advocate, military intelligence officer, and military police officer) for further assessment.[65] Release was conditioned on renouncement of violence and existence of a "guarantor", "a prominent person in his community or a religious or tribal leader who will accept responsibility for the good conduct of the individual being set free".[66]

Some have expressed concern about the grounds for holding detainees. An incident in November 2003 drew particular attention. Reportedly, US forces arrested the wife and daughter of General Izzat Ibrahim al-Douri, former Vice-Chair of Iraq's Revolutionary Command Council, in an effort to locate the general. A US military spokesperson asked about the incident was quoted as saying "they may be able to shed light on any situation that will improve our general position of finding al-Douri or anyone else". The incident generated a letter from Human Rights Watch Executive Director Kenneth Roth to the Secretary of Defense. Roth voiced concern that the family members remained in US custody and that "US officials have provided no information as to the reason for taking these family members of a wanted person into custody".[67]

Coalition forces have progressively turned security duties over to Iraqi organizations.[68] Most significantly, the CPA retained the existing police forces, albeit subject to de-Baathification.[69] Additionally, early in the occupation, Coalition commanders authorized the continued operation of various unofficial protection organizations, many of which had religious connections. This practice proved ill-advised and hastened attempts to bolster the authority of official law enforcement agencies.[70]

In contrast, the CPA disestablished both the regular and special armed forces in May 2003.[71] Citing the Resolution 1483 call for assistance in creating "conditions

---

65   Edward Wong, Iraq Regime to Release 500 Security Detainees, International Herald Tribune Online, Jan. 7, 2004, <http://www.iht.com/articles/123996>.

66   L. Paul Bremer, Conditional Release Announcement, Jan. 7, 2004, <http://www.cpairaq.org/transcripts/Jan7Bremer_Conditional>.

67   Human Rights Watch, Letter to Defense Secretary Donald Rumsfeld, Jan. 12, 2004, <http://www.hrw.org/English/docs/2004/01/12/usint6921_txt>.

68   Coalition forces remaining in Iraq to perform stabilization, security, and relief duties are sizable. As of early February 2004, US troop strength in Iraq was approximately 120,000, whereas 34 other States have contributed an additional 26,500. US Forces Order of Battle, Feb. 11, 2004, <http://www.globalsecurity.org/military/ops/iraq_orbat>; Non-US Forces in Iraq, Feb. 6, 2004, <http:// www.globalsecurity.org/military/ops/iraq_orbat_coalition>.

69   The desired size of the force is 71,000. By August 2004, the force consisted of over 68,000. Anthony H. Cordesman, Nation Building in Iraq: The Good News, the Mixed News, and the Bad News, CSIS Report, Jan. 28, 2004

70   An example is the Fallujah Protection Force that was involved in a mistaken firefight with US forces on 12 September 2003. At least eight Iraqis were killed. Iraqi Police Killed in Confusing Firefight, CNN.com, Sept. 12, 2003, <edition.cnn.com/TRANSCRIPTS/0309/12/nfcnn.01>.

71   CPA Order No. 2, *see supra* note 11.

of security and stability", the CPA subsequently authorized an all-volunteer Iraqi Army,[72] and promulgated a Code of Military Discipline.[73] The "New Iraqi Army" is tasked with "military defense of the nation, including defense of the national territory and the military protection of the security of critical installations, facilities, infrastructure, lines of the communication and supply [sic] and population". Former Iraqi military personnel are eligible for service subject to lack of prior involvement with the Baath Party.[74]

Although only Iraqis hold command positions, "[s]upreme command, control and administrative authority" reside on "an interim basis with the Administrator of the CPA as the civilian Commander-in-Chief pending transfer of such authority to an internationally recognized, representative government, established by the people of Iraq". Further, when operating with Coalition forces, "operational or tactical command . . . may be vested in an officer of Coalition Forces of rank superior to that of the commander of such Iraqi units", as designated by the CPA Administrator.[75]

The CPA has also founded the Civil Defense Corps (CDC), Facilities Protection Service (FPS), and Defense Support Agency (DSA).[76] The CDC is a "security and emergency service agency" intended to "compliment operations conducted by Coalition military forces in Iraq to counter organized groups and individuals employing violence against the people of Iraq and their national infrastructure". It is distinguishable from the police and army in that it "perform[s] operations that exceed the capacity of the police", but "is not subject to the orders of the New Iraqi Army chain of command".[77] Essentially, the CDC is a paramilitary force that operates under the authority of the Administrator and supervision of Coalition forces.[78]

---

72   CPA/ORD/8 August 2003/22, Creation of a New Iraqi Army. The transitional nature of CPA orders is recognized in that the "continued existence of the 'New Iraqi Army' beyond the period of CPA's authority" is made "subject to a decision by the future internationally recognized, representative government, established by the people of Iraq".

73   CPA/ORD/20 August 2003/23, Creation of a Code of Military Discipline for the New Iraqi Army. As with Order 22, the authority cited for creation of the Code was the Resolution 1483 appeal to assist the Iraqi people in the creation of "conditions of security and stability in Iraq".

74   Three divisions are planned by September 2004, but recruiting and training are proceeding slowly. Cordesman, *see supra* note 69.

75   CPA Order No. 22, *see supra* note 72.

76   The CPA also established a Department of Border Enforcement within the Ministry of Interior to coordinate all border related functions previously conducted by a range of ministries. These include border police, customs police, customs inspections, immigration inspections, and passport issuance and inspections. CPA/ORD/24 August 2003/26, Creation of the Department of Border Enforcement. Order 16 sets forth the policies the department will implement. CPA/ORD/1 December 2003/16 (revising Order of 27 June).

77   CPA/ORD/3 September 2003/28, Establishment of the Iraqi Civil Defense Corps.

78   The desired CDC force structure is 40 battalions (40,000 troops) by March 2004. As of January 2004, it consisted of nearly 20,000 personnel. Cordesman, *see supra* note 69.

More benign, the FPS consists of "trained, armed, uniformed entities charged with providing security for ministry and governorate offices, government infrastructure, and fixed sites under the direction and control of government ministries and governorate administrations".[79] By contrast, the DSA lacks an operational role. Rather, it is a civilian entity charged with administrative and logistic support of the New Iraqi Army.[80]

3.1. *Legal Assessment*

Human rights law and domestic criminal law govern detention of common criminals. In light of the hearing before a law-trained judicial officer, access to counsel, and transfer to Iraqi authorities for investigation and prosecution, CPA policy complies with both. It is worthy of note that Coalition authorities do not exercise criminal jurisdiction themselves, thereby rendering inapplicable various Geneva Convention IV provisions.[81]

However, Geneva Convention IV also addresses detention of civilians for security reasons. Article 78 provides that "[i]f the Occupying Power considers it necessary, for imperative reasons of security, to take safety measures concerning protected persons, it may, at the most, subject them to assigned residence or internment." Such determinations "shall be made according to a regular procedure" which "shall include the right of appeal". There is furthermore a requirement for a periodic review "if possible every six months".[82]

Internees have specific rights of communication and family visits.[83] However, "a person under definite suspicion of activity hostile to the security of the Occupying Power . . . shall, in those cases where absolute military security so requires, be regarded as having forfeited rights of communication" under Geneva Convention IV, although they must be "treated with humanity"[84] and "granted the full rights and privileges of a protected person . . . at the earliest date consistent with the security of the . . . Occupying Power".[85]

Despite some confusion over terminology (detainees v. internees), the provi-

---

79   CPA/ORD/4 September 2003/27, Establishment of the Facilities Protection Corps.
80   CPA/ORD/19 September 2003/42, Creation of the Defense Support Agency.
81   Geneva Convention IV, *see supra* note 5, arts. 66-77.
82   The convention lays down detailed provisions on conditions of internment. *Id.*, arts. 79-135.
83   Geneva Convention, *see supra* note 5, arts. 106-108, 116.
84   Attention is drawn here to Article 75 of Protocol Additional I, which lays down certain fundamental guarantees for persons "who do not benefit from more favorable treatment" under the Geneva Conventions or Protocol. This provision is now accepted as customary international law.
85   Geneva Convention, *supra* note 5, art. 5. Protocol Additional I, *see supra* note 5, art. 45, limits the forfeiture only to cases where the person is held as a spy.

sions of Memorandum No. 3 fulfill these requirements. Yet, because there is little public information on the conditions under which detainees are being held, it is difficult confidently to assess their legality. This is particularly apposite regarding communication rights, in light of reports of detainees being held incommunicado.[86] Also problematic are reports of detention of family members of wanted individuals. If true, it is hard to see how such detentions can be brought within the terms of Geneva Convention IV.

Establishment of the various security organizations is generally well-based in either humanitarian or UN law. Clearly, occupiers have an affirmative duty to fill the security vacuum left by the absence, removal, or ineffectiveness of the indigenous security forces, for Hague Regulation IV, Article 43, specifically requires an occupant to "take all the measures in his power to restore, and ensure as far as possible, public order and safety".

Security Council resolutions provide an even firmer basis for the CPA measures. Resolution 1483 charges the CPA with "working towards the restoration of conditions of security and stability". More to the point, Resolution 1511 authorizes "a multinational force under unified command to take all necessary measures to contribute to the maintenance of security and stability in Iraq", and calls upon "Member States and international and regional organizations to contribute to the training and equipping of Iraqi police and security forces". On the specific issue of the police, Resolution 1483 tasked the UN Special Representative, working with the CPA, to encourage "international efforts to rebuild the capacity of the Iraqi civilian police force". Although the UN withdrew most of its expatriate staff after the bombing of its Baghdad headquarters, the provision implicitly acknowledges the civilian police force's legitimacy and CPA's support thereof.

Also relevant is the Hague Regulations prohibition on compelling "nationals of the hostile party to take part in the operations of war directed against their own country, even if they were in the belligerent's service before the commencement of the war".[87] Geneva Convention IV widens the prohibition by forbidding individuals from being impressed into the occupier's armed or auxiliary forces.[88] Although the convention does not prohibit creation of indigenous security organizations (or

---

86 In July 2003, for instance, Amnesty International expressed concerns on both the lack of family visits and the Coalition forces' "failure to notify the families of detainees of their arrest and place of detention". It expressed dissatisfaction with Coalition assurances that "Humanitarian Assistance Centers" were being established throughout Iraq at which on-line information about detainees would be available. Amnesty International, Memorandum on Concerns Relating to Law and Order, MDE: 14/157/2003, July 23, 2003, <http://web.amnesty.org/library/Index/ENGMDE141572003>.

87 Hague Regulations, *see supra* note 5, art. 23.

88 Geneva Convention IV, *see supra* note 5, art. 51. It also forbids recruitment efforts for this purpose.

recruiting for existing ones), the official Commentary states that the prohibition "referred generally to all enlistment in the armed forces of the Occupying Power, whatever the theater of operations and whoever the opposing forces might be – the armed forces of the non-occupied portion of the territory, of a government in exile, of an allied State, or of resistance movements operating within the occupied territory".[89]

In light of this interpretation, retention of supreme command by the CPA Administrator might make use of the New Iraqi Army or other Iraqi security organizations in a counter-resistance role problematic. Obviously, occupation authorities must retain some control over indigenous armed units operating within the occupied zone. However, under occupation law, their creation must not be a subterfuge for augmenting the occupying military with additional combat forces. Whether or not the Iraqi military's intended usage rises to this level appears to have been rendered moot by Resolution 1511's emphasis on "the importance of establishing effective Iraqi police and security forces in maintaining law, order, and security and combating terrorism". Given resistance attacks not only on Coalition forces, but also international organizations, non-governmental organizations, and interim Iraqi governmental entities such as the police, counter-resistance operations fall within 1511's ambit.

4.   Relief

In May 2003, Administrator Bremer established the Development Fund for Iraq (DFI), held by the Central Bank of Iraq.[90] The Security Council noted the Fund's establishment in Resolution 1483, and directed 95% of future Iraqi oil and gas export sales revenue into it. It further authorized transfer of $1billion from the Oil for Food Programme established in 1995 to support humanitarian relief of the Iraqi people.[91] Resolution 1483 provided for eventual closure of that program, transfer of residual funds to the DFI, and shift of responsibility for on-going operations to the CPA within six months.[92] The same day, President Bush issued an Executive Order protecting the fund from attachment and other judicial processes.[93] Administrative guidance for DFI's operation was promulgated in June.[94]

---

89   Commentary, *see supra* note 52, at 293.
90   Action cited in Executive Order Protecting the Development Fund for Iraq and Certain Other Property in which Iraq has an Interest, May 22, 2003.
91   UNSC Res. 986 (April 14, 1995).
92   Termination of the program occurred in November 2003.
93   Executive Order, *see supra* note 90.
94   CPA/REG/15 June 2003/2, Development Fund for Iraq.

Fund disbursements have supported the "wheat purchase program, the currency exchange program, the electricity and oil infrastructure programs, equipment for Iraqi security forces, and Iraqi civil service salaries and ministry budget operations".[95] By late January 2004, the Fund balance stood at $8.5 billion, with nearly $2 billion already disbursed.[96]

The CPA has actively sought further relief commitments on behalf of the Iraqi population. To "support, encourage and facilitate participation of the international community in relief, recovery and development efforts", it established the Council for International Coordination in June 2003.[97] The Council, consisting of representatives from various States, is appointed by, and works under the direction of, the Administrator. Additionally, the CPA established a "Strategic Review Board", with primarily Iraqi membership, to "provide overall policy guidance with respect to multilateral and bilateral financial and economic development assistance for Iraq" in a prioritized and non-discriminatory manner.[98]

US relief efforts are managed by the Agency for International Development (USAID), albeit under CPA control.[99] In 2003, the United States government provided over $2 billion for direct emergency relief and reconstruction.[100] The Department for International Development runs the British programs, to which £248 million has been committed through April 2004. A further £296 million is pledged through 2006.[101]

The European Union has promised 100 million euros in support, climbing to 200 million by the end of 2004.[102] Aid has flowed in from such other sources as individual States (particularly via the Madrid Donors' Conference),[103] the UN, ICRC, national Red Cross societies, and non-governmental organizations. Total aid funds available as of January 2004 are $58.7 billion, $22.7b of which has been committed.[104]

---

95 Coalition Provisional Authority, The Development Fund for Iraq,<http://www.cpa-iraq.org/budget/DFI_intro1.htm>.

96 Coalition Provisional Authority, DFI Balance, <http://www.cpa-iraq.org/budget/DFI_03feb2004.xls>.

97 CPA/REG/17 June 2003/5, Council for International Coordination.

98 CPA/REG/5 December 2003/7, International Donor Assistance.

99 For a discussion of USAID efforts, *see* <http://www.usaid.gov>.

100 USAID, Iraq Reconstruction and Humanitarian Relief, Weekly Update 17, Feb. 3, 2004, <http://www.usaid.gov/iraq/updates/feb04/iraq_fs17_020304>.

101 For a discussion of DFID efforts, *see* <www.dfid.gov.uk>.

102 Department for International Development, Iraq Update No. 72, Feb. 2, 2004, <http://www.dfid.gov.uk/News/PressReleases/files/iraq_update72_2feb04>.

103 Held 23-25 October 2003. More than $33 billion was pledged. Major commitments were made by: Japan, $5 billion; World Bank, $3-5 billion in loans; IMF, $2.5-4.25 billion in loans; Korea, $200 million; Canada, over $150 million. Department of State, Madrid Donors' Conference: Helping the Iraqi People Build a New Iraq, Nov. 6, 2003, <http://www.state.gov/r/pa/ei/rls/26038>.

104 Cordesman, *see supra* note 69.

Many signs of recovery are promising. For instance, health care exceeds that available before the war. Nevertheless, problems remain. Water treatment plants function at 65% of pre-war levels; sewer facilities, irrigation water, and telecommunications assets fall below the level required; agricultural reform proceeds slowly; and although electrical production has reached pre-war levels, supply falls well below need. A major concern is transportation, for recovery in other areas depends on reliable lines of communication. Unfortunately, roads are insecure, commercial air traffic is limited, and petrol prices on the black market are 10 times that authorized.[105] Complicating matters is the security environment, which has caused many relief entities to downsize or cancel their programs.

To coordinate allocation of relief and reconstruction resources (whether seized, loaned, or granted), the CPA established the Program Review Board, which ensures "that funds available to the CPA for providing relief to, and the recovery of Iraq, are managed in a transparent manner and consistent with applicable law, for and on behalf of the Iraq people".[106] The Board consists of the relevant CPA department heads, the Coalition Force Commander, representatives from Coalition countries, and the Iraqi Ministry of Finance.[107]

4.1. *Legal Assessment*

Occupation law regarding relief is relatively explicit, particularly Geneva Convention IV. Under the convention, the occupying power must ensure "the food and medical supplies of the population; it should, in particular, bring in the necessary foodstuffs, medical stores and other articles if the resources of the occupied territory are inadequate."[108] Additional provisions require the occupier to permit other sources to provide relief when the population is inadequately supplied.[109] However, it may reasonably limit aid delivery for "imperative reasons of security".[110]

Occupation forces must further ensure and maintain "to the fullest extent of the means available to it . . . with the cooperation of national and local authorities, the medical and hospital establishments and services, public health and hygiene in

---

105 *Id.*
106 CPA/REG/15 June 2003/3, Program Review Board.
107 There are a number of non-voting members, including representatives of the International Monetary Fund, World Bank, and UN Special Representative.
108 Geneva Convention IV, *see supra* note 5, art. 55. Protocol Additional I, *see supra* note 5, art. 65, lists the following additional material that must be provided: "clothing, bedding, means of shelter, other supplies essential to the survival of the civilian population of the occupied territory, and objects necessary for religious worship". This provision is applicable to the occupation of Iraq as a restatement of customary international law.
109 *Id.*, arts. 59-61.
110 *Id.*, art. 62.

the occupied territory".[111] Additionally, they must permit "special organizations of a non-military character" to continue operating "for the purpose of ensuring the living conditions of the civilian population by the maintenance of the essential public utility services by the distribution of relief and by the organization of rescues".[112] Specific mention is made of the national Red Cross/Red Crescent Society and "other relief societies".

It is worth noting that a decade of sanctions had substantially reduced the Iraqi living standard. This is relevant because humanitarian law requirements vis-à-vis the civilian population are objective in nature. A minimum level of care is required, not simply a return to the *status quo ante bellum*. On the other hand, both the prevailing security environment and the humanitarian situation at the time occupation commenced condition the adequacy of the occupier's actions.

The Security Council has echoed occupation law's concern with care of the civilian population. Resolution 1483 calls upon "all Member States in a position to do so to respond immediately to the humanitarian appeals of the United Nations and other international organizations for Iraq and to help meet the humanitarian and other needs of the Iraqi people by providing food, medical supplies, and resources necessary for reconstruction and rehabilitation of Iraq's economic infrastructure". To assist in this end, it lifted trade sanctions (other than on armaments). The resolution also noted the CPA's establishment of the DFI, underlining that it "shall be used in a transparent manner to meet the humanitarian needs of the Iraqi people [*inter alia*] . . ., " and acknowledging that the CPA Administrator disburses Fund proceeds at his discretion.

Contextual evaluation of US and UK relief and reconstruction efforts, even applying the requisite objective standard, leaves little doubt that the impressive efforts to provide emergency relief and long-term reconstruction, as well as the great pains taken to involve many additional sources of aid, meet the requirements of humanitarian law and comply with Security Council dictates. Indeed, the DFI has received direct approval and lines of funding from the Security Council. The transparency and oversight offered by the Program Review Board is further indication of the Coalition's commitment to effective relief, as is establishment of the Council for International Coordination and Iraqi Strategic Review Board.

---

111 *Id.*, art. 56. Protocol Additional I, *see supra* note 5, art. 14 places limitations on the requisition of civilian medical units, a restatement of customary international law. Further, art. 15 requires the occupying power to "afford civilian medical personnel in occupied territories every assistance to enable them to perform, to the best of their ability, their humanitarian functions". Coalition forces have not requisitioned Iraqi medical material, but instead have provided extensive medical care to the Iraqi population and undertaken efforts to restore the Iraqi medical system.
112 *Id.*, art. 63. *See also* Protocol Additional I, *see supra* note 5, art. 17.

5.   Property Concerns

As a practical matter, every occupying force must make some use of pre-existing facilities in the occupied territory. The CPA has recognized its "obligation to responsibly manage Iraqi public property on behalf of the Iraqi people" in CPA Order No. 9.[113] The order provides for a Register of Property and Assets "documenting relevant information concerning all public property occupied, used, managed and assigned by the CPA". A "Facility Manager" is charged with administering CPA activity and working "with the Iraqi Ministry of Housing and Construction, in order to facilitate the transfer of public property management responsibilities to the future government of Iraq".

Baath Party property and assets are treated separately, in CPA Order No. 4.[114] The order encompasses "all movable and immovable property, records and data, cash, funds, realizable assets and liquid capital, in whatever form maintained and wherever located, used, possessed, or controlled by the Baath Party, its officials and members, and all residences occupied by Baath officials or members assigned to them by the Party, a member of the Baath Party or other State instrumentality and that were not purchased for full value by those officials or members". Characterized as State assets, all such property is made "subject to seizure by the CPA on behalf, and for the benefit of the people of Iraq". Anyone in possession or control of Baath Party property is required to "preserve those assets, promptly inform local Coalition authorities, and immediately turn them over, as directed by those authorities. Continued possession, transfer, sale, use, conversion, or concealment of such assets following the date of [the] order is prohibited and may be punished". Appeals to a Confiscation Appeal Tribunal are possible, although only on the basis that the property or assets were purchased at full value or are not Party property. The order authorizes penalties for noncompliance.

Individuals or groups deemed to be in illegal occupation of State real property, including Baathist Party property, may be evicted.[115] The Commander of Coalition Forces makes these determinations, with appeal possible to the CPA Administrator.

As Coalition forces and the CPA have primarily used public property,[116] private

---

113 CPA/ORD/8 June 2003/9, Management and Use of Iraqi Public Property.
114 CPA/ORD/25 May 2003/4, Management of Property and Assets of the Iraqi Baath Party.
115 CPA/ORD/8 June 2003/6, Eviction of Persons Illegally Occupying Public Buildings.
116 Both Coalition forces and CPA officials are operating from former governmental or party property. For instance, CPA headquarters is located in the Presidential Palace in Baghdad, whereas the UK Divisional Headquarters in Basra is contained within the Airport Terminal Buildings. In many cases, military forces have created camps to house their operations, particularly around the international airport in Baghdad. CPA officials are often housed in private hotels, for which they pay.

property issues center on claims for damage caused by Coalition forces, destruction of residences, and reconciliation of contested ownership. With regard to the first, both the US and UK armed forces have well-established claims programs; neither includes reimbursement for legitimate war damage, but both parties are actively paying occupation claims.[117]

In a troubling matter, Coalition forces have reportedly bombed and otherwise destroyed residences as a "collective punishment" in areas where attacks have taken place. For example, it is reported that on 10 November 2003 US soldiers ordered individuals living in a farmhouse near the town of *al-Mahmudiya* to leave. Shortly thereafter, two F-16s destroyed the building, in which weapons had supposedly been found. This action was "apparently carried out in retaliation for an attack a few days earlier by Iraqi armed groups against a US convoy which resulted in the killing of a US Army officer". Amnesty International has further reported that US forces destroyed at least 16 houses in Tikrit during November 2003.[118] US Central Command confirmed that during Operation Ivy Cyclone II, which was underway in the area, counter-insurgency forces destroyed twelve "anti-Coalition safe houses and buildings".[119]

Resolving private property lease and ownership disputes during the occupation has been especially complex. Poor economic conditions have placed heavy rental payment burdens on tenants. Concerned that "widespread eviction of tenants will have a destabilizing effect on security and well-being of Iraqi citizens", but desiring to balance fairly rights and obligations of landlords and tenants, the CPA has amended the Law of Estate Lease to preclude immediate eviction for rent non-payment.[120]

Additionally, Baathist policies over the past decades had caused substantial population shifts. For instance, many Kurds were forcibly resettled in the South, while Arabs had been compelled to reside in the northern Kurdish region. Additionally, considerable extrajudicial confiscation and reallocation of private property had taken place, particularly in the case of property owned by opponents of the regime.

Viewing conflicting assertions of property ownership as a threat to public order and security, in June 2003 the CPA proposed an Iraqi Property Reconciliation Facility to collect real property claims and promptly resolve them "on a voluntary basis in a fair and judicious manner".[121] Although envisaged as run by a UN agency, withdrawal

---

117 E.g., US Army Regulation 27-20, Claims, July 1, 2003. In January 2004, for instance, the Coalition Commander in Iraq reported that over 15,000 claims had been submitted, with 11,000 settled for a total in excess of $2.2 million Combined Joint Task Force 7 Briefing, Jan. 29, 2004, <http://www.defenselink.mil/transcripts/2004/tr20040129-0381>.

118 Both reports are contained in Amnesty International Press Release, MDE14/177/2003(Public), Nov. 20, 2003.

119 CENTCOM News Release 03-11-34, Nov. 19, 2003, <http://www.centcom.mil/CENTCOMNews/News_Release.asp?NewsRelease=20031134>.

120 CPA/ORD/7 September 2003/29, Amendment to the Law of State Lease.

121 CPA/REG/26 June 2003/4, Establishment of the Iraqi Property Reconciliation Facility.

of UN staff following the bombing of its headquarters precluded this step. In January 2004, the CPA filled the void by delegating to the Governing Council the authority to create by statute the Iraqi Property Claims Commission (IPCC).[122]

The IPCC will consist of regional commissions in each governorate, with an Appellate Division established as a chamber of Iraq's Court of Cassation. Regional commissions are comprised of a judge appointed by the Council of Judges, the governorate Office of Property Registration Director, and the governorate State Property Director (or their representatives). The process is entirely written, claims may be filed regarding property in the hands of either the government or private individuals, and the period covered stretches back to 1968.[123]

An early concern regarding property arose from reported widespread damage to, and looting of, cultural property. Retrospectively, such accounts appear exaggerated. Nevertheless, they drew international attention to the plight of Iraq's cultural heritage after decades of neglect, sanctions, and conflict. Coalition forces, particularly US forces in Baghdad, were criticized for failing to prevent looting in the immediate aftermath of the regime's collapse. However, most looting appears to have taken place at a time of tenuous Coalition control of the main population centers; thus, it is debatable whether the strict obligations of occupation law applied at that time. Moreover, once criticism surfaced, Coalition forces acted quickly to remedy the situation.

One of the CPA's earliest actions was to appoint a "Civil Administrator for Iraqi Cultural Heritage", who in turn chose former Iraqi officials in the Ministry of Culture and Department of Antiquities as advisers.[124] Soon thereafter, UNESCO sent an experts mission to report on the situation. Since then there have been numerous follow-up missions and meetings to assess damage and loss, secure cultural sites and property, and attempt recovery of unaccounted for items and those taken from the country during the previous regime or in the immediate aftermath of its collapse. Additional UNESCO measures include fund-raising, appointment of a Liaison to the CPA, establishment of "an International Coordination Committee for the Safeguarding of Iraqi Cultural Heritage", and finalization of a needs assessment. Throughout, the CPA has cooperated closely with UNESCO. In September 2003, the Governing Council appointed an interim Minister of Culture with the CPA's approval.

---

122 CPA/REG/14 January 2004/8, Delegation of Authority Regarding an Iraq Property Claims Commission. This Regulation rescinded Regulation 4, *see supra* note 121. The terms of a statute had been previously negotiated between the Governing Council and the CPA.
123 CPA/REG/14 January 2004/8/ANNEX, Iraq Property Claims Commission.
124 Report of the UNESCO First Assessment Mission to Baghdad, 17-20 May, 2003. Reports on all missions and meetings are available at <portal.unesco.org>.

5.1. *Legal Assessment*

Both the Hague Regulations and Geneva Convention IV address the treatment of public property during occupation. The Regulations allow an occupier to seize "cash, funds, and realizable securities" belonging to the State, as well as its movable State property.[125] By contrast, the occupier may use public buildings, land, and other public immovable property, but only as an administrator thereof, and must safeguard its value and condition.[126] This implicitly recognizes that the property will be returned to the indigenous government as it resumes authority.

Under the Hague regulations, an occupier may requisition private property and services, but only when so ordered by the Occupation commander, and solely for the needs of occupation forces. If cash payment is impracticable, a receipt must be provided, with reimbursement thereof as soon as possible.[127] Seizure or unnecessary destruction of property belonging to municipalities or institutions dedicated to religion, charity, education, or the arts and sciences is prohibited.[128]

Geneva Convention IV bars the destruction of either real or personal public and private property unless "rendered absolutely necessary by military operations".[129] The convention also forbids collective punishment such as destroying the property of an individual for an offense he or she has not committed. Similarly, any form of reprisal against a protected person or their property is prohibited.[130]

Cultural property is subject to a special protection regime during occupation. The Hague Regulations forbid "seizure, destruction or willful damage" to institutions dedicated to religion, charity and education [and] the arts and sciences", as well as "historic monuments [and] works of art and science".[131] Resolution 1483, given the looting of cultural property that had previously taken place, requires Member States to "take appropriate steps to facilitate the safe return to Iraqi institutions of Iraqi cultural property and other items of archeological, historical, cultural, rare scientific, and religious importance illegally removed from the Iraq National Museum, the National Library, and other locations in Iraq since . . . including by

---

125 Hague Regulations, *see supra* note 5, art. 53.
126 *Id.*, art. 55.
127 *Id.*, art. 52.
128 *Id.*, art. 56.
129 Geneva Convention IV, *supra* note 5, art. 53.
130 *Id.*, art 33. Reprisals are illegal actions taken to cause someone to cease and desist from their own illegal conduct.
131 Art. 56. Although Iraq is a party to 1954 Convention for the Protection of Cultural Property in the Event of Armed Conflict, the United States and United Kingdom are not. The First Protocol thereto deals specifically with occupation. Hague Protocol for the Protection of Cultural Property in the Event of Armed Conflict, May 14, 1954, 249 U.N.T.S. 358.

establishing a prohibition on trade in or transfer of such items and items with respect to which reasonable suspicion exists that they have been illegally removed".

There is little doubt that the bulk of Coalition policy regarding Iraqi public and cultural property complies with occupation law. While the CPA policy on eviction relief might appear to violate the Hague Regulations, Article 46, stipulation that "private property . . . must be respected", as well as Article 43's requirement to respect the laws in force, the fact that the relevant order was founded on a security concern justifies its issuance. Further, the stability that eviction relief results in fosters Resolution 1483's mandate to "promote the welfare of the Iraqi people through the effective administration of the territory".

By contrast, the policy of treating the property of Baathist officials as State property is problematical. The definitions used in Order No. 4 are extremely broad; to characterize property purchased at less than full value as State property merely because its purchaser was a Party official or member appears to go too far. In cases where the amortization of the property's value indicates the transaction was a sham, this may be appropriate, but to categorize all amortized transactions together fails to distinguish cases where there may be a genuine reason for reduction. Rather, the proper course would be a claim by the disadvantaged party that title did not pass as a matter of law because of duress or other obstacle. The Iraq Property Claims Commission provides a convenient forum for making such assertions, at least with regard to private property transactions.

US and UK claims procedures for compensating owners of private property damaged during the occupation fulfill occupation law requirements. On the other hand, the reported destruction of private property as a form of collective punishment or reprisal, if true, would be a direct violation of Geneva Convention IV. Indeed, "extensive destruction and appropriation of property, not justified by military necessity and carried out unlawfully and wantonly" is a "grave breach".[132] Of course, if the houses were being used for hostile purposes at the time of destruction, or if future use was highly likely and only destruction could preclude it, then they were military objectives subject to destruction.[133]

Insofar as the Coalition has sought to resolve private property disputes arising out of the activities of the previous regime, it would appear to be going well beyond

---

132 Geneva Convention IV, *see supra* note 5, art. 147. The article requires States Party search for those alleged to have committed or ordered the grave breach and try them, regardless of nationality, in their own courts. Alternatively, they may hand such persons over to another State Party once that State has made out a prima facie case.

133 Military objectives are "objects which by their nature, location, purpose or use make an effective contribution to military action and whose total or partial destruction, capture or neutralization, in the circumstances ruling at the time, offers a definite military advantage". Protocol Additional I, *see supra* note 5, art. 52.2.

anything required under humanitarian law. However, if the failure to settle such disputes would have a detrimental effect on public order, then there may be an obligation on the occupying authority to take some action. Given the pervasiveness of the problem across Iraq, this appears to be the case.

Finally, although there were initially difficulties with respect to cultural property, particularly as regards charges of inaction during looting of the Baghdad Museum, the CPA has since actively cooperated with UNESCO and the Governing Council in safeguarding Iraq's cultural heritage.

6.   The Economy

In June, the CPA suspended most tariffs, customs duties, import taxes, licensing fees, and similar surcharges for goods imported into or exported from Iraq for 2003.[134] Later, it imposed a 5% "reconstruction levy" on imports from 1 January 2004; resulting revenue may only be used "to assist the Iraqi people and support the reconstruction of Iraq".[135] Certain goods, such as food, clothing, and books, were exempted from the levy.

The CPA set forth its initial tax policy in September 2003.[136] Order No. 37 began by recognizing that tax collections "are for the benefit of the Iraqi people, and, as far as possible, are in accordance with the rules of assessment and incidence in effect under existing law". Most taxes from 16 April through year's end were suspended and individual and corporate income tax rates for 2004 were capped at 15%. The CPA retained existing tax procedures, unless and until amended by the CPA Administrator or an "internationally recognized, representative government".

Because the previous regime interfered with the banking system for its own purposes, the CPA acted to ensure the Central Bank of Iraq's (CBI) independence. Specifically, it granted the CBI authority to "determine and implement monetary and credit policy without the approval of the Ministry of Finance".[137] After revising banking law generally in September 2003,[138] the CPA tasked the CBI with converting the existing Iraqi currency into the "New Iraqi dinar".[139] This measure was

---

134 CPA/ORD/8 June 2003/12, Trade Liberalization Policy.
135 CPA/ORD/19 September 2003/38, Reconstruction Levy. Subsequently, this date was changed to 1 March 2004 by CPA/ORD/31 December 2003/47, Amendment to Coalition Provisional Authority No. 38.
136 CPA/ORD/19 September 2003/37, Tax Strategy for 2003. Excepted were hotel and restaurant taxes, transfer of real property taxes, car sale fees, and petrol excise duties.
137 CPA/ORD/7 July 2003/18, Measures to Ensure the Independence of the Central Bank of Iraq.
138 CPA/ORD/19 September 2003/40, Bank Law, with the law set forth in Annex A thereto.
139 CPA/ORD/14 October 2003/43, New Iraqi Dinar Banknotes. The CPA set the conversion rate.

necessary not only to remove Saddam Hussein's image from currency, but also because two types of notes were in circulation, thereby sowing confusion.[140]

To facilitate reintegration into the world economy, the CPA created the Trade Bank of Iraq to provide "financial and related services to facilitate the importation and exportation of goods and services to and from Iraq in order to benefit the economy of Iraq".[141] Its capital was initially drawn from the DFI and profits generated are returned thereto. Further, the CPA has replaced the existing foreign investment law.[142] The new law effectively opens investment to foreign investors on terms no less favorable than those applicable to an Iraqi investor, except as specifically provided to the contrary. This move caused some Iraqis to express concern regarding foreign control of their economy.

Finally, a particular problem facing the CPA was the fact that salaries for government workers were largely reflective of loyalty to the former regime rather than performance or responsibility. Thus, the CPA imposed a "transparent" compensation system, in particular, by creating a salary table based on the grade of the employee, with allowance made for positions of "risk".[143]

6.1. *Legal Assessment*

The Hague Regulations require retention of the preexisting tax structure "as far as is possible", but in return the occupier is "bound to defray the expenses of the administration of the occupied territory to the same extent as the legitimate Government was so bound".[144] Additional taxes may be levied only "for the needs of the army or of the administration of the territory in question".[145] Any taxes or money contributions so raised "shall only be effected as far as possible in accordance with the rules of assessment and incidence of the taxes in force".[146] CPA tax policies meet these requirements.

As to labor matters, under Geneva Convention IV the local population may be compelled to work, but only tasks necessary "either for the needs of the army of occupation, or for the public utility services, or for the feeding, sheltering, clothing, transportation or health of the population of the occupied country".[147] Additionally,

---

140 At the time of the order, the "Swiss dinar", issued until 1989, and its replacement, the "1990 dinar", were in circulation.
141 CPA/ORD/17 July 2003/20, Trade Bank of Iraq.
142 CPA/ORD/19 September 2003/39, Foreign Investment.
143 CPA Order No. 30, *see supra* note 34.
144 Hague Regulations, *see supra* note 5, art. 48.
145 *Id.*, art. 49.
146 *Id.*, art. 51.
147 Geneva Convention IV, *see supra* note 5, art. 51.

creating unemployment or restricting employment opportunity to induce the population to work for the occupying power is forbidden.[148] Most significantly, existing
labor law remains applicable. Coalition policies comply with these requirements
generally, while appropriately discarding prior discriminatory policies.

There is no specific mandate in occupation law for economic reconstruction.
Resolution 1483, on the other hand, recognized the pressing need to rebuild Iraq's
economy. Amongst the responsibilities it gave the Special Representative was, "in
coordination with the Authority, . . . promoting economic reconstruction and the conditions for sustainable development, including through coordination with national
and regional organizations, as appropriate, civil society, donors, and the international financial institutions".[149] The resolution also called upon "international financial institutions . . . to assist the people of Iraq in the reconstruction and development
of the economy". In Resolution 1511, the Security Council reemphasized the development imperative and appealed "to Member States and the international financial
institutions to strengthen their efforts to assist the people of Iraq in the reconstruction and development of their economy". Unquestionably, Resolutions 1483 and
1511 provide the CPA authority for activities going well beyond the mere preservation of existing economic structures and conditions.[150]

7.   Legal System

In early June, the CPA turned its attention to the legal system.[151] Its first step was
to recognize in Order No. 7 that "the former regime used certain provisions of the
penal code as a tool of repression in violation of internationally recognized human
rights standards".[152] The CPA therefore ordered the last penal code in force before

---

148 *Id.,* art. 52.

149 The US decision to limit US-funded reconstruction contracts to companies from the United States,
Iraq, Coalition partners and troop-contributing States has generated much controversy. However,
occupation law imposes no limitation on the manner in which relief and reconstruction funds are
expended. Deputy Secretary of Defense, Determination and Findings, Dec. 5, 2003, <http://www.useu.be/
Categories/GlobalAffairs/Iraq/Dec1003IraqReconstrContracts>.

150 Tellingly, both the Bank Law and the Foreign Investment orders referred to specific provisions of
Resolution 1483 as their authority.

151 Note that the CPA, Coalition forces, and foreign liaison missions, together with their personnel and
assets, are immune from any form of Iraqi legal process. Coalition contractors and their sub-con-
tractors not normally resident in Iraq are immune with regard to activities performed in the course
of their duties. In all other matters, proceedings may only be initiated with the consent of the
Administrator. CPA/ORD/27 June 2003/17, Status of the Coalition, Foreign Liaison Missions, their
Personnel and Contractors.

152 CPA/ORD/10 June 2003/7, Penal Code.

Saddam Hussein seized power, that of July 1969, to be put back into effect.[153] The order suspended parts thereof, such as the death penalty, and adjusted others, for example by enacting the principle of non-discrimination. Additionally, provisions unreasonably restricting freedom of expression and the right of peaceful assembly were separately suspended, although new provisions were enacted consistent with the requirement to restore and maintain order.[154] Other penal provisions enacted dealt with forfeiture of property used, intended for use, or acquired in the commission of criminal offenses involving natural resources or utility infrastructure,[155] and black-marketing of oil and other petroleum products.[156]

In mid-June, the CPA also introduced various human rights standards regarding investigations, pre-trial custody, and trial into criminal procedure law.[157] Continuing insecurity in the country, however, led the CPA to increase sentences for certain crimes as "deterrence to such conduct". Affected offenses included kidnapping, rape and indecent assault, damage to public utilities or oil infrastructure, and theft of means of transportation. A full life sentence was authorized for each, with the exception of indecent assault, for which the maximum was 15 years imprisonment.[158]

As noted, the CPA disestablished the revolutionary, special, and national security courts; however, the ordinary criminal and civil courts continued to operate insofar as the security situation allowed. The CPA gave a high priority to enabling the judicial system to function effectively.[159] Coalition force judge advocates were charged with assessing the legal system in their area of operations and implementing measures necessary get it functioning again. Their remit included personnel, logistic, financial, and security matters.

Due to the unstable security situation, including threats and violence against judges trying cases involving either regime crimes or offenses against the Coalition, as well as Coalition unwillingness to employ military courts, the CPA created the Central Criminal Court of Iraq in July 2003.[160] Jurisdiction extends to crimes of a

---

153 Together with its amendments.

154 CPA/ORD/10 July 2003/19, Freedom of Assembly. For instance, various limitations were imposed on demonstrations and other public gatherings.

155 CPA/ORD/3 September 2003/25, Confiscation of Property Used In or Resulting from Certain Crimes.

156 CPA/ORD/3 Oct 2003/36, Regulation of Oil Distribution.

157 Memorandum 3, *see supra* note 62. These included the right to remain silent and the right to an attorney.

158 CPA/ORD/10 September 2003/31, Modifications of Penal Code and Criminal Proceedings Law.

159 An interesting side note is that under the old regime no provision was made for pensions for families of judges and prosecutors who died or were killed in office. Following the murder of two judges, the CPA reacted by granting such pensions. This measure was made retrospective to 1 June 2003. CPA/ORD/8 January 2004/52, Payment of Pensions for Judges and Prosecutors Who Die While Holding Office.

160 CPA/ORD/18 June 2003/13, The Central Criminal Court of Iraq (Revised).

transnational character, those that present special security concerns, and offenses that hinder reconstruction, including breach of CPA orders that fall within these areas.[161] The Administrator appoints its judges, who are Iraqis, for a one year term following recommendations from the Judicial Review Committee, a body established in part as a facet of the de-Baathification process.[162]

In the aftermath of de-Baathification, the reestablished Council of Judges assumed responsibility for administering the judicial and prosecutorial systems.[163] The Council is responsible for nominating candidates for judicial appointment; promoting and transferring existing judges; investigating allegations of misconduct or professional incompetence; and judicial discipline. The Supreme Court's Chief Justice serves as Council President, with other members drawn by position from key judicial and administrative posts in the Iraqi government.

Even before occupation began, and especially in light of the Guantanamo situation, the Coalition was forced to address the accountability of former regime members for complicity in genocide, crimes against humanity, and war crimes. At issue was the nature of the body that would conduct trials. The United Nations favored an international tribunal such as those established to handle such offenses emanating from former Yugoslavia and Rwanda. In contrast, the Governing Council pushed for an indigenous tribunal. Occupation forces sought to avoid the possibility of military tribunals, such as the Guantanamo Commissions.

Ultimately, the Governing Council prevailed. In December 2003, the CPA delegated authority to set up the "Iraqi Special Tribunal", and promulgate its statute, to the Governing Council.[164] The statute, the terms of which had been "discussed extensively between the Governing Council and the CPA", was annexed to the order.

The Tribunal will consist of "one or more" trial chambers and an appeals chamber. Jurisdiction extends to "any Iraqi national or resident of Iraq" accused of genocide, crimes against humanity, war crimes, and certain violations of Iraqi law

---

161 One of its earliest cases involved two Ukrainians convicted of smuggling Iraqi diesel fuel out of the country. CPA Press Release, "Iraq's Central Criminal Court convicts two oil smugglers, Oct. 13, 2003, <http://www.cpa iraq.org/pressreleases/20031014_OCT-14-Conviction>. In another, the court sentenced the former Governor of Najaf to 14 years imprisonment for illegal arrest, destruction of a government document, and misuse of office. CPA Press Release, "Iraq's Central Criminal Court Sends Former Governor of Najaf to Prison for 14 Years, Nov. 3, 2003, <http://www.cpa-iraq.org/pressreleases/20031103_Nov-03-ConvictionPR>.

162 CPA Order No. 7, *see supra* note 152. The Committee consists of three Iraqi and three international lawyers appointed by the Administrator to "investigate and gather information on the suitability of judges and prosecutors to hold office". It may remove judges and prosecutors from office and appoint suitable successors. CPA/ORD/23 June 2003/ 15, Establishment of the Judicial Review Committee.

163 CPA/ORD/18 September 2003/35, Reestablishment of the Council of Judges.

164 CPA/ORD/10 December 2003/48, Delegation of Authority Regarding an Iraqi Special Tribunal.

committed between 17 July 1968 and 1 May 2003. Because no specific Iraqi legislation existed on the international crimes, the Statute drew from the International Criminal Court Statute in defining offenses.

While primarily an Iraqi domestic court, the Governing Council (or successor body) may appoint non-Iraqi judges "if it deems necessary". In addition, the Tribunal President must appoint international advisers/observers to its various components, including the judiciary, investigative judges, and Office of the Prosecutor. Iraqi criminal trial procedure will apply, but a majority of the Tribunal's judges may approve rules of procedure that override the provisions thereof. To date, no trials have taken place, although it is this tribunal that will likely conduct the trials of Saddam Hussein and other senior Iraqi leaders.[165]

7.1. *Legal Assessment*

The fundamental principle governing the legal system during occupation is laid down in Article 43 of the Hague Regulations, which requires the occupier to respect "unless absolutely prevented, the laws in force in the country". Geneva Convention IV expands on this requirement vis-à-vis penal law. Article 64 provides that penal laws should "remain in force, with the exception that they may be repealed or suspended by the Occupying Power in cases where they constitute a threat to its security or an obstacle to the application of the present convention". However, where "essential to enable the Occupying Power to fulfill its obligations under the present Convention, to maintain the orderly government of the territory, and to ensure the security of the Occupying Power", its personnel and facilities, the occupier may introduce additional penal provisions.

Retention by occupation authorities of the existing penal law, except as necessary to ensure security or to comply with international human rights standards, complies with these standards. On the other hand, the Geneva IV requirements that penal provisions be published in the language of the inhabitants and brought to their knowledge before coming into force have not been met.[166]

The preexisting court system must also remain in place during occupation, except to the extent that it impedes either application of the Geneva Convention IV provisions protecting the population or the "effective administration of justice".[167] In other words, no requirement exists to retain elements of the court system that are dysfunctional or offend against basic human rights principles. With regard to enforce-

---

165 The Statute of the Iraqi Special Tribunal, effective Dec. 10, 2003, <http://www.cpairaq.org/ human_rights/Statute.
166 Geneva Convention IV, *supra* note 5, art. 65. See text accompanying fn 59 *supra*.
167 *Id.,* art. 64.

ment of penal laws promulgated by the occupier, offenders may be handed over to the "properly constituted, non-political military courts" of the occupier.[168] Thus, the existing military courts of an occupier may assume jurisdiction over occupation penal law. This does not prevent the indigenous courts dealing with such offenses where they are capable of doing so, although they may only apply "those provisions of law which were applicable prior to the offense".[169]

Disestablishment of the revolutionary, special, and national security courts appears fully justified in the light of their past abuses. In that the CPA established the Central Criminal Court for valid security reasons, it too would appear justified by occupation law, particularly given its application of existing Iraqi law. Further, in that Resolution 1483 requires the UN Special Representative, working with the CPA, to encourage "international efforts to promote legal and judicial reform", the Security Council clearly anticipated and approved of changes in the legal system.

The Iraqi Special Tribunal poses different issues. Delegation of authority to create the tribunal by the CPA to the Governing Council comported with both the legislative primacy of the CPA and Resolution 1511's recognition that the Governing Council embodies Iraqi sovereignty during the transitional period. Resolution 1483 provides further support by affirming "the need for accountability for crimes and atrocities committed by the previous Iraqi regime". In doing so, it implicitly recognizes the legality of trials for crimes under international and domestic law committed by the Baathist regime.

That the offenses over which the Tribunal exercises jurisdiction are drawn from the ICC Statute is strong evidence of their customary international law status. However, because the ICC Statute was concluded in 1998, but the Tribunal's jurisdiction extends back to 1968, the question as to whether the various crimes listed were of a customary international law nature before 1998 (and if so, as of when) remains.

Human Rights Watch (HRW), while reserving its position on the legitimacy of the Tribunal, has raised a number of concerns on procedural and other matters.[170] These include investigative protections and guarantees of fair trial. Many are likely to be met by the forthcoming promulgation of the Tribunal's rules of procedure. HRW has also criticized the Tribunal Statute's failure to explicitly require judges and prosecutors to "have experience managing complex criminal trials and trials involving serious crimes". While Tribunal proceedings would certainly benefit from

---

168 *Id.*, art. 66.

169 *Id.*, art. 67.

170 Human Rights Watch, Memorandum to the Iraqi Governing Council on "The Statute of the Iraqi Special Tribunal", December 2003, <http://www.hrw.org/backgrounder/mena/iraq121703.htm#5>.

experienced judges, inclusion of such a requirement in the legislatively mandated qualifications of domestic (as opposed to international) judges is rare.

Finally, with regard to the provisions of CPA Memorandum No. 3, the Geneva Convention IV sets forth extensive procedural requirements for occupation courts. They include, *inter alia*, the rights to notification of charges, trial before conviction, speedy trial, presentation of evidence, representation by counsel, interpretation of proceedings, and appeal.[171] However, Memorandum No. 3 deals only with Iraqi, not occupation, courts. As it extends many of the Geneva Convention IV provisions to their courts for the first time, it advances the interests of the Iraqi people beyond the strict requirements of humanitarian law, and contributes to their treatment by those courts in accordance with human rights standards.[172]

8.   Termination of Occupation

As noted above, the CPA is moving rapidly towards return of governmental authority to the Iraqi people. The 15 November 2003 agreement between the Governing Council and CPA on the *Timeline to a Sovereign, Democratic and Secure Iraq* sets 30 June 2004 as the day occupation will end and full sovereignty passes to an Iraqi government. It is at this point that the CPA's authority over Iraq will end, although Coalition authorities will continue to provide extensive assistance, aid, and advice to the government and Coalition forces will contribute to maintaining internal security. To date, the Security Council has not embraced the agreement, and the Secretary-General has recognized that there are some difficulties with it.[173]

In assessing this agreement, it is necessary to recall the status of the Governing Council under Resolution 1511 as the embodiment of Iraq's sovereignty until "an

---

171 Geneva Convention IV, *supra* note 5, arts. 70-73. Moreover, representatives of a Protecting Power must be notified with details of proceedings and have the right to attend trials, although this latter right may be limited if, as an exceptional measure, a trial is being held in camera "in the interests of the security of the Occupying Power". *Id.*, arts. 71 & 74. Protecting Powers are States (or a humanitarian organization) designated by the individual belligerents to perform certain duties set forth in humanitarian law. In the case of Iraq, no such entities have been designated. Therefore, most Protecting Power responsibilities have devolved to the International Committee of the Red Cross.

172 In light of the situation in Guantanamo, it should be noted that "individual or mass forcible transfers, as well as deportations of protected persons from occupied territory to the territory of the Occupying Power or that of any other country, occupied or not, are prohibited, regardless of their motive". Geneva Convention IV, *supra* note 5, art. 49. This would prohibit individuals detained by Coalition forces, except POWs, from being taken from Iraq even for trial purposes.

173 Secretary-General, Office of the Spokesman, Secretary-General's Press Encounter with President George W. Bush of the United States of America, Feb. 3, 2004, <http://www.un.org/apps/sg/offthe-cuff.asp?nid+534>.

internationally recognized, representative government is established and assumes the responsibilities of the Authority". Thus, the Governing Council is the appropriate body for the CPA to negotiate turnover of responsibility with, but the termination of occupation will depend on the emergence of a government meeting the Resolution 1511 criteria. Presumably, international recognition will come in the form of a Security Council resolution. Absent such a resolution, a unilateral withdrawal and termination of occupation could only legally be achieved once the Hague Regulations, Article 43, duty to "restore and ensure" public order and safety has been complied with. Humanitarian law does not permit occupation forces to leave a security and safety void in territory they have occupied. Indeed, while application of Geneva Convention IV ceases "one year after the general close of military operations",[174] this is subject to the continuation of most articles governing occupation.[175]

9.   Conclusion

As this article is being written, Coalition and Iraqi authorities are encountering tragic obstacles to restoring order and safety to Iraq. Moreover, serious disagreements exist on how the Iraqi government will be selected.[176] The likelihood of effective return of sovereignty to Iraq by 30 June 2004 remains highly debatable. Nevertheless, despite some instances of possible non-compliance, the CPA's policies have generally been well within its rights and duties under occupation and UN law.

What is most interesting about the occupation of Iraq is the extent to which the coexistence of UN and occupation law has benefited the civilian population. It has permitted Coalition authorities to go far beyond the strict terms of occupation law when necessary, particularly with regard to reconstruction and development of the country. The extent to which this dynamic identifies actual deficiencies in humanitarian law that should be resolved through further codification of humanitarian law remains to be seen.

---

174 Geneva Convention IV, *supra* note 5, art. 6. The phrase "general close of military operations" is unclear. While the Commentary to Geneva Convention IV is unhelpful, its Protocol Additional I counterpart states that "the general close of military operations may occur after 'cessation of hostilities,'" thereby indicating that the general close of military operations implies the absence of any combat with remnants of the defeated State's military. Commentary on the Additional Protocols of 8 June 1977 to the Geneva Conventions of 12 August 1949, para 153 (Yves Sandoz, Christophe Swinarski & Bruno Zimmerman eds. 1987). Protocol Additional I, by contrast, ends application "on the general close of military operations and, in the case of occupied territories, on the termination of the occupation". Protocol Additional I, *supra* note 5, art. 3(b).

175 Excepted are Articles 1-12, 27, 29-34, 47, 49, 51-53, 59, 61-77, 143.

176 Some favor a caucus system, others propose direct elections. Negotiations under UN auspices appear stalemated, suggesting resolution of the matter may be delayed. Should that occur, the CPA may turn authority over to an interim Iraqi government.

Warfighter and Traditional Peacekeeper Attributes for Effective Performance: Applied Psychological Theory and Research for Maximizing Soldier Performance in 21st Century Military Operations

Matt C. Densmore and Harvey Langholtz *

Examining psychological dimensions of the soldier in both traditional peacekeeping and warfighting is relevant and important for 21st Century military forces. The increased importance placed on international relations and diplomacy, the global economy, and human rights, coupled with the proliferation of international and regional alliances (e.g., the United Nations, North Atlantic Treaty Organization, European Union, Association of South East Asian Nations, Organization of American States, Organization of African Unity, Arab League of Nations) and continued inter and intrastate conflicts, has led many nations to call on their armed forces to perform across a widening spectrum of operations. In today's post-Cold War environment characterized by an end to super power rivalry and an increase in international cooperation, modern militaries rarely exist solely to defend borders or to fight and win their nations' wars. For instance, the importance of military operations other than war (MOOTW), including peace operations, in international diplomacy is clearly reflected in the United States Department of Defense (DOD) mission statement.[1] The DOD is responsible for fielding and sustaining the military capabilities needed to meet the demand for U.S. forces, not only to protect the U.S. from direct threats

* Captain Matt C. Densmore is a psychology instructor at the United States Military Academy, West Point, New York. He has seven years of active duty service in the US Army infantry. He has a Masters Degree in Psychology from the College of William and Mary in Virginia. Dr. Harvey Langholtz is the editor-in-chief of *International Peacekeeping – The Yearbook of International Peace Operations* and Director of the United Nations Institute for Training and Research Programme of Correspondence Instruction (UNITAR POCI). He also is an Associate Professor at the College of William and Mary in Williamsburg, Virginia, where he teaches Decision Theory.

1 United States Department of Defense. *DoD 101*, available at <http://www.defenselink.mil/pubs/dod101> 18 Nov. 2002.

Harvey Langholtz, Boris Kondoch, Alan Wells (Eds.),
International Peacekeeping: The Yearbook of International Peace Operations, Volume 9, 2004, pp. 63-76.
© *Koninklijke Brill N.V. Printed in the Netherlands*

and to help maintain peace and stability in regions critical to U.S. interests, but also to help support multinational efforts to bring peace to regions torn by ethnic, tribal, or religious conflicts and to ameliorate human suffering. In fulfilling these objectives, the DOD has deployed U.S. military forces to more than 30 troubled areas around the world to conduct peace operations ranging from disaster relief to peace enforcement in the last decade alone. Since 1988, The UN has established 38 peace operations, nearly three times as many as in the first 40 years of the organization's existence. Over 50,000 U.S. soldiers deployed to major peace operations, both UN and non-UN, in 1998.[2] With nearly 13 million people living as refugees and another 22 million internally displaced, armed conflicts continue to uproot more people worldwide than any other cause. Recent dramatic events in the Ivory Coast, Liberia, and Haiti further emphasize the importance of political and military preparedness to prevent or shorten such conflicts.

Past and ongoing military deployments to conduct operations other than war provide evidence that the individual soldier in modern militaries is expected to perform in ever-changing roles far more diverse than as a traditional warfighter. In many instances, soldiers have to be resocialized to accept the position that their traditional mission is not simply to fight and win wars, but rather to do what their nation asks them to do.[3] The varying nature of warfare and the increased use of militaries as instruments of policy have raised a number of questions and arguments as to the changing psychological dimensions concerning the modern soldier. Many nations strive to establish optimum selection and training processes for their soldiers to ensure they perform their duties effectively. The psychological health, and thus the readiness, of military personnel can be directly measured and quantified, thereby providing a useful framework for the development of psychological and psychosocial measures.[4] Examining psychological dimensions of the soldier in both traditional peacekeeping and warfighting is relevant and important for 21st Century military forces. Identifying and measuring the attributes predictive of soldier performance could ultimately lead to enhanced readiness and performance through more effective methods of selection, screening, and training. This in turn could add to overall mission success when these findings are applied to the understanding that effectively performing individual warfighters and peacekeepers contribute to the unit's overall performance.

A detailed investigation of these separate ends of the conflict continuum, warfighting and traditional peacekeeping, can aid in identifying, comparing, and solidify-

2   United States Congressional Budget Office. *Make peace while staying ready for war: The challenges of U.S. military participation in peace operations*, available at <http://www.cbo.gov> Dec. 1999.

3   *See* A. Adler, B. Litz, and P. Bartone, "The nature of peacekeeping stressors". In T. Britt & A. Adler (Eds.), *The Psychology of the Peacekeeper: Lessons from the Field* (2003), 149-168.

4   *See* C. Castro, A. Adler, and A. Huffman, "Psychological screening of U.S. peacekeepers in Bosnia" (1999), available at <http://www.internationalmta.org/1999/99a04.pdf> Nov. 1999.

Conflict Intensity Continuum and Proposed Dichotomous Framework of the Soldier's Role

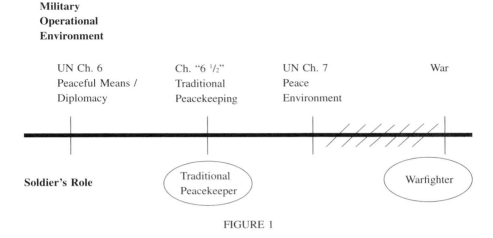

FIGURE 1

ing the psychological aspects of the warrior ethos and the peacekeeper ethos and will allow for further development of valid and reliable measures that can aid in determining what level of psychological fitness a soldier must possess to successfully perform his duties in these respective environments. As presented in Figure 1, examining and differentiating among the psychological attributes in these two contexts will not only provide insight into the psychological dimensions contributing to military members' effective performances as warfighters or traditional peacekeepers, but will also provide a framework in which to view the psychological dimensions of soldiers in modern operational settings. Rather than attempt to examine the psychological attributes required for effective performance across a potentially infinite number of conditions military personnel may face during current and future deployments, exploration of the two differing operational environments of war and traditional peacekeeping will provide a more useful framework. This dichotomous perspective will allow for further understanding of the attributes required to meet the multiple psychological challenges soldiers face in 21st Century military operations, which are often characterized by increased ambiguity, varying levels of conflict, and ill-defined parties and objectives; those operations that lie in the "gray areas" between traditional peacekeeping and warfighting.

1.   Warfighters and the Warrior Ethos

Despite the multitudes of interpretations, most will agree that war involves the aggressive application of force to impose the will of one group on another. Whatever term is chosen for the individuals performing the acts of war, the warfighter, warrior or combatant lie at the crux of human experience as wars and conflict have shaped and molded the texture of history. In the words of Marshall Saxe: "The human heart is the starting point in all matters pertaining to war".[5] Soldiers of all nations are trained to prevail in combat over a clearly defined foe and the traditional soldier's psychology is one of force and intimidation.[6] Though the meanings, tactics, and weaponry of war are constantly changing and becoming more complex, nations continue to train, equip, and deploy their combat soldiers for the purpose of fighting and winning on the battlefield. Even in an age when the strategic posture of deterrence can sometimes mislead armies into forgetting that, even if war prevention is their most usual function, warfighting is their ultimate task.[7] General Douglas MacArthur summed up the warfighter mission in his speech to West Point Cadets in 1962:

> Through all this welter of change and development, your mission remains fixed, determined, inviolable. It is to win our wars.Everything else in your professional career is but corollary to this vital dedication.

Many nations invest vast resources in developing weapons systems and training soldiers to maintain their ability to win in war. Technological, tactical, and strategic advances do not however cancel out the need for courage, endurance, resolution, cool-headedness, and audacity.[8] The intangible factors, especially the psychological fitness of warfighters, are equally vital to wartime victories. The study of soldiers in war and armed conflict has played an important role in understanding the psychology of human behavior. As J.F.C. Fuller pointed out in his personality study of Generals Ulysses S. Grant and Robert E. Lee, "at base, seven-eighths of the history of war is psychological. Material conditions change, yet the heart of man changes but little".[9] Psychological research in the area of armed conflict has led many nations to realize the value of soldier testing. Psychological testing of soldiers' cognitive, social, and personality attributes, usually at the entry level, has become a useful human resource management tool allowing for enhanced individual readiness and performance through better recruiting, placement, and training programs. The psychological dimensions contributing to warfighters' effective performance and battlefield success is commonly referred to as the *warrior ethos*.

---

5   *See* J.F.C. Fuller, *Grant and Lee. A Study in Personality and Generalship* (1957), p. 97.
6   *See* H. Langholtz and P. Leentjes, "U.N. peacekeeping: Confronting the psychological environment of war in the Twenty-First Century". In D. Christie, R. Wagner, and D. Winter (Eds.), *Peace, Conflict, and Violence. Peace Psychology for the 21st Century* (2001), 173-182.
7   *See* R. Holmes, *Acts of War: The Behavior of Men in Battle* (2001).
8   *See* J.F.C. Fuller, *supra* note 5.
9   *See* J.F.C. Fuller, *supra* note 5, p. 7.

The warrior ethos is a concept embodying the will to fight, persevere, and win in the most demanding of combat situations. The idea of a warrior ethos has its origins in the Greek phalanx of Hellenic military tradition at the dawn of decisive warfare in which battles and wars were decided by men who closed on one another face-to-face, stabbed, struck, or shot at close range and physically drove the enemy from the battlefield.[10] Buckingham defines the warrior ethos as the character, values, behaviors, and attributes developed within groups of warriors over centuries of armed combat which are essential to closing with and destroying an enemy.[11] According to U.S. Army doctrine, the warrior ethos is a mindset characterized by mental toughness, courage, dedication, and a winning attitude that is developed in soldiers through realistic and demanding training.[12] It is the sum of the distinguishing characteristics that describe what it means to be a Soldier: committed to, and prepared to, close with and kill or capture the enemy.[13] Burbelo & Zinsser suggest that the warrior ethos is not only built through the experience of tough, realistic training, but is an internal mindset for success and achievement on the battlefield which can be trained to ensure a mental edge.[14]

Studies of the warrior ethos aid in examining the psychological dimensions of individual performance associated with the highest levels of conflict intensity. In general, militaries view past performance and individual experience as the key indicators for future performance: How many real combat operations, live-fire exercises, training center rotations, and military schools has the unit or individual soldier successfully completed? In this sense, an individual soldier's past performances in military environments, including military schools, field training exercises, and especially real-world deployments show potential for effective future performance. Beyond individual experience, several psychological studies provide insight into warfighter effectiveness. One of several studies exploring the psychological dimensions concerning how and why soldiers fight includes the Stouffer & Lumsdaine study of combat-experienced soldiers during World War II.[15] This in-depth study of individuals in combat was instrumental in establishing quantitative measures for combat attitudes and behavior. White & Olmstead conducted content analysis of behavioral

---

10   *See* V. Hanson, *Carnage and Culture* (2001).

11   *See* D. Buckingham, "*The Warrior Ethos*", available at <http://handle.dtic.mil/100.2/ADA366676> Dec. 1999.

12   *See* United States Department of the Army, *Field Manual 22-100: Army Leadership*. (1999).

13   *See* R. Honore and R. Cerjan, "Warrior ethos. The Soul of an Infantryman", (1999). *News from the Front Jan.-Feb. 2002*, available at <http://call.army.mil/products/nftf/janfeb02/honore.html>.

14   *See* G. Burbelo and N. Zinsser, "The ultimate weapon: Harnessing the combat multiplier of a warrior mindset" (2003). *Infantry Online April 2003*, available at <http://www.benning.army.mil/OLP/InfantryOnline/issue_28>.

15   *See* S. Stouffer and A. Lumsdaine, *The American Soldier: Combat and its Aftermath* (1949).

event interviews of 375 combat-experienced U.S. Army soldiers to develop a list of 25 Combat Effectiveness Variables (CEVs).[16] This study borrowed from five previous studies of U.S. Army soldier attributes in selecting the resulting CEVs which remain an important contribution to understanding individual behaviors and attributes that contribute to combat effectiveness. Kilcullen, Mael, Goodwin, & Zazanis used rational biodata scales and panels of experienced military personnel to establish four main categories used in predicting U.S. Army Special Forces field performance. The authors investigated 30 attributes organized into cognitive, communication, interpersonal and motivational, and physical abilities and found that motivational attributes (e.g., achievement orientation, initiative, perseverance, dependability) were most predictive of field performance.[17] Dispositions for combat motivation and the willingness to volunteer for foreign combat missions have also been measured in many studies using nine different military deployment scenarios of the Combat Ethic scale. The Combat Ethic scale has been used in several instances to predict individual combat orientation.[18] Studies along these lines provide insight into the individual in combat and further the examination of the psychological attributes that potentially contribute to the warrior ethos and effective warfighter performance.

2.   Peacekeepers and the Peacekeeper Ethos

The changing nature of international relations and peacekeeping operations over the last 50 years has led to several varying views in defining the peacekeeping operational environment. One of the factors contributing to the complexity of peace operations is that there is no common perspective or standard taxonomy for defining the missions. The word "peacekeeping" does not exist in the UN Charter. However, peacekeeping operations are those missions broadly defined and undertaken within Chapter VI (Pacific Settlement of Disputes) and Chapter VII (Actions with Respect

---

16   *See* R. White and J. Olmstead, *Identification of Potential Combat Effectiveness Variables* (1997). U.S. Army Research Institute for Behavioral and Social Sciences Report No. 98-01.

17   *See* R. Kilcullen, F. Mael, G. Goodwin, and M. Zazanis, "Predicting U.S. Army Special Forces field performance" (1999). 4 *Human Performance in Extreme Environments*, 53-63.

18   For studies using the Combat Ethics Scale *see* C. Brown and C. Moskos, "The American volunteer soldier: will he fight?" (1976), 56 *Military Review*, 8-17; D. Burrelli and D. Segal, "Definitions of mission among novice Marine Corps officers" (1982), 10 *Journal of Political and Military Sociology*, 299-306; W. Cockerham and L. Cohen, "Volunteering for foreign combat missions: An attitudinal study of U.S. Army paratroopers" (1982), 24 *The Pacific Sociological Review*, 329-354; D. Segal and B. Meeker, "Peacekeeping, warfighting, and professionalism: Attitude organization and change among combat soldiers on constabulary duty" (1985), 13 *Journal of Political and Military Sociology*, 167-181.

to Threats to Peace, Breaches of Peace, and Acts of Aggression) of the UN Charter.[19] It is generally understood that peacekeeping operations lie along a continuum encompassed by the definitions found within Chapters VI and VII, in which Chapter VI peacekeeping includes diplomatic negotiation as the mainstay of conflict settlement and Chapter VII peacekeeping is the forceful enforcement of a settlement. This view can be problematic however in modern application, especially as peacekeeping has evolved and the international community has had to confront the issue of State sovereignty and rethink the UN role in securing peace in what has come to be known as the "failed State".[20]

Soon after the UN was founded, early peacekeeping operations, referred to now as traditional, first generation, or "chapter six and a half" peacekeeping, responded to inter-state conflicts and were characterized by sovereign nations with organized armies consenting to a cease-fire. UN mandated forces monitored the agreed-upon cease-fire and separation of forces while a permanent peace was brokered through diplomatic and political means. Operationally, a traditional peacekeeping mission is a static operation with the purpose of monitoring activities and reacting in a way that will de-escalate the conflict by peaceful means. Several current international and regional operations fit within the first generation or traditional peacekeeping operation definition, including the Multinational Force and Observer Mission in Sinai, Egypt (MFO-Sinai), United Nations Observer Mission in Georgia (UNOMIG), the United Nations Mission in Ethiopia and Eritrea (UNMEE), the United Nations Truce Supervision Organization (UNTSO) in Palestine, the United Nations Peacekeeping Force in Cypress (UNFICYP), and the United Nations Mission for the Referendum in Western Sahara (MINURSO).

The traditional peacekeeping soldier, or peacekeeper, will remain the physical representation of the world's effort to maintain international peace and security. His or her effective performance is essential for current and future peace operations and will continue to play a critical role in international security into the 21st Century. Though many varying names and definitions are used to describe soldiers fulfilling the roles of a peacekeeper, the term peacekeeper is used here to denote the soldier who performs in the narrowly defined environment of traditional or first generation peacekeeping operations in which he or she is an impartial third party to a conflict. Soldiers serving on traditional peacekeeping operations are called upon to use a different set of psychological approaches. Instead of using force to achieve their ends, they use the tools of persuasion and trust to limit fighting between the armies engaged

---

19   *The Charter of the United Nations* (1945), available at <http://www.un.org/aboutun/charter/index> 20 Oct. 2002.

20   *See* United Nations, *Blue Helmets. A Review of United Nations Peace-keeping* (1996).

in the conflict.[21] A peacekeeper is focused on maintaining, building, restoring, or stabilizing peace and non-violent conflict resolution, as opposed to the warfighter who is a direct combatant focused on missions directed toward a clear objective defined in terms of an enemy, terrain, or resources. The peacekeeper is a third party to someone else's conflict who strives to prevent the use of force and limit conflict intensity, whereas the warfighter is a direct participant in the conflict who is expected to willingly use force to overcome a clearly defined foe. Principals of the *peace-keeping ethos* include the concept of impartial application of the techniques of conflict resolution to contain and limit violence.[22] To properly examine the peace-keeping ethos it is important to understand the operational environment and psychological demands that a peacekeeper will likely face. Like war, peacekeeping is a military enterprise serving political ends; but unlike war, it is typically conducted in an environment that is not well defined, lacks a focal enemy, and may lack clearly defined mission objectives.[23]

Military operations in general present many psychological challenges to the individual soldier. Peacekeeping places special demands on military members and these should be taken into account when suitability for deployment is being assessed.[24] Though a few nations organize and train units for the sole purpose of conducting peacekeeping operations (e.g., Canada, Ireland, and Norway), the majority of national military forces do not consider peacekeeping a primary mission. Peacekeeping generally receives lower priority in training time and resources, compounding the difficulty in soldiers' abilities to operate in the complex environment. The peace-keepers' role is like many other temporary roles that are not involved in fighting wars that military personnel are asked to play, often with little structure; while they are constructed and played, they are not psychologically internalized and do not become part of the soldier's identity.[25] Many peacekeeping operations require soldiers to perform tasks far removed from the ones they would be expected to perform during conventional warfare. Inherent tension exists for the soldier in traditional peacekeeping operations because they require the peacekeeper to achieve the unit's objectives through visible, overt, and coordinated performance, which conflicts with the familiar tactics of the combat role. Unlike conventional combat operations, which place a premium on stealth during patrol, peacekeeping operations generally use

21   *See* H. Langholtz and P. Leentjes, *supra* note 6.
22   *See* H. Langholtz (Ed.), *The Psychology of Peacekeeping* (1996).
23   *See* V.C. Franke, "The social identity of peacekeeping". In T. Britt and A. Adler (Eds.), *The Psychology of the Peacekeeper: Lessons from the Field* (2003), 31-52.
24   *See* F.C. Pinch, "Screening and selection of personnel for peace operations: A Canadian perspective". In D. Segal (Ed.), *Peace Operations: Workshop Proceedings* (1994), 57-80.
25   *See* D. Segal, "Is a peacekeeping culture emerging among American infantry in the Sinai MFO?" (2001), 30 *Journal of Contemporary Ethnography*, 607-636.

patrols to demonstrate a visible presence and to obtain vital intelligence or to assess the situation in a particular area.[26]

Traditional peacekeeping presents a unique psychological challenge for many nations' combat-trained soldiers who must as peacekeepers adhere to measured and restrained responses to hostility. The potential for incompatibility exists between a soldier's combat training and martial orientation as a warfighter on the one hand, and the restraint and impartiality required of the peacekeeper on the other. The prescriptions associated with the identity images of "peacekeeper" and "warrior" are themselves conflicting, and soldiers are often expected to adopt both types of identities during a single operation.[27] This contradiction and role ambiguity between aggressive warrior identity and the mission objectives of a traditional peacekeeping operation can be distressing and may present the soldier with cognitive dilemmas in resolving identity tensions to fulfill the role of a peacekeeper. Personal accounts of U.S. peacekeepers still confirm the suggestion that participating in peacekeeping operations may challenge the stability of established self-conceptions.[28] Peacekeeping involves a psychological change from an adversarial to a pacific role; from confrontation to third-party presence. In peacekeeping there is often no physical enemy force: the objective is to avoid hostilities, to improve communication between the parties, and to advance the process of reconciliation. Further, effective performance in peacekeeping operations demands a fair-minded and impartial approach while operating in an atmosphere of distrust and suspicion between the protagonists, often under difficult and provocative circumstances.

Peacekeepers also face the psychological challenges of building trust and maintaining impartiality in dealing with the many parties involved, while protecting the force through security and deterrence. It is often a delicate balancing act between diplomacy and security. Peacekeepers must always operate along that uncomfortable border between peaceable and forceful settlement of disputes.[29] Soldiers face the challenges of dealing with multiple agendas of members of other militaries, refugees, noncombatants, non-governmental organizations (NGOs), the media, and the multiple belligerents or warring factions. This necessitates a full understanding of the causes of the conflict – political, military and economic – as well as the social and cultural environment. Peacekeeping is characterized by more players and

---

26 *See* M. Hardesty and D. Ellis, "Training for peace operations. The U.S. Army adapts to the post-cold war world". *Peaceworks 12* (1997).

27 *See* T. Britt, "Psychological ambiguities in peacekeeping". In H. Langholtz (Ed.), *The Psychology of Peacekeeping* (1998), 111-128.

28 *See* V.C. Franke, *supra* note 24.

29 *See* D. McLean, "Peace operations and common sense: Replacing rhetoric with realism". *Peaceworks 9* (1996).

significantly less precise definitions of relationships.[30] Maintaining impartiality between two or more warring parties taxes the mental apparatus of the individual peacekeeper, thereby also possibly increasing the risk of psychological effects.[31]

Peacekeepers may experience an extremely fluid and complex operational environment, in which they face varying mission tasks and levels of possible conflict. The variety of peacekeeping definitions and multiple stressors noted earlier are indicators of the environmental complexities the peacekeeper faces. Rules of engagement (ROE), or the norms and regulations that define the legitimate use of force and guide behavior during an operation can add further psychological strain during an operation.[32] ROE limit peacekeepers to certain kinds of responses and reoccurring ROE changes can lead to further confusion and frustration for the peacekeeper. Stress levels even within one operation can change dramatically depending on the time period and the rotation.[33]

Research in the psychological aspects of the peacekeeper has increased over the last two decades just as the frequency of peacekeeping operations and their complexity have increased. Understanding the unique stressors soldiers encounter while deployed on peacekeeping operations has become increasingly critical for many nations considering the preparation and deployment of their military forces to effectively complete peacekeeping missions. Many studies have closely examined psychological stressors unique to peacekeeping operations to gain a better understanding of the environmental and social factors that affect soldiers and units.[34] Other psychological studies have investigated soldier attitudes about the appropriateness and challenges of operations other than war, such as peacekeeping.[35] Though these studies provide insight into the psychological challenges peacekeepers face and their perceptions, opinions, and attitudes toward post-Cold War military operations, they

---

30   *See* D. Eyre, "Cultural awareness and negotiation skills in peace operations". In D. Segal (Ed.),
      Peace Operations. Workshop Proceedings (1994), 101-114.
31   *See* L. Weisaeth, "The psychological challenge of peacekeeping operations". In T. Britt and
      A. Adler (Eds.), *The Psychology of the Peacekeeper: Lessons from the Field* (2003), 207-222.
32   *See* V.C. Franke, *supra* note 26.
33   *See* L. Weisaeth, *supra* note 31.
34   Studies exploring psychological stressors of peacekeeping include, P. Bartone, A. Adler, and
      J. Vaitkus, "Dimensions of psychological stress in peacekeeping operations" (1998), 163 *Military
      Medicine*, 587-593; T. Britt, "Psychological ambiguities in peacekeeping". In H. Langholtz (Ed.),
      The Psychology of Peacekeeping (1998), 111-128; C. Harleman, "Psychological aspects of peace-
      keeping on the ground". In H. Langholtz (Ed.), *The Psychology of Peacekeeping* (1998), 101-110.
35   Studies of soldiers' attitudes towards peacekeeping include, D. Avant and J. Lebovic, "U.S. mili-
      tary attitudes toward post-Cold War missions" (2001), 27 *Armed Forces and Society*, 37-52;
      L. Miller, "Do soldiers hate peacekeeping? The case of preventive diplomacy operations in
      Macedonia" (1997), 23 *Armed Forces and Society*, 415-450; L. Miller and C. Moskos, "Humanitarians
      or warriors? Race, gender, and combat status in operation Restore Hope" (1995), 21 *Armed Forces
      and Society*, 615-638.

do not point to psychological attributes required for effective performance in those operational environments.

Studies that examine individual soldier attributes are relatively few in the peace-keeping literature, but are worth considering. In *Peace Soldiers*, Moskos surveyed the military and civilian participants deployed in support of the UNFICYP peace-keeping operation and measured soldiers' constabulary ethic and internationalist atti-tudes. Constabulary ethic was defined as "the minimal use of force shading into noncoercion" and internationalism as the "commitment to use and be bound by political institutions transcending the nation state".[36] Moskos was able to find a pos-itive correlation between constabulary ethic and internationalism scores and the overall evaluation of the peacekeeping operation's success. Segal & Meeker con-ducted surveys of U.S. Army paratroopers before, during, and after deployment to the MFO Sinai peacekeeping mission.[37] The researchers used the multiple item indexes of combat ethic and orientation in showing an incompatibility of strong combat orientation and constabulary mission performance. They did not however argue for combat orientation as a negative predictor of peacekeeping performance. In a study of U.S. Army reserve soldiers deployed as part of the MFO Sinai, Mael, Kilcullen, & White developed a model of individual attributes relevant to peace-keeping based on soldier surveys, interviews, and job knowledge tests.[38] The model includes 22 attributes concluded to be especially useful for soldier participation in the MFO Sinai peacekeeping mission. Data revealed general agreement on attribute importance for both officers and soldiers. The authors also noted that enlisted sol-diers viewed stress tolerance and tolerance for boredom as more important than did officers, perhaps reflecting the greater stretches of time soldiers spent in observa-tion posts. Schmidtchen of the Australian Army Psychology Corps presented a model of three major psychological dimensions that define what makes a successful peace-keeper.[39] From his qualitative study of Australian Defense Force soldiers who had peacekeeping operation experience, Schmidtchen determined that individual quali-ties (stability, maturity, reliability), problem-solving skills (flexible application of skill base, developing innovative solutions), and team skills (interpersonal abilities), were key measures in predicting an individual soldier's success as a peacekeeper.

Though the basic individual and small unit collective tasks and the psychological

---

36   *See* C. Moskos, *Peace Soldiers: The Sociology of UN Military Forces* (1976).

37   *See* D. Segal and B. Meeker, "Peacekeeping, warfighting, and professionalism: Attitude organiza-tion and change among combat soldiers on constabulary duty" (1985), 13 *Journal of Political and Military Sociology*, 167-181.

38   *See* F. Mael, R. Kilcullen, and L. White, "Soldier attributes for peacekeeping and peacemaking". In H. Phelps and B. Farr (Eds.), *Reserve Component Soldiers as Peacekeepers* (1996), 29-50.

39   *See* C. Schmidtchen, *What makes a successful peacekeeper?* (1997), available at <http://www.inter-nationalmta.org/1997/97IMTAproceedings.pdf> 14 Sep. 2002.

challenges share similarities across the varying duties and locations of peacekeeping operations, psychological assessments or predictors remain extremely varied.
Australians may test a soldier for certain attributes that might predict peacekeeping
performance, while the Austrians, Belgians, Canadians, Irish, Swedish, United
Kingdom, and U.S. each look for something different. As a further complication,
many national militaries conduct soldier testing at different times during their careers.
For instance, the assessment of knowledge, skills, and abilities (KSAs) and physical fitness in both the U.S. and Canadian militaries is intense at the entry-level, but
lacking throughout soldiers' career progression.[40] The ability to identify and measure individual attributes critical to peacekeeper performance is clearly advantageous for future peacekeeping operations. Valid and reliable measures that can aid
in determining what level of psychological fitness a soldier must possess to successfully perform his or her duties while deployed on a peacekeeping operation
could ultimately lead to enhanced readiness and performance through more effective methods of selection, screening, and training.

3.   Psychological Aptitude Assessment for Effective Performance

An in-depth review of existing research and findings will provide conceptual, theoretical, and empirical support for the development of psychological aptitude, or
suitability assessment instruments which can aid military commanders in assessing
soldiers' psychological strengths and weaknesses in relation to particular operational
environments. Empirical findings such as those sited here can improve soldier selection and training systems by identifying suitable attributes for effective performance
and measuring them with greater precision. The crucial challenge of developing and
implementing a psychological instrument to determine a soldier's best fit for a mission, whether traditional peacekeeping or warfighting, remains the lack of objective
and measurable standards for what constitutes "effective performance" by a soldier
in each level of conflict intensity. Just because a soldier, or the unit he or she happens to be assigned to, is deployed to conduct duties in a peacekeeping or warfighting mission does not mean that his score on a psychological instrument will necessarily
reflect his true performance as gauged by an objective standard. To address this
deficiency, psychological research of the concepts presented here would have to
exercise a set of assumptions: that warfighters and peacekeepers from the field know
what attributes are reflected in soldiers' effective performance and can provide a
pool of subject matter experts to judge the most important attributes; and that sol-

---

40   *See* F.C. Pinch, *Lessons from Canadian Peacekeeping Experiences* (1994).

diers who take a psychological attribute test are accurate judges of their own abilities.

Established assertions based on an extensive review of the literature and existing tests are needed to select and operationalize the attributes associated with peacekeeper and warfighter performance. Identifying and defining these attributes should be based on a synthesis of relevant attributes compiled from existing research concerning the psychological dimensions of military performance in the peacekeeping and warfighting environments. It is widely agreed that a prerequisite for being an effective peacekeeper is being a good soldier, which is inherently linked to being an effective warfighter as well. Peacekeepers are expected to maintain the ability to interchange peacekeeping roles to the combat abilities of a warfighter in the fluid environment of peacekeeping operations. Thus, overlap should be expected in assessment dimensions for traditional peacekeepers, warfighters, and the general military population and it will be beneficial to measure attributes relevant to all. For example, Britt's study of aspects of identity that relate to individual levels of job engagement found a negative, significant correlation between warriorism and peacekeeper identity among U.S. Army Rangers.[41] However, the correlation was not very strong, indicating that U.S. Army Rangers may "possess a high level of warriorism and a strong peacekeeper identity".

A psychological assessment instrument along these lines should not be intended as a one-stop answer for military selection and screening. Rather, it could complement any number of other useful cognitive, personality, and social tests that militaries use to make personnel decisions. Most importantly, the aptitude test will provide a commander with a snapshot of his soldiers' psychological aptitude based on attributes that were found to contribute to effective performance in the warfighting or traditional peacekeeping operational environments. Results may give a commander, or recruiter, a general picture of a group, whereby the group can be examined for higher or lower warfighting or peacekeeping aptitude, or for individual outliers. For example, an individual outlier may be a soldier within a unit preparing for, or engaged in a traditional peacekeeping operation that scores significantly higher for warfighting aptitude than for the peacekeeping aptitude. This is not to say that the soldier cannot be an effective peacekeeper, but does give his or her commander insight into the psychological dimensions associated with his or her soldier's performance. Based on the aptitude test results, a commander may find that his or her unit or individual soldiers within the unit need further training focused on the specific attributes examined in the instrument. Such an instrument will certainly be useful to national militaries that screen individual soldiers to perform duties in specific operational environments such as traditional peacekeeping (e.g., Ireland, Norway).

---

41   *See* T. Britt, "Aspects of identity predict engagement in work under adverse conditions" (2003), 2 *Self and Identity*, 36.

The U.S. does not currently mandate units for the sole purpose of performing peace-keeping operations. Doctrinally, U.S. military forces exist to fight and win the nation's wars, while peacekeeping operations are secondary. In the U.S. case, an instrument developed from this type of psychological research and findings could still play a useful role in assessing the unit's overall mindset, or "psychological readiness", to tailor the unit's training in the planning and predeployment phases of an operation.

4.   Summary

As seen in the existing research, traditional peacekeepers and warfighters perform their duties using differing sets of psychological attributes as a result of the military operational environment's requirements. Differentiating among the attributes for both peacekeepers and warfighters will allow for the development of valid and reliable tests that can aid in determining what level of psychological fitness a soldier must possess to successfully perform his or her duties in these respective environments. Such an instrument is clearly advantageous for establishing a framework to build an understanding of the increasingly complex psychological challenges that soldiers face in modern military operations, and may help military commanders improve their abilities to screen soldiers and develop training programs. The application of psychological research and principles to the investigation of military personnel will aid in answering the real-world need to examine individual soldiers' psychological makeup in terms of those attributes closely tied to effective performance. As the demands of modern warfare become more complicated, an established foundation and instrument by which to judge attributes as psychological criteria in recruiting, screening and selecting, and training becomes increasingly important.

Refugees International Report on the United Nations Organization Mission in the Democratic Republic of the Congo MONUC: A Misunderstood Mandate

Clifford Bernath*

"MONUC was never intended to make peace. The parties must make the peace. There has been no request from the region for MONUC to make the peace. MONUC has no capacity to do that. There is not a single state willing to provide combat forces".

Senior Official from a P-5 Member Country
January 2003

"The mandate is a function of what member states are likely to bear, and what donating states are willing to commit to. I haven't heard any member of the P-5 say they want to commit more troops or expand the mandate".

United Nations Official
January 2003

"While the rebels are killing us, MONUC takes notes and makes reports. What good is that?"

Congolese citizen, Kisangani
November 2002

1.   Introduction

Blessed with natural resources and cursed by nations willing to do anything to obtain them, the Democratic Republic of Congo (DRC) has never been the master of its own fate. From 1908 to 1960, the country was colonized by Belgium, which ruthlessly exploited the Congo for its rubber and ivory and other resources. The exploitation

---

*   Clifford Bernath is the Director of Special Projects for Refugees International.

Harvey Langholtz, Boris Kondoch, Alan Wells (Eds.),
International Peacekeeping: The Yearbook of International Peace Operations, Volume 9, 2004, pp. 77-92
© *Koninklijke Brill N.V. Printed in the Netherlands*

of the DRC's resources has continued ever since, by neighboring countries and by western nations as well.

In its October 2002 report "Final report of the Panel of Experts on the Illegal Exploitation of Natural Resources and Other Forms of Wealth of DR Congo", the United Nations focused on diamonds, gold, coltan, copper, cobalt, timber, wildlife reserves, fiscal resources and trade in general. One of the report's findings was:

> The regional conflict that drew the armies of seven African States into the Democratic Republic of the Congo has diminished in intensity, but the overlapping microconflicts that it provoked continue. These conflicts are fought over minerals, farm produce, land and even tax revenues. Criminal groups linked to the armies of Rwanda, Uganda and Zimbabwe and the Government of the Democratic Republic of the Congo have benefited from the microconflicts. Those groups will not disband voluntarily even as the foreign military forces continue their withdrawals. They have built up a self-financing war economy centered on mineral exploitation.

Not all of the exploitation has been from other nations. From the time of its independence in 1960, the country has been ruled by despots more interested in personal wealth and power than in the welfare of their people or the good governance of the nation.

Today, the DRC is a nation without a strong central government; a nation consumed by wars with many of the combatants funded and armed by neighboring countries; a nation with hundreds of thousands of displaced people; a nation whose population is under constant threat of being killed, raped, plundered, kidnapped, forced into military service, and being driven from homes and villages; a nation with almost no paved roads; a nation that has lost almost four million people to the ravages of war, sickness and hunger; a nation whose people pray for the United States or the United Nations to militarily impose peace in their country so they can make a living and provide for their families.

Into this maelstrom, MONUC (United Nations Organization Mission in the Democratic Republic of the Congo) was deployed in 1999. From the time of its deployment, it has been heavily criticized (primarily by Congolese, but also by non-government organizations (NGOs) in the country and by many MONUC personnel themselves) for not doing enough to stop the fighting and bring peace to the DRC. United Nations officials and members of the UN Security Council nations point out, however, that MONUC is an observer force, not a combat force; and its mandate has never been, and never will be, to forcibly bring peace to the DRC. This dichotomy between the mandate many people believe MONUC *should* have, and the mandate that the UN and its member nations have imposed and are willing to support is key to people's assessment of the mission. A senior MONUC representative put it this way: "The UN has to coax troop-contributors by downplaying the 'robust-ness' of MONUC's mandate at the same time as it has to fight for as robust a role as reasonable in order to gain ground on the security front".

2. *RI*'s Interest in UN Peacekeeping Operations

Since early in 2000, *Refugees International* has been promoting effective peace-keeping operations as a means of preventing or shortening military conflicts that are the primary causes of refugees and displaced persons worldwide. In that year, *RI* co-founded the Partnership for Effective Peace Operations, which is a working group of NGOs that supports improvement of United Nations peace operations. In 2001, we began a series of studies on UN peacekeeping operations. In October 2001, we published our first report on the UN mission in Sierra Leone, "UNAMSIL – A Peacekeeping Success: Lessons Learned".

This report on MONUC is the second in the series. The purpose of these studies is to help develop a list of factors that enhance the effectiveness of UN peace operations, and also a list of factors, based on lessons learned, that are not conducive to effective peace operation.

3. Brief History of *RI* Engagement in the Congo

RI has advocated in the war-torn Great Lakes region consistently since the Rwandan genocide in early 1994. The current humanitarian crisis in the Congo has its beginnings in that same war. RI has repeatedly called for increased attention, assistance and a regionalized response to the crises in this region, frequently visiting Eastern Congo along with Rwanda and Burundi, and the refugee camps in Western Tanzania.

In December 2000, RI called for donors to make greater efforts to provide humanitarian aid to needy Congolese by utilizing an extensive network of Congolese civil society, churches, and NGOs.

In Spring 2001, we identified a food shortage for Congolese and Burundian refugees in Tanzania due to insufficient donor contributions. We then published a bulletin on child soldiers in the Congo, bringing to light the continuing recruitment and use of child soldiers, highlighted by specific stories of children recruited by armies operating there. We testified on this before Congress, and we advocated with international NGOs who demobilize child soldiers to demobilize girls as well as boys.

In January 2002, RI was on the scene when a well-publicized volcanic eruption destroyed one half of the city of Goma. We pointed out that as destructive as the volcano was, the devastation of its impact paled in comparison to the consequences of the ongoing conflict in the region: that the war, a human disaster of unimaginable proportions, is the equivalent of daily volcanic eruptions. We also continued our reporting on the plight of children affected by the war, including the growing population of street children in urban areas of the Congo. We were requested to testify before the Senate Foreign Relations Committee's Sub-Committee on Africa about these issues. Despite progress toward peace, the people of Congo and its Great Lakes neighbors, especially Burundi, are still very much in need of protection and humanitarian aid.

Our November 2002 mission focused on analyzing the MONUC mission. We conducted more than 50 interviews with MONUC personnel, NGOs and Congolese citizens. We also interviewed senior officials in the U.S. Department of State, the Department of Defense, at the UN Department of Peacekeeping Operations in New York, and representatives from various countries that comprise the UN Security Council. These interviews and historical research form the basis of this report. Our latest mission to the DRC was February 2003.

4.   Historical Overview

4.1.   *The Belgian Congo*

The seminal history of the colonization of the Congo by Belgium is Adam Hochschild's *King Leopold's Ghost: A Story of Greed, Terror, and Heroism in Colonial Africa*, (Mariner Books, 1999). The book chronicles the period from the 1880s until the death of King Leopold II in 1909. As the title indicates, the book describes Leopold's personal obsession with obtaining a colony, focusing on the availability of the Congo, and then, once his goal was achieved, how he systematically plundered the resources of the Congo for his personal gain. It also chronicles the extreme cruelty he inflicted on the Congolese people. By some estimates, he was responsible for the deaths of half the population of the Congo. Belgian colonization of the Congo continued until international pressure caused it to grant independence in 1960.

According to a BBC World Service Report,

> On the eve of independence, the Congo, a territory larger than Western Europe, bordering on nine other African colonies/states, was seriously underdeveloped. There were no African army officers, only three African managers in the entire civil service, and only 30 university graduates. Yet Western investments in Congo's mineral resources (copper, gold, tin, cobalt, diamonds, manganese, zinc) were colossal. And these investments meant that the West was determined to keep control over the country beyond independence.

One of the seeds Belgium planted still germinates today: it failed to educate the Congolese population and to train Congolese leaders to govern and lead the nation in its transition to freedom and democracy. Instead, leaders arose who continued to exploit their power and gain personal fortunes.

4.2. *Joseph Kasavubu*

When the Congo declared independence in 1960, Joseph Kasavubu assumed the presidency on the recommendation of the Belgians; and Patrice Lumumba was appointed Prime Minister and Minister of Defence. Lumumba wanted a strong centralized state free of outside interference and hoped to make the Republic of the Congo the leader of a Pan-African Union of African States. Kasavubu, a federalist, took a more moderate stance and wanted to maintain close connections with Belgium and the West. In September 1960, both were unseated by a military coup led by Joseph Desire Mobutu. Kasavubu was reinstated in February 1961 and remained president until 1965. In 1965, he was removed in a second coup d'état by Mobutu and retired from politics.

Lumumba was not that fortunate. In November 1960, Lumumba sought to travel from Leopoldville (currently Kinshasa), where the United Nations promised him protection, to Stanleyville (Kisangani), where his supporters had control. With the active complicity of foreign intelligence sources, Mobutu sent his soldiers after Lumumba. He was caught after several days of pursuit and was delivered on January 17, 1961 to the Katanga secessionist regime, where he was executed on the night of his arrival.

4.3. *Joseph Desire Mobutu*

Mobutu, who also called himself Mobutu Sese Seko, had served as Lumumba's private secretary and then as chief of staff of the army.

In 1965, Mobutu seized power permanently, declaring himself president. He was one of Africa's most tenacious and ruthless dictators, ruling the country for the next 32 years. Mobutu generally relied on a system of government described as "kleptocracy", which meant staying in power by diverting the nation's wealth to his own coffers, sharing that wealth with his political allies, and controlling their personal access to government revenue. Anyone in any position of power was authorized to extract fees/bribes for the delivery of services. Those who were not willing to participate in the kleptocracy and others who could not be trusted were often executed or murdered.

Mobutu was particularly successful at taking advantage of the Cold War rivalry between the United States and the Soviet Union. Both sides were so intent on preventing the other from gaining advantage in Africa that both paid enormous amounts of money to Mobutu to keep him from going over to the other side.

By the last few years of his regime, Mobutu was sick and was growing increasing removed from running the country. As he loosened his grip on the sources of his power – control over the wealth of the country and control over the distribution of that wealth – he, too, became susceptible to being overthrown. That happened on May 17, 1997 in a rebellion led by Laurent Kabila.

4.4. *Laurent Kabila*

Kabila was also a disciple of Patrice Lumumba. He came to prominence in October 1996, when he emerged to lead a revolt by ethnic Tutsis in South Kivu. With support from the government in Uganda and the Rwandan military – then headed by Major General Paul Kagame, another Kabila associate – Kabila united the Tutsis with veteran anti-Mobutu guerrilla groups to mount a full-fledged rebellion. Kabila's forces were known as the Alliance of Democratic Forces for the Liberation of Congo-Zaire (ADFL).

Kabila had a great deal of popular support at the time of the coup. Mobutu had devastated the nation over the past three decades and people looked to Kabila to restore good governance and order. In a May 22, 1997 broadcast of "Newshour", Jim Lehrer described the situation:

> The Republic of Congo's new rulers have inherited a nation transformed from one of the richest countries in Africa to one of the poorest, a country the size of Western Europe with only 300 kilometers of paved roads. In a city where unemployment is over 90 percent, manual workers wait by their piles of tools for casual labor. Less than a week of the new regime hasn't changed conditions, but it has raised expectations.

Those expectations were never realized. On January 16, 2001 Laurent Kabila was shot in an incident that initially had the hallmarks of a failed putsch. His most trusted bodyguard, identified at the time as one Kasereka Rashiri, reputedly shot him. Later reports had it that the assassin was killed.

Kabila's reign was described in a BBC News Profile written the day after his assassination:

> It is the Congolese people who have suffered most, reduced to even greater poverty. And their hopes of freedom, of full inclusion in the international community, have remained unfulfilled. Laurent Kabila quickly alienated himself from aid donors and investors as he surrounded himself with friends and family members and became increasingly secretive. After coming to power he banned all political parties except his own and promised elections that were never held, and he refused to restart payments on the country's $14 billion debt. When he blocked a United Nations investigation into the massacre of tens of thousands of Rwandan refugees during his march to power, the international community lost much faith in him too.

A few days after the assassination, it was announced that Joseph Kabila had assumed his father's role. Kabila, the son, is the DRC's current ruler.

5.   Roots of DRC's Current Problems

The DRC's current problems are rooted in the 1994 genocide in Rwanda. After an estimated 800,000 Tutsis and some Hutu conservatives were killed by Hutus in Rwanda, then-Major Paul Kagame led an exiled army against the Rwandan Hutu government. Hutus fearing retaliation for the killings fled en masse to Congo. These Hutus consisted of military units, family members, civilians who took part in the genocide and a number of civilians who were either forced to flee or who fled for fear of the incoming Tutsi army. The Hutu camps they set up in the DRC were located mostly in the provinces of North and South Kivu. In North Kivu, they reverted to old habits and began to harass the province's Congolese Tutsis. Tutsis in South Kivu (known as Banyamulenge), fearing they'd share the same fate, launched a preemptive strike in October of 1996 against the Hutu militias and Mobutu's Congolese army.

Mobutu had granted amnesty and impunity to the Hutu militias, as he had to rebel groups fighting the governments of Angola and Uganda for the past 30 years. Mobutu himself was in a struggle with Kabila, the father, to maintain power and was enlisting the aid of former Rwandan military units.

Rwanda's Paul Kagame joined forces with Uganda's Yoweri Museveni, and dispatched several units to South Kivu in support of the Banyamulenge and to clear the DRC-Rwandan border of the Hutu camps. Mobutu's army refused to fight back and fled. Kagame and Museveni began preparations to oust Mobutu. They put together a coalition of Congolese exiles called the Alliance of Democratic Forces for the Liberation of Congo-Zaire (AFDL), headed by Laurent Kabila.

By 1998, less than a year after Kabila reached Kinshasa, both Kagame and Museveni were frustrated by the lack of progress in rooting out the Hutu militias, who remained in Congo. They demanded a free hand to take care of the problem, but to their surprise, Kabila refused. He had replaced most of the Rwandan and Ugandan advisors who had initially eased him into Kinshasa with his own men, who assured him that the rebuilt Congolese army could hold its own. But it could not hold its own. Very quickly, the Rwandan and Ugandan units and their local proxies seized half the country up to the gates of Kinshasa itself.

Sensing an opportunity for enrichment, the Angolans, Namibians and Zimbabweans threw their support behind Kabila. The Rwandans and Ugandans were gradually pushed back, though they retained control of about half of the country.

6.   Description of the Current Situation for Refugees and the Displaced

In many ways, little has changed in the DRC since that time. Despite a number of ceasefire agreements and the deployment of the most expensive United Nations peacekeeping operation, Joseph Kabila is still the leader of the DRC Kinshasa government, although there have not been any national elections. The eastern part of the country remains under various rebel faction control. And most important, the Congolese people are still suffering from war, poverty, lack of government services, sickness, and hunger. Families are still being driven from their homes. Children are still being pressed into military service. Women are still being raped.

Much of the conlict is now centered in the Ituri district of eastern DRC. Ituri is an area the UPDF (Ugandan-backed forces) have occupied since 1998. The most recent rounds of clashes involve new groups and breakaway factions that have all, at one time or another, received support from Uganda, as reported in the UN panel of Experts on the Illegal Exploitation of Resources, and also by Human Rights Watch. Six Red Cross workers were targeted and killed in this area in 2001, prompting the ICRC to withdraw all of its work in Ugandan-held territories pending an investigation.

The rebel groups operating in the area, each seeking power on its own behalf, represent an alphabet soup of acronyms and a spaghetti highway of links to foreign governments. Rather than try to explain each group in the body of the report, a list of acronyms and brief descriptions is attached.

Since August 2002, the areas of N. Kivu have been subject to successive population displacements on a massive scale. In two health zones of Ituri, an estimated 85% of the population is displaced. As RI has reported on elsewhere in the conflicts in the Congo, civilians are targets of much of the violence. In September, a massacre in a hospital in Nyakunde provoked the flight of 100,000 people. In January 2003, reports of cannibalism and rape motivated some media attention, and mobilized MONUC and UN investigations. Insecurity still prevents much of the humanitarian response from reaching the populations. Reports currently reaching RI state that levels of malnutrition among the displaced are catastrophic. For the entire region, estimates are that 500,000 IDPs are on the move or trying to get home.

7.   Enter MONUC

7.1. *Lusaka Ceasefire Agreement*

On July 10, 1999 at Lusaka, Zambia, the heads of state of the DRC, Namibia, Rwanda, Uganda and Zimbabwe, and the Minister of Defence of Angola, signed an agreement for a cessation of hostilities between all the belligerent forces in the DRC. The RCD and the MLC declined to sign.

The ceasefire included:

- All air, land, and sea attacks as well as all actions of sabotage;
- Attempts to occupy new ground positions and the movement of military forces and resources from one area to another, without prior agreement between the parties;
- All acts of violence against the civilian population by respecting and protecting human rights. The acts of violence include summary executions, torture, harassment, detention and execution of civilians based on their ethnic origin; propaganda inciting ethnic hatred; arming civilians; recruitment and use of child soldiers; sexual violence; training of terrorists, massacres, downing of civilian aircraft and bombing the civilian population;
- Supplies of ammunition and weaponry and other war-related stores to the field;
- Any other actions that may impede the normal evolution of the cease-fire process.

A key element of the agreement was the establishment of a United Nations force for the DRC:

> The United Nations Security Council, *acting under Chapter VII* of the UN Charter and in collaboration with the OAU, shall be requested to constitute, facilitate and deploy an appropriate peacekeeping force in the DRC to ensure implementation of this agreement; and taking into account the peculiar situation of the DRC, mandate the peacekeeping force to track down all armed groups in the DRC. In this respect, the UN Security Council shall provide the requisite mandate for the peacekeeping force.

Thus was MONUC born. And from its conception, it was flawed. According to a senior representative of the Permanent Mission of Belgium to the United Nations, "The Congo file started in Africa, not in the United Nations. The Lusaka Agreement called for UN forces. They didn't know what they were writing. The UN wasn't there. The UN came in with a framework that wasn't theirs".

The Lusaka signatories (also referred to as "parties") were expecting a military force that would be in addition to observing and verifying elements of the agreement:
- Providing and maintaining humanitarian assistance to and protect displaced persons, refugees and other affected persons;
- Tracking down and disarming armed groups;
- Screening mass killers, perpetrators of crimes against humanity and other war criminals;
- Handing over "genocidaires" to the International Crimes Tribunal for Rwanda;
- Repatriation;
- Working out such measures (persuasive or coercive) as are appropriate for the attainment of the objectives of disarming, assembling, repatriation and reintegration into society of members of the armed groups.

On August 6, 1999, the UN Security Council issued Resolution 1258, authorizing:

the deployment of up to 90 United Nations military liaison personnel, together with the necessary civilian, political, humanitarian and administrative staff, to the capitals of the States
signatories to the Ceasefire Agreement and the provisional headquarters of the JMC (Joint
Military Commission), and, as security conditions permit, to the rear military headquarters of
the main belligerents in the Democratic Republic of the Congo and, as appropriate, to other
areas the Secretary-General may deem necessary.

The mandate was basically to assist the JMC, provide information to the Secretary
General, and to lay the groundwork with the signatories for possible deployment of
military observers in the DRC.

Next came UN Security Council Resolution 1273, date November 5, 1999.
UNSCR 1273 extended the mandate until January 15, 2000. A few weeks later,
November 30, 1999, UNSCR 1279 was adopted. It said that personnel authorized
under resolutions 1258 and 1273 "shall constitute the United Nations Organization
Mission in the Democratic Republic of the Congo (MONUC) until 1 March 2000".
It also established a Special Representative of the Secretary-General to lead MONUC.
Added to its mandate was "to maintain liaison with all parties to the Ceasefire
Agreement to facilitate the delivery of humanitarian assistance to displaced persons,
refugees, children and other affected persons, and assist in the protection of human
rights, including the rights of children". Lastly, the resolution requests that the UN
Secretary-General, "with immediate effect", take the administrative steps needed to
equip up to 500 military observers for the DRC.

MONUC's current mandate and manpower authorizations are contained in
UNSCR 1291 dated February 24, 2000. It authorized the expansion of MONUC to
consist of up to 5,537 military personnel, including up to 500 observers, or more,
provided that the Secretary-General determines that there is a need and that it can
be accommodated within the overall force size and structure, and appropriate civilian support staff in the areas, inter alia, of human rights, humanitarian affairs, public information, child protection, political affairs, medical support and administrative
support, and requests the Secretary-General to recommend immediately any additional force requirements that might become necessary to enhance force protection.

7.2. *Analyzing the MONUC Mission*

The difficulty of analyzing the MONUC operation in terms of what is working, what
is not working, and what can we learn that can help future operations succeed is
that definitions of "success" and "failure" depend on who and where you are. If
you are in New York with a UN Mission or DPKO, there are some small problems
but, basically, everything is going according to plan. If you are an NGO or a part
of the MONUC organization in the DRC, particularly outside Kinshasa, MONUC
has its successes but there's a lot of frustration about how little it's doing and how
hard it is to do more. If you are a Congolese, you are wondering why armed sol-

diers either sit around in their bases or drive their UN vehicles on your dirt roads and don't lift a finger to protect them or stop the fighting. All three perspectives are equally valid and invalid, depending on your perspective. This report will analyze strengths and weaknesses of the MONUC mission from each of the three applicable perspectives and make recommendations to bridge the perspective-gaps as well as MONUC operations.

7.3. *The Mandate*

The most contentious element of the mandate is the last one pertaining to protection under Chapter VII of the UN Charter – "Action With Respect To Threats to the Peace, Breaches of the Peace, and Acts of Aggression". Article 42 of Chapter VII is the operative article. It states:

> Should the Security Council consider that [non-military] measures would be inadequate or have proved to be inadequate, it may take such action by air, sea, or land forces as may be necessary to maintain or restore international peace and security. Such action may include demonstrations, blockade, and other operations by air, sea, or land forces of Members of the United Nations.

The vast majority of UN peacekeeping operations fall under Chapter VI of the UN Charter – "Pacific Settlement of Disputes". Other than for self-protection, Chapter VI mandates generally prohibit the use of force.

The MONUC mandate is referred to both in New York and in the DRC unofficially as a "Chapter 6-1/2". Although it is primarily an "observer" mission under Chapter VI, it clearly has a Chapter VII provision. Many of the people and parties who disagree on the success or failure of MONUC do so based on how they interpret this particular element of the mandate.

The current MONUC mandate is at Figure 1.

A close reading of that element shows how vaguely it is written:

> Acting under Chapter VII of the Charter of the United Nations, decides that MONUC *may* take the ***necessary*** action, ***in the areas of deployment of its infantry battalions*** and *as it deems it within its capabilities*, to protect United Nations and co-located JMC personnel, facilities, installations and equipment, ensure the security and freedom of movement of its personnel, and ***protect civilians under imminent threat of physical violence***.

The best example, and consequences, of the mandate's lack of clarity occurred on May 14-17, 2002, in Kisangani. According to an OCHA report on July 22, 2002:

> A report by a UN expert has detailed "the massacres" of at least 183 people in Kisangani, eastern Democratic Republic of Congo, allegedly committed by one of the main rebel groups in the country, the Rwanda-backed Rassemblement congolais pour la democratie (RCD-Goma).

MONUC Mandate

➤ to monitor the implementation of the Ceasefire Agreement and investigate violations of the ceasefire;

➤ to establish and maintain continuous liaison with the field headquarters of all the parties' military forces;

➤ to develop, within 45 days of adoption of this resolution, an action plan for the overall implementation of the Ceasefire Agreement by all concerned with particular emphasis on the following key objectives: the collection and verification of military information on the parties' forces, the maintenance of the cessation of hostilities and the disengagement and redeployment of the parties' forces, the comprehensive disarmament, demobilization, resettlement and reintegration of all members of all armed groups referred to in Annex A, Chapter 9.1 of the Ceasefire Agreement, and the orderly withdrawal of all foreign forces;

➤ to work with the parties to obtain the release of all prisoners of war, military captives and remains in cooperation with international humanitarian agencies;

➤ to supervise and verify the disengagement and redeployment of the parties' forces;

➤ within its capabilities and areas of deployment, to monitor compliance with the provisions of the Ceasefire Agreement on the supply of ammunition, weaponry and other war-related matériel to the field, including to all armed groups referred to in Annex A, Chapter 9.1;

➤ to facilitate humanitarian assistance and human rights monitoring, with particular attention to vulnerable groups including women, children and demobilized child soldiers, as MONUC deems within its capabilities and under acceptable security conditions, in close cooperation with other United Nations agencies, related organizations and nongovernmental organizations;

➤ to cooperate closely with the Facilitator of the National Dialogue, provide support and technical assistance to him, and coordinate other United Nations agencies' activities to this effect;

➤ to deploy mine action experts to assess the scope of the mine and unexploded ordnance problems, coordinate the initiation of mine action activities, develop a mine action plan, and carry out emergency mine action activities as required in support of its mandate;

Acting under Chapter VII of the Charter of the United Nations, decides that MONUC may take the necessary action, in the areas of deployment of its infantry battalions and as it deems it within its capabilities, to protect United Nations and co-located JMC personnel, facilities, installations and equipment, ensure the security and freedom of movement of its personnel, and protect civilians under imminent threat of physical violence.

Figure 1

The killings started following a mutiny in Kisangani on Sunday, involving troops of the RCD-Goma, the de-facto authority in eastern Congo. The group briefly occupied a local radio station and appealed to the public to expel Rwandan troops from the country. A number of people were immediately killed by a mob, after which RCD-Goma troops retaliated.

In a briefing to the UN Security Council on Tuesday, UN High Commissioner for Human Rights Mary Robinson cited accounts by witnesses in Kisangani detailing the shooting of police and soldiers who were ordered to lie down, with their hands bound; others were hacked to death with machetes or had their throats slit on the Tshopo Bridge in the city.

"It appears that some of the bodies were decapitated before being thrown in the river. Some of the bodies were reportedly put in plastic bags", she said.

Among the dead were 103 civilians and at least 60 soldiers and police officers. But the report indicated that a further 20 unidentified bodies were also observed in the Tshopo River after the mutiny.

A Congolese woman who lives in Kisangani told *RI* her experience on May 14, 2002. "I was in my house listening to the radio about what the military was saying. I was staying calm. At high noon, a military person came to the door and said the Commandant wanted to *see* me". She refused to go. "He came back with a second soldier and they threatened to beat me up if I didn't come. I was very afraid and ran to the Moroccan (MONUC) camp. I told them that the RDC was menacing me and I asked for their help". After waiting on the sidewalk outside the MONUC base, she returned to her home. "Two days later, Rwandans passed through my house and found my 20 year old son. They told him that if he didn't help them find the civil president they would recruit him into their army. We went into hiding after that". *Despite the presence of a Moroccan Infantry Battalion and a Uruguayan Infantry Battalion in Kisangani, MONUC commanders there did not believe they had the mandate to protect the citizens, or to even help this woman.*

Yet on June 12, 2002, Amos Ngongi, the Secretary-General's Special Representative to the country, told reporters after briefing the Council behind closed doors, that "There were discussions on the protection aspect of MONUC's work, and clearly it is understood that MONUC does not have the capacity to be able to ensure full protection of the civilian population in the DRC – that's not possible", he said. "But clearly MONUC has the responsibility and the mandate to be able to protect those whose lives are in imminent danger, especially in the areas in which MONUC is fully deployed, like Kisangani". He went on to say "We can take dissuasive action, rather than proactive protection. We don't have the troops or the appropriate equipment for that. But that's no excuse for not coming to the rescue of people whose lives are imminently in danger".

7.4.   *The New York Perspective*

If MONUC's first problem was that the UN was not present at the Lusaka Ceasefire Agreement to weigh in on what the signatories were asking for, MONUC's second problem was the UN was responsible for the mandate the signatories were going to get. This is not an indictment of the United Nations, but rather an acknowledgement of the realities under which it operates.

New York is the Headquarters of the United Nations. In addition, each member country has a Mission to the UN in New York. The office responsible for peace-keeping operations is the Department of Peacekeeping Operations (DPKO). The mission and scope of operations of the DPKO are:

> The United Nations Department of Peacekeeping Operations (DPKO) is responsible for the planning, preparation, conduct and direction of UN peacekeeping operations. As an operational arm of the Secretary General, it formulates policies, procedures and contingency planning, based on Security Council decisions, for peacekeeping operations and certain other operations, such as election monitoring. While DPKO has a core of its own staff, supplemented by seconded military and civilian staff, it does not have military forces permanently under its direct control. Instead, each operation utilizes troop contingents provided by various governments, normally headed in the field by a Force Commander chosen from one of the troop contributing nations".

What the Lusaka parties asked for was a force to restore and enforce the peace. What they got was the UN reality. "The mandate is a function of what member states are likely to bear and what troop-donating countries are willing to commit to", said a Humanitarian Affairs Officer with the Office of the Commissioner for Humanitarian Affairs (OCHA). Or as another member of the Permanent Mission to the UN Security Council put it, "There is no such thing as a bad mandate. The mandate is what the Security Council makes it. Simply put, there was no willingness among the UN member states to commit combat troops to a Chapter VII mission in the DRC".

A senior military official in DPKO said "Mandates are political. Mandates are the result of taskings. The wishes of a commander on the ground are different from those in New York. Here we have the problem of the dollar sign". Another senior DPKO official said "The UN knows it can't do military missions without military assets".

"The enormity of the task of deploying a peacekeeping force to the DRC whatever its mandate was clear from the outset", according to a report from the International Crisis Group (ICG), "From Kabila to Kabila: Prospects for Peace in the Congo", dated March 16, 2001.

> Security Council officials in New York were loath to accept responsibility for what they expected to be a disaster. The U.S. Congress, which contributes one-third of any peacekeeping operation's budget, was equally wary of what appeared to be a dangerous Congolese quagmire. Compelled to placate these conflicting concerns, the UN Secretary General decreed that the force deployed to the Congo must be both militarily credible and cheap.

An OCHA Humanitarian officer told *RI* that the "mandate was written the way the members wanted it. It was essentially set up with the idea that essentially the Africans need to sort things out themselves". He explained that there are really three types of conflict in the DRC: Interstate (belligerents from neighboring countries fighting in the DRC), Interstate (Congolese rebel factions fighting with the Kinshasa government and among themselves), and Ethnic (Hutu-Tutsi, Lendu-Hema). "The [MONUC] mandate accounts primarily for the interstate conflict", the OCHA official said. "And from that perspective, MONUC has succeeded in separating the belligerent parties. The mandate really doesn't affect the situation in the east. I know this is a sore point for people who don't like the mandate".

"MONUC was never intended to make peace", said a representative from the Permanent Mission of France to the UN. "The parties [to the Lusaka Ceasefire Agreement] must make the peace. MONUC has no capacity to do that. There is not a single state willing to provide combat forces. MONUC must use political instruments, not military ones. But if MONUC were not doing what it does, no one else would be doing it. Things would be much worse".

And yet another DPKO perspective: "Mandates are political. Canada, Norway and others pushed the protection mission into the mandate. But no troops were provided for that part. That's why there are so many caveats. We are basically an observer mission. They created the expectation of protection but couldn't fulfill it".

Ultimately, the debate about the mandate boils down to two questions: Is the mandate too weak, or is the MONUC leadership interpreting the mandate too conservatively? The view from DPKO, the UN missions (including the United States) favors the latter. A U.S. State Department official told *RI* that the current mandate is robust enough to accomplish the mission and to protect citizens. "But the MONUC leadership is risk-averse", he said. "Risk-averse" is a term that came up frequently in meetings an UN Missions and at DPKO.

One country's Mission said, "The current mandate would support deployment in Ituri. Mr. Ngongi [the Senior Representative to the Secretary-General – SRSG] has a very conservative view of the mandate, just like his bosses in New York. There is no need to provide the military with more aggressive equipment. They only need to be equipped for deterrence". "Our country", he said, "supports a more proactive role. We support more presence in the east. All this is possible within the current mandate".

An OCHA Humanitarian Officer asked, however, if the SRSG is risk-averse, or is he getting a risk-averse message from the P-5 (the Permanent Members of the UN Security Council: UK, U.S., France, Russian Federation and China)? At least one P-5 country representative agreed. "The problems are not linked to one person", he said. "They are cautious because we keep saying 'no' to them. There is not good communication between New York and Kinshasa".

A senior military officer in DPKO argues that MONUC's ability to pursue a Chapter VII initiative is very limited. "The UN military system is complex. We have rotating leadership and contingents. Some are rotated every six months. Some don't speak English. Some don't speak French. This leads to problems in understanding the mandates", he said. "Beyond that, the troop strength in MONUC is a drop in the bucket. You say 'Why not send troops with MILOBS (Military Observers) and security officers?' What if those troops are attacked? We can't get troops from Kinshasa or other places for hours or days. You can't send in troops without plans for helping them if they run into problems. That's a basic military strategy. All they are trained or equipped or manned to do is protect their bases and equipment".

In summary, the point of view of the leadership in DPKO and the UN Missions is pragmatic. The current MONUC mandate is the right mandate because it's the best mandate they are going to get. There is no support among UN member states to send combat troops to the DRC to enforce a peace.

International Police Forces in Peace Operations

*Thorsten Stodiek**

1.   Classifying the International Police in the Area of Conflict Management

International police components have been playing an increasingly important role within the framework of peace missions led by the UN and regional security organizations such as the EU and the OSCE. While during the Cold War, the UN generally operated only in inter-state conflicts by stationing blue helmet soldiers as a buffer between two enemy armies, since the 1990s, this world organization has almost without exception been confronted with intra-state conflicts. To solve these conflicts, which often took place in an anarchic environment, it was necessary to go through the complex process of building democratic structures under the rule of law, and it was of fundamental importance that these be protected by an international police force. Soldiers can, by their very presence, prevent the extensive outbreak of violence between conflict parties, however, because of inadequate training and equipment, they are not able, or willing, to perform the tasks that civilian uniformed police forces, criminal police departments or the traffic police are capable of. Therefore, missions in countries in which the local police have been disbanded, or discredited – due to serious violations of (human) rights committed against their people – need international police forces, which, through consistent implementation of the laws and operating under the principles of the rule of law, are able to win over the confidence of the people, thus forestalling arbitrary vigilantism (one need not even mention that a functioning judicial system is a fundamental prerequisite).

---

*   Dr. Th. Stodiek is a researcher at the Institute for Peace Research and Security Policy at the University of Hamburg (www.ifsh.de). He is also a co-editor of the quarterly "Sicherheit und Frieden. Security and Peace (S+F)". This article is the result of studies conducted as part of the research project "International Police as an Instrument for Conflict Management" funded by the Volkswagen Foundation, respectively the result of the author's dissertation "Internationale Polizei. Ein empirisch fundiertes Konzept der zivilen Konfliktbearbeitung". Baden-Baden, 2004.

Harvey Langholtz, Boris Kondoch, Alan Wells (Eds.),
International Peacekeeping: The Yearbook of International Peace Operations, Volume 9, 2004, pp. 93-107.
© *Koninklijke Brill N.V. Printed in the Netherlands*

The increase in the importance of the police component in international peace operations has been reflected in the development of the peacekeeping missions since the end of the Cold War in quantitative as well as qualitative terms. While, in the Namibia Mission from 1989 to 1990, about 1,500 UN police were deployed only to monitor local police forces,[1] in the following missions, new tasks, such as the creation and training of local police units, were also added to their responsibilities. This took into account that the success of a peacekeeping mission was, to a large extent, dependent on the "performance" of the local police after the withdrawal of international security forces. At the end of a mission, these local police had to be capable and willing to prevent violations of human rights, protect democratic institutions and take resolute action against corruption, organized crime and terrorism. At the end of the day, the capability to guarantee domestic security is a basic prerequisite for the socio-economic stabilization of crisis regions.

The quantitative and qualitative high point in the history of international police missions was the deployment of the *United Nations Civilian Police* (UNCIVPOL) as a component of the *United Nations Interim Administration Mission in Kosovo* (UNMIK, since 1999). In addition to the usual monitoring and training tasks, UNCIVPOL was entrusted with armed law enforcement responsibilities. This 4,718 strong UN police force comprises, by far, the largest police contingent in UN peace operations to date. Because the police contingent, which was sent to East Timor (*United Nations Transitional Administration in East Timor*/UNTAET) a couple of months later, was also vested with armed law enforcement competencies, one can assume that this kind of mandate (at least within a UN framework) will increasingly appear on the daily agenda alongside the traditional tasks of training and monitoring local police. This is a fact that must be taken into consideration in setting up international police contingents.

2.   Experiences and Problems in Deploying Police Components in International Peace Operations

2.1.   *Problems of Quantity*

Up to now, all missions have had to tackle logistical problems in their initial phases. There has often been a lack of office supplies, computer and communications technology or there have not been enough police cars available. These problems became even more severe, when UNCIVPOL was deployed to mission areas, where the

---

1   See F.-E. Hufnagel, UN-Friedensoperationen der zweiten Generation. Vom Puffer zur neuen Treuhand (Berlin 1996), pp. 62ff.; and A.S. Hansen, From Congo to Kosovo: Civilian Police in Peace Operations, Adelphi Paper 343 (New York 2002), p. 20.

whole infrastructure had been destroyed during the civil wars, as for example in Kosovo and in East Timor.[2]

However, the most difficult and most persistent problem in all the missions – at least those requiring a large number of personnel – has been the recruitment issue, respectively the lack of qualified personnel. In 2000, 25 percent of the 8,641 police positions authorized for UN police missions remained vacant.[3] The grave consequence of these personnel shortcomings became most obvious in Kosovo, when UNCIVPOL was, for the first time in UN history, entrusted with the complex task of armed law enforcement, requiring police officers with various specific skills. In December 1999, half a year after the Mission started, there were only about 2,000 of the 4,718 police that UN Secretary-General Kofi Annan had requested to the deployment area. After the withdrawal of all Yugoslav security forces, this number was far too low to adequately support and relieve the overstretched NATO-led *Kosovo Force* (KFOR) soldiers, who were also faced with fulfilling genuine police tasks. During November 1999 alone, KFOR reported 379 murders. Over 180,000 Serbs and Roma (over half of these ethnic groups) had left the country for Montenegro and Serbia for fear of being attacked by Albanians.[4] More than four years after the start of the Mission, the security situation in Kosovo has improved considerably, however, very few Kosovo Serbs dare to take the risk of returning to their home villages.[5] The UNMIK police contingent, which has never reached its full authorized strength (its peak was about 4,500 officers in 2001–2002) has rather been reduced to about 3,770 in September 2003. UNMIK hoped that the newly established Kosovo Police Service with around 5,020 officers on duty in September 2003 would compensate for this reduction in UNCIVPOL personnel.[6]

---

2   Cf. J. Traub, Inventing East Timor, in: Foreign Affairs, vol. 4, No. 79/2000, pp. 82-89; and Th. Stodiek, "International Police. An Empirically Based Concept of Civilian Crisis Management" (Baden-Baden) 2004, forthcoming.

3   Cf. Brahimi-Report, Report of the Panel on United Nations Peace Operations, A/55/305-S/2000/809, 21 August 2000, p. 20.

4   Cf. Th. Stodiek, Internationale Polizeimissionen und die Herausforderungen auf internationaler und nationaler Ebene, in: Vierteljahresschrift für Sicherheit und Frieden (S+F), 1/2000, p. 66.

5   According to the UNHCR, only 4,000 Serbs had returned to Kosovo until Summer 2003, cf. Institute for War and Peace Reporting, Come back, Serbs, Balkan Crisis Report No. 441, 4 July 2003, at: http://www.iwpr.net/index.pl?archive/bcr3/ bcr3_200307_441_1_eng.txt. During the first five months of 2003, 437 Serbs returned home, see United Nations Security Council, Report of the Secretary-General on the United Nations Interim Administration Mission in Kosovo, 26 June 2003, S/2003/675, p. 9.

6   For personnel figures see UNMIK Police Daily Press Update, 7th September 2003, p. 6, at: http://www.unmikonline.org/civpol/archive/DPU080903.htm. least 6.300 local police officers shall have received basic training at the OSCE run police academy in Vucitrn at the End of 2003, see Organization for Security and Co-operation in Europe. Mission in Kosovo, Media Advisory, 10 April 2003, at: http://www.osce.org/news/generate.pf.php3?news_id=3193.

2.2. *Problems of Quality*

Apart from the purely quantitative aspect of the lack of personnel in UN police missions, the qualitative deficits in the UN police missions, and cultural problems within the ranks of the UN police as well as those between UN police and local police and/or the local population are great impediments to the successful implementation of police mandates which are becoming increasingly complex. Many police officers lack the basic prerequisites for an international mission: They do not speak English, they have no mastery of weapon use (necessary in armed executive missions) and cannot drive the all-terrain vehicles of the UN police. Many officers – especially from developing countries – have been forced into service by their governments without any consideration of their training, equipment and motivation.[7] In addition, some of these officers come from countries, where human rights are routinely violated in daily law enforcement.[8] Their behaviour in missions is therefore often unsatisfactory. As a consequence, they are looked upon negatively by the local police and the local population; this, in turn, can give the whole mission a bad image. Although few, there are even cases of gross misconduct (torturing of detainees)[9] and misbehaviour (black-marketeering, corruption, promotion of prostitution)[10] involving UNCIVPOL officers.

Moreover, cultural differences in behaviour and attitudes towards work can lead to tensions within units which are composed of mixed nationalities. The problem begins with the different approaches to the way in which superiors deal with their subordinates. This can lead to relatively harmless exasperation or someone's honour being wounded, and, at times, ends with fatal consequences because of differing attitudes on the application of physical force during interrogations, or different approaches to arrest and detention.[11]

2.3. *Legal Problems*

In addition, there is the pressing problem of inconsistent legal and procedural foundations and guidelines for law enforcement missions, which hampers equitable, con-

---

7   Interview with UNCIVPOL representatives in Kosovo in June 2000 and in July 2001 in New York.

8   Cf. Hansen, p. 53.

9   For example there has been one case in Kosovo where the international prosecutor has accused an UNMIK police officer of having tortured and abused a Kosovo-Albanian detainee, see Amnesty International Press Release, 18 June 2002, at: http://web.amnesty.org/ library/print/ENGEUR700052002; and UNMIK Chronicle – Issue no. 26, at: http//www.unmikonline.org/pub/chronicle/uc26htm.

10   See for example T. Findlay, Cambodia. The Legacy and Lessons of UNTAC, SIPRI Research report No. 9, (New York) 1995, p. 144; S. R. *Ratner*, The New UN Peacekeeping. Building Peace in Lands of Conflict after the Cold War, (New York) 1995, p. 172; E.A. Schmidl, Police in Peace Operations (Informationen zur Sicherheitspolitik, Nr. 10), (Vienna) 1998; pp. 41ff.; and Hansen, p. 50.

11   Interview with UNCIVPOL representatives in June 2000 in Kosovo and in July 2001 in New York.

sistent and efficient performance by the international police staff. Although, in principle, all UN police must follow the same Code of Conduct, UN guidelines are interpreted differently by different officers and often not implemented uniformly.[12] Moreover, it is often not clear to the police which law is to be enforced in a given mission. Basically, UNCIVPOL must apply and enforce the law of the host country in a mission, insofar as the local law conforms with internationally recognized human rights standards. But as in the case of Kosovo, ethnic Albanian judges refused to accept the current Yugoslav law of 1999, because they felt discriminated and oppressed by it. It took almost half a year before the then head of the UNMIK mission, Bernhard Kouchner, decided that the Yugoslav law of 22 March 1989 – the law applicable before the removal of the Kosovar autonomy by Slobodan Milosevic – would be applicable, however subordinate to several regulations promulgated by Kouchner himself.[13] It took even longer to develop coherent Serbian, Albanian and English translations of the applicable law and to release these translations to the local as well as international judiciary and police. In East Timor, the judiciary and police faced similar problems with respect to the compilation and translation of the applicable law.[14] Furthermore, it has been difficult for officers in law enforcement missions to combine the *Standard Operating Procedures* (SOPs) and criminal provisions issued by the UN Interim Administrations with the specific legal regulations of the host countries. The regulations for investigative activities, for example, can be different from country to country and the resultant insecurity and possible infringements of legal rights can interfere with solving crimes in an efficient manner.[15]

Up to now, there have only been very weak approaches toward creating uniform training programmes for law enforcement officials, developing standardized penal and criminal codes and preparing national police contingents for international missions, which could eliminate the above-mentioned problems. More on this later.

Alongside the UN, regional organizations such as the OSCE and the (W)EU have also engaged in international civilian policing missions. They have concentrated

---

12   Cf. ibid.

13   See C. Rausch, The assumption of authority in Kosovo and East Timor: legal and practical implications, in: R. Dwan (ed.), Executive Policing. Enforcing the Law in Peace Operations, SIPRI Research report No. 16, (New York) 2002, pp. 13ff.; H. Strohmeyer, Collapse and Reconstruction of a Judicial System: The United Nations Missions in Kosovo and East Timor, in, American Journal of International Law, vol. 95, no. 1, 2001, pp. 58f.; and Interview with UNCIVPOL representatives in June 2000 in Kosovo and in July 2001 in New York.

14   Cf. Rausch, p. 17f.

15   For example, the Yugoslav law which was to be applied in Kosovo demanded UN police officers to call an investigating judge when approaching the scene of a crime and searching for traces of evidence. Because many international police officers did not know this fact or, because in some cases, there was simply no investigative judge available a lot of crime evidence material, which had been collected by the police, was later not accepted in court due to procedural errors. See Interview with UNCIVPOL representatives in June 2000 in Kosovo.

on monitoring tasks as well as recently reforming and/or totally rebuilding local, and partially ethnically mixed police forces in Albania, Eastern Slovenia, Kosovo, Southern Serbia, Macedonia as well as Bosnia and Herzegovina, where missions have generally been evaluated as successful. Because the missions of these regional actors have and have had relatively small staffs (not exceeding several hundreds instead of several thousands), the contingents in most cases have generally been provided with well-trained personnel (although they also have had to struggle to receive professional training personnel from the contributing countries).[16] In addition, the cultural problems mentioned within the framework of UN missions do not appear to have played a very big role in (W)EU and OSCE missions, because all the officers in these missions came from similar cultural environments.

In principle, the OSCE and the EU would have the same recruitment problems as the UN if they had to raise police forces to a size as large as those of the UN in Bosnia, Kosovo or East Timor, because their member states in general have to cope with the same problem of seconding police officers out of their – due to necessary budgetary restrictions – already thinned out and overloaded domestic police forces.

3.   Programmes and Activities to Increase the Efficiency of International Police Missions

3.1.   *UN Measures*

With the "Agenda for Peace", Secretary-General Boutros Boutros-Ghali began comprehensive reforms in 1992 in the area of peacekeeping. During the following years, structural changes were introduced to the *Department of Peacekeeping Operations* (DPKO) to be able to achieve timely and comprehensive plans for peace operations.[17] However, especially in the area of preparing police missions, there have been considerable structural deficits in the DPKO: Up until 2001, there were, for example, only nine police officers dealing with planning and support tasks.

In order to be able to deploy peacekeeping units more rapidly, the UN has concluded *Memoranda of Understanding* (MOU) with 41 member states[18] within the framework of *United Nations Standby Arrangements System* (UNSAS), which has been in existence since 1995. In these MOU, the states established how many troops and how much material they will conditionally make available for UN missions. As

---

16   Interview with representatives of the OSCE in Vienna in May 2001 and April 2003.
17   Cf. Th. Stodiek, Der deutsche Beitrag zu den "Standby Forces" der Vereinten Nationen, Hamburger Beiträge zur Friedensforschung und Sicherheitspolitik, No. 113 (Hamburg 1999), pp. 9, 30f.
18   Figures as of June 2003, cf. DPKO, unsas – dates mou signed, at: http: www.un.org/Depts/dpko/milad/fgs2/unsas_files/status_report/mousigndate.htm

of September 2000, the UN had 2,150 police on standby within this framework.[19] In view of the approximately 6,800 UN police, which were required for missions in the Balkans and East Timor alone during the summer of 2001, these 2,150 police have only been proverbially a drop in the ocean.

To be able to achieve a common performance standard for multinational police units – some missions include police from over 50 countries – the United Nations has issued rules of conduct that regulate dealing with (suspected) criminals (arrest, interrogation, detention, use of firearms) in compliance with human rights and with the use of as little violence as possible. In addition, a catalogue of minimum requirements was developed for UNCIVPOL officers. These include adequate knowledge of the mission language, the capability to drive an all-terrain vehicle and – where armed law enforcement is authorized – the safe handling of weapons. In addition, the UN offers training programmes and supplies training centres with teaching material, mobile training and monitoring teams. Moreover, a screening programme, which is run by *Training Assistance Teams* (TATs), screens seconded police officers in their respective home countries prior to their deployment.[20] Nevertheless – as already mentioned – even in the most recent police missions in the Balkans, there are considerable differences in the qualifications of the mission members from various nations, and still a certain degree of seconded personnel has to be sent home because they are not qualified at all for the missions.[21]

In March 2000, UN Secretary General Annan appointed a commission of experts who published the Brahimi Report on 21 August 2000 in which there were extensive recommendations for improving UN peacekeeping operations. This report, which the UN Security Council and the UN widely affirmed, but which up to now has not been adequately put into practice, also contains a series of remarkable recommendations for making missions more effective in the area of civilian police:

-   To be able to guarantee the faster deployment of civilian police units, a pool of at least 100 senior police officers is to be established within the framework of UNSAS. This pool is to be deployable within seven days, to be integrated into the planning phase of a mission, to act as a forward command in a mission area to set up the necessary structures and to brief new arrivals on their specific duties during the course of the mission.[22]

---

19   Cf. DPKO, Monthly Summary of Contributors as of 30 September 2000, at: http://www.un.org/Depts/dpko/dpko/contributors/index.htm.
20   Cf. Hansen, p. 52.
21   For example, 15 per cent from time to time in Bosnia and Herzegovina, see J.M. Stiers, Testimony at the Hearing before the Commission on Security and Cooperation in Europe. Civilian Police and Police Training in Post-Conflict OSCE Areas, Washington, September 5, 2001, p. 9, at: http://www.csce.gov/ witness.cfm?briefing_id=197&testimony_id=192.
22   Cf. Brahimi-Report, p. 21.

- To be able to remedy the problem of the huge lack of personnel, UN member states will be asked to ensure that more than the 2,150 police, as of September 2000, are placed in national standby pools ready for deployment in UN missions.[23]
- Further, member states are to set up joint training programmes for their officers, so that police from different countries can already get to know one another during the preparation phase and be brought up to the same level of training. States that already possess the necessary training experience and resources are to offer courses to other states.[24]
- Furthermore, the report recommends that police officers make contact with other components of peacekeeping missions during these courses, for example, with military and legal experts or with aid organizations.[25]
- The report also calls for a division between the military and police departments of the DPKO as well as a comprehensive increase in personnel in the police division, so that police planners can fulfil their responsibility towards the 8,000 deployed colleagues.[26]
- To eliminate legal uncertainties in a mission, the report recommends that a commission of legal experts be appointed to examine the feasibility and use of a general transitional criminal law code, which would be adaptable regionally, until local laws and legal bodies are restored. As a result, Kofi Annan tasked an expert group consisting of legal experts from the UN headquarters and the missions in Kosovo and East Timor to examine the commission's recommendation. Although this committee of experts questions whether, in view of the differing legal traditions in the member states, a model law would be feasible and desired in the mission countries, it concludes that at least the development of practical guidelines to fight crime would be useful, provided that these guidelines do not interfere with local laws and are in accordance with international legal standards. However, these reservations would lead in practice to time-consuming compromise agreements and thus would not leave room for much improvement. Annan made reference to the fact that the *Centre for International Crime Prevention*, the office of the *UN High Commissioner for Human Rights* (UNHCR) as well as the office of the *UN Development Programme* (UNDP) and *UN International Children's Emergency Fund* (UNICEF) had already performed extensive preparation work on the question of general UN guidelines. Therefore, he tasked the above-mentioned subordinate UN organizations and the expert group to jointly identify areas in which general guidelines to fight crime need to be drawn up.

---

23   Cf. ibid., pp. 20f.
24   Cf. ibid., p. 21.
25   Cf. ibid.
26   Cf. ibid., p. 31.

Upon the implementation of this demand, it must be said that the unsatisfactory personnel situation in the police pool did not change, so that insiders have described this part of the Standby Arrangements System as a "joke".[27]

Within the DPKO, however, structural improvements have meanwhile taken place: the police department was separated from the military department and the CIVPOL Adviser is now directly subordinate to the Under-Secretary for Peacekeeping and no longer to the head of the Military Division. Moreover, the personnel has been increased by eight people. By the end of 2002, a work force of 20 officers had been deployed.[28]

In contrast, the development of an International Criminal Code looks bleak. There is no one at the UN who really wants to deal seriously with this topic. In particular, the Non-Aligned Movement (NAM) is against the development of this transitional criminal law code. The EU and the US, however, support the idea. The UNDP has, jointly, with Canada begun to merely tackle the development of a Correctional Code.[29]

Conclusion: In the area of mission planning there has been improvement, however, efficient mission implementation still faces many obstacles.

3.2. *OSCE Measures*

As a consequence of the serious recruitment problems in the course of the Kosovo Verification Mission and in face of the fact that, also within the OSCE, police components in the framework of peacekeeping missions have gained ever-increasing importance, the Heads of State or Government of the (then) 54 OSCE participating States at the Istanbul Summit in November 1999 agreed to measures on strengthening the operational area of the Organization. The following measures were considered significant for future police missions:

- the establishment of *Rapid Expert Assistance and Co-operation Teams* (REACT);
- building up capabilities for the implementation of police activities like training, developing and monitoring local police as well as perhaps also implementing police executive measures;
- the establishment of an *Operation Centre* in the *Conflict Prevention Centre* to plan and implement OSCE missions.[30]

Similar to the UN, the OSCE would also like to build up a pool of experts from which they can rapidly recruit the required personnel for a peace mission. Also, in

---

27   Interview with DPKO representatives in New York in June 2001.
28   Cf. ibid., 26.
29   Interview with DPKO representative in New York in June 2001.
30   Cf. Organization for Security and Co-operation in Europe, Charter for European Security, Istanbul, November 1999, in: Institute for Peace Research and Security Policy at the University of Hamburg/IFSH (Ed.), OSCE Yearbook 2000 (Baden-Baden 2001), pp. 425-443, here: p. 426.

the Operation Centre, which has a central file listing its personnel pool, future missions are to be prepared in due time – that is, before the Permanent Council has actually passed a decision to mandate a mission. Even before a mission has begun, potential mission members are to be prepared for future mission work through OSCE training programmes.

However, in the following months little was done to develop police capacities at the OSCE level, aside from setting up the Operation Centre (in operation since September 2000) and starting the Internet-accessible REACT database in April 2001. Therefore, at the insistence of the United Kingdom, the issue of the creation of the position of a Senior Police Adviser was undertaken at the Vienna Ministerial Council in November 2000.

An Open Working Group on Police Matters, to which all the 55 OSCE participating States were able to contribute, was tasked with solving this issue. The working group eventually submitted a report for consultation and decision-making to the Permanent Council. After the Permanent Council had decided on 4 December 2001 to create the post of Senior Police Adviser,[31] the high ranking police officer Richard Monk, on secondment from the UK, assumed office in this new position in February 2002. One of the main tasks of the Senior Police Adviser is to establish relations regarding co-operation between the OSCE and the UN, NATO, the EU and the European Commission, on the one hand, and between the OSCE Secretariat, the participating States and the OSCE missions and actives in the field, on the other.[32]

In May 2002, the Permanent Council also established the first contracted and seconded posts of Police Affairs Officers[33] for the new *Strategic Police Matters Unit* (SPMU). The main tasks of the SPMU are to support and to analyse the police-related activities of the OSCE missions in the Balkans and to increase or promote co-operation among participating States, which coincides with the OSCE's new focus on the security situations in the countries of Central Asia and the Caucasus.[34] As of September 2003, the SPMU has been increased to 9 posts.

Whereas the OSCE police missions in the Balkans are dealing primarily with the tasks of training and reforming multiethnic police forces in war-torn societies, the activities in Central Asia and the Caucasus concentrate on assisting local law enforcement agencies in their efforts to augment the professional capacity of law enforcement personnel, thereby introducing new techniques and skills for address-

---

31   CF. Organization for Security and Co-operation in Europe. Permanent Council, Decision No. 448. Establishment of the seconded post of senior police adviser in the OSCE Secretariat, PC.DEC/448, 4 December 2001.

32   Cf. OSCE Newsletter, Vol. 9, No. 3, p. 5f.

33   Cf. Organization for Security and Co-operation in Europe. Permanent Council, Decision No. 478. Enhancing Resources dealing with Challenges to Security, PC.DEC/478, 23 May 2002.

34   Cf. Organization for Security and Co-operation in Europe, Office of the Secretary General, Annual report of the Secretary General on Police-related Activities, 9 December 2002, p. 8.

ing contemporary policing issues as well as developing institutional capacities for training personnel in human-rights oriented techniques.[35]

While there have been substantial developments in police capacities within the OSCE Secretariat, the recruitment of mission personnel is still confronted with difficulties. Many potential candidates do not meet the selection criteria of the REACT database. In addition, it has been shown that the OSCE Permanent Council is not ready to finance prospective police missions which are personnel-intensive. Therefore, the OSCE will probably concentrate on support programmes for police training – such as the ones that are currently running in Central Asia, where small groups of training experts are recruited for short-term assignments. Personnel-intensive law enforcement and monitoring missions will be entrusted to the UN and the EU (as in the case of Bosnia and Herzegovina).[36]

3.3. *EU Measures*

At the EU Summit in Feira, Portugal in June 2000, the Heads of State and Government passed the decision to set up a European Police Force of up to 5,000 police officers for international missions, of which 1,000 would be deployable upon the request of the UN, the OSCE or the EU within 30 days, and able to attend to the whole spectrum of police work in the frame of peace operations like, for example, providing police advice, training, monitoring as well as executive policing. It was also clearly stated that an armed executive mandate could be given and gendarmerie-type units deployed.[37]

The development of a personnel pool was to be co-ordinated with the OSCE and the UN to avoid duplication.[38]

In November 2001, the foreign ministers of the EU states met in Brussels to announce the number of police they would provide for an EU Police Force. The number was even slightly higher than the previous goal of 5,000 police officers. Germany announced it would make available a maximum of 960 officers.

In July 2001, a police unit was founded under the Secretary General of the Council of the EU and High Representative for Common Foreign and Security Policy, Javier Solana. As of September 2003, this unit consists of eight police officers

---

35 Interview with OSCE representatives in Vienna in April 2003.
36 Interview with OSCE representatives in Vienna in April 2003.
37 Cf. EU Law and Policy Overview, European Security and Defense Policy, Brussels, 15 June 2000, Presidency Report to the Feira European Council on "Strengthening the Common European Policy on Security and Defence", in particular see Appendix 4: Concrete Targets for Police, A.1. Overall EU Capabilities A.2. Rapid Deployment Capability, at: http://www.eurunion.org/legislat/Defense/ESDPFeira.htm.
38 Cf. ibid., Appendix 4, A.3 Raising Standards for International Police Missions.

and one political advisor.[39] It has been tasked with co-ordinating the development of the EU Police and defining its missions.

The baptism of fire for the EU Police Force or its first challenging experience was seen as the taking over of the mandate of the UN *International Police Task Force* (IPTF) in Bosnia and Herzegovina (BiH) on 1 January 2003. By 2005, approx. 500 international police officers from the 15 EU and 18 non-EU member states are to be assisting police officials of the BiH police, not least with the fight against organized crime and corruption. As the former IPTF, the *European Union Police Mission* (EUPM) has no executive mandate.[40] In September 2003, the foreign ministers of the EU approved the deployment of another police mission, this time to the former Yugoslav Republic of Macedonia. The mission, which has been called "Proxima", was to be deployed by mid December 2003 and was to initially have a duration of one year. Similar to Bosnia, the mandate of the 200 police-officer contingent is to assist the local police in the fight against organized crime, reform the interior ministry and strengthen border security.[41]

In order to form a network of the training institutions for senior police officers in each individual state, the Council of Europe passed the decision in December 2000 to create the *European Police Academy* (EPA). This academy was meant to primarily offer training programmes to senior police officers. However, the ultimate goal was also a joint training programme for middle-ranking officers, police officers in the field, for the trainers themselves, as well as for the officers of the EU crisis management police force – who would all be brought up to a uniform level of professional competence. However, the member states, up to now, have not been able to agree on establishing a permanent institution, so that for the time being international training programmes will be held at national academies within the network of the *Colleges of the European Police* (CEPOL). Currently, 500 senior officers are to be trained for a future EU police pool with courses held alternately in various European states. As of September 2003, eight multinational CEPOL-courses have taken place (in Germany, Spain, France, Denmark, Italy, Portugal, Austria and Ireland), bringing the total number of course participants to 160.

---

39   Interview with a representative of the General Secretariat of the Council of the European Union in Brussels in September 2003.
40   Cf. EUPM Overview, at: http://ue.eu.int/eupm/pdf/EUPMoverview.pdf.
41   Cf. euobserver.com of September 30, 2003, at: http://www.euobserver.com/index.phtml? print=true&sid==24aid=12856; and Financial Times of September 28, 2003, at: http://financial-times.../cpt?action=cpt&expire=&urlID=7716090&fb=YpartnerID=170.

4.   Conclusion

Since the end of the 1990s, the UN and its regional partner organizations, the EU and the OSCE, have undertaken great efforts to build up their capacities and capabilities for conducting CIVPOL missions. However, the measures taken, especially in the operational field, have so far shown few real increases in the efficiency and effectiveness of police missions in the early phases of peace missions.

The aim of the following recommendations is to improve the short- and medium-term effectiveness of future international police missions.

4.1.   *Recommendations to Further the Effectiveness of Future Police Missions*

4.1.1.   *At the UN Level*
1. To be able to guarantee more rapid deployment of civilian UN police units, the UN member states should, within the framework of UNSAS, provide personnel to the senior police team mentioned in the Brahimi Report as well as to their own police pool.
2. In developing a standby pool, the importance of female police officers should be taken into account more seriously than it has been up to now. Female police officers could play an important role, in particular, in building up the confidence of the female population with regard to international police forces. Especially women who have been the victims of sexual violence during times of conflict would have more trust in a female police officer in investigations of this kind of crime. The examples of trafficking in women and forced prostitution in Bosnia and, in particular, currently in Kosovo, or the cases of mistreatment in families, make it clear that also during the post-conflict period there are many scenarios in which the female population is dependent upon assistance which only a qualified female police officer can offer.
3. UN member states should become actively engaged in developing joint training programmes for officers of different nations. Especially personnel from developing countries could profit from this type of joint programme.
4. It is true that the Brahimi Report – in view of the continually increasing complexity of the mandate – recommends hiring officers who are better qualified and more specialized, however, it does this only with respect to the area of actively building up local police structures. Nevertheless, it is of utmost importance, for the success of future missions, that UNCIVPOL officers have the capabilities and equipment for armed law enforcement. In addition to the adequate number of patrol officers and *Criminal Investigation Department* (CID) officers, an appropriate number of officers are required, who, as closed units, are able to ensure that law and order at is maintained at large political and cultural events and, who, at the outbreak of political unrest, are able to bring

the situation under control by implementing police operations. In Kosovo, the hundred-strong *Special Police Units* (SPU) from Argentina, Jordan, India, Pakistan, Poland, Spain and the Ukraine have already proved their worth in this respect. Because in many countries in Europe there are police units that are optimally equipped for this type of job (i.e. the Italian Carabinieri, the French Gendarmerie, the Spanish Guardia Civil and the German Federal Border Police), these countries should also be willing to set up hundred-strong police units or joint units. However, countries such as Italy or France would have to be convinced to temporarily disembody these units from their military structures and allow them to take action under civilian UN command. Through their routine duties in their home countries, these units prove continually that they are also used to operating in a civilian sphere.

5. Gendarmerie-like units must also be part of a rapidly deployable multinational police force. The *Standby High Readiness Brigade* (SHIRBRIG) could be used as a model for this. In this brigade, nine nations from Europe as well as Canada and Argentina are represented. If one were to take SHIRBRIG as a model, several nations would have to put together a joint senior police staff. Each member country would make the required personnel and equipment available for specific police activities. Special contributions for certain task areas would be conceivable, for example, in logistics, communications, fighting organized crime, criminal investigation, protection of person and property, riot control, border police, traffic police etc. The police officers of each country would train jointly several times a year, but would fulfil their regular duties at home until mission deployment. To achieve high acceptance of this police force, personnel would have to be recruited from all over the world. This rapidly deployable police force – totalling around 4,000 officers – would, within a period of 30 days, act as a forward command for the international police in the mission area, and would be withdrawn from the mission – after that, at the latest six months – once the main police contingent has actually arrived. This kind of force would have the inestimable advantage over the multinational UN contingents up to now, in that its officers would all have received standardized training and have the experience required that comes from working with police officers from different cultures.

6. It is after all absolutely necessary – also as a measure against the current resistance, primarily from the non-aligned countries – that a general transitional police law as well as criminal and penal law be developed, which is regionally adaptable (to different legal systems, traditions and cultures, and thereby acceptable to the local societies) and which can be exercised by a UN police force and an international judiciary, until local law and legal bodies are restored. The realization of this requirement is imperative if the legal uncertainties in international police executive missions are to be reduced.

4.1.2. *At the OSCE and EU Level*

It is also true for the OSCE and the EU area that an adequate number of police personnel must be made available by the participating States and member states of these organizations.

7. In consultation with the EU, the foreseen 5,000 officers of the future EU Police should also be entered into the personnel files of the REACT database and be earmarked for OSCE missions. The OSCE should thus have, including the officers from non-EU states, over 10,000 police officers ready for deployment, who would also be available for UN missions.

8. Joint training programmes – consistent with the application of UN peacekeeping guidelines – must be offered to police from EU states and other OSCE participating States. These programmes should bring all police officers up to the same level of training. The international CEPOL courses, which have been running since 2001 and focus on the training of senior European police officers, should also be offered in the future to middle-ranking grades. Officers from OSCE participating States, who do not belong to the EU, should also be allowed to participate in these multinational EU training programmes. The additional expenses incurred by the EU should be paid by the more prosperous OSCE nations. In the course of these joint training programmes, those police officers who do not meet the specifications to fulfil specialized positions should not be deployed in future missions. Shortcomings that have occurred at the UN level, due to the principle of the balance of nations in distributing senior positions, could in this manner be prevented.

At present, some of these demands are still being met with rejection by several states. In pointing towards their lack of financial resources, some of these states limit the scope of personnel and material capacities in international police forces; and other states which have a Gendarmerie or Gendarmerie-like police units at their disposal refuse to let these operate under civilian command in international operations. Above all, members of the Non-Aligned Movement are reluctant to accept the introduction of a UN code of police, criminal and procedural law (to be applied in peace operations), because they perceive their sovereignty, and the cultural and traditional features of their national police and criminal law as being threatened by it. These obstacles and concerns must be overcome and/or cleared. Otherwise, the international police will not be able to live up to its increasing importance within the framework of civil conflict management.

Simulating Crises:
A Peacekeeping Teaching Technique

*Elizabeth Griffin and Anthony Verrier**

Abstract

Teaching the practical aspects of peacekeeping is an activity that is mainly restricted to military staff colleges. However, for a number of years, students studying for the LL.M in International Human Rights Law and the MA in The Theory and Practice of Human Rights at the University of Essex (United Kingdom) have had the opportunity to participate in a unique exercise which is designed to examine the practical dilemmas faced by military and civilian personnel deployed as a part of peace support operations. This exercise, know as the SIMULEX, is staged at Colchester Garrison, headquarters of the 16 Air Assault Brigade. The SIMULEX provides participants with an opportunity to act out a number of scenarios which civilian and military personnel are likely to face when working within the context of peace support operations. Students and participating military personnel are assigned various "roles" and they engage in a number of joint problem solving exercises which are conceived with the aim of providing students with a real taste of the tough dilemmas faced by civilian and military personnel working on the ground and with the intention of fostering mutual understanding of the military and civilian perspectives. The origins, evolution and value of the SIMULEX as a teaching technique are described in this article.

*   Elizabeth Griffin, Lecturer in International Human Rights, Law Department of Essex University. Dr. Anthony Verrier, former Director, MA in International Peacekeeping, Essex University.

Harvey Langholtz, Boris Kondoch, Alan Wells (Eds.),
International Peacekeeping: The Yearbook of International Peace Operations, Volume 9, 2004, pp. 109-121.
© *Koninklijke Brill N.V. Printed in the Netherlands*

1.   Introduction

It is doubtful whether any academic or vocational course in peacekeeping can ever hope to fully prepare individuals for the complex and dangerous assignments that they face when they are deployed in, or along side, peace support operations. Moreover, even personnel who have received training in preparation for deployment within the context of complex emergencies, acute crises or post-conflict situations have little time to reflect on the academic and theoretical debates which underpin international peacekeeping. Rather, their time is taken up with formulating responses to a range of tough dilemmas and problems that require immediate and decisive action. Nevertheless, the need for training and preparation for the 'real world' remains a key component of Essex University's peacekeeping curriculum, which is geared towards providing students not only with a sound theoretical and legal knowledge of peacekeeping operations, but also a taste of the real scenarios they are likely to encounter on the field. Along side academic teaching of 'the international law of peacekeeping', students at Essex University are offered the opportunity of participating in a simulated peacekeeping exercise – the SIMULEX. The aim of the SIMULEX is to foster convergence of military and civilian perspectives and to prepare students for the field. The methodology, achievements and benefits of this innovative teaching technique are the subject of this article.

2.   Fostering Convergence of Civilian and Military Cultures

"We need you as much as you need us". With these words, in the autumn of 1995, Brigadier Robin Brims defined the basic objective of the SIMULEX which the University of Essex and Colchester Garrison were preparing to initiate. The objective of the SIMULEX was – and still is – to bring students and soldiers together, to jointly "role play", or simulate, an actual or probable crisis involving United Nations mandated or franchised out police and military forces and the plethora of international and non-governmental civilian agencies who are engaged in the broadest range of civilian professional tasks, including humanitarian relief and human rights field work.

The sub-text to General Brims' statement should be clearly understood. Civilians and soldiers operate in different spheres and are ingrained with different cultural values. Experience from the field tells us that these two cultures do not easily harmonise. While many of the objectives to be pursued in peace support operations, such as establishing and maintaining security, relieving human suffering and protecting and promoting adherence to international human rights standards may be readily defined, the philosophical underpinnings and methodologies applied by civilian and military personnel in the field to achieve these ends often diverge, and frequently clash. Experience shows that convergence of both objectives and methods is hard to achieve and maintain in practice.

Yet it is precisely this convergence that the SIMULEX is designed to foster. Members of the University and successive Garrison Commanders have co-operated in that aim because they believe, and have come to understand through experience, that when students enter or return to the field, and when members of the Garrison are deployed in peace support operations, they will have benefited from participation in the SIMULEX and they may be more effective in executing their tasks on the field. This is because, in the real world of peace support operations, convergence is both desirable and necessary in order to maximise the chances of successful execution of mandates. Ultimately, it is hoped that the benefits of participation in the SIMULEX are reflected in better security arrangements, less suffering on the part of the local population, increased respect for human rights and, above all, better co-operation between military and civilian components of peace support operations to achieve these ends.

Military and civilian culture differ significantly. With regard to military culture: a soldier may be "a citizen in uniform",[1] but there is no escaping the fact that he, or she, *is* in uniform. In his or her uniform, the soldier is subject to command, liable to punishment for disobedience or failure to comply with orders – the soldier is a part of a precisely defined hierarchy and organizational structure. In the field, the soldier is armed with a weapon. The soldier has, under certain circumstances, the right to coerce, enforce and, in the last resort, to kill. Soldiers, as a former Colchester Garrison Commander has stated, "live in a finite world".

The civilian experience differs markedly. A civilian engaged in peace support operations, whatever his, or her, tasks may also be subject to some form of authority. However, the nature of authority is significantly different than that experienced by the soldier. At times it can seem as though civilians working within the context of intergovernmental and non-governmental organisations face seemingly infinite choices. For the civilian, individual and organizational accountability for acts is often lacking. "Punishment" in sense of disciplinary action for incompetence or negligence is rare. Moreover, Civilian hierarchies are often confusingly elaborate as is illustrated by the organizational structure of the United Nations Department of Peacekeeping Operations and UN Specialist Agencies. Today there is a complex web of civilian actors on the ground with various mandates, functions and political allegiances that operate on a horizontal, rather than vertical level. For the average soldier, civilian agencies and personnel working within the context of a peace support operations appear to lack discipline and take unnecessary risks – factors

---

1   English constitutional law prescribes this definition, which is also found in other constitutions.

which often lead to a perception on the part of military personnel that civilians lack professionalism.

Lack of mutual understanding of the different hierarchies, structures and mandates often leads to tension and mistrust between military and civilian actors in the field and this has ramifications for the overall success of a mission. Profound differences between the two cultures regarding issues such as whether the resort to force is *ever* justified often exasperate simmering tensions. The SIMULEX have paid much attention to this rather fundamental issue. Interpretations of "force", of course, vary but there are civilians deployed in peace support operations who object to "enforcement", even if resorting to it does not cause bloodshed. Through an examination of the fundamental issues such as when to use force, the SIMULEX aims to lesson tension by bridging the gap in understanding between soldiers and civilians.

3.   Teaching Techniques

The Department of Law and the Human Rights Centre at the University of Essex are well known for their expertise in teaching and researching the theory and practice of peacekeeping and international human rights. The University of Essex is located in the town of Colchester. The town also houses a large military Garrison which is an important military facility for the UK. The Garrison is a base where many soldiers prepare for participation in peace support operations and they are subsequently deployed from Colchester Garrison to peace support operations around the world, including those in Bosnia, Kosovo and Afghanistan. The Garrison's resident formation, 16 Air Assault Brigade is a key element in the UK Joint Rapid Deployment Force, the British Army's "Spearhead" establishment for peace support operations. The Brigade comprises three infantry battalions, a regiment of field artillery; support units; other units, including armour, as required. The concept behind the SIMULEX was to pool these resources available in the town and fuse the University's expertise in the theory and practice of peacekeeping and human rights with the Garrisons' many years of experience in providing personnel and equipment to peace support operations.

With the primary aims of fostering convergence between these two different cultures and confronting the difficult dilemmas faced by all field staff, the essence of SIMULEX teaching is sharing. The SIMULEX is conducted over the course of two and a half days in Colchester Garrison's Study Centre. The Garrison Study Centre is well equipped to host the SIMULEX – considerable ingenuity is often to be found in staging mock situations – for example, a village in Kosovo and the headquarters of a peacekeeping force have been recreated at the Garrison. During the SIMULEX, civilian and military participants act out scenarios together. Bringing military and civilian personnel together in non-threatening environment and creating an atmosphere in which they are able to talk and listen to each other is the first important step towards promoting convergence of the two cultures. Fundamentally, civilian and military personnel rarely have an opportunity to interact on the field except in times of crisis. During crisis the differences in culture, philosophy and *modus operandi* are magnified. One of the central philosophies underpinning the SIMULEX is the creating a forum for the exchange of views and opinions outside of the stressful confines of the field. It is hoped that by setting the SIMULEX within this context, the level of mutual understanding will be increased and that this will, in turn, improve relations between military and civilian personnel when they meet for real on the ground.

3.1. *SIMULEX Scenarios*

Every year, a complex scenario for the SIMULEX is devised. The scenario contains details of the specific political, historical and geographic setting within which that year's simulated peace support operation is to be mounted. The scenario also includes information on the mandates of the organizations and actors on the ground as found in Security Council Resolutions, resolutions of regional organizations or in the statutes of civilian agencies and organizations. The scenarios are fictional. However, as the SIMULEX aims to prepare students for the "real world", it is no coincidence that the scenarios are often very similar to real situations. For example, the fourth SIMULEX, "Kosovo Restored", addressed the situation which actually existed in the province during the winter of 1999-2000. Considerable deprivation amongst the civilian population was relieved by civilian agencies and civilians were also protected against occasional assault by military units. Differences of opinion as to which security measures were most appropriate rapidly surfaced between the students playing representatives of the agencies and officers of the Garrison playing, as it were, "themselves". The characters of the individuals in question would have been at once recognised by those in the field, all the more so as an increasing number of civilian agencies were on the ground at the time in question. Each SIMULEX scenario also contains information about the specific actors who will appear in the SIMULEX and it provides the actors with an indication of the views and opinions that they will express.

To date, the following scenarios have been created for the SIMULEX:

Dates	Operation Name	Scenario
1996-1997	"REBUILD"	Municipal elections in Bosnia
1997-1998	"RESTORE ORDER"	Threatened disintegration of a Central African State

Table (*cont.*)

Dates	Operation Name	Scenario
1998-1999	"RAPID RESPONSE"	Responding to refugee flows into Macedonia
1999-2000	"KOSOVO RESTORED"	Humanitarian aid and internal security in Serb and Albanian villages
2000-2001	"MONTENEGRO SECURED"	Threatened secession of Montenegro from the Yugoslav Federation
2001-2002	NO CODE NAME[2]	The tasks of the International Security Assistance Force in Kabul
2002-2003	"MONTENEGRO SECURED"	Threatened secession of Montenegro from the Yugoslav Federation[3]
2003-2004	"IRAQ REFORGED"	Security Dilemmas in Iraq

Participants in the SIMULEX are assigned various roles. Some of the roles which have been played by students over the past seven years include; the head of an EU mission in Montenegro; a UN Special Representative of the Secretary-General (SRSG) who is struggling to direct a UN mission deployed in a fictional African state that has descended into violence and is heading towards disintegration; a UNHCR protection officer deployed on the Macedonian border and responsible for dealing with a major influx of Kosovar refugees; representatives from Medicines Son Frontiers working in Central Africa who are trying to ensure that humanitarian aid is delivered to internally displaced persons and other vulnerable victims of conflict; a human rights officer working of the Office of the High Commissioner for Human Rights in Montenegro who is mandated to monitor and report on the human rights situation in the country and the newly appointed Prosecutor of the Iraqi Special Tribunal who is faced with the dilemma of how to collect evidence without co-operation from co-alition forces. In each case, the SIMULEX illustrates not only the situation on the ground, but also the differences which invariably arise between a civilian "Head of Mission" and the Commander of a UN or franchised force over the basic question of "whose running the show". For example, in "Restore Order", the SRSG and the Commonwealth Force Commander differed sharply as to who should be responsible for the supervision of refugee camps in the area of Equitoria, the African state threatened by secession. The issue was resolved, to the extent that it was, by initiatives taken by military subordinates in the area concerned – as indeed happens in actuality. Some of the military roles scripted to date include the commander of UN Peacekeeping force in a Central African; the Chief of Staff of a

---

2   *See* Annex 1 for an explanation.
3   After discussion between the Director of the SIMULEX and the Garrison Commander it was agreed
    to "re-run" the 2000-2001 SIMULEX, as it raises questions of current political importance in the
    European context.

NATO led operation in Kosovo; Head of ISAF The NATO Supreme Allied Commander Europe (SACEUR) who seeks to initiate air strikes as a means of ensuring that municipal elections in Bosnia go ahead.

3.2.   *SIMULEX Structure*

The SIMULEX is divided into three phases: A preliminary analysis of the overall scenario, the acting out of certain sub-scenarios and an overall evaluation of SIMULEX. Initially, on the first morning of the SIMULEX, the atmosphere is a little aloof. Clearly, some students arrive at the SIMULEX convinced that soldiers don't understand, and are not interested in, human rights and humanitarian relief issues or any of the principles that underpin civilian action in situations of crisis, conflict and post-conflict reconstruction. At this stage, it is also evident that some soldiers are convinced that the students are impractical idealists or even 'peace-nicks'. However, during the first morning the atmosphere changes quickly as the participants throw themselves into critical debates and animated acting.

3.2.1.   *Preliminary Analysis of the Overall Scenario*

The first morning of the SIMULEX is spent discussing the general issues raised by the scenario. The focus of this discussion is an analysis of the overall security, humanitarian and human rights situation on the ground, the scope of the mandates of the various military and civilian actors, the political factors at play and an assessment of the operation priorities of the different agencies and actors and the operation as a whole. During these discussions, students and soldiers are in role. Divergence of the two cultures is often evident at this stage as the crucial dilemma of how to reconcile the often seemingly conflicting priorities of the military and civilian components of peace support operations are thrashed out. Every year, during this phase of the SIMULEX, military and civilian actors struggle to reach consensus on issues such as how to balance the maintenance of security with the provision of humanitarian assistance and the protection of human rights and how to act effectively to ensure lives are protected given the constraints of the mandate(s). Invariably, discussions focus on how to interpret the mandate, how to meet the needs on the ground, given the constraints of the mandate, and how military and civilian personnel can best work together to fulfil the mandate(s). Students have become progressively aware, over the past six years, of the evolutionary nature of peace support operations, and that a combination of mediation and enforcement is necessary if any kind of success is to be attained in the provision of security, protection and humanitarian relief.

3.2.2. *Role Playing – Selected Incidents*

The first afternoon and the whole of the second day are taken up with role playing three or four "incidents" which occur within the context of the wider scenario. It is this stage of the SIMULEX that provides the students and military alike with the greatest insight into the others' motivations and *modus operandi*. All the SIMULEX incidents which have been staged over the years, illustrate the inherent uncertainty of peace support operations, and the importance of understanding the influence of personalities and experience upon the ebb and flow of events. For example, in "Rebuild", Commander SFOR insisted on the application of the doctrine of minimum necessary force in the context of the local municipal elections and did so against SACEUR's belief in the validity and necessity of "overwhelming force".[4] In the end, the doctrine of "minimum necessary force" prevailed, executed above all, through vigilant foot patrols by day and night in the municipal areas with the aim of deterring isolated acts of violence from escalating into major armed clashes.

In "Restore Order", an incident occurred which forced the various actors on the ground to deal with the issue of how many refugees from Equatoria could be given sanctuary. A triangular argument prevailed between the representatives of the International Committee of the Red Cross and Crescent (ICRC); a "secession leader"; and the Commander of a military battalion deployed in the area of greatest potential communal violence. The fact that the officer who played the battalion commander had served in Rwanda (Commanding the Garrison's Field Ambulance), gave him the edge in the debate as to how many refugees could be given sanctuary, but the students who played the other two roles (from Ireland and Croatia) were vocal enough to make for a very dramatic incident.

During "Rapid Response", comparable exchanges took place between two students (from the UK and Turkey) who had led a party of refugees in the hope of finding sanctuary for them in Macedonia. The Corporal commanding the section at one of the observations posts (played by an NCO from the Garrison) politely but firmly, denied the refugees entry and on the order of a higher authority who would not allow the Corporal to make an independent decision. This incident was given credibility by some imaginative reconstruction of the observation post and by some ingenious simulation of crying children and wailing babies! The understandable emotional context of the incident was dramatically evoked. The incident was fur-

---

4   The clash of doctrine and principle reflects, of course, the dilemma which has been pursued in the UN and regional organizations since the early days of peacekeeping – when, if ever, is recourse to force justifiable? And if so, how much? This dilemma has never been resolved, but it is important to note here that Heads of mission and civilian agencies remain, on the whole, adverse from the application of force under any circumstances, whereas military forces, understandably, are prepared to invoke it.

ther developed in some barbed exchanges between a Macedonian police officer (played by a student from Cameroon who is, in fact, a police superintendent) and the Commander of one of MFOR's infantry battalions. The Macedonian policeman stated that no refugees should be able to enter Macedonia, relying on his "higher authority", the Minister of the Interior. The Battalion Commander argued that a certain number of refugees should be allowed to enter the country provided they were firstly screened for arms and other unwelcome possessions. His view prevailed in the end.

In "Montenegro Secured", the issue of the application of force, or the threat to invoke it, in order to deter troublemakers from ruining the secession referendum was the central issue. The NATO Commander, Regional Command South, argued, as had SACUER in "Rebuild" that "these people only understand force when it is severely applied". Commander MFOR, insisted, has had Commander SFOR in "Rebuild", that force had to be threatened or invoked, it should be on a graduated scaled, whereby the level of potential violence would be met by an equivalent level of response, a concept which would be credible if there was sufficient manpower margin among the units concerned.

In "Montenegro Secured", the concept of the SIMULEX was widened somewhat, to include a political dimension which extended beyond the political factors on the ground and operational considerations which complimented the situation further. The fact that the European Union (EU) has been considering for sometime now, the establishment of a Rapid Reaction Core, and that this has been met with mixed reactions from a US dominated NATO, was debated in the preliminary phases of the SIMULEX by recourse to the devise of syndicates. All participants became members of either the political syndicate, which debated the EU's mixed aspirations and objectives in sponsoring a Rapid Reaction Core, and an operational syndicate which considered the credibility of a rapid reaction core in relation to manpower, armaments and logistical requirements.

All the aforementioned incidents role-played during successive SIMULEX were created with the aim of demonstrating the difficult and often intractable problems faced by military and civilians in the field. The incidents played out as a part of the SIMULEX highlight the problems and often life or death decisions that have to be made in the heat of the moment.[5] It is important to emphasise that while there is an element of scripting to the SIMULEX, scripts are not texts which are to be

---

5   The Simulex has also attempted to examine the effect that the presence of international personnel has on the local community. However, we are aware that this issue has yet to be fully explored as a part of the SIMULEX. The effect of peace support operations on the local community and the manner in which interaction takes place between international and local persons will be explored to a greater extent in forthcoming SIMULEX.

adhered to at all times; extemporise and *ad lib* intervention are encouraged and often lead to the most valuable exchanges. The discussions are also greatly enhanced by contributions from students who have experience of being in the field, of which there are a number every year. Indeed, many of the student and military participants in the SIMULEX have substantial field experience in, or alongside, peace support operations. Shared experience of those students with field experience benefits those who lack it. The "old hands" know that nothing in a peace support operation ever goes as planned, and that all personnel in the field suffer from the remoteness and incomprehension of the "high command", be it the all to often dysfunctional UN in New York, NATO or the EU in Brussels; or in fact, the headquarters of any organisation involved. Those with field experience also understand that lives can depend upon certain outcomes and as a consequence they bring depth, understanding and sensitivity to the discussions.

3.2.3. *SIMULEX Evaluation*

The final morning of the SIMULEX is taken up with a discussion of "lessons learned". This extremely important session provides time for mutual reflection and analysis and also forms the basis for a subsequent report written by the Director of the SIMULEX and distributed to all SIMULEX participants. Evaluation of the SIMULEX is a key element of the exercise as it allows student and military participants the opportunity to elaborate upon the reasons that motivated them to act in a particular way. The evaluation session often sheds light on why convergence was not achieved and how, if at all, compromise was finally reached. By attempting to identify the barriers to convergence, it is hoped that mutual understanding and respect for the position of the "other side" is achieved. In particular, discussion of issues and role playing of incidents leads participants to an increased understanding not only of the frequently diverging aims of "Head of Missions" and Force Commanders but as to there sphere of responsibilities but what might be called a "given divergence" as to how "mediation" should, or should not be complimented by enforcement. The need to strike a balance between mediation and enforcement is a prevailing element in actual peace support operations. Participants and observers disperse after the lessons learnt session with a conviction that they have seen things from a different perspective.

4.   Conclusion

There is one absolutely paramount conclusion: "We need you as much as you need us". For both the Law Department of the University and Colchester Garrison the SIMULEX is, after seven years, an integral, not an incidental element in their education and training. The enthusiasm with which students and soldiers who are very fully stretched in their studies, and in their training, exercises, and operations bring to the SIMULEX reflects the shared conviction that it has a direct relevance to a world "out there", to what the soldiers aptly call "the sharp end". No simulation of a crisis, of a conflict, and of what the international community does about it can be more than an imaginative and intelligent attempt to enlighten. But that the attempt is necessary is attested by those who have participated in this unique peacekeeping teaching technique. Teaching peacekeeping can be approached from various perspectives – it can focus on an analysis of the legal framework of peacekeeping operations, a political analysis of the motivations which underpin intervention or it can concentrate on a historical analysis of the reasons why the situation in a given geographical area has escalated to a level where the peacekeepers are deployed. However, one perspective that should never be omitted when teaching peacekeeping is the practical nature of the tasks and challenges faced by military, civilian and police personnel on the field. International peacekeeping is about responding to a particular and unique situation and success depends upon effective co-operation between military and civilian personnel. In peace support operations military and civilian components need to work together and respond creatively and effectively to pressing developments on the ground – this fact should never be forgotten when teaching peacekeeping.

ANNEX 1: SIMULEX Scenarios 1996-2002

REBUILD: The scenario for REBUILD was set in selected "municipal districts" of Bosnia-Herzegovina, where elections were due to be held (these elections were in fact held in Bosnia in September 1997). In REBUILD violence threatened the elections. In attempting to formulate a response to this violence, the NATO Stabilisation Force (SFOR), which was mandated to maintain security, was influenced by the view of the NATO Supreme Allied Commander Europe (SACEUR) that trouble in the municipal districts should be deterred by the threat of air strikes. SACEUR's view was that mounting air strikes would contain the violence. Commander SFOR, however, argued to the NATO Council that "minimum necessary force" was preferable to "overwhelming force". Eventually, Commander SFOR's view prevailed. SFOR units in the "municipal areas" were reinforced and vigilant foot patrols by day and night eventually contained and curtailed violence and the elections took place in conditions of relative security.

RESTORE ORDER: The scenario in RESTORE ORDER was set in a province of a fictional Central African State of Equatoria. Equatoria was experiencing considerable violence as a result of competing claims for control of oil revenues (the similarity of this situation with that of Nigeria during the 1967-70 Civil War was not coincidental). Violence could well lead to provincial secession and the loss of oil revenue by the Equatorian Government. After debate in the Security Council, a Commonwealth Force was deployed to Equatoria. The Force Commander soon found himself at odds with the United Nations Special Representative of the Secretary-General (SRSG), not only regarding the issue of priority tasks, but also regarding who should have responsibility for executing them. The SRSG argued that in the troubled province priority should be given to the provision of humanitarian assistance. However, the Force Commander argued that the priority task should be the restoration of law and order. The issue was *not* resolved, and relief agencies and the Commonwealth Force units in the province had to cope with problems as best they could.

RAPID RESPONSE: The scenario was the "Black Line" on the northern borders of Macedonia, manned by troops from the NATO Prevention Force (NAPFOR). The situation is one which would have confronted the UN Preventative Deployment Force (UNPREDEP) had it not been withdrawn by the time in question. Albanian refugees from Kosovo were seeking sanctuary in Macedonia and NAPFOR units had to decide whom to admit and whom to reject. Humanitarian relief agencies pleaded for most of the refugees to be admitted. However, the Macedonian Government insisted that only a very small number of refugees should be admitted. NAPFOR sought to hold the balance. Compromise was achieved through the exercise of humanity and common sense, tempered with caution. All refugees who did cross the boarder were searched and those found to be possessing weapons were not admitted.

KOSOVO RESTORED: The scenario for Kosovo Restored was set in four villages in Kosovo (two Albanian and two Serb). The villages were garrisoned by a company belonging to one of KFOR's battalions. The scenario was set in winter during particularly sever weather conditions – heavy snowfall was preventing relief agencies from transporting food, medicines and other supplies to vulnerable regions. The company Commander had the task of maintaining basic internal security. The Commander also had to deal with an alleged murder, and with attempted looting in one of the villages. The alleged murderer is seized under the authority of CIVPOL; a looting attempt is deterred – the looter is shot, dead. This incident brings the company commander into verbal conflict with representatives of the relief agencies. They deplore such acts, which strike them as provocative. But the representatives are forced by circumstances, specifically the severe weather, to accept, reluctantly, the company commander's authority.

MONTENEGRO SECURED: The scenario was a growing demand in Montenegro for secession from the Yugoslav Federation. The Government in Belgrade decides that the issue must be settled by a referendum, to be monitored by teams from the Organisation for Security and Co-operation in Europe (OSCE), and supervised by a force drawn from European members of NATO (M-FOR). As most of the anti-secessionist sentiment is in the north of Montenegro and pro-secessionist sentiment is in the south, Commander M-FOR, acting under instructions from the EU Council of Ministers, establishes a demilitarised zone (DMZ) in the centre of the country. The DMZ is to be controlled by M-FOR, but too few troops are available to prevent the seizure of an OSCE team by an anti-secession faction. The hostages are rescued by Special Forces, and the referendum takes place.

2001-2002 MINI-SEMINAR: Owing to the deployment of Headquarters 16 Air Assault Brigade (the operational formation in Colchester Garrison) to Afghanistan, it was not possible to conduct a SIMULEX on the usual scale. Instead, students and such members of Garrison Headquarters debated the tasks of the International Security Assistance Force (ISAF). One officer from 16th Air Assault Brigade had returned to Colchester by the time this debate took place, and described ISAF's tasks. Particular attention was paid to humanitarian relief work being carried out by ISAF in the absence of civil agencies.

IRAQ REFORGED: The scenario was set in Iraq a year into the occupation. The central theme was how to move ahead with political and security reforms in the absence of a basic level of security. Representatives of the Co-alition insisted on pushing ahead with electoral registration while the security situation deteriorated. However, UN and NGO representatives insisted that the delivery of humanitarian assistance, human rights initiatives and development programmes were impossible given the security situation. Tensions between the military and civilian actors came to boiling point after the death of 40 UN Volunteers who had been deployed to register voters. These tensions were exasperated after Co-alition forces in Basra conducted an arrest operation and detained 100 civilians, including women and children. The arrests lead to mass demonstrations on the streets of Basra which were eventually dispersed peacefully after a lengthy meeting between community leaders, UN representatives and Co-alition forces.

Ireland Withdraws from Participation in EU Peacekeeping Mission to Macedonia

*Ray Murphy**

Introduction

After making a commitment to the first ever European Union (EU) preventive deployment force, Irish Defence Force personnel were allocated a number of positions on the EU lead mission in the former Yugoslav Republic of Macedonia ("Macedonia"). Soon after Ireland withdrew its commitment to contribe personnel to the operation. This was a source of significant embarrassment to Irish diplomats at the Department of Foreign Affairs and the Defence Forces.[1] The Irish Attorney General advised the government that Ireland could not contribute troops to this mission, as it did not satisfy commitments made by Ireland as part of the Seville declaration prior to the Nice Treaty referendum. This has serious consequences for Irish foreign policy, both within the EU, and with regard to participation in future peacekeeping operations. In December 2003, Ireland dispatched around 470 troops to participate in the United Nations Mission in Liberia (UNMIL).[2] This marked an important shift in Irish foreign policy in relation to peacekeeping operations in general. This article examines the background to Irish involvement in peace support operations, and to recent developments that reinforce Ireland's policy regarding non-participation in missions that have not been approved or mandated by the UN.

---

*   Dr. Ray Murphy is Director, LL.M. in International Peace Support Operations, Irish Centre for Human Rights, National University of Ireland, Galway, Ireland.
1   Personal interview, Department of Foreign Affairs official, Dublin, March 2003.
2   *See* M. Hennessy, "Risks facing soldiers on UN Liberia mission raised by Smith", *The Irish Times*, 11 November 2003, p. 15; "Troops for Liberia", leader article, *The Irish Times*, 17 November 2003, p. 15, and M. Hennessy, "500 soldiers set for mission in Liberia", p. 10.

Harvey Langholtz, Boris Kondoch, Alan Wells (Eds.),
International Peacekeeping: The Yearbook of International Peace Operations, Volume 9, 2004, pp. 123-138.
© *Koninklijke Brill N.V. Printed in the Netherlands*

Background to Irish Participation in Peacekeeping

Membership of the United Nations (UN) has been a cornerstone and determiner of Irish foreign policy since 1955.[3] For many years, prior to accession to the European Community, the UN was the only forum where Ireland could express its concerns across a wide range of international issues. The building and maintenance of a strong and effective UN, especially in the area of conflict prevention, forms a key objective of Irish foreign policy within which peacekeeping operations have come to play a central role.[4] As a small country, Ireland had a vested interest in the promotion of multilateral diplomacy and collective security. Despite the deficiencies in the UN Charter and the general framework of the UN, the advantage to a small state was apparent from the beginning. Eager to participate fully in every aspect of the Organization, Ireland was not hesitant about committing its defence forces to UN command in far flung lands largely unknown to most Irish people at the time.

Today participation by Defence Forces and Gardai (police) in a range of UN sponsored activities is commonplace.[5] This involvement has become a significant element of Irish foreign policy, and a concrete manifestation of commitment to the UN and the maintenance of world peace.[6] A tradition of active membership of both the League of Nations and the UN has assisted in establishing a peacekeeping tradition.[7] Furthermore, the effects of Ireland's policies over a range of issues including decolonisation, disarmament, human rights, and its history under colonial rule and non-membership of a military alliance, combined to make it acceptable as a contributor to peacekeeping and related activities.[8]

---

3   Department of Foreign Affairs, *Challenges and Opportunities Abroad, White Paper on Foreign Policy*, Dublin, (1996), 149-167, and Department of Defence, *White Paper on Defence*, Dublin, (February, 2000), 59-70.

4   *Ibid.*

5   *See* Department of Defence, *Defence Forces Annual Report*, Dublin, (1999), 32-38 and Department of Justice, Equality and Law Reform, *Ireland's Involvement in International Police Missions – A Discussion Paper*, Dublin, (November, 1999). *See also* J.P. Duggan, *A History of the Irish Army*, Dublin: Gill and Macmillan, (1991), 249-278 and *An Cosantoir – The Defence Forces Magazine*, UN Anniversary Edition, (October 1995).

6   *See* J. Morrison Skelly, *Irish Diplomacy at the United Nations, 1945-65*, Dublin: Irish Academic Press, (1997).

7   Skelly, *op. cit.* and Michael J. Kennedy, *Ireland and the League of Nations*, Dublin: Irish Academic Press, (1996). *See also* Norman J.D. McQueen, "Irish Neutrality: the United Nations and the Peacekeeping Experience 1945-1969", D. Phil. thesis, New University of Ulster, 1981, esp. the Introduction 1-13. Nina Heathcote, "Ireland and the United Nations Operation in the Congo", 111 *International Relations*, (May 1971), 880. Patrick Keatinge, *The Formulation of Irish Foreign Policy*: Dublin, Institute of Public Administration, (1973), 7 and 83-86; and *A Place Among the Nations*: Dublin, Institute of Public Administration, (1978), 158-161.

8   *Ibid.*

Despite the ongoing involvement in peace support operations, there is surprisingly little debate on the issue in Ireland. In 1993, Ireland revised and updated the municipal legal basis for troop participation in UN operations to allow Ireland to contribute soldiers to UNOSOM II in Somalia. This brought about a fundamental change in policy, after which participation in peacekeeping forces not specifically of a police nature was permitted.[9] At the time this did generate some debate as to whether Ireland should contribute forces to new kinds of military action by the UN. Since then the debate about future Irish participation in peace support operation has become more controversial owing to the foreign policy and security implications of the recent EU Amsterdam and Nice Treaties.

The most significant political development on Irish participation in peace support operation in recent years was the publication of the Government White Paper on Foreign Policy, and a White Paper on Defence.[10] The White Paper on Foreign Policy was strong on ideals, but weak in identifying Ireland's interests and the practical implications of foreign policy decisions. Likewise, the White Paper on Defence was dominated by bland descriptive passages, mixed with cost cutting suggestions disguised as expenditure analysis.[11] The Paper lacked policy analysis and vision.[12] The surprise decision to reduce the Defence Forces even further to around 10,500 sparked off the most serious public dispute ever between the Department of Defence and the Defence Forces.[13] This had the unfortunate consequence of detracting attention from other defence and security issues discussed in the White Paper. Although both the Foreign Policy and Defence Forces White Papers were vague in many respects, the chapters dealing with overseas peace support operations did set out the background to Irish involvement, and the factors that will inform the government's consideration of requests for troops were enunciated in clear terms. They also spelled out the guiding principles the government should consider in deciding whether or not to participate in enforcement operations in the post Somalia era.[14] What is most surprising about the criteria and guidelines is how little reference is actually made to them in the Dáil (Irish Parliament) debates seeking approval for

---

9   The Defence (Amendment) Act, 1993. *See infra* and R. Murphy, "Ireland: Legal issues arising from participation in United Nations operations", 1 *International Peacekeeping* (Kluwer), No. 2, (March May 1994), 61-64.
10   *See* M. Hennessy, *supra* note 2.
11   *See White Paper on Defence, op. cit.*, 12.
12   *See* criticisms by Mr. T. Murray, a former government consultant who reviewed the Defence Forces, *The Irish Times*, 4 March 2000, 10. He was especially critical of the treatment of the Naval Service and Air Corps. For the view of the Minister for Defence, M. Smith, *see The Irish Times*, 26 April 2000, 16.
13   *See*, for example, Jim Cusack, *The Irish Times*, 9 February, 2000, 3, where a former Chief of Staff asked the Taoiseach to intervene in the dispute.
14   *See infra.*

participation.[15] Part of the problem may be the need to respond quickly to humanitarian emergencies.

The key issue relating to peacekeeping and Irish foreign policy arising from the White Paper on Foreign Policy was the focus on maintaining military neutrality while fostering a security role within Europe.[16] The security role within Europe was expanded upon in the White Paper on Defence with a commitment to pledge troops to the European Rapid Reaction Force.[17] The participation in UN led and sponsored operations is not a controversial issue, but the growing trend of recent years to contract out peace support operations to regional organizations such as the North Atlantic Treaty Organization (NATO) may present problems for a country that has up to now shied away from difficult or controversial decisions on security and defence issues.

The debate stimulated by the publication of the White Paper on Foreign Policy was a welcome attempt to engage the Irish public in the formulation of foreign policy, and it has assisted in identifying and clarifying some key issues. The importance of maintaining a clear distinction between traditional peacekeeping and operations involving some degree of enforcement action is not just important for the UN, but also contributing states like Ireland. The intra state conflicts of today present complex and dangerous situations for all peacekeepers, and while there is general support from the Irish public for participation in such operations, they are not prepared to accept any significant casualties or unnecessary exposure to risk. Politicians in Ireland are not unlike their counterparts elsewhere, they will respond to public opinion and may even succumb to a media driven agenda. The real risks are not well understood, although Ireland contributed to UNIFIL for over twenty years, there was still a large degree of ignorance among the Irish general public of the dangers and general situation prevailing there for UN peacekeepers.[18]

The decision to apply for membership of the UN was probably motivated by a fear of Ireland being isolated and denied any role on the world stage. In this way, the decision was based on pragmatic considerations, rather than any idealistic or similar commitment to the UN itself.[19] There are interesting parallels with the debate

---

15   *See*, for example the debate on participation in KFOR, Dáil Debates 507, (852-869), 1 July 1999.
16   *White Paper on Foreign Policy*, *op. cit.*, 191-205. In considering the constitutional implications of a policy of neutrality, the *Report of the Constitution Review Group* stated that neutrality has "always been a policy as distinct from a fundamental law or principle, and the Review Group sees no reason to propose a change in this position," *Report of the Constitution Review Group*, May 1996, Dublin: Government Publications, 93.
17   *White Paper on Defence*, *op. cit.*, 15-18, *The Irish Times*, 31 October and 1 November 2000, 16, 17. At the Helsinki EU Summit of December 1999, it was agreed that by 2003, the EU would be in a position to deploy a 60,000 military force, *see Presidency Conclusions Helsinki European Council Annex IV*, Brussels, European Council 1999, and P. Gillespie, *The Irish Times*, 20 May 2000.
18   *See* the comments by Pat Kenny and others on "Kenny Live", 25 April 1998. The two hour RTE television show was exclusively devoted to the Defence Forces and UN peacekeeping.
19   "We in the Government have balanced the pros and cons [of membership]. In our circumstances,

regarding membership of the NATO sponsored Partnership for Peace and Irish participation in the UN mandated but NATO commanded Stabilisation Force (SFOR)
and Kosovo Force (KFOR) missions in the former Yugoslavia. There was a very
real fear among officials in the Department of Foreign Affairs and the military that
if Ireland did not join the Partnership for Peace programme, it would be isolated
and out of touch with international developments in peacekeeping.[20] Those fears
echoed similar concerns expressed by the then Taoiseach (Prime Minister) de Valera
some fifty years earlier in relation to membership of the UN.[21]

Although the Irish commitment to the UN forces in Somalia (UNOSOM II) was
quite small and numbered around one hundred and eighty personnel, the decision
to participate had significant political and military implications.[22] It was the first
time Irish soldiers participated in a Chapter VII peace enforcement operation of this
kind and it set a precedent that helped pave the way for the current participation in
the Stabilisation Force in the former Yugoslavia.[23] It marked a watershed in Irish
involvement in peacekeeping activities, and a realisation that Ireland could be left
behind in the changing nature of the international security environment unless it
too adapted to events. Though the UN operation in the Congo (ONUC) in the 1960's
did involve a degree of enforcement action to which the Irish contingent was a
party, the recent decisions to participate in SFOR, KFOR, UNAMET (East Timor)
and UNOSOM II were conscious decisions made in response to the changed international environment. In the case of SFOR, KFOR and UNAMET, the government
has also agreed to pay all the expenses associated with Irish participation. More
significantly, the participation in the NATO led, albeit UN mandated operations,
placed Irish troops under the *de facto* command of NATO for the first time.[24] There

---

although it is impossible to be enthusiastic, I think we have a duty as member of the world community to do our share in trying to bring about general conditions which will make for the maintenance of peace", Dáil Debates, 102 (1325), 24 July 1946.

20 Personal interview, senior Department of Foreign Affairs official, Department of Foreign Affairs,
Dublin, May 1997; and personal interview, senior serving Defence Forces officer, Department of
Defence, Dublin, May 1997. *See also* the article by Lt. Gen. G. McMahon, retired Chief of Staff,
in *The Irish Times*, 8 October 1998, 16 and the statements by the General Secretary of the Department
of Foreign Affairs, Mr. P. MacKernan, quoted in *The Irish Times*, 29 October 1998, 9.

21 Ireland's willingness to participate in SFOR, despite reservations, was also based upon pragmatic
considerations and a desire to play as full a role as possible in world affairs for a country of its
size and resources, *see* Dáil Debates 479 (514-539), 14 May 1997.

22 Figures supplied by Military Archives, Department of Defence, Dublin, August 1997.

23 This is not to deny that the ONUC operation in the Congo did involve a number of mandate
changes and enforcement operations on the ground. *See* Roselyn Higgins, *The United Nations
Operation in the Congo (ONUC) 1960-1964*, London: Royal Institute of International Affairs,
(1980); Ernest W. Lefever, *Crisis in the Congo*, Washington: The Brookings Institute, (1965) and
Alan James, "The Congo Controversies", 1 (1) *International Peacekeeping* (Kluwer), (Spring
1994), 44-58.

24 *See generally* R. Murphy, "Legal Framework of UN Forces and Issues of Command and Control

are significant legal and constitutional difficulties involved in command and/or control of Irish forces by non-defence force personnel, but successive governments to date have quietly ignored these.[25] Despite this, Irish military and other personnel have adapted successfully to such missions, but there remains an ongoing need to keep up to date in training, and to ensure equipment levels and standards complement this.

At one time there was controversy regarding Irish participation in UN peacekeeping owing to the backlog in reimbursement of expenses from the UN.[26] Reports gave the impression that Ireland was losing considerable sums of money, especially in Lebanon.[27] The financial implications are not as simple as might appear at first glance, and it can be argued that, far from being a loss making exercise, UN operations can be a net contributor to the Irish exchequer, especially as commitments were met from within existing resources.[28] In contrast, recent UN approved operations in Bosnia, Kosovo and East Timor were paid for entirely from the states own resources, and it is intended to finance the European Rapid Deployment Force along similar lines.[29] Despite Ireland's withdrawal from the EU mission to Macedonia, it still paid its share of the operating costs. The current trend is towards delegation of by the Security Council of its powers to establish peace support operations to "coalitions of the willing".[30] However, this is dependent on a powerful state agreeing to take the lead, and others agreeing to contribute. It is when states are unwilling to form such coalitions that the UN often falls back on peacekeeping or peace enforcement operations under Chapter VII, in the latter case, not always successfully. Participation in "coalitions of the willing" can have serious political implications and raises policy issues for countries like Ireland that to date have avoided participation in formal military alliances.

---

of Canadian and Irish Forces", 4 *Journal of Armed Conflict Law*, (June 1999), 41-73; and R. Murphy, "Ireland: Legal issues arising from participation in United Nations operations", 1(2) *International Peacekeeping* (Kluwer), (March-May 1994), 61-64.

25 *Ibid.*

26 *See* comments by Ireland to the Special Committee on Peacekeeping Operations, UN General Assembly, Document A/AC.121/36/Add.1, 4 April 1989, 4-9.

27 *See The Irish Times*, 15 April 1993, and 15 and 17 May 1993.

28 This was especially evident in 1986 when a former Secretary of the Department of Defence informed the Committee of Public Account that Ireland had made some five million pounds profit from its involvement in UNIFIL, and would at that time have made a further net gain of nearly sixteen million if defaulting nations had paid their dues at the UN. This was confirmed by the Secretary of the Department of Foreign Affairs who said: "There has been no additional cost to the Irish taxpayer for keeping troops stationed in Lebanon over and above what it would have cost to keep them in Ireland", *see The Irish Times*, 10 September 1986.

29 Training and re-equipment for this is planned to be completed by 2003, *see* speech by Lt. Gen. C. Mangan, Chief of Staff, reported in *The Irish Times*, 15 November 2000, 9.

30 *See generally* D. Sarooshi, *The United Nations and the Development of Collective Security*, Oxford: Clarendon Press, (1999), esp. Chapters 6 and 7.

In contrast to the situation pertaining in Ireland, Austria, a country that is traditionally seen as neutral, amended its laws to facilitate full participation in European Union (EU) Common Foreign and Security Policy, including sanctions by the EU against other states.[31] This included participation in peacekeeping and peace enforcement operations without a UN mandate.

Guidelines for Participation in Peace Support Operations

The Irish government has committed itself to supporting the unique role and authority of the UN in the field of conflict resolution and peacekeeping. However, in view of the number, size and complexity of current peace support operations, it was deemed necessary to develop a selective response to requests from the UN based on certain factors. The factors that will inform consideration of such requests will include:
- an assessment of whether a peacekeeping operation is the most appropriate response to the situation;
- consideration of how the mission relates to the priorities of Irish foreign policy;
- the degree of risk involved;
- the extent to which the particular skills or characteristics required relate to Irish capabilities;
- the existence of realistic objectives and a clear mandate which has the potential to contribute to a political solution;
- whether the operation is adequately resourced;
- and the level of existing commitment to peacekeeping operations and security requirements at home.[32]

The *White Paper on Defence* outlined additional factors for consideration, including on-going developments in UN peace support operations, the evolution of European security structures, and the resource implications for the defence budget.

The guideline are very broad and imprecise, so much so that it could be said that all peacekeeping forces established will fall foul of at least one or more of them, and they could thus be used to avoid participation in, or even to deny the legitimacy or raison d'être of certain operations. These are legitimate factors for any sovereign state to take into account, and each request must be considered on its own merits. Had they been rigidly applied in the past, Ireland might not have

---

31   Article 23f Bundes-Verfassungsgesetz 1929 (Federal Constitution of 1929) amended on 1 February 2003.

32   *See White Paper on Defence, op. cit.*, 63 and *White Paper on Foreign Policy, op. cit.*, 194-195.

contributed to a number of missions. In this regard they are somewhat unrealistic, and they do not reflect precedent or practice to date. Nonetheless, they are potentially useful guidelines in assessing the nature and extent of what Ireland's support should be for any UN peace support operation.

The UN operations in Somalia have had a profound impact on peace support missions since then, and Ireland's policy was also modified in response to events there. Although Ireland was not tarnished by the policies pursued by other contributors to the UN operation in Somalia, participation in any enforcement mission is risky. Taking into account the experience of Somalia, the Irish government's approach to participation in future enforcement operations will be guided by certain criteria. The criteria are as follows:

- that the operation derives its legitimacy from decisions of the Security Council;
- that the objectives are clear and unambiguous and of sufficiency and urgency and importance to justify the use of force;
- that all other reasonable means of achieving the objectives have tried and failed; that the duration of the operation be the minimum necessary to achieve the stated objectives;
- that diplomatic efforts to resolve the underlying disputes should be resumed at the earliest possible moment;
- that the command and control arrangements for the operation are in conformity with the relevant decisions of the Security Council and that the Security Council is kept fully informed of the implementation of its decision.[33]

While there is nothing radical or innovative about the criteria, and they are broadly similar to those adopted by Canada around the same time, the level of public knowledge and debate has been increased by their publication.[34] They also set down the factors to be taken into account before a decision is made to participate, and they allow for the political and military implications of individual missions to be assessed and evaluated on an ongoing basis. Then, an informed decision can be taken on the basis of all the facts. This may lead to accusations of naiveté, especially as Ireland must now compete with other states to participate in such operations.[35] The end of the cold war has witnessed the industrial-military complex of both camps searching for a new identity and raison d'être. The recent UN sponsored military operations have provided a means for armed forces to resist pressure to rationalise and

---

33   *White Paper on Foreign Policy, op. cit.,* 199-200.
34   Lt. Col. Ernest Reumiller, "Canadian Perspectives and Experiences with Peacekeeping" paper delivered to seminar on Conflict Resolution and Peacemaking/Peacekeeping: the Irish and Canadian Experiences, Dublin, Association of Canadian Studies in Ireland, May 1997.
35   *See* reported warning by Defence Forces Chief of Staff that Irish peacekeepers are facing competition, *The Irish Times,* 5 October 1995; and the Defence Strategy Statements, *op. cit.,* 15.

reduce their capacity. Proposals from smaller states indicate that this is not simply a concern of the larger powers.[36] Nonetheless, Ireland should not be afraid to decline to participate in any UN operation when this is the right course of action to take.

The guidelines were applied for the first time in 1996, when the Irish government decided to contribute troops to the proposed Canadian led UN intervention force planned for Central Africa.[37] In the event, the troops were not required. When the matter of contributing troops to the NATO led SFOR and KFOR was being considered, the guidelines were applied again. There was general support for the proposal from the main political parties.[38] The Defence Forces and the Department of Foreign Affairs were strong advocates of the proposal.[39] In July 1999, Ireland agreed to send a transport company to Kosovo as part of KFOR. There was nothing radical or new in this decision, and their role is very similar to that performed by the Irish contingent with UNOSOM II.[40] Nonetheless, Irish involvement in SFOR and KFOR appeared to set the scene for a longer-term re-orientation of Irish participation in international peace support operations. If the Defence Forces are to retain the skills and reputation acquired to date in the new context of European security, then it may be necessary to participate in the organizations where best contemporary practice is developed. This is all the more so with the UN move from traditional peacekeeping to more complex peace support operations conducted by regional organizations with UN approval. This was a significant development for Ireland that should assist in ensuring that the prominent role played by the Defence Forces to date in peacekeeping operations is not diminished in the future. This is an important consideration as some of Ireland's attributes for traditional peacekeeping, namely the non-membership of NATO and the small armed forces, could be barriers to participation in future UN but NATO led regional operations.

The guidelines were most recently applied in the decision by the Irish Government to participate in UNMIL. According to the Minister for Defence, the decision to

---

36   The Irish Defence forces established a UN Training School in 1993, and agreed to participate in UN Stand-By forces in 1996. *See also* "Improving the UN's Rapid Deployment Capability: A Canadian Study", February 1995; "A UN Rapid Deployment Brigade: the Netherlands Paper", January 1995; and "A Multifunctional UN Stand By Forces High Readiness Brigade: Chief of Defence, Denmark", 25 January 1995.

37   *See* Dáil Debates 472 (701-725), 4 December 1996 and *The Irish Times*, 22 and 28 November 1996.

38   Dáil Debates 479 (514-539), 14 May 1997 and *The Irish Times*, 23 January, 28 April and 8 May 1997.

39   Personal Interview, *op. cit*, n. 1. *See also* Department of Foreign Affairs, *Ireland and the Partnership for Peace*, an explanatory guide, Dublin, 1999. It had been hoped to send a company strength contingent to SFOR, but some fifty personnel in a military police capacity was ultimately agreed.

40   Dáil Debates, 507, (852-86), 1 July 1999. *See also The Irish Times*, 31 August 1999 and 1 and 2 July 1999.

send Irish troops to Liberia was not taken lightly.[41] There was cross party support
fort the initiative, and the media and commentators in general welcomed the decision.[42] This is in contrast to what occurred in respect of the Irish decision to contribute to the EU military mission to Macedonia in early 2003.

Background to EU Mission to Macedonia

The UN in general, and the Secretary-General in particular, has made conflict prevention the cornerstone of the Organization's quest to promote a more peaceful,
equitable and prosperous world. There have been numerous reports and resolutions
stressing that conflict prevention lies at the heart of the mandate of the UN in the
maintenance of international peace and security. The Secretary-General is on record
as stating that the time has come to translate the rhetoric of conflict prevention into
concrete action. Nowhere was this more apparent than in Macedonia, where deployment of UN troops succeeded in containing the violence, and preventing a spill over
of tensions from neighbouring Yugoslavia and Kosovo. The situation in Albania
during 2003 remained unstable, and there was the ongoing problem of preventing
arms trafficking to Kosovo. In addition, there were problems along the Albanian-
Yugoslav border, and in the demarcation of the country's border with the Federal
Republic of Yugoslavia.

 In March 1995, the UN established the United Nations Preventive Deployment
Force (UNPREDEP), to replace an earlier UN mission in Macedonia.[43] The mandate of UNPREDEP remained essentially the same: to monitor and report any developments in the border areas that could undermine the confidence and stability in
Macedonia and threaten its territory. This was regarded as a very successful mission, and the military component of UNDREDEP cooperated with civilian agencies
and offered *ad hoc* community services and humanitarian assistance to the civilian
population. It maintained close co-operation with the Organisation for Security and
Co-operation in Europe (OSCE) and the then European Commission Monitoring
Mission in Macedonia. Unfortunately, the functions of the Force came to an end in
February 1999, when the Security Council failed to renew the mandate due to the
veto of China.[44] Speaking after the vote, the Chinese delegate said his Government
had always maintained that UN peacekeeping operations, including preventive

---

41   *See* statement by Irish Minister for Defence, Mr. Smith, to the Irish Senate (Seanad Eireann), 13
     November 2003.
42   *See The Irish Times*, 20 January 2004, p. 10 and 15 November 2003, p. 15.
43   Security Council Resolution 983 (1995), UN Doc. S/RES/995, 31 March 1995.
44   Press Release SC/6648 25 February 1999.

deployment missions should not be open ended. China considered the situation there to have stabilized. This view was not shared by other members of the Security Council, who especially feared a spill over of violence from Kosovo across the border. In reality it had more to do with the issue of Macedonia's policy regarding Taiwan than any issue related to peacekeeping.[45]

As a result of the inability of the UN to act in this case, the Secretary-General stated that a new approach would have to be adopted by the Government of Macedonia and its neighbours, in consultation with regional organizations. Macedonia is a small country occupying a pivotal position in the geo-political map of the region. In has a large ethnic Albanian population, and there continues to be a serious threat posed to the external and internal security of the country. Ethnic fighting has broken out on more than one occasion in the recent past.

In January 2003, EU foreign ministers approved the first ever EU peacekeeping mission (operation Concordia), and agreed to replace the NATO peacekeeping operation that took over when the UN mission was vetoed by China.[46] This deployment was at the express invitation of the Macedonian president, Boris Trajvoske. However, some Macedonian parliamentary deputies were skeptical about the EU's ability to replace the NATO presence.[47] About 700 NATO troops were deployed there in August 2001 following the peace agreement that put an end to the six-months long conflict between ethnic Albanians rebels and Macedonian authorities. In December 2003, operation Concordia was terminated and replaced by the launch of an EU police mission "Proxima" in Macedonia.[48]

The Irish Decision not to Participate

Although Ireland's policy regarding participation in peace support operations has undergone significant progressive development to take account of the changed international security environment, important legal restrictions on what the government may agree to remain in force. Policy changes reflect an acknowledgement that there will always be a need for traditional peacekeeping, but there may not always be need for Irish personnel to form part of such operations. The support from Ireland for the inclusion of the so called Petersburg tasks of peacekeeping and similar

---

45   *See* "China – Macedonia Set to Cut Ties with Taiwan", *People's Daily*, 1 June 2001.

46   *See* Agence France Presse (AFP), 27 January 2003 and 13 December 2002.

47   *See* E. Saskova, "Macedonia: Debut for Euro Troops", *Institute for War and Peace Reporting*, 25 February 2003.

48   The EU police mission "Proxima" will cover an initial period of twelve months. It will monitor, mentor and advise the local police. It will promote European standards of policing in general, and comprise around 200 police officers and civilians. *See* <http://www.eupol-promixa.org/>.

humanitarian tasks into the Amsterdam Treaty on Europe indicated a growing awareness of the need to respond to the changing international security environment. The
White Paper on Defence also recognized the changing trends in international peace
support operations, while at the same time the government has consistently stressed
that participation in UN approved European peace support initiatives does not change
Ireland's traditional policy on military neutrality. This may well be official government policy, but it is hard to reconcile with the fact of participation with other
European states in military operations of whatever nature, and the increasing cooperation envisaged for EU states under the common foreign and security provisions of the Nice treaty.[49]

At about 350 soldiers from a wide range of countries, the EU mission was
described as small but significant.[50] The origin of Ireland's dilemma regarding participation in the peacekeeping mission in Macedonia are clear in the criteria outlined above, especially the need for the operation to derive its legitimacy from a
decision of the Security Council. Ireland reneged on its initial commitment, as the
EU mission did not have a UN mandate. Under the so-called "triple lock" mechanism, before Ireland can participate in a peacekeeping mission it must be UN authorized, and approved by the Dail (Irish parliament) and Government.[51] At the Seville
European Council in June 2002, the Irish Government made a National Declaration.
This stated, *inter alia*, that the Treaty of Nice does not affect Ireland's policy of
military neutrality, and that a referendum will be held in Ireland on joining any
future common defence. However, it is paragraph 6 of the declaration that is most
relevant to the current debate. It provides that Ireland reiterates that the participation of contingents of the Irish Defence Forces in overseas operations, including
those carried out under European security and defence policy, requires (a) the authorization of the operation by the Security Council or the General Assembly of the
United Nations, (b) the agreement of the Irish Government and (c) the approval of
Dail Eireann, in accordance with Irish law.

No one can take issue with the necessity for parliament and government approval,
but what is to happen when a permanent member of the Security Council prevents
UN authorization. One of the many interesting aspects of the declaration is that

---

49   *See* the *Nice Treaty White Paper*, Dublin: Government Publications, (2001), and *The Irish Times*,
     29 March 2001, 8. *See also* J. Maguire, *Defending Peace – For an Alternative to NATO/PfP and
     a Militarized Europe*, Afri, Dublin, (1999); and Afri Position Paper No. 2, *Towards Real Security –
     A Contribution to the Debate on Irish Defence and Security Planning*, Dublin, (1999), and Comhlamh,
     Focus, Issue 62, Dublin, (Aug./Sep. 2000), 16-24.
50   Statement attributed to German Vice-Admiral Rainer Feist, who was selected to lead the mission,
     see E. Saskova, "Macedonia: Debut for Euro Troops", *Institute for War and Peace Reporting*, 25
     February 2003.
51   *See* Department of Foreign Affairs Press Release, Wednesday, June 19, 2002. <www.gov.ie/iveagh/>.

when the Minister for Foreign Affairs first mentioned this "triple lock" mechanism, the Minister referred to "UN endorsement".[52] Sometime later this became UN authorization, this is a very significant change that is especially relevant to the current situation in Macedonia.[53] The UN Security Council has adopted a resolution that "welcomes" and "endorses" the involvement and support of the European Union for the Framework Agreement to consolidate a multi-ethnic society within Macedonia.[54] However, from a legal perspective, this falls short of authorizing the EU mission to Macedonia, especially when the veto by the Chinese in the Security Council is taken into account.

The Declaration has added another legal dimension to Irish participation in peace support operations. The legal basis for Irish participation in peace support operations was the Defence (Amendment) (No. 2) Act, 1960, as amended by the Defence (Amendment) Act, 1993.[55] The scope of the 1960 Act was confined to matters concerning the contribution of an Irish contingent to a UN force established by the Security Council, or the General Assembly, for the performance of duties of a police character only. There is no elaboration in the Act on what these police duties involve. The most likely purpose for its use was to distinguish between "peacekeeping" and "enforcement action". The term could be construed as somewhat misleading when some of the events in which the UN Force in the Congo were involved, particularly in the Katanga Province, are taken into account.[56] The term also reflects the ambiguous and compromised role in which UN forces can find themselves, and was epitomized by the UN peacekeeping forces in Lebanon during the 1982 Israeli invasion. The Defence (Amendment) Act, 1993 amended and extended the 1960 Act in significant respects. The principle amendment is contained in Section 1 which by defining an "International United Nations Force" as an international force or body established by the Security Council or General Assembly of the UN, goes beyond the previous definition contained in the 1960 Act which had limited Defence Force

---

52   Statement by the Minister for Foreign Affairs, Brian Cowan, Adjournment Debate on Seville Declaration on Neutrality, 19 June 2002, available from <www.gov.ie/iveagh/>.

53   Second Stage Speech by the Minister for Foreign Affairs, Brian Cowan, 26 th. Amendment to the Constitution Bill, 4 September 2002, available from <www.gov.ie/iveagh/>.

54   Security Council Resolution 1371 (2001), UN DOC S/RES/1371, 26 September 2001, paras. 4 and 5. *See also* Framework Agreement signed at Skopje on 13 August 2001 by the President of the Former Yugoslav Republic of Macedonia and the leaders of four political parties.

55   *See* R. Murphy, "Ireland: Legal issues arising from participation in United Nations operations", 1(2) *International Peacekeeping* (Kluwer), (1994), 61-64; and R. Murphy, "Legal Framework of UN Forces and Issues of Command and Control of Canadian and Irish Forces", 4. *Journal of Armed Conflict Law*, (1999), 41-73.

56   R. Higgins, *The United Nations Operation in the Congo (ONUC) 1960-1964*, London: Royal Institute of International Affairs, (1980) and E.W. Lefever, *Crisis in the Congo – A United Nations Force in Action*, Washington DC: Brookings Institute, (1965), 72-121.

participation to UN peacekeeping operations. This brought about a significant change in Irish defence and foreign policy that was not reflected in the level of public or parliamentary debate at the time. Although the Dáil debate indicated that at least some did appreciate the wider ramifications of the change in Irish municipal law, it seemed that the Dáil as a whole did not.[57] It is unlikely that the new legislation would have had such an uncontroversial passage but for the humanitarian considerations in sending an Irish army transport unit to Somalia and the presence of Irish aid workers in that country.

Irish participation in peace support operations is now governed by both the Defence Acts, and the Seville Declaration. However, on this occasion, the Seville Declaration was the decisive issue. There has been much debate in Ireland in recent years about European security and defence issues. The decision to join the NATO sponsored Partnership for Peace (PfP) was controversial, especially as the government of the day reneged on a commitment to hold a referendum on the issue. It is likely the perceived militarization of Europe and a fear that the Nice Treaty would lead to Irish involvement in European defence issues contributed to the decision of the Irish electorate to reject the Nice Treaty in the first referendum on the issue in early 2001.[58] In order to reassure the Irish electorate on the issue of Irish military neutrality and participation in EU military operations during the second referendum campaign, the Government made the Seville Declaration, which was accepted by all the EU member states. The problem that will confront Ireland in future years is participation in UN approved, but not formally mandated operations. If the UN hands over the responsibility of peacekeeping operations such as SFOR or KFOR to the EU without a formal Security Council or General Assembly mandate, this will present Ireland with the same problem as has arisen with the mission to Macedonia.

The situation with regard to Finland is analogous to that of Ireland. Finnish legislation does not permit Finnish troops to take part in peace enforcement operations, as opposed to traditional peacekeeping under Chapter VI of the UN Charter where hostilities have ended and there is agreement between the parties to the conflict.[59] Furthermore, the legislation requires that Finnish troops can only be involved in peacekeeping operations when there is a UN or Organization for Security and Co-operation in Europe (OSCE) mandate. Consequently, Finnish troops were also with-

---

57   Dáil Debates 433, (309, 363, 376), 29 June 1993.
58   A second referendum was held in 2002, and on this occasion a clear majority voted in favour of Irish ratification of the Nice Treaty thus clearing the way for enlargement of the EU.
59   T. Archer, "Keeping out of it: the hangover of Finnish neutralism and the limits of normative commitments", Finnish Institute of International Affairs and Manchester Metropolitan University Seminar, 8-9 March 2002, pp. 2-3.

drawn from the EU mission to Macedonia despite the fact that their assistance was expressly requested.[60] The Finnish Ministry of Defence has suggested that an EU mandate could be added to Finnish law, but the Ministry of Foreign Affairs opposed this on the grounds that there had already been changes in Finnish peacekeeping law recently.[61]

The resistance to amending the law in Finland is, like that of Ireland, political. Many within the parliament and government want to avoid any political risks involved in advocating change. In some ways this is even more restrictive than that of Ireland in that Finnish troops are precluded from participation in missions outside of Finland other than traditional peacekeeping.

The current deployment of Irish troops to Liberia indicates a commitment by Ireland to UN mandated and commanded peacekeeping operations consistent with Irish foreign policy in support of the UN Secretary General. It is the biggest commitment by Ireland to any mission since participation in the United Nations Interim Force in Lebanon (UNIFIL) in 1978. The commitment to the missions in Liberia, Kosovo and elsewhere will permit Ireland to decline any invitation to contribute to a force in Iraq without offending US sensibilities.[62] There are also the cost implications to the Irish exchequer, in that the costs incurred as part of UNMIL will be met from UN funds.

Conclusion

During the summer of 2002, the United States threatened to veto the renewal of crucial mandates for UN peace operations unless a mechanism was agreed to prevent US personnel on UN related missions coming under the jurisdiction of the International Criminal Court ("ICC"). The solution was the adoption of Security Council Resolution 1422 which effectively exempts officials and personnel part of UN authorised or established operations and from a State not a party to the ICC Statute, from the jurisdiction of ICC for twelve months.[63] The resolution then goes on to provide that it is the intention to renew this on an annual basis for as long as may be necessary in the future. The power of the permanent members to veto Security Council mandates at their instigation or renewal remains a real threat to

---

60 *Helsingin Sanomat International Edition*, 2 November 2001.
61 *Ibid.*
62 *See* R. Murphy, "Liberia mission involves significant risks", *The Irish Times*, 26 November 2003, p. 18.
63 Security Council Resolution 1422 of 12 July 2002. This was renewed by Security Council Resolution 1487 of 12 June 2003.

UN authorized peace support operations. At the time Irish troops part of UN operations had to prepare to return home if the necessary mandate was not renewed. Finland and Sweden faced a similar dilemma. Such events are quite likely in the future for a variety of reasons. The legal and political loops Ireland has chosen to apply to participation in this EU mission to Macedonia are a source of some bewilderment and irritation to our EU partners, and are characteristic of Ireland's inept posturing on issues of European foreign policy and security co-operation. The Seville Declaration would not have been necessary had the Irish government been more honest and communicative with the electorate in the first instance. There is also the matter of participation in other EU monitoring missions and under the auspices of the OSCE. Ireland is likely to face similar dilemmas in the future. The EU military mission to Macedonia was a lightly armed preventive deployment of peacekeepers in the European theatre. It would be difficult to find a more worthy and less controversial peacekeeping operation, but Ireland found itself sidelined from the EU's first tentative steps to play a meaningful role in support of this small and vulnerable European country. It is regrettable that Ireland and other states have effectively allowed any permanent member of the Security Council determine future participation in peace support operations, irrespective of the merits involved.

Peace Operations and Counter-Terrorism:
A "Challenges of Peace Operations Project" Seminar*

*Michael Sahlin and Annika Hilding Norberg***

The seminar that took place in Krusenberg, Sweden[1] on 23 May 2003 was the twelfth in a series of meetings held by the "Challenges of Peace Operations: Into the 21st Century', a project that is a multinational and joint undertaking by a group of leading organizations from around the world in the field of peace operations.[2] Phase I, from 1997-2002, ended with the presentation of a Concluding Report to Secretary-General Kofi Annan at UN headquarters, New York, in April 2002. Phase II began with a conference in November 2002 in Melbourne, Australia, (described in last years volume) and is expected to embrace four or five meetings and end in July 2005 with a further report to the UN Secretary-General.

The tragedy of 11 September 2001 occurred in the closing months of Phase I of the Challenges Project and there was insufficient time to address the implications of this new dimension of security threat before the finalization of the Concluding Report of Phase I. The Partner Organizations of the Project decided that the topic should be the opening item in Phase II, with the aim of elaborating on how and to what extent, if any, the recent global terrorist dimensions of threats to security might in the years to come have an impact on the way in which peace operations are being conducted.

---

*   Note: this summary draws heavily on the report of the seminar. Michael Sahlin and Annika Hilding Norberg, editors, *Report on the XII International Challenges Seminar: Peace Operations and Counter-Terrorism*, Elandars Gotab, Stockholm, 2003.

**   Ambassador Michael Sahlin is Director General of the Folke Bernadotte Academy, Sweden. Ms Annika Hilding-Norberg is the project leader of the Challenges of Peace Operations Project at the Folke Bernadotte Academy, Sweden.

1   Hosted by the Folke Bernadotte Academy in association with the Swedish National Defence College, Swedish Armed Forces and the Swedish National Police Board.

2   For further information about the Project and this seminar, *see* <http://www.peacechallenges.net>.

Harvey Langholtz, Boris Kondoch, Alan Wells (Eds.),
International Peacekeeping: The Yearbook of International Peace Operations, Volume 9, 2004, pp. 139-144.
© *Koninklijke Brill N.V. Printed in the Netherlands*

The Krusenberg seminar took place less than three months before the act of terrorism in Baghdad on 19 August 2003 that took the lives of Sergio Vieira de Mello
and more than 20 of his UN staff and colleagues. The opening statement at Krusenberg
was given by the Foreign Minister of Sweden, the late Anna Lindh, who soon afterwards was herself brutally attacked and killed by an assailant in a department store
in Stockholm.

The presentations at the seminar considered the topic from the political, legal,
military and police perspectives of United Nations peace operations, and from the
more detached academic and policy points of view. As underlined by Anna Lindh,
the problems that we face today require multilateral solutions and joint effort. A key
to a more secure future is successful peace operations. Some of the main issues
raised and points made by speakers and seminar participants at Krusenberg are highlighted below.

In opening the seminar, Michael Sahlin made a number of observations. There
are some who believe that peace operations must inevitably be affected by counter-
terrorism in one way or another, and must therefore adapt to the new reality. But
the title of the seminar topic implied no value judgement. There are others who take
the view that, while there may be terrorist acts committed by Al Qaeda or other
groups in various parts of the world, they are in fact directed against policies or a
way of life practiced by a particular country or group of countries. As such, they
are of less direct relevance to the circumstances in which most peace operations are
currently carried out.

Another aspect concerns definitions. What do we mean by "terrorism"? There
are those who define terrorism as "violence, or the threat of violence, calculated to
create an atmosphere of fear and alarm in the pursuit of political aims",[3] which
implies that the terrorists are a sub-national group seeking to change the policies
of the state, such as in Colombia or the Philippines. A somewhat broader definition
is that of the U.S. Department of Defense: "The calculated use of violence or the
threat of violence to inculcate fear; intended to coerce or to intimidate governments
or societies in the pursuit of goals that are generally political, religious or ideological".[4] But even this definition does not fully embrace the actions of such groups
as the Aum Shinrikyo that carried out the sarin attack in the Tokyo subway in 1995,
nor – at the other end of the scale – the terror caused by Pol Pot and the Khmer

---

3   RAND-St.Andrews Chronolgy of Terrorism. *See also* Bruce Hoffman, Vice-President of External
     Affairs and Director of the RAND Corporation Office, Washington, D.C., noted expert on terrorism,
     author of Inside Terrorism.
4   U.S. Institute of Peace, *Teaching Guide on International Terrorism: Definitions, Causes and Responses.*
     See also <http://www.terrorism.com/terrorism/def.shtml>.

Rouge in Cambodia, or the genocide committed by the Hutus in Rwanda. Bearing in mind these differences, seminar participants were cautioned not to run aground on the shoals of definitions.

The seminar discussion was not intended necessarily to seek agreement on terminology, but rather to consider what effects and implications, if any, terrorism and counter-terrorism have on the nature, planning and implementation of peace operations. Are the actions of counter-terrorism limited to those of the military and security services? To the extent that terrorism is the problem, is strengthening the sinews of the state an answer? – or *the* answer? Or do they include civil actions to promote better governance, improve societal stability, build sustainable peace and thereby isolate militant factions to the minority fringe where they belong and where they are unable to recruit followers? In such efforts, do counter-terrorism activities compete with peace operations, or are they compatible and complementary with them?

Among the presenters, Arthur Mbanefo observed that the UN Special Committee on Peacekeeping Operations had yet to address directly the issue of terrorism and counter-terrorism, although other organs of the United Nations were seized with the subject and the Security Council had established a Counter-Terrorism Committee. Ralph Zacklin explored the serious implications for collective security of the United States and some of its allies taking actions to use force in Iraq without the specific support of the Security Council. In his view, following that conflict it was even less likely that peace operations would be mandated for counter-terrorism actions and it could be argued that many of the internal conflicts, ethnic rivalries, unsettled borders and weak governments that provided the backdrop to current peace operations posed at least as dangerous a threat to peace and security as terrorism. He opined that if the UN agenda on peace operations was to be taken over by counter-terrorism it would almost certainly orphan many existing operations and reduce the resources available for new operations. It was not through the deployment of peacekeepers that terrorism could be effectively countered.

Timothy Ford looked at the issue specifically from a military standpoint. He reminded participants that over the history of UN peacekeeping, UN peacekeeping missions had often been exposed to terrorism, either directly or collaterally. Under the new focus, planning for UN peacekeeping operations must be seen to address the possibility of terrorism and mission preparation must include a comprehensive and effective counter-terrorism policy. At the strategic level, in the mission planning the UN needed to ensure that it had the necessary information sources to correctly assess the threats to the peace process and the risk of terrorism acts against the various players and the UN presence. At the operational level, the best defence against terrorism was a capable and credible security force with appropriate rule of engagement, and in turn this meant effective integration of all components of a mission, particularly the security components, and sound security procedures. At the tactical level, any counter-terrorism plan must be implemented effectively by all concerned and personnel would need to be provided with appropriate protection equipment, vehicles and secure communications.

William Durch addressed several issues: the definitional question; the issue of the sources of terrorist violence that might be directed against peace operations personnel; and the potential threat posed by weapons of mass destruction in post-conflict situations. In a comment that unknowingly presaged the tragedy that would occur three months later in Baghdad, he observed that although the Iraq operation was primarily an American operation, there was growing international participation. It offered something of an ideal, highly distributed target for terrorism, not all elements of which could be protected equally well, for attack by Al Qaeda or other radicals.

Satish Nambiar advised that the scope and extent to which the phenomenon of global terrorism and its dimension needed to be introduced into the Challenges Project should be deliberated upon with some care. The Challenges Project was focused on "peace operations" within the terms of Chapter VI of the UN Charter and should remain that way. In his view it would be unwise to consider the application of peace operations in a scenario that envisaged operations against Al Qaeda type of organizations. He drew attention to the conclusions of a Policy Working Group on the United Nations and Terrorism[5] which did not believe that the UN was well placed to play an active operational role in efforts to suppress terrorist groups, to pre-empt specific terrorist strikes, or to develop dedicated intelligence gathering capabilities.

From a police perspective, Lars Nylén felt that issues of terrorism could affect peace operations in several ways, among which was the fact that a conflict area where an international mission was deployed could be a transit area or a hiding place for terrorists, and also targets in a mission area could suffer terrorist attacks without there being any immediate correlation with the ongoing mission as such. In sum, the rise of terrorism meant that there would be a greater load on the police component of a peace operation which in turn placed yet greater importance on the need for all the actors in the security sector to cooperate more closely.

Giving further breadth to the consideration of law and order aspects, Michael Dziedzic argued that reliance on local police and judiciary to deal effectively with extremist elements was a fundamental mistake. Interlocking civil and military strategies should be implemented by the international community to dislodge violent obstructionists and to deal effectively with terrorism in its various manifestations. He believed that integrated efforts of military and civilian personnel were required to complete what he called the "intelligence-to-incarceration" continuum and he

---

5   Established in October 2001 by the Secretary-General, its report was annexed to UN document A/57/273-S/2002/875 – *see* <http://www.un.org/terrorism/a57273/htm#in>.

called for the following actions: the identification of personnel with appropriate skills and experience; the allocation of the necessary resources by key governments, international organizations and NGOs; the facilitation of international coordination of such efforts; and the development of training and induction programmes for international civilian personnel serving in critical capacities based on the lessons of previous experience.

The seminar topic and presentations gave rise to wide-ranging discussion. Some of the issues that were discussed included comments on the matter of international law. One participant, recalling the tribunals set up for former Yugoslavia and Rwanda and the establishment of the International Criminal Court, wondered whether it might be possible to criminalize the terrorist actions and then deal with the perpetrators in some form of UN arena. There was also an exchange of views on the importance of intelligence and information-gathering in a peace operation for the purpose of effective force protection, although a counter view was that in many cases the threats to the security of UN missions were not terrorism but the activities of criminal gangs.

Another comment was that in some of the situations in which peace operations had to be conducted, they were not post-conflict as conflict was still continuing and terrorism was a part of the violence; therefore there was a need to address what kind of capabilities were needed to achieve a successful outcome in such circumstances. Sometimes, it was the political negotiators and civilian administrators, rather than the military, who would be first involved and so there should be appropriate training for them. This drew a comment that often the civilians were not well coordinated and the different civilian elements were perhaps not quite as professionally prepared to go into a complex mission as the military or certain police forces.

Several participants felt that the Challenges Project could not avoid the implications of terrorism to peace operations. In dealing with terrorism – notwithstanding the absence of an agreed definition of terrorism – force would have to be used, and this would present difficulties. It would be essential to make sure that forces were well prepared, coherent, able to protect themselves and carry out their mandate. In the circumstances of the use of terror as a deliberate tactic, would a Chapter VI operation be adequate?

In his concluding remarks, General John Hederstedt, Supreme Commander of Swedish Armed Forces, underlined that sight must not be lost of the real challenges of a world in which the security of individuals, groups and countries are constantly being threatened. In order to be able to address current and forthcoming challenges, he pointed to two dimensions that he saw as urgent:

- The need for close and open-spirited cooperation between military, police and other civilian functions, and
- The need for close cooperation between global and regional organizations and arrangements.

He singled out the critical need for efficient cooperation between the military and police with the common aim to foster efficient security. Regarding interaction between global and regional organizations, he observed that the interplay between different organizations is much too often characterized more by wasteful competition and duplication than by complementary cooperation. Regional organizations are well suited to take on some of the challenges of dealing with regional conflicts, and he recalled the stricture of Ambassador Lakhdar Brahimi that "the challenge rests in how to engage and involve regional organizations without regionalizing peace-keeping".[6]

---

6   Brahimi Lakhdar, Key Note speech, 9th Challenges Seminar, Buenos Aires, August 2001.

The Ankara Seminar on Peace Operations:
The Challenges Project Phase II

Challenges of Change: The Nature of Peace Operations and the
Continuing Need for Reform 18-20 November 2003, Ankara

Murat Bilhan*

1. International Ankara Seminar was held under the framework of the Challenges Project conducted by Partner Organizations with the coordination of Folke Bernadotte Academy in Stockholm. It was first initiated in 1997, under the title of "Challenges of Peace Operations into the 21st Century" to contribute to the success, efficiency and legality of complex peace operations by developing practical recommendations in an unofficial environment open to all experts from different parts of the world. In the Final report of Phase I (1997-2002) of the Project, education and training, military-civilian relations and cooperation were identified as prominent factors contributing to the success of peace operations.

Cooperation and coordination which has been an important cross cutting theme in Challenges Project Report Phase I, has also constituted the common point of the discussions in Ankara. Attaining higher levels of cooperation and coordination among parties involved in peace operations has been referred to as a primary element of success in multi-disciplinary and complex peace operations. Moreover, Project Partners taking into consideration the increasing references made to cooperation and coordination issues, contemplated on making it a general framework for findings of Phase II.

2. The Partner organizations targeted identification of the problems of complex peace operations and searching for their possible answers at the Ankara Seminar. The Seminar, with the importance of its topic, brought together experts from different

---

* Ambassador, Chairman of The Center For Strategic Research.

Harvey Langholtz, Boris Kondoch, Alan Wells (Eds.),
International Peacekeeping: The Yearbook of International Peace Operations, Volume 9, 2004, pp. 145-147.
© *Koninklijke Brill N.V. Printed in the Netherlands*

parts of the world coming from different national, regional and international organizations. In consequence, one of the main objectives of the Challenges Project, the
promotion of a culture of partnership in peace operations, was promoted.

According to Ankara Seminar presentations and discussions, the main focus
of Member States, regional organizations, non governmental organizations, relevant institutions and experts, is on strengthening interaction with the UN, the right
universal body to carry out the peacekeeping operations. Their common aim is to
develop ways to help and support UN capacity to carry out successful peace operations.

On the other hand, during the panels on case studies and institutional prospects,
it was observed that, in addition to the UN, regional organizations, with their particular views and potentials do play important role in complex peace operations.

The Seminar also displayed that key players of peace operations, while acting
with the motives of preventing conflict, maintaining and building sustainable peace,
are also highly concerned with alleviating human suffering during the process.

The Report by the high-level Panel (Brahimi Report) on the problems of complex peace operations, and the on-going UN reform process carried out within its
framework were points of reference in most of the presentations. The Report's
findings which constitute the minimum threshold of change needed to give the UN
system the opportunity to be effective and operational were largely commended. On
the other hand, some blurred areas in the Report were also highlighted. Particularly,
it was stated that strategic planning and doctrinal issues concerning protection of
civilian populations were not adequately considered. In addition, it did not address
what should peace operations do when genocidal acts are occurring or likely to
occur.

Secondly, the report prepared by the "Commission on International Intervention
and Sovereignty of the State" formed by Canada was also mentioned and used in
the presentations. This report titled "Right to protect" focuses and elaborates on
humanitarian intervention issues.

Thirdly, references were made to the Final Report of Challenges Project Phase
I, particularly on its education and training issues. It was reiterated that Member
States are the main partners in Peace Operations, and if success is achieved in bringing more states to a level of both "willing and able to do", then the project shall
serve its purposes to the benefit of the international community.

It was stated that each peace operation is unique in its own characteristics and
requirements. But, they have also the following common elements for success: open
and clear mandate; unity of command; strong planning; cooperation and coordination between the military-police-civil elements; good leadership; relevant education
and preparation; rule of law.

In addition to the above, it was emphasized that at the strategic level, planners
must take into consideration that what to be carried out is a multi-national and multi-
disciplinary complex operation; it must have an exit strategy comprising the clo-

sure of the mission; nuances between the relevant provisions of UN Charter Chapters VI, VII and VIII should be well understood; the dilemmas posed by the military-humanitarian relations should also be addressed.

3. The Ankara Seminar, after examining the most critical issues affecting one way or another contemporary peace operations, reflected a growing consensus on "The importance of cooperation and coordination to the success of peace operations" as a possible central theme for Phase II. Complex multi-dimensional peace operations of our time require "cooperation at strategic, operational and tactical levels during all phases of peace operations, from the planning stage, through its many transitions during the implementation phase, and on to the achievement of lasting peace and stability". While cooperation is necessary at all levels to enhance capabilities, it is hard to achieve effective cooperation because of the multinational and multicultural differences. Cooperation and coordination issues have preoccupied the UN since the early 1990s. Although the World Organization has made meaningful progress in cooperation at all levels with various actors ranging from regional organizations to NGOs and local administrations, effective cooperation has remained a serious challenge not only to the UN but also to member states, regional and non-governmental organizations, local administrations, and professionals of different cultural and organizational environments.

As a central theme for Phase II, "cooperation and coordination" is broad and flexible enough to be examined from the perspective of all the critical issues underlined in the Krusenberg and Ankara meetings. Since the general objective is to increase the effectiveness of peace operations by enhancing UN potential and abilities "cooperation and coordination" appears to be a very significant way of easing or solving the problems that the UN is facing in a complex and changing international system.

Contemporary Legal Issues:
The Rule of Law in Conflict and Post-Conflict Situations Garmisch (15-19 September 2003) Conclusions

Dieter Fleck*

The conference on the Rule of Law in Conflict and Post-Conflict Situations, co-sponsored by the George C. Marshall European Center for Security Studies, the German Ministry of Defence (International Agreements & Policy Directorate), and the U.S. European Command (Judge Advocate's Office), dealt with a variety of topics relevant for legal advisors to political and military decision-makers. Participants from NATO Member States and its new Partners were engaged in discussing controversial issues in this field, realising that the task of identifying, interpreting and implementing the law has become as complex as it remains essential to exchange ideas for further developing existing rules.

1.   Preemption and Humanitarian Intervention Today

The 2002 National Security Strategy of the United Sates of America, together with supplementary documents such as the Joint Vision 2020 and the National Strategy for Combating Terrorism, were presented by Professor *Michael N. Schmitt* (George C. Marshall Center). The speaker explained that in situations where law enforcement activities alone would be insufficient, the necessity criterion of self-defense applies. He provoked controversial discussions on the legal validity of preemption as opposed to anticipatory self-defense. But it was widely felt that in the absence

---

*   Dr. iur., Director, International Agreements & Policy, Federal Ministry of Defence, Germany, e-mail: DieterFleck@t-online.de.

Harvey Langholtz, Boris Kondoch, Alan Wells (Eds.),
International Peacekeeping: The Yearbook of International Peace Operations, Volume 9, 2004, pp. 149-154.
© *Koninklijke Brill N.V. Printed in the Netherlands*

of firm Security Council decisions no bright line rule could be offered for adopting the relevant criteria of necessity, imminence and proportionality. Issues of Preemption and Weapons of Mass Destruction were discussed by *Sir Franklin Berman* (Former Legal Advisor, Foreign and Commonwealth Office, London), considering that "preemption" could either be understood as an application of the established law of self-defense to new circumstances, or as an attempt to develop the law so as to cope with new circumstances. These two alternatives were left open, in particular in light of the fact that a legal right of self-defense has to trigger on the premise of a self-judgment by the threatened State. It was stressed that weapons of mass destruction have a potential for large-scale casualties from a single attack and also the likely potential for indiscriminate effects. Threats to survival can be of the kind to strike an instant blow that amounts to a survival threat. Professor *Torsten Stein* (Universität des Saarlandes) explained that the notion of preemptive military action is not altogether new in legal doctrine to respond to threats that are "instant, overwhelming, and leaving no choice of means and no moment of deliberation". Evaluating recent state practice and legal opinion, he suggested that in modern international law doctrine one cannot expect what is unreasonable from the affected state, when it comes to the imminent threat of an actual attack. He suggested that some concessions were required in the context of Preemption and Terrorism, as the consistent pattern of violent terrorist action embraces both already committed attacks and future attacks. Nevertheless, the speaker emphasized that existing limits to the right of self-defense including the principle of proportionality must be stressed and Security Council authorization sought, in particular in operations where one of the objectives is a regime change.

Legal deliberations were effectively challenged by philosophical contributions: Professor *Martin Cook* (United States Air Force Academy) assessed the Ethical Dimension of the New US "Preemption" Strategy. He did not exclude critical questions as to whether true self-defense acts or rather activities defending national interests were at stake and whether a superpower had failed to capitalize on great international support after September 11. Professor *James T. Johnson* (Rutgers University) offered a Just War Concept in 2003 under the self-chosen sub-title "Back to the Future?" The speaker contemplated on the questions "who has authority to use force, for what substantive reason and for what end to be achieved?" He provoked critical debates when relating the just cause of a military operation to the question, how should force be used. Yet he agreed that the application of the law of armed conflict may not be made subject to a condition of a just cause to be fought, as its obligations apply irrespective of the observance of existing rules by the adversary.

Controversial discussions on the recent Operation Iraq Freedom and Ius Ad Bellum were provoked by Professor *Robert F. Turner* (University of Virginia, Center for National Security Law). He referred both to the right of self-defense and the cause for humanitarian intervention, confirming an instant threat to use weapons of mass destruction and referring to clearly established material breaches of Iraq's obligations under the long list of relevant Security Council Resolutions (678, 687, 707, 949, 1441). He also revoked Iraqi non-compliance with essential human rights obligations. Participants expressed certain doubts, whether the conditions of self-defense were truly met. They also voiced concerns with the suggested resort to humanitarian intervention, particularly in the light of the present post-conflict situation. The very different opinion polls in the US, in Europe and in particular in Iraq itself were considered as indicative for the absence of shared interpretations and common legal opinions. In contrast to such arguments, Professor *Yoram Dinstein* (Tel Aviv University; U.S. Naval War College, Newport, RI) submitted that the use of force was lawful due to Iraq's material breach of the cease-fire which was established under SC Res. 687 (1991).

The presentation of Humanitarian Intervention and International Law by Major General (ret.) *Anthony P.V. Rogers* (Lauterpacht Research Centre for International Law, University of Cambridge, formerly Director of Army Legal Services, Ministry of Defence, United Kingdom) was received with particular attention, as the issue is dividing experts and policy makers alike. Evaluating the more recent practice of military interventions abroad, and commenting on various schools of legal doctrine and current official statements by governments, he concluded that legal opinions remain controversial, ranging from a right not absolutely excluded to an action tolerated by the international community even in the absence of Security Council decisions, if certain excessive conditions, such as the case of genocide, are met. The speaker provided ten specific requirements for justifying humanitarian intervention and he referred to the Report of the International Commission on Intervention and State Sovereignty (ICISS), *The Responsibility to Protect* (International Development Research Centre, Ottawa, December 2001) which considers the responsibility to prevent, to react and to rebuild as inherent in the concept of sovereignty. The Report also establishes main principles for military intervention such as the just cause threshold, precautionary rules, the right authority (the most appropriate being the Security Council), and rules for the professional performance of any such operation.

2. Targeting and Modern Warfare

Targeting issues were addressed with extensive expertise from three different theatres. Mr. *William Fenrick* (International Criminal Tribunal for the former Yugoslavia, Office of the Prosecutor) explained the history and working methods for the preparation of the Final Report to the Prosecutor by the Commission Established to Review the NATO Bombing Campaign against the Federal Republic of Yugoslavia (2000). The Report concluded that complaints that NATO tactics and methods of warfare had amounted to violations of the laws of war were not of sufficient weight to be worthy of investigation. The speaker commented on the application of existing definitions of military objectives, the avoidance of collateral damage and the use of specific weapons including depleted uranium and cluster bombs.

Colonel *David L. Hayden* (Staff Judge Advocate, United States Northern Command) briefed on Targeting During the ongoing Operation Enduring Freedom in Afghanistan, where lawyers are posted in Bagram, Kabul and Kandahar, tasked to assist in the targeting process on a 24 hours basis. He explained problems of identifying enemy forces, specific tasks arising from the high mobility on the battlefield and problems deriving from Afghanistan-Pakistan border ambiguities. The prime concern to minimize civilian casualties was underlined with detailed examples and critical assessments were given for attacks executed by mistake (Deh Rawood wedding party, Mandrassa religious school and Tarnak farms).

Targeting During Operation Iraqi Freedom was explained by Colonel *Richard Gordon* (Staff Judge Advocate, Coalition Forces Land Component Command – CFLCC –). He referred to the continuous review of potential targets, including the non-strike list (such as hospitals, mosques, schools, UN and NGO facilities) and the restricted strike list (infrastructure, lines of communication, economic objects), the development of rules of engagement (ROE) and special instructions and their daily implementation. Particular attention was paid to the collateral damage methodology which requires each commander to specifically verify that the target is authorized by the ROE, to examine whether a protected facility, civilian object or environmental concern is within the effects range of the weapon, and to consider the use of different weapons and different approaches in case of potential collateral damage.

3. Conflict Termination, Legitimization, and Establishing the Rule of Law

Presenting legal Factors in War to Peace Transitions, Professor *Wolff Heintschel v. Heinegg* (Europa Universität Viadriana, Frankfurt/Oder; U.S. Naval War College, Newport, RI) distinguished between termination of war and mere suspension of hostilities, referring also to several examples of more recent armistices which were concluded to ensure the complete cessation of all hostilities. He identified legal rules applicable to the different phases in the transition from war to peace, referring to the law of armed conflict, to express or implicit special agreements between former belligerents and to Security Council Resolutions under Chapter VII, a list which was amplified in Seminar C. An insight View From Baghdad was offered by Commander *Gregory P. Belanger* (Assistant Judge Advocate, US European Command, Stuttgart), informing on judicial reconstruction, the establishment of Iraqi security organizations, detention operations and the prosecutions of war crimes. The speaker described Iraqi attitudes following liberation and undertook a comparison between Germany 1945 and Iraq 2003.

In his presentation on Just Peace and the Asymmetric Threat: The UN and National Self Defense In Uncharted Waters, Professor *Michael J. Novak* (American Enterprise Institute, Former US Representative at the UN Human Rights Committee and the OSCE) distinguished between the religion of Islam and the political doctrine of Islamicism. He explained misgivings concerning the just war concept and addressed the problem of legitimacy in terms of the ius ad bellum, the transitional supervision and the resulting post-war government.

In a broad historic overview of The State of the State: Redefining Sovereignty in the 21st Century, Colonel *Thomas W. McShane* (US Army War College, Department of National Security and Strategy) stressed his conviction that multilateral efforts should be preferred to unilateral action, diplomatic, economic and informational tools should be fully used and states should not intervene in external crises of limited local importance. He convincingly argued that multilateralism reflects also American values and visions for the future.

The Effectiveness and Role of Non-State Actors in Establishing the Rule of Law was addressed by Ms. *Lisa L. Davis* (Freedom House, Washington D.C.), Professor *Debora Spar* (Harvard Business School) and Professor *Michel Veuthey* (Fordham University, New York). Speaking from different background and experience, they instructively showed existing synergies in efforts undertaken by NGOs, economic firms and the Red Cross movement. Mr. *Anthony Dworkin* (Crimes of War Website, London), reinforced such perspectives by an evaluation of wider expectations of public opinion.

The conference work was considerably enhanced by three seminars on

A: Modern Warfare and *ius ad bellum*: Humanitarian Intervention and Preemption, lead by Lieutenant Colonel *Justin McClelland* (Joint Doctrine and Concepts Centre, Ministry of Defence, United Kingdom),

B: Humanitarian Protection and *ius in bello*: Targeting Norms and International Humanitarian Law, lead by Commander *Gregory P. Belanger* (Assistant Judge Advocate, HQ USEUCOM), and

C: The Rule of Law in Post-Conflict Situations: Conflict Termination, Legitimacy, and Peace Building, lead by Ms. *Ulrike Froissart* (Assistant Director, Legal Department, Federal Ministry of Defence, Germany).

on which the attached comprehensive reports were delivered.

In providing this forum for discussion of timely legal issues arising from past and present armed conflicts and post-conflict situations, the conference has again enhanced the collective knowledge among legal advisors of NATO Member States and its Partners and effectively promoted interoperability and interaction. Presenters and participants offered a wide spectrum of expertise on current issues of international security law. Selected conference papers will be prepared for publication.

The co-sponsors and participants expressed their gratitude to the Marshall Center for the professional work dedicated to this project and for the encouraging support provided for extensive information, frank co-operation and sincere confidence-building in a growing community of legal experts involved in the wider field of security. A next conference, under the suggested working title "Civil-Military Co-operation in Post-Conflict Situations", is envisaged for September 2004.

Preemption and Terrorism

*Torsten Stein**

1.   Introduction: The Question of "Anticipatory Self-Defense" As Discussed in Public International Law and State Practice

One of the decisive passages of the new *National Security Strategy of the United States of America*, published in September 2002, reads as follows:

> For centuries, international law recognized that nations need not suffer an attack before they can lawfully take action to defend themselves against forces that present an imminent danger of attack. Legal scholars and international jurists often conditioned the legitimacy of preemption on the existence of an imminent threat – most often a visible mobilization of armies, navies, and air forces preparing to attack. We must adapt the concept of imminent threat to the capabilities and objecties of today's adversaries. Rogue states and terrorists do not seek to attack us using convential means [. . .]. Instead, they rely on acts of terror and, potentially, the use of weapons of mass destruction – weapons that can easily be concealed, delivered covertly, and used without warning. [. . .] The United States has long maintained the option of preemptive actions to counter a sufficient threat to our national security. The greater the threat, the greater is the risk of inaction – and the more compelling the case for taking anticipatory action to defend ourselves, even if uncertainty remains as to the time and place of the enemy's attack. To forestall or prevent such hostile acts by our adversaries, the United States will, if necessary, act preemptively.[1]

The new National Security Strategy of the United States has met mainly with criticism and rejection by independent international lawyers, political commentators

---

*   Professor of Public Law, Director, Institute of European Studies, University of Saarland, e-mail: t.stein@mx.uni-saarland.de.
1   The White House, President George W. Bush, The National Security Strategy of the United States of America, V. Prevent our Enemies from Threatening Us, Our Allies, and Our Friends with Weapons of Mass Destruction <http://www.whitehouse.gov/nsc/nss5.html> (visited September 24, 2003).

Harvey Langholtz, Boris Kondoch, Alan Wells (Eds.),
International Peacekeeping: The Yearbook of International Peace Operations, Volume 9, 2004, pp. 155-171.
© *Koninklijke Brill N.V. Printed in the Netherlands*

and the interested public. In public international law, this new doctrine has stirred up the discussion about preventive or even "preemptive" self-defense. On the other hand, the debate on the permissibility of preemptive strikes is not at all new, but as old as public international law itself. The right of self-defense by forestalling an attack appears already in Hugo Grotius' The Law of War and Peace.[2] Recognizing the need for protection against "present danger" and threatening behavior that is "imminent in a point of time", Grotius indicates that self-defense is permitted not only after an attack has already been suffered but also in advance, where "the deed may be anticipated".[3] Or, as he says a bit further on in the same chapter: "It be lawful to kill him who is preparing to kill . . ."[4]

The customary right of anticipatory self-defense has its modern origins in the *Caroline incident*, which concerned the unsuccessful rebellion of 1837 in Upper Canada against Britain. Following this case, the serious threat of armed attack has generally justified militarily defensive action. In an exchange of diplomatic notes between the governments of the United States and Great Britain, then United States Secretary of State Daniel Webster outlined a framework for self-defense that did not require an actual attack. Here, the framework permitted military response to a threat so long as the danger posed was "instant, overwhelming, and leaving no choice of means and no moment for deliberation."[5]

After the UN-Charter entered into force in 1945, discussion began on whether the classic *Caroline*-Doctrine could remain in existence alongside Art. 51 UN-Charter. One interpretation – voiced especially by those representing the Anglo-Saxon and US-doctrine – is to give Art. 51 UN-Charter a broader interpretation in this context by claiming that Article 51 did not suppress the pre-existing (customary) rule of anticipatory self-defence, which was, therefore, left unaffected by the charter.[6] However, this argument has been opposed. A number of distinguished authors support a more restrictive view:[7] In their opinion, recourse to

---

2   *Hugo Grotius*, "Of the Causes of War; and First of Self-Defense, and Defense of Our Property", reprinted in 2 *Classics of International Law* 168-75 (Carnegie Endowmen Trust, 1925) (1625).

3   *Id.* at 173-174.

4   *Id.* at 177.

5   *See* R.Y. Jennings, "The Caroline and McLeod Cases", 32 *AJIL* 83, 89 (1938)

6   *See*, e.g., D.W. Bowett, *Self-Defence in International Law* (Manchester: Manchester University Press, 1958), at 187-192; M.S. McDougal and F.P. Feliciano (eds.), *Law and Minimum Public Order* (New Haven, Conn.: New Haven Press, 1961), at 232-41; R. Higgins, *Problems and Process – International Law and How to Use It* (Oxford: Clarendon Press, 1994), at 242-3; O. Schachter, *International Law in Theory and Practice* (Dordrecht, Boston, London 1991), at 151; M.S. Schwebel, "Aggression, Intervention and Self-Defence in Modern International Law", 136 *HR* 479 ff. (1972); J. Stone, *Aggression and World Order* (London: Stevens, 1958), at 44; H.G. Waldock, "The Regulation of the Use of Force by Individual States in International Law", 82 *HR* 489 (1951); *see also* M.S. Schwebel, Dissenting Opinion, ICJ, Nicaragua, *ICJ Reports* (1986), at 347.

7   *See*, e.g., A. Randelzhofer, Article 51, in *The Charter Of The United Nations: A Commentary*

customary public international law as supposedly going beyond the wording of the Charter runs contrary to the progress achieved by codification. According to them, the right of self-defense constitutes "culturally transformed natural law"[8] within the Charter, while at the same time its prerequisites and obligations need to be observed. Under the regime of the Charter and its system of collective security, self-defense is only permissible when reacting to an actual attack. Otherwise, the system of collective security, as foreseen by the Charter, would be undermined and eroded.

Without entering further into the details of this conflict of opinions, I would like to comment briefly on state practise concerning this issue. Repeatedly, reference has been made to the Six-Days-War of 1967 and its evaluation by the international community in order to affirm the permissibility of preventive self-defense, whereas, the evaluation of the use of violence by the USA against Libya in 1986 is taken as an example to negate such a right.[9] Also, Israel's numerous military actions in the neighbouring Arabic states, which have regularly been condemned by Resolutions of the Security Council, have been mentioned in this context as demonstrating that preventive self-defense is simply not supported by state practice.[10]

However – and in my view this is crucial for the issue discussed here – a closer look at state practice does by no means give a clear picture. This may be illustrated by the Israeli bombing of the Iraqi nuclear reactor at Osirak in 1981. The UN harshly condemned the destruction of the reactor in its Resolution 487 (1981).[11] The Israeli action has been often taken as an outstanding example of

---

(B. Simma ed., Oxford: Oxford University Press 2002), at 803 (para 39); I. Brownlie, *International Law and The Use of Force by States* (Oxford: Oxford University Press, 1963), at 272 ff.; A. Cassese, *International Law* (Oxford: Oxford University Press 2001), at 307-311; Wright, "The Cuban Quarantine", 57 Am.J.Int'l L. 546, 559 ff. (1963); H.J. Kelsen, *The Law of the United Nations* (London 1959), at 797-8; H. Wehberg, "L'interdiction du recours à la force. Le principe et les problèmes qui se posent", 78 *HR* 81 (1951); *see also* Y. Dinstein, *War, Agression and Self-Defence*, 2nd edn. (Cambridge: Cambridge University Press, 1994), at 188-191, who propounds a middle-of-the-road-view: *Dinstein* has advanced a theory in which a distinction is made between two varieties of anticipatory self-defense. He coins the term "interceptive self-defense" which he defines as taking place "after the other side has commited itself to an armed attack in an ostensibly irrevocable way". It counters an attack that is imminent and practically unavoidable. *Dinstein* reserves the term "anticipatory self-defense" to describe a strike to prevent an armed attack which is merely foreseeable.

8   M. Kotzur, "Krieg gegen den Terrorismus – politische Rhetorik oder neue Konturen des 'Kriegsbegriffs' im Völkerrecht", 40 *AVR* 454, 469 (2002).

9   *See* M. Reismann, "International Legal Responses to Terrorism", 22 *Hous. J. Int'l L.* 3, 33 ff. (1999).

10   *See*, e.g., C. Kreß, *Gewaltverbot und Selbstverteidigungsrecht nach der Satzung der Vereinten Nationen bei staatlicher Verwicklung in Gewaltakte Privater* (Berlin: Duncker und Humblot, 1995) at. 82 ff.

11   S.C. Res. 487 (June 19, 1981), 36. U.N. SCOR (2288th mtg) at 10, U.N. Doc. S/1 UF/37 (1981); 36 U.N. GAOR Supp (No. 51) at 17, U.N. Doc. A/36/51 (1981).

an unlawful preventive measure, whereas the content of Resolution 487 (1981) is not at all clear.[12] Anticipatory self-defense as such was not condemned in general, nor has this been the case in any other UN-Resolution. Merely two states – Egypt[13] and Mexico[14] – voiced their generally negative attitude towards anticipatory self-defense. On the contrary, Great Britain for example indicated that it condemned the Israeli action since it did not conform to the criteria set out in the Caroline-Doctrine.[15] The USA implicitly condoned Israel's action, but voted in favour of the Resolution solely for political reasons.[16] Reismann[17] even asserts that in the wake of Iraq's conduct during and after the second Gulf War, many states in hindsight now believe that Israel's attack on the Iraqi nuclear reactor in 1981 was justified after all.

Concluding this analysis, it can be maintained that, up to the 1990ies, state practice in confirming the legitimacy of anticipatory self-defense bas been inconsistent and influenced heavily by international politics. Literature gives us further examples: it is argued that the universal condemnation of South Africa's pursuit of African National Congress (ANC) terrorists in Angola "seemed to arise more from revulsion at South Africa over apartheid than from a considered legal judgement of the lawfulness of pursuing terrorists into the territory of the state in which they have found [save] haven".[18] The high level of dependency on political considerations in state practice has led some authors to believe that anticipatory self-defense is not a very satisfactory legal basis for conducting anti-terror operations; a state should not attempt to justify an anti-terror operation as anticipatory self-defense "unless no other credible justification exists".[19] From a political point of view, this is undoubtedly correct, but on the other hand it needs to

---

12 *See* B.M. Polebaum, "National Self-Defense in International Law: An Emerging Standard for a Nuclear Age", 59 *N.Y.U.L. Review* 187, 205 (1984); D. Brown, "Use of Force against Terrorism after September 11th: State Responsibility, Self-Defense and other Responses", 11 *Cardozo J. Int'l & Comp. L.* 1, 43 (2003); A. Cassese, *International Law*, supra note 7, at 309-10.

13 ILM, 19 (1981), at 980.

14 ILM, 19 (1981), at S. 991-2.

15 "It was not a response to an armed attack on Israel by Iraq. There was no instant or overwhelming necissity for selfdefence. Nor [could] it be justified as a forcible measure of self-protection.", ILM, 19 (1981), at 977.

16 In the Security Council, the USA (implicitly) indicated that it backed the Israeli concept of self-defense. Nevertheless it voted in favour of the SC resolution condemning Israel, due to Israel's failure to exhaust peacefuls means for the resolution of the dispute, *see* ILM 19 (1981), at 985, 996; A. Cassese, *supra* note 7, at 309-10. For futher discussion of internatonal political influence on state practice, *see* B.M. Polebaum, *supra* note 12, at 205-206; D. Brown, supra note 12, at 43.

17 *See* W.M. Reisman, *supra* note 9, at 18.

18 However, Uganda's pursuit of guerrilla fighters, who massacre tourists into the Democratic Republic of the Congo (DRC) in 1999, apparently drew no protest; *see* W.M. Reisman, *supra* note 9, at 18.

19 *See* D. Brown, *supra* note 12, at 43.

be emphasized that states have deliberately refrained from condemning anticipatory self-defense as such. Obviously, the option of a preventive military strike, last but not least with regard to new forms of threats, should be left open.

2. Anticipatory Self-Defense and the Fight Against Terrorism

Hence, the question is whether and how the new threat arising from Al-Qaeda and other terrorist groups of the so-called "3rd generation"[20] can influence or change the interpretation of anticipatory self-defense in international law. Like no other event before, the attacks of September 11 have demonstrated the vulnerability of the Western World. It became obvious that the fundamental change of strategy in international security strucutures would have to have an effect on public international law. Basic, longstanding and undisputed principles of public international law – i.e., the legal classification of terrorism and the measures permitted and demanded in fighting it – were suddenly called into question.[21] Only a few days after September 11, intensive discussion sparked off in literature on the rules of self-defense and how to apply them to terrorist threats.[22]

At first, the main focus was on the assessment of the attacks.[23] After the war on Afghanistan had begun, the discussion centred on the permissibility of operation "Enduring Freedom" directed against AlQaeda and the Taliban-regime in Afghanistan, a theme connected with the interpretation of the requirements of Art. 51 UN-Charter.[24] The discussion about fighting terrorism is, of course, not a new one. An extensive doctrine focussing on the matter already existed before the assaults on the World Trade Center took place.[25] However, a

---

20 *See* Th. Bruha/M. Bortfeld, "Terrorismus und Selbstverteidigung", 49 *Vereinte Nationen* 161 (2001)

21 *See* Th. Bruha, "Neuer Internationaler Terrorismus: Völkerrecht im Wandel?", in H.-J. Koch (ed.), *Terrorismus – Rechtsfragen der äußeren und inneren Sicherheit* (Baden-Baden 2002), at 51-2.

22 *See* the numerous contributions on the Web Pages of the American Society of International Law, ASIL Insights, <http://www.asil.org/insights/insigh77html> and the European Journal of International Law (EJIL World Trade Venter Forum), <http://www.ejil.org/forumWTC/index.html> (visited September 24, 2003).

23 *See*, e.g., on the Web Pages of ASIL Insights (*supra* note 22): F. Kirgis, "Terrorist Attacks on World Trade Center and the Pentagon"; J. Paust, "Addendum: War and Responses to terrorism"; J. Cerone, "Comment: Acts of War and State responsibility" in *Muddly Waters: the None-State-Actor Dilemma; see* also on the Web Pages of the EJIL World Trade Venter Forum (supra note 22): A. Pellet, "No, This is not War!"; G. Gaja, "In what sense was there an 'Armed Attack'?".

24 *See*, e.g., D.O' Sullivan, "The bombing of Afghanistan", 151 *New Law Journal*, 1778, 1782; T. Bruha/M. Bortfeld, *supra* note 20; G. Stuby, "Internationaler Terrorismus und Völkerrecht", 46 *Blätter für internationale Politik* 1330 (2001); M. Krajewski, "Terroranschläge in den USA, Krieg gegen Afghanistan – Welche Antworten gibt das Völkerrecht?", 34 *Kritische Justiz* 363 (2001).

25 From the literature before September 11, *see*, e.g., R.J. Beck /A.C. Arend, "'Don't Tread On Us': International Law And Forcible State Responses to Terrorism", 12 *Wis. Int'l L.J.* 153 (1994); Y.Z.

clearly changed shift of emphasis can be recognized in literature after September 11.[26] One could, though reservedly, interpret this development in the sense that public international law cannot any longer ignore the new risk potential of terrorism of the 3rd generation, as it has materialized in the assaults of Al Quaeda.

The threat of the New International Terrorism is only one aspect of the situation. Moreover, it has been mentioned in literature before September 11, that "anticipatory self-defense" would perhaps come to full flowering in counter-terrorism theory.[27] The decisive characteristic of terrorist attacks that supports this thesis is their temporal limitation: Due to the "hit-and-run" tactics of terrorists, any military reaction inevitably comes close to a repressive measure prohibited under international law. On account of the "ceasefire" normally following an attack once the terrorists have gone into hiding, the requirement of an "actual attack" is usually – at least at first glance – not fulfilled.[28] Against this background, the boundaries between preventive, punitive-repressive measures and classic self-defense become indistinct.

Blum, "State Response to Acts of Terrorism", 19 *GYIL* 223 (1976); R. Higgins/M. Flory, *Terrorism and International Law* (London, New York 1997); O. Schachter, "The Lawful Use of Force by a State against Terrorists in another Country", 19 *Israel Yearbook on Human Rights* 209 (1989); K. Schmalenbach, "Die Beurteilung von grenz-überschreitenden Militäreinsätzen gegen den internationalen Terrorismus aus völkerrechtlicher Sicht", 42 *NZWehrR* 177 (2000); T. Stein, "International Measures Against Terrorism and Sanctions By and Against Third States", 30 *AVR* 38 (1992); G. Zimmer, *Terrorismus und Völkerrecht, Militärische Zwangsanwendung, Selbstverteidigung und Schutz der internationalen Sicherheit* (Aachen 1998).

26 From the literature after September 11 *see*, e.g., Th. Bruha, *supra* note 21; A. Cassese, "Terrorism is Also Disrupting Some Crucial Legal Categories of International Law", 12 *EJIL* 993 (2001); J. Dellbrück, "The Fight Against Global Terrorism: Self-Defence or Collective Security as International Police Action?", 44 *GYIL* 9 (2001); Ch. Greenwood, "International law and the 'war against terrorism'", 78 *International Affairs* 301 (2002); M. Krajewski, "Selbstverteidigung gegen bewaffnete Angriffe nichtstaatlicher Organisationen", 40 AVR 183 (2002); S. Murphy, "Terrorism and the Concept of Armed Attack in Aricle 51 of the UN-Charter", 43 *Harvard International Law Journal* 41 (2002); E. Rosand, "Security Council Resolution 1373, The Counter-Terrorism Committee, and the Fight against Terrorism", 97 *American Journal of International Law* 333 (2003); M.N. Schmitt, *Counter-Terrorism and the Use of Force in International Law* (Garmisch-Partenkirchen: The Marshall Center Papers, No. 5, 2002); N. Schrivjer, "Responding to International Terrorism: Moving the Frontiers of International Law for 'Enduring Freedom'?", 48 *Netherlands International Law Review* 271 (2001); C. Stahn, "International Law at a Crossroads? The Impact of September 11", 62 *ZaöRV* 183 (2002); C. Stahn, "'Nicaragua is dead, long live Nicaragua' – the Right to Self-defence under Art. 51 UN Charter and International Terrorism", to be published in C. Walter/S. Vöneky/V. Röben/ F. Schorkopf (eds.), *Terrorism as a Challenge for National and International Law: Security versus Liberty?* (Berlin, Heidelberg: Springer 2003); C. Tietje/K. Nowrot, "Völkerrechtliche Aspekte militärischer Maßnahmen gegen den internationalen Terrorismus", 44 *NZWehrR* 1 (2002).

27 *See* G.M. Levitt, in Damrosch/Scheffer (eds.), *Law and Force in the New International Order*, (1991), at 224 ff., 227.

28 *See* K. Schmalenbach, *supra* note 25, at 179.

2.1. *The Doctrine of "Consistent-Pattern-of-Violent-Terrorist-Action"*

Recognizing this difficulty, literature – mainly from the USA – has tried to interpret the requirement of an "actual" attack in such a way that it would not only include each and every terrorist act, but also, and what is more, the overall strategy of terrorism.[29] According to this opinion, terrorism, in its basic conception, is directed towards a uniform threatening behaviour over a significant period of time. Terrorists hence create latent danger and aim at generating fear within the population. As a consequence, a single terrorist act should merely be seen as part of a concept of permanent threat – literature therefore speaks of a *"consistent pattern of violent terrorist action"*.[30]

Based on this concept of a "consistent pattern", self-defense against terrorist acts presents itself from a significantly different perspective. Military reaction to those acts will be neither punitive, since not only a single terrorist attack is concerned, nor solely preventive with a view to avoiding future attacks. Repeated aggressions by a terrorist organization are rather interpreted as a single, uniform *"ongoing armed attack"*.[31] Such an attack is, so to speak, "permanently present". The interval between the attacks means only a temporary pause in the ongoing aggression without interrupting the "armed attack" in the sense of Art. 51-UN-Charter.

The doctrine of "consistent pattern" indeed exactly specifies the characteristics of terrorism as a special form of "indirect violence". The tactics of "hit-and-run" and of pauses in between attacks are, as *Michael N. Schmitt* puts it, "the rule and not the exception".[32] The so-called "ceasefire" is regularly a result of terrorist tactics or logistic necessities.[33] To regard those tactical pauses of terrorists as blocking self-defense, is to deny the right of self defense to the respective states during those phases and means nothing less than to let the terrorists direct over the course of events.

---

29 *See* G.M. Levitt, *supra* note 27, at 227; O. Schachter; "The Extraterritorial Use of Force Against Terrorist Basis", in: 11 *Hous. J. Int'l. L.* 311-12 (1989); M. Baker, "Terrorism and the Inherent Right of Self-Defense", 10 *Hous. J. Int'l L.* 25, 47 (1987); O'Brien, "Reprisals, Deterrence and Self-Defence in Counterterror Operation", *Vanderbilt Journal of Transnational Law* 460, 472, 477 (1990); *see also* Zimmer, *supra* note 25, at 80.
30 *See* Zimmer, *supra* note 25, at 79 ff.
31 *See* M.N. Schmitt, *supra* note 26, at 24.
32 *See* M.N. Schmitt, *supra* note 26, at 24.
33 *See* Zimmer, *supra* note 25, at 80; Levitt, *supra* note 27, at 227; *see also* Schachter; *supra* note 29, at 311-312; M. Baker, *supra* note 29, at 47.

2.2. *Does State Practice Confirm the "Consistent Pattern" – Doctrine?*

Needless to say, the "consistent pattern"-doctrine did not stay undisputed.[34] The main point of criticism was and is that the doctrine does not respect the clear dividing line between repressive and preventive measures. Moreover, it is pointed out that the doctrine runs counter to state practice: The Security Council has, with good reasons that go beyond the fear of abuse of the doctrine, based its judgement on the proportionality of a measure of self-defense on the individual case rather than on the accumulative formula.[35] And by doing so, it expressly rejected to support such accumulative viewpoint.

Indeed, the Security Council repeatedly disapproved of the so-called "accumulation of events" – doctrine propagated by Israel: Between 1965 and 1982, Israel had tried to combine the various "minor" PLO attacks from the South of Lebanon in such a way that they would constitute one "single" heavy armed attack, against which self-defense would be permissible, in order to justify military retaliation.[36] In applying this doctrine, the criteria of "scale" and "effects" set down by the ICJ in the Nicaragua-case[37] in order to determine the level of intensity of an armed attack were to be complied with. The Security Council, though, condemned Israel's actions in numerous Resolutions[38] and thereby declined to "add up" the individual terrorist attacks.

However, the respective Security Council Resolution only dealt with the problem of scattered bagatelle attacks, whereby the terrorists applied a tactic of "pinpricks",[39] so that one could say that the attacks in question, despite of their undisputed tragic results in some cases, were rather "minor" ones. It is therefore questionable whether the Security Council would uphold its opinion in similar cases in the face of the New International Terrorism and its undoubtedly higher risk potential, as shown in the attacks of September 11.

There are significant signs of changed state practice from the beginning or mid 1990ies on, directed towards fighting terrorism with military force. Three, partly parallel, lines of development in state practice can be distinguished: Firstly,

---

34 *See* the criticism made by Zimmer, *supra* note 25, at 80 ff., 83 ff.
35 *See* Zimmer, *supra* note 26, at 86 for further reference.
36 *See* D. Schindler, "Die Grenzen des völkerrechtlichen Gewaltverbotes", 26 *BDGV* 11, 33 ff. (1986).
37 Military and Paramilitary Activities in and against Nicaragua (Nicaragua v. United States of America), Merits, Judgment, I.C.J. Reports 1986 at 103, para. 195.
38 *See*, e.g., S.C. Res. 490 (July 21, 1981), in: SCOR, 36th year, Resolutions and Decisions 1981 (S/INF/37), at 5; S.C. Res 501 (February 25, 1982) in SCOR 37th year, Resolutions and Declarations 1982 (S/INF/38), at 2-3; S.C. Res. 509 (June 6, 1982) in SCOR 37th year, Resolutions and Decisions 1982 (S/INF/38), at 6.
39 *See* K. Schmalenbach, *supra* note 25, at 180.

the international cooperation in fighting terrorism on the police and judiciary level needs to be mentioned. This cooperation had to face difficulties in finding cross-border solutions, a problem that is expressed in the fact that there is still no definition for "terrorism" in international law. "One person's terrorist is another person's freedom-fighter", as *Ronald Reagan* correctly characterized the long-standing status quo of international cooperation:[40] as a result of the differing opinions, the fight against terrorism on the international level presented a very poor picture at the beginning of the 1990ies.

It was not until the New International Terrorism – the terrorism of the third generation, as represented by Al-Qaeda – arose, that the international community changed its view. In the 1994 "Declaration on Measures to Eliminate International Terrorism", which was passed as Annex to General Assembly Resolution 49/60, terrorist activities were unreservedly condemned for the first time without referring to the right of self-determination or to national liberation movements.[41] This new attitude was confirmed in subsequent Security Council Resolutions.[42] From this time on, the General Assembly and the UN Secretary General initiated several activities in order to establish a comprehensive legal regime for the fight against international terrorism.[43] Most recent examples are the 1997 International Convention for the Suppression of Terrorist Bombings,[44] and the 1999 International Convention for the Suppression of the Financing of Terrorism.[45] The fact that "terrorism" was not expressly included in Art. 5 of the ICC's Rome-Statute as a most serious crime of concern to the international community as a whole does not hinder us to say that terrorism – however motivated, be it politically or religiously – is internationally condemned today[46] due to the clear statements and measures of the UN and their specialized organizations,[47] as well as of other international organizations, like the EU.[48] Simultaneously, a comprehensive legal regime was created in order to fight terrorism.

---

40 *See* R. Friedlander, "Terrorism", in: R. Bernhardt (ed.), *Encyclopedia of Public International Law*, Vol. 9 (Amsterdam 1986), at 372.
41 *See* Tietje/Nowrot, *supra* note 26, at 3.
42 *See* G.A. Res. 51/210 (December 17, 1996); G.A. Res. 53/108 (January 26, 1999); G.A. Res. 54/110 (February 2, 2000).
43 Tietje/Nowrot, *supra* note 26, at 3.
44 G.A. Res. 52/164, Annex.
45 G.A. Res. 54/109 (February 25, 2000). The convention attempts to formulate a general definition of "Terrorism" for the first time, *see* Article 2 sec. 1 b); *see also* J. Finke/C. Wandscher, "Terrorismusbekämpfung jenseits militärischer Gewalt", 49 *Vereinte Nationen* 168, 169-70 (2001).
46 Tietje/Nowrot, *supra* note 26, at 4.
47 As, for example, the IMO and the ICAO.
48 *See* T. Stein/Ch. Meiser, "Die Europäische Union und der Terrorismus", 76 *Die Friedens-Warte* 33 (2001).

Secondly, a remarkable development in the practice of the Security Council took place. For the first time, the Security Council determined that state support of terrorist activities was a threat to peace in the sense of Art. 39 UN-Charter in its Resolution 748 (1992) against Libya,[49] while until then terrorist attacks had merely been condemned.[50] The Security Council has affirmed this new attitude in a number of subsequent Resolutions, concerning, inter alia, Sudan, Afghanistan, Kosovo and the bombing of the U.S. embassies in Kenya and Tanzania.[51] A further qualitative level was reached by Security Council Resolutions 1368 (2001)[52] and 1373 (2001),[53] which were passed as an immediate reaction to the events of September 11, 2001. For the first time a *single* terrorist attack, carried out by a *private* terrorist organization, was interpreted as a threat to world peace without a state pulling strings from behind.[54]

The third course of developments in state practice refers directly to the right of self-defense as enshrined in Art. 51 UN-Charter and its application to terrorist threats. Already before September 11, a significant change could be perceived. In particular the *U.S. military action against Iraq in June 1993*, which was a reaction to the planned assassination of then U.S. President George Bush sen., an attack assumably supported by Iraq, is of high importance. The US justified their military action not alone on the basis of Art. 51 UN-Charter; the nature of the U.S. measure was clearly rather marked by repressive and preventive elements.[55] During the following discussion in the Security Council, the majority of the Council members acknowledged that the U.S. attack was in compliance with international law, a view that was shared by a majority of other states.[56] Further examples of state practice are the U.S. *attacks on Sudan and Afghanistan in August 1998 (*using cruise missiles). This military action was a response to the attacks on the U.S. embassies in Nairobi, Kenya, and Darussalam, Tanzania, in which almost 300 people, among them 12 U.S. citizens, were killed. While the action was criticized as far as targeting – especially in Sudan – was con-

---

49   S.C. Res 748 (March 31, 1992).

50   For an overview *see* Bailey, 11 *International Relations* 553 ff. (1992/3).

51   S.C. Res. 1044 (1996); 1054 (1996) concerning Sudan; S.C. Res. 1214 (1998); 1267 (1999); 1333 (2000) concerning Afghanistan; S.C. Res. 1160 (1998); 1199 (1998); 1203 (1998) concerning Kosovo; S.C. Res 1189 (1998) concerning the terrorist attacks in Kenya and Tanzania.

52   S.C. Res 1368 (September 12, 2001).

53   S.C. Res 1373 (September 28, 2001).

54   *See* Th. Bruha, *supra* note 21, at 62-63; *see also* J.D. Aston, "Die Bekämpfung abstrakter Gefahren für den Weltfrieden durch legislative Maßnahmen des Sicherheitsrates – Resolution 1373 (2001) im Kontext", 62 *ZaöRV* 257 (2002).

55   Tietje /Nowrot, *supra* note 26, at 14.

56   *See* Kreß, *supra* note 10, at 100 ff.; M. Reismann, 5 *EJIL* 120 (1994);

cerned, it was as such approved in the end.[57] Here, the position of the League of Arab States[58] deserves special attention, since it condemned the attacks on Sudan but refrained from judging the attack on the Al-Qaeda training camps,[59] which took place almost simultaneously.

Which conclusions can be drawn from this – if not yet changed, then at least changing – state practice, even if it is the practice of only one nation? First, there is a tendency of growing acceptance of unilateral measures in fighting the New International Terrorism. Second, this acceptance seems also to include the anticipatory elements of self-defense.

And third, it seems to support the "consistent-pattern"-theory. If public international law stipulates a comprehensive, absolute ban of terrorism and its support by states, then it must also allow for its enforcement in order to be able to claim effectiveness. A narrow interpretation of "actual attack", or "imminence of threat" as preconditions for the defense against terrorism would yield the possibilities of fighting it. One might even go as far as saying that such an orthodox understanding would rule out the right of self-defense. One only needs to recall the characteristics of a terrorist attack: On the one hand, the target of such an attack is mostly known only after the attack has taken place; on the other hand, ascertaining who is responsible or at least involved might pose great difficulties, so that a prompt reaction is nearly impossible.[60]

Perhaps we can formulate the following interim result: The criterion of "actual attack" or "imminence of threat" is not adequate to the phenomenon of latent danger, which is inherent in terrorism. A limitation in time of the right of self-defense against terrorist acts would, in its last consequence, actually deprive the states of this right.[61] In contrast, giving states that are massively affected by terrorist attacks the possibility of using military force against terrorist groups supported or tolerated by other states, even if the Security Council does not take any measures, could be seen as complying both with state practice and with the *ratio* of Art. 51 UN-Charter. – If it wants to be taken serious in the 21st century, public international law must base it's expectations of states' conduct, should they be realistic, on what the states still consider to be *reasonable*.[62]

---

57 *See* Wedgwood, "Responding to Terrorism: The Strikes Against Bin Laden", 24 *Yale Journal of International Law* 559 (1999); Campbell, "Defending Against Terrorism: A Legal Analysis of the Decision to Strike Sudan and Afghanistan", 74 *Tulane Law Review* 1067 (2000).

58 *See* D. Brown, *supra* note 12, at 15.

59 Letter Dated 21 August 1998 from the Chargé d'Affaires of the Permanent Mission of Kuwait to the United Nations Addressed to the President of the Security Council, U.N. Doc. S/1998/789 (1998).

60 *See* M.N. Schmitt, *supra* note 26, at 24-5.

61 *Id.*, at 25.

62 Tietje/Nowrot, *supra* note 26, at 9.

But recourse to military force against terrorists and their save havens is not admissible under each and every circumstances, it has to meet certain preconditions and is subject to legal restraints.

2.3. *The Burden of Proof*

One central problem of anticipatory measures against terrorism is the burden of proof: Does a state – who has reason to believe that it might become the target of terrorist attacks – has to prove the planning of such an attack (or further ones after an initial attack)? Is full proof of the terrorist organization's responsibility for the attack or the involvement of a state required, or is reasonable suspicion sufficient?

With regard to operation *"Enduring Freedom"*, some criticism arose on the issue of Al-Qaeda not being clearly identified as responsible for the attacks of September 11 at the time of the attack on Afghanistan. A suspicion, "even if well justified" would "not [be] sufficient according to international law in order to identify an organization as responsible for an armed attack".[63] And the U.S. bombing of terrorist camps in Afghanistan and of the factory in Sudan – Operation "Infinite Reach" in 1998 – was equally criticized due to the weakness of proof: On the one hand, it was said that the U.S. government had not provided any proof of the production of chemical weapons. On the other hand, it was said that the allegation that a certain group of terrorists ("Islamic Army for the Liberation of the Holy Places") was planning further attacks against U.S. institutions and citizens, was never sufficiently substantiated.[64] Here we might have to distinguish.

If terrorists have attacked already once, the burden of proof may well shift to their side. The "consistent pattern of violent terrorist action"-theory justifies a *prima-facie case* for an "ongoing attack". Since the terrorists have attacked once, experience tells that they will attack again. A terrorist organization supposedly responsible for previous attacks, or a state that has presumably supported them, can refute the suspicion by distancing themselves from these and further attacks. And they must be given the possibility to do so. However, this needs to be affirmed by concrete measures, like disarming the terrorist organization or extraditing their members. A mere lukewarm statement like that of the Taliban – who half-heartedly condemned the attacks of September 11,[65] but at the same time refused to extradite *bin Laden* – is by no means sufficient.

---

63 H.M. Empell, "Ist der Krieg gegen Afghanistan vom Selbstverteidigungsrecht gedeckt?", in: B. Schoch/C. Hauswedell/C. Weller/U. Ratsch/R. Mutz (eds.), *Friedensgutachten* 2002 (HSFK; BICC;FEST;INEF;IFSH), Münster, Hamburg, London 2002, at 158, 160.
64 Schmalenbach, *supra* note 26, at 182.
65 *See* "Palestinian Joy – Global Condemnation", *The Guardian*, 12 September 2001, Guardian Unlimited, <http//www.guardian.co/uk> (visited September 24, 2003).

There have already been other examples in which the international community assumed such a *change in the burden of proof* by using a well-founded suspicion as justification for resorting to concrete measures. This was the case in
Resolution 748 (1992) against Libya,[66] in which the Security Council explicitly
held, "that the failure by the Libyan Government to demonstrate by concrete
actions its renunciation of terrorism [. . .] constitute[s] a threat to international
peace and security". To apply this assessment also to the right of self-defense
under Art. 51 UN-Charter might – in the light of the recent state practice in fighting terrorism –, be a logical consequence. Therefore, as far as proof of the involvement of a private organization or a supporting state in terrorist acts is concerned[67]
it should be deemed sufficient if the threatened or already affected state *has a
reasonable suspicion*, and if the suspects do not dispel it. Full proof of state
involvement in acts of international terrorism can hardly ever be achieved. Again,
International Law cannot expect what is unreasonable from the affected states.
On the other hand, states under suspicion can well be asked to exonerate themselves, and in the vast majority of cases – i.e. if one does not face a "failed state"
– they have both the opportunity and the means to do so.

3.   The Limits on the Right to Anticipatory Self-Defence

The "consistent pattern"-doctrine leads to necessary, but also significant changes
of the actus reus of Art. 51 UN-Charter: The criteria of "actual attack" or "imminence of threat" are not given up, but interpreted and applied in a wider manner, while the burden of proof might be in favor of the threatened or affected
state. In order to compensate this "softening" of the preconditions of Art. 51
UN-Charter, and at the same to avoid its abuse, the limits on the right of self-
defense will gain additional importance. Undoubtedly, the danger of abuse or
"erosion" of the Charter system, especially in the area of fighting terrorism with
military force – an area under pressure from both politics and the public – is
extremely high.

The Charter system might rapidly disintegrate, if the use of military force
not authorized by the Security Council is not subject to some further conditions.
In that respect, the lessons learned from "Operation Allied Force" during the

---

66   Res. 748 (March 31, 1992).

67   The question of the burden of proof in that case is rarely discussed in literature, *see* Zimmer, *supra*
      note 25, at 42 ff.; A.D. Sofaer, "Terrorism, the Law, and National Defence", *Military Law Review*
      1989, at 95 ff., 105; R. Erikson, *Use of Military Force Against State-Sponsored International
      Terrorism* (1989), at 103-106.

Kosovo crisis and the proposals made for future comparable situations might be called to mind, although they could certainly not be applied "one-to-one" to the fight against terrorism. In the context of the discussion on the legitimacy of "humanitarian interventions" without UN participation, a number of criteria were named, designed to prevent an erosion of the UN-Charter system.[68] According to those criteria,

(1)   The procedure of the UN-Charter must have been followed by calling upon the Security Council (or the General Assembly according to the "Uniting for Peace"-Resolution) to deal with matter[69] and to act, not only talk.

(2)   Neither the Security Council nor a convincing majority of the General Assembly must have condemned the (preventive) military action or called upon its cessation.[70]

(3)   Unless time does not allow it, political and diplomatic solutions to the conflict vis-á-vis the state assumably supporting the terrorist action, including non-forcible sanctions (embargos), must have been tried without success.

(4)   The military intervention needs to be suitable for stopping the (terrorist) attacks.

(5)   The operation has to be strictly limited to eliminating the terrorist danger and must comply with the principle of proportionality.

(6)   The military operation needs to comply with the rules of humanitarian law applicable in armed conflict.

These criteria were meant – in view of possible future forcible humanitarian interventions – to prevent the Security Council from being circumvented or marginalized. In this context, it needs to be emphasized once more that the UN-Security Council did not stay inactive after the events of September 11, 2001. Resolution 1368 (2001) was already passed on September 12, 2001, just one (!) day after the attacks on the World Trade Center and the Pentagon.

Furthermore, strict compliance with the principle of proportionality will gain additional importance. However, the application of this principle is not without problems in cases where a measure of self-defense not only responds to an attack already committed, but is also directed towards preventing future attacks. I only have to refer to the controversial debate on the U.S. Operation *Enduring Freedom*, as it was held within parts of international law literature.[71]

---

68   *See* T. Stein, "Welche Lehren sind aus dem Eingriff der Nato im Kosovo zu ziehen?", in: Ch. Tomuschat/T. Stein (eds.), *Eingriff in die inneren Angelegenheiten fremder Staaten zum Zwecke des Menschenrechtsschutzes* (Heidelberg 2002), at 21 ff., 32.

69   *Id.*, at 27.

70   *Id.*, at 27.

71   *See supra* note 26.

Within the framework of the principle of proportionality, both range and con-sequences of the attack and the measure of defense have to be in proportion to one another. Therefore, a valuing comparison has to be carried out, primarily taking into account the estimated amount of civilian victims.[72] The lack of such an evaluation was one of the main points of criticism of Operation *"Enduring Freedom"*, since exact numbers of civilian victims of the war against the Taliban-regime are not available. Careful estimates speak of alone more than 3,700 casu-alties from the beginning of October 2001 until the beginning of December 2001.[73] It can be assumed that the number of civilian victims of the bombings in Afghanistan is approximately of the same scale as that of the attacks of September 11, 2001, which was less than 3,000. Literature draws its criticism of the U.S. military action as being disproportionate from this number: If self-defense results in more victims than the attack has caused, then – it was said – its proportionality is doubtful.[74] On the other hand one might have doubts as to whether "counting heads" does make much sense in that context.

Other authors consider Operation "Enduring Freedom" to be (unproblematic) proportionate, but base their view on a different standard: It is not the direct con-sequences of the single terrorist attack that are compared to the consequences of a war, but the definitive elimination of the latent danger posed by Al-Qaeda. *Michael N. Schmitt elaborates on this* as follows:

> Were the strikes against Al Quaeda proportionate [. . .]? Clearly, they were. Al Quaeda forces in Afghanistan numbered in the thousands and were widely dispersed. Moreover, to be disproportionate, the use of force would have had to be excessive in relation to the degree of force actually needed to prevent continuation of Al Quaeda's campaign.[75]

The diverging views concerning "Enduring Freedom" demonstrate a basic under-lying problematic of the preventive fight against terrorism. The "consistent pat-tern of violent terrorist action" embraces both already committed and future attacks. Hence, the question is which criterion is relevant for carrying out the proportionality test: is it the dimension of the attacks already committed or that of the future ones?[76]

Some authors recommend an overall assessment of this issue: The proportionality of an act of self-defense should be valued considering its intention, namely

---

72   *See* M. Krajewski, *supra* note 26, at 208.
73   *See* M.W. Herold, *A Dossier on Civilian Victims of United States' Aerial Bombing of Afghanistan: A Comprehensive Accounting*, University of Hampshire, December 2001, <http://www.cursor.org/sto-ries/civilian_deaths.htm> (visited September 24, 2002).
74   *See* M. Krajewski, *supra* note 26, at 209.
75   M.N. Schmitt, *supra* note 26, at 30.
76   For an overview of this debate *see* Zimmer, *supra* note 25, at 80-1.

defense against an "ongoing attack". Accordingly, the overall past behavior of the respective terrorist organization needs to be taken into account in order to be able to predict future attacks.[77] Already in 1987, an american author, M. Baker, has hence placed the main emphasis on the probability and the size of future attacks:

> If each of the terrorist attacks is viewed in isolation, then responses such as the Libyan bombings can easily be seen as disproportionate. But, when responding to a continuing series of attacks such a myopic view is inappropriate. The self-defensive measure should be weighed against all attacks immediately prior to the response and more importantly, the probability and size of future attacks. In light of these considerations it would be hard to classify the target state's response as either disproportionate or excessive.[78]

This opinion has met objections. A proportionality test that is to such an extent based on the future lacks measurable criteria, or an assessable standard.[79] An ex-ante prognosis of expected terrorist attacks is open to subjective assessments. In principle, the only reliable standard ist that of previous terrorist attacks.[80] The prognosis of a "latent" danger not yet existent should, however, to the maximum amount possible be left to the international community.

4.   Conclusions

In the fight against terrorism, and in view of the right to self-defense under Art. 51 UN-Charter, international law doctrine needs to make concessions. It cannot close its eyes to the danger related to today's terrorism, and it cannot expect what is unreasonable from the affected state. Criteria like that of an "actual attack" or "imminent threat" have to be modified as far as they are not sufficient to deal with changed reality. At the same time, the other limits on the right of self-defense have to be maintained and perhaps also to be strengthened. One of these is the principle of proportionality. In all cases where military force is used against another state, the attempt must be made to have the action authorized by the UN Security Council, in particular if one of the objects of the operation is a regime change. Here we find a significant difference between the wars against Afghanistan

---

77   *See* O'Brien, *supra* note 29, at 477; Schachter, *supra* note 29, at 315.
78   *See* M. Baker, *supra* note 29, at 47.
79   G. Roberts, "Self-Help in Combatting State-Sponsored Terrorism: Self Defense and Peacetime Reprisals", 19 *Western Case Reserve Journal of International Law* 243, 282 (1987).
80   *Id.*, at 282; *see also* Zimmer, *supra* note 25, at 81.

and against Iraq. To bring about a regime change is, in principle, even ruled out for the UN under Art. 2/7 of the Charter.

In the second Gulf war, Security Council Resolution 678[81] said: "Free Kuwait and restore peace and international security in the area," not: "Oust Saddam Hussein". Afghanistan is different, because the Taliban and Al Qaeda were so intertwined that international security could hardly be restored if the Taliban had stayed in power and were only obliged to tolerate some isolated foreign military operations on their territory. In Afghanistan, the fight against terrorism cannot avoid a regime change. Let us hope that we will see it one day; we are still far away from it.

The fight against terrorism was not among the original motives for the war against Iraq, nor was the oppressive character of the regime. There was no plausible indication that the Iraqi government supported international terrorism; mass graves were found later. The primary motive were weapons of mass destruction – which we have not found yet.

Today we hear that the war against, and the occupation of Iraq are part of the global war against terrorism. But it makes a lot of difference whether a State supports terrorism or whether terrorists infiltrate a State whose government has been forcibly overthrown.

For not being misunderstood: Weapons of mass destruction pose an enormous danger. If it can be shown that a State is prepared to use them other than in self-defense, the possible target State could hardly wait for the attack; one single of those weapons could – depending upon its size – end its existence. The danger is even greater if terrorist groups dispose of weapons of mass destruction; this would always constitute an "imminent threat". States normally do not commit suicide, terrorists do. Here lies, by the way, another difference: the one regarding North Korea.

New threats require new answers, and international law has to adjust to them. But "adjusting" international law cannot mean that we go back to the era of "just wars". No new system will be better than the one governed by the Charter of the UN, so we have to try to keep the necessary changes within that system.

International law can be changed through practice and opinio iuris, even against written norms as long as they do not constitute ius cogens. The prohibition of the use of force is ius cogens, but the preconditions for the exceptions to this principle are not. Customary law might even emerge out of the practice of one or a few States, if they are the most affected ones. But we must keep in mind that such a new rule will be one for all States, not for one or a few. And such a rule might turn one day against its creator.

---

81 S.C. Res. 678 (November 29, 1990).

Preemption and Weapons of Mass Destruction

*Franklin D. Berman**

'Preemption' is necessarily associated in our minds nowadays with President Bush's National Security Strategy sent to Congress on 17 September 2002. Despite what some commentators have claimed, that document hardly represents an abandonment of international law. On the contrary there are signs that the document seeks to situate the notion of 'preemption' within the broad mainstream of the international law on the use of force. Specifically, it says (in Section V):

> For centuries, international law recognized that nations need not suffer an attack before they can lawfully take action to defend themselves against forces that present an imminent danger of attack. Legal scholars and international jurists often conditioned the legitimacy of preemption on the existence of an imminent threat – most often a visible mobilization of armies, navies, and air forces preparing to attack.

Later in the same section the Document says:

> The United States will not use force in all cases to preempt emerging threats, nor should nations use preemption as a pretext for aggression. . . . . The purpose of our actions will always be to eliminate a specific threat to the United States or our allies and friends.

Those passages look to be equating the notion of 'preemption' with the older and more familiar category of *anticipatory self-defence*. In other passages, though, the notion is made to appear something much newer. For example, President Bush says in his Introduction to the document:

> The gravest danger our Nation faces lies at the crossroads of radicalism and technology. Our enemies have openly declared that they are seeking weapons of mass destruction, and evidence

---

* Professor of International Law, Oxford University; Judge Ad Hoc, International Court of Justice; Formerly Legal Adviser of the Foreign and Commonwealth Office. E-mail: Fberman@essexcourt.net.

Harvey Langholtz, Boris Kondoch, Alan Wells (Eds.),
International Peacekeeping: The Yearbook of International Peace Operations, Volume 9, 2004, pp. 173-182.
© *Koninklijke Brill N.V. Printed in the Netherlands*

indicates that they are doing so with determination. The United States will not allow these efforts to succeed . . . as a matter of common sense and self-defense, America will act against such emerging threats before they are fully formed.

And the Document itself says at one point:

We must be prepared to stop rogue states and their terrorist clients before they are able to threaten . . . weapons of mass destruction against the United States and our allies and friends.

The discussion in this paper will therefore be based on the premise that "preemption" should either be understood as an application of the established law of self-defence to new circumstances, or as an attempt to develop the law so as to cope with new circumstances. Let me add, as an interesting aside at this point, a reference to the famous Webster correspondence in the *Caroline* case. It seems that, immediately *before* the listing of the criteria for self-defence that we all learn by rote from our text-books, Webster's Note ran: "It must be remembered that preventive action in foreign territory is justified only in cases of . . .". That sounds to me very much like an early invocation of "preemption"!

In approaching the analysis, two things are clear – though (as I hope to show) the two things tend to merge into one. The first is that the classic law of self-defence is a set of rules that balances *response* against *threat*. That is certainly true so far as the law on anticipatory self-defence is concerned. And I have no need to go into the argument, so beloved of my fellow academics, that the UN Charter somehow wiped anticipatory self-defence off the legal screen. Not even a sufficiently close *textual* analysis of Article 51 of the Charter can climb that mountain. Moreover, it is an argument which I find as arid as it is wholly unrealistic. But in any case, the law on self-defence against *actual* armed attack is itself a law which itself balances *response* against *threat*; it is just that the "threat" to the defending State is differently defined.

The second thing which is clear is that President Bush's "preemption" doctrine likewise bases itself on a balancing out of *threat* and *response*. The premise on which the doctrine is based is that the threats are new, or at least that they are known threats which take on a new colour in a changed context. And, if that is true (so the argument runs), then the range of permitted responses has to be re-thought, and if necessary revised.

So I propose not to look at "preemption" as if it were some new legal doctrine of its own. It seems to me better to look at it as proposal to develop the law on self-defence, and in the light of the rules and principles that have become established in that context. That, as I have said, appears to be what the National Security Strategy document itself intends. To do otherwise – to treat "preemption" as if it were some newly minted legal doctrine – would entail assembling sufficient evidence of general State practice, and of *opinio juris*, to enable its proponents to show that a new rule of customary international law had come into being. And I only have to state the proposition in that form for it to become obvious that the enterprise would be doomed to failure.

The essence of this afternoon's enquiry is therefore to relate weapons of mass destruction (or at least a particular weapon of mass destruction) to the established categories of the law of self-defence, in order to *see* whether the threat they pose is one which justifies a response which, in turn, can properly be thought of as "preemption". It's as well to begin, though, by making sure that we understand what we mean by "weapons of mass destruction".

The term is much used, and even has its own acronym (WMD), but seems not to have a generally understood definition – at least not a qualitative definition, i.e. one which specifies more precisely what characteristics a weapon has to display to enter within that class. Such definitions as we have are purely descriptive, or enumerative: they *list* the weapons we have in mind. The most common list includes three weapons: nuclear, chemical, biological – though from time to time people come up with suggestions for new additions, these usually being futuristic weapons not (or not yet) in any national arms planning. The listing does not however do a great deal to bring out the special characteristics these weapons have in common, and there has indeed been scepticism about whether they do actually form a common class. So, it is said, nuclear weapons are weapons of strategic deterrence, chemical weapons are battlefield weapons and biological weapons are weapons of terror. Chemical and biological are inherently anti-personnel weapons; nuclear not necessarily so.

The International Court of Justice clearly took the view that nuclear weapons are unique; in its Advisory Opinion of 1966 (which will be referred to in greater detail in a moment) it summarized their essential nature in the phrase "the unique characteristics of nuclear weapons, and in particular their destructive capacity, their capacity to cause untold human suffering, and their ability to cause damage to generations to come". So I propose to leave aside the terrorism scenarios – in particular given that Torsten Stein has just dealt with the it – and take nuclear weapons on the basis that they are, in fact – and possibly in law, unique.

One could at least say that there are two elements in common amongst all three kinds of weapons. One is the potential for large-scale casualties, or presumably fatalities, from a single attack. The other (not unconnected with the first) is the likely potential for indiscriminate effects. I say "potential" for large-scale casualties, and "potential" for indiscriminate use, and do so deliberately, because one of the problems that lies in *listing* weapons in descriptive terms based on the method by which they destroy but *grouping* them in terms of the magnitude of destruction is that it immediately obscures the question of *method* of use: in what circumstances, in what concentration and against what objective do we envisage the actual use being made?

This question is one that lurked in the background of the Advisory Proceedings before the International Court of Justice on the Legality of the Use of Nuclear Weapons in 1995-96. But in the background only; no doubt because the Nuclear Weapon Powers deliberately avoided any detailed discussion of their nuclear arsenals in case it opened a temptation to the judges to declare the strategic nuclear option unlawful while allowing that battlefield uses of tactical weapons might in appropriate circumstances be lawful. The issue broke surface here and there, but did not attain any great importance in the proceedings. The Court preferred instead to proceed on the basis of what it called "certain unique characteristics of nuclear weapons", namely:

> that nuclear weapons are explosive devices whose energy results from the fusion or fission of the atom. By its very nature, that process, in nuclear weapons as they exist today, releases not only immense quantities of heat and energy, but also powerful and prolonged radiation. According to the material before the Court, the first two causes of damage are vastly more powerful than the damage caused by other weapons, while the phenomenon of radiation is said to be peculiar to nuclear weapons. These characteristics render the nuclear weapon potentially catastrophic. The destructive power of nuclear weapons cannot be contained in either space or time. They have the potential to destroy all civilization and the entire ecosystem of the planet.

Although the Advisory Proceedings did not raise the issue of pre-emption as such, they are notable for two aspects which are relevant to the present enquiry. The first is that the Nuclear Powers – or at least those amongst them who made submissions to the International Court – unanimously took the view that the "ordinary" rules, both of *jus ad bellum* and *jus in bello*, applied to the use or threat of use of nuclear weapons. In this, they joined the overwhelming opinion of the non-nuclear weapon States, and the Court was happy to endorse it. It did so in these terms:

> A threat or use of force by means of nuclear weapons that is contrary to Article 2, paragraph 4, of the United Nations Charter and that fails to meet all the requirements of Article 51, is unlawful; . . . [a] threat or use of nuclear weapons should also be compatible with the requirements of the international law applicable in armed conflict, particularly those of the principles and rules of international humanitarian law, etc. etc.

It might of course be objected that that position (some apparently saw it as a "concession") refers to the *use of* the weapon, not to *defence against* it. But that would seem to be too narrow a view. On the one hand, the question put to the Court covered the *threat* of use in equal terms with actual use, and the Court dealt with the matter accordingly. On the other hand, if one is thinking in preemptive terms, while the nuclear weapon may certainly not be only means of removing a nascent nuclear (or indeed chemical or biological threat), it must be amongst the *range* of possible preemptive means. It follows that, if preemptive use of conventional weaponry may be lawful, then it must also be potentially lawful for nuclear weaponry as well; and *vice versa*, if pre-emption by nuclear means is unlawful, it is hardly likely to be potentially lawful by conventional means.

At all events the ICJ proceedings seem clearly to have proceeded on the footing that, so far as the *jus ad bellum* was concerned, the law regulating the threat or use of nuclear weapons was the law of self-defence. That is however subject to one proviso, which relates to the theory and practice of deterrence. In their argumentation the Nuclear-Weapon States, quite understandably, made much of the fact that the principal purpose of their nuclear weapons was deterrence, i.e. that they were weapons designed not to be used, but the threat of whose potential use had nevertheless to be real. France went so far as to describe them as "political weapons". If that represented an intention to suggest that different legal rules (or perhaps no legal rules at all?) applied to them, then it was a suggestion which the Court's Opinion flatly rejected. In fact, the Court seems to have gone out of its way not to consider or to pronounce on the doctrine of deterrence as such. All that it says – in a famously Delphic utterance – is: "Nor can it [the Court] ignore the practice referred to as 'policy of deterrence', to which an appreciable section of the international community adhered for many years."

Judge Shi – currently the President of the ICJ – responds to this in pretty vehement terms in his separate Declaration:

> Undoubtedly, this practice of certain nuclear weapon States is within the realm of international politics, not that of law. It has no legal significance from the standpoint of the formation of a customary rule prohibiting the use of nuclear weapons as such. Rather, the policy of nuclear deterrence should be an object of regulation by law, not *vice versa*. The Court, when exercising its judicial function of determining a rule of existing law governing the use of nuclear weapons, simply cannot have regard to this policy practice of certain States as, if it were to do so, it would be making the law accord with the needs of the policy of deterrence. The Court would not only be confusing policy with law, but also take a legal position with respect to the policy of nuclear deterrence, thus involving itself in international politics – which would be hardly compatible with its judicial function."

So I think one must conclude that, even at the level of deterrence, i.e. at the phase lying in time between threat and attack, the Court was nervously ambivalent about facing up to offering a legal endorsement to massive counterforce capabilities.

Let's now pass however to another aspect of the right of self-defence that has been rather mocked by many of the text-writers, namely the 'inherent' character of the right. We have to recall not just that the formulation in Article 51 of the Charter is cast in terms of a saving clause ("Nothing in the present Charter shall impair. . . ."), but also that what is not to be impaired is referred to as the "inherent right of self-defence". The French text calls it a "droit naturel", the Spanish text has "derecho inmanente" (which I understand to mean the same thing), the Russian text, so I am told, gives the sense of 'imprescriptible' – and I'm sure there is somebody in the room who can explain the Chinese text to us!

There seem to be two aspects to this question of inherency. On the one hand it explains *why* nothing in the Charter impairs it: because it is something so basic to the existence of a State that it is simply not possible to take it away – much the sense of the Russian text as just described. At other points in its Nuclear Weapons Advisory Opinion, the International Court said something similar about certain of the laws of war, which it described as "intransgressible", much as it had done in the *Teheran Hostages* case for the inviolability of diplomats and diplomatic premises. Now, you could of course say much the same about domestic jurisdiction as well, yet, as we know, the Charter does affect that, and in a double sense: because the concept itself, as enshrined in Article 2(7), shifts as international law develops; and because the Security Council is specifically empowered to override it under Chapter VII. It would seem, however, that there *is* something special about self-defence – perhaps because it touches on the very existence of the State and not simply on the extent of its rights. And that something special is captured in turn in the actual wording used in Article 51, inasmuch as it talks in terms of the right being "impaired", not about it being "affected" or even "limited" in some way; and impaired carries the connotation of spoiling the essence of the right itself.

This leads to the second aspect of inherency, which goes to the substantive content of the right itself. The idea is a difficult one to express with a proper degree of delicacy and precision. To express it at all is to risk being howled down by one side or another. But the idea is tied up with what may be the true nature of the right of self-defence: if its "inherency" means that the right to act in self-defence is inextricably tied up with the very existence of the State, this would seem to entail that the right may represent one of those intransgressible limits which simply may not be crossed by international law, whether by the development of new rules or by the interpretation of existing rules. The idea is certainly not without controversy; it is not dissimilar to the argument raised by Bosnia-Herzegovina in the Security Council and in the interim measures phase of the *Genocide Case*, where the reasoning ran that it was simply not open to the Security Council, by maintaining the arms embargo on the whole of the former Yugoslavia, to deprive Bosnia of the *means* to defend itself effectively. It may be that this argument failed in any case on the facts, and the ICJ found that it was without jurisdiction to pronounce on the point; although Judge *ad hoc* Sir Elihu Lauterpacht does confront the argument more directly in his separate Declaration, he looks at it in the context of "ethnic cleansing" and of the duty on the Security Council to reconsider the embargo, rather than as a matter impinging on the right of self-defence as such.

The issue therefore remains open in the jurisprudence of the ICJ except to the extent that the Advisory Proceedings on the Legality of the Use or Threat of Use of Nuclear Weapons touched upon it. The key reference is that in paragraph E of the dispositif where the Court talks about "an extreme circumstance of self-defence, in which [the State's] very survival would be at stake". The same phrase is used in paragraph 97 of the main body of the Advisory Opinion, where it appears almost out of the blue, not as part of the main discussion of the right of self-defence earlier on, but as an addendum to an equally lapidary reference to "the fundamental right of every State to survival, and thus its right to resort to self-defence, in accordance with Article 51 of the Charter, when its survival is at stake". It may be that the Court was at this point picking up (but without attribution) part of the argument made by States before it: cf., for example, the Written Statement of the United Kingdom, which posed the case in which the destruction of a particular military objective was "essential to the survival of a State which was under attack", and the use of a nuclear weapon offered the only means of destroying that objective. It should immediately be pointed out however that the *context* in which the UK was making that particular argument was a quite different one, namely the proportionality calculation for collateral civilian damage under the laws of war.

But something else should be pointed out as well, namely that the references just made to the Advisory Opinion relate directly to that notorious and most controversial paragraph in the *dispositif* in which the Court purports to decide, by an equality of votes, that it cannot decide at all as to the legality of the use of nuclear weapons in the extreme circumstance in which the very survival of the State is at stake. There is no call to rehearse in this context the barrage of criticism of every kind to which this particularly Delphic non-finding has since been subjected. The point of interest is simply the glimmering the Court gives that some special form of reasoning may be needed where the self-defence situation under consideration is the outright survival of the State under attack.

It is this point which seems to be taken one stage further still in the Separate Opinion by Judge Fleischhauer, which has been equally the subject of considerable subsequent comment. It will be recalled that Judge Fleischhauer expressed the view

> that, although recourse to nuclear weapons is scarcely reconcilable with humanitarian law applicable in armed conflict as well as the principle of neutrality, recourse to such weapons could remain a justified legal option in an extreme situation of individual or collective self-defence in which the threat or use of nuclear weapons is the last resort against an attack with nuclear, chemical or bacteriological weapons or otherwise threatening the very existence of the victimized State.

To recall the proposition in those bald terms does less than justice to the subtlety of Judge Fleischhauer's reasoning, including the way he derives his conclusion from what he sees as the need to find a balance between conflicting legal rules and principles, all of which have equal rank. But again, the point of interest for today is his postulate, namely that it is a legally relevant fact that the threat is a threat to the very existence of the victim State.

It is time now to try to relate those indicators, thin and indefinite as they may be, to the precise situation of preemption against a future nuclear threat. It seems to me that the materials do at least justify an argument that – within the context of anticipatory self-defence – a sliding scale operates according to the gravity and immediacy of the threat. To say that is, in fact, to do no more than to restate the "Caroline" conditions in slightly more generalized form. The limiting case is that of a threat to the survival of the State as such. Threats to survival can be of two kinds: a massive mismatch of relative military power allied to aggressive intent (Iraq vs. Kuwait, for example); or the ability to strike an instant blow that amounts to a survival threat. The first requires no special consideration; it is the second that is in issue here, and strategic nuclear weaponry is the classic example, for the reasons given by the ICJ and already cited above. In relation to that second case, there does appear to be an element of legal authority for the idea that a threat of that magnitude and immediacy would justify an exceptional anticipatory response – or could justify such a response so long as proportionality could be satisfied, both in *ius ad bellum* and in *ius in bello* terms.

The question is, however, how far that reasoning takes us. Can it serve as a platform for the establishment of a right of preemption in they sense I have described earlier. The $64 dollar question, in other words.

To my mind, it is perfectly clear that it does not – for a whole series of reasons, of which the most important are the following three:

First amongst them is the question of "threat". As I have said, the whole of the law of self-defence is a balancing of *response* against *threat*. And the line of reasoning sketched out above – if accepted – tells us no more than that a particularly vicious threat may justify an exceptionally strong response. But the essence of the doctrine of preemption is surely that it seeks to justify dealing with a future possibility before it becomes an actual threat. That is exactly what the Bush Introduction says: "America will act against such emerging threats before they are fully formed." We can go back at this point to the whole discussion of deterrence in the ICJ proceedings. The opponents of nuclear weapons made a spirited attempt to turn the deterrence posture of the major nuclear Powers – consisting in the possession of nuclear arsenals with a stated determination to use them in defined circumstances – into a sort of standing threat, the lawfulness of which was therefore subject to Article 2(4) of the UN Charter. But the Court would have none of it, stating that the answer depended on various factors, including "whether, in the event that it were intended as a means of defence, it would necessarily violate the principles of necessity and proportionality". And this was, if anything, more cautious than the positions of the nuclear Powers themselves, who roundly denied that their deterrence posture was an Article 2(4) 'threat' at all. The two cases are not exactly parallel, but this brief discussion clearly shows how formidably difficult it would be – except perhaps in the most extreme of special circumstances – to elevate the construction, or acquisition of nuclear weapons, or attempts to construct or acquire them, into a "threat" strong enough to trigger anticipatory self-defence. This is hardly a surprising conclusion, since otherwise a preemptive strike against the Soviet Union (as advocated by Edward Teller and others), or against China, or more close to our present day by either of India or Pakistan against the other, could have been argued to have been legally permissible.

My second reason is as follows. I don't want to tread back at this point over the ground so challengingly covered by the International Court in the *Nicaragua* Judgment. Whether the Court did or did not leave open, under customary international law, the possibility of an armed riposte to an imminent *threat* of use of force, will continue to be argued over endlessly. My personal view is that the way in which the paradigm was enunciated by the Court will not stand the test of time. But on one point it is impossible to disagree with the Court, namely that (whatever its outer limits may be) the strength of the permissible riposte is governed by the extent of the threat, and the use of force is a measure of last resort; so, once again, we have a balancing of *response* against *threat*. And while an actual armed attack may be, in classic Caroline terms, so "instant and overwhelming" that the defending State has no other choice open to it, in the case of anticipatory self-defence (the threatened attack) – and much more strongly even in the case of preemption against a threat not yet fully formed – there is a far wider range of responses open to the State which feels itself under present or future threat. And this is where Article 51 of the Charter does come in, in a big way. I am not one of those who believe that self-defence and collective security under the Charter operate in separate watertight compartments. The language of Article 51 itself says something quite different. Nor have I ever been able to see any sense in the argument that, under Article 51, there is only a limited time-window for self-defence. The language of Article 51 itself plainly does not say that at all. What Article 51 is striving for is surely a harmonious blending of individual rights and collective measures (what Judge Lachs, in another context, called a "fruitful interaction") – provided that the powers of the Security Council always take precedence. The relevance of that analysis to the present case is this: that it is pretty well impossible, within the structure and spirit of Chapters VI & VII of the Charter, to find a valid justification for unilateral preemptive measures at long remove without having attempted the UN route, and if (the UN route once having been attempted) the Security Council takes the matter into its own hands, that is that.

My third and final reason is a little more jurisprudential. One of the inherent characteristics of a legal right of self-defence is that it has to trigger on the premise of a self-judgement by the threatened State. No-one else can be in a position to determine a State's security needs for it. The matter may start there but it can't end there. Whereas the Security Council's collective judgement as to what constitutes a threat to international peace and security, and what measures are necessary to deal with it, can be final and conclusive, the same simply can't be true of unilateral self-defence. If the defending State were the sole and absolute judge, it would render meaningless the twin limiting conditions of *necessity* and *proportionality*. The very existence of these conditions has to imply the possibility of authoritative judgement after the fact as to whether the defending State's claims were well-founded or not. There is room for such a judgement to be made *ex post facto* in the case of direct or anticipatory self-defence – and perhaps it happens more frequently than we tend to notice, though mostly in a rather attenuated form. But there is no room for it in the case of preemption; what manageable standards would there be by which to judge whether a future danger would develop into a direct and pressing threat (to a particular State, of course), and that the military measures employed were the only or best way to deal with it effectively? The case could never be proved. And that is, to my mind, the fatal flaw in preemption as a supposed legal doctrine – even in relation to the most menacing of the weapons of mass destruction.

The State of the State:
Redefining Sovereignty in the 21st Century

*Thomas W. McShane**

> We have before us the opportunity to forge for ourselves and for future generations a new
> world order, a world where the rule of law, not the law of the jungle, governs the conduct of
> nations.
>
> President George H. Bush

World events since 1648 have reflected the political, social, economic and military aspirations of people organized into sovereign states. Increasingly, they reflect the influence and authority, both real and perceived, of international law and international organizations. This development has become evident since the end of the Cold War, but its roots go back much further. Recent international interventions in places as diverse as Somalia, East Timor, Haiti, Kosovo and Liberia, conducted under the auspices of the United Nations, regional organizations such as NATO, or by ad hoc coalitions, are shaped by a large and growing body of treaties, practice and custom that we collectively refer to as international law.

The world's leading states, and the United States in particular, have advanced the development of international law for more than a century.[1] At the same time,

---

*   Director, National Security Legal Studies, Department of National Security and Strategy, United States Army War College. E-mail: Thomas.McShane@carlisle.army.mil. The views expressed in this paper are those of the author and do not necessarily reflect the official policy or position of the U.S. Government, the Department of Defense, or any of its agencies.
1   U.S. War Department, General Orders No. 100, Instructions for the Government of the Armies of the United States in the Field, April 24, 1863. The first comprehensive summary and codification of the humanitarian rules governing land warfare. Frequently called the "Lieber Code" after its author, Dr. Francis Lieber, G.O. No. 100 furnished inspiration for the Geneva Conventions of 1864 and 1929 and the Hague Conventions of 1899 and 1907.

Harvey Langholtz, Boris Kondoch, Alan Wells (Eds.),
International Peacekeeping: The Yearbook of International Peace Operations, Volume 9, 2004, pp. 183-208.
© Koninklijke Brill N.V. Printed in the Netherlands

states become frustrated when international law restrains or limits the pursuit of important national and global interests. This was vividly illustrated in the debates and reactions surrounding American-led efforts against Iraq throughout 2002 and 2003. The debate, in fact, continues. Regardless, its is essential that strategic leaders and their legal advisors understand the global environment as it exists today. International law is a critical component of the current geopolitical environment, and we ignore its impact on state practice at considerable risk.

To put this discussion into context, this paper briefly reviews the development and evolution of international law, its principal components and characteristics, and its relative influence on global politics and state practice over time. It proposes that international law competes with sovereignty as an organizing principal of international relations. Although sovereignty is likely to remain a critical component of the international system, it faces a growing threat from international organizations and institutions that pursue international order and individual rights at the expense of traditional rights enjoyed by sovereign states.

This paper refutes conventional wisdom that this phenomenon sprung to life after the collapse of the Soviet Union and the end of the Cold War in 1990. Instead, it will argue, the ascendancy of international law represents evolutionary developments in politics, philosophy and law over centuries, further shaped by the cataclysmic wars and associated excesses of the Twentieth Century. Important elements of today's international system matured in relative obscurity during the Cold War as groups and nations sought self-determination, peace, democracy, and individual freedoms. It is important that we examine how developments in international law are subtly but certainly redefining sovereignty and how states are adapting to this reality.

The Search for Order

Humans seek order in life. Traditionally, religion reflects our search for meaning and purpose, but social institutions also address these basic needs. In ancient times, families organized themselves into tribes, then cities, states and empires. Social order implies security and a sense of predictability. Order promotes prosperity and growth – both individual and collective. At the same time, order discourages destructive social behavior and competition for scarce resources.[2] Order requires a degree of cooperation and sacrifice, and by definition some inherent limitation on individual freedom. The political process is the means usually used to create order and

---

2   Werner Levi, *Contemporary International Law*, (Boulder, Westview, 1991), 14.

determine social rules and mores. Laws are crafted to facilitate and support this process.

Order may be imposed within groups or nations or states. On occasion, international order may be imposed by hegemonic powers, for example the Roman Empire, the British Empire at its height in the Nineteenth Century, and by American power since 1945. But scholars typically describe the international system as unstructured, or anarchic, in nature. States strive for supremacy, or hegemony, over other states. International politics is a "ruthless and dangerous business . . . [t]his situation, which no one consciously designed or intended, is genuinely tragic".[3] Others analyze the international system in different terms: the dynamic of how states establish international order e.g., balance of power, bipolar, or hegemonic systems; the nature of state actors as determining state behavior, e.g. democracies act one way, revolutionary states another, etc.; and the influence of individual decision-makers, e.g., great men drive events – Churchill, Hitler, etc.[4]

Rule of law is widely regarded as an indispensable predicate for international order and the freedom and prosperity that flow from it. The National Security Strategy of the United States tells us that the "nonnegotiable demands of human dignity" include "the rule of law; limits on the absolute power of the state; free speech; freedom of worship; equal justice; respect for women, religious tolerance; and respect for private property".[5] Establishing the rule of law was a stated objective of international efforts in Bosnia, Kosovo and Afghanistan, among others. Efforts to establish rule of law in places such as Kosovo, and more recently Iraq, illustrate a growing tension between international law and sovereignty which we will examine in detail later.

Defining International Law

Law prescribes norms of proper behavior, or as Blackstone says in his *Commentaries*, "a rule of civil conduct, commanding what is right, and prohibiting what is wrong".[6] These rules may be prescribed by the sovereign, but they are usually based on reli-

---

3   John J. Mersheimer, *The Tragedy of Great Power Politics*, (New York, W.W. Norton & Company, 2001), 2-3.

4   John W. Spanier and Robert L. Wendzel, *Games Nations Play*, 9th Ed. (Washington, D.C., Congressional Quarterly, Inc., 1996), 22.

5   George W. Bush, *The National Security Strategy of the United States of America*, (Washington, D.C., The White House, September 2002), 3.

6   Blackstone, *Commentaries on the Laws of England*, Book One, Chapter One, p.118. Available from The Avalon Project, Yale Law School at <www.yale.edu/lawweb/avalon/blackstone>. Accessed 11 April 2003.

gious, cultural and moral values. As such, the law often depends upon voluntary compliance, or more precisely on social pressure to conform. Sanctions may be imposed in cases where individuals will not or cannot comply.

Others feel that laws by definition require sanctions:

> It is essential to the idea of a law that it be attended with a sanction; or, in other words, a penalty or punishment for disobedience If there be no penalty annexed to disobedience, the resolutions or commands, which pretend to be laws will, in fact, amount to nothing more than advice. . . .[7]

Regardless, law provides a foundation for order, stability, predictability, and enjoys general acceptance by the population at large. Laws not generally accepted, perhaps because they do not reflect widely-held beliefs or morals, or serve no constructive purpose, are often ignored and prove particularly difficult to enforce.[8] Lastly, law evolves; it is not static. Laws change regularly, and considerably over long periods of time. While all this is true with respect to municipal, or domestic, law, does it apply equally to international law?

International law has been defined as "the body of rules and principles of action which are binding upon civilized states in their relations with one another".[9] Critics question, and we will examine later, whether international law can be "binding," and the efficacy of its application outside its historical Western European incubator – the so-called "civilized" states. Yet a closer look reveals that international law plays an essential role in global trade and commerce, regulating disputes, compensation, banking, and laws applying to a given transaction. It is indispensable to international transportation, regulating sea and air routes, privileges and immunities, and claims for loss or damage.[10] International treaties establish standards for the sciences, health, and the environment.[11]

The law of war is most familiar to us as that branch of public international law regulating armed conflict between states, and increasingly within states suffering from civil war, or intrastate conflict. This body of law provided the foundation for the war crimes tribunals at Nuremberg and Tokyo following World War II, and later

---

7   Alexander Hamilton, "The Federalist, No. 15," *The Federalist*, (New York, The Modern Library, 1941), 86.

8   E.g., The prohibition of alcohol, U.S. Constitution, amendment 18. It was repealed by the Twenty-First Amendment fourteen years later.

9   J.L. Brierly, *The Law of Nations*, 6th Ed. (Oxford, Oxford Press, 1991), 1.

10 E.g., Convention on International Civil Aviation (Chicago Convention) (1944); United Nations Convention on the Law of the Sea (UNCLOS III) (1982).

11 E.g., The United Nations Framework Convention on Climate Change (9 May 1992); Kyoto Protocol to the United Nations Framework Convention on Climate Change (11 Dec 1997).

for the international tribunals organized to adjudicate war crimes and crimes against humanity in former Yugoslavia and Rwanda. Even more recently, the Rome Statute established the International Criminal Court, a standing rather than ad hoc tribunal which recently became operational and whose jurisdiction may be universal.[12]

In most respects, international law serves the same purposes as municipal law and shares many common attributes: it provides a foundation for order, is founded on religious, cultural and moral values, serves to provide stability and predictability, and enjoys general acceptance among the international community. International law protects rights of states and individuals alike. In one important particular, however, the international legal system differs from municipal systems – there is no sanction for noncompliance, if by sanction is meant imposition of penalty by a higher authority. This theme recurs in any discussion of international law, although its relevance is often overstated.[13]

Sources of International Law

Historians frequently comment upon the "laws" of ancient Greece and Rome and their influence on modern western institutions. Although recognizing that a sophisticated legal system provided the foundation for domestic order and stability, and underpinned a wide-ranging commercial system that stretched from Britain to Asia Minor and ringed the Mediterranean, neither civilization understood the concept of international law as we apply the term today.[14] Ancient Greeks, Romans, and their Chinese imperial contemporaries did not customarily treat outsiders as their equals in an international system of equals. Greeks regarded non-Greeks as uncivilized; The Roman Empire didn't negotiate acquisitions, it simply took them. The Chinese considered any group of peoples outside the "Middle Kingdom" as barbarians not worthy of their full attention.[15]

Elements of modern international law existed before the creation of the Westphalian system in 1648. Ancient Greek philosophers, the Romans, and their heirs believed in "natural law," a higher law of nature that controlled all human endeavors, and to which all are bound, even kings and rulers. An expression of this concept is found

---

12   Rome Statute of the International Criminal Court, (United Nations Diplomatic conference of Plenipotentiaries on the Establishment of an International Criminal Court, 17 July 1998).

13   Horace B. Robertson, Jr., "Contemporary International Law: Relevant to Today's World?" *U.S. Naval War College International Law Studies, Volume 68*, ed. John Norton Moore and Robert F. Turner (Newport, Naval War College Press, 1995), 3.

14   *See* J. Brierly, *supra* note 9, 17.

15   *See* W. Levi, *supra* note 2, 6.

in the term *ius gentium*, meaning a principle of universal application that all follow because it has been independently discovered by application of reason, a "natural law." Our contemporary use of the phrase "human rights," examined in this context, becomes for us a form of natural law or *ius gentium*, and a fundamental principle of international order.[16]

Other elements of international order evolved during the Middle Ages, particularly concepts of property rights and loyalty to the sovereign, key ingredients of modern nation-states. The property rights of the ruler and the ruling class shaped feudal society, and dictated a network of complicated, but well-understood, relationships that provided stability and order. Feudalism depended upon loyalty up and loyalty down the social hierarchy. All were bound by reciprocal responsibilities. While the Catholic Church provided legitimacy and support of feudal institutions, these principles survived the Protestant Reformation. The idea that states enjoy sovereignty and the right to control territory is a feudal legacy.[17]

Finally, following the self-destructive upheaval of the religious wars of the 16th and 17th centuries, the Treaty of Westphalia in 1648 provided badly needed order in Europe, stabilizing borders and relationships. Kings could dictate any religion they wished within their borders, but foreswore any rights to interfere in the religious affairs of other sovereign states. Rulers frequently violated this principle for political, if not religious, reasons, but the Treaty achieved its purpose.

Once states were recognized as sovereign, a way had to be found for them to interact on a nominal basis of equality. Guiding principles of relations between sovereign states rested on five basic assumptions. States had the right to: make laws; act independently in international affairs; control their territory and people; issue currency; and utilize the resources of the state. Sovereignty thus became the organizing element of modern history.

International Law Hierarchy

Most authorities recognize four categories of sources for international law, arranged in a hierarchy.[18] At the top are conventions, treaties and agreements, such as the United Nations Charter, or the Law of the Sea Treaty. These represent contractual relationships between sovereign states, and states are bound by their obligations freely undertaken.[19]

---

16   *See* J. Brierly, *supra* note 9, 17.
17   *Ibid.*, 3. *See also* Levi, 6-9.
18   Statute of the International Court of Justice, Article 38.
19   The *SS Lotus Case*, (Fr. v. Turk.), 1927, Permanent Court of International Justice, 1927,

The second category of international law is the practice of states, referred to as customary international law. No hard and fast rule governs customary international law. It reflects the behavior of states over time, acting in accordance with what they believe to be the dominant, binding rules of international order. Customary law exists independently of treaty law, although treaty law may help to shape customary law.[20]

The third category consists of principles of law recognized by the leading, or so-called "civilized" nations. International politics help to define these principles, which are further shaped by the municipal law of states.[21]

The fourth and final category of international law represents judicial decisions and the writings of jurists and scholars. These include the opinions issued by the International Court of Justice, its predecessor the Permanent Court of International Justice, the European Court of Human Rights, and the International Criminal Tribunals for the Former Yugoslavia (ICTY) and Rwanda (ICTR). Writings of scholars supplement these decisions, illustrating and explaining the state of the law based on their experience and study. Changes in the law are often preceded by debate among jurists and scholars over what the law should be. Their authority is persuasive and influential, not substantive.[22]

International Law and Sovereignty – An Evolutionary Relationship

International law has never existed in a vacuum. It reflects existing norms and mores, and illustrates the difficulty of constructing international order in a disordered world. The Westphalian system has provided the fundamental framework for order for over three centuries and has greatly influenced the development of international law. Over time sovereignty has ebbed and flowed, as prevailing practices and international

---

(Ser.A), No. 10, at 18-19 (7 September): "The rules of law binding upon States therefore emanate from their own free will as expressed in conventions or by usages generally accepted as expressing principles of law. . . ." International law scholars disagree on the fundamental nature of law. There are two distinct schools of thought. The Monist view holds that international law and municipal (state) law are simply parts of an integrated system. The focus is on the individual. Dualists believe that international law and municipal law are two distinct systems. The focus of domestic law is the individual; the focus of international law is on states. These views influence contemporary debate. *See* Levi, 22-23.

20 *See* W. Levi, *supra* note 2, 35. Levi cites as an example the launching of Sputnik by the Soviet Union, which claimed that artificial satellites could fly unimpeded over state territory, and the general acceptance of this proposition.

21 *Ibid.*, 5.

22 *See* J. Brierly, *supra* note 9, 66.

politics shaped the behavior of the leading states. To the extent these practices and politics establish binding precedent, they help to define international law.

This portion of the paper examines how modern principles of international law and sovereignty developed simultaneously over time. Although sovereignty has provided the dominant basis for international order, it has consistently adapted to accommodate evolving concepts of government, freedom, human rights, and the quest for predictability and stability,[23] the historical attributes of international law.

Early models of sovereignty were based on the prevailing form of government in 17th Century Europe – monarchies ruled by hereditary dynasties of kings or emperors. Consistent with historical political and religious practice, individuals were subordinate to the state, represented by the King. Other precedents existed, going back to classical Greece and its democratic ideals,[24] but the prevailing norm made Kings the absolute rulers of their states, and they exercised their authority with little regard for the sensibilities of their subjects.

Contemporary writers described the nature of this relationship. Jean Bodin wrote in 1576 that law comes from the King, who although not bound by his own laws, was not above the law of nature, an important exception bearing on future developments.[25] Thomas Hobbes wrote in *Leviathan*: "It appeareth plainly that the sovereign power . . . is as great as possibly men can be imagined to make it."[26] Louis XIV of France, the "Sun King," epitomized the classical sovereign – not merely the head of the state, but its very embodiment, anointed by God to rule. Subjects owed unquestioning loyalty to the King, who might or might not act in their best interests. More precisely, the King's interests were the state's interests. Hence the dynastic wars of Louis XIV waged to expand the glory of France and of Louis XIV were the business of the King and his advisors, not the people of France. As characterized in popular culture: "It's good to be the King!"[27]

Not everyone regarded sovereignty this way. Hugo de Groot, also known as

---

23   Although both predictability and stability are encompassed in the phrase "rule of law," the phrase is itself of fairly recent origins, representing the triumph of the western democracies since World War II. Historically, international law has concerned itself more with creating a stable, predictable world, rather than with a particular technique used to accomplish these ends.

24   Democracy in ancient Greece, notably Athens, was real and vibrant but limited in modern terms: only citizens could exercise political rights or hold land; women had few rights; slavery was an essential institution. None of this, however, diminishes the power and influence of Greek thought on leaders of the Enlightenment. *See* William Y. Elliott and Neil A. McDonald, *Western Political Heritage*, (New York, Prentice-Hall, 1955), 63-74.

25   *See* J. Brierly, *supra* note 9, 7.

26   *Ibid.*, 13.

27   Mel Brooks, Director, *History of the World, Part I*, Fox Films, 1981.

Grotius, is referred to as the father of international law for his treatises on international law and the law of war. He was also a proponent of the law of nature and reason. He saw excesses in unbridled sovereignty:

> I saw prevailing throughout the Christian world a licence in making war of which even barbarous nations should be ashamed; men resorting to arms for trivial or for no reasons at all, and . . . no reverence left for divine or human law, exactly as if a single edict had released a madness driving men to all kinds of crime.[28]

As the culminating act of the English Civil War and the Thirty Years' War, the British throne of Charles I fell to the reformist Protestant armies of Oliver Cromwell. In 1649, one year after Westphalia, Cromwell had King Charles beheaded. Sovereignty was no longer coexistent with monarchy.[29]

During the 18th Century, philosophers, scholars and popular writers rediscovered the writings of the ancient Greeks, combining them with Christian philosophy and natural law into a doctrine of Enlightenment. Locke, Rousseau and Jefferson, among others, emphasized individual rights and the obligations of sovereigns toward their citizens.[30] Their beliefs were incorporated into the Declaration of Independence and the American and French Revolutions.

The established order elsewhere did not change, but regime change in America and France, replacing monarchies with democratically-based governments, was a harbinger of things to come. It advanced the idea that sovereignty vested in the people, rather than in the government or the ruler, and demonstrated the efficacy of a higher law, themes that would resurface periodically in the Nineteenth Century and erupt in the latter half of the Twentieth. International agreements and treaties began to recognize that individuals as well as states have rights.[31]

Following the twenty-five year struggle to suppress Revolutionary France and Napoleon Bonaparte, the major powers of Europe in 1815 sought to reestablish order, stability, and a balance of power. In response to Napoleon's imperial ambitions, the political leaders who met in Vienna created a system firmly grounded in sovereignty and balanced so as to preclude a return to revolution. Under the leadership of Prince Metternich of Austria and Lord Castlereigh of Great Britain, they succeeded in establishing a framework for peace that would survive essentially intact for a hundred years.[32]

---

28 *See* W. Levi, *supra* note 2, 10.
29 Bernard Grun, *The Timetables of History*, 3rd Ed. (New York, Touchstone, 1991), 294.
30 *See* W. Levi, *supra* note 2, 8.
31 *Ibid.*, 9.
32 Henry Kissinger, *Diplomacy* (New York, Touchstone, 1994), 78.

Other influences shaped the Nineteenth Century. Charles Darwin's scientific work on evolution stimulated development of a social philosophy known as social Darwinism, extrapolating Darwin's theories of natural selection and survival of the fittest species into international relations and politics. Those nations which were strongest were most likely and best suited to survive. Social Darwinism heavily influenced political leaders such as Bismarck and Theodore Roosevelt.[33] Sovereign states exerted a sort of muscular self-interest in their international relations, demonstrating their superiority by economic growth and territorial acquisition. The last great era of Colonialism was the result, as France, Great Britain, and Germany competed to acquire overseas colonies. The United States too, succumbed to temptation at the end of the century, acquiring overseas interests in the Hawaii, the Phillipines, Cuba, and Panama, among others.[34] The sovereign rights of underdeveloped, militarily weak states counted for little in this environment.

Facilitating economic expansion in an era of relative peace were the modern technologies of steamships, railroads and telegraphs. The speed of communication and transportation caused the world to "shrink," as trade, commerce and banking connected the continents, creating the first era of "globalization." The modern unified industrial state came into its own as the United States, Germany, and Italy consolidated their territorial boundaries and joined the ranks of the great powers.[35] In many regards, it was the apogee of sovereignty.

At the same time other, largely unseen, developments reflected the dark side of unbridled sovereignty and hinted at issues that would rise to prominence in the Twentieth Century. The industrial revolution prompted upward mobility and increased the size of the middle class in most western nations, yet it also created a new urban underclass, with associated problems of disease, family breakup and child labor. Visible disparity in wealth and power in developed states caused socialism to flourish, creating revolutionary pressures that threatened the established order. Karl Marx promulgated his economic theories preaching class warfare. Modest political reform helped to defuse tensions and postpone the final accounting for at least another generation.

Public international law played an important role in international affairs, particularly through treaties regulating trade, communication and finance. In 1863, Henri Dunant founded the International Red Cross in Geneva to mitigate the destructive effect of modern war.[36] The first Geneva Convention covering treatment of sick

---

33   *Ibid.*, 40, 127.
34   *See* Fareed Zakaria, *From Wealth to Power* (Princeton, Princeton University Press, 1998), Chapter 5: "The New Diplomacy, 1889-1908."
35   *Ibid.*
36   Eric. S. Krauss and Mike O. Lacey: "Utilitarian vs. Humanitarian: The Battle Over the Law of War," *Parameters*, 32 (Summer 2002): 73, 76.

and wounded on the battlefield was signed in 1864.[37] Based largely on the Lieber Code of 1863,[38] which promulgated laws of war for Union armies in the American Civil War, the Hague Conventions of 1899 and 1907[39] attempted to prescribe means and methods of warfare consistent with then-existing humanitarian principles. A century later, law of war concerns over certain acts in the recent war with Iraq – use of civilian hostages, fighting from protected places such as hospitals or mosques, combatants not wearing military uniforms – can be traced directly to the Hague Conventions.[40]

The Twentieth Century – Age of Conflict and Ideology

The Twentieth Century was marked by tremendous highs and abysmal lows. The best and the worst of human nature were on public display, often at the same time. The era was marked by three major world wars, two hot and one cold, and the clash of powerful ideologies. Socialism, Communism, Nazism, and Fascism emerged fully-grown on the world stage, competing with Democracy for primacy in the hearts and minds of nations. Tentative steps to form world government were taken. Natural law resurfaced in the guise of anticolonialism, self-determination of peoples, the human rights movement, and demands for equality by the non-western world. Change accelerated development, redefining political and cultural priorities. The second great era of globalization and progress brought the world closer, yet left others even farther behind. The similarities between 1903 and 2003 are striking, as are the differences. The maturation of international law and sovereignty's accommodation to change is one major highlight of the century.

---

37   *Ibid.*

38   General Orders No. 100, *supra* note 1.

39   The Hague Conventions of 1899 were largely incorporated in the Conventions of 1907, of which five are important: (1) Convention Relative to the Opening of Hostilities, 18 October 1907, 36 Stat. 2259; (2) Convention Respecting the Laws and Customs of War on Land and Annex, 18 October 1907, 36 Stat. 2277; (3) Convention Respecting the Rights and Duties of Neutral Powers and Persons in Case of War on Land, 18 October 1907, 36 Stat. 2310; (4) Convention Concerning Bombardment by Naval Forces in Time of War, 18 October 1907, 36 Stat. 2351; and (5) Convention for the Adaptation to Maritime Warfare of the Principles of the Geneva Convention of 6 July 1906, 18 October 1907, 36 Stat. 2371.

40   Kenneth Anderson, "Who Owns the Rules of War?," *New York Times Magazine*, 13 April 2003, 38.

The Great War – Changing of the Guard

The period immediately following World War I is essential to understanding the rest of the Twentieth Century. The issues facing the allied powers in Versailles, and the choices made then and over the next decade dictated the course of events for the remainder of the century. International law emerged as a critical component of international order and would play a major role in international politics.

World War I, The Great War, caused tremendous upheaval in the established order. The victorious allies attempted to address these problems at Versailles in 1919. First was the unexpected scope of violence and destruction, prompting calls for vengeance – war reparations to be paid by the losers and trials of those responsible for the conflict. Second was the collapse of major empires – the German, Austrian-Hungarian and Ottoman Empires on the losing side, and the Russian Empire in 1917 on the allied side – and the emergence of the United States as the predominant military and economic power.[41] The third problem was the creation of new nation-states out of the former empires. Lastly, lack of consensus concerning the goals of the war and what the allies had won plagued the peace and designs for international order.

Revolutionary efforts to create a world government fell short – the League of Nations was a start, but not a sufficient one. President Wilson's visions for the postwar order clashed with the national interests of the allies and frustrated effective, unified action. The Versailles Treaty became a compromise. Complicating matters, Wilson failed to persuade the American public or the United States Senate to ratify the treaty creating the League of Nations, and without American participation the League proved too weak to enforce Wilson's vision of collective security – peace through the rule of law supported by military force when necessary.[42] Wilson's vision would be revived in 1945 and again in 1990 with relatively greater success.

Attempts to try the Kaiser and others for War Crimes encountered similar problems. The allies could not agree, and the Germans would not cooperate. Ambitious plans drawn up at the Paris Peace Conference in 1920 called for some 900 war criminals to be tried, but allied disunity and German recalcitrance prevailed. As a compromise, 12 German soldiers ranging from Private to Lieutenant General were tried in German courts; six were convicted, with the most severe sentence being four years. The Leipzig trials undoubtedly influenced allied actions at Nuremberg in 1945.[43]

---

41   *See* H. Kissinger, *supra* note 32, 259.

42   *Ibid.*, 247.

43   Department of the Army, *Pamphlet 27-161-2, International Law, Volume II* (Headquarters, Department of the Army, 1962), 221. These trials, known as the Leipzig trials, demonstrated

One encouraging development at Versailles was public debate over whether the rule of law and ethics would supersede national interests and replace international politics-as-usual. The conflict between these poles of international order would continue throughout the Twentieth Century and still exists. As Kissinger characterizes it:

> At the end of the First World War, the age-old debate about the relative roles of morality and interest in international affairs seemed to have been resolved in favor of the dominance of law and ethics. Under the shock of the cataclysm, many hoped for a better world as free as possible from the kind of *Realpolitik* which, in their view, had decimated the youth of a generation.[44]

Efforts to enforce peace through rule of law continued for over a decade following Versailles. Arms control agreements took the place of serious collective security enforcement. Examples include the Naval Conferences at Washington in 1922 and London in 1930, regulating the number and size of battleships, cruisers, destroyers and submarines, then considered the major strategic weapons of the great powers.[45] In the Kellogg-Briand Pact of 1928 the signatory parties agreed to renounce war as an instrument of national policy.[46]

In the end, sovereignty and national interests proved too strong for the Wilsonians. International law became just another diplomatic tool as the great states re-armed themselves for World War II. Former President Theodore Roosevelt, still a keen observer of world events, captured the essence of power politics when he said: "As yet there is no likelihood of establishing any kind of international power ... which can effectively check wrong-doing ... I regard ... trusting to fantastic peace treaties, to impossible promises, to all kinds of scraps of paper without any backing in efficient force, as abhorrent".[47]

---

the problem obtaining jurisdiction over war criminals – Germany was not defeated and occupied as in World War II. The Leipzig trials did motivate the allies in 1945 to establish an international tribunal at Nuremberg.

44 *See* H. Kissinger, *supra* note 32, 247.

45 *Ibid.*, 373. The Washington Conference of 1922 attempted to regulate capital ships; the London Conference of 1930 attempted to regulate submarines as well. *See* Department of Army Pamphlet 27-161-2, supra, at 16. For a detailed study of the Naval Treaties *see* W. Hays Parks, "Making Law of War Treaties: Lessons from Submarine Warfare Regulation," *U.S. Naval War College International Law Studies, Volume 75*, ed. Michael N. Schmitt (Newport, Naval War College Press, 2000), 339.

46 The Kellogg-Briand Pact, or Pact of Paris, is formally known as The General Treaty for the Renunciation of War, (27 August 1928), 46 Stat. 2343.

47 *See* H. Kissinger, *supra* note 32, 40.

World War II and the Search for Institutional Order

The world got a second chance in 1945 to recreate international order. The unprecedented destruction of the second major war in a generation dwarfed that of 1914-
18 and brought modern war to the home front with a vengeance. Millions of
noncombatants became casualties of war. The discovery of nuclear fission at the
end of the war threatened even greater destruction in any future conflict. Sovereignty
had to be checked, and international law was applied to the task. The problem was
neatly defined by one study:

> A sovereign state at the present time claims the power to judge its own controversies, to
> enforce its own conception of its rights, to increase its armaments without limit, to treat its
> own nationals as it sees fit, and to regulate its economic life without regard to the effect of
> such regulations upon its neighbors. These attributes of sovereignty must be limited.[48]

The creation of the United Nations in 1945 and the proceedings of the Nuremberg
Tribunal immediately following were watershed events that permanently altered the
nature of the debate regarding a state's right to wage war and its treatment of its
citizens. Together they announced to the world that aggressive war would no longer
be tolerated and that individuals who commit aggression and crimes against humanity will be held criminally responsible for their acts. It was a sincere effort and a
good start, enjoying almost universal support.

One of the United Nations' early proclamations, the Universal Declaration of
Human Rights,[49] outlined fundamental human rights in terms reminiscent of the
American Declaration of Independence and the Bill of Rights. It was intended as
common standard for "all peoples and all nations".[50] Although aspirational in tone
and lacking an enforcement mechanism, it has served for more than fifty years as
a beacon for people in search of freedom and justice. Over the following decades,
International agreements outlawing genocide, recognizing the rights of minorities,
and emphasizing humanitarian concerns consistently advanced individual rights at
the expense of state sovereignty.[51]

---

48   *See* J. Brierly, *supra* note 9, 47, quoting from the International Conciliation Pamphlet, 1941.
49   Universal Declaration of Human Rights, United Nations General Assembly, 10 December
     1948.
50   *Ibid.*, Preamble.
51   *See*: the Convention on the Prevention and Punishment of the Crime of Genocide, 9 December
     1948, 78 U.N.T.S. 277, art.VI; the Geneva Conventions of 1949 (four separate conven-
     tions – on the Amelioration of the Condition of the Wounded and Sick in Armed Forces in
     the Field, on the Amelioration of the Condition of Wounded, Sick and Shipwrecked Members
     of Armed Forces at Sea, the Geneva Convention Relative to the Treatment of Prisoners of

Collective security acquired new life after World War II with the creation of the United Nations, the North Atlantic Treaty Organization (NATO), the Organization of American States (OAS), and other international and regional organizations. Although the Cold War provided the initial impetus for NATO, it survives as a viable, productive organization. With expanded membership and new missions, NATO today provides collective security while extending democracy and prosperity to the nations of Eastern Europe, a development unimagined a generation ago.

The Rule of Law and Human Rights Center Stage

The rule of law in international affairs is manifest in many ways: by actions of the United Nations Security Council and other UN organizations;[52] by Nongovernmental Organizations (NGO's) advancing collective western values and international humanitarian law; by treaties regulating strategic nuclear weapons, conventional weapons, and chemical/biological weapons;[53] by international agreement on global warming; by creation of an international criminal court;[54] and by the number of "coalitions of the willing" contributing forces to intervene in intrastate conflicts.

A common misperception is that these developments emerged suddenly in 1990 with the collapse of the Soviet Union and the end of the Cold War.[55] In reality, the incorporation of international law and human rights into international relations since 1945 stems from historical trends and events described earlier. It reflects timeless values, classical and modern philosophy, and the common experiences of mankind over centuries. Although it is true that the bipolar system and threat of great power veto limited the ability of the United Nations Security Council to take effective

---

War, and the Geneva Convention Relative to the Protection of Civilian Persons in Time of War); and Protocols to the Geneva Conventions of 1949 (1977). These conventions form the nucleus of what is commonly called "International Humanitarian Law."

52   E.g., The Food and Agriculture Organization, the World Health Organization, the International Civil Aviation Organization, the United Nations Educational, Scientific and Cultural Organization, the International Labor Organization, and the International Monetary Fund, to name only a few.

53   E.g., the START and SALT strategic arms negotiations and Anti Ballistic Missile (ABM) treaties with the U.S.S.R, and multilateral international agreements, including the Conventional Weapons Treaty (1980), the Chemical Weapons Convention (1993), and the Ottawa Treaty on Anti-Personnel Land Mines (1997).

54   Notes 11 and 12, *supra.*

55   E.g., Ivo H. Daalder, "The United States and Military Intervention in Internal Conflict," in *International Dimensions of Internal Conflict*, ed. Michael E. Brown (Cambridge, MIT Press, 1996), 461.

action throughout the Cold War, the quest for international order based on the rule
of law consistently influenced political developments and discourse.

The struggle to end colonialism and promote self-determination of peoples following World War II is illustrative. The UN Charter, firmly rooted in sovereignty,
contemplated the end of Western colonialism.[56] The United States advocated renunciation of overseas imperial holdings and supported self-determination by their populations.[57] During World War II, the U.S. stance on this issue periodically created
rifts within the Anglo-French-U.S. partnership.[58] After the war, when the U.S. was
leading western efforts to develop a Containment Policy against Communism,
American leaders demanded an end to British and French rule in Africa and Asia.
When newly independent colonial states subsequently lapsed into Communism, as
happened in Vietnam, Americans suddenly found themselves with a new problem
on their hands, one as much political as military in nature.[59] The search for order,
justice, and democracy stumbled on the rock of great power politics. International
law alone could not preserve the peace.

Cold War arms control agreements[60] reflected not so much American and Soviet
optimism as they did global public opinion, uneasy over the prospect of annihila-
tion at the hands of the two superpowers. With the advent of intercontinental ballistic missiles, mutual assured destruction became a fact. With satellite technology,
the U.S. and the U.S.S.R. acquired the capacity to place nuclear weapons in earth
orbit.[61] Many states became fervent practicioners of international law for purely
parochial reasons, but the success of the international community, particularly non-
aligned states, in framing global debate demonstrated the force of western values
and the rule of law. These trends emerged in the 1950s and acquired prominence
in the 1960s and 1970s. Neither the United Nations nor the international commu-

---

56   United Nations Charter, Chapter I, Article 2, para. 1 and Chapter XI.
57   Eric Larabee, *Commander in Chief*, (New York, Touchstone, 1987), 632.
58   *Ibid.*
59   E.g., Vietnam. Our efforts to combat aggressive communist expansion encountered interna-
      tional opposition both at the UN and in other international forums. Agreements such as
      Protocols I and II to the Geneva Conventions of 1949 and the United Nations Convention
      on Law of the Sea displayed a distinct anti-Western and anti-American bias, yet reflected
      the considered opinion and practice of many states. International law was no longer the sole
      province of the great powers and the "civilized" states, and traditional American leadership
      in international law began to fade.
60   SALT, START, ABM, START II, etc.
61   Nuclear weapons (and other weapons of mass destruction) have been banned from space,
      although space has not been "demilitarized." Treaty on Principles governing the Activities
      of States in the Exploration and Use of Outer Space Including the Moon and Other Celestial
      Bodies (Outer Space Treaty) (1967).

nity could force the great powers to take specific actions against their interests, but this does not mean that the great powers, notably the U.S. and U.S.S.R., were free to do as they pleased. Pressures to conform with world opinion were subtle and often invisible, but real nonetheless.

Contributing to the force of international law was the proliferation of NGOs capable of global operations in the decades following World War II. These NGOs pursued their own special interests, but most had an underlying humanitarian agenda, advancing the cause of human rights and promoting "International Humanitarian Law".[62] The International Committee of the Red Cross is the oldest and best-known of the NGOs.[63] Human Rights Watch, Doctors without Border, CARE, and thousands of other organizations effectively precipitated international intervention in what had been considered previously the internal affairs of sovereign states.[64]

Two examples illustrate the power and influence NGO's have acquired. The first is the UN intervention in Somalia in 1992, under American leadership, to ensure delivery of relief supplies and avert a humanitarian disaster forecast by NGOs and highlighted on television screens around the world. UN intervention alleviated the immediate problem, but failed to address the underlying problem of stability. When it did, too little and too late, it led to the battle of Mogadishu and eventual withdrawal of U.S. forces.

The second example of NGO influence is the Ottawa Treaty banning landmines.[65] The preamble to the Treaty states in part:

> *Stressing* the role of public conscience in furthering the principles of humanity as evidenced by the call for a total ban of anti-personnel mines and recognizing the efforts to that end undertaken by the International Red Cross an Red Crescent Movement, the International Campaign to Ban landmines, and numerous other non-governmental organizations around the world, *Basing* themselves on the principle of international humanitarian law that the right of the parties to an armed conflict to choose methods or means of warfare is not unlimited . . .[66]

---

62   International Humanitarian Law essentially encompasses the principles enunciated in the Geneva Conventions of 1949 and Protocols I and II of 1977.

63   *See* Joint Pub 3-08, *Interagency Coordination During Joint Operations*, Vol. II, 9 October 1996, Appendix B for a detailed listing of NGOs and countries in which they operate.

64   There are many examples. International support of the Palestinians is one; international efforts to remove white racist governments in Rhodesia and South Africa are another.

65   The Ottawa Treaty, formally known as the "Convention on the Prohibition of the Use, Stockpiling, Production and Transfer of Anti-Personnel Mines and Their Destruction," December 1997. The Ottawa process featured active participation by NGOs and international celebrities. Their priorities were humanitarian, not utilitarian in nature. *See* Krauss and Lacey, *supra*, note 36 at 81.

66   Preface to the Ottawa Treaty, *ibid.*

NGOs and international celebrities like Princess Diana of Britain actively participated in the Conference process, dismissing security concerns raised by the United
States. Humanitarian concerns over civilians killed or maimed by abandoned land
mines preoccupied the Conference and carried the day. While not a party to the
treaty, the United States has since conceded substantial compliance by policy.[67]

The State of the State – Sovereignty in the New Millenium

Trends evident in 2003 reflect the foregoing discussion. In advanced states, post-
industrial society replaced basic industry and manufacturing in the last decade of
the Twentieth Century. These activities migrated to less-developed countries with
lower labor costs, contributing to global commerce and prosperity. Banks, utilizing
the Internet, operate anywhere in the new global economy. Globalization draws
nations and peoples closer, despite recent economic setbacks and the war on terrorism. The World Trade Organization is a powerful international force capable of
influencing decisions by the leading economic powers, including the United States.[68]
International labor organizations demand basic standards and benefits for workers
and workplaces located on all continents. These trends undermine sovereignty and
reflect a highly structured international environment that constrains even the strongest
states to behave in ways promoting international order.

   Human rights concerns influence international agendas and domestic actions.
International humanitarian intervention as practiced in Kosovo, East Timor, and possibly Iraq, has emerged as a precedent for the use of international force against or
within the territory of sovereign states that demands our attention. It has likely not
reached the status of customary international law, but lively debate on the subject
tends to re-define how we view sovereignty.[69] This development, ironically enough,

---

67   On 17 September 1997, President Clinton announced that the United States would develop
     alternatives to anti-personnel land mines by 2003, and would replace all "dumb" land mines
     in South Korea by 2006. The principle U.S. objection to the Ottawa Process was its failure
     to acknowledge U.S. fielding of "smart" or self-destructing land mines. The Conventional
     Weapons Convention of 1980 prohibits indiscriminate laying of mine fields and requires
     mapping, marking and removal, among other requirements. The Ottawa Process is unlikely
     to stop rogue states and revolutionary movements from indiscriminately laying and aban-
     doning mines.

68   World Trade Organization sessions have attracted enormous demonstrations by diverse groups
     ranging from environmentalists to religious organizations to unrepentant communists.

69   *See*, e.g., George K. Walker, "Principles for Collective Humanitarian Intervention to Succor
     Other Countries' Imperiled Indigenous Nationals," *American University International Law
     Review*, Volume 18, Number 1, 35; John C. Yoo, "The Dogs That Didn't Bark: Why Were

represents the triumph of values advanced by Woodrow Wilson at Versailles almost a century ago. The principles of the American and French revolutions have become universal, though not all states concede that individual rights supersede the welfare of the state, most notably China, the world's most populous nation.

Themes for the 21st Century and Implications for Strategic Leaders

International law will play an important role in addressing issues and trends likely to persist for decades to come. The most important of these include: a globalised economy; urbanization; intrastate conflict; clash of cultures; unequal distribution of wealth; environmental degradation; transnational crime; collective security; multilateralism; and humanitarian intervention. Global problems require global solutions; sovereign states cannot solve them, although they can address symptoms within their borders. Most, eventually, will require international cooperation to resolve.

International law challenges strategic leaders to think globally, not nationally. The positivist approach to international law expressed in the S.S. Lotus case: "Restrictions upon the independence of States cannot therefore be presumed",[70] is threatened by a new paradigm: "a law more readily seen as the reflection of a collective juridical conscience and as a response to the social necessities of States organized as a community".[71] United Nations Secretary General Kofi Annan articulated this new paradigm as follows:

> State sovereignty, in its most basic sense, is being redefined – not least by the forces of globalization and international cooperation. States are now widely understood to be instruments at the service of their peoples, and not vice versa.[72]

The implications of this principle are staggering. Yet Kofi Annan is no revolutionary; his language is reminiscent of Thomas Jefferson's in the American Declaration of Independence: "That to secure these rights, Governments are instituted among

---

International Legal Scholars MIA on Kosovo?," *Chicago Journal of International Law*, Spring 2000, 149, accessed on line at <www.proquest.umi.com/pqdweb?TS> on 27 January 2003.

70   *Supra* note 19.

71   *Legality of the Threat or Use of Nuclear Weapons*, International Court of Justice, 8 July 1996, Declaration of President Bedjaoui at para. 13, quoted in Robert F. Turner, "Nuclear Weapons and the World Court: The ICJ's Advisory Opinion and Its Significance for U.S. Strategic Doctrine," *U.S. Naval War College International Law Studies, Volume 72*, ed. Michael N. Schmitt (Newport, Naval War College Press, 1998), 309, 312.

72   Kofi A. Annan, "Two Concepts of Sovereignty," *The Economist*, 18 September 1999, p. 49.

Men, deriving their just power from the consent of the governed." States exist, as many believe, to promote and protect individual rights and freedoms. The challenge for international leaders is what action the international community should take in those cases where states deliberately and systematically violate the human rights of their citizens.[73]

None of this implies that sovereign states cannot guarantee, promote, and advance human rights. To the contrary, the American experience teaches that individual rights and rule of law are mutually supportive and thrive in a democratic environment. Ironically, the American experience also encourages internationalism in the promotion of democratic values. As President Bush has stated in his National Security Strategy: "We will defend the peace by fighting terrorists and tyrants. We will preserve the peace by building good relations among the great powers. We will extend the peace by encouraging free and open societies on every continent".[74] This sentiment resembles Woodrow Wilson's and, indeed, those of most American presidents since 1918. Kissinger portrays this as an essential element of American altruism motivating our actions abroad: "Wilson put forward the unprecedented doctrine that the security of America was inseparable from the security of *all* the rest of mankind. This implied that it was henceforth America's duty to oppose aggression *everywhere . . .*".[75] This is a truly ambitious goal given the competing strain of American isolationism manifest in the interwar years.

The current world situation encourages debate over the scope and authority of international law. Recent American actions in Iraq, taken contrary to international public opinion, without the endorsement of the United Nations Security Council, and against the wishes of longstanding allies such as France, Germany, and Turkey, support Mersheimer's proposition that great powers behave as their interests dictate.[76] Perhaps sovereignty is alive and well after all. Unilateral action can, at least in certain cases, achieve the same results as multilateral efforts.

Proponents of international order and rule of law argue that lasting order cannot be imposed unilaterally. The Congress of Vienna in 1815, which created the "Concert of Europe," was a collective, multilateral effort, albeit predicated on sovereignty. But it took enormous cooperation to maintain international order for a hundred years. Even the British Empire at its height in the 19th Century realized its limitations and attempted to construct a favorable balance of power. John Ikenberry,

---

73 *See* Thomas W. McShane, "Blame it on the Romans: Pax Americana and the Rule of Law," *Parameters* 32 (Summer 2002): 57.

74 Bush, National Security Strategy, *supra*, note 5, Preface.

75 *See* H. Kissinger, *supra* note 32, 47.

76 *See* J. Mersheimer, *supra* note 3.

in his book *After Victory*, analyzes the rebuilding of international order after major wars. He says the diplomats of 1815 created a "constitutional order," which are "political orders organized around agreed-upon legal and political institutions that operate to allocate rights and limit the exercise of power".[77]

Ikenberry's concept of "constitutional order" helps to explain how the current international system evolved after World War II, and how it operates today. At its heart was the sharing of power by the United States, by far the most powerful state in the world in 1945. The framework was an extensive system of multilateral institutions, including alliances, which bound the United States and its primary partners in Europe together.[78] The Cold War may have accelerated this process, but it did not create it.[79]

If this theory is correct, then the primacy of international law and institutions is no accident, but instead the direct and expected result of efforts to create a framework of mutually supporting and binding ties. As we have seen, these international institutions have performed as designed. It should come as no surprise, viewing the international system in this way, that international organizations and politics restrain the choices and actions of sovereign states. From this perspective, international order displays many of the characteristics of municipal order.[80] Ikenberry explains this: "if institutions – wielded by democracies – play a restraining role . . . it is possible to argue that international orders under particular circumstances can indeed exhibit constitutional characteristics".[81]

The New World Order and American Hegemony – Who Owns International Law?

What is America's role as the sole superpower in the current environment? How should the international system respond to the threat of global terrorism? Can it maintain the security and prosperity created by American leadership since 1945? Can the rule of law accommodate the national interests of the great powers and protect the interests of weaker states threatened by demagogues, genocide, civil war

---

77   G. John Ikenberry, *After Victory: Institutions, Strategic Restraint, and The Rebuilding of Order after Major Wars*, (Princeton, Princeton University Press, 2001), 29.

78   *Ibid.*, 163. These institutions included the United Nations, NATO, The Marshall Plan, and the World Bank, among others.

79   *Ibid.*, 166.

80   *Ibid.*, 4.

81   *Ibid.*, 6.

and internal armed conflict? The remainder of this paper will attempt to suggest answers to these questions.

Dynamic, disparate forces challenge the international order. Globalization promises prosperity and freedom, but failed states, disease, pollution and rising birthrates hold large segments of the world's population hostage. Furthering individual rights and enforcing collective security requires international cooperation, but depends at present upon the good will and determination of powerful sovereign states.

A brief look at two recent developments illustrates the nature of the challenge and provides insights as to possible courses of action. The first of these is the creation of the International Criminal Court; the second is the American-led war on terrorism.

The International Criminal Court is an idea whose time has come. It fulfills the hopes and aspirations of a majority of the world's nations. Eighty years in the making, from Versailles in 1919 to the Rome Statute in 1997, it reflects a new consensus on international justice and the rule of law. Recognizing that sovereignty protected rulers and their agents from accountability for crimes ranging from aggressive war to democide,[82] the ICC provides a permanent forum for prosecution when state courts cannot or will not act. As of this writing 139 nations have signed the treaty, and 89 have ratified it. The Court commenced operations on July 1, 2002, and according to its charter enjoys almost universal jurisdiction.[83] Its potential impact is enormous, even without United States participation.[84]

At the same time, the United States leads international efforts to locate, isolate

---

82   Democide refers to the torture and killing of citizens by their own governments, generally despotic and totalitarian in form. One figure attributes 170 million deaths to democide over the course of the 20th Century, a number two to four times greater than the total number killed in war. *See* John Norton Moore, "Opening Comments," 149 *Military Law Review*, 7, 10 (1995). Professor Moore, Director of the Center for National Security Law at the University of Virginia School of Law, made these comments in a symposium on "Nuremberg and the Rule of Law: A Fifty Year Verdict" at the U.S. Army Judge Advocate General's School, 17 November 1995.

83   Universal Jurisdiction is based upon the principle that certain crimes violate international interests and norms and that states may take action regardless of the location of the crime or the nationality of the perpetrator or the victim. At present international law recognizes universal jurisdiction for certain offenses (e.g., crimes against humanity, war crimes) covered by the Geneva Conventions of 1949. The apprehension of Nazi war criminal Adolf Eichmann in Argentina and his trial in Israel in 1961 is often used to illustrate the concept. Others would extend the principle further, to cover domestic crimes that violate humanitarian principles not formally recognized in international law. *See The Princeton Principles on Universal Jurisdiction*, the Princeton Project on Universal Jurisdiction, (Princeton, Program in Law and Public Affairs, 2001).

and destroy international terrorist groups with global reach. These groups threaten international order and prosperity. They promote extremist views and promise false hopes to states and individuals left behind on the road of progress. While most states support and encourage American efforts to eradicate this plague, the international system is not well-suited for the struggle. There is no international agreement on terrorism, and none that even attempts to define the term. Several treaties address individual terrorist acts – hijacking, murder, money laundering, illegal crossing of borders, etc., but their solutions require state action – apprehension, extradition and prosecution of individual terrorists.[85] As some commentators, such as Ruth Wedgwood, have suggested, perhaps the current situation is so unique that existing models and laws need to be re-examined and updated. How does international law address a war waged on states by an amorphous group of non-state actors? What rules apply?

To date, therefore, the international response to terrorism depends upon American leadership, moral and physical. Coalitions are formed to fight terrorism, but they form and reform constantly depending on where American efforts are focused. In Afghanistan a multilateral effort enjoyed broad international support;[86] in Iraq, another theater in this new global war, the coalition fell short of expectations, and the intervention remains controversial.[87] The search for order and the rule of law means different things to different states. America may lead, but others need not follow.

These events are closely related. They represent opposite poles of debate over how we are to pursue Ikenberry's "constitutional order" on a global scale. While most states agree in theory with the efficacy of multilateral institutions, the utility of the United Nations, and the need for rule of law within and among states, international law must contend with the "friction" of sovereignty.[88] This uneasy rela-

---

84 President Clinton signed the treaty on behalf of the United States on 31 Dec 2000. It was never sent to the Senate for ratification, and on 6 May 2002 the United States officially notified the United Nations of its intention not to become a party. *See* U.S. Department of State Press Statement containing the official notice, accessed on line at <www.state.gov/r/pa/prs/ps/2002/9968pf.htm> on 29 October 2002.

85 *See*, e.g., Convention on Offenses and Certain Other Acts Committed on Board Aircraft, 14 Sept. 1963, 20 U.S.T. 2941; Convention for the Suppression of Unlawful Seizure of Aircraft (Hijacking), 16 Dec. 1970, 22 U.S.T. 1641; Convention for the Suppression of Unlawful Acts Against the Safety of Civil Aviation (Sabotage), 23 Sept. 1971, 24 U.S.T. 564.

86 The United Nations Security Council endorsed, although it did not direct, efforts to remove the Taliban and destroy Al Qaeda bases in Afghanistan.

87 The United Nations Security Council did not support intervention in Iraq beyond weapons inspectors. With at least two of the permanent members, France and Russia, likely to veto any Security Council Resolution sanctioning invasion, the United States led a "coalition of the willing."

88 As Undersecretary of State Marc Grossman stated on 6 May 2002, as he explained why the United States withdrew from the ICC Treaty: "We believe that states, not international insti-

tionship is likely to continue. By way of example, some states and prominent individuals have called for the ICC to investigate American intervention in Iraq as an "illegal" use of force in violation of treaty and customary law.[89]

Unilateralism: What Price Sovereignty?

This status quo is not particularly healthy. The new world order described in preceding sections of this paper is real and it is here to stay. The ties that bind the international community are strong and enduring, and international institutions enjoy unprecedented support and influence. Perhaps the most amazing point of all is that American values and leadership were instrumental in creating this environment. We are reminded once again that we have to be careful what we wish for.

American actions are well-intended, although many people sympathetic to American interests do not accept this proposition at face value. To the extent that American national interests must be served, the U.S. can continue to make unpopular decisions and execute American grand strategy without broad international support. But it cannot do so indefinitely. America may act unilaterally on a case-by-case basis, weighing costs and benefits; however it should harbor no illusions regarding the consequences – others may perceive these actions as excessive and bullying.

The cost of military intervention can be high: proponents must establish a legal basis, a jus ad bellum, for action; they must apply force consistent with the laws of armed conflict and possible mandates of the UN Security Council; the fighting must be controlled both in time and in space; fallout and political reactions must be anticipated; and, lastly, those advocating intervention must expect the unexpected. Murphy's Law applies to all human endeavors. Given the national interest in defeating terrorism and preserving international order, some degree of risk is normal and expected.

---

tutions are primarily responsible for ensuring justice in the international system." Remarks at the Center for Strategic and International Studies, distributed via e-mail by <Listmgr@PD.STATE.GOV> on 6 May 2002.

89   This represents politics as much as law. UN Security Council sanction is not a prerequisite for intervention. Article 51of the Charter permits state action in self defense and customary law provides an independent basis for action. The Kosovo precedent of international humanitarian intervention without Security Council approval also supports American intervention to remove the rogue regime of Saddam Hussein. International law scholars do not agree on these points.

The Road Ahead: Surviving in the New World Order

No state operates in a vacuum. The international environment outlined in this paper demands American attention if not cooperation. It provides several useful lessons to guide conduct in the 21st Century.

First, multilateral action is preferred in most cases. America lacks the political and military strength to go it alone in every instance. U.S. economic and military power provides the mobility and ability to go anywhere, but coalitions provide additional resources, political support, and legal justification and legitimacy for international operations. If international relations theorists are correct, states that pursue hegemonic order motivate other powers to combine to frustrate their efforts. Although such a backlash against American hegemony is not evident at present, no one can guarantee that further unilateral adventures will not produce one.

Second, the United States has tremendous capabilities at its disposal without employing the military element of power. Diplomatic, economic and informational tools provide enormous flexibility in formulating strategy and handling complicated problems as they arise. Infrequent demonstration of American military power will suffice to remind opponents of military capabilities while diplomats pursue peaceful resolution of disputes by other means.

This approach will also reassure friends, allies and critics alike of American intentions and demonstrates a willingness to exhaust all reasonable alternatives before applying force. It will preserve valuable goodwill.

Third, every crisis does not require international intervention or the use of military forces. Acknowledging the threat posed by global terrorist networks, most international crises are local and have little impact on terrorism or global security. Many of them, we need to remind ourselves, may be safely ignored and left to others to solve. Unless international stability is seriously threatened, mobilizing the international community and its resources might prove counterproductive. We've learned, since the heady days of 1991, of the great Gulf War Coalition forged by President Bush, that the new world order promised by the collapse of the Soviet Union and the end of the Cold War has not come to pass, at least not in the way we imagined it. But there is a new world order and states have to live in it.

The fourth and final lesson we can draw from this analysis of international law and sovereignty is that the international system as it exists (and as it was designed) reflects American values and American visions for the future. It is a legitimate national heritage. To presume that all institutions oppose American interests because some do, or presume that all treaties are suspect because some are, is to deny that heritage. More often than not, international institutions and agreements further American interests.

It is important to remember that democracies tolerate differences, and in fact thrive on them. If the core of "constitutional order" in the world is Western democracy, then we must expect that there will be disagreements and heated debate among states. We will not always agree on everything. But in a constitutional system everyone must play; the rules don't allow a state to simply takes its ball and go home whenever it doesn't get its way. True, no referee will step in to impose a penalty, but true international order, just like domestic order, depends upon mutual respect, cooperation, and responsible behavior. Those who claim global leadership within the system have the greatest responsibilities to ensure the system works. It is time to reassess America's global role, reassert American leadership of the world community, and cease struggling against the ties that bind, like a modern Gulliver.

Iraq Legal Issues: Perspectives from the Field

Gregory P. Belanger*

Military lawyers play a key role as advisors to Commanders during military operations planning and execution. They provide Commanders expertise to help ensure compliance with the international and domestic laws that regulate military activities, and are also problem solvers as professionals trained in fact gathering, research and analysis. In post conflict State building and reconstruction operations, the role of the military lawyer is especially crucial in missions focused on building institutions that establish the rule of law.

I was assigned to Combined Joint Task Force SEVEN (CJTF7), the Land Component Commander for Iraq, as a Judge Advocate from late May 2003, to the middle of August 2003. This paper presents a few of the legal issues confronted by Military Judge Advocates engaged in the State building mission in Iraq during that time period. Currently, there are over 100 Judge Advocates deployed to Iraq, in support of the mission to establish the rule of law, and a new Democratic Iraqi government to replace the tyrannical legacy of the Baath Party.

My office was located in Baghdad with the CJTF7 headquarters staff. The CJTF 7 Office of the Staff Judge Advocate consists of 17 uniformed attorneys. The legal staff also maintained offices at the Coalition Provisional Authority (CPA) Headquarters in Baghdad, about 8 kilometers from my location. The CJTF7 Judge Advocate, with 3 other attorneys worked closely with the CPA to ensure our common efforts between the military and the civil governing authorities were fully coordinated.

As of one of many lawyers involved in the Coalition military mission in Iraq, my professional observations experiences were unique, and derivative of my responsibilities and position. My principal responsibilities related to the management of legal advice from my office to subordinate commands on administrative law matters,

---

*   Commander, US Navy, Assistant Judge Advocate, United States European Command, Stuttgart, Germany, e-mail: belangeg@eucom.mil.

Harvey Langholtz, Boris Kondoch, Alan Wells (Eds.),
International Peacekeeping: The Yearbook of International Peace Operations, Volume 9, 2004, pp. 209-217.
© *Koninklijke Brill N.V. Printed in the Netherlands*

operational law, and military justice issues, and staffing work for the CJTF7 Command Staff Judge Advocate necessary to carry out his responsibilities as the legal advisor to the Commander.

The military mission Iraq is organized into sectors. There are Multi-National Brigades (MNB) under CJTF7 that command specific geographic areas of responsibility, or sectors. Under UK Command is MNB South East (SE), which included the cities of Al Basrah and Umm Qasr. The main contributors to this MNB are the United Kingdom, Italy, and the Netherlands. MNB Central South, (CS) which includes the cities of An Najaf, and Al Nasaririyah, and south to the Saudi Arabia boarder is currently under the command of the Poles, with Poland, Ukraine, Spain, Slovakia, and Romania contributing the bulk of the forces. The units outside of the MNB sectors are under direct U.S. Command. There are U.S. sectors Central, North and West, with some multi-national participation in these areas, all under U.S. command. Coalition operations bring unique challenges to the battlefield, with different communications systems, doctrine, and national rules and restrictions.

Understanding and tracking the differences in the domestic rules that governed each Coalition member became a Judge Advocate responsibility, so that the Commander could be advised on issues that effect force employability, and other operational planning considerations. For example, some coalition partners were not prepared or allowed to handle the detention of persons for anything beyond a few days. This required coordination and assurances between Coalition Partners to ensure that further detention would be handled properly, if for example there were a need to turn over detainees to another Coalition Partner. Other limitations and differences may exist in the ROE context, which needed to be understood and reconciled.

The number of troops that were deployed to Iraq during the time of my assignment was less than 150,000 troops, including all of the MNB's. With modern technology, principally communications and transportation, you would that expect less troops would be required to complete the mission than in prior occupation operations, for example in Germany and Japan. The Kosovo operation used close to 40K troops by comparison during the initial phases of the intervention. Kosovo's population, and land area is much smaller, and the Coalition there had a greater troop concentration advantage. There is great public debate on what the right number is, but the US position is that additional troops are not required, however, more international participation is certainly desired. The key of course is getting the Iraqi people to take responsibility for their new freedom and they are participating in greater numbers every day.

A comment on the security situation is warranted as I am asked about this frequently. My headquarters was located on a compound in Baghdad. I did travel and spend time in both Al Najaf, and Al Fallugia, slightly North West of Baghdad and frequently sited as a hot spot. I can report that over the three months that I was working in Iraq, I was never shot at directly to my knowledge, and the closest mortar round exploded over 800 meters from my position. There were of course security precautions undertaken before we moved about. While I was there the rules required that ground travel would always be with two vehicles, with body armor, and helmets, as well as personal weapons.

In my opinion, and as many of you should suspect, the media tends to sensationalize the amount of violence. It is important to keep in mind that we have a large number of troops spread over a country of 25 million. That said, I do admit that there is some confusion that was caused by the announcement in May that "major combat operations" had ended. Combat operations continue in Iraq, as Baath Party sympathizers and other terrorist that oppose Coalition efforts to bring peace and stability to the area continue to fight. Addressing the security situation was the primary focus of the mission, with State building underway contemporaneously.

The principal international law legal authorities for the law of occupation are Hague Convention IV, (18 October 1907) (the Hague Rules), and United Nations Security Council Resolution (UNSCR) 1483. The Coalition Provisional Authority is a defacto occupier in Iraq as recognized under UNSCR 1483. UNSCR 1483 and the Hague Rules are the controlling black letter law, and are the most on point tools which guide CPA actions and initiatives in establishing civil order in Iraq.

Military Judge Advocates, line officers, and all soldiers receive training in the Law of War throughout their careers. Law of war references, including the Hague Rules, The Geneva Convention Relative to the Protection of Civilian Persons in Time of War (1949), the 1977 Protocols, and Department of Army Field Manual 27-10, The Law of Land Warfare (1956) are readily available to the deployed Judge Advocate to execute their mission to provide legal support to operations. These references are in use daily by Judge Advocates at various levels in planning and execution of operations in Iraq and around the world to help insure law of war compliance in U.S. military operations. I would note that the 1977 Protocols, although not binding on the United States, are a useful reference a recognized restatement of customary international law.

Due to the complexity of the operation, all sources of law were consulted. For example, to determine the extent of Coalition authority in the territorial seas of Iraq, Oxford Manual of Naval Warfare 1913, an accepted statement of customary international law was instructive. Article 88 in particular of that reference clearly extends the terrestrial limits of the law of occupation to the territorial waters of the occupied territory. Also, the Hague Cultural Property Convention of 1954, which has occupation provisions, was considered in certain matters. With regard to evidentiary standards for hearings, and due process considerations, standards incorporated from the domestic law of the United States were applied to many of the issues that relate to search, apprehension and detention.

I will address a few of the more significant contributions of military and civilian Coalition lawyers during the period I was in Iraq. Specifically, I would like to

speak about judicial reconstruction in Iraq, the establishment of Iraqi security organizations, detention operations, law of war and international law considerations, to
include war crimes. Along with these special and important contributions, Judge
Advocates every day are supporting the mission by carrying out traditional judge
advocate responsibilities such as military justice, claims, and other administrative
law advice.

Briefly, I will point out that with regard to the investigation and reporting of
such matters as friendly fire incidents, claims, and other mishaps, Judge Advocates
serve a central role not only as legal advisors, but in many instances as investigating officers. During this conflict, Judge Advocates in many case were assigned
directly to fully investigate and provide reports on various mishaps. The ordinary
practice of assigning non-lawyers to these details was by-passed so that line officers
remained unburdened, and could pursue the more pressing mission of continuing
with the fight. The commander's choice of assigning these sometimes time con-
suming and administratively intensive responsibilities to military lawyers is a great
choice in practice, as lawyers have the professional training to complete the necessary and sometimes complex fact finding, research, and analysis quickly and
accurately.

A major task of the Coalition following entry into Iraq was the reconstruction
of the judicial infrastructure and systems. Prior to the arrival of Coalition Forces,
Court infrastructure was dealt a heavy blow. Most court houses in the country were
looted by criminals, and some, in particular in the Baghdad area were completely
destroyed. Nearly all of this damage is attributable to the wide spread looting that
took place as the Baath Party collapsed. The destruction not only included the court
houses, but court records as well. Of the over 300 Courts in operation prior to April
2003, none were in operations following the liberation of the Iraqi people.

Judge Advocates were quick to establish contact with former Iraqi judiciary and
assess immediate needs to get the courts up and running. In some districts, in addition to the requirement for basic infrastructure improvements, orders from the CPA
were required to get the dockets up and moving. The Judiciary in some instances
required an order to reestablish jurisdiction under the CPA. This process was facil-
itated by Judge Advocates all over Iraq in conjunction with the in coordination with
the overall civil affairs effort. Also, money was provided to court officials to make
necessary repairs, all done under the supervision of military lawyers. In the Baghdad
area, four lawyers from the CJTF7 staff, and three enlisted personnel were assigned
to this critical task.

Docket coordination, logistics, and evidence production were some of the many
tasks necessary for the reestablishment of the courts that were handled by Judge
Advocates throughout Iraq. Working on a daily basis with the judiciary, the Courts
in Iraq were largely reestablished prior to the completion on my tour.

Another important structural development following the arrival of the Coalition was the establishment of the Central Criminal Court (CCC), which is the beginning of the institutionalization of an independent judiciary for Iraq. The CCC was established by CPA Order 13 and has at its bedrock the principle of Judicial Independence. This court was established to adjudicate felonies intended to destabilize the government, to include violence or other crimes that transcend provincial boundaries.

The Judges appointed to the CCC are to make decisions "independently, impartially, and in accordance with [the law]." Judges are prohibited from participating in political activities. The criminal procedure and code is pursuant to Iraqi law which with a few exceptions is the same as it was prior to the arrival of coalition forces. Requests for referral can come from almost anywhere, and the Administrator submits matters for referral. The Administrator receives advice for referral from the Coalition Provisional Authority General Counsel.

Prior to my departure, a case involving the illegal transportation of weapons began at the initial investigative hearing stages. This was the first case to be tried before the Central Criminal Court. The case involved the transportation of a cache of weapons in a Red Crescent ambulance. The case was charged under laws prohibiting the possession of weapons, as opposed to a war crime for misuse of the red crescent emblem.

Staffing for a special tribunal to address war crimes is ongoing, however the CPA order for its establishment has not been promulgated. Drafts of the establishment order reflect that this court will have jurisdiction domestically over Iraqi nationals accused of War Crimes from July 1968 up until the present. The list of crimes is similar to those delineated by the International Criminal Court, including genocide, war crimes, and other crimes against humanity. In addition, the special tribunal will be able to charge the underlying violations of the Iraqi Criminal Code in conjunction with the universal crimes.

Judge Advocates and civilian CPA lawyers were also involved in the establishment of the various Iraqi security organizations that are integral to the establishment of security and the rule of law in Iraq. By Coalition Provisional Authority Order's 1 and 2 of May 2003, the Iraqi Army was disestablished, and all Baathist Party Security related apparatus in Iraq was made illegal. Because of the large effect these orders had on civil security structure in Iraq, new security organizations were required to be established to fill the security void. The establishment of new security organizations and structures remains a priority and is an ongoing project. The Iraqi Police Force was the immediate priority.

The establishment documents for these organizations were drafted during the summer of 2003. The legal challenge was to fit the organizations within the existing legal framework of Iraq. With respect to internal security, the Iraqi Police Force, Site Security and the Iraqi Civil Defense Corps (ICDF) are all subject to the Criminal Law of Iraq. Their authority is specified under their CPA Charters. The police and Facilities Protection Services are under the ministry of the Interior. The ICDF is under coalition forces command and control. The forces assist Coalition troops, providing interpreter service and other advice, as well as providing security. They have no powers of arrest, but may detain persons temporarily. Iraqi nationals have been retained by Coalition military to fill these purposes since the arrival of U.S. Forces. The formalization of the organizational structure and establishment of these forces clarifies their legal status as full participants in the Iraqi security forces mix.

The New Iraqi Army is at it infancy, and has a revamped code of discipline. The work in drafting the new code of discipline was undertaken by coalition lawyers, and was complete in July of 2003.

As these new security organizations were and continue to be stood up, Coalition Forces are the main provider of law enforcement and security services in many areas of Iraq. The law enforcement mission, and in particular, evidence collection procedures and detention quickly became one of the main efforts following Coalition forces arrival. This presented a challenge for our troops as our soldiers are not trained in evidence collection and police procedures. A large effort was undertaken to quickly train our forces to preserve evidence necessary for prosecutions.

If you compare NYC to Baghdad, there are over 50,000 police in New York. At the beginning of my tour, we were attempting to police Baghdad with about 15,000 troops. This placed a large strain on resources, as well as making policing and patrols a primary mission for U.S. Forces, necessary to carry out the international law obligation to maintain public safety.

Every member of Coalition forces suddenly became responsible for evidence collection, a law enforcement mission in which most soldiers have no training or experience. Procedures were put in place to preserve evidence for later use in prosecutions. These orders in large measure were the result of CJTF7 Judge Advocate effort.

As an adjunct to the law enforcement mission, and a large burden on force was the requirement to carry out detention operations. Most will freely admit that the Coalition was unprepared to meet the burdens imposed by the scope of this task. Shortly before the arrival of Coalition Forces in Iraq, Saddam ordered the release all of the criminals held in Iraqi custody (approximately 115,000 Prisoners). With a population of over 25 Million people, it has been estimated that statistically at least 100,000 persons could be expected to be incarcerated at any one time. Needless to say, the release of these prisoners, for whatever purpose, greatly enhanced the degree of lawless throughout Iraq.

Imagine the security situation in your own country if all criminals currently incarcerated were released. There is no question that this tactic created a chaotic situation, resulting in considerable pain and suffering inflicted upon Iraqi citizenry. As a consequence of Saddam's action which most likely was calculated to create chaos and terror in his own country, nearly all prisons, prison records, and infrastructure were destroyed.

Coalition Judge Advocates were quick to jump in and help create a system in conformance with international law responsive to the detainee issues, to not only safeguard those rights provided under the Conventions, but to also ensure those who present a threat to the coalition or could assist by providing valuable intelligence remain under coalition control. Military lawyers were involved in every aspect of these operations, from drafting the controlling orders for the coalition in detention operations, to serving as magistrates making recommendations for release of retention of detainees. The complexity of these tasks was substantial, complicated by the different categories of detainees, and the differing procedures and rights associated with their treatment.

There are three categories of detainees currently held in Iraq; Enemy Prisoners of War (EPW's), Criminals and Security detainees. Some detainees may be a combination of all three. EPW's are afforded all protections under Geneva Convention III Relative to Treatment of Prisoners of War (GC III (PW)). Such detainees are granted access by the IRC and are generally eligible for release at the cessation of hostilities. Criminal detainees, on the other hand, remain in detention until they can be tried by a competent Court. Finally, security detainees, those held for intelligence purposes or because of the threat that they pose, are only detained so long as an imperative security inertest makes detention necessary.

Prisoner status determinations under GC III (PW), Article's 4 and 5 were administered by Judge Advocates and were underway throughout the summer of 2003 in Iraq. The criteria for determining EPW status is specified by Article 4. Due the nature of operations and tactics currently employed by forces opposing the coalition, the requirements for a command structure, fixed distinctive sign recognizable at a distance, and conduct of operations in accordance with the law of war all create issues that many times favor findings that detainees are not EPW's.

There are other difficult issues. For example, is the former Baath Party still a party to the ongoing conflict, or did the Baath Party's defeat and disestablishment render all resistance currently in Iraq to criminal status? Do civilians that have direct command and control over military forces under the Iraqi regime organization get EPW status as a member of the military component, or are they really civilians within the meaning of the Convention?

Criminal detainees, those detained persons reasonably suspected of having committed a crime against Iraqi nationals or property, presented another set of problems. As mentioned before, evidence collection procedures needed to be instituted to ensure chain of custody, and to preserve basic facts such as names of witnesses, and photographs. Given the security situation and language barriers, the preservation of crime scene evidence was extraordinarily difficult in most cases, and sometimes impossible. The Iraqi Courts ultimately review these cases, and where there is insufficient evidence, detainees are released. Release determinations were made by military magistrates in many cases before the involvement of the Iraqi Courts.

Within 72 hours of induction into a Coalition detention facility, criminal detainees are informed of the basis of their detention and the right to remain silent. They are afforded access to counsel prior to trial.

Security Internees are another category of persons detained by the Coalition, that are either interned for their own protection or because they pose a threat to the security of coalition forces, its mission, or are of intelligence value. This category of detainee includes persons committing crimes against coalition forces, the provisional government, state infrastructure, war crimes or crimes against humanity, and therefore, one can see how there can be a crossover of categories, criminal, EPW, or security detainee. Security detainees are afforded magistrates reviews, and are granted an automatic right to appeal, in conformance with Article 78 of Geneva Convention IV, Article 78.

Every step of the way in the detainee process, there is Judge Advocate involvement. From case development, magistrate reviews, to assisting with Iraqi the Iraqi Courts in evidence production, or in the administration of the Article 5 process, military lawyers are fully engaged. This is a team effort involving a team effort with Provost authorities, military and civilian Iraqi authorities. Given the numbers of detainees, approximately 5000, this is a huge task.

I will now turn to a couple of points on other International Law issues that arose during my assignment to Iraq. Procedures were put in place from the planning stage during the targeting process to ensure protected places under the Conventions were not harmed. Again, during the state building phase of operations currently underway, special attention and procedures were put in place to ensure that sensitivities to religious and other places of cultural significance were properly respected. In order to establish a stable and secure environment, the law allows Coalition Forces to search all places under Coalition control, to include military places. This power is not exercised arbitrarily, and is done in cooperation with Iraqi police authorities in most instances. Military lawyers provide advice in planning these operations, and standard operating procedures were developed and published from CJTF7.

Judge Advocates at the CJTF7 Headquarters stand watch 24 hours per-day, 7 days a week. They provided advice on a broad range of operational law related issues, in particular the sometimes difficult issues related to targeting and the rules of engagement. For example, a cross border hot pursuit situation developed around 18 or 19 June of 2003, which has since been publicized in the news. The CJTF7 legal team was consulted and involved in providing advice during this sensitive operation and in its aftermath. Other emergent issues are addressed by watch standers, to include such first impression matters as legal regulations/restrictions that may relate to the media's access to deceased regime leadership, in particular, Saddam's sons.

The problem of foreign fighters is a continuing one. Coordination with the national's embassy is undertaken in these cases consistent with State practice in other contexts where foreign citizens are arrested outside their country. These situations, and the disposition of such detainees, are largely controlled by political factors.

Of major concern is the problem of persons engaging Coalition Forces without a distinguishing uniform, and using other tactics that endanger the civilian population. From the beginning of Coalition forces entry into Iraq, opposition forces adopted this tactic, using civilians as shields, using protected places, schools hospitals, and religious places as operating bases, and always wearing civilian cloths. These tactics are a violation of the law of war, and raise the issue of combatant immunity, which will likely be raised and resolved in cases brought before the CCC, or the Iraqi Special Tribunal.

It has yet to be determined how the Coalition interests in justice will be vindicated. On such possibility is a Uniform Code of Military Justice (UCMJ) Article 21 Tribunal under U.S. military law. Should there be authority to litigate these cases before an UCMJ Article 21 tribunal, like those now hearing cases in Guantanamo Bay, Cuba; arguments will likely be heard concerning combatant immunity. Currently, there are no military courts authorized to try civilians in Iraq, however, these matters are under consideration.

In order to stabilize and establish the rule of law in Iraq, the delivery of justice for the manifold crimes and serious human rights abuses committed by the former regime will need to be vindicated. It is likely these matters will be resolved by the Iraqi people themselves, through the Special Tribunal for such matters now under consideration. Coalition Forces are securing mass grave sites currently, so that appropriate forensic examination can be conducted. The most conservative estimate provided by British Organization INFORCE, estimates the loss of life at the hands of the Iraqi Regime as evidenced by mass graves to be approximately 300,000.

As one travels through Iraq, a day does not pass by without a citizen expressing their gratitude for the liberation, and current coalition efforts to rebuild the country. We will prevail with and for these patriots. It is difficult to imagine this is the case given the frequency of attacks on Coalition forces; however, there is underlying support for Coalition efforts. The public remains intimidated by the thugs previously in power, and they continue to terrorize with impunity. With continued pressure, the tide will turn, and more Iraqis will join us to reclaim their country.

To conclude, the military judge advocate will continue to be a key player in Iraq's reconstruction. From my experiences in Iraq and interaction with the Iraqi people, the Coalition will succeed in creating a strong and stable Iraq, and the goals of the war on terror will be advanced. Iraq will no longer be a safe haven for terrorists, and it will be possible for Iraq to realize its great potential as a peaceful member of the community of nations.

Targeting Issues in Afghanistan

*David L. Hayden**

I intend to convey a practical look at the background of our deployment to Afghanistan, with particular focus on the unique nature of combat in *Operation Enduring Freedom* (OEF). I will also address, in general terms, the Rules of Engagement (ROE) we were operating under to the extent I can given their classified status, the targets and threats we faced in my year there, and some of the more significant issues I personally observed and dealt with in my capacity as the Staff Judge Advocate for Combined Joint Task Force-180 (CJTF-180), from May 2002 until April 2003.

Let me begin by recounting an exchange I observed in a press conference in Kabul, Afghanistan in July 2002. A CJTF-180 aircraft had fired on several antiaircraft positions near the village of Deh Rawod, causing substantial civilian casualties. A joint CJTF-180 and Afghanistan investigation team had just finished debriefing President Karzai and his cabinet in the Presidential Palace on their findings. In response to a reporter's question regarding whether the United States was now targeting civilians as part of their Global War on Terrorism, Lieutenant General Dan K. McNeill, commander of CJTF-180, responded with the following words: "There is only one group of people in this world that intentionally target civilians and those would be the terrorists that we are pursuing in the Global War on Terrorism." I could not have been prouder to see my commander point to the single most distinguishing factor between our forces and the terrorists we were pursuing. As the senior lawyer for the entire theater in a command that included forces from 32 different countries engaged in the Global War on Terrorism, I was challenged in ways I never

---

* Colonel, US Army, Staff Judge Advocate for NORAD and US Northern Command; formerly Staff Judge Advocate for the 82d Airborne Division, for XVIII Airborne Corps and Fort Bragg, and, most recently, for Combined Joint Task Force – 180 in Bagram, Afghanistan. E-mail: David.Hayden@northcom.mil. The opinions expressed in this article are those of the author and do not necessarily reflect the position of the Department of the Army or any other federal agency.

Harvey Langholtz, Boris Kondoch, Alan Wells (Eds.),
International Peacekeeping: The Yearbook of International Peace Operations, Volume 9, 2004, pp. 219-227.
© *Koninklijke Brill N.V. Printed in the Netherlands*

thought possible, and saw aspects of the modern battlefield that directly affected the paradigms of legal support that I had been taught, trained on, and expected.

All of our lives changed on September 11th with the attacks in the US. As a soldier in our XVIII Airborne Corps, I expected to be involved very quickly in the Global War on Terrorism, but never expected to find myself on the plains of Afghanistan living in a tent at a base surrounded by minefields and individuals with a desire to do harm to our forces. I had a robust team of lawyers and paralegals assigned to our command, primarily located at three locations to better serve the forces throughout the theater; in the capital of Kabul; at our base at Bagram Airfield north of Kabul; and another base in the South at Kandahar, in the middle of the most contentious area of the conflict.

Afghanistan is a land of contrast with beautiful landscapes that have witnessed some of the most violent aspects of modern warfare and, even today, holds the danger of uncharted landmines. Warfare covered the full spectrum. The fighting was sometimes primitive in nature (some Special Forces rode into battle on horseback), and at other times the fighting was with technologically advanced weapons and other systems that were not even in our inventory 10 years before. The one significant result of all this technology was a significant increase in the need for legal advice to commanders regarding the Law of War (LOW) and targeting in particular.

Our Bagram airfield base was the primary headquarters for CJTF-180, located on a previous Soviet base from two decades earlier. The area surrounding the base had been a veritable battlefield for those intervening years, strewn with numerous minefields, a constant danger that our forces were clearing all the time. Civilian relief agencies were also involved in clearing minefields and we coordinated our efforts with them. One of the most heartbreaking aspects of my tour was the almost indifference of some of the local villagers and nomads who traveled the area as part of their annual migration. There were so many minefields, many of which were unmarked, that civilian mine clearing agencies resorted to painting rocks red alongside the roadway to signify a minefield that had not been cleared. It was not unusual to see a long row of red painted stones and local Afghans living and walking through that same minefield, seemingly indifferent to the risks. Unfortunately, the risks were always there and we had many innocent mine strike victims from the adjoining communities that were brought into our base hospital for emergency treatment. Most of them appeared to be children. I know there was always an aggressive campaign by our civil-military affairs sections to educate the civilian populace wherever they could, but the problem never seemed to diminish during my year.

Bagram airfield was located at the base of the majestic Hindu-Kush Mountains and was a stopping place of Alexander the Great during his conquests many centuries ago. The local rural areas were dotted with small compounds. I likened them to small French Foreign Legion forts that were the subject of many Hollywood movies in my youth. I understood that the compounds were primarily to allow extended families to be protected and grow their own gardens or groves within the walls. They were made of mud and straw and extremely durable, lasting years. This is significant to know because much of our combat action involved sweeps and searches of these compounds and they could be very dangerous without significant forces. The people living in the Bagram area were very supportive for the most part and welcomed our arrival. They had been primarily associated with the Northern Alliance that opposed the Taliban and suffered terribly under the Taliban government when the Northern Alliance forces were driven north years before. The greatest dangers and majority of the combat activity was primarily confined to the small section of the countryside along the Eastern Border with Pakistan and to the South where the Pashtun tribes were located. The Pashtun were the largest ethnic population. The Taliban movement originated in that area and the Pashtuns still harbored sentiment of support for the Islamic fundamentalism advocated by the Taliban. Interestingly, President Karzai is also Pashtun. All together, these portions of the country were a very small fraction of the entire country.

Unique aspects of combat in Afghanistan impacted on our ROE and legal advice. First and foremost was the difficulty in identifying the enemy, whether Taliban, Al Qaeda, or other forces opposed to the new Afghan administration and our efforts in the country. This placed a premium on accurately identifying any targets before engaging. We had a distinct advantage of mobility because of our aviation assets. We also used every technologically advanced system we could field during that time. Unmanned aerial vehicles (UAV) were significant in that arsenal. These gave us the opportunity to better identify targets and a loiter capability in the vicinity of any operations for long periods of times. Your view, however, could become narrow because you focused only on what the UAV cameras saw. Nonetheless, UAVs gave commanders a precise real-time picture that further enhanced their ability to make informed decisions on targeting, a definite improvement to the process. I envision future battlefields with many more systems available to small unit commanders to provide them improved battlefield eyes and ears.

Improved guidance systems on ordnance and advanced targeting methods created some unbelievably precise capabilities to hit targets. The use of guided precision munitions in Afghanistan was significantly higher than in any previous conflict. Commanders, and to a great extent the media and the public, came to expect that our targeting methods and procedures would always be that precise. Whether that leads to a movement to impose higher law of war standards on superpowers with precision munitions to expect and demand lower collateral damage remains to be seen. I certainly hope not. Besides, apart from our obligations under LOW to engage in our proportionality assessments to minimize collateral damage when targeting otherwise lawful and valid targets on the battlefield, we also face the ever increasing expectations of the public and the media to avoid most, if not all, collateral damage. War is an inherently dangerous and often times unfortunate experience.

Terms such as precision munitions and surgical strikes convey unrealistic notions of antiseptic environments that arguably mislead the public.

Our radar systems were also able to record and analyze incoming trajectories of indirect fire weapons. These radar systems could tell you with amazing precision where the rockets or mortars were coming from. They would, however, occasionally provide false readings when, in fact, no launch had occurred. Moreover, they did not, by themselves, normally provide the necessary "eyes on the target" to satisfy our requirements of identification or allow counter-fire. As a practical matter, most of these rockets were fired by time-delayed fuses to allow the enemy to leave the area before the launch actually occurred. They were notoriously inaccurate and probably caused more casualties to the enemy than they ever did to coalition forces. On more than one occasion, we would hear of an incident where a rocket or other explosive would go off prematurely and kill the person setting it off.

Other unique aspects of combat in Afghanistan included a small footprint by our forces. We rarely had over 12,000 total US forces in the theater at any given time, which is a small contingent given the enormous size of the country. Artillery was generally impractical due to the inhospitable terrain. Our forces had to rely on air delivered munitions as their primary form of fire support

The country's transportation system infrastructure was almost nonexistent with few roads. The practical effect was that short journeys on the ground took long and difficult routes. We were forced to use an air link for most of our support and travel. We had a large runway that was constantly under repair. This also meant that we could not easily move forces in response to any threats. They had to be prepositioned and located where they were most likely to be needed, such as along the Pakistani-Afghan border.

The Afghan population was also hard to communicate with. Media options were limited or impractical. Much of the population was illiterate, in large part due to the interruption of basic education due to war for many years. Radio was about the only effective means to communicate, but even that was severely hampered by a lack of radios in the countryside.

Finally, Afghanistan-Pakistan border ambiguities contributed to some unusual situations. In some areas, there was no mutually accepted international border. Differences of up to 2 kilometers were not unusual. Many of these border areas were at extremely high altitudes and presented substantial challenges to forces attempting to control movement between the two countries. There was at least one incident where a Pakistani border post was several kilometers inside of Afghanistan.

These were not the only unusual aspects of combat in Afghanistan, but certainly some of the major considerations in our operations. Planning and operations had to develop new tactics, techniques and procedures to adapt to these new paradigms.

There were numerous threats against our forces and the future of a stable and democratic Afghan government. Most of these were the typical weapons of war found in a combat environment, from rockets and small arms to improvised explosives. In my opinion, however, the greatest threat to the stability of the Afghan government and the efforts of our forces were the regional leaders, sometimes referred to as warlords. These were the power brokers in each of the regions who assisted in the overthrow of the Taliban regime and subsequent efforts to stabilize their respective regions. They exerted the most power in those regions through their Afghan militia forces and their other resources. Many were reputed to be corrupt and involved in illegal activities such as the drug trade. They did prove to be cooperative for the most part with our coalition forces. This was due, in large part, to our commander's ability to communicate personally with each one of them and ensure they understood their individual continuation as a regional leader was dependent upon their cooperation. In order for the central government to succeed, these regional warlords had to concede power over time, something not in their best interest. Dealing with this "threat" was as frustrating to our efforts at times as dealing with Taliban and Al Qaeda remnants.

The OEF Rules of Engagement (ROE) applied to all US forces in the theater and were classified; therefore, they cannot be discussed specifically in this forum. They can be addressed in general terms and that will be my focus for the remainder of this article. Two aspects of our ROE that can be addressed is the significant, though necessary emphasis on target identification and the inherent right that our forces retain to defend themselves when confronted by hostile acts or hostile intent. Both ideas reflected in our ROE are essentially the same wherever US forces operate, but particularly important in Afghanistan.

The technologically enhanced ability to observe the battlefield combined with precisely delivered ordnance, placed greater emphasis on correctly identifying the target to minimize the risk of collateral damage. Our forces were directed from the beginning of hostilities to take as many steps as possible to minimize collateral damage, especially casualties to noncombatants. The Afghan environment, as detailed before, complicated our ability to accurately identify potential targets. Nonetheless, our expectations were higher because of our technological capabilities. I would venture to say that no other force has imposed such a high standard of target identification on its forces. Some would argue that our restrictions were unreasonable and allowed some enemy elements to escape. Conversely, incidents did occur that involved collateral damage and the public outcry at those incidents underscored the need to carefully review all targets. In my opinion, the requirement to positively identify all our targets as lawful and valid struck the right balance. This was increasingly a public relations war and that element could not be ignored in our conduct of the war.

A second aspect of our ROE was the inherent right of our forces to exercise self-defense in response to hostile acts and hostile intent. US forces always have a right to self-defense. The OEF ROE simply restated that principle. Some of the coalition forces were more restrictive of their own forces' ability to exercise self-defense than the US forces. US forces, however, did not have to wait for opposing elements to engage us first. Ultimately, most of our combat actions on the ground and in the air were done in self-defense. Despite greater flexibility in their ROE, US forces repeatedly exercised incredible restraint when they could have responded with force in self-defense or even anticipatory self-defense. This is understandable given the difficulty in identifying legitimate enemy targets absent some kind of hostile act or demonstrated hostile intent.

Pivotal in ensuring compliance with the ROE and avoiding mistakes in the use of force were the procedures used to clear and use fires. We referred to these procedures as the Targeting Process. The prime concern remained all along to minimize civilian casualties and other collateral damage. This was a legal requirement under the Geneva Conventions and associated Protocols, but also a moral imperative for our forces. It is the way we have always been trained. We also recognize the practicality of modern day warfare and the instantaneous access of the media to events as they unfold. Events involving high collateral damage and civilian casualties become instant news items and could turn public opinion very quickly if ignored or given minimal attention.

The Targeting Process occupied our thoughts before, during and after operations. During my tenure, very little deliberation or preplanned targeting occurred. We were primarily focused on targets that arose during the course of operations such as when units were receiving fire. In theory, our operational planning would use targeting boards to identify protected areas and people and areas of possible collateral damage in order to be prepared should a request for fire on those locations occur. Judge advocates were members of the targeting boards and intimately involved in the planning process, vetting potential targets and providing legal advice on potential courses of actions. These targeting meetings became part of our battle drills that were rehearsed frequently. When an actual request for fire would arise, an almost daily occurrence, all of the participants in the Targeting Process knew their roles and responsibilities and were able to provide appropriate advice when necessary. This was particularly effective when responding to time-sensitive targets that arose during operations. A judge advocate had to be available 24 hours a day in the operations center to ensure no delay was caused by searching for members of the targeting boards. In addition to complying with the ROE and international standards on targeting, the commanders were equally dedicated towards avoiding friendly fire incidents. Requests for fire support, therefore, had to be cleared by beforehand. The judge advocate had a pivotal role in that process.

A unique problem from our perspective involved targeting near the border with Pakistan. Most of our hostilities involved enemy forces crossing over to attack coalition bases, then returning to their safe havens in the Pakistan countryside. It was a politically sensitive issue as you can imagine. It was unacceptable to CJTF-180 for enemy forces to have a sanctuary along the border. Hot pursuit of enemy forces into Pakistan, would have strained relations with the Pakistani government, absent their prior approval. A Pakistani Army Colonel was assigned as a liaison to our staff to address this problem, but that solution never quite solved all the complicated issues. Coordination with the Pakistani authorities, however, was the key to any hope of addressing this problem. Significant efforts were made to coordinate with the Pakistani border authorities. We provided them cell phones to improve communication links. We also engaged in joint patrols to monitor cross border incursions. Unfortunately, the Pakistani authorities had limited control of major portions of the Pakistani countryside near the border. This problem never went away and was a constant source of concern for our forces.

Three particular engagements we experienced in Afghanistan may help to understand the complexities and the extent of our efforts to address targeting issues. These include the friendly fire incident resulting in the deaths of several Canadian soldiers at Tarnak Farms, a potential cross-border fire mission on a religious compound, and a reported attack by coalition aircraft on a "wedding party" that allegedly resulted in numerous civilian casualties. Each of these engagements highlighted certain aspects of the targeting issues that have been discussed so far.

In the spring of 2002, two US fighter jets were returning from a mission over Afghanistan when one observed tracers rounds shooting into the air towards their aircraft. One pilot requested authority from his command center to attack the source of the tracer rounds. The other pilot almost immediately declared he was going to attack out of self-defense. He dropped ordnance on the source of the tracer fire, resulting in the deaths and injuries to numerous Canadian soldiers who were simply firing their weapons on a practice range in Afghanistan. The difficulty in identifying the source of the tracer rounds underscored the reasons behind requiring positive identification of targets in our ROE. This was almost always the primary issue when vetting calls for fire. In this particular incident, a joint investigation was conducted to identify the cause of the tragic friendly-fire incident and assess any responsibility or other action necessary to prevent a reoccurrence. On the modern battlefield, especially in the fog of combat, target identification is always going to be extremely difficult. Today, however, expectations are much higher on accurate determinations and much less tolerance exists for mistakes such as this.

In another instance, a small joint Pakistani-Coalition patrol received fire near the Pakistani border. One US soldier was seriously injured. The apparent source of the firing was an individual located in a Mandrassa, an Islamic religious center. We quickly tried to acquire as much information as possible concerning the event before responding to the request for fire support. Aircraft with ordnance were circling above the proposed target, the Mandrassa itself. A Mandrassa, a Holy place under local culture, would normally be considered a protected place under the law of war. This protected status would cease once used by enemy forces for military purposes. The first issue was the location of the Mandrassa. Initial reports placed it just inside the

Pakistani border. Our ROE would allow our forces to defend themselves from attacks from anywhere, but the sensitivity of a cross-border response was foremost in our minds, especially if this was not a self-defense scenario. Another major concern was the imminence of the threat. Initial facts were indicating our forces were no longer under any attack. Under those circumstances, any offensive action on our part was more difficult to justify without more evidence of an imminent threat from the individual in the Mandrassa. Another serious legal issue concerned the status of a protected place under the law of war when used for military purposes and the possibility of collateral damage from other people, if any, in the facility. A subsequent report indicated hostile fire was originating from the Mandrassa. The entire targeting process became academic, however, when the senior patrol member on the ground declared a self-defense emergency and brought the circling aircraft down to attack. The Mandrassa was finally determined to be in Afghanistan so the cross-border issue became irrelevant. Fortunately, the Mandrassa was essentially unscathed by the attack and no civilian casualties were reported. The enemy firing stopped immediately after the aircraft attack and local authorities took control of the scene. The conclusion drawn from our experience in this particular scenario was that the Targeting Process continued to work, despite the incomplete reporting. Absent the declaration of self-defense by the ground force commander, our command would have been hard pressed to give consent for the attack absent more facts or evidence of hostile intent or imminent threat.

The most serious targeting issue during my deployment occurred within months of my arrival, in July of 2002. A US Air Force AC-130 gunship was supporting an ongoing operation in the vicinity of Deh Rawod. A CJTF-180 ground force was about to be inserted aboard CH-47 Chinook helicopters and conduct a cordon and search of suspected Taliban compounds. While circling one particular compound, observers on the aircraft noticed an anti-aircraft weapon firing directly at them from within the compound. The AC-130 then provided suppressive fires on that compound. It subsequently attacked several other compounds that had fired anti-aircraft weapons that night.

It was later reported in various news media a "wedding celebration," including traditional celebratory rifle fire into the air, had been attacked in one of the compounds in Deh Rawod. Casualties were estimated to be more than a hundred, including many woman and children. The international attention given to the incident prompted an immediate response from the coalition. An initial Afghan-CJTF-180 joint fact-finding investigation was conducted within 3 days of the attack, interviewing victims and other witnesses. A more comprehensive Afghan-CJTF-180 joint formal investigation was also conducted. The assessment of the investigations concluded that the attack by the AC-130 probably did result in significant civilian casualties, but was a reasonable response in self-defense under our ROE. There was ample evidence of hostile acts and hostile intent at each of the targeted compounds.

The unfortunate civilian casualties and collateral damage was tragic under any circumstances, but the immediate efforts to jointly investigate and meet with the local Afghans served to mitigate the associated fallout from the incident. War can be unbelievably violent and unpredictable. This particular example underscored that point in the extreme. It also demonstrated that even in a modern battlefield with the latest technology available, tragic events with collateral damage are often unavoidable.

An interesting observation made during the investigation into the tragic incident at Deh Rawod revealed some insight on the attitudes and perceptions of the local population who lived near one of the targeted compounds. One of the fact-finders was gathering information by walking around the compound where most of the casualties allegedly occurred. In one small room, there were two drawings on the hardened mud walls that appeared to depict an Afghan firing a machine gun at helicopters. The local representatives said it was a picture from years previously when the Russians were in Afghanistan. Local nationals repeatedly denied any animosity towards coalition or support for the Taliban. The fact-finder touched the painting and noted it was still wet from having been drawn in the preceding days. Someone had rubbed berries on the wall and the debris from the crushed berries lay beneath the pictures on the ground. It was arguable the pictures represented animosity towards coalition aircraft in the area, contrary to the comments of the local representatives. Conversely, it may mean nothing at all but was an interesting observation nonetheless.

In conclusion, several points concerning targeting can be drawn from the experiences of CJTF-180 during OEF in Afghanistan. The main learning point is recognizing the modern battlefield requires more legal advice and support than ever contemplated. Greater use of precise munitions heightened expectations of commanders and the public in the coalition's ability to strike when and where it wanted with minimal risk of collateral damage. Neither precision munitions nor human judgment are perfect and mistakes will occur. When they do occur, public outcry will be as vocal as ever, often pointing to the failure to meet the heightened expectations. Moreover, access to the battlefield is much greater and the flow of information much quicker than at anytime in our history. Information sent through the Internet or direct feeds of visual media through satellite technology ensures the world will have the quickest and most complete access to events unfolding in the world. An expectation has been placed on commanders making correct targeting decisions every time. Our operations in Afghanistan were not an anomaly, but the new norm of the modern asymmetric battlefield.

Seminar A:
Humanitarian Intervention and Preemption

*Justin McClelland**

Both Humanitarian Intervention and Pre-emption are controversial issues in international law. The Seminar discussions reflected in many ways the tension that exists between what was felt instinctively as being morally right or unequivocally sensible on the one hand and what current international law was equipped to deal with or able to bear on the other. This presented as sharp but cordial divisions within the group regarding both concepts. In essence the group "agreed to disagree agreeably".

Humanitarian Intervention

The group began by considering our understanding of the term "Humanitarian Intervention". There was a consensus that, despite it not possessing any legal significance itself, it had negative connotations as it struck at the heart of state sovereignty. Alternative terms suggested initially drew upon the ICISS project entitled "Responsibility to Protect" which assisted in shifting the focus away from the controversy regarding intervention with sovereignty. Additionally, "Humanitarian Rescue" was considered as encapsulating to some extent the nature of the emergency that Humanitarian Intervention concept symbolised.

There was agreement that in the understanding of the group, a Humanitarian Intervention would be considered to have taken place only if it had been conducted without UN authorisation, as with UN SC authorisation it would be considered as a Chapter VII action. Acknowledging the that the UN SC had difficulties in addressing

*   Lieutenant-Colonel, Joint Doctrine and Concepts Centre, Ministry of Defence, United Kingdom, e-mail: mcclellandjustin@hotmail.com.

Harvey Langholtz, Boris Kondoch, Alan Wells (Eds.),
International Peacekeeping: The Yearbook of International Peace Operations, Volume 9, 2004, pp. 229-232.
© *Koninklijke Brill N.V. Printed in the Netherlands*

humanitarian situations in the past, the group was almost unanimous in its view that there would be situations in which humanitarian catastrophes would occur which would require action by the international community in the absence of action by the sovereign state in which the catastrophe was taking place.

The group was split, however, on the question of whether Humanitarian Intervention, as it would always be without UN SC authorisation would ever be legal. A view held by a significant number of participants was to the effect that Humanitarian Intervention runs counter to the UN Charter.

Assuming that the UN SC had not addressed the problem (for whatever reason) and considering in the abstract the problem of what could be done, the group addressed the thresholds at which such catastrophes would warrant Humanitarian Intervention. A number of variations of the possible criteria were discussed including those of the ICISS, the UK Foreign and Commonwealth Office, and academics including those of Major General (ret.) APV Rogers (from his presentation to the conference). The criteria adopted by the group included:

- a humanitarian catastrophe in progress which was exceptional in nature and extent. This would be characterized by large-scale loss of life or the imminent threat of such large scale loss of life. It was noted that the media had in the past played a significant role in raising awareness of the international public to situations that states had been "blind" to;
- a failure by the sovereign state in which the catastrophe was occurring to address the situation;
- preferably some form of UN acknowledgement/resolution/determination that the situation had reached such levels (but without UN SC resolution authorizing response as otherwise it would not fit the group's understanding of Humanitarian Intervention);
- all UN "routes" had to have been exhausted;
- intervention in the situation by the "international community", i.e. collective action by *ad hoc* or regional security organisation;
- exhaustion of all non-military force options in addressing the situation i.e. military force be the last resort;
- use of force must be necessary and proportionate.

The determination of whether these thresholds had been met could not be left to individual states. The requirement for collective action would go some way to easing this problem. Additionally, the potential for the UN SC to reach a compromise solution of determining the nature of the situation without authorizing action could provide a common "start point" for action. The information provided by OSCE in re Kosovo was cited as an example of such an independent approach to information-gathering on a developing situation.

Previous examples of Humanitarian Interventions had been conducted upon the basis, *inter alia*, of self-defence. This had contributed to two problems: the lack of any unambiguous precedent for Humanitarian Intervention, and; the fuelling of scepticism regarding the ulterior motives of the states involved in the Humanitarian Intervention. Accordingly, in order to eradicate these problems the humanitarian basis of the intervention should be unequivocally declared from the outset.

Allied to this was the need to generate a long-term plan to address the humanitarian problem. Without a holistic approach it would be difficult to demonstrate that the Humanitarian Intervention had a realistic prospect of success, a factor considered important in assuring the international community that the Humanitarian Intervention would alleviate and not exacerbate the situation. One example was the need, where appropriate, to consider the prosecution of persons involved in creating or perpetuating the humanitarian crisis so as publicly and legitimately to remove them from the "equation".

Finally, the conclusions reached in respect of Humanitarian Intervention represented an uneasy compromise in a situation where politics had the potential to "outshine" morality. Whilst recognised as unrealistic some called for the UN Charter to be revisited, whether by reference to a Code of Conduct for the UN SC or by a wholesale re-engineering of the mechanisms within the UN.

Pre-Emptive Self Defence

Those divisions that existed within the group regarding Humanitarian Intervention again showed themselves regarding pre-emptive self defence. The divisions mirrored what had been described within presentations as the "literalist" and the "creativist" (vis-a-vis the interpretation of the UN Charter), namely a prohibition against using pre-emptive self-defence and a limited authority for such action.

Several different terms had been used to describe what the term "pre-emptive self defence" was meant to convey. Such terms included "preventive", "anticipatory" and "interceptive". The relationship between these terms was deliberately avoided owing to constraints of time. However, it was noted that the proliferation of such terms could only serve to complicate an already controversial area of law. Further, the use of terms which were also military in nature (e.g. pre-emptive strike) in what is essentially a military context (i.e. the use of military force) introduced unwelcome cross-pollination of understanding.

Agreement existed that any pre-emptive self defence should be preceded by a period of preventive diplomacy. This could take the form of negotiation through appropriate media with the source of the threat. This would be possible whether the threat was state or non-state actor-related.

Whilst pre-emptive self-defence had been discussed in the context of states the group was particularly concerned to explore the concept with respect to non-state actors adopting terrorist methods. This accorded with the tenor of the presentations at the conference as well as that of international discussions. It was important in dealing with such a situation post-Sept. 11 to retain sight of the "basic principles". Whilst Sept. 11 in many ways marked a watershed regarding the international approach to terrorism, it also had the potential unduly to skew thinking on this area. It was viewed by some as lowering the levels of tolerance of terrorism internationally.

Noting such basic principles, if non-state actors acted within a state then the matter was essentially domestic in nature. Orthodox policing measures would therefore be required. State support of terrorist non-state actors, which could manifest itself in a variety of forms, would raise the issue to one of international importance. At the international level a number of options existed before resort to the use of military force. Transnational policing which it was noted was increasing and successful and should be considered.

The use of military force in a 3rd state in respect of non-state actors terrorists generated division along the lines of the "literalist" and "creativist" schools. Those of the literalist school could not countenance pre-emptive self defence. Those of the creativist school welcomed the scope for proactive self preservation that pre-emptive self defence provided.

The sharp division within the group over the legality of pre-emptive self-defence dominated and limited discussion of the threshold of threats that would warrant such pre-emptive action being taken against NSAs in 3rd states. However, dealing with the issue hypothetically, if such action was ever to be considered as legal then there was some agreement that it would be exceptional and in response to an extreme threat. Further, there had to be some evidence to justify such action which would withstand international scrutiny, most notably by the UN SC.

Seminar B:
Targeting Norms and International Humanitarian Law

David Jividen*

Seminar B set forth two goals, one general and one specific. First, we tried to identify those factors that have had an affect on selection of targets, and hence perhaps on targeting norms in the past, and those which will have an effect in the future. Then, we took one of the factors that we envisioned having a direct effect on the practice of targeting in the future, (either via a change in interpretation of current law, or a change in the law itself) and analyzed it a little more in depth.

The Seminar's first meeting identified several factors bearing on the selection of targets in the past. One was selection of the targeting objectives keeping in mind "post-war reconstruction" requirements. Targets such as the electrical power grids, communication and command infrastructure, as well as other essential transportation infrastructure needed for reconstruction purposes were, and likely will be, very closely scrutinized for appropriateness despite the validity of some of these target sets under targeting law. This restrictive approach to targeting, characterized by one participant as "extremely restrictive" also helps relieve tactical logistic pressure on the attacking force, that is, the more of an opponents logistical structure that remains intact, the less resources the attacking force will need when that area of a country is captured. Finally, one factor that directly impacts target selection is a particular county's adherence to multilateral treaties or conventions that impose a stricter standard on target selection then otherwise permissible under customary law or the laws of war.

This last factor led the seminar group to consider factors that will continue to affect targeting in the future, coalition operations; differing capabilities, and differing interpretation of targeting law. With regard to the first factor, coalition operations,

---

*   Lieutenant-Colonel, Assistant Judge Advocate, Joint Staff, Pentagon, e-mail: david.jividen@js.pentagon.mil.

Harvey Langholtz, Boris Kondoch, Alan Wells (Eds.),
International Peacekeeping: The Yearbook of International Peace Operations, Volume 9, 2004, pp. 233-236.
© *Koninklijke Brill N.V. Printed in the Netherlands*

the fact that in one coalition two nations may have two different targeting guide-lines stemming from different international obligations, presents unique issues that bear study. One, for example, is the extent of cooperative responsibility for a tar-get an ally might destroy, which would have been prohibited by the other ally adher-ing to a regional multilateral treaty. Other factors looming larger in the future that could create disparate targeting guidelines between allies, and changes in targeting law generally, include dual use targets and the whole area of information operations.

The group concluded the first meeting with a discussion of the role individual judgment plays in proportionality decisions with regard to the permissibility of tar-geting, and the effect, if any, of the increased use of precision munitions on the a state's ability to revert to the use of "dumb munitions" in its arsenal. The group concluded that the collateral damage and proportionality rules, under the law of armed conflict, will not become bifurcated, with two potential standards or a slid-ing scale, depending on the ability of the state of use of precision munitions, rather, the law should continue to have one standard.

During the second seminar meeting, the group decided to focus on the legal concept of proportionality. This rule, which prohibits incidental excessive death and injury to civilians and/or excessive damage to civilian objects in relation to the destruction of a military target, is simple to state but difficult to use *a priori* to a specific targeting situation, battle, campaign, or war. Nevertheless, the seminar agreed that the proportionality process itself, that is, actively enunciating the target, the military advantage anticipated from attacking the target, and an analysis of the resul-tant collateral damage due to the attack – is central to the decision maker and the rule of law. This holds true whether the person performing the proportionality test is a military or political official. As one participant put it with regard to the rule of law, "the process is $^1/_2$ the battle."

Similarly, some in the seminar noted that the proportionality test and the prin-ciple of discrimination (which attempts to identify and distinguish proper military objectives) often overlap in practice. This occurs at the point when the type and amount of collateral damage is being calculated – property and persons have to be clearly demarcated as non-military targets in order to correctly assess the amount of collateral damage.

The seminar also noted that the proportionality weighing test is affected by the choice of weapon, and angle of attack, and weather etc., and it was in this context of the discussion that the participants raised the issue of whether, for types of weapons and uses of weapons not explicitly prohibited in the law of armed conflict, there is any one weapon system that would never pass the proportionality test, that is, is there an "upper level of collateral destructiveness" caused by a weapon that would ever preclude attacking a particular target set with a particular weapon. After some lively discussion, the seminar decided there was, in fact, no upper limit. This is because proportionality tests, including particular ceilings or civilian collateral damage, are made before or during a particular conflict, that is, they are fundamentally "attack-dependent." This is true whether one is talking about the irreducible *legal* minimum on civilian damage imposed by the proportionality test, or the cap on civilian damage imposed due to *political considerations*. The former legal limitation is set by the military objective and potential collateral damage within the totality of the circumstances at the time of the targeting, the latter limitation is set by policy makers making political decisions after weighing a myriad of factors, such as the "CNN factor." A citation was made also to the ICJ Advisory Opinion on the Use of Nuclear Weapons, wherein the court refused to declare the mere possession or use of nuclear weapons illegal.

Finally, the seminar participants identified fighting methodologies, increasingly raised by current conflicts that have complicated the proportionality-weighing test. These include dual use targets, suicide bombers, and perfidy.

During the last two seminar meetings, the group focused on effects-based targeting, especially as it relates to information operations or warfare. The seminar first tackled "effects-based" targeting as it related to *jus ad bellum*, inquiring whether an non-kinetic "electronic" "computer" attack, or a kinetic "effects-based" "attack" would fall into the international legal category of "armed attack" triggering a nation's right of self-defense under customary law as recognized by the UN Charter. The majority of the seminar agreed that an attack on a country's vital functions via an electronic or similar effects based "attack," for example, shutting down the whole of, or a portion of a nation's electronic grid, banking system, water supplies etc., could constitute an "armed attack" under international law. Some in the seminar, however, opined that they would require a direct or immediate loss of life as a result of the attack before they would characterize such an action as a "attack" permitting an armed response. Some in the seminar, although they disagreed with this requirement nonetheless noted that in such a case, it would wise for those making targeting decisions to consider the "CNN factor" when selecting targets for attack in self-defense.

These latter points lead the seminar to analyzed effects-based targeting as it relates to the proportionality test. Specifically, once a nation is involved in a war or conflict, how does effects-based targeting relate to proportionality balancing test? The issue identified at the onset of this discussion revolved around the difficulty in properly identifying collateral damage and weighing this against the advantage achieved through the destruction of the military objective. What "effects" caused by an effects-based attack is the attacking party legally responsible for (and thus should enter into the proportionality calculation). Should "collateral damage" estimates only attempt to measure the primary effect of an attack, or does responsibility extend to secondary, or even tertiary effects. Are these effects resulting from an effects-based attack even calculable? Even more fundamentally, can a proper weighing of an effects-based attack ever take place under a proportionality test, given the subjective nature of the proportionality test and the fact that effects-based targeting is measuring collateral damage of a nature more removed then traditional collateral damage estimates.

The seminar came to several conclusions with regard to these questions. First, the seminar noted that identifying effects-based collateral damage is a difficult endeavor, but not impossible in some cases. Intelligence should be used to identify critical nodes of a civilian community, such as a communicative, or transportation, or health systems, and, using statistical analytical techniques, attempt to assess and perhaps reduce the primary damage to these facilities as a result of an effects-based attack. At some point however, the group noted that such an analysis becomes progressively more difficult as the effects analysis proceeds to the secondary and tertiary effects. The group noted that perhaps the international legal community could import concepts found in civil law to determine at what point responsibility of an effects-based attack would end. "Reasonable forseeability" is one such concept identified by the group. Some in the group also sounded a note of caution, advising against wholesale importation of civil law concepts into the laws of war involving targeting absent adjustment to recognize the unique nature of war. Finally, the seminar concluded that the increasing urbanization of nations and communities, and the increasing reliance on computers for critical functions, is sure to keep effects-based targeting questions in the forefront of future military operations.

Seminar C:
The Rule of Law in Post-Conflict Situations:
Conflict Termination, Legitimacy, and Peace Building

*Lewis Bumgardner**

Using the seminar's title as a thesis statement and recent events in Kosovo, Afghanistan, and Iraq as case studies, the group attempted to identify significant legal concepts illustrated by these conflicts. Referencing primary documents such as UN Security Council Resolutions, accords like the Bonn Agreement that re-established permanent government institutions in post-conflict Afghanistan, and the scholarly knowledge of the participants, the group developed by consensus nine broad criteria to compare the post-conflict situations in Kosovo, Afghanistan, and Iraq. The first two meetings considered these nine criteria. The final session considered the influence of history and other factors for state building and the rule of law in post-conflict situations.

In list form, the nine criteria identified and examined were: 1) the legal framework of the post-conflict state; 2) the reason for the international presence on the territory of the post-conflict state; 3) the chapter of the UN Charter that provides authority for actions; 4) specific tasks of the international presence; 5) the role of the United Nations; 6) the role of agreement by the post-conflict state; 7) identification of who is in charge; 8) the role of local institutions; and 9) the timeframe for post-conflict resolution. In the three meetings held by the group the sharp contours of each topic graphically presented themselves.

In describing the *first* criteria, the legal framework of the post-conflict state, the interplay of multiple layers of law quickly became apparent. In addition to UN Security Council resolutions, cease-fire agreements, armistices, and peace treaties that attempt to control or characterise actions in the post-conflict state, other laws

---

* Colonel, US Marine Corps, Staff Judge Advocate, US Marine Corps Forces Atlantic, e-mail: bumgardnersl@marforlant.usmc.mil.

Harvey Langholtz, Boris Kondoch, Alan Wells (Eds.),
International Peacekeeping: The Yearbook of International Peace Operations, Volume 9, 2004, pp. 237-240.
© *Koninklijke Brill N.V. Printed in the Netherlands*

have important effect. These start with international humanitarian law (the law of war or the law of armed conflict) that specifically describes expected conduct and processes during an occupation. Human rights law may require actions where obligations created in international humanitarian law do not control. International treaties establish legal responsibilities either because they were acceded to and have continuing effect on the post-conflict states or because they bind forces of sending states. Status of forces agreements also formalise and create legally enforceable relations between the post-conflict state and sending state forces. Customary international law is always present in the interactions of states during a post-conflict period. So also is the pre-existing domestic or municipal legal code of the post-conflict state, the domestic law of any sending states of foreign military forces, and any emerging law established by the creation of a new constitution or domestic and municipal codes.

While the sources of law for a post-conflict state may be rich and numerous, it was recognised that this legal tapestry can be accurately described by only referencing the political and historical context in which it exists. To this end the *second* criteria used by the group posed the question, "What were the reasons for an international presence on the territory of the post-conflict state?" For each of the three case studies considered, circumstances produced a unique answer. In *Kosovo* the reason given for the international intervention was to prevent the continuance of a humanitarian disaster. In *Afghanistan* the international presence sprang from the response to the devastating attacks of 11 September 2001 on the United States. With regard to *Iraq*, the United States and Great Britain described their reason for the conflict in 2003 as an exercise of pre-emptive self-defence in response to threatening a rogue regime.

The *third* criteria used by the group – what chapter of the UN Charter authorised action – found Chapter VII was cited by states in all three cases although only in the case of Afghanistan did Security Council resolutions precede the conflict. However, inquiries about the specific tasks of the international presence on the territory of the post-conflict state, the actors, and the role played by various international organisations including the UN – the *fourth* and *fifth* criteria; agreement by the post-conflict state concerned – the *sixth* criteria; the question of who was in charge – the *seventh* criteria; the role of local institutions – the *eighth* criteria; and, finally, a timeframe for post-conflict resolution – the *ninth* criteria; all produced distinctly different results for the three post-conflict situations examined.

In *Kosovo* the primary actors were found to be NATO and the United Nations. The concrete tasks of security and demining were determined to be military responsibilities undertaken by NATO. The task of reconstruction was found to be a civilian responsibility conducted by various international humanitarian organisations generally co-ordinated and controlled by an Interim Authority appointed by the United Nations. The date of a hand-over of these military and civilian tasks to an established local government in Kosovo was hard for Seminar C to determine or predict.

In *Afghanistan* a local government was needed quickly. With this need foremost, the primary actors were found to be Afghan Interim Authority (established by the Bonn Agreement), the International Security Assistance Force, and the Special Representative of the Secretary General (SRSG). The concrete task of providing security in Kabul was identified as a task of the Afghan Interim Authority supported by the International Security Assistance Force. The SRSG was also identified as having an assisting role with the Afghan Interim Authority by overseeing implementation of all elements of the Bonn Agreement, investigating human rights violations, and implementing human rights education. Specific dates for the conclusion of the activities of the Afghan Interim Authority and the transfer of all authority to a newly organised and permanent government are contained in the Bonn Agreement.

In *Iraq* the primary actors were the United States and the United Kingdom for all tasks, military and civilian. While the Security Council is to be briefed periodically concerning the progress of post-conflict activities and a Special Representative of the Secretary General (SRSG) was assigned, the group concluded the UN's role to be neither significant nor strong. Unlike Afghanistan where consent to activities by the post-conflict state was built into the Bonn Agreement, the United States and the United Kingdom have not effectively established a representative of the Iraqi people. Consequently, like Kosovo, no clear date or certain timetable exists for the transfer of post-conflict activities from the United States and the United Kingdom to a newly organised post-conflict Iraqi government.

At its final meeting the returned to a consideration of the influence of historical events and numerous other factors critical to the successful establishment of the rule of law in post-conflict reconstruction. Appreciating that events as remote as the 1389 Battle of Kosovo Polje, as recent as the decade of Security Council Resolutions aimed at Iraq following the Gulf War, or as sudden as the 9/11 attack had a continuing and powerful effect on post-conflict states, Seminar C concluded the rule of law in post-conflict situations must specifically address history. This acknowledgment quickly led to the identification of a large number of other topics necessary for successful state building in post-conflict situations. A listing of these include: sociological, cultural, and religious factors; the creation of state institutions based on the rule of law, economic factors, psychological factors; the role of print and broadcast media; the role of multinational regional alliances; the role of non-government organisations, experts, local people and; threats to the peace process.

While many of these topics raise matters outside of the direct competence of a military legal office or even a Ministry of Defence legal office, all are important factors for the establishment of the rule of law in a post-conflict situation. The sociological, cultural, and religious factors that include ethnic and religious differences have to be addressed in a manner that effectively provides security and fairness for all in the post-conflict country. Informal networks or so-called shadow governments that may once have exercised significant authority over citizens have to be confronted in post-conflict activities to ensure transparency exists during the peace building

process. Economic factors ranging from needs springing from individual poverty to
the settling of debts incurred by the former regime or exacted as compensation for
the cost of the war, to the distribution of natural resources all require solutions found
in the rule of law. Psychological factors such as the identification of the population
with the "new" post-conflict state, public acceptance of foreign forces, and the
important issue of a culture collectively moving beyond the conflict also requires
considerable legal attention.

Participants recognised the means used to address the sociological, economic,
and psychological factors that exist in a post-conflict state always would be scruti-
nised for their legality and legitimacy. Would criminal trials or truth and reconciliation commissions be used to sanction and resolve past misconduct? How would
print and broadcast media be governed to permit the free flow of information and
opinion building while controlled to ensure accuracy and the participation of all
groups? As these questions are answered the vigorous interaction would continue
between the people, the existing government, armed forces of sending states, and
international and domestic organisations and entities. Only by the constructive interplay of these many topics and factors a post-conflict state can move from negative
peace – the mere cessation of hostilities – to positive peace and return to the community of nations as an effective and self-sustaining partner.

Three conclusions arose from these discussions. *First*, while every post-conflict
situation is different, goals, resources, and risk form the boundary where the rule
of law must build legitimacy. In this context unique sociological, cultural, religious
and other factors must be appreciated and acted upon for the creation of an effective state system based on the rule of law. *Second*, common lessons learned from
the too numerous post-conflict situations of the 20th Century must be considered.
The costly experiences in Iraq, Somalia, Afghanistan, East Timor, Bosnia, Chechnya,
Germany, Japan, and Italy have value only if remembered. To that end, the web-
sites of the U.S. Army War College <http://carlisle-www.army.mil/>, The Carr Center
For Human Rights at the John F. Kennedy School of Government, Harvard University
<http://www.ksg.harvard.edu/cchrp/>, and others might be consulted as resources
for these lessons learned. *Finally*, participants specifically acknowledged one of the
conclusions reached by the International Commission on Intervention and State
Sovereignty in its 2001 report titled, *The Responsibility to Protect*, <http://www.dfait-
maeci.gc.ca/iciss-ciise/00_Intro-en.asp>. In this report the limits to occupation and
post-conflict obligations are considered under the title of "The Responsibility To
Rebuild." Although complete agreement was not reached concerning which actors
in post-conflict situations should have the greatest role in fulfilling this obligation,
the group accepted the responsibility to rebuild as integral to the creation of positive peace, legitimacy, and the rule of law in post-conflict situations.

Reflections on the War in Iraq

Noëlle Quénivet*

On 27 June 2003 the Institute for International Law of Peace and Armed Conflict (IFHV) of the Ruhr-University of Bochum organised, in collaboration with the German Red Cross, a conference entitled "Reflections on the War in Iraq" in The Hague. The conference aimed to present different political and legal perspectives on the recent armed conflict waged by the United States and its allies against Iraq. In this regard the organisers of the conference opted for an interesting setting, thereby offering the audience a bigger choice in presentations.

First, all participants to the conference met in the plenary session where Prof. Dr. Joachim Wolf, the director of the IFHV, welcomed the audience and introduced the various speakers before leaving the floor to the keynote speaker, Mr. Howard Roy Williams, President of the Center for Humanitarian Cooperation (USA) and Former Director of the Office of Foreign Disaster Assistance at USAID.

Mr. Williams started his presentation by pondering on the recent changes in the provision of humanitarian assistance.[1] From the very beginning of his speech, Mr. Williams began discussing the most current hot issue, namely the relationship between international humanitarian law, humanitarian assistance, military action and political discussions. Without a shimmer of doubt this issue is probably the most topical, especially in the light of the recent operations led by the US in Iraq and in Afghanistan.

First, Mr. Williams described the connections between the four aforementioned topics, stressing that, until recently, they had followed separate lines, baring the

---

*   Noëlle Quénivet is research associate at the Institute for International Law of Peace and Armed Conflict of the Ruhr-University of Bochum in Germany. She is also a PhD candidate in international law at the University of Essex in the United Kingdom.
1   Howard Roy Williams, "The Changing Understandings of the Nature of Humanitarian Assistance and the Longer-Term Implications for the Role of International Humanitarian Law", (2003) 3 *Humanitäres Völkerrecht-Informationsschriften* 119-121.

241

Harvey Langholtz, Boris Kondoch, Alan Wells (Eds.),
International Peacekeeping: The Yearbook of International Peace Operations, Volume 9, 2004, pp. 241-251.
© *Koninklijke Brill N.V. Printed in the Netherlands*

exception of international humanitarian law which was always linked to the existence of military action in the field.

Then, turning to humanitarian assistance, a field in which the speaker has an
impressive knowledge, Mr. Williams pointed out that the scope of and the circumstances surrounding humanitarian assistance have greatly changed the situation on
the ground. The growing number of organisations involved in this field and the rising amounts of money spent in providing humanitarian assistance led many to question their work and their efficiency. Part of the problem lies in their co-operation
on the ground with international organisations. An excellent example of this global
humanitarian system is provided by the armed conflict in Bosnia-Herzegovina where
UNHCR became the leading agency for purposes of providing assistance, thereby
working hand in hand with NGOs.

Relief workers are, according to the statute of the organisation for which they
work, impartial and neutral. This is particularly underlined in the Code of Conduct
for the International Red Cross and Red Crescent Movement and NGOs in Disaster
Relief. Another trait of character of relief workers is the moral imperative to assist
populations in danger. According to Mr. Williams, this means that workers take
decisions based on assessments and subsequent determination of needs without referring to a particular political agenda or to international humanitarian law. In the mind
of workers, their job needs to be and is clearly separated from military operations
and political decisions.

In the 90s the NGO commitment to the humanitarian imperative was severely
tested. By taking the situation in refugee camps in Goma (Zaire), Mr. Williams convincingly showed how NGOs were caught in the crossfire. Pointing at the perva-
sive human rights violations and at the psychological consequences to the individual
relief worker, many NGOs pulled out of Goma, leaving behind the population they
were supposed to be helping. For the first time, one spoke of "humanitarian disasters" referring to a situation where, because NGOs had failed, the international community, looking for a responsible and leading actor, pointed at the failure of political
will. Suddenly the politicians understood the importance of humanitarian assistance
when taking decisions.

Another step in the evolution of the provision of humanitarian assistance is the
growing misuse of the word "humanitarian" in order to provide the international
community with a friendly perception of the situation on the ground. The behaviour of the international community is consequently highly influenced by immediate events and perceptions and not by law. For example, much of the public attention
was focused on the plight of the Afghan people rather than on the operations carried out against terrorists.

The latest relief operations carried out by the international humanitarian assistance community showed the growing interaction between the military and the
NGOs. The major clash concerns the application of the principles of neutrality,

impartiality and independence that are so dear to the NGO community. The new formula applied to Afghanistan but incorporating elements of the civilian authorities with the military in a leading role met the initial reluctance of NGOs. Yet, with time passing, the co-operation turned out to be fruitful, the complaint being now that the security is still not assured. Much of what was going in Iraq at that time could be see as a repetition of the Afghan scenario. Mr. Williams stressed that "relief is an objective and accomplishing it seems to be increasingly a matter of an engineering approach".

After this excellent introduction to the conference, the audience split into three groups, each of them offering three presentations. The first group focused on issues discussed before the operations were launched in Iraq, the second group dealt with the armed conflict itself and the third concentrated on the consequences of this armed conflict.

The first group started with the presentation of Dr. Mark Gose, the political advisor to the Commander of the US Air Forces in Europe. Dr. Gose convincingly presented to the audience the National Security Strategy of the United States adopted in September 2002 following the tragic event of September 11th.[2] Dr. Gose clearly presented the American standpoint on the reasons for waging war against Iraq. His remarkable skills as a honest and accurate speaker appealed to even the most engaged anti-American person. It was, in fact, refreshing and intellectually challenging to listen to a neat and rational presentation of the US strategy, far away from the typical anti-American discourse that had swept Europe in the last few months.

The reasoning behind the adoption of this new doctrine is the massive changes to which the US and more generally the world have recently been exposed. "The world face dangers much different from those traditional threats of the past." Nevertheless, Dr. Gose points out that this strategy was designed well before September 11th, already taking shape in 1997 when a report elaborating a new strategy was published in the Quadrennial Defense Review.

A characteristic of this new world is the increasing link between radical actors and technology, notably that of weapons. The new enemy is supranational in the sense that it is without borders, does not share common views on national, societal or international behaviour and is able to strike anywhere at any time. Dr. Gose admits that this threat is not new; it existed in the past but its dimension revealed by the September 11th attack calls for a new strategy.

The US has moved from the threat-based model to the capabilities-based model which aims to identify, develop and then use all necessary abilities, systems and

---

2   Mark N. Gose, "The New US National Security Strategy: Meeting New Challenges in a Changed World", (2003) 3 *Humanitäres Völkerrecht-Informationsschriften* 121-124.

methods to ensure the survival of the American State. The new strategy is based on five pillars, each of them thoroughly examined by Dr. Gose. The first and main goal of the US is to defend itself, its population and its interests by pinpointing and destroying the threat before it harms. The second aim is to transform the instruments of national defence. The third and the fourth encourage the US to strengthen alliances and work with other nations in the fight against terrorism and to enhance agendas for co-operative action with other big powers. Last but not least the US aims to prevent enemies from threatening friends and allies with weapons of mass destruction.

Turning to the major disagreements that raged between the US and its European allies before the inception of the conflict in Iraq, Dr. Gose explains that, in his opinion, the differing views relate to the differing perceptions of "the true nature of these dangerous threats" and "the continued utility of trying to deter these adversaries". Whereas the US sees Iraq as part of the terrorist parcel, European States tend to conceive of Iraq and Al Qaeda as two separate issues that need to be handled differently. Western States are also reluctant to accept the terminology of deterrence as understood by the US. Deterrence, in the past, worked because the enemies were rational and both aware of and averse to the consequences of the use of certain weapons. Yet, the current enemy is nowhere near this shared understanding and, therefore, deterrence cannot work. In conclusion, Dr. Gose stressed that what is feasible and workable is a preventive strategy of defence in case of an imminent threat.

The next presentation discussed the resolutions adopted by the UN Security Council pertaining to Iraq and the US operation.[3] Dr. Erika De Wet, an expert in international law attached to the Amsterdam Centre for International Law in the Netherlands, has been working much on the role and powers of the UN Security Council and was, hence, a suitable speaker on such a controversial issue. Convincingly, Dr. de Wet demonstrated that neither the principle of self-defence nor resolution 678 (1990) in combination with resolution 687 (1991) provided a legal basis for the full scale operation launched by the US and the United Kingdom on 17 March 2003. In her opinion, the operation could only have been considered as legally justified, had a UN Security Council resolution explicitly authorised these States to use all necessary measures to disarm Iraq. Such a reference cannot be found in the last resolution adopted prior to the intervention since the text only mentioned the establishment of an enhanced inspection regime. Even the wording relating to the "serious consequences" if Iraq would violate its international obligations cannot be considered as an authorisation to use force.

---

3   Erika de Wet, "The Illegality of the Use of Force Against Iraq Subsequent to the Adoption of Resolution 687 (1991)", (2003) 3 *Humanitäres Völkerrecht-Informationsschriften* 125-132.

In addition, the failure of the Security Council to act did not mean that the US were free to act. To the claim that the US acted in self-defence to the Iraqi threat, Dr. De Wet answered that it could not form, under the given circumstances, a legal basis for military action because no armed attack had occurred.

Unlike the operations led by NATO in Kosovo in 1999, the military operations that took place in Iraq could not be justified on the basis of an *ex post facto* authorisation. Resolution 1483 adopted on 22 May 2003 merely recognised the US and the UK as the occupying "authority" and authorised their administration. Yet, it does not refer to the earlier operations and hence does not grant them either legitimacy or legality.

Dr. De Wet, although near to speaking of aggression, never used that word and, instead, referred to it as an invasion by the US and the UK. It is regrettable that the speaker did not further elaborate on the use of these terms although it must be admitted that her presentation did not aim at qualifying the operations but at investigating whether their legality could be grounded in the UN Security Council resolutions.

The last speaker on pre-intervention issues was Prof. Dr. Wolf, director of the Institute for International Law of Peace and Armed Conflict and holder of the Chair of Public Law of the University of Bochum. Prof. Wolf took up an important issue, that is of the role played by the media in the global anti-terror war started by the US. There is no doubt that the images of the attacks of September 11th will stay in the memory of many viewers. According to the speaker, this event endowed the media with a new task, namely to support the US in its campaign against terrorism. In order to do so, the media are simply reiterating facts and opinions expressed by either the US government or its military personnel without any further analysis. He contended that the Bush administration had followed the US military warfare manual on information warfare and hence was able to ensure that all news broadcast adhered to the views expressed by the authorities.

Prof. Wolf argued that while most media were made pliable to the opinions of the US authorities, others disregarded or criticised them. The consequences were almost immediate. Several journalists and members of media crew fell victims to the military campaign. Whereas some contend that they were directly targeted, more moderate speakers believe that the targeting was to remind journalists that they should not be on the ground. Prof. Wolf clearly articulated the view that deliberate targeting of journalists infringed international law and more particularly the right to freedom of expression.

Further, the speaker, having analysed the media coverage since September 11th in the most significant press media in the US, Switzerland and Germany came to the conclusion that even ordinary media coverage had been influenced by the US in friendly States. In the speaker's opinion the straightforward propaganda for purposes of the media coverage by friendly States, including NATO allies, is not only illegitimate but also incompatible with the rules of international law.

After the presentations, the debate in the audience focused on Dr. De Wet's presentation of the Security Council's resolution. Also, one participant questioned whether the overall "good will" history of the US in undertaking international actions should be given great weight.

While the first group discussed issues that arose prior to the US intervention in Iraq, the second group delved into the intricacies of the application of international humanitarian law during the armed conflict in Iraq. It must be said that, from the very beginning, it was clear to the audience that this conflict was of on international character and hence the Geneva Conventions were applicable to it in their entirety. Only two presentations were held in this group as Mr. Dworkin, the second speaker on the list, could not, at the last moment, join the participants to the conference.[4]

The first presentation on targeted killings was made by two members of the IFHV, Ms Noelle Quénivet, research associate, and Mr. Bernard Dougherty, guest researcher.[5] After a general introduction on the rules pertaining to legitimate targets as contained in the Geneva Conventions of 1949 and the additional protocols of 1977 as well as in customary international law, Ms Quénivet delivered the first part of the presentation on targeting objects and more precisely TV stations.

There is no doubt that in the last few years there has been an increased number of buildings used by the radio and the television damaged or destroyed by a party to an armed conflict. This targeting practice undoubtedly questions whether the rules of targeting have changed by way of interpretation by the parties or whether the new interpretation is so far away from the original text that the adoption of new rules should be considered. On the other hand, the issue relating to targeting so-called dual-use objects is not new in international humanitarian law. Ms Quénivet stressed that it must be borne in mind that, despite the common usage of the word "dual-use" objects, humanitarian law only knows of military and non-military objects.

It holds that in order to determine whether a particular building can be the object of a military attack, a certain number of requirements need to be fulfilled. First, it must be determined whether the object makes an effective contribution to military action and second, whether the striking of this object would offer a definite military advantage. Whereas Ms Quénivet agreed that, in some instances, TV stations were contributing to military action notably by their use as relay stations, she expressed her doubts as to the fulfilment of the second requirement. Indeed, more and more often, political actors assert that the destruction of such a building would

---

4   Anthony Dworkin, "Grey Areas in the Laws of War: Lessons from Iraq", (2003) 4 *Humanitäres Völkerrecht-Informationsschriften* 197-199.

5   Bernard Dougherty & Noëlle Quénivet, "Has the Armed Conflict in Iraq Shown once more the Growing Dissension regarding the Definition of a Legitimate Target? What and Who can be Lawfully Targeted?", (2003) 4 *Humanitäres Völkerrecht-Informationsschriften* 188-196.

undermine the capacity of the enemy to gather the support of the population and, therefore, would weaken its military capacity. The bone of contention is whether it is lawful to attack the morale of the population. According to a strict interpretation of article 51 of the Additional Protocol, it is unlawful. Yet, some States such as the US contend that customary international law permits such attacks. This clearly shows a major shift in the US policy of targeting "military" objectives, a change that is even more remarkable when it comes to persons.

Mr. Dougherty then undertook to describe and analyse the policy of targeted killings that has become the latest course of action followed by several States in situations that do not seem to fit within the traditional definitions of armed conflict and peace. Such killings have been officially recognized by the United States in its "war against terrorism" and by Israel in its actions in the occupied territories. After leading the audience through a historical review of acts of targeted killings since the Second World War, Mr. Dougherty dealt into the core of the subject, namely the legality of such acts. To gauge the lawfulness of these individual attacks, one must first determine which set of laws applied, that of armed conflict or that of peacetime. If the laws of war or also called international humanitarian law applies, then it must be proven by the attacker that the person was a legitimate target, i.e., a combatant. Unfortunately, often, it is difficult to make such a pronouncement and the only body which would have the right to do so is a national or international court. However, these individuals are targeted before such a determination can be made. There is consequently a danger that the killed individual is a civilian protected by the Geneva Conventions and their additional protocols and by customary international law that assert the principle of distinction between combatants and civilians.

In times of peace, human rights law applies as do national laws. There is no doubt that such killings can be considered as murder, as an infringement on one's right to life. Further, human rights law and jurisprudence establish that before using deadly force against an individual, the State is under the obligation to arrest the person and bring him/her to court that will provide him with a fair trial.

Mr. Dougherty discussed the following recurrent issues in targeted killings: the lack of clear identification of the targeted individual, the total lack of a judicial procedure to determine guilt (and the lack of appeal), the encouragement of loose investigation methods and eventually the deaths of other individuals during the attack. Mr. Dougherty concluded that the policy of targeted killings was in clear contravention to norms of international law.

The second presentation focused on the status of the "Free Iraqi Forces" during the armed conflict in Iraq.[6] To an audience, which had only heard about the

---

6   Roberta Arnold, "The US Uniformed Iraqi 'Freedom Fighters': Regular Combatants or Traitors of the Homeland?", (2003) 4 *Humanitäres Völkerrecht-Informationsschriften* 199-202.

existence of such individuals, Ms Arnold, from the Swiss Ministry of Defence, gave
first a broad picture of the situation. In December 2000, Hungary gave permission
to the US to use a military base to train Iraqi volunteers recruited from the Iraqi
opposition. The first volunteers were sent to Iraq in April 2003 under the training
programme of the so-called "Free Iraqi Forces". One of the major issues raised during the presentation was the nature and the status of the such forces. Whereas initially these troops were only trained for civilian tasks, it appeared that, once on the
ground, they were also entrusted with military tasks. This undoubtedly questions
whether, if captured, they can claim prisoner of war status or they are to be treated
as criminals for having unlawfully participated in combat.

The first theme tackled was their nationality. Most of them were American citizens but some still held an Iraqi passport and, hence, could have been considered
as traitors by the Iraqi armed forces. Whether the FIF qualified as either a volunteer corps *forming part* of the US armed forces under paragraph (A)(1) of Article
4 III GC, or a volunteer corps *belonging* to the US under paragraph (A)(2) of the
same provision was also dealt by Ms Arnold at length. Ms Arnold also very well
presented the alternative, which is whether the members of the FIF fulfilled the criteria listed in Article 4(A)(2) III GC.

Another extremely important part of Ms Arnold's presentation centred upon
their relationship to the US armed forces. In fact, the Free Iraqi Forces were wearing American uniforms, yet distinct by a small patch indicating that they belonged
to the FIF. Also mentioned was that the FIF could be considered as spies or mercenaries or be tried for perfidy. Ms Arnold's presentation shed some interesting light
on the use of foreigners in one's armed forces, an issue that is again gaining
significance in modern armed conflicts.

Most of the discussion which took place after these two presentations concentrated on two issues inextricably linked issues, the definition of a military target and
of the status of combatants/civilians.

In the third group, the speakers developed themes relating to post-conflict Iraq.
The armed conflict that took place in Iraq had recently occurred and, hence, the
speakers could only conjecture about the possible problems Iraq and the occupying
powers would face in the next few months.

Dr. Heintze, research associate and currently Acting Executive Director of the
Institute for International Law of Peace and Armed Conflict of the University of
Bochum, started this group of presentations by examining the then current situation
in Iraq regarding the protection of human rights and more particularly of minority
rights. First, Dr. Heintze stressed that, contrary to what many believe, Iraq is a State
party to many fundamental human rights treaties of the United Nations. There is no
doubt that these instruments were violated during the time of Saddam Hussein's
leadership. Yet, from time to time, the government submitted reports to the bodies
responsible for the implementation of these human rights treaties. Unfortunately,

the scope of these reports was rather limited and, therefore, did not provide a good insight into the human rights situation in Iraq prior to the intervention of the United States.

One question of utmost relevance raised by Dr. Heintze was whether the occupying powers, the US, the United Kingdom and Poland at that time, were under the duty to abide by the provisions of the human rights treaties signed and ratified by Iraq. More interestingly, he discussed the issue whether these powers were obliged to report to the bodies responsible for the implementation of these treaties. To answer this question Dr. Heintze drew a parallel with the situation of Israel in the occupying territories, arguing that there was such a duty upon the occupying powers.

Further, Dr. Heintze underlined that, in assessing the future of the Iraqi population, one needs to take into account its ethnical and religious composition. At the time of his presentation, Dr. Heintze argued that it would have a considerable impact on the internal structure of Iraq, especially if democracy were to be applied and, thereby, enable all elements of the Iraqi population to express their opinions. Another point noted was the right to self-determination and the influence that the neighbouring countries could have on an internal or external self-determination process. In particular, the speaker warned that self-determination should not allow these ethnic and/or religious groups to separate from Baghdad or to declare an Islamic State since it would automatically infringe other rules of international law such as the principle of sovereign integrity and of territoriality.

The next speaker, Mr. Heinsch from the Law Centre for European and International Cooperation of the University of Cologne, focused on the eventual prosecution of individuals involved in past atrocities.[7] From the outset, he pointed out that a distinction must be drawn between criminal offences during the conflict in Spring 2003 and those committed under the regime of Saddam Hussein.

First, Mr. Heinsch examined whether it would be possible to prosecute alleged perpetrators before the international criminal court in The Hague. Due to the *rationae temporis* jurisdiction of the ICC, only crimes perpetrated after the Statute came into force, i.e., after 1 July 2002, could be investigated by the ICC. This would automatically preclude the prosecution of most crimes committed under the regime of Saddam Hussein and, particularly, during the two Gulf wars, the first against Iran and the second against Kuwait. Yet, the main argument against a trial at the ICC is the personal and territorial jurisdiction since neither Iraq nor the US has ratified the ICC Statute. However, since the United Kingdom is a State Party to the ICC Statute, members of its armed forces who fought during the Spring 2003 intervention in

---

7   Robert W. Heinsch, "Possibilities to Prosecute War Crimes Committed in Iraq: The Different Forum Options", (2003) 3 *Humanitäres Völkerrecht-Informationsschriften* 132-138.

Iraq could face a trial before the ICC. Another means to haul perpetrators to court is by a Security Council referral. Unfortunately, as Mr. Heinsch underlined, this is very unlikely since the US has been a long-time opponent of the ICC and is endowed with veto power in the Security Council. That a case is judged before the ICC is all the more improbable as the Court must demonstrate, before it takes up a case, that a State is not able or willing to prosecute the alleged perpetrator.

Consequently, Mr. Heinsch delved into the possibilities to use other judicial mechanisms. In his view, there were four possible options warranting examination. The first option consisted in establishing an *ad hoc* tribunal, under the auspices of the UN Security Council using its Chapter VII powers, similar to the ICTY or the ICTR. Many NGOs had, in June 2003, lent their support to the proponents of this option. The second possibility was to opt for a mixed tribunal that would be composed of both national and international lawyers and that would be based on an either multilateral or bilateral treaty. Examples of such tribunals are the Special Court for Sierra Leone and the Serious Crimes Panel of the Dili District Court in East Timor and the future Court in Cambodia. A third option would be the prosecution through national courts, whether they are in Iraq or in any other country which took part in any of the three Gulf wars. At that period of time, the US seemed to favour a fourth option, that of the prosecution of war crimes by military tribunals or military commissions. In June 2003, when Mr. Heinsch presented his thoughts on the possibilities of prosecution of violations of international humanitarian law in Iraq, all options appeared to be open.

Last in the group, Ms Michaela Schneider, Associate at the Institute for International Law of Peace and Armed Conflict of the University of Bochum, took up the issue of the protection of humanitarian staff in Iraq.[8] In the past few decades, there has been a routine of attacking the life, health and freedom of humanitarian staff. Despite numerous resolutions condemning such acts on the universal level, these attacks continue unabated.

Ms Schneider started her presentation by analysing Security Council resolution 1472 of 28 March 2003 that urged all parties to the conflict "to promote the safety, security and freedom of movement of United Nations and associated personnel and their assets, as well as personnel of humanitarian organizations in Iraq." In her opinion, it was the first time that the Security Council used such a terminology. This indicates a major shift in the attitude of the international community towards the protection of humanitarian workers. The attacks on humanitarian personnel that occurred since the end of the cold war find their roots in the increased number of

---

8   Michaela Schneider, "Die Sicherheit humanitärer Helfer im Irak", (2003) 3 *Humanitäres Völkerrecht Informationsschriften* 138-141.

so-called new armed conflicts taking place in failed States and involving the participation of non-State actors who are aloof to most principles of international law and only pursue their own agendas. Another reason for the proliferation of such attacks is closely linked to the concept of "humanitarian assistance" which from the mere provision of basic commodities turned into a full political and military package including the protection of civilians, the media, and the inclusion of the armed forces. A third reason mentioned by Ms Schneider is the lack of proper management in matters relating to security in organisations involved in humanitarian assistance. A fourth explanation is the relative lack of pertinent international law norms dealing with humanitarian assistance.

In the particular case of Iraq, Ms Schneider noted that few humanitarian workers were killed during the military operations and that it was probably due to the fact that the conflict was of an international character and, hence, there were few independent factions engaged in the fighting. Another reason for this low rate of casualties is that, since all humanitarian organisations needed to register with the US prior to the intervention and few did so, they were very few organisations on the ground. In post-war Iraq, the general disorder has led to an increased rate of criminality. Attacks on humanitarian workers need to be considered in this context. The question is then related to the obligation of the occupying power to ensure peace and security in Iraq, a duty which the US seem to find difficult to fulfil.

The focus of the discussion was the relationship between the US and the international criminal court, especially the activities of the US to exclude their soldiers from the scope of criminal responsibility before the newly established ICC. Doubts were also articulated that the state of occupation in Iraq would be terminated in a short term. Therefore, many participants underlined the future responsibilities of the occupying powers in Iraq.

After the internal discussions, all participants gathered again in the plenary where three students of the master programme in humanitarian assistance of the Institute for International Law of Peace and Armed Conflict of the University of Bochum summarised the presentations as well as the debates that took place in the workshops. The ensuing discussion centred upon the current American policy and more particularly upon the unilateralist approach of the US in dealing with issues that appear to be of international concern: the international criminal court, the Tokyo Protocol on the protection of environment, international terrorist networks, etc. Overall, it can be said that the conference enabled better understanding of the situation in Iraq and of the American policy in the "war against terror".

2003 Annual Meeting of the IAPTC

Victoria Firmo-Fontan[1]

The 2003 annual meeting of the IAPTC was be held during the period 19-24 October 2003 at the Baden-Wurttemberg Police Academy in Wertheim, Germany. Its theme was "Enhancing the Effectiveness of Peace Operations through Education and Training". Three sub-themes included "Creating Common Ground", "Building Partnerships", and "Evaluating Success".

1. Creating Common Ground

This sub-theme was intended to examine core or foundation education and training for peace operations. It examined standards and guidelines developed by several organizations – the United Nations (UN), the European Union (EU), the Partnership for Peace Program of the North Atlantic Treaty Organization (NATO/PfP), and various others. In particular the conference examined the latest developments in the UN's Standardized Generic Training Modules (SGTMs). Military, Civilian and Police training centers were encouraged to bring copies of their basic course programs to exchange and compare with others. The preparation of civilians for deployment to peace operations was of particular interest to several participating organizations in 2003. The need to mainstream topics such as gender, culture and human rights in all peace operations' training was also emphasized. The exchange of ideas and practices presented between various participants allowed the participants to understand how various centers are dealing with some of today's key challenges in peace operations from an education and training perspective: for example rule of law; secu-

---

1 Visiting Assistant Professor of Peace Studies, Colgate University, United States. The author wishes to thank Clemens Bohnbacker, Roland Kuhn, Ralf Trez and Arnaud LeGuiffant for gathering group proceedings.

Harvey Langholtz, Boris Kondoch, Alan Wells (Eds.),
International Peacekeeping: The Yearbook of International Peace Operations, Volume 9, 2004, pp. 253-265.
© *Koninklijke Brill N.V. Printed in the Netherlands*

rity sector reform; governance and interim administrations; disarmament, demobilization and reintegration; and, civil-military-police cooperation.

The discussion surrounding the question of creating common grounds in peacekeeping training focused on two central issues pertaining to a) the input of common grounds in the 3rd Standardized General Training Manual for Strategic Level Management, and b) common grounds in individual training. After the plenary session, three working groups were established to reflect on these issues.

1.1.   *Input to 3rd SGTM (Standardized General Training Manual) for Strategic Level Management*

Different working groups approached the question in various manners.

In the first group, it was agreed that the UN Training and Evaluation Service (TES) should consult with Peacekeeping Training Centers as well as with member states and strategic level education institutions such as war colleges and university programs. NORDCAPS UNSMAS was identified as a relevant model. NORDCAPS is the military cooperation between the Nordic countries (Denmark, Finland, Norway and Sweden) and was established in 1997 by Nordic Ministers of Defense. The aim was to strengthen and expand the already existing cooperation in the Nordic Cooperation Group for military UN matters (Nordisk samarbetsgrupp för militära FN-ärenden – NORDSAM-FN) with regard to military peace support operations (PSO), focusing on the foreseen requirements for political as well as military consultations. The need for joint military, police and civil management in creating common grounds was also highlighted. The following management topics were identified: decision making, guidance supplying, benchmarking, goal setting, the appreciation of Peace and Conflict impact on decisions and actions, and the anticipation of the complex dynamic of a given situation. The necessity to embed human rights as well as other types of mainstreaming in all programs was also raised.

The second group chose a progressive approach to the question. It first identified two sets of STM for Senior Managers. The first one was functional, and aimed at preparing STM to senior mission managers in their own area, i.e. separate tasks for military, police and civil/diplomatic senior managers. The second was managerial; it focused on exposing the different senior functional managers to the key issues that impact on each others' areas of responsibility as well as establishing mechanisms for co-ordination and co-operation. Mediation and negotiation were identified as potential tactics to reach common grounds with regards to the aforementioned issues. While the necessity of a basic joint training between civilian and military was mentioned, the exclusion of civilian components in specific training was formulated. After a common approach between civilian and military instruments both at strategic and operational levels was agreed upon, it was decided that a consolidation, then the inclusion of specific subjects should be taken into account. These are: operations management – including identification requirements, resource allocation and operational concepts; programming and budgeting within the UN system – requiring an interaction with member states; mission and mandate formation – including force generation and civilian recruitment; interagency co-ordination – based on models such as those provided by the Inter-Agency Standing Committee (IASC), established in June 1992 in response to General Assembly Resolution 46/182 that called for strengthened coordination of humanitarian assistance; and an emphasis on humanitarian law – especially with regards to Human Rights, host nations judicial issues and Treaty law; finally, information management was identified as a comprehensive subject.

In its debate, the Third group emphasized the need to determine what constitutes Senior level of management. Where should a line be drawn? Who should be trained? Force Commanders, Section/Sector Commanders, CMO's and equivalent for other components, i.e. Police Commissioners and their deputies, were identified as Senior management, this along with CAO's and civilian equivalent in Agencies and NGO's. According to this stratification, it can be understood that functions have been identified as more important than ranks. Moreover, it was agreed that if NGO's or other civilian Agencies are willing to attend training, this should be decided on behalf of NGO's. The rationale lying behind this conceptualization is unambiguous: a common training course is important to understand each other. A second part of the group's debate on the raised was areas of content to be included in the program. Here, it was decided to build on member's previous experience in peacekeeping operations. Attendance to a basic course for non-experienced members was highlighted as necessary, however, it was agreed that most Senior Level personnel would have acquired previous field experiences. According to the group, the contents of the training should include: planning, management, leadership, etc.; background information on mission areas, cultural awareness (at a deeper level of knowledge); legal aspect of peace operations; mandates of all components; negotiation and mediation (not just techniques); human rights; stress management, and finally coordination exercises and international diplomacy skills. Finally, a challenge was highlighted, that of identifying the level of proficiency of a given individual, that is to say: finding the right person for the right job.

1.2. *Issues of Individual Training*

The first group agreed that it was difficult for civilians to find both time and funds to attend training sessions. It was also mentioned that lesser rich countries have difficulties funding civilian training. A solution identified to lessen these concerns was a consensus according to which richer countries ought to invite civilians from less rich countries to participate in their trainings, this in order to achieve a state of mutual benefit for all parties concerned. A question was then raised: should the military, the police and civilians always train together or should they focus on individual competencies? According to a member of the group, the experience of Slovenia would indicate the limitations of such a combination. In a conclusion therefore, it was agreed that there is a need to separate training, this while recognizing the necessity for joint training in some areas.

The third group focused on the need for assessment of the people who are trained as well as the necessity to include qualified training staff. Issues concerning the lack of time to dedicate to training were acknowledged, especially with regards to civilians. Finally, methodological approaches, technology and training facilities and infrastructures were deemed as crucial to comprehending issues of individual training.

2.   Building Partnerships

This sub-theme examined the importance of training together for peace operations. The session focused on ways of bringing various groups and professional cultures and disciplines together to assist in overcoming the many challenges posed by differing mandates, cultures, resources, operational procedures, attitudes, and training standards. Organizations were encouraged to bring information on joint courses, joint exercises and other activities designed to contribute to overcoming the many different approached to peace operations, and to building effective cooperation and coordination mechanisms.

The discussion surrounding the issue of building partnerships in peacekeeping training focused on two central questions: a) what should be done together in joint training overlapping Military, Police and Civilians, and b) provide examples of good experiences of joint activities. Again, the plenary audience was split into three working groups.

2.1.   *What Should Be Done Together in Joint Training Overlapping Military, Police and Civilians?*

The first working group decided first on themes that should be covered in joint training. These were identified as: mine awareness, UN System and values, roles and mandates, cultural & religious awareness, rules of engagement, refugee issues, gender issues, child protection, human rights, disarmament, demobilization and reintegration, mediation/negotiation, mission briefings/lessons learned, medical issues, security and protection, case study exercises, live exercises, ethics, legal framework, conditions of employment, leadership & management, logistics, humanitarian Law, communication, information management, media relations – this with regards to concept of operations, stress management, CIMIC, mission analysis – and finally political implications. During the collecting of the points mentioned above, some questions were raised, and ought to be taken into consideration. First, what type of training should be involved? A consensus was reached on Generic Training, Mission Specific Training, Pre-mission-training and In-mission-training. Second, on the question of resources versus benefits, it was agreed that different agencies ought to be given tasks that fit their normative mandates. On the question of levels that should be catered for, all were mentioned: Junior, Senior, and Mission Management levels. The type of mission and its feasibility was also part of the discussion dynamic. After deliberation, it was agreed that most of the themes mentioned above should form joint training.

The second chose to look at different levels of approach, whether they be tactical, operational or strategic. In the field of tactics, it was decided that training ought to remain separated, this for based on the following grounds: the danger of overwhelming civilians with details, the need of special training for the role, all this enhancing the functional competence of some parties over others. In the operational field the consensus was to integrate lectures on other components and functions, this as different components may eventually lead common processes. Finally, with regards to higher levels of management it was agreed to focus more on education than on training.

Group three initiated its discussion on four original assumptions: a) training is a responsibility of the member states, not of the UN, and b) SGTM (Standard General Training Manual) forms the kind of training that ought to be undertaken, c) training of forced bodies needs to be done as a single task and is too difficult to be done collectively, and d) a focus needs to be placed on middle management. Ideally all training should be done collectively, however the group realised that this is not possible at all times due to financial constraints as well as co-ordination issues. It was agreed that level 1 SGTM type of training should be done collectively, but that, conversely, skill specific training ought to be carried out separately. To best combine the generic and specific training, a combined field training exercise/command post exercise (CPX) should be completed. Moreover, the use of simulation in training should be developed. The consensus was that training should be done just prior to deploying if possible. However, in case of impossibility, training should then be done whenever the highest number of personnel can be involved. According to the group, the three main challenges to training are the availability of personnel, that of appropriate civilian personnel, and also a commonly encountered of English skills. In addition to actual training, the group raised the idea of information to be disseminated online, this in order for other potential participants to access valid information.

2.2. *Provide Examples of Positive Experiences of Joint Activities*

Group one provided the following examples of viable joint activities: PKO South/North, Strong Resolve (NATO), Viking 03 (Sweden), NORDIC PEACE (northern countries), Invited Instructors, KABANNAS, and evidently the IAPTC. Viking 03, for instance, has been established by the Swedish military to enhance the interoperability for Peace Support Operations, including civil-military co-operation, and to further develop the PSN (Peace Simulation Network) Concept, while the Nordic Peace aims at promoting interoperability and civil-military cooperation in international Peace Support operations. A number of international and domestic organizations also participate in the exercises that they provide.

Group Two mentioned civil-military partnerships, and also the need for some civilian partners to overcome their reluctance to train jointly with the military. The establishment of advisory councils was promoted, encouraging the involvement of ministries, NGO's as well as academic institutions. Operational professional networks were mentioned, such as the IAPTC, APSTA, GTZ, PPC, SW, NO, CIMIC and GPS. Bilateral and trans-national partnerships were mentioned and finally regional training initiatives were reviewed, such a UNSMAS in Bangladesh, soon to be passed on to Sri Lanka, and the Nordic Joint event in Copenhagen.

Group three emphasized the need for combined training with Military, Police and Civilians, and also the fact that all are doing so in some form or another. The IAPTC was mentioned as an example of collective efforts, although it was recommended that NGO representative should also attend. NORDCAP was mentioned as a viable example of joint training, this with also the joint SLOVAKIAN and AUSTRIAN training for UNO, held twice a year at the Austrian UN-training centre. Joint SLOVAKIAN and HUNGARIAN training for UNFICYP was also mentioned. It is currently held twice a year, once in Slovakia, once in Hungary. The UN Police Commander Course organized by Sweden every year was brought up. It lasts for three weeks and is intended for the training of senior police personnel and has a CPX (Command Post Exercise) at end that includes military and civilian aspects. Finally, the EU Police Commander course for senior staff of EU member states was mentioned, where participants are to be trained for future EU police missions i.e. EUPM in Bosnia. This course lasts for three weeks and completes with an exercise that has military and civil aspects such as rule of law, civilian administration and civil protection.

2.3. *General Discussion*

Time allowed for a plenary discussion on the results of group sessions. The debate that emanated from the Theme 2 presentation of results added on the overall topic on several grounds. It was advised that an evaluation of the joined-basis training necessity be evaluated, this at a pre and post deployment level. Moreover, the question of generic or mission specific training was re-iterated. As was presented, one is not necessarily aware of what one does need before one gets back from a mission. It was pointed that one way of looking at the question, of training when and to whom, was from the point of view of the motivation and background knowledge and experience of audience members. To this respect, experience has shown that courses which mix students with a great variance in levels of interest, experience and knowledge can be problematic, this for several reasons. First, a student coming to the subjects for the first time can feel intimidated and therefore not fully participate in the course activities. Second, the experienced course members can often feel under-challenged and can consider that they are being "used as a training aid" when they actually come to learn. Civilians who generally self-identify or volunteer for deployment are, in general, more likely to have a greater interest and background knowledge then other groups. In sum, peacekeeping centres which offer courses to public access should make sure to depict the course structure accurately and precisely. The aforementioned description should reflect the level of the course. Moreover, registrars ought to monitor closely the level of individuals taking the course, and, if the level of the candidate does not match that of the course, contact the individual in question.

The question of inter-agency meeting and co-operation was also raised. The point was made that in different circumstances, various agencies might not interact with each other automatically. An example was provided from Norway, where the co-operation of different sectors of peacekeeping personnel has generated the NOR-CAPS initiative. The Pearson Centre raised awareness towards the reluctance of civilians to engage in joint training, this for different reasons ranging from the lack of financial and time resources to the lack of attraction for a military-based method of training. Another member of the group expressed the need for military personnel to understand how civilians conduct peacekeeping operations, mentioning the fact that, often, civilians are more experienced within time in comparison to their military counterparts. The question of levels of training was also raised, expressing the need to re-iterate training expectations, different at national and international level, as well as hierarchically within the agencies solicited. A change in the semantic component of training was also encouraged, this in order to attract a greater civilian attendance. The point was made that civilians do need training also within the UN agencies, and that although their time presence in different missions might be greater than that of military personnel, different missions warrant different training. Also, the transposition of certain standards expected in a mission to another mission might not be automatically advisable. In a concluding statement, it was mentioned that training institutions ought to look for opportunities instead of being overcome and at times blinded by impossibilities.

3.   Evaluating Success

The issue of determining the effectiveness of education and training is a difficult one. The conference will look at how certain peacekeeping centres evaluate their individual training, how specialized training is followed up, and the success of international organizations in evaluating their collective training. Hopefully through presentations and discussion the group will be able to identify the principal challenges in evaluating the effectiveness of training and education in preparing individuals and groups for missions, and best practices for those who have procedures and systems in place.

The discussion surrounding the issue of evaluating success in peacekeeping training focused on two central questions: a) what different processes and challenges exist with regards to debriefing/evaluation of peacekeeping training, and b) ways and approaches of debriefing.

Group one focused on three specific categories: military, civilian and police. It then raised the following question: what could be utilised for next rotation and new countries? A common theme was identified, in that there are processes that are available and are commonly utilised. It was concluded that resources are lacking with regards to databases. Furthermore, there might be classification problems with regard to databases. NATO for instance might not be able to share all information. It was said that the UN seems to be the best place to look for databases at the moment. For the military component, evaluation represents a key issue that alleviates the possibility of problems for the future. According to the group, staffing through the command system alleviates the possibility of being useful. It was then concluded that each institution has problems in this area. From the police perspective, it was stated that in the case of a young nation developing a recently reformed police component, a problem might arise concerning modalities of evaluation. Finally, from the civilian perspective, there are evaluation reports done with respect to quality control. Databases are also available. To this respect, the difficulty to ascertain whether training is good enough upon completion was raised.

Group two suggested that the current challenges to evaluation lie in the fact that they are carried out one year to 18 months after a given training session, thus generating the response of a mere 20% of participants. The formation of a database was therefore mentioned, as well as the extraction of lessons learned, the hiring of exterior consultants to evaluate, the elaboration of questionnaires. However, one problem remained; that of financial cost. The elaboration of regional evaluation groupings was proposed as a way to alleviate potential financial burdens.

Group three initially discussed the meaning of the term debriefing. It was agreed that the term should be used to qualify a post training session, and that it should not involve any type of psychological burdening or strain. It was then discussed that the results on debriefing depend on the learning conditions and the environment in which the training is bring carried out. It was concluded that post-training sessions should be part of the learning process, and that they ought to be documented in a database. Participants should be given the option to exert their feedback prerogative with the possibility to analyse or change the training process. The current state of affairs was analysed according to the following: mission members judge the value and content of the pre-mission courses after their mission. It was therefore declared that part of the evaluation process should be to have the possibility to brief the next contingent with the achieved information, the latter may be represent a comprehensive feedback from the host nations (culture, attitude). The necessity of an ongoing dialogue between students and trainers was emphasized. It was then concluded that others ought to be able to benefit form feedback information, so that constructive alternatives may be sought. The concept of an on-going dialog was stressed with regards to evaluation. An additional kind of feedback that was mentioned consists in sending trainers in the mission-area, this to debrief the mission members there. However, the issue of lack of resources was emphasised, this particularly in the case of civilian organisations. The group then discussed the idea of debriefing sessions to be carried out in partnership with other organizations such as armed forces, police or civilian organisations. However, representatives of various armed forces saw problems with the possible dissemination of military secrets. However, it was concluded that an exchange of students and an exchange of instructors would be to evaluation as a concept of growing importance, this also for representatives of the armed forced. Collaboration in this direction will represent a heightened sense of international trust and respect.

4.   Professional groups results

In order to optimise the various debates prompted by the plenary sessions and group discussions, professional groups were put together to reflect on the conferences' various sub-themes. These groups were made of, a) civilian practitioners, b) military personnel, c) police staff.

4.1.   *Civilian Group: Sharing Training Centres' Experiences – Key Challenges*

A report on ZIF with regards to the sharing of training centres experiences was presented by Ms. Wibke Hansen. With respect to recruitment into ZIF, the question asked was: how do we get senior personnel that are needed in peace operations? Moreover, how to recruit senior level individuals who have professional and personal commitments? ZiF's policy on the matter is to encourage individuals to apply for training, who then upon successful completion of training will be added to ZIF's active roster.

A report was then given by the US/Hawaii Peacekeeping Training Centre where it was mentioned that external consultants were hired to run evaluations throughout the year, before reports back to the institution itself. It was also mentioned that instructors were sent to other organizations' courses, and that staff include internationals as well. Moreover, at times, courses are given with no US staff involved. The centre employs different skill sets; library, research, as well as information technology. IT specialists assure that methods are up to date. A challenge identified was: how to get to trained individuals after they have been deployed, kowing that an estimated 70% of people trained wihtin the centre are deployed. A possible solution identified was to promote the use of online resources. However, access and cost were identified as potential impediments.

A report was then given by the institute Training for Peace, based in Norway, this with a special focus on Southern African Development Community (SADC) region. A problem was identified with regards to measuring training outcomes. With respect to the number of individuals to have been deployed, the use of an externally run database was highlighted, this in conjunction with the fact that a high demand for civilian experts remains within UN missions. The question on whether to adopt training to job profiles was raised, among other quesitons. How to assure that trainees are motivated for deployment; that they will be deployed? Is training broad enough to allow trainees to apply to general UN and other courses? To the question concerning "per diem hunting" on part of the participants, it was concluded that the application process ought to be made exclusive so that applicants should put in an effort. On the questions pertaining to the monitoring of deployment as well as possible feedback after training, it was concluded that a new context may not require feedback in revised training curricula. Even those who are not deployed it was decided that there are spin-off benefits that need to be communicated to funders; e.g. police officers that do not get deployed but can use those skills at home. To the question concerning the random pick of students, it was answered that, ideally, students are already landmarked for deployment. However, how does one get the end users more involved in selection/recruitment? A first step identified was the custom-tailor building training to end user's needs. To the issue of "measurement of success", a more flexible definition beyond "deployment" was wished, this in the context that training may facilitate better performance in related profession. The it was mentioned that most civilian trainees are women. An important factor to be highlighted with regards to the importance of training was the maximization of the "utilization" of good trainees. It was concluded that creative ways to ensure completion of the latter ought to be found, this through a renewed focus on qualitative, not only quantitative ways.

Overall, it was discussed that in-mission training needs assessment, this in a context within which the discussion of needs with section chief is not very productive. It was highlighted that informal discussions with Mission Members are more fruitful, the latter being in the process of starting to design their own training program on the mission specific needs. These needs were identified as generic training on administrative and logistic tasks, specific training, e.g. in the fields of Human rights, Child protection, gender issues, political affairs, etc. The group concluded that training is great opportunity for "lessons learned" exercise. It gives important input to best practises unit, as well as productive feedback on quality of staff (quality control). Remarks were made with regards to in-mission training, as there seems to be limited time allocated to this type of training. It was proposed to limiit training to one or two days to the benefit of in-mission training, this while staff on in-mission training cell may be limited at times, for instance, as little as 4 staff, incl. 2 trainers can be allocated to full-time training in some fully-developped missions. It was also mentioned that in practice, limited are the people deployed who have been exposed to pre-mission training. As a result, in-mission training has to be conducted very creatively; using abundantly case studies, hands-on and content-driven training. While this option remains highly demanding on part of the staff as well as the trainees, materials have to be customized, driven by cases and be directly related to the trainees job in the field. It was also mentioned that at times, training gives staff the impression of "expertise" to the participants, who may feel overly confident and may apply "skills" they do not have. This could eventually be dangerous. For instance, misperceptions can be applied to what serious skills can really be accomplished in a matter of days, a skill which requires practise. An example was given with regards to negotiation training, where it was mentioned that it would be irresponsible to apply those "skills" immediatly after training.

With regards to evaluation, it was concluded that trainee feedback has only limited meaning, and that real feedback comes from the "impact" of the field. Could a possible solution to fill this gap be the utilisation of pre-trained civilian staff right before deployment? Time between assignment and deployment might be too brief. A crucial fact was raised: 20% of vacancies are left unfilled in many missions. It was concluded that training ought to also link up with missions to prepare potential candidates.

A brief thought was finally given to the role of distance-learning for in-mission training.

4.2. *Military Group: Sharing Training Centres' Experiences – Key Challenges*

A presentation was given by Lt. Col Taubeneder about the NATO working group TEPSO, including 26 Training Modules for PSO, available for NATO/PfP countries. A discussion then followed, where proposals were made in order to have more time for and in the Military Subcommittee for discussion and to have fewer presentations instead. Col. McDonald proposed to the secretary to have precise themes to work on at an earlier time to be able to reach better results. The IAPTC answer was that the aim of that conference is not to produce results primarily, but to build up a global network of all International Peacekeeping Training Centres. Carolyn BRAND, DPKO, offered to serve as an information point for PTC on any requests about training material or information material for preparing any UN-mission. A presentation of the German bundeswehr about SIRA/SIRA is a computer based simulation system for training and education in PKO. A new chairman for the Military Subcommittee was appointed. After some discussions about the rotation process Lt. Col Ibrahim NASRON, Malaysia, volunteered and the subcommittee agreed on him.

4.3. *Police Group: Sharing Training Centres' Experiences – Key Challenges*

The session started with the appointment of a new Police Chairman. Mr. Superintendent Lars Egerstad (Sweden) was appointed by the group to be elected at the next meeting of the executive committee.

To the question regarding the exchange and interchange of experiences, the following statements were made. The DPKO requested support from its other police counterparts. It was mentioned that the DPKO will have to train 7000 people next year and that they have only two trainers. So they cannot do a real training, only a kind of co-ordination. The DPKO is currently searching for mentors/advisors/trainers for the UN-training. The trainers have also to do evaluation of the courses and to create new concepts and programs for peacekeeping training.

Invitations were made on part of Slovakia for the session-members to join their trainings and train with them. Hungary also invited other training centers to train or to monitor their courses. They also invited people from the neighboring states to join the training as participants.

On the question pertaining to the selection of mission-participants, the session members discussed the assessment of the different countries. They agreed that a good selection was important to enhance the performance of the mission. The DPKO stated that selection depends on the countries, and they ought to be more transparent and in their choices, privileging the deployment of confirmed police officers.

Discussion about the different assessments of the countries was initiated. It was concluded that there are different systems of assessment. An example was provided by Singapore, which claims to apply a very stringent assessment: at last 7 people out of 100 pass the examination. Germany exposed some problems with regards to the federation system, leaving assessment prerogatives to the 16 German states individually, hence prompting differences in methods and precedents.

The last discussion in the morning was about the Contingent Commanders. There are different practices on how to install the commanders. In some countries it depends on the ranks, while not in other countries. In some countries it depends in the mission experience of the commanders and in other countries deployment is offered to new mission participants.

In the early afternoon the discussion was focused on the demonstration provided by the armed forces earlier on. A few of the session members provided constructive criticism towards the field exercise, especially with regards to the exposed anti-riot practices. It was pointed out that this was a typically military response to a civilian-based problem, and that therefore advisors of the police may be helpful in defusing a potentially lethal situation. It was also said that it might be dangerous to mix police and military competences. The question that emerged was: Should there be police-advisers in a military unit? The group did not come to an agreement on this question. While it could be workable in a military mission of the EU, such as the EUPM, it would be more complex in a NATO mission. Another problem in that case could be that the mandate from the armed forces can be radically different from that of the police. It was therefore identified as crucial to have a clear mandate for both military and police components of a given mission, this as early as possible in the mission.

Book Reviews

The Psychology of the Peacekeeper: Lessons from the Field, **Britt, T.W. and Adler, A.B.**
Praeger: Westport, Connecticut, August 2003 (Psychological Dimensions to War and Peace Series), 344 pp.
Hardback, ISBN 0-275-97596-7, $59.95; £33.99

*Matt C. Densmore**

Examining psychological dimensions of the soldier in peacekeeping operations is relevant and important for 21st Century military forces. The increased importance placed on international relations and diplomacy, the global economy, and human rights, coupled with the proliferation of international and regional alliances (e.g., the United Nations, the North Atlantic Treaty Organisation, the European Union, the Association of South East Asian Nations and the Arab League of Nations) and continued inter- and intra-state conflicts, has led many nations to call on their military personnel to perform across a widening spectrum of operations. Past and ongoing deployments to conduct peacekeeping operations provide evidence that the individual soldier in modern militaries is expected to perform in ever-changing roles far more diverse than as a traditional warfighter. In many instances, military personnel have to alter their mind-set to accept the idea that their traditional mission is not strictly fighting and winning wars, but rather doing whatever their nation asks them to do. The varying nature of warfare and the increased use of militaries as instruments of policy have raised a number of questions and arguments as to the changing psychological dimensions concerning the modern soldier. The peacekeeping soldier, or peacekeeper, will remain the physical representation of the world's effort

---

*   Captain Matt C. Densmore is a psychology instructor at the United States Military Academy, West Point, New York. He has seven years of active duty service in the U.S. Army infantry. He has a Masters degree in Psychology from The College of William and Mary in Virginia.

Harvey Langholtz, Boris Kondoch, Alan Wells (Eds.),
International Peacekeeping: The Yearbook of International Peace Operations, Volume 9, 2004, pp. 267-268.
© *Koninklijke Brill N.V. Printed in the Netherlands*

to maintain international peace and security. His, or her, effective performance is essential for current and future peace operations and will continue to play a critical role in international security and stability into the 21st Century.

Much of the published work on peacekeeping operations is concerned with aspects of conflict resolution, diplomacy, and geopolitics, but *The Psychology of the Peacekeeper* focuses largely on the individual soldier. Rather than spending a great deal of space on the semantic arguments over what constitutes a peacekeeping operation, their histories, or varying types, this book arranges unique psychological research from several fields to provide a useful framework for examining the multiple challenges military personnel face in performing their duties as peacekeepers. Understanding that healthy peacekeepers, who perform effectively, contribute to the overall success of peacekeeping operations, the book is guided by the detailed examination of the peacekeeper role – the challenges and demands of coping with the complex, stressful environment of peacekeeping operations. Most importantly, the research in this volume draws heavily on studies using military personnel conducting real-world peacekeeping operations, offering a greater potential for application of psychological principles to current and future operations.

From the outset, the editors' framework of hypothesised factors influencing peacekeeper well-being and performance, which includes operational, unit, and individual factors, helps direct the reader through this comprehensive investigation of the peacekeeper and his environment. The book is divided into five subchapters, each of which present research from varying areas of psychology: social, industrial-organisational, health, clinical, and cross-cultural psychology.

Within these multidimensional contexts, one begins to gain a clear perspective of how demanding the peacekeeping environment can be on the individuals performing the operational tasks. An in-depth examination of the potentially traumatic psychological distress soldiers encounter while performing peacekeeping duties, and reviews and recommendations concerning various psychological interventions and treatments, are offered in the health and clinical psychology subchapters as well. Peacekeeping operations call on soldiers to perform their duties among unfamiliar people and cultures and often times within a multinational force. Citing lessons from several past peacekeeping operations, the editors, who contributed to the cross-cultural psychology subchapter, also present very insightful considerations associated with the cross-cultural issues present in modern day peacekeeping operations.

The editors' organisation of each of the contributor's materials provides a high degree of utility. Military commanders and personnel, diplomats and policymakers, and psychological researchers who are interested in examining current peacekeeping operations, or are preparing for future ones, will benefit greatly from the psychological perspectives offered in this volume. *The Psychology of the Peacekeeper* is a very valuable contribution to many varied fields of theoretical debate and research, and is a timely and useful tool for anyone seeking insight into the demands and effects of peacekeeping operations on the individual soldier.

Humanitarian Intervention. Ethical, Legal, and Political Dilemmas, **J.L. Holzgrefe
and Robert O. Keohane (eds.)**
Cambridge University Press 2003,
Paperback – ISBN 0 521 52928 X, £ 18.95; US $ 25.00
Hardback – ISBN 0 521 82198 3, £ 50.00; US $ 70.00

Dieter Fleck*

The discussion on humanitarian intervention has been controversial for centuries.
It has become even more acute, as in 1994 the international community failed to
intervene in the genocide in Rwanda[1] and in 1999 the Security Council was unable
to take a decision to stop gross human rights violations in Kosovo which culmi-
nated in systematic killings and genocide, until a group of states intervened without authorisation under Chapter VII of the UN Charter. After a wealth of previous
publications, in particular the Report of the Independent International Commission
on Kosovo[2] and the Report of the International Commission on Intervention and
State Sovereignty,[3] J.L. Holzgrefe and Robert O. Keohane, together with a group
of experienced political scientists, philosophers and lawyers, have undertaken the
task of developing a thorough and truly interdisciplinary assessment of the ethical,
legal and political dilemmas of humanitarian intervention. This book may be expected
to considerably influence state practice and legal opinions in the forthcoming years.

Humanitarian intervention is defined by Holzgrefe (p. 18) as:

---

*   Dr. iur., Director, International Agreements & Policy, Federal Ministry of Defence, Germany,
    E-mail: DieterFleck@t-online.de.

1   *Report of the Independent Inquiry into the Actions of the United Nations During the 1994 Genocide
    on Rwanda*, 15 December 1999 [S/PV.4127 of 14 April 2000, SC/6843], <www.un.org/news/dh/
    latest/rwanda.htm>.
2   Independent International Commission on Kosovo: *Kosovo Report: Conflict, International Response,
    Lessons Learned* (Oxford 2000), <http://www.reliefweb.int/library/documents/thekosovoreport.htm>.
3   International Commission on Intervention and State Sovereignty, *The Responsibility to Protect:
    Report of the International Commission on Intervention and State Sovereignty* (International
    Development Research Centre, Ottawa, 2001), <http://www.dfait-maeci.gc.ca/iciss_ciise/>.

Harvey Langholtz, Boris Kondoch, Alan Wells (Eds.),
International Peacekeeping: The Yearbook of International Peace Operations, Volume 9, 2004, pp. 269-272.
© *Koninklijke Brill N.V. Printed in the Netherlands*

> the threat or use of force across state borders by a state (or group of states) aimed at pre-
> venting or ending widespread and grave violations of the fundamental human rights of indi-
> viduals other than its own citizens, without the permission of the state within whose territory
> force is applied.

Not formally excluded by this definition are actions taken under Security Council
decisions which all Members of the United Nations agreed to accept and to carry
out under Art. 25 of the UN Charter. Thus the deliberations developed in this project are as relevant for the decision-making of the Security Council as for the evaluation of actions taken without a Security Council mandate. Holzgrefe shows that
the dispute about pros and cons of humanitarian intervention is much more complex as the ethical divide between realist and liberal, moral and legal, or rule-ori-
ented and consequence-oriented arguments. With this complexity in mind, he develops
the principal theories of humanitarian intervention: utilitarianism, natural law, social
contractarianism, communitarianism, and legal positivism. But results remain as
unclear as the situation is complex: if there is a right to humanitarian intervention,
the potential of abusing such a right is notoriously high and there is certainly not
a corresponding duty to make use of it. Thus victims of gross human rights violations may wait in vain for remedies and the US, as the only remaining superpower
which can be expected to act, will, as Tom Farer convincingly explains (p. 87), find
itself operating flagrantly outside the normative consensus.

The most controversial recent case, the intervention in Kosovo, is addressed in
this book from different viewpoints and, as could be expected, without agreement.
Fernando R. Tesón, taking the NATO intervention as justified, is developing his
position from the argument that governments who seriously violate fundamental
human rights undermine the one reason that justifies their political power and thus
should not be protected by international law. His definition of permissible humanitarian intervention (p. 94) is as follows:

> the proportionate international use or threat of military force, undertaken in principle by a
> liberal government or alliance, aimed at ending tyranny or anarchy, welcomed by the victims,
> and consistent with the doctrine of double effect.

As admitted by the author (pp. 115/16), the latter doctrine is, in fact, a doctrine of
proportionality which requires that for legitimate interventions three conditions must
be met:
(1)   the act must have good consequences;
(2)   the actor must aim to achieve the good consequences and
(3)   the act's good consequences must outweigh its bad consequences.
These are fine principles, but even people of good will can interpret and implement
them in quite different ways. As Tesón rightly states (p. 109), the contrast is between

international lawyers who uphold human values and those who uphold state values. Allen Buchanan, taking a more cautious approach, considers the intervention in the case of Kosovo as unjustified *de lege lata*, but justified as a dire moral emergency to avert a humanitarian disaster. He does not exclude that the act may also be justifiable with the aim of contributing to the development of a new, morally progressive rule of international law for which he coins the term of "Illegal Legal Reform Justification" (p. 132). He develops interesting guidelines to respond to this justificatory issue (p. 160), but concludes that NATO's intervention was not credible as an act directed towards reform of the international law of humanitarian intervention (p. 170). In the words of Michael Byers and Simon Chesterman, however, the intervention in Kosovo could be justified under an alternative approach of exceptional illegality, but at the end the legal debate is considered as sterile and unhelpful, as "it is extremely unlikely that workable criteria for a right of humanitarian intervention without Security Council authorization will ever be developed to the satisfaction of more than a handful of states" (p. 202).

Looking for ways to resolve – or at least manage – the conundrum, Thomas M. Franck considers that unauthorised interventions may be tolerated or retroactively validated by the Security Council (which had then to admit that it had failed to act in the right moment). He convincingly calls for extreme caution and diligence in any effort of "promoting synthesis and synergy between legality and legitimacy: between what is lawful and what is right" (p. 231).

Jane E. Stromseth underlines the fact that the uncertain legality of humanitarian intervention puts a very high burden of justification on those who would intervene without Security Council authorisation. In her opinion this is helpful to provide consensus, based on case-by-case practice. Convincingly, she prefers a "customary law evolution approach", aiming at the identification of emerging new norms, to more static alternatives which are characterised in her contribution as "status quo approach" or "excusable breach" approach. Yet she admits that the customary law approach has some drawbacks, as relatively few cases exist and they are hardly comparable (pp. 253-54). In any event, the effectiveness of using military force for humanitarian purposes is a decisive element for any meaningful assessment. Failing effectiveness may not only influence the judgment on the particular invention, but have also serious spill-over effects on other potential interventions of equal or greater need. In this context the author explains that the severe problems encountered in the mission in Somalia during 1992 had generated such adverse reactions in the US Congress that in 1994 a significant military operation in Rwanda which could have saved so many lives was viewed by policy-makers as a non-starter (p. 270). She convincingly advocates in favour of practical decisions on a case-by-case basis rather than in a doctrinal formulation abstractly in advance, thus accepting results which may be short of what is acceptable under existing law, but could have an impact on *opinio iuris* nevertheless.

Robert O. Keohane strongly endorses the requirement to make policies to be followed after intervention as an integral part of any overall assessment. "Evaluations of the legitimacy, or prudence, of humanitarian intervention should be conditional on estimates of eventual political success. Decisions 'before intervention' should depend, to some extent, on prospects for institution-building 'after intervention'" (p. 276). This of course requires a departure from traditional conceptions of sovereignty as a serious barrier to effectiveness of post-conflict peace building. The author deliberately takes a radical position in developing the notion of limited sovereignty in modern international relations. But such radicalism may rather be considered as a realistic approach, considering many examples, in particular Germany after World War II and the US trade policy over the past 70 years, which are ably developed in Keohane's chapter. The specific influence of international institutions and good neighbourhoods remain essential mot only for the outcome of any intervention, but also for proper decision-making in advance.

The issue of sovereignty was deepened and expanded by Michael Ignatieff, considering that all recent interventions were in weak states spinning apart in the fission of civil war and secession. Rethinking the real conditions for effective domestic sovereignty, he compares protectorates and opportunities for UN administration in various relevant regions, stressing that an intervention policy that takes sides is very different from one premised on neutrality, casualty-avoidance and exit strategies.

Far from discussing this controversial topic in a merely result-oriented manner, the ten contributors were influencing each other in establishing criteria for evaluation rather than quick decision-making, which often fails to stand the test of long-term developments. This excellent piece of scholarship vigorously responds to UN Secretary-General Kofi Annan's vision that sovereignty of the people, accountability of leaders, individual rights and the rule of law deserve particular attention vis-à-vis old thinking in traditional terms of state sovereignty and non-interference in domestic affairs of other states.[4] It should be extensively consulted by experts and decision-makers alike.

---

4   UN Secretary-General, Annual Report 2001, General Assembly, Official Records, Fifty-Sixth Session, Suppl. N°. 1 (A/56/1).

Books Received

Regions of War and Peace

Douglas Lemke

This book asks whether the causes of war among great powers apply to other countries, examining regions around the world and was described in the Journal of Peace Research as ". . . deserves to be read by everyone interested in regional subsystems."
Cambridge University Press, paperback, January 2002, £15.95

Africa: A Continent Self-Destructs

Peter Schwab

Peter Schwab is an authority on human rights and a Professor of Political Science at SUNY Purchase. He has published extensively on the politics of Africa. In this book he asks: can Africa survive? Many of the nations of sub-Saharan African have all but ceased to exist as organised states: tyranny, diseases such as AIDS, civil war, ethnic conflict and border invasions threaten the complete disintegration of a region. Peter Schwab, says his publisher, offers a clear, authoritative portrait of a continent on the brink. Globalisation and an accompanying level of economic health have passed over Africa. Added to these factors is a patronising attitude from the West that change in Africa must take place within Western parameters; a UN that lacks any real power; and a US foreign policy in Africa that is unclear. Looking to South Africa as an example of successful Western support of an African nation, Schwab suggests that the US should use its leverage to help democrats into positions of power and then work with them under a framework dictated by the leaders themselves. It is, he argues, only with a distinctly African approach to African problems that the survival of the continent can be assured.

Contents

The Slave Trade, Colonialism, and the Cold War; Civil Wars, Wars, and Political Collapse; Whither Human Rights?; African Poverty and the AIDS Crisis; Globalisation and Africa; Will Africa Survive?

Harvey Langholtz, Boris Kondoch, Alan Wells (Eds.),
International Peacekeeping: The Yearbook of International Peace Operations, Volume 9, 2004, pp. 273-281.
© *Koninklijke Brill N.V. Printed in the Netherlands*

Reviews

"Offers brief, invaluable descriptions of several countries' circumstances . . . readers will gain much from this astute analysis." – *Publishers Weekly.*

"Peter Schwab has written this book with courage, honesty, and enormous insight, as well as with a deep sense of humanity. For anyone interested in the reality of Africa, this is the book to read." – Amos Sawyer, President of Liberia, 1990-1994
Palgrave Macmillan, paperback, May 2003, 212 pages, ISBN 1403960534, £12.99.

Worlds in Collision: Terror and the Future of Global Order
Ken Booth, Tim Dunne
Professor Ken Booth is Head of the Department of International Politics, University of Wales, Aberystwyth. In 2001 he was elected a member of the Academy of Leaned Societies in The Social Sciences. Tim Dunne is Senior Lecturer in International Politics at Aberystwyth. He has co-edited five books and is the author of *Inventing International Society: A History of the English School.* By bringing together an outstanding group of thinkers, they seek in *Worlds in Collision* to provide the essential book for understanding the debate about the future of global order in the wake of international terrorism and the war in Afghanistan.

For years to come, if not decades, the "war on terrorism" will be the defining paradigm in the struggle for global order. When the victim of such horrific terror attacks happens to be the world's only superpower, the agenda is set for the future global order. This book, offering a comprehensive and provocative collection of viewpoints from leading intellectuals from a number of countries, will help readers understand the ways in which our worlds collided on September 11, 2001. Not only does it comprehensively address the first phase of the war against international terrorism, the book also looks at the wider regional and global ramifications. Worlds in Collision is ultimately about more than the war on terrorism, it concerns itself with the possibilities for re-shaping global order on the basis of new kinds of politics.

Contents
Preface; Worlds in Collision; *K. Booth & T. Dunne*; **Part One: Terror**; History and September 11, *F. Fukuyama*; A New Type of War, *L. Freedman*; Unanswered Questions, *S. Smith*; Desperately Seeking Bin Laden: The Intelligence Dimension of the War Against Terrorism, *D. Ball*; Targeting Terrorist Finances: The New Challenges of Financial Market Globalization, *T. Bierstekker*; Who may we Bomb?, *B. Buzan*; Mr Bush's War on Terrorism: How Certain is the Outcome?, *I. Wallerstein*, *In Terrorem*: Before and After 9/11, *J. Der Derian*; Terror and the Future of International Law, *M. Byers*; Who are the Global Terrorists?, *N. Chomsky*
Part Two: Order; The Public Delegitimation of Terrorism and Coalition Politics, *R.O. Keohane*; The Meanings of Victory: American Power after the Towers,

M. Cox; Upholding International Legality: Against Islamic and American *Jihad, A.A. An-Na'im*; American and the Israeli-Palestinian Conflict 1991-2001, *A. Shlaim*; The Reconstruction of Afghanistan, *W. Maley*; State-Society Relations: Asian and World Order After September 11, *A. Acharya*; Catharsis and Catalysis: Transforming the Subcontinent, *R. Mohan*; Political Violence and Global Order, *P. Rogers*; Realism Vindicated? World Politics as Usual after September 11, *C. Gray*; A New Global Configuration, *F. Halliday*

Part Three: Worlds; Democracy and Terror in the Era of Jihad vs McWorld, *B. Barber*; How to Fight a Just War, *J. Bethke Elshtain*; Terrorism and Intercultural Dialogue, *B. Parekh*; Rethinking Common Values, *S. Bok*; Narratives of Religion, Civilization and Modernity, *C. Brown*; Unnecessary Suffering, *A. Linklater*; Governance Hotspots: Challenges we must Confront in the Post September 11 World, *S. Sassen*; Testing Patriotism and Citizenship in the Global Terror War, *R. Falk*; Peace, Poetry and Pentagonese, *P. Williams*; The Continuity of International Politics, *K. Waltz*.

Reviews

"This provocative and timely collection contains rich diversity in both method and content. The average quality of contributions is remarkably high, and the best are gems." – Henry Shue, Professor of Ethics and Public Life, Cornell University.

"This is a very timely and high quality collection of essays on the contexts, causes and consequences of September 11. Booth and Dunne have brought together a star-studded galaxy of authors – intellectuals, academics and thinkers who explore the myriad facets – terror, power, culture – of the attack on the twin towers from the viewpoints of international relations and international political economy. The essays are tightly argued and form a valuable collection for students, teachers, policymakers and policy watchers." – Lord Meghnad Desai.

"As we try to understand September 11, 2001, it would be hard to find a more diverse and interesting set of authors than those assembled here. Agree or disagree, you are bound to learn from them." – Joseph S. Nye, Jr. author of *The Paradox of American Power* and former, Assistant Secretary of Defence.

"This fascinating and well-written collection of essays provides abundant evidence that scholars sharply disagree not only about the causes of the September 11 terrorist attacks on the United States, but also about how best to combat the problem." – John J. Mearsheimer, R. Wendell Harrison Distinguished Service Professor, University of Chicago.

"Worlds in Collision is probably the most impressive academic symposium to appear since the World Trade Centre attack". – *The Age*.

"The editors have managed to garner contribution from a genuinely stellar group of scholars". – Navraj Singh Ghaleigh, *German Law Journal*.

"For all their academic orientations, the contributors have kept it both simple and palatable for the reader . . . the book's greatest strength is that it shifts the spotlight on to a range of questions that have been marginalized, sidelined and kept outside of policy discourse by governments across the world". – Pranab Dhal Samanta, *The Hindu.*

"As we try to understand September 11, 2001, it would be hard find a more diverse and interesting set of authors than those assembled here. Agree or disagree, you are bound to learn from them." – Joseph S. Nye, Jr. author of *The Paradox of American Power* and former Assistant Secretary of Defence.

"This fascinating and well-written collection of essays provides abundant evidence that scholars sharply disagree not only about the causes of the September 11 terrorist attacks on the United States, but also about how best to combat the problem". – John J. Mearsheimer, R. Wendell Harrison Distinguished Service Professor, Political Science Department, University of Chicago.

Palgrave Macmillan, paperback, June 2002, 384 pp., ISBN 0333998057, £15.99.

Islam and the West: Conflict or Cooperation?

Amin Saikal

A broad-ranging assessment of relations between the Muslim and Western worlds in the contemporary era set in the context of the way these have evolved historically. Arguing that the relations have been marked by long periods of peaceful coexistence, but also by many instances of tension, hostility and mutual recrimination, Amin Saikal (Director of the Centre for Arab and Islamic Studies and Professor of Political Science, Australian National University) assesses the impact of the continuing Arab-Israeli conflict, the consequences of the Iranian revolution and of the wars in the Gulf and Afghanistan, and charts a course for future co-existence.

Contents

Introduction; September 11 and its Aftermath; Shared Values and Conflicts: The Historical Experience; US Globalism and Regional Domination; The Great Issues; Democratisation in the Muslim World; *Conclusion*: The Way Forward

Reviews

"Dismissing as an oversimplification the 'clash of civilizations' view that Islam and the West are engaged in an inevitable and irreversible conflict, this book – written by a distinguished Afghan-born, Western-educated scholar – analyses the specific political, economic, and cultural roots of Islamicist terrorism. Anyone who wishes to understand the contemporary world, must heed Professor Saikal's argument." – Professor Robert G. Gilpin Jr., Princeton University.

"This is a book with a brave agenda addressed at a wide intelligent audience of non-specialists which succeeds on many levels. Covering with equal assuredness the Middle East and Central, South, and Southeast Asia, Amin Saikal provides a masterful analysis of the complex relations of Muslim polities with the non-Muslim

West. He is especially convincing in showing how the lone superpower at the end of the 20th century, the United States, has allowed itself to be drawn into, or has purposely pursued, policies that serve to undermine its professed democratic values and even-handedness in foreign relations." – R.D. McChesney, Professor of Middle Eastern Studies, New York University and editor *Iranian Studies.*

"A sober and sobering examination of what has emerged as the most critical fault-line in world affairs since 11 September 2001. All who pick up this book, including those who take issue with the author's interpretations, analyses and recommendations, are likely to put it down the richer in informed reflection for having read it." – Professor Ramesh Thakur, Vice Rector, United Nations University.

"At once engagingly written and worthy of the most serious scholarly attention, Amin Saikal's book provides an illuminating portrayal of Islam as a world historical force and a devastating account of the American response to the September 11 attacks. He concludes with a series of policy guidelines that offer the world its best chance of overcoming the intertwined challenges of mega-terrorism, religious extremism, and Western hegemonic geopolitics. All in all, a stunning achievement!" – Professor Richard A. Falk, Princeton University.

". . . a book with brave agenda addressed at a wide intelligent audience of non-specialists . . ." – R.D. McChesney, Professor of Middle Eastern Studies, New York University and editor Iranian Studies.
Palgrave Macmillan, paperback, April 2003, 184 pp., ISBN 1403903581, £13.99

Issues in Peace Research 2002 – Challenge to Non-violence
Edited by Michael Randle
Over a period of six years, from 1994-1999, the Non-violent Action Research Project brought together activists, journalists and academics – and some who were two or three of these things at once – to reflect on issues in international politics and, in particular, on non-violence and its relevance to the modern world. This book assembles a selection of the presentations, and the subsequent discussions which raise issues of enduring concern.

The result, says the publisher, is a stimulating and provocative book which is essential reading for anyone interested in contemporary politics and the role non-violence might play in shaping them in the future.
Department of Peace Studies, University of Bradford, September 2002, 304 pp., ISBN 1 85143 189 6, £15.00

All for One: Terrorism, NATO and the United States

Tom Lansford

This detailed examination of the role of the Transatlantic Alliance in support of the America-led military and intelligence operations against the Taliban and the Al-Qaida network since the terrorist attacks on the United States provides the first in-depth analysis of NATO's historic first invocation of Art. V of the Washington Treaty.

Including a substantial overview of NATO's place in the broad security framework of the Western Atlantic powers and both the shared history and ideals that form its common basis, the book specifically analyses the political machinations behind the decision to invoke Art. V and the impact of political differences among the Alliance partners. The book also looks at efforts to prevent future incidents by expanding the security framework of the Alliance.

The publisher describes this work as an essential reference source for military and foreign policy academics, courses and practitioners, offering the reader an unprecedented insight into NATO's response to this most significant event.

Tom Lansford works at The University of Southern Mississippi, USA.

Contents

Introduction: The First Test of Art. 5; Regime Formation and the Formation of NATO; NATO's role in the Transatlantic Security Regime; Building a Consensus; The Call to Arms; The Military Response to 11 September; Burdensharing; *Conclusion*: NATO's Post-11 September role
Bibliography
Index.

Reviews

". . . an opportune and telling evaluation of a complicated topic . . . Dr. Lansford's study is a sophisticated, exhaustive analysis of the NATO Alliance's role in the global war on terror . . . will repay a close reading by the scholar and the general reader alike." Henry E. Mattox, Ed. *American Diplomacy.*

". . . All for One comes highly recommended. Tom Lansford has captured the essence of the emerging debate . . . offering a timely, thoughtful voice on this momentous event . . . a well-written and balanced account . . . quite rare . . ." Robert P. Watson, Florida Atlantic University, USA.

"Lansford offers an invaluable contribution to political and military history. Highly recommended." *Choice.*

"[Tom Lansford] is to be strongly commended for pulling together the mass of details required to analyse NATO's response to 9/11 and the details of transatlantic relations as the US sought to generate a coalition and mount the military operation in Afghanistan, and for setting them out in a coherent manner in support of his analysis." *International Affairs.*

Ashgate, hardback, August 2002, 222 pp., ISBN 0 7546 3045 5, $59.95/£39.95

America's War on Terror

Patrick Hayden, Tom Lansford and Robert P. Watson

9/11 has become more than a date. It has become a noun, an idea shaped and moulded by the media and the American political establishment, and the rationale for the subsequent 'War on Terror'. But what are the real factors that have motivated the world's sole remaining superpower to engage in a permanent war declared on an often elusive and abstract enemy and risk the very relationships that have augmented that global status?

While the tragic events of 11 September 2001 caused a sea-change in the perception and realities of American security interests and its ability to project a foreign policy agenda; simplistic views that the resulting War on Terror is merely 'reactionary warfaring' no longer carry any credibility. To fully understand the direction of contemporary US foreign policy requires a detailed understanding of the complex political, historical and personal processes which influence America's new sense of itself and its view of the world. Written by a collection of leading analysts in the field, *America's War on Terror* is said by its publisher to shed new light on the causes of the War on Terror, the domestic and foreign policy implications and the forthcoming challenges for the United States and the global community.

Features include:

- Four specifically designed sections analysing the origins and the implications of the War on Terror for the United States and the broader global community.
- Historical background on the US relationship with militant Islamic extremism and the contemporary policy choices of the United States.
- Wide-ranging and diverse perspectives presented by a varied collection of contributors.
- A wealth of new original studies providing the analytical means with which to understand both the factors behind the attacks and the nation's response to them.

The publisher describes this as an engaging volume which will be essential reading for all those seeking to understand the background to the War on Terror, contemporary US foreign policy, security, Islamic terrorism and international relations.

Contents

Origins of the War on Terror: Debates and Issues: Osama bin Laden, radical Islam and the United States, Tom Lansford and Jack Covarrubias; The fight against terrorism in historical context: George W. Bush and the development of presidential foreign policy regimes, Neal Allen; Why Bush should explain 11 September, Kristin Andrews. US Domestic Implications: National security, budgeting, and policy priorities: the role and importance of candidate and President Bush, Michael G. Dziubinski and Steve A. Yetiv; The war on terrorism and President Bush: completing his father's legacy and defining his own place in history, John Davis; The loyal foot soldier: Vice President Cheney in the war on terror, Jack Lechelt. International

Implications: The politics of the Middle East peace process and the war on terror, Vaughn P. Shannon; The war on terrorism and the just use of military force, Patrick Hayden; Why identify and confront the "Axis of Evil"?, Robert J. Pauly, Jr; Conclusion: Reframing the War on Terror: "Terrorism" in the moral discourse of humanity, Mark Evans; Appendices; Select bibliography; Index.

Patrick Hayden is Lecturer in Political Theory at Victoria University of Wellington, New Zealand, Tom Lansford is Assistant Professor of Political Science at the University of Southern Mississippi, Gulf Coast, USA and Robert P. Watson is Associate Professor of Political Science at Florida Atlantic University, USA. *Ashgate, August 2003, 184 pp., ISBN 0 7546 3799 9, hardback $99.95/£55.00, paperback $24.95/£17.00*

Building Peace in West Africa: Liberia, Sierra Leone, and Guinea-Bissau
Adekeye Adebajo
Among all of Africa's troubled regions, West Africa has gone the furthest toward establishing a security mechanism to manage its own conflicts. The ECOMOG intervention in Liberia in 1990-1997 was the first by a subregional African organisation relying principally on its own personnel, money, and military materiel; and ECOMOG's 1998 intervention in Sierra Leone to restore a democratic government to power was equally unprecedented. Adekeye Adebajo explores these two cases, as well as the brief and unsuccessful intervention in Guinea-Bissau in 1999, in this study of regional peace-building efforts.

After discussing the political, economic, and security contexts of West Africa since independence, Adebajo assesses the domestic and external dynamics of the three conflicts and examines the roles and motivations of the full range of actors. Dissecting the successes and failures of external intervention in each case, he draws crucial policy lessons for building peace through the ECOWAS Mechanism for Conflict Prevention, Management, Resolution, Pecekeeping, and Security.

Adekeye Adebajo is director of the Africa Programme at the International Peace Academy and adjunct professor at Columbia University's School of International and Public Affairs. Dr. Adebajo has served on UN missions in South Africa, Western Sahara, and Iraq. He is co-editor (with Chandra Sriram) of *Managing Armed Conflicts in the 21st Century*.

Contents
Introduction; West Africa Since Independence: A Griot's Tale; Liberia: A Banquet for the Warlords; Sierra Leone: A Feast for the Sobels; Guinea-Bissau: Lilliputians Without Gulliver; The ECOWAS Security Mechanism: Toward a *Pax West Africana*.

Reviews

"Adebajo's analysis of the historic hegemonic rivalry between Nigeria and France in the region is superb." – Lansana Gberie, *African Affairs*.

"A definitive study of subregional intervention and is ideally suited for both graduate and undergraduate readings." – John Boye Ejobowah, *International Journal*.

"Provides both a sound introduction for newcomers to the region's security issues and, largely because of the interviews Adebajo has conducted with some of the region's key actors and analysts, some novel insights for more specialist audiences." – Paul Williams, *International Affairs*.

Ashgate, 2002, 191 pp., ISBN 1-58826-077-1 PB $14.95

Explorations in Themes of Conflict and Peace

Edited by Ranabir Samaddar

With the publication of this collection of essays, this series on South Asian Peace Studies begins. The first volume is therefore a general one covering a broad range of issues involving South Asia.

The essays have looked into ideals and notions of democracy, human rights and justice in the light of social and political realities of the colonial and post-colonial world. In a world characterised by structures of dominance, inequality and received notions of freedom, peace studies have to be of a critical nature. This volume is a collection of such critical writings that have emerged in this region in the last decade.

The growing militarisation of the South Asian region, arms competition, recurrent coups, ethnic conflicts, brutal suppression of popular movements and the general erosion of civil liberties and human rights have given birth to a widespread concern for peace, thus making this series in general and the volume in particular relevant and timely.

The essays in the volume cover such issues as the definition of peace studies, war and conflict situations, and peace and dialogue.

Sage Publications, November 2003, 392 pp., ISBN 0761996605, cloth, £35.00

Bibliography

Abiew, F.K., *NGO-Military Relations in Peace Operations*, International Peacekeeping (Frank Cass), Vol. 10, No. 1, 2003, p. 24.

Adomeit, H., *Putins Militärpolitik*, 2003, 43 pp. (SWP-Studie; S 2003/16).

Aggestam, K., *Conflict Prevention: Old Wine in New Bottles?*, International Peacekeeping (Frank Cass), Vol. 10, No. 1, 2003, p. 12.

Albright, M.D., *Why the United Nations Is Indispensable*, Foreign Policy, September/October 2003, p. 16.

Ali, T., *Bush in Babylon. The Recolonisation of Iraq*, Verso, 2003, 214 pp.

Ambos, K., *"Freiburg Lawyers' Declaration" of 10 February 2003 – On German Participation In A War Against Iraq*, German Law Journal, Vol. 4, No. 3, 2003, http://germanlawjournal.com/article.php?id=246.

Amnesty International, *Iraq. Memorandum on Law and Security*, AI Index MDE: 14/157/2003, 2003, 26 pp.

Amnesty International, *Iraq. On Whose Behalf?*, AI Index MDE: 14/128/2003, 2003, 23 pp.

Amnesty International, *Iraq. The Need for Security*, AI Index MDE: 14/143/2003, 2003, 16 pp.

Angel, H.-G., *Ethische Grundsätze militärischer Reaktionen*, Humanitäres Völkerrecht-Informationsschriften, Vol. 16, No. 2, 2003, p. 83.

Ansari, A.M., *Continuous Regime Change from Within*, The Washington Quarterly, Vol. 26, No. 4, 2003, p. 53.

Harvey Langholtz, Boris Kondoch, Alan Wells (Eds.),
International Peacekeeping: The Yearbook of International Peace Operations, Volume 9, 2004, pp. 283-313.
© *Koninklijke Brill N.V. Printed in the Netherlands*

Aragao, E.J.G. de, *Ein internationaler Strafgerichtshof für den Irak?*, Humanitäres Völkerrecht-Informationsschriften, Vol. 16, No. 1, 2003, p. 22.

Archer, S.E., *Civilian and Military Cooperation in Complex Humanitarian Operations*, Military Review, Vol. 83, No. 2, 2003, p. 32.

Atlantic Council of the United States, *A Winning the Peace: Managing a Successful Transition in Iraq*, Chair: R.W. Murphy, Rapporteur: C. Richard Nelson, 2003, 29 pp. (Policy Paper Series/Atlantic Council of the United States).

Atlantic Council of the United States, *New Capabilities: Transforming NATO Forces*, Co-chairs: R. Hunter; G. Joulwan, Project Director and Rapporteur: C.R. Nelson, 2002, 14 pp. (Policy Paper Series).

Aust, S., Schnibben, C. (Eds.), *Irak. Geschichte eines Modernen Krieges*, 2003, DVA, 224 pp.

Azimi, N., In, C.L., *The United Nations Transitional Administration in East Timor (UNTAET)*, Academic Publishers Brill, 2003, 320 pp.

Baimu, E., Sturman, K., *Amendment to the African Union's Right to Intervene*, African Security Review, Vol. 12, No. 2, 2003, p. 37.

Bandow, D., *Bring the Troops Home: Ending the Obsolete Korean Commitment*, 2003, 20 pp. (Policy Analysis/CATO Institute).

Barton, F.D., *Winning the Peace in Iraq*, Washington Quarterly, Vol. 26 No. 2, 2003, p. 7.

Baskin, M., *Post-conflict Administration and Reconstruction*, International Affairs, Vol. 21, No. 1, 2003, p. 161.

Bazergan, R., *Intervention and Intercourse: HIV/AIDS and Peacekeepers*, Conflict, Security and Development, Vol. 3, No. 1, 2003, p. 27.

Beestermöller, G. (Ed.), *Die humanitäre Intervention – Imperativ der Menschenrechtsidee?: rechtsethische Reflexionen am Beispiel des Kosovo-Krieges*, W. Kohlhammer, 2003, 169 pp.

Beestermöller, G., Little, D. (Eds.), *Iraq: Threat and Response*, Lit. Verl., 2003, 151 pp. (Studien zur Friedensforschung).

Bello, W., *Pax Romana versus Pax Americana: Contrasting Strategies of Imperial Management*, 2003, 4 pp. (Foreign Policy in Focus).

Bennis, P., *Before and After: US Foreign Policy and the September 11th Crisis*, Olive Branch Pr., 2003, 246 pp.

Berman, E.G., *The Multinational Force for the Congo*, African Security Review, Vol. 12, No. 3, 2003, p. 97.

Berman, E.G., *The Provision of Lethal Military Equipment: French, UK, and US Peacekeeping Policies towards Africa*, Security Dialogue, Vol. 34, No. 2, 2003, p. 199.

Berman, P., *Terror and Liberalism*, Norton, 2003, 214 pp.

Bestermöller, G., *Die USA – legitime Autorität für einen Krieg gegen den Irak?*, Vierteljahresschrift für Sicherheit und Frieden, Vol. 21, No. 1, 2003, p. 20.

Betts, R.K., *Striking First: a History of Thankfully Lost Opportunities*, Ethics & International Affairs, Vol. 17, No. 1, 2003, p. 17.

Bhatia, M.V., *War and Intervention: Issues for Contemporary Peace Operations*, Kumarian Press, 2003, 222 pp.

Bieber, F., Daskalovski, Z. (Eds.), *Understanding the War in Kosovo*, Frank Cass, 2003, 350 pp.

Blumenwitz, D., *Die völkerrechtlichen Aspekte des Irak-Konflikts*, Zeitschrift für Politik, Vol. 50, No. 3, 2003, p. 301.

Boshoff, H., Francis, D., *The AU Mission in Burundi. Technical and Operational Dimensions*, African Security Review, Vol. 12, No. 3, 2003, p. 41.

Bothe, M., *Der Irak-Krieg und das völkerrechtliche Gewaltverbot*, Archiv des Völkerrechts, Vol. 41, 2003, p. 255.

Bowman, S.R., *Iraq: US Military Operations*, updated 14 April 2003, 13 pp. (CRS Report for Congress).

Brecher, J., *Unite for Peace: What Can the World Do with US Troops in Baghdad?*, 2003, 4 pp. (Foreign Policy in Focus).

Bredel, R., *The UN's Longterm Conflict Prevention Strategies and the Impact of Counter-Terrorism*, International Peacekeeping (Frank Cass), Vol. 10, No. 2, 2003, p. 51.

Briscoe, N., *Britain and UN Peacekeeping, 1948–67*, Palgrave Macmillan, 2003, 288 pp.

Britt, T.W., *The Psycology of the Peacekeeper: Lessons from the Field*, Greenwood Pub. Group, 344 pp.

Broomhall, B., *International Justice and the International Criminal Court: Between Sovereignty and the Rule of Law*, Oxford Univ. Press, 2003, 215 pp.

Brown, C., *Self-defense in an Imperfect World*, Ethics & International Affairs, Vol. 17, No. 1, 2003, p. 2.

Brown, D., *Use of Force against Terrorism after September 11th: State Responsibility, Self-defense and Other Responses*, Cardozo Journal of International and Comparative Law, Vol. 11, No. 1, 2003, p. 1.

Bruha, T., *Irak-Krieg und Vereinte Nationen*, Archiv des Völkerrechts, Vol. 41, 2003, p. 295.

Bruhacs, J., *The Iraqi War and International Law: Surrealist Questions?*, Foreign Policy Review, Vol. 2, No. 1, 2003, p. 3.

Bury, J., *The UN Iraq-Kuwait Observation Mission*, International Peacekeeping (Frank Cass), Vol. 10, No. 2, 2003, p. 71.

Butler, R., *Improving Nonproliferation Enforcement*, The Washington Quarterly, Vol. 26, No. 4, 2003, p. 133.

Byers, M., *Letting the Exception Prove the Rule*, Ethics & International Affairs, Vol. 17, No. 1, 2003, p. 9.

Call, C.T., *Challenges in Police Reform: Promoting Effectiveness and Accountability*, 2002, 17 pp. (IPA Policy Report/International Peace Academy).

Calliess, J. (Ed.), *Zivile Konfliktbearbeitung im Schatten des Terrors*, 2003, 322 pp. (Loccumer Protokolle).

Cameron, F., Herrberg, A., *What Security Capabilities for the EU?*, 2003, 5 pp. (Security Trialogue Project/EastWest Institute).

Carey, H.F., *Conclusion: NGO Dilemmas in Peace Operations*, International Peacekeeping (Frank Cass), Vol. 10, No. 1, 2003, p. 172.

Carey, H.F., Richmond, O.P., *Mitigating Conflict: the Role of NGOs*, Frank Cass, 2003, 196 pp. (International Peacekeeping, London).

Carlowitz, L. von, *UNMIK Lawmaking between Effective Peace Support and Internal Self-Determination*, Archiv des Völkerrechts, Vol. 41, 2003, p. 336.

Carpenter, T.G., *Options for Dealing with North Korea*, 7 pp. (Foreign Policy Briefing/CATO Institute).

Center for Defense Information, *Security after 9/11: Strategy Choices and Budget Tradeoffs; a Briefing Book*, 2003, 45 pp.

Center for Policy Analysis on Palestine, *The Conflict in the Middle East: the Breakdown of Peace: Compendium of Publications July 2001 to June 2002*, 2002, 296 pp.

Chesterman, S., *Justice under International Administration: Kosovo, East Timor and Afghanistan*, 2002, 15 pp. (Transitional Administrations/International Peace Academy).

Chesterman, S., *Tiptoeing through Afghanistan: The Future of UN State-building*, 2002, 11 pp. (Transitional Administrations/International Peace Academy).

Chubin, S., Litwack, R.S., *Debating Iran's Nuclear Aspirations*, The Washington Quarterly, Vol. 26, No. 4, 2003, p. 99.

Chuter, D., *War Crimes. Confronting Atrocity in the Modern World*, Rienner, 2003, 299 pp.

Clawson, P., *How to Build a New Iraq after Saddam*, A Washington Institute for Near East Policy Book, 2003, 93 pp.

Coipuram, T. Jr., *Iraq: United Nations and Humanitarian Aid Organizations*, updated 2 June 2003, 9 pp. (CRS Report for Congress).

Colangelo, A.J., *Manipulating International Criminal Procedure: The Decision of the ICTY Office of the Independent Prosecutor Not to Investigate NATO Bombing in the Former Yugoslavia*, Northwestern University Law Review, Vol. 97, No. 3, 2003, p. 1393.

Copson, R.W. (Coordinator), *Iraq War: Backround and Issues Overview*, 22 April 2003, 55 pp. (CRS Report for Congress).

Council on Foreign Relations, *Afghanistan: Are We Losing the Peace?: Chairmen's Report of an Independent Task Force*/Co-Chairs: F.G. Wisner II, N. Platt, M.M. Bouton, Project Directors: D. Kux and M. Ispahani, New York, 2003, 24 pp.

Council on Foreign Relations, *Drastically Underfunded, Dangerously Unprepared: Report of an Independent Task Force*, Chair: W.B. Rudman. Senior Advisor: R.A. Clarke, Project Director: J.F. Metzl, 2003, 57 pp.

Crawford, N.C., *The Slippery Slope to Preventive War*, Ethics & International Affairs, Vol. 17, No. 1, 2003, p. 30.

Cronin, A.K., *Al Quaeda after the Iraq Conflict*, 2003, 6 pp. (CRS Report for Congress).

Czaplinski, W., *Crimes against Humanity v. Immunity of State Officials Revisted – Some Remarks on the Congo v. Belgium Case*, Die Friedens-Warte, No. 1, 2003, p. 63.

Czernecki, J.L., *The United Nations' Paradox: the Battle between Humanitarian Intervention and State Sovereignty*, Duquesne Law Review, Vol. 41, No. 2, 2003, p. 391.

Dalpino, C.E., *From Paris to Bonn: Lessons for Afghanistan from the Cambodian Transition*, 2002, 48 pp. (Working Paper Series/Asia Foundation).

Daniel, D.C., Caraher, L.C:, *NATO Defense Science and Technology*, 2003, 5 pp. (Defense Horizons/Center for Technology and National Security Policy).

Dawisha, A., Dawisha, K., *How to Build a Democratic Iraq*, Foreign Affairs, Vol. 82, No. 3, p. 35.

Dawn, R. (Ed.), *Executive Policing: Enforcing the Law in Peace Operations*, SIPRI Research Report, No. 16, OUP, 2003, 144 pp.

Debiel, T., Klein, A., *Fragile Peace. State Failure, Violence and Development in Crisis Regions*, Zed Books, 2002, p. 234.

Debiel, T., *UN-Friedensoperationen in Afrika: Weltinnenpolitik und die Realität von Büergerkriegen*, Dietz, 2003, 308 pp.

Deller, N., Makhijani A., and Burroughs, J. (Eds.), *Rule of Power or Rule of Law?: an Assessment of US Policy and Actions Regarding Security-related Treaties*, Apex, 2003, 272 pp.

Dickinson, L.A., *The Promise of Hybrid Courts*, The American Journal of International Law, Vol. 97, No. 2, 2003, p. 295.

Dobriansky, P.J., *Women and the Transition to Democracy: Iraq, Afghanistan, and Beyond*, Heritage Foundation, 2003, 8 pp. (Heritage Lectures).

Dobson, H., *Japan and United Nations Peacekeeping: New Pressures, New Responses*, Routledge, 2003, 188 pp.

Donald, D., *Neutral is Not Impartial: The Confusing Legacy of Traditional Peace Operations Thinking*, Armed Forces & Society, Vol. 29, No. 3, 2003, p. 415.

Donell, B.T., Kraska, J.C., *Humanitarian Law: Developing International Rules for the Digital Battefield*, Journal of Conflict & Security Law, Vol. 8, No. 1, 2003, p. 132.

Dörmann, K., *Völkerrechtliche Probleme des Landmineneinsatzes: Weiterentwicklung des geltenden Vertragsrechts durch das geänderte Minenprotokoll, vom 3. Mai 1996 zum UN-Waffenübereinkommen von 1980*, Berlin-Verl. Spitz, 2003, 534 pp.

Dougherty, B.J., *Rogue States, the Axis of Evil, and the Ethical Debate*, Humanitäres Völkerrecht-Informationsschriften, Vol. 16, No. 2, 2003, p. 87.

DSS, *Gewaltfrieden nach dem Willen der einzigen Weltmacht?: Wege aus der Gefahr*, Beiträge zum 11. Dresdner Friedenssymposium am 22. Februar 2003, 86 pp. (DSS-Arbeitspapiere).

Durch, W.J., *Picking Up the Peaces: The UN's Evolving Postconflict Roles*, The Washington Quarterly, Vol. 26, No. 4, 2003, p. 195.

Dürr, H., *Öl-M(m)acht-Raum- geopolitische Optionen*, Humanitäres Völkerrecht-Informationsschriften, Vol. 16, No. 1, 2003, p. 14.

Engelbrecht, G., *The ICC's Role in Africa*, African Security Review, Vol. 12, No. 3, 2003, p. 61.

Ehteshami, A., *Iran-Iraq Relations after Saddam*, The Washington Quarterly, Vol. 26, No. 4, 2003, p. 115.

Einsiedel, S. Graf von, Chestermann, S., *Doppelte Eindämmung im Sicherheitsrat. Die USA und Irak im diplomatischen Vorfeld des Krieges*, Vereinten Nationen, Vol. 51, No. 2, 2003, p. 47.

Eisnaugle, Carrie J. Niebur, *An International "Truth Commission": Utilizing Restorative Justice As an Alternative to Retribution*, Vanderbilt Journal of Transnational Law, Vol. 36, No. 1, 2003, p. 209.

Eitelhuber, N., *Europäische Streitkäfte unter dem Zwang der Bescheidung: Partner der USA nur bei friedenssichernden Einsätzen*, 2003, 35 pp. (SWP-Studie; S 2003/8).

Eland, I., Gourley, B., *Why the United States Should Not Attack Iraq*, 2002, 10 pp. (Policy Analysis/CATO Institute).

Eland, I., *Is Chinese Military Modernization a Threat to the United States?*, 2003, 14 pp. (Policy Analysis/CATO Institute).

Eland, I., *The China-Taiwan Military Balance: Implications for the United States*, 2003, 9 pp. (Foreign Policy Briefing/CATO Institute).

Ethics and Public Policy Center, *Iraq: Making Ethnic Peace after Saddam*, a Conversation with K. Makiya and P. Clawson, 2003, 8 pp.

Ethics and Public Policy Center, *Religion and Terrorism*, a Conversation with B. Hoffman and J. Goldberg, 2002, 14 pp. (Center Conversations/Ethics and Public Policy Center).

Evans-Kent, B., Bleiker, R., *NGOs and Reconsructing Civil Society in Bosnia and Herzegovina*, International Peacekeeping (Frank Cass), Vol. 10, No. 1, 2003, p. 103.

F Hay, William Anthony, *A Preliminary Reckoning: Prospects for US-European Relations after Iraq*, 2003, 7 pp. (Watch on the West/Foreign Policy Research Institute) http://www.fpri.org/ww/0401.200304.hay.useuropepostiraq.html.

Farer, T.J., *The Ethics of Intervention in Self-determination Struggles*, Human Rights Quarterly, Vol. 25, No. 2, 2003, p. 382.

Farrell, B., *The Role of International Law in the Kashmir Conflict*, Penn State International Law Review, Vol. 21, No. 2, 2003, p. 293.

Fasulo, L., *An Insider's Guide to the UN*, Yale University Press, 2003, 272 pp.

Fischer, H, *Der Irak-Krieg: Herausforderungen für die Humanitäre Hilfe im Schatten des Regimewechsels?*, Humanitäres Völkerrecht-Informationsschriften, Vol. 16, No. 3, 2003, p. 116.

Fischer, H., *Zwischen autorisierter Gewaltanwendung und Präventivkrieg: Der völkerrechtliche Kern der Debatte um ein militärisches Eingreifen gegen den Irak*, Humanitäres Völkerrecht-Informationsschriften, Vol. 16, No. 1, 2003, p. 4.

Fontanini, F., *Liberia's Child Soldiers Relive. Lost Childhood in Sierra Leone*, Conflict Trends, No. 2, 2003, p. 30.

Foot, R. (Ed.), *US Hegemony and International Organizations: the United States and Multilateral Organizations*, Oxford Univ. Pr., 2003, 296 pp.

Frank, H., *NATO und Europäische Union im Lichte des Irak-Kriegs*, Sicherheit+ Stabilität, Vol. 1, No. 1, 2003, p. 13.

Friedenszentrum Burg Schlaining, *Post-conflict Peacebuilding: Foundation Seminar*, 2002, 78 pp.

Frostad, M., *Good Guys Wearing Cuffs – The Detention of Peacekeepers*, German Yearbook of International Law, Vol. 45, 2002, p. 291.

Frowein, J.A., . . . (Eds.), *Verhandeln für den Frieden: Liber Amicorum Tono Eitel = Negotiating for Peace*, Springer, 2003, 866 pp.

Gaer, F.D., *Human Rights NGOs in UN Peace Operations*, International Peacekeeping (Frank Cass), Vol. 10, No. 1, 2003, p. 73.

Gajazova, O., *International Law and the Just and Justiable in Secessionist: the Cases of Tatarstan and Chechnya 1990–94*, 2002, 44 pp. (Working Papers/Copenhagen Peace Research Institute).

Gallagher, M.M., *Declaring Victory and Getting out [of Europe]: Why the North Atlantic Treaty Organization Should Disband*, Houston Journal of International Law, Vol. 25, No. 2, 2003, p. 341.

Gallis, P.E., *NATO Enlargement*, updated 5 May 2003, 6 pp. (CRS Report for Congress).

Gallis, P.E., *NATO's Decision-making Procedure*, updated 5 May 2003, 6 pp. (CRS Report for Congress).

Gardiner, N., *Limit the Role of the United Nations in Post-war Iraq*, 2003, 2 pp. (WebMemo/Heritage Foundation).

Gardiner, N., Rivkin, D.B., *Blueprint for Freedom: Limiting the Role of the United Nations in Post-war Iraq*, 2003, 9 pp. (Backgrounder/Heritage Foundation).

Gareis, S.B., *Das Ende der Weltordnung? Die Vereinten Nationen nach dem Irak-Krieg*, Humanitäres Völkerrecht-Informationsschriften, Vol. 16, No. 3, 2003, p. 142.

Gasser, H.-P., *International Humanitarian Law and Human Rights Law in Non-international Armed Conflict: Joint Venture or Mutual Exclusion?*, German Yearbook of International law, Vol. 45, 2002, p. 149.

Gokay, B., Walker, R.B.J., *11 September 2001*, Frank Cass, 2003, 160 pp.

Gompert, D.C., Nerlich, U., *Shoulder to Shoulder: the Road to US-European Military Cooperability, a German-American Analysis*, 2002, 69 pp. (RAND).

Gose, M.N., *The New US National Security Strategy: Meeting New Challenges in a Changed World*, Humanitäres Völkerrecht-Informationsschriften, Vol. 16, No. 3, 2003, p. 121.

Gow, J., *The Serbian Project and Its Adversaries: a Strategy of War Crimes*, Hurst, 2003, 322 pp.

Graham, T., *National Self-defense, International Law, and Weapons of Mass Destruction*, Chicago Journal of International Law, Vol. 4, No. 1, 2003, p. 1.

Green, L.C., *Criminal Responsibility of Individuals in Non-international Conflicts*, German Yearbook of International Law, Vol. 45, 2002, p. 82.

Green, L.C., *Enforcement of International Humanitarian Law and Threats to National Sovereignty*, Journal of Conflict & Security Law, Vol. 8, No. 1, 2003, p. 101.

Grobe-Hagel, K., *Irakistan. Der Krieg gegen den Irak und der "Kreuzzug" der USA*, ISP, 2003, p. 237.

Gupta, A., *South Asia*, 2003, 13 pp. (Strategic Effect of the Conflict with Iraq/Strategic Studies Institute).

Gyarmati, I., Walker, C., *Reconceptualizing NATO*, 2002, 7 pp. (Policy Brief/EastWest Institute).

Hadar, L.T., *Pakistan in America's War against Terrorism: Strategic Ally or Unreliable Client?*, Cato Inst., 2002, 22 pp. (Policy Analysis/CATO Institute).

Hadden, T., Harvey, C., *Local Conflict, Global Intervention: a Handbook of Human Rights, Armed Conflict and Refugee Law*, Oxford University Press, 2003, 300 pp.

Häusler, B., *Gerechtigkeit für die Opfer: eine juristische Untersuchung der indonesischen Menschenrechtsverfahren zu den Verbrechen auf Osttimor im Jahre 1999*, Justitia et Pax, 2003, 272 pp. (Gerechtigkeit und Frieden: Arbeitspapier/Deutsche Kommission Justitia et Pax).

Hagan, J., *Justice in the Balkans: Prosecuting War Crimes in the Hague Tribunal*, University of Chicago Press, 2003, 272 pp.

Hamzeh, M., May, T., *Operation Defensive Shield. Witnesses to Israeli War Crimes*, Pluto Press, 2003, 208 pp.

Hardegger, S., *Cimic-Doktrin im Spannungsfeld zwischen humanitärer Hilfe und militärischer Krisenintervention*, 2003, 86 pp. (Beiträge/Forschungsstelle für Internationale Beziehungen).

Harris, G., *The Case for Demilitarising Sub-Saharan Africa*, Conflict Trends, No. 2, 2003, p. 49.

Hauser, G., *Sicherheit in Mitteleuropa: Politik, Kooperation, Ethnizität*, 2003, 112 pp. (Schriftenreihe der Landesverteidigungsakademie).

Hawkins, V., *Measuring UN Security Council Action and Inaction in the 1990s. Lessons for Africa*, African Security Review, Vol. 12, No. 2, 2003, p. 61.

Headley, J., *Sarajevo, February 1994: the First Russia-NATO Crisis of the Post-Cold War Era*, Review of International Studies, Vol. 29, No. 2, 2003, p. 209.

Heinsch, R.W., *Possibilities to Prosecute War Crimes Committed in Iraq: The Different Forum Options*, Humanitäres Völkerrecht-Informationsschriften, Vol. 16, No. 3, 2003, p. 132.

Heintschel von Heinegg, W., *Fusion or Co-existence of International Human Rights Law and International Humanitarian Law*, German Yearbook of International Law, Vol. 45, 2002, p. 55.

Heintze, H.-J., *Zerfällt der Irak unter amerikanischen Bomben?*, Humanitäres Völkerrecht- Informationsschriften, Vol. 16, No. 1, 2003, p. 16.

Heintze, H.-J., *The European Court of Human Rights and the Implementation of Human Rights Standards during Armed Conflicts*, German Yearbook of International Law, Vol. 45, 2002, p. 60.

Higgins, N., *The Protection of United Nations & Associated Personnel*, The Journal of Humanitarian Assistance, 14 April 2003, http://www.jha.ac/articles/a116.htm.

Hillgruber, C., *Das Verhältnis von Frieden und Gerechtigkeit-völkerrechtlich betrachtet*, Zeitschrift für Politik, Vol. 50, No. 3, 2003, p. 245.

Hinde, R., Rotblat, J., *War No More. Eliminating Conflict in the Nuclear Age*, Pluto Press, 2003, 208 pp.

Hiro, D., *Iraq: In the Eye of the Storm*, Thunder's Mouth/Nation Books, 2002, 271 pp.

Hiro, D., *War without End: the Rise of Islamist Terrorism and Global Response*, Routledge, 2002, 513 pp.

Hirschmann, K., Leggemann, C. (Eds.), *Die Kampf gegen den Terrorismus: Strategien und Handlungserfordernisse in Deutschland*, Berlin Verl., 2003, 406 pp.

Hitchcock, N., *Complex Emergencies*, Conflict Trends, No. 2, 2003, p. 7.

Holzgrefe, J.L., Keohane, R.O., *Humanitarian Intervention: Ethical, Legal and Political Dilemmas*, Cambridge Univ. Pr., 2003, 350 pp.

Howard, J., Oswald, B. (Eds.), *The Rule of Law on Peace Operations. A Challenges of Peace Operations' Project Conference*, Asia-Pacific Center for Military Law, 2002, 289 pp.

Human Rights Watch, *Hearts and Minds: Post-war Civilian Deaths in Bagdad Caused by U.S. Forces*, Vol. 15, No. 9 (E), 2003, 62 pp.

Human Rights Watch, *Violent Response: The U.S. Army in Al-Falluja*, Vol. 15, No. 7 (E), 2003, 21 pp.

International Alert, *Ensuring Progress in the Prevention of Violent Conflict: Priorities for the Greek and Italian EU Presidencies*, 2003, 29 pp.

International Crisis Group, *A Middle East Roadmap to Where?*, 2 May 2003, 2003, 41 pp. (ICG Middle East Report).

International Crisis Group, *Aceh: Why the Military Option Still Won't Work*, 9 May 2003, 10 pp. (ICG Indonesia Briefing).

International Crisis Group, *Afghanistan's Flawed Constitutional Process*, 12 June 2003, 34 pp. (ICG Asia Report).

International Crisis Group, *Baghdad: a Race against the Clock*, 11 June 2003, 18 pp. (ICG Middle East Briefing).

International Crisis Group, *Congo Crisis: Military Intervention in Ituri*, 13 June 2003, 19 pp. (ICG Africa Report).

International Crisis Group, *Islamic Social Welfare Activism in the Occupied Palestinian Territories: a Legitimate Target?*, 2003, 31 pp. (ICG Middle East Report).

International Crisis Group, *Kosovo's Ethnic Dilemma: the Need for a Civic Contract*; 28 May 2003, 29 pp. (ICG Balkans Report).

International Crisis Group, *Myanmar Backgrounder: Ethnic Minority Politics*, 7 May 2003, 30 pp. (ICG Asia Report, 52).

International Crisis Group, *Nepal Backgrounder: Ceasefire – Soft Landing or Strategic Pause?*, 10 April 2003, 27 pp. (ICG Asia Report).

International Crisis Group, *Nepal: Obstacles to Peace*, 17 June 2003, 30 pp. (ICG Asia Report).

International Crisis Group, *Sudan's Other Wars*, 25 June 2003, 20 pp. (ICG Africa Briefing).

International Crisis Group, *Tackling Liberia: the Eye of the Regional Storm*, 30 April 2003, 41 pp. (ICG Africa Report; 62).

International Crisis Group, *Taiwan Strait I: What's Left of, 'One China'?*, 6 June 2003, 59 pp. (ICG Asia Report).

International Crisis Group, *Taiwan Strait II: the Chance of Peace*, 6 June 2003, 41 pp. (ICG Asia Report; 55).

International Peace Academy, *A Framework for Lasting Disarmament, Demobilization, and Reintegration of Former Combatants in Crisis Situations*/Rapporteurs: L. Hagman, Z. Nielsen, 2003, 13 pp. (IPA Workshop Report/International Peace Academy).

International Peace Academy, *Creating Conditions for Peace: What Role for the UN and Regional Actors?*, Rapporteur: D. Carment, 15 pp. (IPA Workshop Report/ International Peace Academy).

International Peace Academy, *Economic Agendas in Armed Conflict: Defining and Developing the Role of the UN*, Rapporteur: A. Guaqueta, 2002, 24 pp. (International Peace Academy).

International Peace Academy, *Lessons Learned: Peacebuilding in Haiti*, Rapporteur: L. Hagman, 2002, 15 pp. (IPA Seminar Report/International Peace Academy).

International Peace Academy, *Operationalizing the ECOWAS Mechanism for Conflict Prevention, Management, Resolution, Peacekeeping, and Security*, Rapporteurs: D. Bekoe, A. Mengistu, 2002, 37 pp. (Program on Developing Regional and Sub-Regional Security Mechanisms in Africa/International Peace Academy).

International Peace Academy, *Peacemaking in Southern Africa: the Role and Potential of the Southern African Development Community (SADC)*, Rapporteur: D.A. Bekoe, 2002, 30 pp. (Program on Developing Regional and Sub-Regional Security Mechanisms in Africa/International Peace Academy).

International Peace Academy, *Policies and Practices for Regulating Resource Flows to Armed Conflict*, Rapporteur: J. Sherman, 2002, 23 pp. (IPA Conference Report/ International Peace Academy).

International Peace Academy, *Responding to Terrorism: What Role for the United Nations?*, 25–26 October 2002, 60 pp. (International Peace Academy).

International Peace Academy, *Security and Development in Sierra Leone*, Rapporteur: L. Hagman, 2002, 15 pp. (IPA Workshop Report/International Peace Academy).

International Peace Academy, *Sharing Best Practices on Conflict Prevention: the UN, Regional and Subregional Organizations, National and Local Actors*, 2002, 18 pp. (IPA Policy Report/International Peace Academy).

International Peace Academy, *You, the People: Transitional Administration, State-building and the United Nations*, Conference Report/Rapporteur: S. von Einsiedel, 2002, 19 pp. (Transitional Administrations/International Peace Academy).

Ishizuka, K., *Ireland and International Peacekeeping*, Frank Cass, 2003, 320 pp.

Ismael, T.Y., Haddad, W.W. (Eds.), *Iraq. The Human Cost of History*, Pluto Press, 2003, 256 pp.

Israeli, R., *Islamikaze*, Frank Cass, 2003, 472 pp.

Israeli, R., *War, Peace and Terror in the Middle East*, Frank Cass, 2003, 256 pp.

Jenkins, B.M., *Countering al Qaeda: An Appreciation of the Situation and Suggestions for Strategy*, 2003, 30 pp. (RAND).

Jennings, R.S., *After Sassam Hussein: Winning a Peace If It Comes to War*, 2003, 15 pp. (Special Report/United States Institute of Peace).

Jennings, R.S., *The Road ahead: Lessons in Nation Building from Japan, Germany, and Afghanistan for Postwar Iraq*, 2003, 38 pp. (Peaceworks/United States Institute of Peace).

Jinks, D.P., *September 11 and the Laws of War*, The Yale Journal of International Law, Vol. 28, No. 1, 2003, p. 1.

Johnson, M.T., *The American Servicemembers Protection Act: Protecting Whom?*, Virginia Journal of International Law, Vol. 43, No. 2, 2003, p. 405.

Jones, D.V., *Toward a Just World: the Critical Years in the Search for International Justice*, Univ. of Chicago Pr., 2002, 270 pp.

Jonge Oudaat, C., *Combating Terrorism*, The Washington Quarterly, Vol. 26, No. 4, 2003, p. 163.

Kagan, R., *Macht und Ohnmacht: Amerika und Europa in der neuen Weltordnung*, 2003, 126 pp.

Kaplan, L.F., Kristol, W., *The War over Iraq: Saddam's Tyranny and America's Mission*, Encounter Books, 2003, 153 pp.

Katzman, K., *Afghanistan: Current Issues and US Policy*, updated 12 June 2003, 38 pp. (CRS Report for Congress).

Katzman, K., *Iraq: US Regime Change Efforts and Post-war Governance*, updated 12 June 2003, 25 pp. (CRS Report for Congress).

Katzman, K., *Iraq: Weapons Programs, UN Requirements, and US Policy*, updated 16 April 2003, 14 pp. (CRS Issue Brief).

Kaul, H.-P., *Der Internationale Strafgerichtshof: Eine Bestandsaufnahme im Frühjahr 2003*, Die Friedens-Warte, No. 1, 2003, p. 11.

Kent, V., Malan, M., *The African Standby Force*, Progress and Prospects, African Security Review, Vol. 12, No. 3, 2003, p. 71.

Kiesow, I. (Ed.), *From Taiwan to Taliban: Two Danger Zones in Asia*, Co-authors: I. Oldberg, FOI, 2002, 407 pp. (Scientific Report/Swedish Defence Research Agency).

Kimmerling, B., *Politicide. Ariel Sharon's War against the Palestinians*, Verso, 2003, 234 pp.

Klerk, B. de, Ngubane, S., *Some Reflections on the Role of Civil Society in Conflict Prevention*, Conflict Trends, No. 2, 2003, p. 33.

Klerk, B. de, *Poverty and Peace: The Internally Displaced and Refugees in Angola*, Conflict Trends, No. 2, 2003, p. 21.

Kolko, G., *Another Century of War?*, New Press, 2002, 165 pp.

Korb, L.J., *Reshaping America's Military: Four Alternatives*, Council on Foreign Relations, 2002, 96 pp.

Korhonen, O., *"Post" As Justification: International Law and Democracy-Building after Iraq*, German Law Journal, Vol. 4, No. 7, 2003, http://germanlawjournal.com/article.php?id=292.

Kosiak, S.M., *Analysis of the Administration's FY 2003 Supplemental Request for the War with Iraq*, 2003, 5 pp. (Center for Strategic and Budgetary Assessments).

Kosiak, S.M., *Potential Cost of a War with Iraq and Its Post-war Occupation*, 2003, 8 pp. (Backgrounder/Center for Strategic and Budgetary Assessments).

Kovács, A. (Eds.), *NATO, Neutrality and National Identity: the Case of Austria and Hungary*, Böhlau, 2003, 494 pp.

Krasno, J., Hayes, B.C., Daniel Donald C.F. (Eds.), *Leveraging for Success in United Nations Peace Operations*, Praeger, 2003, 288 pp.

Krasno, J.E., Sutterlin, J.S., *The United Nations and Iraq. Defanging the Viper*, Praeger Publishers, 2003, 238 pp.

Kröning, V, *Prävention oder Präemption?*, Humanitäres Völkerrecht-Informations-schriften, Vol. 16, No. 2, 2003, p. 82.

Ku, C., Brun, J., *Neutrality and the ICRC Contribution to Contemporary Humanitarian Operations*, International Peacekeeping (Frank Cass), Vol. 10, No. 1, 2003, p. 56.

Kühnemund, M., *Die Vereinten Nationen und der "Krieg gegen den Terrorismus"*, 2003, 108 pp. (Arbeitspapiere zu Problemen der internationalen Politik und der Entwicklungsländerforschung).

Kull, S.P., *Americans on Iraq after the UN Resolution*, 3 December 2002, PIPA, 2002, 10 pp. (The PIPA/Knowledge Networks Poll).

Kull, S.P., *The Potential for a Nonviolent Intifada II: a Study of Palestinian and Israeli Jewish Public Attitudes*, PIPA, 2002, 32 pp. (Program on International Policy Attitudes).

Kunig, P., *Das Völkerrecht als Recht der Weltbevölkerung*, Archiv des Völkerrechts, Vol. 41, 2003, p. 327.

Kunzmann, K., *Reconstructing Iraq and Who Pays: Is There an International Responsibility to Reconstruct a Country Destroyed by War?*, German Law Journal, Vol. 4, No. 7, 2003, http://germanlawjournal.com/article.php?id=293.

Laqueur, W., *Krieg dem Westen: Terrorismus im 21. Jahrhundert*, Propylaen-Verl., 2003, 420 pp.

Laurenti, J., *Iraqi Threats: What Common Cause across the Atlantic?*, 2002, 13 pp. (United Nations Association of the United States of America).

Lawyers Committee for Human Rights, *Refugees, Rebels and the Quest for Justice*, 2002, 295 pp.

Lepel, O.M. Frhr. von, *Die präemptive Selbstverteidigung im Lichte des Völkerrechts*, Humanitäres Völkerrecht-Informationsschriften, Vol. 16, No. 2, 2003, p. 77.

Levitt, M., *Targeting Terror: US Policy toward Middle Eastern State Sponsors and Terrorist Organizations, Post-September 11*, Washington Institute for Near East Policy, 2002, 141 pp.

Limpert, M., *Auslandseinsatz der Bundeswehr*, Duncker & Humblodt, 2002, 155 pp.

Long, W.J., Brecke, P., *War and Reconciliation: Reason and Emotion in Conflict Resolution*, MIT Pr., 2003, 235 pp.

Lüder, S.R., *Zum verfassungsrechtlichen Umfeld einer Beteiligung der Bundeswehr an Maßnahmen des Internationalen Strafgerichtshofes*, Humanitäres Völkerrecht-Informationsschriften, Vol. 16, No. 1, 2003, p. 25.

Lutz, D.S., Gießmann, H.J. (Eds.), *Die Stärke des Rechts gegen das Recht des Stärkeren*, Nomos, 2003, 430 pp.

MacDonald, N., Sullivan, S., *Rational Interpretation in Irrational Times: the Third Geneva Convention and the "War on Terror"*, Harvard International Law Journal, Vol. 44, No. 1, 2003, p. 301.

MacInnes, C., *A Different Kind of War?: September 11 and the United States' Afghan War*, Review of International Studies, Vol. 29, No. 2, 2003, p. 165.

Mackinlay, J., Cross, P. (Eds.), *Regional Peacekeepers: the Paradox of Russian Peacekeeping*, United Nations University Press, 2003, 224 pp.

MacQueen, *A Community of Illusions? Portugal, the CLP and Peacemaking in Guiné-Bissau*, International Peacekeeping (Frank Cass), Vol. 10, No. 2, 2003, p. 1.

Madelin, A., *For a New Alliance*, Heritage Foundation, 2003, 6 pp. (Heritage Lectures).

Mair, S., *Einsatzgebiet Kongo: die EU-Friedensmission in der Ituri-Provinz*, 2003, 4 pp. (SWP-aktuell, 2003/22).

Makins, C.J., *'Power and Weakness' or Challenge and Response?: Reflections on the Kagan Thesis*, 2003, 13 pp. (Atlantic Council of the United States).

Maley, W., Sampford, C. and Thakur R. (Eds.), *From Civil Strife to Civil Society: Civil and Military Responsibilities in Disrupted States*, United Nations University Press, 2003, 369 pp.

Maley, W., *The Afghanistan Wars*, Palgrave, 2002, 340 pp.

Malone, D.M., Khong, Y.F., *Unilateralism & U.S. Foreign Policy. International Perspectives*, Lynne Rienner Publishers, 2003, 477 pp.

Manske, G., *Verbrechen gegen die Menschlichkeit als Verbrechen an der Menschheit. Zu einem zentralem Begriff der internationalen Strafgerichtsbarkeit*, Duncker & Humblot, 2003, 400 pp.

Manwaring, M.G., *Latin America*, 2003, 15 pp. (Strategic Effect of the Conflict with Iraq/Strategic Studies Institute).

Marauhn, T., *The Debate about a Revolution in Military Affairs – A Comment in the Light of Public International Law*, Die Friedens-Warte, No. 4, 2002, p. 411.

Mark, C.R., *Palestinians and Middle East Peace: Issues for the United States*, updated June 12, 2003, 16 pp. (CRS Issue Brief).

Matthews, J., *Women and War*, Pluto Press, 2003, 192 pp.

Matveeva, A., Hiscock, D. (Eds.), *The Caucasus: Armed and Divided: Small Arms and Light Weapons Proliferation and Humanitarian Cosequences in the Caucasus*, 2003, 169 pp. (Report/Saferworld).

Maull, H.W., *Sicherheit und Macht in den Zeiten der Globalisierung*, Sicherheit+ Stabilität, Vol. 1, No. 1, 2003, p. 17.

McDougall, W.A., *What the US Needs to Promote in Iraq (Hint: It's Not Democratization Per Se)*, 2003, 12 pp. (FPRI Wire/Foreign Policy Research Institute), http://www.fpri.org/fpriwire/1102.200305.mcdougall.uspromoteiniraq.html.

McIntyre, A., *Rights, Root Causes, and Recruitment. The Youth Factor in Africa's Armed Conflicts*, African Security Review, Vol. 12, No. 2, 2003, p. 91.

McIntyre, A., Thusi, T., *Children and Youth in Sierra Leone's Peace Building Process*, African Security Review, Vol. 12, No. 2, 2003, p. 73.

Mégret, F., Hoffmann, F., *The UN As a Human Rights Violator?: Some Reflections on the United Nations Changing Human Rights Responsibilities*, Human Rights Quarterly, Vol. 25, No. 2, 2003, p. 314.

Meiers, F-J., *Die Auswirkungen des 11. Septembers 2001 auf die transatlantischen Beziehungen*, 2003, 72 pp. (Zentrum für Europäische Integrationsforschung-Discussion Paper).

Mekenkamp. M. (Ed.), *Searching for Peace in Central and South Asia: an Overview of Conflict Prevention and Peacebuilding Activities*, Rienner, 2002, 661 pp.

Migdalovitz, C., *The Middle East Peace Talks*, updated 12 June 2003, 16 pp. (CRS Issue Brief).

Millen, R.A., *The "New" American Way of War: 14th Annual Strategy Conference*, 2003, 4 pp. (Conference Brief/Strategic Studies Institute).

Molukanele, T., *On Being a Refugee in Africa*, Conflict Trends, No. 2, 2003, p. 16.

Monshipouri, M., *NGOs and Peacebuilding in Afghanistan*, International Peacekeeping (Frank Cass), Vol. 10, No. 1, 2003, p. 138.

Moore, D.W., *Fewer Say Iraq Worth Going to War Over: Failure to Find Weapons of Mass Destruction, Continuing Conflict Appear to Have Major Impact*, 1 July 2003, 7 pp. (Gallup Poll Analysis).

Müller, H., *Die IAEA unter Beschuß. Lernprozesse einer Internationalen Organisation*, Vereinten Nationen, Vol. 51, No. 3, 2003, p. 71.

Murphy, R., *United Nations Peacekeeping in Lebanon and Somalia, and the Use of Force*, Journal of Conflict & Security Law, Vol. 8, No. 1, 2003, p. 71.

Murphy, S.D., *International Law, the United States, and Non-military "War" against Terrorism*, European Journal of International Law, Vol. 14, No. 2, 2003, p. 347.

Murphy, R.,Wills, S., *Criminalizing Attacks on United Nations Peacekeepers and the Creation of an Effective International Legal Protection*, Irish Criminal Law Journal, Vol. 11, No. 2, 2001, p. 14.

Murswiek, D., *Die amerikanische Präventivkriegsstrategie und das Völkerrecht*, Neue juristische Wochenschrift, Vol. 56, No. 14, 2003, p. 1014.

Neff, S.C., *The Legal Institution of War: a History*, Cambridge University Press, 2003, 450 pp.

Nelson, C.R., Purcell. J.S. (Eds.), *Transforming NATO Forces: European Perspectives*, a Compendium of Papers Presented at a Conference 18 October 2002, 2003, 143 pp. (Atlantic Council of the United States).

Neukirch, C., *Konfliktmanagement und Konfliktprävention im Rahmen von OSZE-Langzeitmissionen: eine Analyse der Missionen in Moldau und Estland*, Nomos Verl. Ges., 2003, 333 pp.

Newport, F., Carroll, J., *Americans Growing Less Positive about Media's Coverage of War: New Poll Shows Largest Decrease in Ratings of the News Media by War Supporters*, 2003, 5 pp. (Gallup Poll Analysis).

Ngandu, I., Swai, F., *World Refugee Day: What It Means for Africa*, Conflict Trends, No. 2, 2003, p. 11.

Nichols, T.M., *Just War, Not Prevention*, Ethics & International Affairs, Vol. 17, No. 1, 2003, p. 25.

Nienhaus, V., *Kosten eines Irak-Krieges: Wirtschaftliche und politische Aspekte*, Humanitäres Völkerrecht-Informationsschriften, Vol. 16, No. 1, 2003, p. 10.

Ngoma, N., *SADC: Towards a Security Community*, African Security Review, Vol. 12, No. 3, 2003, p. 17.

Nolte, G. (Ed.), *European Military Law Systems*, De Gruyter Recht, 2003, 908 pp.

Noonan, M.P., *The Military Lessons of Operation Iraqi Freedom*, 2003, 5 pp. (E-notes/Foreign Policy Research Institute), http://www.fpri.org/enotes/20030501.military.noonan.militarylessonsiraqifreedom.html.

O' Hanlon, M., Mochizuki, M., *Toward a Grand Bargain with North Korea*, The Washington Quarterly, Vol. 26, No. 4, 2003, p. 7.

Oette, L., *Die Vereinbarkeit der vom Sicherheitsrat nach Kapitel VII der UN-Charta verhängten Wirtschaftssanktionen mit den Menschenrechten und dem humanitären Völkerrecht*, Peter Lang, 2003, 592 pp.

O'Hanlon, M.E., *Defense Policy Choices for the Bush Administration*, Brookings Inst. Pr., 2003, 220 pp.

O'Hanlon, M.E., *Expanding Global Military Capacity for Humanitarian Intervention*, Brookings Inst. Pr., 2003, 125 pp.

Okumu, W., *Humanitarian International NGOs and African Conflicts*, International Peacekeeping (Frank Cass), Vol. 10, No. 1, 2003, p. 120.

Oldberg, I., *Reluctant Rapprochement: Russia and the Baltic States in the Context of NATO and EU Enlargements*, FOI, 2003, 82 pp. (Swedish Defence Research Agency).

Orakhelashvili, A., *The Legal Basis of the United Nations Peace-keeping Operations*, Virginia Journal of International Law, Vol. 43, No. 2, 2003, p. 485.

Orford, A, *Reading Humanitarian Intervention: Human Rights and the Use of Force in International Law*, Cambridge University Press, 2003, 300 pp.

Orjuela, C., *Building Peace in Sri Lanka: a Role for Civil Society?*, Journal of Peace Research, Vol. 40, No. 2, 2003, p. 195.

O'Sullivan, M.L., *Shrewd Sanctions: Statecraft and State Sponsors of Terrorism*, Brookings Inst., 2003, 424 pp.

Paech, N., *Die Rolle der UNO und des Sicherheitsrates im Irakkonflikt*, Vierteljahresschrift für Sicherheit und Frieden, Vol. 21, No. 1, 2003, p. 28.

Pampell, C., *More than Victims: the Role of Women in Conflict Prevention*, a Conference Report, 2002, 55 pp. (Woodrow Wilson International Center for Scholars).

Parachini, J., *Putting WMD Terrorism into Perspective*, The Washington Quarterly, Vol. 26, No. 4, 2003, p. 37.

Perl, R.F., *Terrorism and National Security: Issues and Trends*, updated 6 June 2003, 16 pp. (CRS Issue Brief).

Perthes, V., *Nach Saddam Hussein: politische Perspektiven im Mittleren Osten*, 2003, 17 pp. (SWP-Studie).

Pew Research Center for the People and the Press, *War Concerns Grow but Support Remains Steadfast: 71% Favor Major Post-war Role for US*, 3 April 2003, 17 pp. (Survey Report).

Pew Research Center for the People and the Press, *War Coverage Praised, but Public Hungry for Other News: Overcovered: Protesters, Ex-generals*, 9 April 2003, 11 pp. (Survey Report).

Philips, J.D., *Iranian and Syrian Meddling in Postwar Iraq*, 2003, 2 pp. (Heritage Foundation).

Pickering, T.R., Schlesinger, J.R., *Iraq: the Day after: Chairs' Update*, 2003, 23 pp., http://www.cfr.org/publication.php?id=6075 (Council on Foreign Relations).

Pilch, F.T., *Sexual Violence: NGOs and the Evolution of International Humanitarian Law*, International Peacekeeping (Frank Cass), Vol. 10, No. 1, 2003, p. 90.

Plate, B. von, *Die Zukunft des transatlantischen Verhältnisses: mehr als die NATO*, 2003, 23 pp. (SWP-Studie).

Polman, L., *We Did Nothing. Why the Truth Doesn't Always Come Out When the UN Goes In*, Viking, 2003, 240 pp.

Polyakov, L., *Ukrainian-NATO Relations and New Prospects for Peacekeeping*, RIIA, 2003, 75 pp.

Posner, E.A., *A Theory of the Laws of War*, The University of Chicago Law Review, Vol 70, No. 1, 2003, p. 297.

Preble, C., *After Victory: toward a New Military Posture in the Persian Gulf*, 2003, 15 pp. (Policy Analysis/CATO Institute).

Priest, D., *The Mission: Waging War and Keeping Peace with America's Military*, Norton, 2003, 429 pp.

Program on International Policy Attitudes, *Americans on Iraq and the UN Inspections*, January 2003, 14 pp.

Prosper, P.-R., *Justice without Borders: the International Criminal Court*, Temple International and Comparative Law Journal, Vol. 17, No. 1, 2003, p. 85.

Puttler, A., *Deutschland, der Irak-Konflikt und das Grundgesetz*, Humanitäres Völkerrecht-Informationsschriften, Vol. 16, No. 1, 2003, p. 7.

Quénivet, N., *Who Changed the Road Rules? The ICC and the Security Council Hammering in Conflicting Road Signs*, Die Friedens-Warte, No. 1, 2003, p. 53.

Rabil, R.G., *Embattled Neighbors: Syria, Israel, and Lebanon*, Rienner, 2003, 306 pp.

Rai, M., *Regime Unchanged. Why the War on Iraq Changed Nothing*, Pluto Press, 2003, 256 pp.

Rau, M., *Der aktuelle Fall: Die belgische Justiz als Wächter über die Menschenrechte? Das Urteil der "Cour de Cassiation de Belgique" im Fall Sharon vom 12. Februar 2003*, Humanitäres Völkerrecht-Informationsschriften, Vol. 16, No. 2, 2003, p. 92.

Reisman, W.M., *Assessing Claims to Revise the Laws of War*, The American Journal of International Law, Vol. 97, No. 1, 2003, p. 82.

Reissner, J., *Iran nach dem Irak-Krieg: zwischen amerikanischen Druck und europäischer Annäherung*, 32 pp. (SWP-Studie; S 2003/25).

Reiter, E. (Ed.), *Europas ferne Streitmacht: Chancen und Schwierigkeiten der Europäischen Union beim Aufbau der ESVP*, Mittler, 2002, 296 pp.

Richardson, H.J., *U.S. Hegemony, Race, and Oil in Deciding United Nations Security Council Resolution 1441 on Iraq*, Temple International and Comparative Law Journal, Vol. 17, No. 1, 2003, p. 27.

Richmond, O.P., *Introduction: NGOs, Peace and Human Security*, International Peacekeeping (Frank Cass), Vol. 10, No. 1, 2003, p. 1.

Ropers, N., *Friedensentwicklung, Krisenprävention und Konfliktbearbeitung: technische Zusammenarbeit im Kontext von Krisen, Konflikten und Katastrophen*, 2002, 90 pp. (Deutsche Gesellschaft für technische Zusammenarbeit).

Rosand, E, *Security Council Resolution 1373, the Counter-Terrorism Committee, and the Fight against Terrorism*, The American Journal of International Law, Vol. 97, No. 2, 2003, p. 333.

Rost, C.A., *A Legal War, a Legal Regime? Facts and Statement of the Legality of the War and the "Post-Saddam Iraq"*, Vierteljahresschrift für Sicherheit und Frieden, Vol. 21, No. 1, 2003, p. 14.

Roubini, N., Setser, B., *Should Iraq Dollarize, Adopt a Currency Board or Let Its Currency Float?: a Policy Analysis*, 2003, 14 pp. (Council on Foreign Relations).

Roux, L. le, *Defence Sector Transformation. Challenges for Sub Saharan Africa*, African Security Review, Vol. 12, No. 3, 2003, p. 5.

Rubin, B.R., *Transitional Justice and Human Rights in Afghanistan*, International Affairs, Vol. 79, No. 3, 2003, p. 567.

Rubinstein, R.A., *Cross-cultural Considerations in Complex Peace Operations*, Negotiation Journal, Vol. 19, No. 1, 2003, p. 29.

Rudolf, P., *Der 11. September, die Neuorientierung amerikanischer Außenpoltik und der Krieg gegen den Irak*, Zeitschrift für Politik, Vol. 50, No. 3, 2003, p. 257.

Rupprecht, J., *Frieden durch Menschenrechtsschutz: Strategien der Vereinten Nationen zur Verwirklichung der Menschenrechte*, Nomos, 2003. 363 pp.

Saikal, A., Schnabel, A. (Eds.), *Democratization in the Middle East: Experiences, Struggles, Challenges*, United Nations Univ. Pr., 2003, 211 pp.

Sanford, V., *Eyewitness: Peacebuilding in a War Zone: The Case of Columbian Peace*, International Peacekeeping (Frank Cass), Vol. 10, No. 2, 2003, p. 107.

Sautman, B., *"Cultural Genocide" and Tibet*, Texas International Law Journal, Vol. 38, No. 2, 2003, p. 173.

Schabas, W.A., *Punishment of Non-state Actors in Non-international Armed Conflict*, Fordham International Law Journal, Vol. 26, No. 4, 2003, p. 907.

Schloms, M., *Humanitarian NGOs in Peace Processes*, International Peacekeeping (Frank Cass), Vol. 10, No. 1, 2003, p. 40.

Schmidseder, K., *Internationale Interventionen und Crisis Response Operations: Charakteristika, Bedingungen und Kosequenzen für das internationale und nationale Krisenmangement*, Peter Lang, 2003, 204 pp.

Schmidt, P., *ESVP und Allianz nach dem Vierergipfel*, 2003, 8 pp. (SWP-aktuell).

Schmitt, M.N., *Preemptive Strategies in International Law*, Michigan Journal of International Law, Vol. 24, No. 2, 2003, p. 513.

Schmitz, K., *Durchgriffswirkung von Massnahmen der UN und ihrer Sonderorganisationen unter besonderer Berücksichtigung von Resolutionen des UN-Sicherheitsrates: die Entwicklung supranationaler Strukturen*, Peter Lang, 2003, 282 pp.

Schneider, M., *Die Sicherheit humanitärer Helfer im Irak*, Humanitäres Völkerrecht-Informationsschriften, Vol. 16, No. 3, 2003, p. 138.

Schneider, P., *Internationale Gerichtsbarkeit als Instrument friedlicher Streitbeilegung: von einer empirisch fundierten Theorie zu einem innovativen Konzept*, Nomos Verl.-Ges., 2003, 332 pp.

Schneider, T., *Wasserver- und -entsorgung—ein militärisches Ziel?*, Humanitäres Völkerrecht-Informationsschriften, Vol. 16, No. 1, 2003, p. 23.

Schorlemer, S. von (Eds.), *Praxishandbuch UNO: die Vereinten Nationen im Lichte globaler Herausforderungen*, Springer, 2003, 774 pp.

Schorlemer, S. von, *Human Rights: Substantive and Institutional Implications of the War against Terrorism*, European Journal of International Law, Vol. 14, No. 2, 2003, p. 265.

Schreiber, W., *Das Kriegsgeschehen 2002: Daten und Tendenzen der Kriege und bewaffneten Konflikte*, Leske u. Budrich, 2003, 272 pp.

Schürr, U., *Der Aufbau einer europäischen Sicherheits- und Verteidigungsidentität: Im Beziehungsgeflecht von EU, WEU, OSZE und NATO*, Peter Lang, 2003, 316 pp.

Schütz, C., *Die NATO-Intervention in Jugoslawien: Hintergründe, Nebenwirkungen und Folgen*, 2003, 165 pp.

Scraton, P. (Ed.), *Beyond September 11: an Anthology of Dissent*, Pluto Pr., 2002, 251 pp.

Scruton, R., *The United States, the United Nations, and the Future of the Nation-state*, Heritage Foundation, 2003, 12 pp. (Heritage Lectures).

Sealing, K.E., *"State Sponsors of Terrorism" Is a Question, Not an Answer: the Terrorism Amendment to the FSIA makes Less Sense Now than It Did before 9/11*, Texas International Law Journal, Vol. 38, No. 1, 2003, p. 119.

Serafino, N.M., *Peacekeeping: Issues of US Military Involvement*, updated 12 June 2003, 16 pp. (CRS Issue Brief).

Sewall, G.T., *Textbooks and the United Nations: the International System and What American Students Learn about It*, 2002, 62 pp. (United Nations Association of the United States of America).

Sicherman, H., *The Road to Palestine*, 2003, 9 pp. (Peacefacts: a Briefing on the Middle East Peace Process/Foreign Policy Research Institute), http://www.fpri.org/peacefacts/101.200306.sicherman.roadtopalestine.html.

Sick, G., *Iran: Confronting Terrorism*, The Washington Quarterly, Vol. 26, No. 4, 2003, p. 69.

Siedschlag, A., *Der 11. September, der Irak-Krieg und die Nonproliferation von Massenvernichtungswaffen*, Zeitschrift für Politik, Vol. 50, No. 3, 2003, p. 281.

SIPRI, *SIPRI Yearbook 2003: Armaments, Disarmament and International Security*, OUP, 2003, 847 pp.

Sloan, S.R., *NATO and Transatlantic Relations in the 21st Century: Crisis, Continuity or Change?*, 2002, 56 pp. (Headline Series/Foreign Policy Association).

Smith, A.L., *Southeast Asia*, 2003, 15 pp. (Strategic Effect of the Conflict with Iraq/Strategic Studies Institute).

Smith, D., *"The Regime is Gone": Early Lessons from Iraq*, 2003, 3 pp. (Foreign Policy in Focus).

Smith, D., *The Penguin Atlas of War and Peace*, Penguin Books, 2003, 128 pp.

Smith, D., *The World at War*, January 2003, 17 pp. (Defense Monitor).

Smith, M.A., *Russia and the Israeli-Palestinian Conflict*, 2002, 7 pp. (Occasional Brief/Conflict Studies Research Centre).

Smith, M.G., Dee, M., *Peacekeeping in East Timor: the Path to Independence*, Rienner, 2003, 214 pp. (Occasional Paper Series/International Peace Academy).

Smoljan, J., *Socio-economic Aspects of Peacebuilding: UNTAES and the Organisation of Employment in Eastern Slavonia*, International Peacekeeping (Frank Cass), Vol. 10, No. 2, 2003, p. 27.

Sofaer, A.D., *On the Necessity of Pre-emption*, European Journal of International law, Vol. 14, No. 2, 2003, p. 209.

Sponeck, H. von, *Irak, Chronik eines gewollten Krieges*, Kiepenheuer u. Witsch, 2003, 158 pp.

Sriram, C., Wermester, K., *From Promise to Practice: Strengthening UN Capacities for the Prevention of Violent Conflict*, 2003, 21 pp. (IPA policy report/International Peace Academy).

Sriram, C.L., Wermester, K. (Eds.), *From Promise to Practice: Strengthening UN Capabilities for the Prevention of Violent Conflict*, Rienner, 2003, 427 pp. (International Peace Academy).

Stedman, S.J., Tanner, F. (Eds.), *Refugee Manipulation: War, Politics, and the Abuse of Human Suffering*, Brookings Inst. Pr., 2003, 202 pp.

Stott, N., Meek, S., *Ready, Set, Trace. Making Progress in Trafficking Illegal Arms*, African Security Review, Vol. 12, No. 2, 2003, p. 27.

Stürmer, M., *Welt ohne Weltordnung*, Sicherheit+Stabilität, Vol. 1, No. 1, 2003, p. 9.

Suayna, T.S., *NATO Enlargement: Assessing the Candidates for Prague*, 2002, 6 pp. (Bulletin/Atlantic Council of the United States).

Sutterlin, J.S., *The United Nations and the Maintenance of International Security: a Challenge to Be Met*, Praeger, 2003, 264 pp.

Swart, G., *A Brief Assessment of the Lusaka Ceasefire Agreement and the Inter-Congolese Dialogues: Towards Peace in the DRC*, Conflict Trends, No. 2, 2003, p. 37.

Swart, G., Solomon, H., *The Islamic Fundamentalist State of Sudan*, Conflict Trends, No. 2, 2003, p. 43.

Terrill, W.A, *Prospects for Peace in South Asia*, 2003, 4 pp. (Conference Brief/Strategic Studies Institute).

Terrill, W.A, *The Middle East, North Africa, and Turkey*, 2003, 14 pp. (Strategic Effect of the Conflict with Iraq/Strategic Studies Institute).

Thamm, B.G., *Im Brennpunkt: Die Bedrohung durch nicht-staatliche Akteure*, Sicherheit+Stabilität, Vol. 1, No. 1, 2003, p. 55.

Theiler, O., *Die NATO im Umbruch: Bündnisreform im Spannungsfeld konkurrierender Nationalinteressen*, Nomos Verlagsgesellschaft, 2003, 357 pp.

Thio, L.-A., *Developing a "Peace and Security" Approach towards Minorities' Problems*, The International and Comparative Law Quarterly, Vol. 52, No. 1, 2003, p. 115.

Thürer, D., *Irak-Krise: Anstoß zu einem Neuüberdenken der völkerrechtlichen Quellenlehre?*, Archiv des Völkerrechts, Vol. 41, 2003, p. 314.

Thusi, T., *Assesing Small Arms Control Initiatives in East Africa. The Nairobi Declaration*, African Security Review, Vol. 12, No. 2, 2003, p. 17.

Tomuschat, C., *Völkerrecht ist kein Zweiklassenrecht. Der Irak-Krieg und seine Folgen*, Vereinten Nationen, Vol. 51, No. 2, 2003, p. 41.

Toure, A., *The Role of Civil Society in National Reconciliation and Peacebuilding in Liberia*, 2002, 28 pp. (Project on Civil Society: Case Studies on National Reconciliation and Peacebuilding in Africa/International Peace Academy).

Travalio, G.M., Altenburg, J., *Terrorism, State Responsibility, and the Use of Military Force*, Chicago Journal of International Law, Vol. 4, No. 1, 2003, p. 97.

Tshitereke, C., *On the Origins of War in Africa*, African Security Review, Vol. 12, No. 2, 2003, p. 81.

United Nations Association of the United States of America, *Rebuilding Iraq: How the United States and United Nations Can Work Together*, a Briefing Paper, 2003, 23 pp.

United States Institute of Peace, *Establishing the Rule of Law in Iraq*, 2003, 16 pp. (Special Report/United States Institute of Peace).

United States Institute of Peace, *Unfinished Business in Afghanistan: Warlordism, Reconstruction, and Ethnic Harmony*, 2003, 12 pp. (Special Report/United States Institute of Peace).

United States Institute of Peace, *Would an Invasion of Iraq Be a "Just War"?*, 2003, 15 pp. (Special Report/United States Institute of Peace).

Vagts, D.F., *Which Courts Should Try Persons Accused of Terrorism?*, European Journal of International Law, Vol. 14, No. 2, 2003, p. 313.

Valki, L., *Legal Surrealism: The War against Iraq*, Foreign Policy Review, Vol. 2, No. 1, 2003, p. 17.

Wagner, C., Wilke, B, *Nach dem Irakkrieg: neue Bewegung im Kaschmirkonflikt?*, 2003, 7 pp. (SWP-aktuell, 2003/23).

Weigel, G., *Moral Clarity in a Time of War: the Second Annual William E. Simon Lecture*, 2002, 19 pp. (Ethics and Public Policy Center).

Weiss, T., *A Demand-Side Approach to Fighting Small Arms Proliferation*, African Security Review, Vol. 12, No. 2, 2003, p. 5.

Weiss, T.G., *The Illusion of UN Security Council Reform*, The Washington Quarterly, Vol. 26, No. 4, 203, p. 147.

Weldon, C., *A Korea Peace Initiative*, 2003, 5 pp. (Foreign Policy Research Institute), http://www.fpri.org/enotes/20030626.asia.weldon.koreapeaceinitiative.html.

Wellens, K., *The UN Security Council and New Threats to the Peace: Back to the Future*, Journal of Conflict & Security Law, Vol. 8, No. 1, 2003, p. 15.

Wet, E. de, *The Illegality of the Use of Force Against Iraq Subsequent to the Adoption of Resolution 687 (1991)*, Humanitäres Völkerrecht-Informationsschriften, Vol. 16, No. 3, 2003, p. 125.

Wetzel, J.E., *Der aktuelle Fall: Der Special Court für Sierra Leone*, Humanitäres Völkerrecht-Informationsschriften, Vol. 16, No. 3, 2003, p. 147.

Wiesmann, K., *Die vielleicht letzte Chance der NATO: die Umsetzung der Prager Gipfelentscheidungen*, 2003, 30 pp. (SWP-Studie).

Williams, I., *Will International Law Shape the Occupation or the Occupation Shape International Law?*, 2003, 3 pp. (Foreign Policy in Focus).

Williams, R., *The Changing Understandings of the Nature of Humanitarian Assistance and the Longer-Term Implications for the Role of International Humanitarian Law*, Humanitäres Völkerrecht-Informationsschriften, Vol. 16, No. 3, 2003, p. 119.

Wilson, G., *UN Authorized Enforcement: Regional Organizations versus 'Coalitions of the Willing'*, International Peacekeeping (Frank Cass), Vol. 10, No. 2, 2003, p. 89.

Wirsing, R.G., *Kashmir in the Shadow of War: Regional Rivalries in a Nuclear Age*, Sharpe, 2003, 285 pp.

Woodrow Wilson International Center for Scholars, *Winning the Peace Conference Report: Women's Role in Post-conflict Iraq*, Principal Author and Conference Rapporteur: A. Brennan, 2003, 24 pp.

Wrange, P., *Of Power and Justice*, German Law Journal, Vol. 4, No. 9, 2003, http://germanlawjournal.com/article.php?id=314.

Yadgar, Y., *From "True Peace" to "the Vision of the New Middle East": Rival Images of Peace in Israel*, Journal of Peace Research, Vol. 40, No. 2, 2003, p. 177.

Yoh, J.N., *Peace Procesesses and Conflict Resolution in the Horn of Africa*, African Security Review, Vol. 12, No. 3, 2003, p. 83.

Zagorskij, A.V., *Russia and NATO: Prospects for Cooperation after the Prague Summit, 2002*, 10 pp. (Policy Papers/Institute for Applied International Research).

Zaharna, R.S., *The Unintended Consequences of Crisis Public Diplomacy: American Public Diplomacy in the Arab world*, 2003, 4 pp. (Policy Brief/Foreign Policy in Focus).

Zaharna, R.S., *Winning Round Two: American Public Diplomacy in the Arab and Muslim World*, 2003, 3 pp. (Foreign Policy in Focus).

Zimmermann, D., *The Transformation of Terrorism: The "New Terrorism", Impact Scalability and the Dynamics of Reciprocal Threat Perception*, 2003, 75 pp. (Zürcher Beiträge zur Sicherheitspolitik und Konfliktforschung).

Chronicle of Events – July 2002 – June 2003

Introduction

This Chronicle concentrates on the reporting of actual events rather than confer-ences, debate and supposition. Although there were significant press reports on the following areas they are not covered in any detail:

Anti-Ballistic Missile Treaty; Arms sales; Arms trading; Atomic energy; Biological Weapons Convention; Biological weapons; Bioterrorism; Chemical Weapons Convention; Chemical weapons; Comprehensive Nuclear-Test-Ban Treaty;

Convention on Prohibitions or Restrictions on the Use of Certain Conventional Weapons; Disarmament; Inhumane weapons; International Atomic Energy Agency; Landmines; Mercenaries; Nuclear Proliferation Treaty; Nuclear Test Ban Treaty; Nuclear testing; Nuclear weapons; Sanctions; Small arms; Strategic Arms Reduction Treaty; Terrorism.

Sources:

The following sources have been used in the compilation of this Chronicle:

ABCNews.com
Agence France-Presse
Agencia de LUSA Noticias
al-Bilad
Al-Jazeera
allAfrica.com
Angola Press Agency
Arusha Internews
Asahi Shimbun
Associated Press
Associated Press of Pakistan
Atlanta Constitution-Journal
Baltimore Sun
Bangkok Post
BBC Online

Beirut Daily Star
Boston Globe
Caracas El Nacional
Chicago Tribune
Christian Science Monitor
CNN.com
Corriere della Sera
Cox News Service
Cyprus Mail
Daily Yomiuri
Dar es Salaam Guardian
Dhaka Independent
Diario de Noticias
Earth Times
EFE News Agency

Harvey Langholtz, Boris Kondoch, Alan Wells (Eds.),
International Peacekeeping: The Yearbook of International Peace Operations, Volume 9, 2004, pp. 315-641.
© Koninklijke Brill N.V. Printed in the Netherlands

El Espectador
El Pais
El Tiempo
Emediamillworks Inc
Ethiopian News Agency
Financial Times
Frankfurter Rundschau
Harare Financial Gazette
Human Rights Watch
Integrated Regional Information Networks
Internews
IRIN
Irish Times
IRNA
Islamic Republic News Agency
ITAR-Tass
Johannesburg Independent Online
Jordan Times
Karachi Business Recorder
Karachi Dawn
Korea Times
Kuala Lumpur Star
La Presse
La Repubblica
La Tribune
Le Figaro
Le Monde
Le Temps
L'Observateur Paalga
London Daily Mirror
London Daily Telegraph
London Guardian
London Independent
London Observer
Los Angeles Times
Madrid, El Mundo
Mainichi Daily News
MSNBC.com
Nando Times
New Vision
New York Daily News
New York Times

News 24
News Network International
Norsk Rikskringkasting
Norway Post
NPR Morning Edition
Pacific Islands Broadcasting
Association
Pearson Peacekeeping Centre
Philadelphia Enquirer
Radio Free Europe
Radio Liberty
Regional Integrated News Networks
Reuters
RTL.be
SABCnews.com
South African Press Association
South China Morning post
Straits Times
Sydney Morning Herald
Tehran Times
The Globe and Mail
The Hindu
The Island
The National Post
The Scotsman
Times of India
Tokyo Sankei
TOMRIC News Agency
Toronto Globe & Mail
Toronto National Post
Trust Press of India
UN Newservice
UNWire
United Press International
USA Today
Washington Post
Washington Times
Xinhua News Agency
Xinhua News Agency
Yahoo! News
ZDFonline

Abbreviations

AUC	United Self-Defence Forces of Columbia
BONUCA	UN Peacebuilding Support Office in the Central African Republic
CEMAC	Economic and Monetary Community of Central African States
CAR	Central African Republic
CIA	[US] Central Intelligence Agency
CNDD-FDD	Conseil National pour la Defense de la Democratie-Force pour la Defense de la Democratie
DRC	Democratic Republic of Congo
ECOWAS	Economic Community of West African States
ELN	National Liberation Army
EU	European Union
FAR	Forces Armees Rwandaises
FARC	Revolutionary Armed Forces of Columbia
FDD	Forces pour la Defence de la Democratie
FNL	Forces Nationales de Liberation
FRG	Guatemalan Republican Front
IAEA	International Atomic Energy Agency
ICC	International Criminal Court
ICRC	International Committee of the Red Cross
ICTY	International Criminal Tribunal for the former Yugoslavia
IDF	Israeli Defence Force
IOM	International Organisation for Migration
ISAF	International Security Assistance Force
KFOR	Kosovo Force
LTTE	Liberation Tigers of Tamil Eelam
LURD	Liberians United for Reconciliation and Democracy
MPCI	Mouvement Patriotique de la Cote d'Ivoire
MLC	Mouvement de Liberation du Congo
MINUCI	Un Mission in Cote d'Ivoire
MINUGUA	UN Verification Mission in Guatemala
MINURSO	UN Mission for the Referendum in Western Sahara
MODEL	Movement for Democracy in Liberia
MONUC	UN Organisation Mission in the Democratic Republic of Congo
MPCI	Mouvement Patriotique de la Cote d'Ivoire
NATO	North Atlantic Treaty Organisation
NPT	Nuclear Nonproliferation Treaty
OAU	Organisation of African Unity
OCHA	UN Office for the Coordination of Humanitarian Affairs
OIC	Organisation of the Islamic Conference

PALIPEHUTU-FNL	Parti de Liberation du Peuple Hutu-Force Nationale de Liberation
PLO	Palestine Liberation Organisation
RCD	Rally for Congolese Democracy (Rassemblement Congolais pour la Democratie)
RUF	Revolutionary United Front
SADC	Southern African Development Community
SPLA	Sudan People's Liberation Army
UK	United Kingdom
UN	United Nations
UNAMA	UN Assistance Mission in Afghanistan
UNAMSIL	UN Mission in Sierra Leone
UNDOF	UN Disengagement Observer Force
UNOL	UN Peacebuilding Support Office in Liberia
UNDP	UN Development Programme
UNFICYP	UN Peacekeeping Force in Cyprus
UNHCR	UN High Commission for Refugees
UNIFIL	UN Interim Force in Lebanon
UNIKOM	UN Iraq-Kuwait Observation Mission
UNITA	União Nacional para a Independência Total de Angola
UNMIBH	UN Mission in Bosnia and Herzegovina
UNMEE	UN Mission in Ethiopia and Eritrea
UNMIK	UN Mission in Kosovo
UNMOP	UN Mission of Observers in Prevlaka
UNMOVIC	UN Monitoring, Verification and Inspection Commission
UNOL	UN Peacebuilding Support Office in Liberia
UNOMIG	UN Observer Mission in Georgia
UNRWA	UN Relief and Works Agency for Palestine Refugees in the Near East
UNSECORD	UN Security Coordination Office
UNSCOM	UN Special Commission on Iraq
UNTAET	UN Transitional Administration in East Timor
UNTOP	UN Tajikistan Office of Peace-building
US	United States of America
WHO	World Health Organisation

July 2002

AFGHANISTAN

Two grenades were thrown at an airfield used by US special forces outside the southern Afghan city of Kandahar. No one was injured in the attack. The attack came as US and British forces continued their search for al-Qaeda and Taliban fighters seeking refuge in the mountains along the Afghan-Pakistani border.

United States forces in eastern Afghanistan discovered a large weapons cache during a search of the village of Zarmaki Ghar.

A spokesman for Kandahar Governor Gul Agha said that negligence had been the cause of an explosion in the southern border town of Spin Boldak. Despite the announcement, conflicting reports were coming out regarding the incident.

In Pakistan, the government stepped up the search for al-Qaeda fighters on the run, deploying more than 3,000 troops in the border region and posting wanted posters and reward offers. According to US officials, as many as 1,000 al-Qaeda fighters may still have been in the region. Calling top al-Qaeda officials "dangerous religious terrorists," Pakistan had also called for public support to catch the remaining fighters following a gun battle between Pakistani and al-Qaeda fighters that left 10 Pakistani soldiers dead. The Government offered rewards of up to $320,000 for 10 militants who had been charged with carrying out bombings in the southern Pakistani city of Karachi. The government also offered rewards for information leading to the arrest of those responsible for the murder of US journalist Daniel Pearl.

The UN special representative for Afghanistan sent a letter to ethnic Uzbek warlord and Jumbesh-e-Milli Islami leader Abdul Rashid Dostum complaining about the treatment of ethnic Pashtuns in the north of Afghanistan.

Afghan transitional President Hamid Karzai appointed former interim Women's Affairs Minister Sima Samar (who had been barred from public office by Afghan Chief Justice for allegedly making statements against the interests of Islam in the country) as the country's new human rights commissioner.

United States warplanes mistakenly bombed a mountain village northeast of Kandahar. Forty members of a wedding party were killed and another 100 injured making it one of the deadliest military errors since US-led operations began in the country. Most of those killed were women and children. The US Defence Department announced plans to send a team led by the Air Force and including experts in air traffic control and AC-130 aircraft to investigate. Defence Department officials insisted the AC-130 plane had legitimate cause to shoot because the crew believed it was under fire, even though no anti-aircraft weaponry was found in the area. Governors of the southwestern Farah and Nimruz provinces began to debate a plan by Kandahar Governor Gul Agha under which US forces would need the governors' approval to attack Taliban and al-Qaeda elements in their provinces. The governors of the strategic Helmand, Oruzgan and Zabul provinces were not expected to attend, making it unlikely that Governor Agha's proposals would be approved. Interim President Karzai welcomed another proposal by Gul Agha for a border control force, but he insisted that such a force be under central government and not local control. Governor Agha further called for the creation of a rapid reaction force of 500 men to hunt down al-Qaeda and Taliban fugitives, as well as a 3,000-troop force to guard

Afghanistan's borders with Pakistan and Iran. The United States dismissed Gul Agha's proposal, insisting that Afghans would not be allowed to control US military operations. However, the US Defence Department was reportedly considering changing the makeup of its Afghanistan force in an attempt to foster better ties with Afghan civilians. Some senior officials were advocating the deployment of more conventional forces, while others called for more "civil affairs" and special operations forces. Governor Gul Agha later dismissed reports that he was calling for the approval of US operations by local Afghan commanders; gave his full support to US forces; and said he wanted only to be consulted on operations.

Citing on-site reviews of 11 locations where air-strikes allegedly resulted in the deaths of as many as 400 civilians, the *New York Times* found fault with US commanders' preference for air instead of ground operations and dependence on intelligence from Afghan warlords and others with "unclear" loyalties. The newspaper reported that those aspects of US strategy contributed to the civilian deaths. United States defence officials said they were focusing more on ground forces in an effort to root remaining pockets of al-Qaeda and Taliban elements, but continued reliance on air power was having a "disastrous" effect, the *Times* added.

Pakistani police forces arrested seven suspected al-Qaeda operatives in the remote tribal region on the border with Afghanistan. In a massive air and ground operation, 1,000 Pakistani troops searched the region for 40 al-Qaeda fighters who fled after a gun battle which killed 10 troops.

Afghan police arrested 12 people in connection with the assassination of Vice President and Public Works Minister Abdul Qadir. Those held included 10 of the guards at Qadir's ministry, who allegedly did nothing as 36 bullets were fired at the late vice president's car. Police and soldiers were deployed around Kabul as government officials gathered to mourn Qadir. Afghan ministers decided to ask for the aid of ISAF in investigating the killing. Various theories concerning the killing were circulating, including the possibility of a Taliban hit against the former Northern Alliance commander; that he was killed because he was the highest-ranking Pashtun in the transitional government after transitional President Karzai; that the killing may have been the work of eastern drug barons upset at the poppy eradication campaign Qadir was heading; or that the assassination had been orchestrated by al-Qaeda. The International Security Assistance Force said its officers believed the assassination was an individual attack designed to destabilise the government. It put its 5,000 troops in Kabul on higher alert as a precaution against further violence and increased the number of helicopter patrols over roads through the mountains around Kabul. About 50 US troops were called in to assist in guarding the Afghan presidential palace following the killing. Despite the arrests, questions arose about the transitional administration's ability to maintain security.

In a report to the UN General Assembly and Security Council, the Secretary General called security in Afghanistan a "cause for concern" and expressed support for a limited expansion of the International Security Assistance Force, now deployed only in Kabul. He noted that the Taliban had not formally given up despite its defeat by US-led forces and said the regime's remnants, along with those of al-Qaeda, were still present in the country. He added that other groups – "armed factions that nominally support" the political process begun last year under UN supervision at a meeting near Bonn – also "pose a threat to the consolidation of peace and civil government in the country." Unless viable Afghan security forces were present or the ISAF was expanded, Afghanistan would continue to experience insecurity that "could seriously undermine the political and reconstruction efforts". While UN officials had consistently argued for expansion of the force to other regions of the country, in particular other urban areas, the US and other major powers rejected this option. Afghan Ambassador Ravan Farhadi suggested ISAF consider deploying in only one other location, such as the major northern city of Mazar-e Sharif.

The US Ambassador, John Negroponte, told the Council that US and French trainers were working with the Afghan authorities to train a new army, with the first battalion ready to graduate imminently. Following three months of training, 350 US-trained Afghan army recruits marched at a former Soviet military academy in Kabul.

The London *Observer* reported that the UK and the US were giving "huge sums of money" to Afghan warlords including Agha and Nangahar warlord Hazrat Ali in order to keep them from revolting against Karzai's central government. According to the *Observer*, some warlords receiving such funds had been involved in opium production, human rights abuses and drug trafficking.

Following a move by President Karzai's to secure US military protection for himself and dismiss Afghan guards loyal to Defence Minister Mohamed Fahim, it was reported that Karzai supporters saw the country's 30,000-employee secret service (the National Security Directorate, or *Amaniyat*, run by Fahim) as a threat to national security and a huge, corrupt system that operated outside the President's authority and posed a threat to democracy in Afghanistan. Amid allegations the agency tortured and killed a former refugee who had returned from Pakistan, the President named a high-level commission to investigate charges against the *Amaniyat* and recommend reforms.

Afghan officials foiled a suicide bombing plot in Kabul just 300 yards from the US Embassy. It was unclear whether the alleged bomber was targeting the embassy or top Afghan leaders in their cars. Afghanistan's General Department of National Security said a car packed with more than half a ton of explosives hidden in its doors was meant to collide with one of the vehicles carrying the leader of Afghanistan's transitional Islamic state. However, the car hit another vehicle, wounding one person, before the alleged would-be assassin was arrested.

BOSNIA

The UN Mission in Bosnia and Herzegovina was at this time largely a civilian police operation numbering about 1,500 people with its primary responsibilities being law enforcement and the training of the new Bosnian police force. The Mission was to have been extended until the end of the year, at which time the EU would assume the police duties handled by the UN. As 74 countries had ratified the Rome Statute, the treaty establishing the International Criminal Court (the ICC) was due to come into force on July 1 with genocide, war crimes and crimes against humanity that occur as of that date falling under the jurisdiction of the Court. After failing to get immunity for peacekeepers from prosecution by the new International Criminal Court, the US vetoed a Security Council resolution which would have extended the mandate of the peacekeeping mission in Bosnia. In a separate action, the Council then extended the mission for 72 hours so negotiations could continue on a solution to the standoff. The US did not view the new extension as buying time for negotiations, but rather to allow others, in particular the EU members, to decide how to proceed without a peacekeeping mission.

The US insisted that, since it is not a party to the ICC, its peacekeepers should be beyond the reach of the court. It had made several proposals to guarantee this immunity. However, Court supporters, including the UK and France, said these concerns were unwarranted and that the US proposals would undermine the Court. Since May, the US had lobbied for a paragraph to be included in the resolutions extending the mandates of peacekeeping missions that would grant immunity for peacekeepers from states that are not party to the ICC. The UN Mission of Support in East Timor was the first mission for which the US tried and failed to insert an immunity clause.

The Security Council later gave a third, short-term extension to UNMIBH, delaying a showdown with the US. It unanimously adopted a resolution rolling over the existing mandate of UNMIBH until July 15.

The Council was then considering several options. One would be another rollover. Another would be to do nothing and let UNMIBH expire, in which case the UN would have to start withdrawing all its forces from Bosnia. There was still a possibility that the Council could adopt a resolution calling for an accelerated transfer of police duties from UNMIBH to the EU, which was scheduled to happen by December before the rift developed on peacekeeper immunity. However, none of these options addressed the US concerns about immunity for peacekeepers.

The last day of the new rollover, July 15, was also the day the mandate of the UN Mission of Observers in Prevlaka expired. The mandates of three other missions – in Lebanon, Georgia and Western Sahara – needed to be renewed by July 30.

When the ICC entered into force, the US ordered its three civilian police officers home from East Timor. It did not say what it planned to do about the 46 police officers assigned to UNMIBH.

A landmark meeting of the presidents of Yugoslavia, Bosnia and Herzegovina and Croatia ended with a final declaration announcing a trilateral agreement to rebuild relations and facilitate the return of refugees displaced during the war that ravaged the region during the 1990s. They also pledged full cooperation with the International Criminal Tribunal for the former Yugoslavia in The Hague and not only to right the wrongs of the war years and to improve relations but also to coordinate efforts against organized crime and to develop their economies – requisite tasks for prospective members of the EU. Under the trilateral declaration, the three countries are to settle disputes peacefully, according to the standards of developed European countries.

The Muslim chairman of Bosnia's presidency, said he wanted an apology from Yugoslavia for Serb atrocities inflicted on Bosnian Muslims during the war but that he would not let the issue hold up the normalisation of relations. Yugoslav President Kostunica refused to apologise or to call for former Bosnian Serb leader Radovan Karadzic to surrender to ICTY.

BURUNDI

The UN Security Council voiced its "firm support" for Burundi's transitional government, called on rebels fighting in the country to enter cease-fire negotiations and stressed the importance of early progress ahead of a high-level meeting set to begin in the country. The Council president, British UN Ambassador Jeremy Greenstock, issued a statement expressing the Council's continuing support for "the whole Arusha process" and underlining its "stern warning against any attempts by others to undermine the present coalition." The Council voiced "strong concern" over Burundi's humanitarian situation, expressing hope that the UN High Commissioner for Refugees could soon resume full-scale efforts in the country, despite concerns about the security of UNHCR staff in Burundi. Council members also called on donors to "deliver on their funding promises" and urged the International Monetary Fund to quickly provide post-conflict assistance.

A Burundi army spokesman said 209 rebels had been killed in fighting which he said had also brought in hundreds of combatants from UN refugee camps in western Tanzania. Only two civilians had been killed.

Rebel officials from the Forces in Defence of Democracy agreed to meet with the Government but rebel leaders from the Forces for National Liberation rejected the proposed talks. The peace talks subsequently failed to open as rebel leaders of the Forces for the Defence of Democracy claimed to have been given insufficient notice of the talks.

The UN Security Council called on rebel groups to enter cease-fire negotiations and voiced its firm support for the transitional government. The talks were postponed, however, to give leaders of the main Hutu rebel group, who had made it clear that they were not ready, more time for "material, human and psychological preparations".

The Burundian Foreign Minister criticised a draft cease-fire accord drawn up by experts from South Africa, Tanzania, Gabon and the UN and reiterated his country's claim that Tanzania was supporting the Burundian rebels.

CHEMICAL WEAPONS

Argentine Rogelio Pfirter became director general of the Organisation for the Prohibition of Chemical Weapons following his formal approval by a conference of parties to the Chemical Weapons Convention – replacing Jose Bustani, a Brazilian diplomat who had been voted out in April after the United States said it had lost confidence in him, accusing him of failing to consult with Washington about sensitive issues, including his effort to persuade Iraq to join the organisation.

CONGO, DEMOCRATIC REPUBLIC OF

The International Court of Justice in The Hague rejected a request by the Democratic Republic of the Congo to order a halt to what the country called Rwanda's "war of aggression." In an action filed in May, the DRC accused Rwanda of "genocide against more than 3.5 million Congolese" and demanded the country pay damages. The charges detailed the "killing, massacring, raping, throat-slitting and crucifying" of people in the DRC and asked for an arms embargo and ban on gold sales by Rwanda.

While the Court said it had no legal basis to intervene between the two countries, it also rejected Rwanda's request to strike the case from its docket, and said it would hear allegations by the DRC of "massive, serious and flagrant violations of human rights" by Rwandan forces in the DRC.

The leaders of Rwanda and the DRC signed a peace agreement that was seen as a major step in ending a bloody four-year conflict that had claimed millions of lives in the DRC. According to the terms of the agreement Rwanda would withdraw 20,000 of its troops from the eastern DRC in exchange for security guarantees. The agreement also stipulated that the 12,000 Interahamwe, Rwandan rebels and former Rwandan Hutu soldiers who had been nominal DRC allies and had been accused by the Rwandan government of attempting to destabilise Rwanda (as well as involvement in the 1994 genocide) would be rounded up, disarmed and repatriated to Rwanda. The agreement also called for the UN Organisation Mission in the DRC to be upgraded to a peacekeeping force and said that the DRC government was ready to co-operate with MONUC to assemble and disarm the Rwandan Hutu forces. The main Rwandan-backed rebel group, Rassemblement Congolais pour la Democratie, also threw its support behind the new peace agreement. The Democratic Forces for the Liberation of Rwanda, the key Hutu militia group in the DRC, said that, while it would demobilise, it would also resist any efforts to repatriate its forces. Rwandan diplomats said they wanted the militia members to be extradited either to the International Criminal Tribunal for Rwanda (which sits in neighbouring Tanzania) or to Rwanda. The group called the peace deal a "delaying manoeuvre" and said it would oppose the accord until Rwanda withdrew its troops "unconditionally" and dropped demands for the militias' extradition.

United States Ambassador-at-Large for War Crimes, Pierre-Richard Prosper, was expected to arrive in the DRC capital of Kinshasa to launch a manhunt for several prime suspects of the 1994 Rwanda genocide, which left 800,000 Tutsis and moderate Hutus dead. The suspects, who included Augustin Bizimana, Jean-Baptiste Gatete, Augustin Bizimungu, Idelphonse Hategekimana, Augustin Ngirabatware, Idelphonse Nizeyimana and Callixte Nzabonimana, were believed to be hiding in the DRC or in the neighbouring Republic of the Congo. The United States was reportedly offering up to $5 million for information leading to their arrest.

The UN High Commissioner for Refugees warned the estimated 390,000 people who fled the DRC war to beware of returning home due to continued violence in the east of the country, where the Hutu militias were active. According to the UN agency, most of the DRC refugees were in Tanzania and the Republic of the Congo.

CYPRUS
Talks between Cypriot President Glafcos Clerides and Turkish Cypriot leader Rauf Denktash failed to yield a breakthrough before an end-of-June deadline. The talks, which had been based on the four key issues of governance, security, territory and property, ended with no sign of resolution in sight. A resolution to the conflict was gaining urgency because the Greek Cypriot side of the island was set to join the European Union in 2004, with or without the reunification of the island.

EAST TIMOR
In an early step toward the end of the UN peacekeeping mandate in East Timor, elements of the new country's nascent defence force took over command of the eastern district of Lautem from the UN Mission of Support in East Timor that had been in East Timor since 1999. The UNMISET force, whose troop strength, including police forces, stood at 6,200, was gradually being scaled down as the threat of pro-Indonesian militia incursions into East Timor from the Indonesian region of West Timor declined.

GEORGIA
The UN Security Council extend the mandate of the UN peacekeeping force in Georgia until January 2003 and called on both sides in the country's conflict to work harder for an agreement.

IRAQ
United Nations negotiators sought the return of weapons inspectors to Iraq after nearly four years. Iraq was suspected of continuing development of weapons of

mass destruction despite UN sanctions in place since the Gulf War ended in 1991. United States officials were saying that in the absence of on-site monitoring, Iraqi President Saddam Hussein had made modest progress in advancing Iraq's outlawed chemical, biological and nuclear capabilities, but had not acquired any fissionable material to build a nuclear bomb.

Iraq wished to also discuss the lifting of sanctions as well as an end to the US- and British-enforced no-fly zones over northern and southern Iraq. The US, however, made it clear that further delays were unacceptable and a full accounting of the destruction of Iraq's weapons of mass destruction and missiles had to be completed before sanctions could be lifted, as required by UN resolutions dating back to the Gulf War.

Iraq had managed to open a number of overland routes between Iraq and Turkey, Syria and Jordan, as well as the return of commercial airline flights to Baghdad.

United Nations officials predicted that if they failed to reach the desired solution, they could pave the way for US military action against Hussein's regime.

The UN was ready to move quickly if it got the green light from Iraq. The inspectors' abandoned weapons monitoring headquarters in Baghdad could have been operating within seven to 10 days but two days of negotiations ended with no agreement. The UN Secretary General told members of the Security Council that he planned no further talks with Iraq until it indicated some willingness to allow weapons inspectors to return.

The United Kingdom was reported to be preparing to provide at least 30,000 troops to join a US invasion of Iraq in the early Spring of 2003. The number of British troops in Kosovo, Macedonia, Bosnia and Sierra Leone had been reduced in preparation for an attack against Iraq.

The US President George W. Bush said that it was his firm intention to oust Iraqi President Saddam Hussein from power.

There was, at this time, no indication of an Iraqi military build-up along the border with Kuwait said the UN Iraq-Kuwait Observation Mission, which had been responsible for monitoring the border since the 1991 Gulf War.

KOSOVO

The UN Mission in Kosovo criticised Kosovar media over allegations that UN police committed abuses in connection with the arrest of 10 people for their alleged roles in the killing of a Kosovar family in 2001.

The UN Secretary General said that the UN Mission in Kosovo had still to extend its authority throughout the UN-administered Yugoslav province despite progress in recent months in safety and interethnic relations. Kofi Annan said UNMIK was committed to achieving sustainable returns of refugees and displaced persons in 2002, with increasing returns in coming years. He said almost 1,000 Kosovars had returned from other parts of Yugoslavia so far, about four times as many as over the same period in 2001. He also highlighted a $61 million UNMIK budget cut over the following two years, saying the reduction would "necessitate the transfer of responsibility and authority to the provisional institutions earlier than planned". The World Bank subsequently approved a $15 million grant to UNMIK to aid war-affected Kosovars.

According to the head of UNMIK, the pace at which the UN mission turned over authority to provisional Kosovar institutions would depend on their willingness to assume real responsibility. He emphasised that UNMIK police were working hard to crack down on organised crime and corruption and insisted that UNMIK was trying to establish its authority in the divided city of Mitrovica, calling on authorities in Belgrade to stop financing "parallel structures" in the Serb-dominated northern part of the city.

United States troops began patrolling areas in the province without helmets or bulletproof vests as the US prepared to scale down its military presence in the region. One of 16 outposts was closed by US peacekeepers and they were set to close seven more.

Two KFOR soldiers were injured in explosions in two villages. There were no reported civilian casualties in the incidents, but three houses belonging to Kosovar Serbs were destroyed.

KUWAIT
The UN Compensation Commission released more than $708 million for payment to 33 governments and three affiliates of international organisations as restitution to 961 claimants for losses or damage suffered as a result of Iraq's 1990 invasion and occupation of Kuwait. Approximately $550 million of the approved amount was to go to claimants from Kuwait. After Kuwait, the largest compensation amounts announced yesterday went to Brazil, China, Egypt, France, Germany, India, Israel, Japan, Jordan, Pakistan, Switzerland, Turkey, and the United States. The offices of the UN Development Programme in Egypt and Washington, as well as the Gaza offices of the UN Relief and Works Agency for Palestine Refugees in the Near East also received compensation. The Commission had now approved a total of $15.5 billion in payments to individuals, governments and companies.

LEBANON *see also* MIDDLE EAST
The 3,630-troop UN Interim Force in Lebanon, whose mandate was due to expire on July 31, had been extended every six months since its creation in 1978. Lebanon formally requested a further extension. The US Ambassador to the UN warned that all peacekeeping missions were subject to a US veto in the Security Council because of Washington's fears that peacekeepers could be unjustly prosecuted by the new International Criminal Court.

Meanwhile, military and diplomatic observers questioned the need for UNIFIL, which stood by during Israel's long occupation of southern Lebanon, which ended in May 2000, and had succeeded in preventing neither Israeli raids into Lebanon nor Lebanese-based Hezbollah attacks on Israel. Lebanon had refused to deploy troops along its southern border as the UN had requested.

The UN Secretary General recommended extending the mandate of the UNIFIL until January. He did, however, mention Hezbollah attacks across the Blue Line (and Lebanon's unwillingness to deploy there, despite the urgings of the Security Council) as well as "unjustified Israeli incursions into sovereign Lebanese airspace" that "continued on an almost daily basis." He also expressed concern over restrictions on UNIFIL's movement, describing attacks against UN troops as "unacceptable" and calling on Lebanon to ensure full freedom of movement for the force. Noting UNIFIL's $106.5 million budget shortfall, the Secretary General called on member countries to pay assessments promptly. The shortfall represented money owed to troop-contributing countries.

The UN Security Council unanimously adopted a resolution extending the mandate of the UNIFIL but remained committed to reducing its size despite Lebanese government objections. The Council praised the Lebanese government for increasing its military presence in the south of the country. The resolution did not, however, scrap plans to reduce the 3,600-strong UN force to 2,000 by the end of the year, as Lebanon had earlier requested.

LIBERIA *see also* SIERRA LEONE

The UN offices in Liberia were being relocated from a suburb outside the country's capital, Monrovia, to an area near the city's centre as a precaution to "unconfirmed reports of a possible attack" on the compound.

Diplomats accused Liberian President Charles Taylor of exaggerating and even staging rebel attacks in an effort to persuade the UN to lift its arms embargo against the country. The embargo and other sanctions, however, were extended in May in response to Taylor's alleged gun and diamond trade with rebels in Sierra Leone.

Government forces retook a key northwestern Liberian town, with hundreds of soldiers, many of them children, parading through the town. Human rights groups accused both sides in the Liberian conflict of abuses, including rapes, killings and the forced recruitment of civilians, while local residents said both sides had looted their belongings.

The UN Secretary General appointed a third panel of experts to conduct a follow-up assessment mission to Liberia to probe its compliance with sanctions levied by the Security Council. In a letter to the Council president, Kofi Annan named the four experts to the panel, which would operate for three months. The panel would compile a report covering the potential economic, humanitarian and social impact of sanctions on the Liberian population. The two previous panels appointed by

Annan had recommended maintaining the sanctions, which included an arms embargo, a ban on travel for Liberian officials and a prohibition on the import of rough diamonds from Liberia.

MADAGASCAR

Troops loyal to Marc Ravalomanana, the declared victor in Madagascar's disputed December 2001 presidential election, took full control of the island country following the flight of former President Didier Ratsiraka to France. After seven months of uncertainty and violent clashes, Ravalomanana's troops entered Ratsiraka's last stronghold, Toamasina, and pro-Ratsiraka troops there pledged allegiance to the new leader.

The African Union (formerly the Organisation of African Unity) justified the organisation's decision to bar Ravalomanana from the inaugural summit of the African Union, saying the decision was "a matter of principle and . . . a reaffirmation of our commitment to the ideas of governance."

MIDDLE EAST

The US Secretary of State Colin Powell stepped up his government's refusal to deal with Palestinian Authority Chairman Yasser Arafat, again calling for new Palestinian leadership.

The European Union appeared to be altering its opposition to the US move to oust Mr Arafat, as the Danish Prime Minister (whose nation then held the EU presidency) said he favoured the Palestinian chairman's replacement because Mr Arafat either would not or could not stop suicide bombings against Israelis. Mr Arafat said that terror attacks on Israel were the fault of groups outside the Palestinian territories and repeated his condemnation of all terrorist acts on Israel civilians.

Israeli forces lifted a two-week curfew on several Palestinian cities, prompting a flood of residents to come out onto the street, visiting family and stocking up on food. The army also began dismantling 10 illegal Israeli settlements on the West Bank. Many of the settlements were described as small outposts and were not established with Israeli government permission. Israeli Defence Minister Binyamin Ben-Eliezer promised to dismantle more illegal Jewish settlements in the Palestinian territories, saying he planned to bring the total to 34 within the following two weeks.

Israel dismantled a liaison office with the Palestinians located in the West Bank town of Beit Jala.

A five-kilogram bomb placed along a train track in the Israeli town of Lod blew up as a train carrying 500 passengers passed by on an adjacent set of tracks. Four passengers were reported lightly injured.

Hezbollah guerrillas fired on Israeli jets as they made an incursion into Lebanese airspace. AFP reported that the planes were making a mock attack on a Palestinian refugee camp.

A spokesman for the Palestinian group Hamas promised retaliation after Israeli forces killed a West Bank bomb maker. Israel said he was responsible for the deaths of 121 people. Reports differed over the circumstances of the death, with one account saying he was killed in a tank attack and another saying he had engaged in a shootout with the Israelis.

The al-Aqsa Martyrs Brigades issued a statement vowing to "strike at Zionist and American interests and installations." The group, which had claimed responsibility for a string of terrorist incidents, blamed the US for efforts "to remove the legitimate leader of the Palestinian people," an apparent reference to the US Government's call for the replacement of the Palestinian Authority Chairman. Although the group is part of Mr Arafat's Fatah movement, the Palestinian leader issued a statement distancing himself from the al-Aqsa Martyrs Brigades' threat, saying it was not made in his name.

Israeli forces made more arrests of suspected terrorists, including Nizal Sawiftah, the Islamic Jihad leader for the West Bank town of Tubas.

Both Egyptian President Hosni Mubarak and Jordanian King Abdullah indicated they were seeking clarification of the US position. A diplomatic source was quoted by Beirut *Daily Star* as saying that Egypt, Jordan, Syria, Lebanon, Saudi Arabia and the Palestinian Authority were planning a 'mini-summit' sometime in the near future to work out a unified response to the US stance.

Some 4,000 demonstrators broke into Yasser Arafat's Gaza City compound during a rare protest against the Palestinian leader. The Israeli daily *Ha'aretz*, which put the number of demonstrators at 5,000, said the group was demanding the Palestinian Authority set up an employment fund, which it had promised some years previously. The report said some demonstrators shouted, "Where are the millions?" as an accusation that the authority had stolen donations intended for them. During the past 22 months of violence, unemployed workers had received only "one or two token payments" from the Palestinian government, the report said. Agence France-Presse, meanwhile, said the demonstration was in protest of Israeli military blockades which prevent Palestinians from traveling to work. The report cited UN Middle East coordinator Terje Roed-Larsen as saying that Palestinian unemployment had reached 75 per cent.

The head of the UN Relief and Works Agency for Palestine Refugees in the Near East, said that although Israel had eased its blockade of Gaza's port, Israeli delays and restrictions in issuing transit permits for his staff were hampering humanitarian work and food distribution. UNRWA was at this time the second-largest employer of Palestinians after the Palestinian Authority.

In talks endorsed by Israeli Prime Minister Ariel Sharon and Yasser Arafat, Israeli Foreign Minister Shimon Peres met with new Palestinian Authority Interior Minister Abdel Razik Yehiyeh to discuss Mr Arafat's recent security reforms. A meeting between Mr Peres and Palestinian Authority Finance Minister Salam Fayed marked the first face-to-face contact between the parties at such a senior level in months.

Mr Sharon's Government was reported to be backing a proposed law that would allow Arab Israelis to be barred from living in many Israeli communities. However, after initially endorsing a legislator's attempt to bar Arabs from settling in communities built on state land in Israel, the Israeli Cabinet decided to oppose the bill. More than 90 per cent of Israeli land is state-owned or -controlled. The Cabinet's ruling, which came in response to the petition of an Israeli Arab barred from buying a house in Galilee, followed intense criticism by the country's left, including Foreign Minister Shimon Peres of the Labour Party.

US President Bush said that Israel was justified in occupying the West Bank until "security improves".

Jordan called on countries to support the UN Relief and Works Agency in its relief efforts for Palestinians.

An Israeli F-16 accompanied by Apache helicopters fired missiles on the house of Hamas leader Ahmad Youssef Abdel Wahab in the Gaza town of Khan Yunis, destroying the three-level structure after Wahab escaped from it. During the chaos created by the attack, a suspected informer on trial in a nearby Palestinian security building was shot dead by the relatives of those he allegedly betrayed. Israel said the building it destroyed was a bomb factory and Hamas meeting place.

International Labour Organisation Director General Juan Somavia met with top Palestinian officials and employers' and workers' representatives to discuss job creation in the territories amid high unemployment linked to the difficult security situation. The participants addressed the eventual establishment of a new employment and social protection fund and the need in the meantime for emergency programmes. The talks also addressed the possible return of Palestinian workers to Israel.

The quartet of international leaders working for a Middle East peace settlement established a joint task force to help reform the Palestinian Authority while increasing the delivery of humanitarian aid to the Palestinian people. Unity on that matter, however, did little to mask the differences over other issues, notably the role of the Palestinian leader. The US wanted Mr Arafat sidelined from any negotiations, calling him unreliable, but the other three parties (the UN, the EU and Russia) did not agree. The quartet was also divided over how much the security track should take precedence over the tracks of humanitarian relief and political action. The quartet decided to create a new International Task Force on Reform that would "assist the Palestinians to build institutions of good government, and to create a new governing framework of working democracy, in preparation for statehood." Besides the members of the quartet, the task force was to include Japan, Norway, the World Bank and the International Monetary Fund. The communiqué continued: "For these objectives to be realized, it is essential that well-prepared, free, open and democratic elections take place . . . Implementation of an action plan, with

appropriate benchmarks for progress on reform measures, should lead to the establishment of a democratic Palestinian state characterized by the rule of law, separation of powers, and a vibrant free market economy that can best serve the interests
of its people."

Palestinian gunmen disguised as Israeli soldiers killed nine Israelis and wounded
about 20 in a West Bank attack in which they first detonated a bomb next to a bus,
then fired on passengers as they tried to escape. The operation in the Emmanuel
settlement was the first major Palestinian attack in more than three weeks. Four different Palestinian groups claimed responsibility for the attack, but Israeli military
sources attributed it to a Hamas cell that carried out a similar ambush at the same
site in December 2001. An Israeli soldier and a Palestinian gunman were later killed
near the site of the attack in an exchange of fire that also left three Israeli troops
wounded.

Later in the same week two Palestinian suicide bombers killed three people and
wounded more than 40 others in an apparently coordinated attack in a crowded Tel
Aviv neighbourhood populated by many Romanians and other non-Israelis. The
bombers were about 30 yards apart when they blew themselves up within seconds
of each other. Islamic Jihad claimed responsibility for the bombing.

In response to the bombings the Israeli Defense Minister ordered a freeze on
the planned easing of restrictions on the Palestinians.

Israeli soldiers killed two Palestinians and injured two others in an operation
near the West Bank town of Nablus aimed at al-Aqsa Martyrs Brigades members
and an Israeli plane fired a missile into a factory in the Gaza Strip that Israeli military sources called a Hamas weapons factory.

The Saudi, Egyptian and Jordanian foreign ministers brought forward a detailed
plan for a new Palestinian government with a written constitution, an elected parliament and a prime minister that could be recognised as a state by January 2003.

Israel approved a South African shipment of $500,000 in humanitarian aid for
the West Bank. The shipment had been held up since June 26. A South African
official said Israel had delayed the aid for political reasons, while Israel said the
South Africans had refused to comply with internationally accepted procedures for
the transport of such aid.

An Israeli F-16 fired a missile on a crowded Gaza City neighbourhood, leaving 16 dead and about 150 wounded. The target of the attack was Salah Shehada, the
commander of Hamas military brigades that Israel said had carried out hundreds of
suicide attacks over the previous two years. The Palestinian Authority and numerous countries condemned Israel at an emergency UN Security Council meeting over
the air-strike. The Israeli army opened an investigation of the attack, focusing on
the Israeli secret intelligence operation, which Israeli officials said assured the army
prior to the air-strike that only Shehada was in the building. When the strike took

place, the target's wife and daughter were also inside. Army officials added that it was a mistake to use a 2,000-pound bomb in such a densely populated neighbourhood. Several members of the Knesset criticised the army and government for failing to notify the Security Cabinet before the strike. Israel made several gestures apparently aimed at mitigating the effects of the attack. Before the attack, Peres said he was to release $45 million in blocked tax revenue to the Palestinian Authority and reissued 3,000 work permits for Palestinians with jobs in Israel. He said the offers were still in effect and that his team planned to meet with international monitors seeking to help the Palestinian Authority with police restructuring and democratic reforms. The strike appeared, though, to have scuppered a possible cease-fire on the part of Palestinian militant groups. The al-Aqsa Martyrs Brigades, Islamic Jihad and Hamas announced a revenge campaign following the air-strike.

Under an Arab draft resolution, drawn up by Syria following the air-strike, the Security Council would criticise Israeli actions in the West Bank and Gaza Strip, express sympathy for Palestinian victims and call for an Israeli withdrawal to pre-September 2000 positions, but not mention Israeli victims or Palestinian attacks. The US Ambassador to the UN told the Security Council that the draft resolution was one-sided and that he would oppose it if it came to a vote. The *Jerusalem Post* reported that the move marked a major policy shift, with Washington signaling its intention to support only those council resolutions including condemnation of Palestinian terrorism and calling on both sides to seek a political settlement. The Security Council briefly discussed the draft resolution but was unable to reach consensus. However, the document remained "on the table."

Suspected Palestinian gunmen shot and killed an Israeli rabbi and seriously injured another person in an attack on a car near a Jewish settlement south of Qalqilya in the West Bank.

Armed Jewish settlers returning from a funeral of one of four Israelis killed in a Palestinian attack near Hebron killed a 14-year-old girl and wounded at least 10 other Palestinians when they attacked several houses in the West Bank city of Hebron. Israeli sources said the settlers were first attacked by Palestinians who threw stones and iron rods from rooftops but vowed swift action against the settlers.

A bombing in a crowded cafeteria at the Hebrew University of Jerusalem left at least seven dead and at least 85 injured. Hamas claimed responsibility for the attack. The attack followed a suicide bombing at a downtown Jerusalem falafel stand in which five people were injured.

Residents of Nablus in the West Bank defied an Israeli curfew. Israeli troops in Nablus were taking no action to stop the movement.

RWANDA *see* CONGO

SIERRA LEONE *see also* LIBERIA

The UN Security Council called on Sierra Leone to reform its security and police operations in order to improve stability before the withdrawal of UN troops could begin. The UN force stood at more than 17,000 troops and 90 civilian policemen. The Council expressed concern about the escalation in fighting in neighbouring Liberia, which "could threaten the stability of Sierra Leone" and encouraged efforts by the Economic Community of West African States and others in seeking a solution to the Liberian conflict.

Despite the deployment of the largest UN peacekeeping force, the disarmament of more than 47,000 combatants and the resettlement of hundreds of thousands displaced civilians, Sierra Leone's newly elected government was faced with acting decisively to address the issues that led to the bloody civil war, including steps to establish the rule of law and seek accountability for past abuses.

Human Rights Watch called on two new institutions, the Special Court for Sierra Leone and the Truth and Reconciliation Commission, to objectively investigate members of all warring factions. It also called on donors to ensure the court was fully funded.

Unless urgently and decisively addressed, instability in Liberia was seen as risking reversal of the significant gains made in the peace process in Sierra Leone. That instability could have a further domino effect in the region, destabilising Guinea and Cote d'Ivoire.

United Nations peacekeepers and local security forces quelled anti-Nigerian riots that flared in the capital of Freetown following the death of a businessman who was allegedly murdered by Nigerians involved in fraudulent activities. The local police deployed forces to protect residential areas where Nigerians were living. Nigerians, who operated businesses in Freetown, also comprised the biggest contingent in UNAMSIL, whose head was Nigerian.

SMALL ARMS

Senior government and civil society representatives from 22 countries attended a two-day meeting in Manila on the plan of action approved at the 2001 UN Conference on the Illicit Trade in Small Arms and Light Weapons. The estimated 600 million small arms worldwide (considered the "weapons of choice" in 46 of 49 major conflicts since 1990) had played a part in the deaths of about 500,000 people, 80 per cent of them women and children. Canadian Secretary of State for Asia-Pacific, David Kilgour, called for measures to collect unlicensed firearms, tighten stockpile controls and crack down on regional drug cartels, which had contributed to the illegal weapons trade. He said the illegal trade in guns was not just a national concern since "no borders are completely secure from the problem".

A UN-convened expert group on small arms completed its first five-day session. The 23 experts were charged with studying the feasibility of an international instrument on small arms marking and tracing.

SOMALIA

The Prime Minister of Somali's transitional Government, Hassan Abshir Farah, called on the UN Security Council to dispatch peacekeepers to help disarm the country's warring factions in order to secure a stable government in the Horn of Africa country. He said that a massive number of weapons remained in Somalia, preventing the establishment of a strong central government and destabilising neighbouring countries.

Warlords condemned the appeal which was interpreted by some as an admission by the transitional government that it has failed to exert authority in Somalia.

Fighting broke out in the southwestern Somali town of Baidoa between factions of the Rahanweyn Resistance Army, which controled much of the region. Casualties were reported in the fighting, including the deaths of two religious leaders who died while trying to stop the fighting.

Norway promised more than $820,000 for the new UN Trust Fund for Building Peace in Somalia.

In response to a report by an expert mission to the region, which described Somalia as a "failed state" in which violations of the 10-year-old embargo on weapons and outside military assistance are common, the UN Security Council unanimously adopted a resolution requesting Secretary General to set up within one month a three-person expert panel to monitor violations of the Somali arms embargo. The group would pursue information on the international embargo against Somalia from government, nongovernmental and private sector channels for six months, then report back to the council. In response to the mission's accounts of widespread smuggling from neighbouring states, the new panel would also review customs and other border control regimes along the Somali frontier.

Somali warlord and former US Marines reservist Hussein Aideed, who took over leadership of the armed Somali Reconciliation and Restoration Council from his father (who was held responsible for the deaths of 60 US and UN peacekeepers in 1993) in 1996 and who opposed Somalia's UN-recognised transitional government, offered to provide the US with military bases in exchange for support for his faction. In return for the bases, he said he wanted US monetary support for his faction's efforts to oust the government, which, he claimed, was sheltering members of al-Qaeda and a related terrorist group known as al-Itihaad. The US administration was reportedly reluctant to acknowledge any ties to Mr Aideed.

Members of the international Somali Contact Group, set up by the UN, met for the first time to discuss ways of ending the country's conflicts. The group said that it would seek "to promote the completion of the Arta peace process," referring to the Djibouti conference that established the transitional government.

Fighting continued in the Somali capital, Mogadishu, with 30 dead in two days. The battle involved two rival warlords, both claiming control of the United Somali Congress-Somalia Salvation Alliance faction. One of the leaders had signed an accord with the transitional government, while the other was said to oppose the deal.

SUDAN

The UN Secretary General, on his first official visit to Sudan, commented on flight bans Sudan had imposed in the south of the country. He said the UN was "extremely disturbed if we do not have free and unfettered access to those in need." He expressed confidence, however, that Sudan "will share my concern that we do not want to see anyone in need deprived" of assistance. "I hope during my visit here we will work out concrete arrangements for opening up those areas," he said. He also said that, after two decades of civil war which had left 1.5 million dead and 4 million displaced, a peace deal between the Sudanese government and the rebel Sudan People's Liberation Army was likely imminently, given the pace of talks which started in Kenya in June.

Kofi Annan met with President Omar al-Bashir to discuss the peace process; the delivery of humanitarian supplies; and the role of the UN in ending Sudan's 19-year civil war.

Sudanese government and rebel negotiators subsequently announced a breakthrough agreement in Nairobi, under which southern Sudan would be allowed to vote on independence after a six-year period of autonomy. The deal would also end government efforts to impose Islamic law on the mostly Christian and animist south. The two sides did not sign a formal cease-fire but planned to discuss a permanent cessation of hostilities when talks resumed in August to discuss power and wealth sharing (particularly the sharing of Sudan's large oil resources, located mainly in the rebel-held south) and setting up of institutions for governance of the whole country during the transitional period, security arrangements on what to do about the status of the two armies of the government and SPLA and a comprehensive cease-fire agreement to enable the transition period to start.

VENEZUELA

President Hugo Chavez's government in May had invited the Carter Center to come to Venezuela, which was rocked in April 2002 by a two-day coup, in order to mediate. Opposition groups had previously demanded Organisation of American States or UN mediation and refused to attend a Carter Center-convened meeting with Chavez, officials from the UN Development Programme, the OAS and others.

WESTERN SAHARA

The UN Secretary General welcomed the repatriation of 101 Moroccan prisoners of war released by the rebel Polisario Front on 18 June, but called on the group fighting for the independence of the Moroccan-occupied Western Sahara to free some 1,260 prisoners remaining under its control.

Spain reoccupied a tiny, uninhabited, disputed island (called Perejil by the Spanish and Leila by the Moroccans) 200 yards off the coast of Morocco, evicting six Moroccan soldiers who were part of a detachment that landed on the island. Spain said that it was still willing to start talks to restore "fruitful, friendly and cooperative relations" with Morocco. Morocco had called earlier for dialogue but rejected calls from NATO and the European Union to withdraw its forces from the island, saying that it had occupied the island to better fight terrorism and stem illegal migration across the 12-mile Strait of Gibraltar. Spanish and Moroccan police had chased suspected criminals near the island, which locals say is a drop point for drug traffickers.

Both the EU and the Arab League joined the UN in offering to act as mediators. However, the Spanish Foreign Minister appeared to rule out any kind of mediation, insisting that what was needed was a bilateral agreement. She said she did not expect further military action from Morocco and that a promise from Morocco's King Mohamed VI to respect the neutrality of the island would be enough for a withdrawal of Spanish forces.

Morocco, for its part, protested against Spanish "aggression" to the UN Security Council, the Arab League and the Organisation of the Islamic Conference, demanding the immediate and unconditional withdrawal of Spanish forces from the island.

The Security Council was viewing the dispute as a bilateral issue that should be resolved by the two parties.

The Spanish Foreign Minister and her Moroccan counterpart met in Rabat, to attempt to smooth out relations but the question of what issues would be on the agenda remained in dispute.

Spain subsequently withdrew its 75 troops from the island following an agreement brokered by US Secretary of State Colin Powell. Spanish officials said the deal marked a return to the *status quo* that held before Morocco's attempt to seize the island, while Morocco called the agreement a victory for its king.

Following meetings with the UN Secretary General and members of the Security Council, Polisario Front leader Mohamed Abdelaziz reiterated the Front's rejection of UN Western Sahara envoy James Baker's "framework agreement" for the disputed territory, under which Western Sahara would be a part of Morocco with substantial autonomy. He expressed support for another UN plan under which a referendum would determine the territory's future.

The US presented to the Security Council a revised text of a proposal for resolving the future status of Moroccan-occupied Western Sahara that envisioned autonomy for the former Spanish colony within Morocco. The plan, similar to another US-supported proposal devised by James Baker, failed to garner sufficient support in the Council during earlier consultations on the region in April. The new proposal called for Baker to revise the so-called "framework agreement" plan that would make Western Sahara an autonomous region of Morocco for five years, and would then be followed by a referendum on self-determination, but made no mention of what the next course of action would be if either party rejected it. The British U.N. Ambassador said the new US proposal would now form the "base" of negotiations on Western Sahara while the Polisario Front reiterated its opposition to the proposal.

The UN Security Council extended the mandate of MINURSO until 31 January 2003, calling on both parties in the conflict to cooperate in efforts to reach a political solution to the dispute over the region.

August 2002

AFGHANISTAN
The June *loya jirga* that selected Afghanistan's transitional government was marked by manipulation and intimidation, the International Crisis Group said. The group said the "undemocratic" grand council was "from a narrow perspective, a success" but that "an all-consuming concern for short-term stability caused key Afghan and international decision-makers to bow to undemocratic sectarian demands." Cited in the report were the last-minute inclusion of sometimes unpopular warlords and Afghan and international pressure on would-be Karzai opponents. The group stressed the continuing influence of warlords as a major impediment to stability and democracy.

A UN spokesman commented again on a controversial UN report on a 1 July US airstrike that left 40 Afghan civilians dead at a wedding party in Afghanistan's Oruzgan province. The UN Secretary General's special representative for Afghanistan was "absolutely not" pressured by Washington, either directly or indirectly, to suppress the report. The UN Assistance Mission in Afghanistan insisted that the report was not an investigation of the US strike but an humanitarian assessment. The London *Times* reported that the report indicated the US committed human rights violations in the attack and sought to cover them up afterwards.

The Food and Agriculture Organisation compound in the southern Afghan city of Kandahar was the target of a grenade attack. Although no one was injured or killed, the attack was the first such incident since the December Bonn Agreement, which established the country's interim government and paved the way for the return of UN staff to Afghanistan. All UN premises in Kandahar were under armed guard around the clock.

The Afghan central government broadcast a statement calling on former Paktia province Governor Padshah Khan Zadran, an eastern warlord and US ally, to stop anti-government protests and "subversive activities" in his power base in the eastern city of Khost. Zadran's followers had been protesting against the government of transitional President Hamid Karzai since the end of July, demanding the removal of Paktia Governor Raz Mohamed Dalili and Khost provincial Governor Mohamed

Hakim Taniwal. Since President Karzai sacked him earlier in 2002, Governor Zadran, who claimed to have 3,000 armed men under his control, had occupied the governor's house in neighbouring Khost province and had directly opposed Mr Karzai's administration, accusing the president of being too close to the ethnic Tajik-dominated Northern Alliance.

Tensions continued to rise between Mr Karzai and Defence Minister Mohamed Fahim, who also reportedly controlled the country's secret service. According to the *Post*, the power struggle, which rose to new heights when Mr Karzai replaced guards loyal to Mr Fahim with US special forces units, was smouldering into a potentially explosive confrontation, raising fears of a violent split in the still-fragile government. Mr Karzai met with Mr Fahim and demanded that the he reduce, by 60%, the number of officials in his ministry who were from the Panjshir valley, a Northern Alliance loyalist region. Mr Fahim was reportedly insulted by the move, but eventually partially complied with the order. As Mr Karzai continued to exert his authority in a country ruled by ethnic and regional militias, some officials were saying that the dangers resulting from the personal ambitions of figures such as Mr Fahim were a much more significant threat to stability and progress in Afghanistan than ethnic divisions.

An attack by unidentified gunmen near an Afghan army base south of the Afghan capital, Kabul, left 11 of the attackers, three soldiers and an Afghan civilian dead.

Afghan authorities intercepted a car bomb full of explosives that aimed to target either President Karzai or foreign diplomatic missions.

US soldiers patrolling the eastern Afghan border province of Konar killed four men believed to be members of al-Qaeda when the men began firing on the US troops from a car. Another suspected al-Qaeda member was injured in the clash. US troops patrolling the same area killed two men after they began firing on them from a hilltop.

The brother-in-law of Taliban supreme leader Mohamed Omar was reportedly captured by US forces.

Police in Afghanistan seized weapons and explosives in raids that followed a deadly explosion at a construction company warehouse near the eastern city of Jalalabad. Provincial and national officials disagreed, though, over whether the blast was an accident or a terrorist attack. A UN spokesman said that 11 people were killed in the explosion, which destroyed most of a village near the site, and about 90 people were injured. Afghan figures put the number of those killed at between 14 and 25.

Hazrat Ali, the military commander in Nangahar province, where the explosion took place, said that bombers attacked the warehouse as a second option after military intelligence learned of their plan to bomb a nearby dam and stepped up security there. Foreign Minister Abdullah Abdullah, however, said the blast was an accident caused by explosives stored at the site.

Saudi Foreign Minister Saud al-Faisal said that Saudi Arabia was interrogating 16 suspected al-Qaeda members handed over by Iran and making information obtained available to the United States.

Following reports of a power struggle between the head of the government and his Defence Minister, International Security Assistance Force commander Hilmi Akin Zorlu said President Karzai and Mr Fahim had told him there was "no conflict" between them.

Iranian President Mohammad Khatami paid a one-day visit to the Afghan capital of Kabul, stressing ties with the transitional government there and criticising US policy in the region. During his meeting with President Karzai, President Khatami discussed bilateral security issues, including border control and drug trafficking.

The Iranian president also used the visit to speak against what he described as US "arrogance" in its policies following the 11 September 2001 terrorist attacks. However, Mr Khatami also spoke of common ground between Iran and the US, saying both nations supported Hamid Karzai's government and opposed the Taliban and al-Qaeda. US Defence Secretary Donald Rumsfeld, however, dismissed Mr Khatami's claims of opposing the terrorist network.

Factional fighting surrounding a decades-old dispute in northern Afghanistan took the lives of eight Afghan soldiers. The forces of the two rival local commanders involved in the dispute took 11 other soldiers hostage, but all were released after UN political affairs officer and members of the area's multiparty security commission mediated a truce in the northern town of Gosfandi.

ANGOLA

With the peace process gaining momentum in Angola, the UN Secretary General proposed the creation of a new UN mission for the country that would observe the demobilisation and reintegration of former UNITA rebels and focus on efforts to rebuild the country and deal with its serious humanitarian crisis. Noting that the United Nations had undertaken four separate peacekeeping operations in the past in Angola, the council should now consider setting up a new mission to deal with the responsibilities assigned to the United Nations under the latest government-UNITA agreement. Mr Annan proposed that the UN Mission in Angola (UNMA) be divided into two components: one to deal with political, military and human rights work, and the other devoted to humanitarian, economic and development needs. He also proposed that UNMA be set up for an initial six-month period beginning in mid-August, but also warned that more time may be necessary to allow for demobilisation, reintegration and reconciliation efforts in the country.

UNITA's status as one of Africa's oldest rebel groups was expected to come to a close with the official disbanding of its army and a transition into a political force. Five thousand former rebels were integrated into the country's armed forces and 33 of UNITA's top commanders were expected to join the national armed forces as well. The remaining 80,000 rebels were to be reintegrated into Angolan society as civilians.

UNITA was quickly coalescing into a political force under interim leader Paulo Lukamba Gato, who convinced a dissident UNITA faction represented in the country's parliament to reincorporate itself into the movement. With elections announced for 2004, UNITA was rapidly becoming the second major political force in the country after the ruling MPLA party. Despite such moves, some observers feared that the government was trying to incorporate key UNITA officials into the ruling elite, creating in effect a "two-party dictatorship."

The UN Security Council unanimously adopted Resolution 1433 creating a UN Mission in Angola (the successor mission to the UN Office in Angola) and suspending travel restrictions on UNITA rebel officials in Angola for another 90 days. In addition to assisting UNITA and Angola in implementing the Lusaka Protocol, UNMA's mandate involves land mine clearance, human rights, humanitarian assistance, the reintegration of demobilised UNITA forces and their family members, support for economic recovery and election assistance. UNMA was established for a period of six months i.e until 15 February 2003.

The Council approved Resolution 1432 extending for another 90 days the 17 May suspension of travel restrictions on senior UNITA officials. The Council said that before the end of the extension period, it would consider reviewing the decision based on the implementation of the Angola-UNITA peace accords.

BURUNDI

Two days of talks between Burundi's government and the main wing of the rebel group Forces pour la Defence de la Democratie, the larger of Burundi's two Hutu rebel groups, advanced the possibility of an end to nine years of civil war, said the spokeswoman for South African Deputy President Jacob Zuma, the chief mediator of the negotiations.

A key issue was reforming the ethnic mix of the army. Mediators had prepared a draft text for discussion which called for the returning of army troops to barracks, regrouping rebels in designated areas, disarming all parties and restructuring the army. The Arusha Peace and Reconciliation Agreement of 2000, which the government and rebels signed, had called for an army with equitable representation of Hutus and Tutsis. An estimated 40 per cent of army personnel were at this time Hutu, but the upper ranks were dominated by the Tutsi minority, which had seen itself as the only safeguard against ethnic violence. Despite the signing of the Arusha accord, no cease-fire between the government and rebel groups had ever been signed.

CENTRAL AFRICAN REPUBLIC

The UN Secretary General proposed extending the mandate of the UN Peacebuilding Support Office in the Central African Republic (BONUCA) to the end of 2003 in order to help support national reconciliation and strengthen the country's peace process.

In an exchange of letters with current Security Council President John Negroponte of the US, Mr Annan said he was proposing the extension following a request for its renewal from CAR authorities. He said the renewal would allow BONUCA to "strengthen democratic institutions and the rule of law, and lay solid foundations for sustainable peace and socioeconomic progress in the face of daunting domestic challenges and a volatile subregional environment".

BONUCA was established in February 2000 to support the government's efforts to consolidate peace and national reconciliation following the 1997 Bangui Agreements. There were, at this time, several dozen UN staff at the office, whose mandate was due to expire in December 2002.

COLOMBIA

Colombian President Uribe confirmed that the UN Secretary General had accepted his request that the United Nations continue its "good offices" role and mediate between the government and Revolutionary Armed Forces of Colombia rebels in an effort to bring an end to the country's long-running civil war. Mr Annan insisted negotiations be kept confidential and said the UN was prepared to continue as mediator only if requested to do so by both sides in the conflict.

There were mortar attacks, being blamed on the FARC, in Bogota during Mr Uribe's inauguration as the new head of state. The Bogota office of the UN High Commissioner for Human Rights condemned the attack, calling for authorities to take the "necessary measures" to punish those responsible for the attacks that left at least 19 dead.

The FARC reiterated its conditions for restarting the peace talks that broke down in February following renewed rebel activity. The conditions, similar to those stated on 15 May, include demilitarisation of the southern departments of Putumayo and Caqueta, the end of references to the FARC as "terrorists and narcoterrorists," and clear government policies to eradicate right-wing paramilitary groups, who are reportedly responsible for most civilian deaths in the country.

The Colombian President declared a state of emergency following five days of violence that began with a round of mortar attacks on Bogota that coincided with Uribe's inauguration as the country's new leader. While the newly declared state of emergency would not allow the government to suspend human rights or fundamental freedoms and would respect international humanitarian law, it would allow the government to place restrictions on radio, television, and the right of people to organise and protest. It also allowed the government to negate certain human rights to foreigners.

The President also called for an emergency tax to raise $778 million for military spending.

The upsurge in violence, which had been blamed on the Revolutionary Armed Forces of Colombia, left more than 100 people dead.

Government troops clashed with right-wing paramilitary forces in the northwest of the country, in a sign that President Uribe may have been following through with his promise to fight the paramilitaries with the same determination as he planned to fight the left-wing rebel groups such as the FARC. Twenty paramilitary fighters were killed in the attack, while another 17 were captured. The paramilitaries, which were created by wealthy landowners and cattle ranchers, had been blamed by the UN for the vast majority of human rights atrocities in the country. In July, Carlos Castano, the leader of the former national paramilitary umbrella group, the United Self Defence Forces of Colombia, announced that the group had disbanded because he no longer had control over various regional factions. Mr Castano, however, remained in control of the United Self Defence Forces of Cordoba and Uraba.

The UN High Commissioner for Human Rights reiterated her concern about the critical human rights and humanitarian situation in Colombia, saying the situation had deteriorated amid recent terrorist acts committed since the inauguration of President Uribe The Office of the High Commissioner for Human Rights' field office in Colombia was to continue monitoring and providing advice regarding the adoption and implementation of these exceptional measures.

Ecuadorian officials also expressed concern about the situation in Colombia, with some calling on the UN and the Organisation of American States to collaborate in providing security along the border. Minister of Foreign Relations Heinz Moeller said that the complete closure of the border would be too great an inconvenience because of the high levels of commercial and tourist traffic between the two countries. He said he had already stepped up military and police activities in the area and was planning to meet with his Colombian counterpart.

CONGO, DEMOCRATIC REPUBLIC OF, *see also* RWANDA

Just two days after Rwanda and the DRC signed a peace accord, a UN reconnaissance mission to rebel-held eastern Congo was turned back by unidentified officers wielding machine guns and a rocket launcher. The UN team had hoped to secure access for aid workers in South Kivu's high plateau region, where thousands of people had been displaced by clashes between the Rwandan army, its rebel Hutu allies and militias fighting along the borders of the DRC, Rwanda and Burundi. When more than 100 soldiers in dark uniforms surrounded the UN helicopter, however, doubts were raised about the consolidation of peace in the former Zaire.

Another attempted UN visit to the area was cut short.

Battles in the eastern Congo had intensified in recent months as the Rwandan army and related rebels attempt to crush a popular uprising among fellow ethnic Tutsis.

Five hundred Interahamwe rebels armed with 80 assault rifles were reported to have raided the village of Nyabibwe. A man was killed with a machete when he tried to save his daughter from being kidnapped. In another incident, locals killed three Interahamwe militiamen as they scouted villages in preparation for a looting attack.

In an effort to take the first formal step toward implementing 's peace accord, officials of the DRC and Rwanda were to meet representatives of the African Union and the United Nations at UN headquarters in New York. News of the meeting came after UN special envoy Mustapha Niasse held talks with DRC President Joseph Kabila. During the talks, Mr Niasse briefed Mr Kabila on his tour of countries involved in the DRC war, and they also discussed the possibility of a DRC transitional government. Mr Niasse also met with Jean-Pierre Bemba, head of the Mouvement de Liberation du Congo, a Ugandan-backed rebel group that brokered a separate peace deal with the DRC in April.

At this time Zimbabwe, one of the nations which supported the DRC government against the rebel groups, had already pulled out about half the troops it had sent to the DRC in 1998, leaving around 3,000 troops.

Following the peace deal, the Rwandan-backed rebel group Rassemblement Congolais pour la Democratie said that it was willing to negotiate a power-sharing agreement with the DRC. Analysts, however, expressed concerns about the RCD's willingness to cooperate. Under the peace deal, Rwandan fighters were supposed to be disarmed and repatriated, but they feared returning home to allegations of genocide.

UN observers in northeastern DRC found the remains of 15 people who were hacked to death by machetes, bringing the recent death toll in the area to at least 90. The bodies were discovered in a pit in the town of Bunia, less than 60 kilometers from the Ugandan border, where 75 mutilated corpses turned up.

Reports said fighting around Bunia involved members of the Rassemblement Congolais pour la Democratie-Mouvement de Liberation and ethnic Lendu militias battling ethnic Hemas and elements of the Ugandan army. Another local rebel group accused the RCD-ML of attacking Bunia from the northwest, with the group's leader saying the RCD-ML "forces came and they died".

The Ugandan army seized the town, handing control over to a dissident fringe of former RCD-ML members. The recently discovered corpses reportedly included Ugandan soldiers.

An aid worker said 10,000 families were forced to flee the fighting.

The UN and South Africa established a new secretariat to help implement the peace agreement between the DRC and Rwanda, including facilitating the withdrawal of Rwandan troops. Through the six-person secretariat, the UN and South Africa planned "to work closely together to oversee and verify the implementation of the commitments made by both parties."

Uganda and the DRC signed an agreement re-establishing diplomatic ties after nearly four years of war. Ugandan President Yoweri Museveni said his country planned to withdraw troops immediately from the northwestern Congolese city of

Gbadolite and the northeastern city of Beni. Uganda would maintain troops in the northeastern city of Bunia on one side, ethnic Lendu militias and the Rassemblement Congolais pour la Democratie-Mouvement de Liberation and, on the other side, ethnic Hemas and Ugandan forces.

Fighting in Bunia and surrounding areas had resulted in a new wave of displaced Congolese, as 10,000 families were forced to flee the region.

The Security Council welcomed a Rwandan-DRC agreement on the withdrawal of Rwandan troops from the DRC and the disarming of resident Interahamwe militia and ex-Rwandan armed forces elements, some of whom had been accused of participating in the 1994 genocide in Rwanda.

Human Rights Watch called for the prosecution of commanders of the Rwandan-backed Rassemblement Congolais pour la Democratie rebel group whom the non-governmental organisation blamed for May massacres in the DRC's eastern city of Kisangani. The group issued a 30-page report on the subject, which was compiled during a three-week research trip to the region. Human Rights Watch said the number who died during an RCD mutiny in Kisangani and ensuing crackdown was at least 80 "but probably many more." Its report named at least three RCD commanders involved in the deaths: logistics officer Gabriel "Tango Fort" Amisi and brigade commanders Bernard Biamungu and Laurent Nkunda. It said that all three were seen at Tshopo Bridge – the alleged site of summary executions following the failed mutiny – shortly before those killings were said to have taken place.

The group also questioned whether the UN Organisation Mission in the DRC "failed to carry out its mandate to protect civilians 'under imminent threat of physical violence,'" saying the mission had troops available and was "clearly aware of the killings." While the UN peacekeeping force was commended for its "call for accountability in Kisangani," the Security Council was told that it needed to ensure that the mission had "the means to protect civilians within areas of their deployment, and to increase the number of human rights officers attached to the mission".

The DRC government accused Rwanda of undermining a peace accord between the two countries signed in South Africa on 30 July. In a letter to the UN Security Council, DRC Ambassador to the United Nations Ileka Atoki said Rwandan military takeover of four settlements in the bush country south of the DRC border town of Bukavu was "in flagrant violation of the cease-fire which underpins the whole dynamic of the Pretoria agreement." Mr Atoki added that Rwanda's actions created "a new humanitarian crisis for the people of Kivu region, who have suffered the harmful effects of Rwandan occupation for four years." He called on the Security Council to denounce Rwanda's actions and hold the country to its obligations under the Pretoria agreement.

An RCD spokesman urged the DRC government to abandon its accord with the Ugandan-backed Mouvement de Liberation du Congo rebels, signed earlier in 2002 in Sun City, South Africa.

Rwanda would not withdraw its troops from the DRC until the government there ended its alleged support for Hutu militias, Rwandan UN Ambassador Anatase Gasana said. Mr Gasana said the DRC government still provided arms and munitions to the militias accused of the 1994 Rwandan genocide, in violation of the two nations' peace agreement. The DRC had been provided with a list of those indicted for the genocide but had not taken action to disarm or arrest them, he said.

UN special representative to the DRC Amos Ngongi said that political and economic motivations are involved in the recent conflict in the northeastern town of Bunia. Mr Ngongi said that during a meeting with Ugandan President Yoweri Museveni, he had urged Museveni to be "a little more flexible with regard to the withdrawal of Ugandan troops from Bunia." He added that the Ugandan government had assured him all militia had been expelled from the town.

The UN Organisation Mission in the DRC had reinforced its presence in Bunia and was studying the possibility of installing a civilian police force to safeguard local security.

Mr Ngongi also responded to allegations by the nongovernmental Human Rights Watch that the UN mission was aware of massacres in the eastern DRC city of Kisangani but did nothing to protect civilians there. The peacekeepers "did not have the necessary equipment at the time to deal with the situation" but still managed to protect seven people, offering them refuge at the MONUC compound, he said. The mission's mandate also precluded major action, Mr Ngongi added. "MONUC did what it could at the time," he said. "It is difficult to convince people that MONUC was not in a position to intervene in Kisangani, but that's the reality. . . . MONUC was not created to ensure the security of the population. It is the Security Council that must be asked to change MONUC's mandate."

ETHIOPIA AND ERITREA

The UN Security Council adjusted the UN Mission in Ethiopia and Eritrea's mandate, allowing the mission to assist in the "expeditious and orderly" implementation of the independent Boundary Commission's demarcation of the Ethiopian-Eritrean border. UNMEE was to provide logistical support for the commission's field office and participate in demining in key areas.

The council demanded the two countries give UNMEE unrestricted movement in the region and provide "full and prompt cooperation in the process." It appealed to the parties to exercise restraint, calling on them to refrain from unilateral troop and population movements until the demarcation and transfer of territorial control has been accomplished.

The UN High Commissioner for Human Rights welcomed the 2 August release and repatriation of 15 Ethiopian prisoners of war by Eritrea, assisted by the International Committee of the Red Cross and observed by UNMEE. She called the move a positive development after a long standstill and commended Eritrea for restarting the process. She expressed hope that releases would continue.

GUINEA-BISSAU

The UN Secretary General recommended extending the UN Peacebuilding Support Office in Guinea-Bissau until the end of 2003 after Guinean President Kumba Yala requested the extension in the interest of economic reconstruction and growth.

INDIA AND PAKISTAN

The UN Secretary General appointed a new chief of the UN Observer Group in India and Pakistan amid mutual accusations of attacks between the two nuclear powers.

The Pakistani military said that Indian forces had launched an "unprovoked attack" in Kashmir's northern Gultari sector. An Indian military spokesman dismissed the allegations as "malicious propaganda." The claims of an Indian attack came one day after Indian Deputy Prime Minister Lal Krishna Advani said the hostilities with Pakistan would continue until the Pakistanis cut all support for separatist Kashmiri rebels.

Pakistani Foreign Minister Inamul Haque denied that Pakistan had allowed anyone to enter into Indian-held territory and urged stepping up the UN presence along the Line of Control separating the two sides.

INTERNATIONAL CRIMINAL COURT

The US signed an agreement with Romania giving US troops operating abroad immunity from the International Criminal Court. The agreement was the first of its kind and took advantage of Art. 98 of the Rome Statute that created the international tribunal, which limits the ICC's ability to demand the extradition of suspects if it would conflict with another international agreement.

Observers said the US government was targeting nations seeking to join NATO, such as Romania, for such agreements.

Romania signed the deal with the US despite its status as a party to the Rome Statute.

IRAN *see* AFGHANISTAN

IRAQ

Iraq invited a delegation of UN inspectors to Baghdad for talks, reversing refusals since 1998 to allow such inspectors into the country. It wanted proposed talks with UN Monitoring, Verification and Inspection Commission Executive Chairman Hans Blix to focus on outstanding questions about Iraq's suspected arsenal of weapons of mass destruction and on resolving those questions. Mr Blix had said that UNMOVIC had to return to Iraq to decide on "baselines" for determining whether the country has completed "key disarmament tasks" in accordance with UN resolutions and declined the invitation, saying that he would only consider the trip if Iraq allowed inspectors to return "in accordance with the UN resolutions." Iraq demanded that the UN resolve four issues before it would allow inspectors to return, Mr Blix said: sanctions, no-fly zones, the threat of a US attack and weapons of mass destruction throughout the Middle East. In addition, Iraqi officials had been unwilling to discuss practical issues, such as where inspectors would stay in Iraq, how they would use helicopters, whether they could establish regional offices outside Baghdad, until their political questions had been answered.

In response to concerns that US hawks might be controlling UN leaders and UNMOVIC, Mr Blix acknowledged that "there are in Washington people who do not want the inspections to resume, and there are others such as the US administration's official spokesman who want that to happen . . . but they have no influence on our talks [with Iraq]".

US President Bush said that the US still intended to see the overthrow of Iraqi President Saddam Hussein.

The UN Security Council and Secretary General said that UN weapons inspectors would not visit Baghdad unless Iraq agreed to follow the Council's plan for inspections.

The US Congress refused an Iraqi invitation to inspect suspected Iraqi weapons sites with arms experts for three weeks. Congressional leaders said they would not provide a way for Iraq to avoid allowing UN inspectors to return.

US Middle East and Central Asia commander Tommy Franks briefed President Bush on a new potential plan to invade Iraq with 50,000 to 80,000 troops and heavy air-strikes. The option involves a smaller force than earlier proposals, which have included 250,000 troops and a three-month buildup in the region, a Defence Department official said. Senior Bush administration officials have tended to favour the smaller plan, the official said. US generals, however, have expressed doubts about any plan that would involve less than 100,000 troops.

With the building threat of a US attack on Iraq, Iraqi President Saddam Hussein said that he was ready to allow the return of UN weapons inspectors.

A spokeswoman for the British Foreign Office, however, said, "This changes nothing. It tells us nothing new. Saddam knows what he has to do and that is comply with UN Security Council resolutions."

President Hussein's offer may, nevertheless, have led to dividing the international community, since British policy was aimed at returning weapons inspectors while US policy leaned in the direction of a complete regime change.

Although the US administration had not announced a timetable for military intervention in Iraq, talks between Iraqi opposition leaders and the US administration seemed to indicate that such intervention was a foregone conclusion. The talks seemed to focus on conciliating opposition groups in an effort to garner their support for a US military campaign in Iraq.

Iraqi Information Minister Muhammad Said al-Sahhaf said there was no need for UN weapons inspectors to return to Iraq because they had completed their mission four years before. The US State Department said that Iraq was attempting to confuse the issue and refusing to give an answer on the return of inspectors.

Iraqi crude oil exports under the "oil-for-food" programme, under which Iraq could sell petroleum and use the proceeds for humanitarian relief, fell to 4.4 million barrels, which brought in about $101 million, in one week, down from 8.4 million the previous week, worsening the UN office's budget shortfall. More than 1,000 humanitarian projects worth about $2.4 billion had been approved by the office but lacked funds.

Iraq reiterated its offer to allow the head UN weapons inspector to visit Baghdad and discuss the terms of future inspections. The UN provided no formal response, but diplomats expressed doubt that the latest invitation would persuade UN leaders to send inspectors to Iraq.

As US officials and others debated a possible military strike on Iraq over its alleged non-compliance, the country had been rebuilding chemical weapons facilities near Habbaniyah, northwest of Baghdad, the *New York Post* reported.

The US said that it expected Russia to abide by UN Security Council resolutions in economic dealings with Iraq. Moscow had reportedly undertaken to sign a $40 billion economic cooperation pact with Baghdad. The Russian government defended its expected economic and trade agreement with Iraq, estimated to be worth $40 billion, saying the deal fell within the bounds of UN sanctions against Baghdad. Reacting earlier to news of the planned agreement, the US had called on Russia to stick to Security Council resolutions governing economic deals with Iraq. Iraqi Ambassador to Moscow Abbas Khalaf said the pact would run for five years.

A London *Guardian* report quoted unnamed Western diplomatic sources as saying Russia had made illegal payments to Iraq in order to secure a $270 million oil deal signed in July. The report cited one source as saying the secret Russian payments, made by the country's ministry in charge of emergency aid, was funneled into Jordanian bank accounts and could be used by Iraq to procure weapons. Russian officials denied the allegations.

Foreign Minister Sabri said that UN Monitoring, Verification and Inspection Commission head Hans Blix exceeded his authority by saying that Iraq had to allow inspections to begin before the UN could decide how to verify the country's disarmament. The UN Security Council had no plans to discuss the Iraqi letter, according to a spokesman for the US, which held the Council's presidency this month.

KOREA *see* NORTH KOREA

KOSOVO

Fighting broke out between UN police and ethnic Albanian protesters in Decan, 55 miles from Pristina.

The Spanish UN officers tried to move the protesters, who were blocking a road, and the protesters reacted by throwing stones, injuring one policeman. Police responded by using tear gas, according to a UN Mission in Kosovo spokesman, and hospital officials said some 50 protesters sought medical treatment, mostly for inhalation of the gas. Several protesters were detained.

Some ethnic Albanians accused the UN of pursuing political ends by arresting Kosovar independence leaders, and those in Decan were protesting recent arrests of such figures. The UN participated in the arrest of former rebel commander Rustem Mustafa and indicted former commander Daut Haradinaj and five associates.

The UNMIK head said he was worried about continuing unrest, especially as the International Criminal Tribunal for the former Yugoslavia was expected to seek more arrests in the next few months.

Kosovo's government called on UNMIK to halt a campaign to arrest former ethnic Albanian guerilla leaders in Kosovo. The government criticised UNMIK's detention of six former commanders in the Kosovo Liberation Army for suspected involvement in crimes committed against ethnic Serbs in the late 1990s. UNMIK had no mandate to investigate incidents before the province came under UN and NATO control in 1999, said Kosovo's ethnic Albanian prime minister, Bajram Rexhepi. Mr Rexhepi said the arrests were damaging the political process and aimed at criminalising the ethnic Albanians' attempt to liberate Kosovo.

UNMIK denied it had political motives as the government charged.

MIDDLE EAST

A UN report by the Secretary General (requested by the General Assembly on 7 May after Israel refused to cooperate with a mission endorsed by the Security Council in Resolution 1405) avoided making a conclusion about whether there was a massacre of Palestinians by Israeli troops in the Jenin refugee camp in the West Bank in March and April, but said that "combatants on both sides conducted themselves in ways that, at times, placed civilians in harm's way." The report cited a death toll of approximately 52 Palestinians, a number used by Israel and a hospital in Jenin. However, it was not clear how many of the dead were combatants. An early Palestinian charge "that some 500 were killed . . . has not been substantiated in the light of the evidence that has emerged," the report said.

The report repeated charges the UN made during the incursion that the Israeli Defence Forces used heavy weapons in civilian areas, delayed medical attention to the sick and wounded, and imposed around-the-clock curfews. Concerning other charges made at the time, such as the IDF use of Palestinian civilians as human shields and the booby-trapping of homes by Palestinian militants, the report repeated the charges and counter-charges without drawing any conclusions. The report said 497 Palestinians were killed and 1,447 wounded by the IDF between 1 March and 7 May. In addition to Jenin, the report covered the IDF occupation of Ramallah, Bethlehem and Nablus. Israel maintained that terrorists, including suicide bombers, operated out of all these locations.

The report drew controversy, with some groups, including the Arabic-language press, criticising the document for not condemning Israel over the incident.

A series of Palestinian attacks left at least 12 Israelis dead and dozens injured in Israel and the West Bank. An Israeli couple was killed and their two children injured when their car was ambushed on a main West Bank road; a bus attack near the northern Israeli town of Zefat killed nine, including the suicide bomber who carried out the attack, and injured at least 50; and hours later, a Palestinian gunman jumped onto the running board of a truck in Jerusalem and began firing, killing a passenger in the truck and a cafe customer before he was gunned down by police. Hamas claimed responsibility for the bus attack, calling it revenge for an Israeli airstrike in July on Gaza City that left Hamas leader Salah Shehada and 14 others dead. It also cited its displeasure over the Jenin report because it did not support claims by Palestinians and human rights groups that Israel carried out a massacre earlier in 2002. The al-Aqsa Martyrs Brigades, an armed group affiliated with Palestinian Authority President Yasser Arafat's Fatah movement, claimed responsibility for the Jerusalem shooting spree.

Israeli troops captured Hamas commander Mazan Fukha.

In various West Bank towns Israel destroyed nine houses it said were the residences of Palestinians "who committed or planned murderous acts of terrorism against Israeli civilians".

Israel announced a total ban on Palestinian travel in most of the West Bank and sealed off part of the Gaza Strip, with Defence Minister Binyamin Ben Eliezer pledging to tighten restrictions further.

The UN General Assembly adopted a resolution demanding the end of violence in Israel and the Palestinian territories, an Israeli withdrawal to pre-September 2000 positions and an increase in humanitarian aid to the Palestinians. The body also endorsed the reconstruction of the Palestinian Authority, the reform of Palestinian institutions and the holding of elections in the territories. The Assembly's action followed a day-long meeting (the resumption of a five-year-old, intermittent emergency special session on "illegal Israeli actions" in the territories) requested by the Nonaligned Movement and Arab countries following the release of the Jenin report.

Following a string of Palestinian attacks against Israeli civilians, Israeli helicopters attacked an alleged weapons factory in Gaza City, firing at least three rockets and, according to Palestinian sources, wounding four.

Israeli helicopters killed two Palestinian militants in the West Bank as they returned to a cave hideout. One was a suspect in a 17 July Tel Aviv bombing that left five dead, including several foreign workers. Palestinian sources said both men were members of the al-Aqsa Martyrs Brigades, an armed group affiliated with Palestinian Authority President Arafat's Fatah movement.

The Israeli Defence Minister met Palestinian Interior Minister Abdel Razak Yehiyeh, Palestinian intelligence head Amin al-Hindi and senior Arafat aide Mohamed Dahlan. Mr Ben-Eliezer proposed a security plan under which Israel and the Palestinian Authority would focus on developing a security model in the Gaza Strip and the city of Jericho that could later be extended to other areas. Hamas rejected the plan and accused Israel of stalling.

The Palestinian Authority Cabinet tentatively approved an Israeli plan to withdraw from some of the territories it recently reoccupied in exchange for a Palestinian crackdown on militants. The plan, attributed to the Israeli Defence Minister, would serve as a "pilot project" in which a limited withdrawal would be followed by further troop pullouts if the Palestinian Authority was successful in reining in militant groups. Hamas dismissed the idea as an Israeli public relations ploy.

Israeli troops staged raids in the West Bank town of Tulkarem and the Gaza town of Khan Younis, killing five Palestinians and arresting others. The fatalities included an alleged al-Aqsa Martyrs Brigade leader accused of the execution-style slayings of two Israeli restaurant owners.

In Bethlehem, troops arrested a purported explosives expert said to have organised suicide bombings during a daybreak raid. The Israelis also demolished the man's house, with Palestinian security officials saying the troops had found an explosives belt inside the home.

A bomb in the Tel Aviv suburb of Rishon Letzion blew up a tanker truck loaded with fuel.

The UN special rapporteur on adequate housing urged the international community to intervene to stop Israeli seizure and demolition of houses belonging to suspected Palestinian militants and their immediate relatives.

UN Secretary General appointed former World Food Programme head Catherine Bertini as his personal humanitarian envoy, dispatching her to the Middle East. Citing Palestinian and Israeli reports of a "severe and mounting humanitarian crisis" in the West Bank and Gaza Strip, Mr Annan said Ms Bertini would assess the nature and scale of the problem in the Palestinian territories, reporting her findings to him and through him to the quartet of parties working on Middle East peace – the UN, US, EU and Russia.

Israeli Defence Minister Binyamin Ben-Eliezer and Palestinian Interior Minister Abdel Razak Yehiyeh agreed that Israeli forces would begin pulling out of parts of Gaza and Bethlehem as part of an Israeli plan to withdraw from some recently reoccupied territories in exchange for a Palestinian crackdown on militants. Israeli military commanders were meeting to work out the details of the plan. Under the plan, if the initial pullback was followed by calm, Israel would return other areas to the control of the Palestinian Authority. An aide to Palestinian leader Yasser Arafat said Israel's initial withdrawal would "prepare the atmosphere" for troop pullbacks in other Palestinian areas. Both sides agreed the withdrawal would be complete within 48 hours although an Israeli Foreign Ministry spokesman said no timetable had been set, calling the deal "a glimmer of hope" but saying it was contingent on a halt to attacks on Israelis.

Hamas, Islamic Jihad and other armed Palestinian groups said that attacks would continue. A Hamas spokesman called the plan "nothing but an Israeli plot to sabotage the intifada. The Palestinian uprising is legitimate self-defence." Israeli settlers expressed frustration that Israeli soldiers were planning to pull back "just when the first clear signs of exhaustion and surrender can be seen on the Palestinian side."

The Israeli High Court of Justice issued an interim injunction prohibiting the army from using the so-called "neighbour procedure," in which Palestinian civilians were ordered to approach the houses of those slated for search and arrest operations. The court called for an explanation of the procedure within seven days. The injunction came in response to a petition submitted by seven human rights organisations demanding the army's use of human shields and hostages be abolished. The groups cited activities in which Palestinians had allegedly been forced to walk in front of Israeli troops at gunpoint, going door to door to flush out militants, including a 14 August incident in which a 19-year-old Palestinian was shot and killed after Israeli soldiers allegedly forced him to approach the door of a suspected Hamas member. The petitioners rejected military officials' view that Palestinians deemed by Israeli troops not to be in danger could not be considered human shields.

The Palestinian Authority Ministry of Health released a report warning of a potential health and environmental catastrophe in Palestinian regions due to Israeli security measures.

Israeli troops pulled out of Bethlehem and were replaced by Palestinian Authority security forces as part of a deal worked out earlier between Israeli Defence Minister Benjamin Ben-Eliezer and Palestinian Interior Minister Abdel Razak Yehiyeh.

Israeli moves to ease conditions in Gaza, however, still awaited Palestinian action against shooting and mortar attacks, which continued.

Israel had promised to undertake further measures, including allowing more Palestinians to enter its territory to work and removing other travel restrictions, if it is satisfied with Palestinian efforts to stop attacks against its citizens. The Israeli administration had not set specific conditions, however, referring only to a "reduction in the violence."

The deal brought some criticism from both sides, however, with Israeli Minister Effi Eitam of the National Religious Party saying the agreement was made "behind the government's back" and accusing Mr Ben-Eliezer of using the military for political reasons. Former Palestinian West Bank security chief Jibril Rajoub said the Palestinian people – including Palestinian President Yasser Arafat's own Fatah faction, were "very angry with the agreement," and that any security agreement would need political progress to work. Some Fatah members in the West Bank issued a statement calling the deal "a new conspiracy" and finding fault with Mr Yehiyeh for accepting it. Moderate Fatah leaders, however, said they would wait to see whether Israel was serious about withdrawing from Palestinian territory. Militant groups Hamas and Islamic Jihad voiced their opposition to the deal. The US welcomed the move.

Violence continued, however, with one Palestinian gunman killed by Israeli forces, which pushed into a West Bank refugee camp in the city of Tulkarem.

The Palestinian daily *al-Ayyam* reported that purported terrorist Sari al-Bana, better known by his pseudonym Abu Nidal, shot himself in his Baghdad apartment. The suicide reportedly stemmed from an addiction to painkillers and his battle with leukemia. Leader of the militant organisation bearing his name, Abu Nidal was accused of orchestrating attacks that killed almost 1,000 people in 20 countries.

Israeli and Palestinian officials said they would continue to adhere to their current truce despite more violence in the region. Israeli troops killed two alleged Palestinian militants in as many days, while a Palestinian sniper killed an Israeli soldier.

Israeli undercover forces in Ramallah shot and killed Mohammed Saadat, the brother of a Popular Front for the Liberation of Palestine leader. Israeli sources said they had planned to arrest Saadat, whom they accuse of being a militant, but said Saadat fired on them, wounding two soldiers. Mr Saadat's brother Ahmed was the Ramallah leader of the PFLP and has been jailed by the Palestinian Authority for taking part in the killing of an Israeli tourism minister.

The Israeli military said it had also killed a Palestinian militant leader in Tulkarem named Assam Salim, whom it accused of masterminding suicide attacks against Israelis.

An Israeli solider was also shot dead by a Hamas sniper in the Gaza Strip refugee camp of Khan Younis. Hamas sources were quoted as saying the move was meant to disrupt the truce. Israel responded by demolishing two apartment buildings, which they said could be used to fire at nearby Jewish settlements. The operation took the life of a Palestinian struck by falling debris and badly damaged eight nearby homes.

While Palestinian and Israeli officials traded accusations, both sides promised to uphold their agreement. They said an Israeli pullout from Hebron would be the next step in the truce process. Six of the eight main Palestinian population centres in the West Bank remained under Israeli control.

Palestinian officials began talks in Paris with representatives of the UN, the US, Russia and the EU – the "quartet" of powers charged with facilitating the Middle East peace process – on proposals to reform the Palestinian Authority. The participants were expected to discuss a 100-day reform blueprint drawn up recently by the Palestinian government. The Paris talks – also scheduled to include the World Bank, the International Monetary Fund, Norway and Japan – followed two meetings over the previous month in the West Bank city of Ramallah dealing with international financing of the reforms and transparency in Palestinian handling of the funds.

Israeli police officials said that they had taken 15 men into custody in connection with the July Hebrew University bombing and seven other recent attacks, adding that the alleged terrorist cell was part of the militant wing of Hamas. The Israeli officials said they did not believe the Palestinian Authority was connected with the group. They identified five of the suspects by name, adding that four were residents of East Jerusalem.

Palestinians living in East Jerusalem were not subject to the restrictions placed on residents of the West Bank and Gaza Strip and were allowed to move about Israel freely. The Israeli government issued a statement expressing concern about the alleged involvement of East Jerusalem Palestinians in terror attacks and warning of consequences for such residents.

MYANMAR
Sources were predicting a major offensive against the Karens in the following few months and Karens were outnumbered by government forces.

NORTH KOREA
North Korean military officials met at the border village of Panmunjom with members of the US-led UN Command overseeing an armistice between the Koreas. The officials discussed preventing clashes (such as the 29 June naval engagement) and agreed to hold regular staff-level talks in the future, with details to be agreed upon later. The meeting was the first of its kind in almost two years.

The UN Command told the North Koreans that the 29 June naval battle was a violation of the armistice accord by North Korea. The North Korean delegation called for a redrawing of the sea boundary.

NUCLEAR-FREE ZONES
After five years of negotiations five Central Asian nations – Uzbekistan, Kazakhstan, Tajikistan, Kyrgyzstan and Turkmenistan – agreed to become the world's fifth nuclear weapons-free zone. It was the first such agreement to be negotiated under the UN.

The treaty would ban all production, testing and admittance of nuclear weapons in the region, including by Russia and the US – which had bases in Kyrgyzstan and Uzbekistan.

PAKISTAN *see* INDIA AND PAKISTAN

RWANDA

Some 100,000 Rwandan fighters in the Democratic Republic of the Congo were ready to surrender to the UN Organisation Mission in the DRC, according to a MONUC spokesman, following the signing of a peace accord to end the four-year conflict that had claimed two and a half million lives.

DRC President Kabila agreed to round up and disarm Rwandan Hutu extremist rebels in the country, while Rwandan President Kagame pledged to withdraw his 20,000 troops from the DRC. The Rwandan-backed rebel group Rassemblement Congolais pour la Democratie called for the immediate arrest of Rwandan Hutu militia leaders in the country.

The UN asked South Africa to send 1,500 troops to the DRC to assist in implementing the pact.

The Zimbabwean Foreign Minister said that his country was closer to withdrawing thousands of its troops in the DRC, expressing optimism in the landmark peace pact. Up to 10,000 Zimbabwean troops were still in the DRC.

SOMALIA

UN officials confirmed reports that a Food and Agriculture Organisation official was kidnapped by unidentified gunmen in the Somali capital of Mogadishu. He was the second UN staff member to be kidnapped since April.

The minister of state for tourism, kidnapped on 26 June, was still being held. His captors demanded a $10,000 ransom.

A Somali employee of the Food and Agriculture Organisation who was kidnapped in Mogadishu on 5 August was released unconditionally and without ransom after mediation efforts by the FAO and family members.

A previous kidnapping of a UN employee in late April prompted the world body to suspend its activities in Mogadishu in May.

The president of the transitional national government expressed disappointment about a lack of support from the international community for rehabilitation of Somalia. Abdiqassim Salad Hassan said that if the international community "keeps neglecting us," Somalia could became "a safe haven" for local terrorists who collaborate with international terrorists. He called on the Security Council and other international bodies to disarm Somali militia groups.

SUDAN

News reports citing rebel representatives indicated a government offensive with an attack on rebels near the village of Tam in the state of al-Wahdah. Sudan denied claims by the rebel Sudan People's Liberation Army that government troops killed more than 1,000 people in a major offensive in the country's southern oil region but admitted that "low-level skirmishes" took place as government- and rebel-allied militias sought to gain territory ahead of a possible cease-fire arising from Sudanese President Omar al-Bashir meeting for the first time with rebel leader John Garang and agreeing on a framework peace deal (without cementing a comprehensive cease-fire). Humanitarian sources said the evidence suggested large numbers of people were killed but that rebel estimates appear inflated.

One of the two German World Vision employees kidnapped in southern Sudan by a regional militia was released and arrived in the town of Lokicoggio, where aid groups in the region were based. The adjunct coordinator of the UN-sponsored umbrella group Operation Lifeline Sudan, said that both Germans were "in good health" but did not comment on a Kenyan abducted at the same time. He confirmed German press reports indicating a nominally pro-government militia headed by Simon Gatwich was responsible for the abductions.

The second round of peace talks between Sudan's government and the rebel Sudan People's Liberation Army opened in Kenya, following the signing in July of the Machakos Protocol in which the government agreed to an independence referendum for southern Sudan in six years.

Despite efforts to achieve a cease-fire between the government in Khartoum and the SPLA in the south, a rebel spokesman said fighting would probably continue until a "comprehensive agreement" could be reached.

The International Crisis Group said the main questions still to be addressed in the negotiations include a geographic definition of southern Sudan, power and wealth sharing arrangements between the two sides and security issues. It added that debate surrounding the government's application of Islamic Shariah law was not fully addressed in the Machakos Protocol and that the issue would remain a live one until an agreement was reached on a constitution for the central government that was neutral on religion.

Neighbouring Egypt had promoted an alternative peace initiative, also supported by the Libyan government, and criticised the Machakos Protocol's planned independence plebiscite, saying a vote to split the country would run counter to its interests.

In a gesture of democratic reform, Sudanese President Omar al-Bashir lifted a ban on political parties, which he imposed after seizing power in 1989. The SPLA's opposition to the then current Constitution, however, barred it from official recognition, and Sudan's main opposition parties – the Umma Party and the Democratic Unionist Party – had refused to register, citing unacceptable conditions. President Al-Bashir had not said whether the country's parliament, dissolved following the coup, would be reinstated.

UGANDA *see* CONGO

September 2002

AFGHANISTAN

A car bomb exploded in the centre of Kabul, leaving at least 26 people dead and 150 injured. The blast destroyed five or six vehicles, shattered windows and ripped doors off hinges. Kabul residents said the explosion was the worst in the city since the government of President Hamid Karzai came to power after the ousting of the Taliban. Kabul's deputy police chief quickly blamed the ousted Taliban, al-Qaeda and former Afghan Prime Minister and leader of the main faction of Hizbe Islami Gulbuddin Hekmatyar for the attack. Peacekeepers with the International Security Assistance Force were assisting with an investigation of the attack. Authorities closed the road leading to the German Embassy and partially closed the main entry to ISAF's headquarters.

President Karzai survived an assassination attempt when an Afghan security guard shot at his vehicle as it was leaving the governor's mansion in Kandahar. His US bodyguards opened fire in response, killing three people, one wearing an Afghan military uniform. Though Mr Karzai escaped unhurt, Kandahar Governor Gul Agha was slightly injured. Afghan security forces arrested 18 suspects in Kandahar, including Sayed Rasoul, who had been in charge of security at the entrance of Agha's former headquarters, where the assassination attempt took place. According to Agha's spokesman Khalid Pashtun, "We think it is the work of the Taliban." Police in Kabul also detained two suspects who were linked to the taxi that concealed the car bomb. President Karzai sought to quell fears of further attacks.

The latest incidents, coupled with the assassination of Karzai's Vice President Abdul Qadir, who was shot dead by unidentified assassins two months previously, and the attempt on another vice president's life in April, underlined fears that extremists remained a potent force in Afghanistan.

The UN authorised its personnel to return to the provinces of Khost, Paktia and Paktika. A few dozen staff had been stationed there in the past, but were withdrawn due to security concerns after US-led forces in the region repeatedly came under fire. The UN also lifted a ban on UN staff traveling the road from Kabul to the eastern city of Jalalabad.

Northern Afghan warlords told UN officials at the end of joint talks that any investigation into the deaths of hundreds of Taliban prisoners in 2001 should include an inquiry into alleged Taliban atrocities. Hundreds of Taliban prisoners allegedly suffocated to death while being transported in unventilated metal containers and were then dumped in mass graves. The UN offered to continue investigations into the incident, but only if given security guarantees by Afghan authorities to protect potential witnesses from reprisals.

Defence Ministry forces said Russia was to sign a five-year agreement that would supply firearms and munitions as well as communication and other equipment to the post-Taliban regime.

UN special representative to Afghanistan Lakhdar Brahimi and UN High Commissioner for Human Rights Mary Robinson said that warlords still posed a threat to Afghan security.

An Afghan guard was injured when two rockets hit a UNICEF compound in the eastern Afghan city of Jalalabad. A third rocket landed elsewhere in the city, but it was unclear if it caused any casualties.

Two weeks after the assassination attempt on President Karzai and the explosion of a powerful car bomb in Kabul, the head of the UN operation in Afghanistan, Lakhdar Brahimi, told the Security Council that the Afghan government did not have the resources to handle its own security while rebuilding the country following decades of war.

AL-QAEDA
International efforts to block al-Qaeda's access to funding had faltered, enabling the terrorist network to obtain tens of millions of dollars, according to a draft UN report.

While $112 million in assets were frozen in the months after the 11 September 2001 attacks against the US, only $10 million in additional funds had been blocked during the past eight months, said the 43-page report by the UN Monitoring Group on al-Qaeda. Al-Qaeda, it said, continued to draw on funds from the personal inheritance of Saudi-born militant Osama bin Laden, and its backers in North Africa, the Middle East and Asia manage as much as $300 million in investments. The UN panel said there were also bank accounts under the names of unidentified intermediaries in Dubai, Hong Kong, London, Malaysia and Vienna, while private donations – estimated at $16 million p.a. – were believed to "continue, largely unabated."

The report also cited US and other governments' failure to provide complete information about the suspected al-Qaeda members and warned that the publication of different terrorist lists by the UN, the EU, the US and other countries was creating confusion and undermining efforts to halt al-Qaeda.

Dutch authorities arrested seven people in several cities suspected of having links to the al-Qaeda network, saying they were thought to have provided material, financial and logistic support to the terrorist group.

US commanders were contending that their troops should be released from the hunt in Afghanistan for bin Laden, whom some believe was killed during a US bombing raid at Tora Bora in December 2001. Pakistani security officials also believed bin Laden was dead, according to their latest assessment of his whereabouts.

The Israeli *Ha'aretz* reported that between 150 and 200 al-Qaeda operatives, including several senior commanders, had taken refuge in a large Palestinian refugee camp in Lebanon. An unnamed source in Jerusalem said the information came from Israeli and Western intelligence agencies. Palestinian Colonel Abu Ali Tanios, the head of Fatah military intelligence, denied the claim.

The head of a Security Council team monitoring sanctions against al-Qaeda said that a more accurate and comprehensive list of suspected terrorists was needed if the network's operations were to be crippled.

The UN had a consolidated list of people and groups suspected of links to al-Qaeda compiled by the Council based on information supplied by governments, containing the names of more than 300 individuals and entities, such as charities and banks that were suspected of being linked to terrorism. Anyone on the list was subject to the sanctions.

ANGOLA

A UN commission set up to supervise peace between Angola and the former rebel group UNITA met for the first time in the Angolan capital, Luanda, with UN special representative Ibrahim Gambari calling for flexibility and commitment in order to attain national reconciliation.

BAKASSI

The UN Secretary General met with the leaders of Cameroon and Nigeria. They agreed to respect a pending International Court of Justice decision on the border dispute between the two countries and expressed their determination to restore "the fraternal and neighborly relations" that had existed until recently.

The case was launched by Cameroon in 1994 over a dispute relating to the question of sovereignty over the Bakassi Peninsula. Cameroon claimed the peninsula was partially under Nigerian military occupation and later extended the case to "the question of sovereignty over a part of the territory of Cameroon in the area of Lake Chad," which it claimed was also occupied by Nigeria. Ownership of the 1,000-square kilometer strip of coastal swamp has implications on the sea border for the countries in the Gulf of Guinea, which has rich fishing grounds and offshore oil. A ruling on the case was expected shortly.

BELIZE

The UN Secretary General welcomed a proposed agreement that could end a long-running territorial dispute between Belize and Guatemala and strongly encouraged the countries' populations to endorse the settlement, which was to be the subject of referendums in both countries before the year was out.

The agreement stipulated the creation of an international shipping lane, exclusive Guatemalan control over a maritime area and the retention of fishing rights by Honduras and Belize in their waters and those of Guatemala. In addition to recognising their border in line with an 1859 treaty, the countries would create an ecological marine park covering coastal areas in Honduras, Belize and Guatemala. The accord would also allow 134 Guatemalan farmers occupying land in Belize either to remain in Belize or to return to Guatemala, where a "model human settlement" was to be established for landless farmers.

To foster development in the border area, the creation of a $200 million trust fund administered by the Inter-American Development Bank was suggested. The US, Mexico, Canada, Spain and the UK pledged money for the fund.

An eventual free trade agreement between the two countries was foreseen.

The deal was to be put before the voters of both countries within 75 days, and the issue would come before an international court or back before the OAS if the agreement was not approved in both polls.

BURUNDI

The UN Security Council urged Burundian rebels to return to peace talks, calling on them to take a "serious approach" to the negotiations. The statement included a condemnation of a recent alleged massacre in the country's Gitega region. Burundian President Pierre Buyoya had called for an investigation into the 9 September incident, in which 183 people were reportedly slain.

CAMEROON *see* BAKASSI

CHECHNYA

Russian President Vladimir Putin sent a letter to UN Secretary General and to the leaders of UN Security Council and Organisation for Security and Cooperation in Europe countries insisting on Russia's right to military intervention against Chechen rebels allegedly operating in Georgia.

Georgia said that "not a single combatant" remained on its territory following a police operation in August in the Pankisi Gorge region, where the Chechens were said to be based.

COLOMBIA

The estranged factions of the United Self-Defence Forces of Colombia signed an agreement to reunify, end their involvement in the drug trade and begin participating in peace talks with an aim to end the country's decades-long civil war. The agreement ended months of division within the 10,000-strong right-wing paramilitary group.

Reuters reported that the move to reunify the AUC and distance itself from the drug trade could have been a move to gain political legitimacy should a peace accord be reached with the government, especially since President Alvaro Uribe came to power vowing to get tough with all the country's illegal armed groups.

El Espectador reported that President Uribe's government was considering backing a programme that gave incentives, including a possible amnesty or pardon, to rebels and paramilitaries to disarm, demobilise and reintegrate into society. The proposal would not include those who participated in or orchestrated acts of terrorism, kidnapping, genocide or extra-judicial killings, meaning in effect that the programme would benefit mostly low-ranking combatants and not, for example, the leaders of the Revolutionary Armed Forces of Colombia, who had pending judicial cases against them.

The Colombian government ordered the arrest of three senior right-wing paramilitary leaders, following a request for their extradition from the US, which considers the paramilitary United Self-Defense Forces of Colombia a terrorist group, accusing the AUC officials of being involved in the drug trade.

CONGO, DEMOCRATIC REPUBLIC OF

The leaders of Uganda and the Democratic Republic of the Congo ratified a bilateral accord brokered in Luanda, Angola, in August 2002 that provided for the withdrawal of Ugandan troops from most of the DRC. Under the deal, Ugandan forces in the DRC were limited to the Ruwenzori Mountains, which straddle the border between the two countries.

The leader of the Ugandan-backed Mouvement de Liberation du Congo rebel group, Jean-Pierre Bemba, voiced approval and said his rebel group was waiting for similar agreements with Zimbabwe and Angola.

Although the UN Security Council welcomed the Luanda agreement, the Council President said that members were concerned about alleged massacres in and around the eastern town of Bunia and believed that as long as its troops were there, Uganda was duty-bound to ensure the protection of the population. UN peacekeepers would be unable "to move ahead with the disarmament, demobilization, reintegration, return or resettlement of armed groups" until the hostilities ended.

UN special envoy to the DRC Amos Ngongi urged the Rassemblement Congolais pour la Democratie-National, a breakaway faction of the rebel Rassemblement Congolais pour la Democratie, to halt an advance toward Bunia and nearby Beni. The towns were previously held by another RCD splinter group, the RCD-Kisangani-Mouvement de Liberation, which Uganda backed. Uganda had reportedly withdrawn 2,000 troops from locations including Beni. He added that Rwanda's armed forces had also been active in the area and urged that country to stop its military advances there. Rwanda had reportedly told UN peacekeeping officials that it was conducting a counteroffensive against extremist ethnic Hutu militias hiding out in the area.

A UN Organisation Mission in the Democratic Republic of the Congo spokesman said the UN was looking into reports that more than 100 people had been killed in a new round of violence in the DRC.

Residents fleeing the town of Nyankunde in Ituri province – where violence erupted as Ugandan troops pulled out under an agreement brokered in August – told UN observers in nearby Bunia of an attack against their village by tribal warriors and fighters from one of several Ugandan-backed rebel factions.

More than 6,000 refugees in Rwandan camps had returned to the Congo under duress since 31 August, less than two weeks after the start of an alleged forced repatriation by the government and RCD forces, the UN High Commissioner for Refugees said, adding that the UN had lodged a protest with the Rwandan government.

The Gihembe camp in northern Rwanda and Kiziba in western Rwanda hosted nearly 32,000 DRC refugees, many of whom said they were being pressured to leave the camps and that local officials were warning that this was their last chance to return home with assistance. UNHCR continued to counter this allegation.

Following a visit to both camps by the minister of state for local government and the UNHCR representative in Rwanda to assure refugees that protection and assistance would continue for those who did not wish to return, the number of returning refugees dropped sharply.

In accordance with terms of a peace agreement signed with the DRC in July, Rwanda began withdrawing its troops.

The Rwandan-backed rebel group Rassemblement Congolais pour la Democratie in the Democratic Republic of the Congo said it had lifted its ban on UN envoy Amos Ngongi. The rebels did not explain the reason for ending the ban, imposed in May amid RCD accusations that Ngongi had spread propaganda against them in connection to a massacre following a failed mutiny in the eastern city of Kisangani

COTE D'IVOIRE
Cote d'Ivoire's interior minister, Emile Boga Doudou, and former military ruler Robert Guei were killed in Abidjan during a mutiny by hundreds of soldiers in cities across the country. The mutineers said they were only protesting plans to force them into retirement under a new military streamlining plan. They had reportedly seized Bouake, Cote D'Ivoire's second largest city, and the northern town of Korhogo, where sources said they had been joined by local youths armed with automatic weapons. Kouassi said loyalist military forces were preparing to move against Bouake.

The coup attempt was staged by about 800 disgruntled former soldiers who had been accused of disloyalty and dismissed from the army. President Laurent Gbagbo had vowed to fight for the rebel-held cities of Bouake and Korhogo, but military officials said concern for civilians delayed action.

French troops sent to conduct a potential evacuation of French nationals and other Westerners arrived in Bouake. The US also sent troops to protect its nationals, including about 100 children at a Bouake school compound that rebels reportedly entered and used as a firing base. The first of about 200 US troops to be sent to Cote d'Ivoire landed in neighbouring Ghana.

Instructing their military chiefs to prepare an intervention force in case diplomacy failed, 11 West African heads of state dispatched a contact group to mediate between Cote d'Ivoire and rebels who staged the failed coup. The Economic Community of West African States summit decided to send a group made up of Ghana, Mali, Nigeria, Togo and Guinea-Bissau to establish contact with the insurgents, prevail upon them to immediately cease all hostilities, restore normalcy to the occupied towns and negotiate a general framework for the resolution of the crisis. If such efforts failed, a regional military force was to be at the ready.

Cote d'Ivoire voiced its opposition to a military intervention, and diplomats said sending such a force would be difficult without Ivorian consent. The rebels, too, expressed opposition to outside military intervention.

CYPRUS

The UN Secretary General met separately with the president of Cyprus, Glafcos Clerides, and Turkish Cypriot leader Rauf Denktash in an effort to break the two sides' impasse over the fate of the divided Mediterranean island. Deutsche Presse-Agentur reported, however, that little real progress was expected from talks with Mr Annan since Turkey was preparing for national elections in November.

DISARMAMENT

Seeking to break a four-year deadlock in the Conference on Disarmament (CD), five ambassadors presented a plan to the Geneva-based conference for a programme of work that would treat four key disarmament issues equally, thus avoiding a debate over which issue should dominate the conference's agenda.

Since it completed negotiations to draft the Comprehensive Test Ban Treaty in 1996, the conference, the only permanent body with the mandate to negotiate disarmament treaties, had failed to agree even on a programme of work. This deadlock was the result of countries placing greater emphasis on one issue over another and some wanting each issue dealt with in isolation while others sought a linkage. The new initiative sought to overcome this problem by dealing with four issues on parallel tracks. In previous years, the CD had focused on only one issue at a time.

The "five ambassadors" plan would set up ad hoc committees on:
1. negative security assurances, or guarantees not to use nuclear weapons against non-nuclear states;
2. nuclear disarmament;
3. a ban on production of weapon-grade fissile materials; and
4. prevention of an arms race in space (PAROS).

Besides the ad hoc committees, the plan called for three special coordinators on other areas "who are only there to seek the views of the states, to see what we can do in those fields," rather than begin negotiations. The topics included radiological weapons, including "dirty bombs," and two areas involving conventional weapons – "transparency in armaments" and a "comprehensive programme of disarmament."

The ambassadors' "nonpaper" (i.e. having no official status) spelt out, in general terms, what each committee would do. For negative security assurances and fissile materials, the initiative called for negotiations, while the nuclear disarmament committee would "exchange information and views on practical steps for progressive and systematic efforts to attain this objective, and, in doing so, examine approaches towards potential future work of a multilateral character."

The PAROS paragraph was more complicated:

> The ad hoc committee shall identify and examine, without limitation and without prejudice, any specific topics or proposals, which could include confidence-building or transparency measures, general principles, treaty commitments and the elaboration of a regime capable of preventing an arms race in outer space. In doing so, the ad hoc committee shall take appropriate account of the need to contribute actively to the objective of the peaceful use of outer space and the prevention of an arms race there, while also promoting international stability and respecting the principle of undiminished security for all.

The US Ambassador welcomed the proposal, but said he was not in a position to make any commitment based on the initiative. The Chinese Ambassador, while not commenting on the "five ambassadors" plan, introduced a revised proposal for PAROS negotiations. Austrian, Australian, Canadian, New Zealand, Spanish and Swiss representatives praised the initiative.

The UN Conference on Disarmament concluded its 2002 session, adopting its annual report but failing, for the fourth consecutive year, to agree on a programme of work.

ETHIOPIA AND ERITREA

The UN Secretary General recommended extending the UN Mission in Ethiopia and Eritrea mandate for six months, appealing to both countries to maintain their commitments to peace and pledging UN support during the border demarcation process.

Senior UN officials in the region worked with Ethiopian and Eritrean authorities to alleviate tensions over cattle rustling along their common border.

The UN confirmed that the International Committee of the Red Cross had accompanied the remaining group of 279 Ethiopian prisoners of war out of Eritrea. Mr Annan said the two countries' pledge to release 1,300 Eritrean and 300 Ethiopian detainees "will no doubt contribute to the successful implementation of the peace process between the two countries." Ethiopia said, however, that the release was a publicity stunt and accused Eritrea of holding more prisoners.

The UN Security Council unanimously voted to extend the mandate of the UN Mission in Ethiopia and Eritrea for six months, until 15 March 2003. The Council left UNMEE troop levels unchanged at 4,200, including 220 military observers, and decided to continue to review the countries' progress in implementing agreements on boundaries and other issues. The decision followed the 10 July report by Kofi Annan in which he recommended that UNMEE's mandate be extended for six months while UNMEE and the Boundary Commission completed demarcating the border.

GUATEMALA *see* BELIZE

IRAQ

UN Secretary General Kofi Annan and Iraqi Deputy Prime Minister Tariq Aziz met to discuss the long-running UN-Iraq impasse on weapons inspections. Mr Aziz said Iraq was ready to discuss allowing UN weapons inspectors back into the country, but only if international officials also discussed broader Iraqi concerns. In particular, he said, talks had to include such subjects as lifting UN sanctions, restoring control of northern and southern Iraq to Baghdad and stopping US threats of ending the rule of Iraqi President Saddam Hussein. He repeated earlier invitations for a US congressional delegation to visit Iraq. Congressional leaders and the Bush administration had dismissed earlier invitations as meaningless.

Readying for the possibility of inspections, the UN Monitoring, Verification and Inspection Commission was preparing to add 80 experts to its staff of 200 inspectors. UNMOVIC officials said the commission's staff differed significantly from past inspection teams belonging to the UN Special Commission on Iraq. UNSCOM inspectors were from about a dozen countries, while the UNMOVIC staff includes people from 44 countries. UNSCOM personnel were employed by their home governments, but current inspectors were employed by UNMOVIC. UNMOVIC Executive Chairman Hans Blix was seeking a final pool of 300 inspectors to be available for three-month rotations in Iraq.

Russian Foreign Minister Igor Ivanov suggested that Russia would veto any UN Security Council measure to authorise the use of force against Iraq. Nevertheless, he also urged Iraq to allow UN weapons inspectors to resume their work.

Other countries from a variety of regions had also been urging the US to avoid a unilateral military action against Iraq. In Europe, German Defence Minister Peter Struck said Germany would withdraw its weapons of mass destruction response units based in Kuwait if the US were to attack Iraq. Germany deployed the specialised forces to contribute to the fight against terrorism, Mr Struck said. In the Middle East, US friends including Qatar, Kuwait and Saudi Arabia were urging caution. Turkey also sought to avoid military confrontation. Even Iran opposed an attack against its old enemy. Outside the Middle East, Pakistani President Pervez Musharraf said a US attack would "alienate the Muslim world."

Examining satellite photographs, weapons inspectors identified several nuclear-related sites in Iraq that had undergone new construction or other unexplained changes since they were last visited by international inspectors.

French President Jacques Chirac proposed a two-stage approach that could result in UN authorisation of a military strike against Iraq. He proposed a UN Security Council resolution that would lay out for Iraq a three-week deadline for readmitting UN weapons inspectors without "restrictions or preconditions." If Saddam Hussein refused to readmit inspectors, or interfered with their work, then a second

UN resolution should be passed on the use of military force. Mr Chirac said he was in favour of a new government in Iraq, but any attempt to remove President Saddam from power without the backing of a UN Security Council resolution would disrupt global affairs.

British Prime Minister Tony Blair said that he believed those nations opposed to military action against Iraq would be convinced once they saw evidence of Iraq's aims regarding weapons of mass destruction.

US officials claimed that Iraq had increased its pursuit of nuclear weapons and had begun a worldwide search for the materials needed to make such weapons. In the previous 14 months Iraq had attempted to purchase thousands of specially designed aluminum tubes, which US officials believed were for use in centrifuges to enrich uranium. Several attempts to purchase the tubes were blocked or intercepted, US officials said, declining to say how the shipments were stopped because of intelligence concerns. The technical specifications of the tubes had convinced US intelligence experts that they were meant for Iraq's nuclear weapons programme, officials said, adding that the last attempt to purchase the tubes had occurred in recent months. President Saddam had also met with Iraqi nuclear scientists and praised their efforts as part of his campaign against Western nations, according to US intelligence. Defectors from Iraq's nuclear weapons programme had said that obtaining a nuclear weapon had again become a top priority for Saddam, according to the *Times*.

Canadian Prime Minister Jean Chretien urged US President George W. Bush to get UN support before launching any attack on Iraq.

The US President's contention that Iraq was reconstructing its programmes for weapons of mass destruction received no support from the UN's chief weapons inspector. Hans Blix told journalists, "If I had solid evidence that Iraq retains weapons of mass destruction, or was constructing such weapons, I would take it to the Security Council."

The UN Secretary General made a strong appeal for multilateral efforts, an obvious response to recent US pronouncements suggesting unilateral action against Iraq.

US President George W. Bush told the UN General Assembly that Iraq was a threat to international peace and that the UN was facing "a defining moment" in the face of Baghdad's defiance of the Security Council. He did not call for a new Council resolution, demand the return of weapons inspectors or explicitly call for a regime change. Yet he methodically laid out a history of Iraq's violation of Security Council resolutions and international law.

A weekend of speeches before the General Assembly revealed support for the US position on Iraq, but also concerns that attention needs to be paid to the issues raised by the US beyond the context of Iraq, including the Middle East, terrorism and weapons of mass destruction.

A panel of nonproliferation experts promoted an alternative approach to going to war to rid Iraq of weapons of mass destruction. Under the "coercive inspections" approach, released by the Carnegie Endowment for International Peace, UN arms inspectors would return to Iraq, but they would be backed by a heavily armed and mobile US-led "implementation" force to ensure unimpeded access. The approach would be made possible by the threat of a US war if Iraqi President Saddam Hussein refused to cooperate. The UN-sanctioned (ideally multinational) force would employ a highly sophisticated intelligence capability, operate under the cover of no-fly and no-drive zones near inspection sites and be supported by US fighter jets, bomber aircraft and surveillance aircraft, the panel said. Once the force concluded Iraq was free of weapons of mass destruction, it would depart, leaving a team of UN inspectors in place to monitor for new activity. The panelists acknowledged the plan would be a difficult one to implement.

As the US sought to shore up support for possible military action against Iraq and President Bush called on the UN to "show some backbone" in its dealings with Baghdad, the UN Secretary General asked Arab League foreign ministers to put pressure on Iraqi President Saddam Hussein to readmit UN weapons inspectors into his country.

The International Atomic Energy Agency had been unable to verify the current states of Iraq's and North Korea's nuclear weapons programmes, IAEA Director General Mohamed ElBaradei said.

At the time of the last IAEA inspections in Iraq in 1998, the agency determined that there were no signs that Iraq had developed a nuclear weapon or that the country had the physical capability to produce weapon-grade materials.

Iraq delivered a letter to the UN Secretary General saying Saddam Hussein's government would accept the return of weapons inspectors "without conditions." The government said it "based its decision concerning the return of inspectors on its desire to complete the implementation of the relevant Security Council resolutions and to remove any doubts that Iraq still possesses weapons of mass destruction." The letter also noted that the resolutions called for nations "to respect the sovereignty, territorial integrity and political independence of Iraq."

Iraqi Foreign Minister Naji Sabri told the General Assembly:

> I hereby declare before you that Iraq is clear of all nuclear, chemical and biological weapons. . . . Our country is ready to receive any scientific experts accompanied by politicians you choose to represent any one of your countries to tell us which places and scientific and industrial installations they would wish to see.

Mr Sabri directly challenged the US's tough position on Iraq.

UN chief weapons inspector for Iraq Hans Blix said that his recent talks with Iraq concerning weapons inspections were about practical manners, not a renegotiation of the terms for those inspections.

Using a variety of 1990s UN Security Council resolutions as their mandate, UN weapons inspectors were to be ready to resume their work in Iraq as soon as 15 October, but US officials said they would block the inspectors from returning on the basis of their existing mandate. Instead, the US was expected to introduce a new, more rigorous resolution.

UN weapons inspectors would have free access to any site they choose to inspect once they return to Iraq, an adviser to Iraqi President Saddam Hussein said.

Iraqi officials held a news conference to refute a British dossier detailing Iraq's suspected weapons of mass destruction capabilities. According to the British report, *Iraq's Weapons of Mass Destruction: The Assessment of the British Government*, Iraq had chemical and biological weapons and its command structure could deploy them within 45 minutes.

In a foreword to the 50-page document, British Prime Minister Tony Blair wrote:

> ... the assessed intelligence has established beyond doubt ... that [Iraqi President] Saddam [Hussein] has continued to produce chemical and biological weapons, that he continues in his efforts to develop nuclear weapons, and that he has been able to extend the range of his bal- listic missile programme. ... [A]s stated in the document, Saddam will now do his utmost to try to conceal his weapons from UN inspectors.

Iraqi officials dismissed the claims in the dossier as "lies."

LIBERIA

During a call for an eventual reduction of UN peacekeeping forces in Sierra Leone the UN Secretary General expressed concern about continuing conflict in neigh- bouring Liberia, which he said could destabilise Sierra Leone and the wider region.

Sierra Leonean President Ahmed Tejan Kabbah sent an open letter to Mr Annan citing the Liberian conflict and urging the UN to keep a peacekeeping presence in his country.

The UN Secretary General hailed the creation of the International Contact Group on Liberia, welcoming a "convergence of views" among concerned countries on cooperation to promote peace and stability in the troubled West African nation. Set up on the sidelines of the UN General Assembly session, the group includes the US, the UK, France, Morocco and Senegal, as well as the UN, the African Union, the EU and the Economic Community of West African States.

In light of the Sierra Leonean peace, the Liberian Foreign Minister called on the UN to lift an arms embargo and a diamond export ban against Liberia and a travel ban on Liberian President Charles Taylor and others. The UN Security Council was to review the sanctions in November, and council members cited by Reuters said the measures were unlikely to be lifted.

MIDDLE EAST

The Israeli-Palestinian conflict was a topic of heated comments at the World Summit on Sustainable Development, with Israeli Foreign Minister Shimon Peres taking the plenary podium and Palestinian Authority Foreign Minister Farouk Qaddumi holding a press conference.

An animated Mr Qaddumi and other Palestinian officials called Israeli Prime Minister Ariel Sharon a "butcher" and blasted the US for supporting Israeli "state terrorism" even as it purported to lead a worldwide anti-terrorism campaign.

In his plenary speech, Mr Peres was more diplomatic, mentioning the Israeli-Palestinian conflict only as it relates to development and the environment. "Terror," he said, "will accomplish nothing."

The statements followed the killing by Israeli troops of at least eight Palestinian civilians, including four children. Israeli Defence Minister Binyamin Ben-Eliezer ordered an inquiry into the killings, which occurred during two separate incidents in the West Bank and Gaza Strip.

Citing the civilian deaths, the Palestinian Authority called for an urgent meeting of the UN Security Council. Palestinian Information Minister Yasser Abed Rabbo said all talks with the Israeli government should be suspended.

The *Washington Post* reported that mutual accusations between the Israeli and Palestinian sides were jeopardising their recent agreement, which included an Israeli pullout from reoccupied territory. The Palestinian Authority cited the recent deaths of its civilians while Israel said not enough had been done to crack down on militants.

A spokesman for Mr Sharon's office said that Palestinian Chairman Yasser Arafat would not be allowed to return to the West Bank if he left the area, adding that Palestinian officials had raised the possibility of Mr Arafat attending international conferences.

Israel's High Court of Justice unanimously ruled that two relatives of an accused West Bank terrorist could be legally deported to the Gaza Strip for up to two years because they aided the man in hiding from Israeli troops and in moving bombs. The court blocked the deportation of a third Palestinian, saying there was not enough evidence to prove he had known of the planning of the attack.

Fighting between Israelis and Palestinians broke out again on the eve of the Jewish New Year, as Israel foiled a major bombing in the north of the country. The Israeli military discovered a bomb containing 1,300 pounds of explosives inside a car headed toward northern Israel from the West Bank.

A Palestinian attack on an Israeli tank in the Gaza Strip killed one of the armored vehicle's crew and wounded three others after it hit a landmine. In a separate attack, a Palestinian gunman shot and killed an Israeli officer in northern Gaza.

Israeli retaliation began with a missile attack on a metalworking factory in the Gaza refugee camp at Khan Younis, with no injuries reported. In the West Bank city of Jenin, gunfire between Israelis and Palestinians killed a Palestinian Authority security officer and a leading member of the Fatah movement's military wing.

Israeli forces also blocked two key road junctions in the Gaza Strip, effectively dividing the territory into three separate zones.

Israeli Prime Minister Ariel Sharon said that the 1993 Oslo peace accord and a subsequent peace deal reached in 2000 during talks at Camp David in the US and Taba, Egypt, no longer existed.

Palestinian President Yasser Arafat accused the Israelis of committing crimes against humanity by expelling two relatives of an accused terrorist bomb-maker from the West Bank to the Gaza Strip.

West Bank Fatah leader Marwan Barghouti said he refused to recognise the Tel Aviv court which began trying him on murder and terrorism charges. Mr Barghouti said the Israeli government should be on trial rather than he, and pointed to his status as an elected official. The *Financial Times* reported that Israel hoped to use the trial to link the Palestinian Authority to terrorism, although the Israeli Justice Ministry denied this.

In his first speech to the Palestinian parliament in 18 months, Yasser Arafat condemned "every act of terror against Israeli civilians" and suggested, in a remark Associated Press reported may have been a joke, he could step down if asked.

Mr Arafat appeared before parliament to seek approval for a new Cabinet and for US- and Israeli-backed reform plans. The session in the West Bank town of Ramallah began at his headquarters, to which he had been largely confined in recent months, and was to move to the parliament building after Mr Arafat's speech. Citing "security reasons," Israel barred 14 Gaza Strip parliamentarians from attending the session.

The Palestinian Fatah movement said that it would oppose and try to prevent attacks on civilians in Israel, but according to Associated Press, it left open the possibility of such attacks within the West Bank and Gaza Strip.

A UN Food and Agriculture Organisation senior nutritionist warned of increasing malnutrition, particularly among children, in the Palestinian territories.

Yasser Arafat said that Palestinian general presidential and parliamentary elections would take place on 20 January 2003. By setting an election date, Mr Arafat dampened the possibility of a no-confidence vote against his Cabinet. He had been concerned about dissent from within his own Fatah movement over his earlier refusal to fire Cabinet ministers accused of corruption and incompetence, according to the Associated Press. With some Fatah members of the Palestinian Legislative Council voicing their opposition to the ministers, Mr Arafat was said to have met with the movement's lawmakers in an attempt to garner their support for the Cabinet.

Cabinet members submitted their resignations, apparently to avoid being ousted.

The "Quartet" of parties working to broker peace between Israel and the Palestinians – the UN, the US, Russia and the EU – released a "road map" that aims to reach a final settlement by 2005.

The UN Secretary General outlined the three phases of the road map:

1. Palestinian security reform, Israeli withdrawals, and support for Palestinian elections to be held in early 2003;
2. during 2003, efforts focused on the option of creating a Palestinian state with provisional borders and based on a new constitution, as a way station to a permanent status settlement;
3. from 2004 to mid-2005, Israeli-Palestinian negotiations aimed at a permanent status solution.

Militant group Islamic Jihad claimed responsibility for a suicide attack at a bus stop in northern Israel that killed an Israeli policeman and wounded two other Israelis. A bomb exploded on a crowded city bus in Tel Aviv in the second Palestinian suicide bomb attack in two days, killing at least five Israelis and wounding 60 people. There was no immediate claim of responsibility.

Israeli forces ended their demolition activities at Yasser Arafat's Muqata compound in the West Bank city of Ramallah after destroying all but the one building he occupied. They maintained their siege of his building, saying they would not withdraw unless dozens of Palestinian security officials inside surrender.

Mr Arafat rejected Israeli demands that he turn over a list of everyone inside his compound.

Palestinians around the West Bank and Gaza territories protested in support of Mr Arafat. Violence broke out during the protests, claiming the lives of four Palestinians. A fifth Palestinian died in disputed circumstances.

Arab and European states called for an end to the siege and the Security Council adopted a resolution calling on Israel to end its siege in Ramallah and calling on the Palestinian Authority to bring terrorist suspects to justice. Israel dismissed the resolution, calling the text unbalanced and pledging the siege would continue until the surrender of the wanted men among the 250 people inside Mr Arafat's compound.

Jordanian Foreign Minister Marwan Muasher challenged Israel to publicly accept the "road map" for peace introduced by the Quartet of parties working on the Middle East peace process and approved by all 22 Arab nations. Israel had not yet offered its official support for the plan.

Israeli troops launched a major incursion targeting suspected militants in the Gaza Strip, killing nine people, including six civilians, according to Palestinian officials. More than 80 armored vehicles, along with helicopters, stormed Gaza City early in the day, sparking a five-hour battle.

Israel lifted its 10-day siege of the Palestinian Authority's compound in Ramallah following mounting pressure from the US and rising international criticism that resulted in UN Security Council Resolution 1435. However, although Israeli forces had withdrawn from the compound, troops had been given orders to examine anyone leaving the area and to detain anyone on the Israeli Defence Forces' list of terror suspects, 18 of whom Israel claims are being sheltered inside the building. Up to 250 Palestinians, including Mr Arafat, former Cabinet members and his senior advisers were inside the besieged building.

In statements following the Israeli forces' withdrawal, Mr Arafat dismissed the pullout as "cosmetic" and insisted that Israel was continuing to defy Resolution 1435.

NIGERIA *see* BAKASSI

NORTH KOREA

The IAEA had been unable to verify that North Korea had declared all of its weapon-grade materials as required under its safeguards agreement with the agency, the IAEA Director General said. Noting North Korean delays in allowing IAEA inspections, Mr ElBaradei said it would probably take three to four years to verify Pyongyang's initial declarations. Further delays could seriously slow construction of two light-water nuclear reactors as agreed to in the 1994 "agreed framework," he said. Under the framework, North Korea agreed to end its nuclear programme in exchange for the reactors.

NUCLEAR WEAPONS

There remained 44 nuclear-capable states that had to ratify the Comprehensive Test Ban Treaty for it to enter into force. Thirty-one had ratified, but the holdouts included the US, China, India, Pakistan and North Korea.

SIERRA LEONE *see also* LIBERIA

The UN Secretary General called for an eventual reduction of UN peacekeeping forces in Sierra Leone as part of a gradual handover of security and other responsibilities to the nation's government. In his recommendation to the Security Council, Mr Annan said the UN Mission in Sierra Leone's military component should be reduced from its current strength of 17,000 peacekeepers to about 5,000 by late 2004. Eventually, that number should be further lowered to 2,000, he said. He also called for increasing the UN civilian police presence to around 185 officers in order to help train Sierra Leonean law enforcement.

The UN Security Council renewed for six months the mandate of the UN Mission in Sierra Leone, but Council members called on UNAMSIL to begin reducing troop numbers in line with proposals by the UN Secretary General.

As the first step toward a gradual handover of responsibility to Sierra Leone, the Council called on UNAMSIL to cut 4,500 troops within eight months. It stressed that Sierra Leone must develop an appropriate police force, army, penal system and judiciary and encouraged continued talks among Sierra Leone and neighbours Liberia and Guinea to attain stability in the region.

The Council hailed the beginning of operations at the Special Court for Sierra Leone, which was responsible for handling war crimes committed during the country's decade-long civil war, and encouraged donors to contribute generously to the court.

SOMALIA

Unidentified gunmen in the southern Somali town of Garbahaarrey shot at an airplane carrying the UN Development Programme's country director as it took off from the runway. No injuries were reported, and the aircraft, suffering minor damage, was able to take off and proceed to the capital, Mogadishu. The motive for the attack was unknown. The shooting followed the kidnapping in Mogadishu of UN Food and Agriculture Organisation staff member Mohamed Farah Omar. The UN condemned the abduction and pulled its international staff from the capital, although local staff workers remained.

The UN Secretary General announced the composition of a panel to monitor the 10-year-old arms embargo on Somalia, in line with a Security Council resolution issued in July 2002. The panel consists of a Senegalese aviation expert, a Norwegian Red Cross official and a US-Dutch weapons expert. Similar arms embargo monitoring groups were in place in Angola, Sierra Leone and Liberia.

The UN announced the temporary closure of Somalia's southwestern Gedo region to UN flights and international staff following an incident in which a UN plane was fired on, but not hit, and no one was injured. Following the incident, 10 international and local UN employees who were unable to board the plane were transported to another area and flown out of the region.

Gedo region was facing a serious humanitarian crisis due to conflict and drought. A July report by the UN-EU Food Security Assessment Unit and US Agency for International Development's Famine Early Warning Systems Network warned that as many as 200,000 people in the region are vulnerable to food insecurity.

The UN welcomed the release in Somalia of a Food and Agriculture Organisation national staff member who was freed nine days after being kidnapped when factional fighting broke out near the building where he was being held. He was released along with five other Somalis after their captors fled the scene. He was the fourth UN worker abducted in Mogadishu in 2002.

The UN independent expert on human rights in Somalia, Ghanim Alnajjar, concluded an 11-day mission to Somalia, calling for greater cooperation in addressing serious human rights problems in the country and advocating a national and regional Independent Human Rights Commission which would "allow people to express concerns and to speak directly and constantly with local authorities to promote human rights." In addition, with most of the 320,000 internally displaced Somalis living in abject poverty and in areas under the control of armed faction leaders, Mr Alnajjar called "upon the international community and local authorities to pay more attention to the internally displaced, and for more coordinated action to alleviate their appalling conditions."

Insecurity prevented Mr Alnajjar's team from traveling to Mogadishu or the southwestern town of Baidoa.

An official with the self-declared republic of Somaliland said that the break-away territory would not send a delegation to the reconciliation talks, to which it had been formally invited.

SRI LANKA

The UN Secretary General welcomed the launch of direct talks between the Sri Lankan government and the Liberation Tigers of Tamil Eelam, saying in a statement that he was "pleased that the two sides have successfully implemented the provisions of their cease-fire signed last February and are now entering substantive peace negotiations."

The talks were the first face-to-face negotiations in seven years and were to focus on establishing the agenda for future talks, along with rehabilitation and reconstruction in the war zones.

The rebel Liberation Tigers of Tamil Eelam and Sri Lanka ended a three-day peace conference with the rebels demanding only autonomy, not independence from Sri Lanka – a development widely reported as a major breakthrough. The talks are aimed at bringing an end to 19 years of civil war. The rebels said, however, that they would not lay down their arms until a full agreement was reached.

SUDAN

Sudan was preparing for new fighting after the collapse of talks to end the country's civil war. Sudanese officials suspended talks, hailed by analysts as the best chance of ending the 19-year civil war, after rebels seized the strategic southern town of Torit.

Sudanese officials accused the Sudan People's Liberation Army of backtracking on agreements made in the talks in July, during which it had agreed on the importance of preserving national unity, according to an embassy statement. The 20 July Machakos protocol called for a six-year period of autonomy for southern regions, followed by a referendum on secession.

Sudan's government accused the SPLA of trying to redraw the boundaries of southern Sudan.

UGANDA *see* CONGO

WESTERN SAHARA

Moroccan politicians were campaigning in Western Sahara ahead of legislative elections in Morocco. Elections had occurred several times in the territory since Morocco held a poll in Western Sahara in 1977, in the midst of a war. The Algerian-backed

Polisario Front, which was seeking independence for the former Spanish colony, called on the UN to stop the Moroccans' "illegal" move. An official with MIN-URSO said the Mission would only act under its mandate, limiting itself to observing the cease-fire and preparing the list of voters for a future referendum.

October 2002

AFGHANISTAN

The UN Assistance Mission in Afghanistan announced that factional fighting in northern Afghanistan, which reportedly left five troops dead and two civilians injured, ended following peace talks involving the mission and factional representatives.

Following the onset of hostilities a commission comprising UNAMA and factional representatives went from Mazar-e Sharif to a town near the site of the fighting, which involved Abdul Rashid Dostum's Jumbesh-e-Milli Islami and Mohamed Attah's Jamiat group. The commission ordered the removal of three commanders from each faction. The UN said the commission has returned to Mazar-e Sharif but remained in contact with the region.

Five people were killed in unrelated factional fighting in the east of the country. A spokesman for Khost province said warlord Padshah Khan Zadran's troops attacked militiamen allied with the government, sparking fighting that left a total of five fighters on both sides dead.

Marking the anniversary of the US presence in Afghanistan, Defence Secretary Donald Rumsfeld said that 10,000 US troops would be kept in the country indefinitely to allow the Afghans time to constitute their own army. Mr Rumsfeld added that the US would hunt down Osama bin Laden and other members of his al-Qaeda terror network.

The *Financial Times* reported that Herat Governor Ismail Khan had expanded his power beyond the province and was cultivating strong economic ties to neighbouring Iran, causing concern in Washington and at the UN. The Herat customs house was thriving as traders sought to profit from a newfound relative stability in Afghanistan, and the UN-backed government in Kabul was concerned that Khan's domain could pose a threat, the newspaper reported. Khan had reportedly used customs revenue to restore mosques and rebuild infrastructure including parks and roads, and the prosperity was said to have made the self-proclaimed "emir" the most independent governor in Afghanistan. In four or five neighbouring provinces, according to the *Financial Times*, Khan held more authority than local governors.

Even as Kabul sought a share of Herat's customs income, Iran was proving to be a source of investment, notably funding a Herat-Iran road and connecting Herat to the Iranian electric grid. Nearly all of Herat's trade went through Iran, prompting concern from the US. Earlier in the year, US President Bush named Iran as one of three countries comprising an "axis of evil." Washington set up a permanent diplomatic post in Herat, a first for an Afghan city.

The precarious peace in Afghanistan continued to be threatened by factional fighting and human rights abuses, Lakhdar Brahimi, the head of the UN operation in Afghanistan, told the Security Council.

BAKASSI

Local leaders in the oil-rich Bakassi Peninsula said that they would declare independence, and possibly take military action, if Nigeria complied with an International Court of Justice ruling to hand the territory over to Cameroon.

BALI *see also* JEMAAH ISLAMIYAH

The Security Council unanimously passed a resolution condemning "in the strongest terms" a terrorist bombing in Bali, Indonesia, which killed approximately 200 people. The resolution called this and other attacks threats to international peace and security and called on nations "to work together urgently and to cooperate with . . . Indonesian authorities in their efforts to find and bring to justice the perpetrators, organisers and sponsors of these terrorist attacks."

The Australian Prime Minister said that there was increasing evidence the al-Qaeda terrorist network was involved in the attack in Indonesia, the world's most populous Muslim nation, along with a Southeast Asian group linked to al-Qaeda, Jemaah Islamiyah.

The Indonesian Defence Minister said there was no doubt that al-Qaeda was connected to the attack.

UN investigators were to join a multinational task force in Indonesia to investigate the bombing in Bali. Australia, New Zealand, the UK, Germany, Japan and the US were also sending investigators.

BURUNDI

The smaller factions of two Hutu rebel groups fighting the Burundi transitional government signed a formal cease-fire, making way for what they called a "new era" in Burundi's peace process.

As minor factions of the Conseil National pour la Defence de la Democratie-Force pour la Defence de la Democratie and the Parti de Liberation du Peuple Hutu-Force Nationale de Liberation formalised their agreements with the transitional government, regional leaders instructed the two main groups to continue negotiations "with a view to concluding the cease-fire agreement within 30 days." According to a statement from the summit, delegates agreed to "meet after 30 days to review the situation" and would "take appropriate measures against the recalcitrant parties" if no cease-fire agreement had been reached.

CAMEROON *see* BAKASSI

CENTRAL AFRICAN REPUBLIC

The UN Secretary General called for a return to peace in the fractious Central African Republic and urged insurgents there to lay down their arms. Mr Annan also appealed to the international community "to provide urgently the logistical and other assistance" needed for deployment of a peacekeeping force agreed to at a summit of the Economic and Monetary Community of Central African States.

The peacekeeping mission would work to ensure the safety of CAR President Ange-Felix Patasse, keep security along the Chadian border and help restructure the country's armed forces. Its 300-350 troops were slated to be drawn from Gabon, Cameroon, the Republic of the Congo, Equatorial Guinea and Mali.

Heavy fighting in the CAR capital of Bangui was reported , with Libyan troops, deployed to protect President Patasse after a failed coup in 2001, reportedly shelling insurgents in the city's northern neighbourhoods, including the area around Mpoko Airport. Two Libyan fighter jets, allegedly based in the DRC, were also reportedly taking part in the fighting.

Former CAR Chief of Staff Francois Bozize, once an ally of President Patasse, claimed responsibility for the uprising and demanded the president open talks with the opposition.

The Minister of State for Posts and Telecommunications said that some of the rebel troops captured by the government were from Chad, where Mr Bozize's supporters were said to be based.

CHECHNYA

A group of about 40 Chechen separatist guerrillas, including masked women with explosives strapped to their bodies, stormed a Moscow theatre and took up to 700 people hostage, threatening to shoot them or blow up the building unless Russian troops pulled out of Chechnya. One hostage had, reportedly, been shot dead.

The Russian Federal Security Service chief said Russia would spare the lives of the hostage-takers if they release their captives.

The guerrillas released a total of 15 people, including eight children, but a reported promise to free an estimated 75 foreign hostages was not fulfilled.

The standoff ended with 118 hostages and 50 hostage-takers dead after Russian special forces pumped an unidentified gas into the building to knock out those inside, then rushed in.

Controversy was brewing in Moscow over the use of the gas, which three top Moscow doctors said was responsible for the deaths of 116 hostages. The capital's chief doctor said authorities did not tell medical officials what the gas was, and Associated Press reported that the lack of information apparently hampered efforts to treat about 750 people affected by the substance.

Interfax reported that 405 of those freed were still in hospitals, with 239 having been released. The death toll stood at 118, with 116 killed by the gas and two shot by the rebels. Officials said three gunmen were captured and 50 were killed, including several reportedly shot in the head as they lay incapacitated from the gas.

COLOMBIA

Colombian President Alvaro Uribe criticised the UN for its rejection of his proposal for a peacekeeping force to aid the return of 30,000 families displaced by Colombia's 38-year conflict with leftist rebels.

The president's efforts had included enlisting the support of countries including the US, which has promised about $450 million this fiscal year for counter-narcotics and security programmes. He had also imposed a tax on the rich to finance a strengthening of state security forces.

Ten people died in Colombia in police raids, fighting between paramilitaries and the army and assassinations attributed to Revolutionary Armed Forces of Colombia rebels.

CONGO, DEMOCRATIC REPUBLIC OF

Over 15,000 foreign troops had left the Democratic Republic of the Congo in recent weeks as the conflict there wound down.

The UN Organisation Mission in the Democratic Republic of the Congo announced that all troops operating under Rwanda's current regime had withdrawn from the country, ending over four years of activity in the troubled central African country. MONUC said the last batch of 1,152 Rwandan soldiers crossed the border from Goma, DRC, to Gisenyi, Rwanda, completing a withdrawal process that began in September 2002. According to MONUC, the troops brought heavy weaponry including anti-aircraft guns and armoured vehicles.

MONUC observers who witnessed the withdrawal said they counted 20,941 Rwandan soldiers leaving the DRC. MONUC said about 2,819 Rwandan troops were still unaccounted for, but Rwandan authorities said the troops were on leave, assignment or training at the time of the withdrawal.

The withdrawal was in line with a Rwandan-DRC peace deal brokered by South Africa in July. The Rwandan troops had been in the country since they invaded in 1998 in pursuit of ethnic Hutu rebels and former Rwandan military elements who were involved in the 1994 Rwandan genocide.

The Rwandan-backed Rassemblement Congolais pour la Democratie rebel group in the DRC immediately issued a statement welcoming the withdrawal and calling on all remaining foreign troops to leave as well. RCD President Adolphe Onusumba urged "the international community and the UN Security Council to exert their influence on other countries still present in the Congo so that they pull out without delay or conditions."

The rebels called on the DRC government to "cease all operations to supply foreign and Congolese 'negative forces' active in eastern DRC and to proceed immediately . . . with the disarmament, demobilization and repatriation of Interahamwe [Hutu militias] and ex- Forces Armees Rwandaises groups responsible for the 1994 genocide in Rwanda." The RCD urged "Congolese political actors, civil society, Mayi-Mayi groups and others to seize the opportunity and resolutely commit themselves to finding a global and inclusive political accord with a view to ending the current crisis."

Nearly all the foreign countries involved in the war in the DRC had been withdrawing. Following the withdrawal of Namibian troops in 2001, Angolan and Zimbabwean troops had started to pull out. Uganda pulled most of its troops out in September 2002, leaving only a contingent of 1,000 in the northeastern town of Bunia at the request of MONUC.

The RCD said that it had reached "agreements in principle" with the Congolese government. According to rebel spokesman a consensus had been reached on several issues, including a formula under which the country would have a president and four deputy presidents and the establishment of a ministerial commission on reconciliation. The RCD and nearly a dozen Congolese opposition parties had not signed the Sun City peace accords.

Peacekeepers with MONUC opened fire following protesters' attacks on three of their vehicles in the rebel-held city of Kisangani, injuring a student. The incident marked the first time MONUC forces had fired in self-defence since the UN mission had begun. According to the Mission, a group of university students blocked the road to Kisangani's airport in protest of a recent rebel assault on a professor. Three MONUC vehicles en route to the airport were attacked, and one MONUC official was injured.

The UN Organisation Mission in the DRC denounced the resurgence of fighting in the east of the country, warning it could put the peace process at risk. MONUC said fighting in towns near the eastern border – particularly Uvira, Bunia and Mambasa – posed "incalculable humanitarian consequences."

The Mayi-Mayi militia, a loose network of pro-government fighters, said they had pushed the Rwandan-backed Rassemblement Congolais pour la Democratie from Uvira, a town of about 130,000 at the northern tip of Lake Tanganyika, following battles. The militia said it had taken 200 RCD prisoners and had seized weapons.

The renewed fighting prompted the RCD to break off its negotiations with the DRC government, accusing it of supporting the Mayi-Mayi attack.

Warning that renewed fighting in eastern parts of the DRC threatened to destabilise the entire country, UN envoy Amos Namanga Ngongi said that the warring parties were ignoring his appeals to uphold the cease-fire.

Rwanda claimed that members of Rwanda's former army, the Forces Armees Rwandaises and Interahamwe fighters blamed for the 1994 Rwandan genocide were the "major force" operating in and around Uvira, a town at the northern tip of Lake Tanganyika, which was captured by a pro-Kinshasa militia.

Foreign corporations, senior African officials and criminal networks were plundering the rich natural resources of the DRC, according to a 59-page report prepared for the UN Security Council by a UN-appointed independent panel. Despite the recent withdrawal of most foreign forces, the exploitation of Congo's resources continues, the report said, with "elite networks" and criminal groups tied to the military forces of Rwanda, Uganda and Zimbabwe benefiting from "micro-conflicts" in the DRC. Many of the individuals and companies accused in a UN report of plundering natural resources in the DRC denied any involvement in wrongdoing and challenged the UN to produce proof of the allegations.

UN-mediated peace talks opened and continued with the aim of bringing peace and a new power-sharing government to the DRC. Government and rebel negotiators were discussing what powers the various posts in the transitional government would have. The talks came amid an upsurge this month in fighting in the eastern DRC. In the proposed power-sharing government, President Joseph Kabila would remain as head of state, but four vice presidencies would be created and filled by representatives of the government, the Rwandan-backed Rassemblement Congolais pour la Democratie, the Ugandan-backed Mouvement de Liberation du Congo and civil society and domestic political parties. Any agreement that emerged from the talks was expected to be endorsed by the Inter-Congolese Dialogue.

UN special envoy Moustapha Niasse said he was optimistic that the warring parties in the DRC could reach a peace deal during the talks. He added that he would push for a resolution of the outstanding issues ahead of a meeting between DRC President Joseph Kabila and Rwandan President Paul Kagame.

Negotiating sessions were canceled as Mr Niasse sought agreement from the Ugandan-backed rebel Mouvement de Liberation du Congo for a proposal under which President Kabila would share power with four vice presidents, drawn from the MLC, the Rwandan-backed rebel Rassemblement Congolais pour la Democratie, opposition parties and his own government.

MLC Secretary General Olivier Kamitatu said that allowing the Kabila regime to appoint one of the vice presidents would give the president too much power, adding that he was consulting with MLC leader Jean-Pierre Bemba.

Other sticking points which Mr Niasse said would be among the hardest to resolve involved amnesties and ensuring security for demobilised rebels, as well as provincial and parliamentary power sharing. The UN envoy said that despite the remaining differences, he was "optimistic" for an accord in 2002.

Reports said fierce fighting had again broken out between RCD groups and pro-government Mayi-Mayi militias south of the border port of Uvira. A Mayi-Mayi source accused Burundi, the border of which fronts on Uvira, and neighbouring Rwanda of supporting the RCD.

Negotiators at peace talks reported a breakthrough, following the decision by one of the rebel groups to accede to a key power-sharing proposal.

The talks had now been postponed to allow the Congolese government more time to deliberate and decide how much power it was willing to share with rebel groups.

The breakthrough reportedly came when the Ugandan-backed Mouvement de Liberation du Congo dropped its previous opposition to a proposal under which President Kabila would share power with four vice presidents.

COTE D'IVOIRE

Ivorian UN Ambassador Djessan Philippe Djangone-Bi joined the chorus of those accusing foreigners of being behind the civil conflict in Cote d'Ivoire, calling rebels who staged a failed coup attempt on 19 September "a bunch of mercenaries and deserters."

Ivorian officials and state press had repeatedly said the rebels were propped up by outside forces, implying, but not stating, that Muslim neighbour Burkina Faso was backing the rebels, whose support came from Cote d'Ivoire's Muslim north. Mr Djangone-Bi said "some country" has helped the rebels but that he could not name the country. He added that captured rebel fighters had said Burkinabe, Sierra Leonean and Liberian mercenaries were among their number, but he did not directly accuse Cote d'Ivoire's neighbours of supporting the combatants.

Reports of clashes continue in various areas, with rebels saying they controlled numerous towns but that French troops had prevented them from advancing on the capital, Yamoussoukro. The US and France had deployed troops to evacuate and protect French nationals and other Westerners, and France had reportedly been providing logistical help to the government.

Cote d'Ivoire had, since the coup attempt, been vowing to launch an all-out war on the rebels but had not yet done so, citing concern for civilians.

Rebels now in control of Cote d'Ivoire's predominantly Muslim north demanded an end to discrimination against northerners, the canceling of military demobilisation plans, amnesty for dissident soldiers who had been jailed or fled the country, and the disbanding of an allegedly ethnic-based police force.

Government troops went on the offensive after President Laurent Gbagbo refused to sign a cease-fire agreement unless rebels in the North first disarmed.

Thousands were reportedly fleeing Cote d'Ivoire's second-largest city of Bouake, taking advantage of a lull in the fighting between the government and the rebel Mouvement Patriotique de la Cote d'Ivoire, said to be in control of the city and other areas in the country's north.

French military officials reported an increase in the number fleeing, with up to 1,000 leaving the city daily. The International Committee of the Red Cross put the total number of displaced people from Bouake at up to 150,000. Most of them were said to be immigrants from predominantly Muslim Burkina Faso, which the government had blamed for the insurgency. Unconfirmed reports also referred to up to 4,000 displaced people around Duekoue in the nation's western region.

Burkina Faso, Niger, Ghana and Nigeria had reportedly made contingency plans to evacuate their nationals.

Rebels halted all talks with West African mediators and accused Angola of sending troops to back the government. Angolan officials denied this claim, while airport sources in Abidjan confirmed the arrival of foreign planes bringing weapons, but said they had not seen troops.

The rebels captured the key cocoa-producing town of Daloa, 400 kilometers northwest of Abidjan.

Government forces appeared to have reclaimed Daloa after hours of heavy explosions and gunfire. Aid workers said they fear a tide of refugees could destabilise the region. Residents said fighting was interfering with cocoa production in the country, which accounts for 40% of the World's supply.

President Laurent Gbagbo said he had appealed to the rebels to withdraw as a sign of good faith and added that his government had accepted a mediator's proposal for rebels to confine themselves to barracks so peace talks to end the month-long crisis could begin.

Anti-riot police patrolled the streets of Daloa after recapturing the strategically important central town from the rebel Mouvement Patriotique de la Cote d'Ivoire.

Sporadic gunfire had quieted, with government forces saying they had repulsed a rebel counter-attack. The population of Daloa, a cocoa-producing centre which had changed hands twice in four days, was divided between Muslim northerners who supported the MPCI and southern pro-government Christians, many of whom belonged to the Bete tribe of President Laurent Gbagbo.

The secretary general of MPCI's political wing repeated his group's refusal to negotiate despite its earlier support for mediation efforts and warned of a protracted struggle.

The rebel Mouvement Patriotique de la Cote d'Ivoire signed a truce in Bouake, their stronghold in the central part of the country, agreeing to a cease-fire and allowing deployment of an Economic Community of West African States mechanism to oversee it. Neither the rebels nor ECOWAS mediators who pressed the rebels to agree to the truce said whether the agreement to lay down arms was dependent on President Laurent Gbagbo's acceptance of the deal. President Gbagbo, however, said that he was prepared to accept the cease-fire agreement.

In the cocoa-producing centre of Daloa, recently recaptured by the government, Ivorian paramilitary police reportedly looted a Muslim-owned store and dispersed crowds at a predominantly Muslim market. Youths, mainly from President Gbagbo's Bete tribe, and others looted businesses.

The UN was evacuating non-essential employees and their families from Abidjan despite a cease-fire reached between President Gbagbo's government and rebel forces. A UN Development Programme spokesman added that UNDP staff members had already begun to leave. He called the situation in Abidjan, the country's main commercial city, "sufficiently tense." Evacuations of Belgian, British, Dutch, Portuguese, Spanish and US nationals had also been ordered.

Heads of state of the Economic Community of West African States agreed to send monitors to war-torn Cote d'Ivoire in the interest of regional stability.

Face-to-face talks began between Cote d'Ivoire and rebels who had staged a failed 19 September coup and had been fighting with Ivorian troops since then.

CUBA
Cuba ratified the 1969 Treaty of Tlatelolco, which established a nuclear weapon-free zone in Latin America and the Caribbean. Cuba signed the treaty in 1995, but was the last of 33 eligible states to ratify the treaty.

CYPRUS
The UN Secretary General opened negotiations with Cypriot President Glafcos Clerides and Turkish Cypriot leader Rauf Denktash on the future of divided Cyprus. According to diplomats, a breakthrough was unlikely during the two days of talks at the UN, but the talks could pave the way for a settlement or an interim agreement before a 12 December EU summit at which EU states would decide which of 13 candidate countries, including Cyprus, to accept as new members.

No settlement was likely before Turkey's November general elections.

Greece had said it would veto the accession of other countries vying for EU membership if Cyprus' application is rejected.

Ending the two days of talks Mr Annan, Mr Clerides and Mr Denktash agreed to create two committees to work on treaties and future "common state" laws for divided Cyprus. UN special envoy Alvaro de Soto said "common state" was a provisional designation meant to indicate the state that would be "at the centre of a reunified Cyprus."

The two ad hoc bilateral committees would be able to explore technical matters without being swayed by the two leaders' opinions on core issues, said Mr Annan, pledging UN help as the parties work together toward a reunified Cyprus and calling on Greece and Turkey to support the process.

ETHIOPIA AND ERITREA
The UN formally protested to Ethiopian authorities following two illegal incursions by Ethiopian militiamen into the Temporary Security Zone that served as a buffer between Ethiopia and Eritrea, which fought a bloody border war that ended less than two years before.

The militiamen, who were armed with AK-47 rifles, fired shots at UN Mission in Ethiopia and Eritrea peacekeepers. UNMEE officials said these were the first-ever clashes involving armed Ethiopian militia and peacekeepers.

Ethiopia's Ministry of Foreign Affairs sent a statement to the UN Mission in Ethiopia and Eritrea, accusing it of leaking information about a border clash involving Ethiopian militiamen while ignoring reports of other incidents involving Eritrean soldiers.

The ministry said a senior UNMEE official had volunteered details of Indian peacekeepers' confrontation with the militia members and the mission's subsequent protest to the Ethiopian government. It specifically cited a BBC interview with the unnamed official, saying that UNMEE and Ethiopia had been dealing with the dispute at the time and that the matter should had been kept private.

The BBC said its report on the incident came from information gathered at a regular news briefing. UNMEE Chief of Staff Rajesh Arya was quoted in several reports concerning the reported clash.

GEORGIA

As Georgia wrapped up five months of scouring the countryside for hundreds of radiological power units from the Soviet era, the government was seeking new international assistance to establish a single storage facility for so-called "orphaned sources" to ensure the materials were properly secured and remained out of reach of potential terrorists.

Georgian officials, in completing an intensive search operation sponsored by the IAEA, were confident they had identified most of the radioactive strontium, cesium, cobalt and other radiological sources located in Georgian territory under the government's control. One continuing concern, however, was the worrisome number of radiological sources located at a primate research facility in the northern Abkhazia region of the country, which was seeking independence and had been largely inaccessible to Georgian and international authorities during the previous decade.

INDONESIA *see* BALI

IRAQ

UN weapons inspectors and Iraqi officials negotiated logistical details related to renewed inspections of Iraq. Negotiators made progress in several areas. Iraqi officials agreed to provide reports on dual-use facilities – sites that had possible uses related to both civilian work and weapons of mass destruction – over the past four years. UN inspectors and Iraqi officials also moved forward on the issues of visa-free entry into Iraq, the nationality of inspectors and transport and security arrangements, but not, however, on whether weapons inspectors would be able to fly over suspect sites located in no-fly zones in northern and southern Iraq.

Talks between the UN and Iraq ended with agreement on technical matters relating to the return of weapons inspectors, as more details emerged about the proposed US resolution that would set new conditions for the inspections.

The Iraqi delegation also turned over to Hans Blix four CD-ROMs containing the backlog of monitoring declarations for sites and items that had dual-use capabilities – both civilian and military applications – covering June 1998 to July 2002.

Chief UN weapons inspector Hans Blix and IAEA Director General Mohammed ElBaradei briefed the Security Council on practical arrangements for returning weapons inspectors to Iraq. Mr Blix said existing Council resolutions provide the requisite authority for the inspectors to return. He had made preliminary plans for inspectors to return to Baghdad on 19 October, UN sources said.

The UN Compensation Commission (the UN body in charge of ruling on compensation issues from Iraq's 1990 invasion of Kuwait) ended its latest session, approving nearly $1 billion in payments for claimants against Iraq. Its largest dispensations during the session involved environmental claims from governments. The body's Governing Council ruled in favour of 22 out of the 31 claims submitted, for a total award of more than $711 million and approved 290 large claims by individuals, totaling over $87 million. Meanwhile, 282 Kuwaiti claims from outside the oil sector also received approval, with a total value of over $143 million. Insurance companies, export credit agencies and various concerns from outside Kuwait also received commission awards.

The US and the UK were using a briefing by the UNs' chief weapons inspectors to press their case for the rapid passage of a new, tougher Security Council resolution on Iraq's weapons of mass destruction.

Iraq's statements that presidential palaces might soon be accessible for weapons inspection and that Iraq was willing to work with the UN were dismissed by US officials as unconvincing.

The Bush administration was preparing a list of 13 Iraqi officials whom it hoped to prosecute for a variety of war crimes, according to the *Tribune*. President Hussein headed the list, which also contained six of his family members, including two of his sons. Ali Hassan Majid, who was alleged to have played a large role in the use of chemical weapons that killed Iraqi Kurds in northern Iraq in 1988, was second on the list.

The CIA released a report saying that since the end of UN weapons inspections in 1998, Iraq had sought to rebuild or further develop its weapons of mass destruction programmes. Many intelligence analysts believed that for the previous four years, Iraq had sought to rebuild its nuclear weapons programme, which was heavily set back because of the 1991 Gulf War and later UN inspections. Iraq had also heavily invested in its biological weapons programme and worked to maintain its chemical weapons programme.

US President Bush again sought public support for possible military action against Iraq over its alleged pursuit of weapons of mass destruction and its refusal to allow UN weapons inspectors back into the country. Mr Bush acknowledged the US did not know how close Iraq was to acquiring a nuclear weapon but stressed the dangers of Baghdad's other weapons of mass destruction and the need to contain any nuclear programme before it was too late.

In a letter sent by Hans Blix to Iraqi presidential adviser General Amir al-Saadi, UN weapons inspectors outlined the rules Iraq would be expected to abide by during inspections. According to the letter, UNMOVIC and the IAEA would have the right to determine the number of inspectors that would be used at each inspection site. Iraq would be informed of new sites once inspectors arrive at a location and would safeguard aircraft in the no-fly zones in northern and southern Iraq.

Iraq had to also allow inspectors to interview anyone they wished, it had to not interfere with any data transmissions and it had to provide inspectors with accommodations and offices, including a northern office in Mosul and a southern office in Basra. The letter spelt out that the agencies "had the right to determine the number of inspectors required for access to any particular site."

A US Defence Intelligence Agency official claimed that Iraq had already begun preparations to conceal equipment and documents related to its weapons of mass destruction programme.

The *Los Angeles Times* reported that the US and the UK could have been getting closer to accepting a compromise UN Security Council resolution that would call for "consequences" if Iraq failed to comply with weapons inspections but would not automatically authorise the use of force. The resolution would reportedly drop references to UN members "automatically" having the right to use "all necessary means" against Iraq.

There was growing agreement on the idea that Iraq should face "appropriate consequences," the US State Department said. Officials said the specific language of the resolution was still being negotiated.

The compromise resolution could have been an attempt to undercut a French proposal calling for a two-stage approach involving one resolution on a new inspections regime and a second on the use of force. The purpose of the compromise resolution was to avoid a long debate on a second resolution.

The US Congress approved a resolution giving President Bush the authority to use military force against Iraq.

The resolution supported Mr Bush's efforts to enforce past UN resolutions on Iraq and supports efforts to secure a new, stricter UN Security Council resolution. The congressional resolution authorised Mr Bush to use military action to "defend the national security of the US against the continuing threat posed by Iraq" and to "enforce all relevant UN Security Council resolutions regarding Iraq."

Mr Bush would now have 48 hours after launching an attack on Iraq to notify
Congress that diplomatic efforts alone would not enforce UN Security Council resolutions or would not "adequately protect the national security of the United States
against the continuing threat posed by Iraq."

The Security Council began a public debate (requested by the Nonaligned
Movement) on Iraq's noncompliance with Council requirements for elimination of
its weapons of mass destruction with the Iraqi ambassador charging the US with
planning to wage a war to colonise his country. The Kuwaiti Ambassador countered
his claims, saying he welcomed this Council meeting "as yet another proof . . . that
the . . . question of Iraq is an issue between Iraq and the UN and not between Iraq
and any particular country or group of countries." The US and France were moving closer to a compromise draft resolution that would set new guidelines for UN
inspectors investigating Iraq's weapons of mass destruction and for how force could
be authorised in the event of Baghdad's resistance, Security Council delegates said
as the Council concluded the two-day open debate. The public speeches by the five
permanent members of the council – the US, the UK, France, Russia and China –
did not give any indication of a meeting of minds, with all five repeating the positions they had held since discussions on a new draft resolution began five weeks
before. The 10 nonpermanent members of the Council all wanted the inspectors to
return but those who addressed the question of the council authorising the use of
force insisted that the decision-making stay in Council hands. The session ended as
it began, with Iraq saying inspectors could return to see that Iraq has no weapons
of mass destruction.

Hans Blix, the head of UNMOVIC, confirmed reports that he had given up on
plans to send inspectors to Iraq by 19 October.

Iraq began handing over Kuwait's national archives, which it took during its
1990 occupation of Kuwait.

As the US prepared for a possible attack on Iraq and the UN Security Council
continued to consider the passage of a new resolution on Iraq's weapons of mass
destruction programmes, Mr Annan said that he hoped "that sometime . . . soon,
there would be a new resolution of the Security Council."

The US presented its draft resolution on Iraq to permanent members of the
Security Council, calling for intensive UN inspections and warning that Iraq could
face "severe consequences" if it failed to destroy its chemical, biological and nuclear
weapons. By formally circulating the draft resolution, the Bush administration was
indicating that its position has firmed up and it was now seeking UN Security
Council approval, according to the *Post*.

In changes from its original draft, the US eliminated language that would automatically authorise military action against the government of Iraqi President Saddam
Hussein if Baghdad failed to cooperate with weapons inspectors and removed a
clause granting permanent council members the right to participate in inspections. The

new draft would allow the chief UN weapons inspector to use "accomplished, dedicated and experienced experts" on UN missions to Iraq.

Other measures in the draft resolution would require Iraq to file a "full, final and complete declaration" of its banned weapons programme within 30 days of the resolution's adoption and to provide "unrestricted" and "immediate access" to any location in Iraq, including eight presidential compounds where special and timely procedures formerly applied.

The text would also allow UN inspectors to invite Iraqi scientists and their families out of the country for interviews and would set up "no-fly" and "no-drive" areas around suspected weapons sites, possibly enforced by US, British or UN forces. In addition, it stipulated that UN security guards would be posted at UN bases in Iraq. The US draft called on Hans Blix to report on Iraq's cooperation after 135 days. In that time period, Iraq would have up to 30 days to submit its declaration. UN inspectors would then have up to 45 days to resume inspections and an additional 60 days to report to the Security Council.

Baghdad would have seven days to accept the new UN resolution, which also called on Mr Blix to report immediately any defiance by Iraq, and empowered the Council to convene immediately to discuss "the need for full compliance with all of the relevant Security Council resolutions in order to restore international peace and security."

It should take UN arms inspectors less than a year to sufficiently account for Iraq's suspected weapons of mass destruction if the inspectors receive full Iraqi cooperation, a UN inspections official said. Ron Cleminson, a commissioner of the UN Monitoring, Verification and Inspection Commission – the team responsible for investigating Iraq's efforts to develop weapons of mass destruction – said it should take "10 months to had a definitive document on the desk of the Security Council."

As the five permanent members of the Security Council continued their closed-door consultations on a draft resolution on Iraq's disarmament, the 10 nonpermanent members were expressing increasing frustration at being left out of the discussions. The US draft that would declare Iraq in "material breach" of its disarmament obligations and set new, tougher rules for weapons inspections was widely distributed to the media, but the 10 elected members still had not officially been given the text.

The debate over a resolution demanding Iraq's disarmament entered a new phase with the US bringing its draft resolution to the entire Security Council, thus shifting the focus of the deliberations from trying to find consensus among the five permanent members of the council to seeking enough votes from the 15-member Council to pass its resolution.

Among the five permanent veto-holding members, the US proposal was supported by only the UK. France, Russia, and China said they opposed any new resolution that set the bar too high for Iraq to comply with a new inspection regime and that would give the US unchecked authority to attack Iraq should

Baghdad not comply. Several rounds of meetings among the five did not result in an agreement.

The US was gaining support among the 10 nonpermanent members of the UN Security Council for its draft resolution on a new inspection regime for Iraq, increasing the possibility that the US draft would receive the nine votes needed for approval, according to the *Washington Post.* The Mexican Foreign Ministry indicated that it was more supportive of the US resolution, saying in a statement that the US was "moving closer to the arguments espoused by Russia, France and Mexico." Other Security Council members, such as Colombia, that opposed the 1991 Gulf War had indicated that they would now support the US.

The chief UN weapons inspector told the Security Council that the decision whether to wage war on Iraq would be up to the Council, not him.

US President Bush told two top UN inspection officials – the chief UN weapons inspector and the Director General of the IAEA – that he wanted inspectors to have maximum authority to hunt for Iraqi weapons of mass destruction.

The full 15-member Security Council completed the first round of negotiations on the US draft resolution on Iraq, with none of the five permanent members threatening a veto. The Council members broadly agreed that they wanted to tell President Saddam he had to comply with weapons inspections or face military action, diplomats said.

The US and France were still negotiating specific provisions of the resolution, with the two countries divided over the method of deciding whether Iraq had violated it.

JEMAAH ISLAMIYAH

Indonesia joined with Australia, the US and Singapore to call for UN action against Jemaah Islamiyah, a militant group accused of involvement in attacks in Indonesia including the 12 October Bali bombing, by including it on its list of terrorist organisations. The call came as Indonesian authorities were searching the country for three suspects in the Bali attack, which took the lives of 180 people.

Inclusion on the UN list would mean that the group's assets would be frozen and the ability of its members to cross borders would be hindered.

A UN Security Council committee did add the Southeast Asian network to its list of al-Qaeda and Taliban operatives, making it subject to sanctions that would require countries to freeze assets, prohibit its members from traveling across borders and prevent the sale of arms, supplies and military training to the group.

The militant group, which was founded by the late Abdullah Sungkar, had been accused of involvement in attacks in Indonesia. Although no formal charges had been brought against the group for the 12 October Bali bombing, the Jemaah Islamiyah network was being investigated for the attack. Singapore authorities first tracked down the group's suspected activists in December 2001.

KOSOVO

The UN Mission in Kosovo head unveiled a seven-point plan to alleviate tensions in the divided northern Kosovar city of Mitrovica. Under his plan, UN police and KFOR forces in ethnic Serb-dominated northern Mitrovica would keep watch to ensure there were no incursions from the southern, ethnic Albanian-dominated part of the city. The UNMIK head added that ethnic Serbs from northern Mitrovica had begun joining the Kosovar police. He also said that a new agreement was necessary to ensure that all decisions affecting the city are taken jointly.

The plan was dismissed by Kosovar Serb leader Oliver Ivanovic, who said the offer amounted to extortion. According to Mr Ivanovic, guaranteeing the security and equality of ethnic Serbs was part of UNMIK's mandate, but the UNMIK head was demanding Serbs vote in the elections in order to attain rights to which they were already entitled.

LIBERIA

The UN Secretary General recommended extension of the UN Peacebuilding Support Office in Liberia mandate for another year, as a continuing civil war had caused serious humanitarian problems.

Despite UNOL'S limited mandate and capacity, Mr Annan said the office continued "to contribute to national efforts at reconciliation, while at the same time monitoring developments and assisting in the promotion of respect for human rights and the rule of law." He also said that, should the Security Council request it, he would be open to a revised mandate for the office. The 22-member office's mandate was due to expire on 31 December.

Liberian press reports said the country planned to devote more than half its $70 million budget to fighting rebels. According to budget director Emmanuel Gardiner, 66% of the previous year's budget was devoted to the same purpose. AFP reports that only $29 million of 2002's budget would be devoted to running the government, while $41 million would go toward the war effort and "national security."

Liberia smuggled more than 200 tons of military equipment into the country in violation of UN sanctions, according to a report in which UN experts detailed "a sophisticated trail of double documentation" designed to show the weapons and ammunition were shipped to Nigeria. UN investigators said they had evidence that six cargo planes landed in the Liberian capital, Monrovia, between June and August 2002 with forged documents listing their cargo as drilling and technical equipment being sent to Nigeria. The cargo – rifles, pistols, hand grenades, missile launchers, machine guns, mines and spare parts – was shipped instead to the Liberian government. The cargo was mostly older Yugoslav army stocks supplied by a Belgrade-based company, Temex, the report said.

The UN panel also uncovered millions of dollars of discrepancies in shipping and timber industry records and expressed concern that the money Monrovia used to buy arms may have been diverted from domestic humanitarian programmes.

The report recommended that the arms embargo on Liberia should continue and be extended to include all armed rebel groups in the region. Investigators believed diamonds continued to be smuggled to neighbouring countries and that the travel ban on Liberian President Charles Taylor and his top associates continued to be violated.

Diplomats said the sanctions – imposed following accusations that Liberia was fueling civil war in Sierra Leone through the illicit diamonds trade – were unlikely to be lifted. The Security Council was scheduled to review sanctions against Liberia in November 2002.

The government was complaining that the embargo had left it defenceless against the rebel Liberians United for Reconciliation and Democracy.

A UN Security Council-appointed panel of experts monitoring the arms embargo against Liberia said it had documented new violations, committed, in part, through the use of bogus end-user certificates. In its report to the Council, the panel said it had discovered six cargo planes containing about 200 tons of weapons and ammunition, drawn mainly from old Yugoslav stocks. The arms reached the country from a Belgrade, Yugoslavia, supplier through the use of the false end-user certificates, with flight authorisation and cargo manifests indicating the shipment was intended for Nigeria.

The panel suggested standardising end-user documentation through all member countries of the Economic Community of West African States.

The rebel Liberians United for Reconciliation and Democracy continued to receive arms through Sierra Leone, Cote d'Ivoire and Guinea, the panel added. One case it cited involved mortar rounds originally supplied by the United Arab Emirates for the Guinean military. Guinea's Defence Ministry claimed the mortar shells had been destroyed in a barracks fire.

MIDDLE EAST

US President George W. Bush said US policy regarding Jerusalem had not changed, even though he signed a bill that recognised the city as Israel's capital. The move threatened to deepen resentment among Muslims and Arabs. In a move meant as a response to the decision by the US to require that Jerusalem be recognised as the capital of Israel, Palestinian Authority President Yasser Arafat signed a law formally declaring Jerusalem as the capital of a future independent Palestinian state.

At least 13 Palestinians were killed and scores wounded following a brief Israeli incursion into the Gaza Strip, a move Israel called "obligatory" but which Palestinians said was intended to derail peace efforts.

Israeli forces invaded a Palestinian neighbourhood near Khan Younis in what it said was a "very important" operation to strike a Hamas stronghold Israel had refrained from attacking in the past. The raid and resulting clashes between Palestinian gunmen and Israeli troops were followed by an Israeli helicopter attack on a crowd of Palestinians who had emerged from their homes following the incursion.

The UN Special Coordinator for the Middle East Peace Process strongly condemned a suicide bombing attack near Tel Aviv that killed an elderly woman and injured dozens of other people. Mr Roed-Larsen reiterated that such repugnant terror attacks were legally and morally indefensible and completely counter-productive to peace efforts. He called on Israelis and Palestinians to show restraint and adhere immediately to Security Council Resolution 1435 adopted in September 2002, which called for a halt to "all acts of terror, provocation, incitement and destruction."

The attack was the second suicide bombing on a commuter bus in the Tel Aviv area within a month. The Tel Aviv police chief praised the driver of the bus and a passenger who had restrained the bomber while the other passengers fled, which he said had averted "a major disaster" and "saved the lives of many people."

Hamas claimed responsibility for the attack.

Israeli forces opened fire in the southern Gaza Strip, wounding 16 Palestinians. The gunfire hit several houses and a UN-administered school for Palestinian refugees, triggering clashes between soldiers and stone-throwing youths.

Israeli soldiers and police backed away from a potential confrontation with Jewish settlers who had created a new settlement near the West Bank town of Nablus, allowing them to remain during daylight hours. Critics had accused the government of Prime Minister Ariel Sharon of tolerating illegal outposts as a way to continue informal settlement without angering the US, which had called these settlements an obstacle to peace efforts in the region.

Israeli Defence Minister Binyamin Ben-Eliezer had also criticised these settlements, ordering the dismantling of two dozen. One recent attempt in Havat Gilad was the first time Mr Ben-Eliezer confronted Israeli settlers.

The UN Secretary General said he deplored the Israeli military's attack on the Rafah refugee camp in Gaza, which left at least seven Palestinians dead and wounded dozens more.

Israel had reportedly decided on a limited, measured response to the suicide bombing of a bus near the northern town of Hadera, which left 14 dead and dozens injured. Islamic Jihad claimed responsibility for the bombing, said to be the worst against a bus since June.

Israel was not living up to pledges made by senior officials to ease the movement of Palestinians through checkpoints, UN Deputy Emergency Coordinator Ross Mountain said.

Israeli officials expressed pessimism about the "road map" peace plan endorsed by the "Quartet" of outside parties involved in the region's peace process: the US, the UN, the EU and Russia. The officials said the proposal, which called for reform of Palestinian democratic institutions and set a timetable for an eventual Palestinian state, was unlikely to move the peace process forward.

NEPAL

UN coordinator in Nepal Henning Karcher said the UN stood "ready to assist in the peace talks" between Kathmandu and Maoist rebels who, since 1996, had pursued an insurgency that had left 5,000 Nepalese dead.

Associated Press reported the world body had never before offered to become directly involved in the conflict. Mr Karcher said neither side had requested UN mediation. Nepalese Prime Minister Lokendra Bahadur Chand had offered to begin peace talks, but the rebels had not responded, and fighting continued. Associated Press added that UN and other aid agencies in the country were facing difficulties stemming from the conflict. The World Food Programme Nepal head said rebels had looted food aid in some cases and the government had blocked the flow of aid to some areas over concerns it could fuel the rebel cause.

NIGERIA *see* BAKASSI

NORTH KOREA

After being confronted by a US delegation during a visit to Pyongyang, North Korean officials acknowledged the existence of a nuclear weapons programme. Such a programme would be a violation of international nonproliferation accords, including the Nuclear Nonproliferation Treaty, the 1994 Agreed Framework between the United States and North Korea and the 1991 denuclearisation agreement between North and South Korea. In light of North Korea's admission of its nuclear weapons programme, the US decided to abandon the 1994 Agreed Framework. Under the framework, North Korea had agreed to end its nuclear weapons programme in exchange for two light-water nuclear reactors.

North Korea's ambassador to the UN said that his country had the right to develop nuclear weapons since the US's policy toward North Korea was "a clear declaration of war."

PREVLAKA

Yugoslav and Croatian authorities were making progress in resolving their long-standing dispute over the strategic Prevlaka peninsula, which could soon make the UN peacekeeping presence in the area unnecessary.

The UN Security Council extended for a final two months UNMOP, which had, since 1996, monitored the demilitarisation of the Prevlaka peninsula, an area disputed by Croatia and Yugoslavia. The mission would end on 15 December.

SMALL ARMS

The Security Council endorsed proposals to curb the flow of illicit small arms, including instituting tighter export controls, monitoring arms brokers, studying the possibility of an international system of marking arms and enforcing arms embargoes in conflict zones.

The unanimous statement was the follow-up to a debate the council held on 11 October. That meeting centred around the programme of action approved by the Conference on the Illicit Trade in Small Arms and Light Weapons in All Its Aspects in July 2001 and on a report by the Secretariat on small arms, written in fulfillment of a request by the Council in August 2001. The Council's statement endorsed many of the proposals included in those two documents.

SOMALIA

The Somali National Reconciliation Conference opened with some 350 Somali delegates bringing hope for the establishment of a decentralised, inclusive government and the end of over a decade of factional fighting and anarchy that arose after warlords overthrew Somali president Mohamed Siad Barre in 1991.

Twenty-two Somali military, political, civil society and clan leaders signed a cease-fire, ending a war that started in 1991 in Somalia, promising to continue talks, to create a federal government, to cooperate with other countries against terrorism, to solve disputes peacefully, to maintain only defensive military positions and to facilitate international arms embargo monitors' work.

The Nairobi *Daily Nation* reported some delegates' complaints that their minority groups were not represented nearly disrupted the signing ceremony but that one was allowed to sign after he began to cry.

SUDAN

The Sudanese government and the rebel Sudan People's Liberation Army/Movement signed a temporary cease-fire agreement in an effort to end the 19-year civil war in Africa's largest country.

The agreement followed intensified fighting in Sudan following the rebels' move to take the strategic town of Torit in September. That caused the last round of peace talks to break down. The new cease-fire would remain in effect as long as peace talks continued or until the end of December, whichever came first. If no final peace agreement had been reached before the end of the year, the temporary cease-fire, which allowed "unimpeded" humanitarian access across Sudan, could be extended.

UN PEACEKEEPING OPERATIONS

The General Assembly's Special Political and Decolonisation Committee began a comprehensive review of UN peacekeeping operations. UN Undersecretary General for Peacekeeping Operations Jean-Marie Guehenno said the previous year had witnessed the first new mission since the issuance of the Brahimi report on peace-keeping operations – the UN Assistance Mission in Afghanistan, which was conceived differently to previous missions. Mr Guehenno said that mission has been successful in bringing together relief, rehabilitation and reconstruction activities under a single pillar. Another innovation, he said, was the assignment of lead nations for tasks such as army and police restructuring, judicial reform and drug control.

While the focus of the past two years had been on the reform and strengthening of the Department of Peacekeeping Operations, Mr Guehenno said, the discussion should now move to the operations themselves and six particular areas:
1. rapid deployment;
2. enhancing African peacekeeping capacity;
3. training;
4. best practices;
5. comprehensive rule of law strategies in the peacekeeping context; and
6. security sector reform and disarmament, demobilisation and reintegration.

The General Assembly's Special Political Committee held its annual debate on the state of UN peacekeeping with governments generally supportive of reforms of peacekeeping operations. However, some states, especially the nations providing the bulk of troops, remained concerned that they were not consulted enough about how missions were conducted.

There was general support for how the UN was implementing the recommendations of the Brahimi Report on improving the effectiveness and responsiveness of peacekeeping operations.

November 2002

AFGHANISTAN
Senior NATO sources told the London *Guardian* that the alliance was ready to take up an official role in Afghanistan for the first time by providing support to the International Security Assistance Force. NATO would assemble a force and provide planning, strategic airlift, logistics, communication and intelligence support for ISAF's next six-month mandate in Kabul.

Immediately after the attacks of 11 September 2001 on the US, NATO had invoked its mutual defense clause, under which an attack on one NATO member was to be considered an attack on all members. When the US launched attacks against the Taliban and al-Qaeda in October 2001, NATO offered its assistance, but the alliance never participated in combat operations in Afghanistan. The US had not asked for NATO's help, instead seeking to maintain flexibility by soliciting help from individual member states.

The UN Assistance Mission in Afghanistan condemned the violent police response to student demonstrations at Kabul University that left two students dead and at least 15 wounded.

The UN Security Council decided to extend for another year the mandate of the 22-country, 4,800-troop International Security Assistance Force in Afghanistan. An early vote was expected to ensure that Germany and the Netherlands, which were set to take over the ISAF command from Turkey, had enough time to garner parliamentary approval.

ISAF's mandate had been set to expire on 20 December. Despite repeated calls from Afghanistan, the UN Secretary General and relief groups, ISAF had not been expanded beyond the Kabul region. The Security Council extended the international peacekeeping force in Afghanistan for another year, starting on 20 December, without changing its mandate of patrolling only Kabul and its environs.

ANGOLA

The Joint Commission charged with overseeing the Lusaka Protocol in Angola formally ended its mandate, issuing a final declaration that all sides had "a lasting obligation to follow the logic of peace in the resolution of differences."

In one of its last actions before disbanding, the commission called on the UN Security Council for "the immediate lifting in totality" of remaining sanctions on UNITA, which included bans on UNITA offices and foreign bank accounts.

BAKASSI

The presidents of Nigeria and Cameroon agreed during meetings with the UN Secretary General to ask a UN-backed commission to consider ways of following up on a September 2002 International Court of Justice ruling awarding the disputed, oil-rich Bakassi peninsula to Cameroon.

The "mixed commission," which would be chaired by Mr Annan's special representative, Ahmedou Ould-Abdallah, would consider all implications of the Court's decision, including its effect on the rights of people living on the peninsula. The body would also work to demarcate the boundary and issue recommendations on confidence-building measures such as regular meetings between local authorities and national officials, joint ventures, the avoidance of inflammatory statements, troop withdrawals, demilitarisation and the reactivation of the Lake Chad Basin Commission.

BURUNDI

At least 14 civilians were killed in Burundi as Hutu rebels and the Tutsi-dominated national army exchanged fire in the north of the capital, Bujumbura, and 30 miles to the east in the Rutegama area. Thousands of Bujumbura residents had fled the city, adding to the 40,000 rural residents in Bubanza province, located north of the capital, who fled their homes earlier after fighting broke out there. The head of the Burundi bureau of OCHA, said that there was widespread confusion but that Bujumbura's centre had not yet been attacked.

Burundi's Tutsi-dominated government and its main Hutu rebel group resumed talks aimed at ending the country's nine-year civil war, which the UN estimated had claimed 300,000 lives.

CAMEROON *see* BAKASSI

CENTRAL AFRICAN REPUBLIC
UN Security Council members called for the quick deployment of an international force to the CAR, condemning recent attempts to seize power violently in the country and stressing the need to "implement without delay" steps to bring back stability.

UN workers had ferried more than 1,000 refugees back to their native Democratic Republic of the Congo from the CAR. Mobs had reportedly been attacking refugees in reprisal for looting and rapes by DRC rebels imported into the CAR to defend the president. According to a UN High Commissioner for Refugees representative the refugees said they were victims of Central Africans who want vengeance because of attacks on the local population by Congolese fighters.

COLOMBIA
The government stepped up efforts to reach accords with two left-wing rebel groups and the right-wing United Self-Defence Forces of Colombia announced a unilateral cease-fire, effective from 1 December and not a "Christmas truce."

CONGO, DEMOCRATIC REPUBLIC OF
Democratic Republic of the Congo President Joseph Kabila suspended six government officials accused in a UN report of involvement in the pillaging of the country's natural resources. President Kabila suspended National Security Minister Mwenze Kongolo, Minister at the Presidency Katumba Mwanke, National Security Agency head Didier Kazadi Nyembwe, Minister of Planning and National Reconstruction Denis Kalume, Ambassador to Zimbabwe Mawampanga Mwanananga and Jean-Charles Okoto, the former chief executive officer of state-run diamond company MIBA. He did not say for how long he was suspending the officials.

A UN-appointed independent panel said in its October 2002 report that 29 companies and 54 individuals, including government officials from Rwanda, Uganda, Zimbabwe and the DRC, were involved in multibillion-dollar scams involving "theft, embezzlement and diversion of 'public' funds, underevaluation of goods, smuggling, false invoicing, nonpayment of taxes, kickbacks to public officials and bribery."

Delegates from the DRC government and rebels had nearly reached an agreement on a deal to end the country's four-year civil war. The remaining stumbling blocks included divisions over power sharing, the composition of the armed forces during a two-year transitional period and security arrangements for Kinshasa.

Government and rebel negotiators from the DRC said that they had reached an agreement on power-sharing but adjourned the negotiations without a formal document for signature.

The negotiations were due to resume on 9 December. Remaining disagreements involved the extent of government-rebel power-sharing. While the government said such arrangements should only apply to the top levels of national government, the rebels wanted a deal involving local posts, police, intelligence and diplomatic services and state enterprises.

Despite reports of progress by the UN mediator, the only major agreement to come out of the talks involved the appointment of four transitional vice presidents to serve under President Joseph Kabila. The vice presidents were slated to represent the government, the opposition parties and the two largest rebel groups, the Rassemblement Congolawas pour la Democratie and the Mouvement de Liberation du Congo.

COTE D'IVOIRE
Negotiators for the rebel Mouvement Patriotique de Cote d'Ivoire walked out of talks with Cote d'Ivoire's government but said that they were not withdrawing entirely from the negotiations.The rebel group's political chief, Guillaume Soro, said the suspension of the talks was only a temporary measure made to alert Ivorian President Gbagbo that his latest actions were compromising good negotiations.

The rebel move was seen as a reaction to the discovery in Abidjanof the bullet-riddled corpse of Benoit Dacoury-Tabley, brother of the rebels' European representative, Louis Dacoury-Tabley. Uniformed men allegedly abducted Benoit Dacoury-Tabley. Louis Dacoury-Tabley was described by the Burkinabe daily *L'Observateur Paalga* as the rebel movement's second-in-command, but his brother was reportedly not involved with the rebels. The Burkinabe newspaper compared the killing to that of former Ivorian military ruler Robert Guei on the first day of the conflict, allegedly as he sought to regain power.

CYPRUS
The UN Secretary General submitted a document to Greek Cypriot leader Glafcos Clerides and Turkish Cypriot leader Rauf Denktash on a basis for agreement for a comprehensive settlement of the Cyprus problem.

He asked the two sides to respond to the document by 18 November and asked the two Cypriot leaders not to take a formal public position, but to exercise discretion and take some time to consider the text.

The new document was the most comprehensive peace plan since a failed 1992 plan. Unlike that plan, it did not include a map with exact borders. Cyprus would had a new constitution, flag and national anthem. In addition, the plan would provide for a central sovereign government and international Cyprus identity, but allow each side to look after its own internal affairs.

Mr Annan's recommendation for a solution to the divided island of Cyprus received a mixed response from the international community, with diplomatic sources, however, calling on both sides to accept the deal as a final move to resolve the problem. Mr Annan said he was encouraged by early reaction to his peace plan.

Turkish Cypriot Prime Minister Dervis Eroglu said that leaders of the break-away northern part of the island wanted more time in view of the complexity and sensitivity of the issues at stake.

Greek Cypriot leaders said they intended to ignore the UN deadline.

Cyprus' National Council announced that it had "suggested" to President Clerides that he tell the UN Secretary General that the ethnic Greek state was willing to enter into talks on the UN peace plan. The move made Greek Cypriots the first of the four parties involved in the dispute over Cyprus to agree to the talks.

Mr Clerides said that he planned to ask for clarification on some aspects of the plan and that he had told the UN he did not support a provision calling for a joint presidency for a three-year transitional period. Over the long term, the plan drew on the Swiss model, with a ruling presidential council and a rotating presidency.

The plan stipulated a resolution by 12 December 2002, in time for EU accession talks aimed at enlarging the Union by 10 states, including Cyprus. Turkey had warned that it could annex the northern, ethnic Turkish part of the island if the Greek Cypriot state joined the EU on its own. Mr Annan had given a deadline for the parties' initial reactions to his plan, but progress had been hampered by the poor health of Turkish Cypriot leader. The Turkish Cypriots did not meet the deadline and had not given an indication when they would respond to the Cyprus peace plan. Mr Annan was "very concerned" that delaying negotiations on the divided island of Cyprus could mean losing an opportunity to resolve the island's status.

The peace plan for Cyprus contained "big traps" and could lead to the destruction of the divided island's Turkish Cypriots Rauf Denktash said. He also criticised maps that accompanied the proposal.

The UN Security Council unanimously adopted a resolution renewing the mandate of the UN Peacekeeping Force in Cyprus until 15 June 2003.

About 5,000 Turkish Cypriots took to the streets in the Cypriot capital of Nicosia, urging Turkish Cypriot leader Rauf Denktash to agree to begin talks on a UN-proposed plan to reunite the divided island of Cyprus ahead of the 12 December EU summit.

EAST TIMOR
East Timorese President Xanana Gusmao was asking the UN to ease its security alert for West Timor.

The UN Security Coordination Office had kept West Timor at its highest rating, Phase 5, since the September 2000 killing of three employees of the UN High Commissioner for Refugees. UNSECORD's ratings range from 0 to 5. Phase 1 means UN staff should exercise caution. Phase 4 means only essential staff with security clearance may work, while West Timor's Phase 5 meant all UN organisations were forbidden from working in the country unless extraordinary measures were taken.

GUATEMALA

The UN Secretary General recommended extending the mandate of the UN Verification Mission in Guatemala for another year, echoing concerns of many Guatemalan human rights groups and UN staff in the country that the implementation of the country's peace accords remained behind schedule in many areas.

Guatemala's demilitarisation was on track, but the country's oligarchy was undermining much-needed reforms, President Alfonso Portillo told *UN Wire*. President Portillo also said that the country's ex-military dictator, Efrain Rios Montt, would be the candidate of the ruling right-wing Guatemalan Republican Front in 2003's presidential elections.

Mr Portillo dismissed suggestions by Nobel Peace Prize laureate Rigoberta Menchu and others that the country was slipping back in implementing the peace accords agreed to in 1996 after 36 years of civil war. He insisted his government was fully committed to implementing the peace accords, but was prevented from doing so by the executive's lack of power.

The UN Verification Mission in Guatemala responded to the controversial new $3.64 billion budget passed by the Guatemalan Congress, noting that while it contained some positive developments, a proposed reduction in the powerful military's budget was only "symbolic" given that the institution continued to spend more than what it was officially allocated. The reduction of the military's war-time budget and role in Guatemalan society were major parts of the UN-brokered 1996 peace accords that ended the country's 36-year armed conflict between the government and left-wing rebels. Guatemala's military still constituted the largest armed force in Central America. The accords also called for the resulting peace dividend to be heavily invested in social spending to offset massive inequality in the country and centuries of neglect among Guatemala's mostly rural and poor indigenous population, who were overwhelmingly the victims of the conflict.

IRAQ

The US was preparing to revise its UN draft resolution on Iraq to better reflect the views of France and Russia without compromising on key points, a move that would delay Security Council action. It would take the US about two days to revise its draft resolution, at which point diplomats would consult with their respective governments.

Discussions among the US, British, French and Russian foreign ministers were believed to have created enough support for a new resolution that required the UN to consider what actions to take if Iraq violated the resolution.

US President Bush alleged that Iraqi President Saddam Hussein had connections to al-Qaeda, calling Hussein a "dangerous man" and saying there had been known contacts between Hussein and terrorist organisations. US Undersecretary of State John Bolton said that Iraq had allowed al-Qaeda to operate within its borders. Several European officials and experts, however, had said the evidence was lacking. European experts had said they had not yet seen any US evidence of connections between Iraq and al-Qaeda, nor had they been able to independently prove such connections. There was little reason to believe there could be any connection because President Hussein represented the type of secular Arab leader that suspected terrorist mastermind Osama bin Laden had said he opposes.

The Security Council held closed-door consultations on a new version of the draft resolution by the US and UK giving Iraq "a final opportunity to comply with its disarmament obligations" or face "serious consequences." The draft left in place the tougher weapons inspection regime, including unrestricted access to eight "presidential sites," but changed wording to take into account the concerns of France, Russia and other states that the draft contained "hidden triggers" that the US could use to justify any military action against Iraq without first getting Council approval.

The Security Council unanimously adopted a resolution giving Iraq "a final opportunity" to disarm or face "serious consequences."

Resolution 1441, sponsored by the US and UK, created a tougher weapons inspection regime, including unrestricted access to eight "presidential sites." Last-minute changes took into account the concerns of France, Russia and other states that earlier drafts contained "hidden triggers" that the US could use to justify any military action against Iraq without first getting Council approval.

After the meeting, the chief UN weapons inspector, Hans Blix, said he would have an advance team in Iraq by 18 November.

Iraqi President Saddam Hussein convened an emergency session of the Iraqi parliament to consider the UN resolution which outlined a new inspections regime.

The parliament was expected to criticise the new UN resolution, echoing official comments that it was "bad and unfair." The source also said that Baghdad was "quietly studying" the resolution, however, indicating that President Hussein could agree to it by the 15 November deadline.

Arab League foreign ministers said that Iraq would probably comply with the new UN resolution and urged President Hussein to accept the new resolution as part of an effort "to solve all standing issues peacefully in preparation for the lifting of sanctions and the end of the [UN] embargo as well as the suffering of the Iraqi people." They asserted their "absolute rejection" of military action against Iraq. US officials had also begun to urge President Hussein to comply with the resolution, raising the threat of military action if he did not, according to the *Los Angeles Times*.

Under the new resolution, President Hussein had until 8 December to declare or surrender all Iraqi weapons of mass destruction programmes and UN inspectors had a 21 February 2003 deadline to report to the Security Council. Colin Powell indicated, however, that the US might not wait until the February report to determine Iraq's compliance with the new resolution.

The Iraqi National Assembly voted unanimously to reject UN Security Council Resolution 1441 demanding the country submit to weapons inspections, but the body said the final decision remained with President Saddam Hussein. Iraq subsequently accepted the resolution on the return of weapons inspectors "without conditions and without reservations." Secretary General Kofi Annan and Security Council members welcomed the letter from Iraq accepting it, saying this paved the way for the return of UN weapons inspectors. The initial reaction from the US was one of scepticism.

The international official responsible for dismantling Iraq's suspected nuclear weapons programme said that he would look for a "pattern" of obstruction before reporting Baghdad's noncompliance with the new inspections regime. His comments – just four days before he was scheduled to arrive in Baghdad in advance of the inspection teams along with Hans Blix, chief of the UN team responsible for locating and destroying chemical and biological weapons – marked the first clear indication of what would be considered a breach of Iraq's pledge to cooperate fully. Mr ElBaradei's views appeared to be at odds, however, with those of the US administration, which had said that any indication of Iraqi intransigence would be considered a breach of its obligations.

The first UN weapons inspectors arrived in Iraq to begin preparations for a new round of weapons inspections as mandated under a new UN resolution. The advance team met with Iraqi officials to discuss preparations for weapons inspections. The meetings focused on a timeline for UN Security Council Resolution 1441. Inspection teams would probably not reach their full complement for several weeks because some inspectors were not able to join immediately.

Meanwhile, the Bush administration had begun requesting contributions of military personnel and support from US allies to aid US troops in the event of a war with Iraq. US embassies in 50 countries had been directed to evaluate the willingness of other national leaders to participate in an attack if Iraq was found to have violated the new UN resolution.

The Iraqi Foreign Minister sent a letter to the UN Secretary General criticising Security Council Resolution 1441 as seeking an excuse to attack his country.

The first group of inspectors flew to Baghdad from a UN base in Cyprus. The contingent included six members from the International Atomic Energy Agency, charged with nuclear weapons inspections, and 12 from the UN Monitoring,

Verification and Inspection Commission, which would seek out chemical and biological weapons.

Two contentious UN activities in Iraq – the search for weapons of mass destruction and the humanitarian aid programme called "oil-for-food" – were discussed in a series of Security Council meetings in which the chief UN weapons inspector reported progress on restarting inspections and the humanitarian programme was extended by only nine days owing to new disagreements between the US and other Council members.

Reporting on his recent trip to Iraq, Hans Blix, the executive chairman of the UN Monitoring, Verification and Inspection Commission, said he told Iraq that "the most important thing [it needed to do] was that whatever there existed by way of weapons programs and proscribed items should be fully declared." Mr Blix said that "the Iraqi side assured us that Iraq intended to provide full cooperation with us."

UN inspectors examined two Iraqi factories, marking the beginning of a new round of searches for weapons of mass destruction. Iraqi officials again cast doubt on their willingness to allow unrestricted inspections, as the UN Security Council had unanimously mandated.

KENYA

News media were reporting growing disagreement among those investigating a suicide attack in Mombasa in which as many as three people reportedly smashed a car bomb into the lobby of an Israeli-owned hotel, killing three Israelis and 10 Kenyans. The attack came just minutes after two missiles were fired at an Israeli plane as it left a nearby airport.

Israeli army radio identified the bombers as two members of the al-Qaeda terror network who had been indicted in the 1998 US embassy bombings in Kenya and Tanzania, in which 224 people were killed and thousands wounded. One was also accused of providing training and assistance to Somali militiamen opposed to UN intervention in the Somali civil war.

KOSOVO

Progress in the UN-administered Yugoslav province of Kosovo was going slowly, and more emphasis on reconciliation between ethnic groups was needed, UN Undersecretary General for Peacekeeping Operations Jean-Marie Guehenno told the Security Council.

Mr Guehenno lamented the continuing existence of parallel government structures in the province. He pointed to problems including slow recruitment into Kosovo's institutions, security concerns, workplace ethnic tensions and an insufficient pool of minority applicants.

He criticised continuing attacks on the province's ethnic Serb minority, but he added that the Serbs' boycott of 26 October elections was to their own detriment because it prevented them from deeper involvement in decision-making, which was now left mainly to the ethnic Albanian majority.

Following an agreement with Yugoslavia, the UN Mission in Kosovo took control of the Serb-dominated northern section of Mitrovica, a divided city in the UN-administered Yugoslav province. The move put UNMIK in charge of the entire province for the first time since the arrival of the mission in 1999.

LIBERIA

The UN Security Council extended international sanctions on Liberia, accusing the government of violating an embargo on the import of weapons.

The Council also made reference to the rebel Liberians United for Reconciliation and Democracy, which it said was also covered by the arms embargo.

The sanctions in place also included a ban on diamond exports, which were believed to provide funds for the country's conflict, and travel prohibitions on President Charles Taylor and others in his administration.

Diplomats on the Council said the sanctions regime would be reviewed again in May 2003.

MIDDLE EAST

In an attack on an Israeli kibbutz near the pre-1967 border with the West Bank five people were shot and killed. The al-Aqsa Martyrs Brigades, a military group associated with Fatah, claimed responsibility for the attack, but the Palestinian Authority quickly condemned it. Subsequently Israel demolished the West Bank house of Mohammed Naefa, a militant believed to be behind the attack. Mr Naefa, whose house was in the city of Tulkarem, was a senior member of Palestinian Authority President Yasser Arafat's Fatah movement and was still at large.

The US reportedly agreed to a request by Israeli Prime Minister Ariel Sharon to freeze implementation of the road map plan until the country had held its general election early in 2003.

An attack in the West Bank city of Hebron resulted in the deaths of nine Israeli police officers and soldiers, including Colonel Dror Weinberg, the highest-ranking Israeli officer to be killed in the current intifada. Three Israeli settlers and three Palestinian gunmen blamed for the attack were also killed. Islamic Jihad claimed responsibility. In the wake of the attack Israeli helicopters struck a Palestinian security base in Gaza City and deployed tanks in Gaza and Hebron. Three Palestinian security troops were injured in the Gaza attack, and Israeli forces left the city before dawn following a clash with local gunmen.

A suicide bombing on a crowded bus in Jerusalem left 11 people dead and scores injured, with numerous children on their way to school among the victims. The bomber was identified as a known supporter of Islamic Jihad, which had not claimed responsibility for the attack.

A senior UN official was shot and killed in the West Bank town of Jenin in an exchange of gunfire between Israeli Defence Forces and Palestinian gunmen at a refugee camp.The victim, Iain Hook, was a British national who headed a UN Relief and Works Agency project to rebuild homes in the Jenin refugee camp. Soldiers fired on Mr Hook inside the compound of the UN Relief and Works Agency after reportedly mistaking him for a Palestinian fighter and the cellular phone he held for a grenade. UN officials say there were no such combatants inside the UNRWA compound. An 11-year-old boy was also killed and an Irish national was wounded in other incidents in the camp. The UN Relief and Works Agency denied claims by a preliminary Israeli Defence Forces investigation that Palestinian gunmen used the UNRWA compound in Jenin to fire at soldiers during the gun battle in which Iain Hook was killed. The UN Secretary General wanted Israel to identify and punish soldiers who shot and killed Mr Hook.

NIGERIA *see* BAKASSI

NORTH KOREA
Meeting for the first time since the US said in October that North Korea had acknowledged a secret programme to enrich uranium, the International Atomic Energy Agency's 35-member board called on the country to drop its nuclear weapons programmes and accept international inspections. The board said North Korea's claim that its sovereignty entitled it to pursue nuclear weapons was a violation of the Nuclear Nonproliferation Treaty.

SIERRA LEONE
Sierra Leone's government had to extend its authority throughout the country, regain control over national resources and begin to take over security responsibilities from the UN in order to secure progress in the post-conflict country, the UN Secretary General said.

SRI LANKA
Negotiators for the Sri Lankan government and the rebel Liberation Tigers of Tamil Eelam agreed to set up a joint committee and together seek aid for rebuilding the war-torn north of the country.

Debate about the authority for rehabilitating the north had centred over whether to place the Sri Lankan prime minister, the parliament or an independent fund in charge. Government minister Rauff Hakeem said the issue had been decided in favour of a committee reporting directly to the negotiating parties.

The sides had also agreed to insure representation on the committee for the island nation's Muslim minority. Mr Hakeem, who headed the Sri Lanka Muslim Congress party, said the move would give the country's more than 1 million Muslims the "feel of peace."

The rebels dropped demands for a separate state in the north of the country.

The latest round of peace negotiations also yielded a deal under which both sides were to work together to resettle over 1 million people displaced by the war.

WESTERN SAHARA

Moroccan King Mohamed VI, on the anniversary of his nation's 1975 annexation of Western Sahara, for the first time publicly dismissed plans for a UN-supervised referendum on the fate of disputed Western Sahara.

Morocco supported a different plan that would give the territory large autonomy but keep it under Moroccan sovereignty.

December 2002

AFGHANISTAN

The UN Assistance Mission in Afghanistan said that disarmament efforts in the north of the country were producing an emerging sense of hope.

A monitoring Mission to the town of Shulgarah in Balkh province reported general adherence to a week-old demilitarisation agreement there.

UNAMA also reported the earlier collection of 103 weapons in the Piroz Nakhjir area, including assault rifles, grenade launchers, a rocket launcher and a mortar. Another 30 weapons were pledged for surrender to the UN Mission.

A suicide bomber attacked the headquarters of the German contingent of the International Security Assistance Force in the Afghan capital of Kabul, marking the second time in 48 hours that foreign troops were targeted and raising fears that a new campaign against WASAF had begun.

In addition to the attacker, two Afghans were killed and two French journalists were wounded.

Two American military personnel and their Afghan interpreter were wounded when a grenade was thrown into their car in Kabul.

The United Nations planned to investigate mass graves in northern Afghanistan but was to allow the Afghan government to decide what action to take on any evidence uncovered. Excavations at three or more sites could have begun as early as April 2003.

A US Army spokesman at Afghanistan's Bagram air base rejected allegations in a *Washington Post* article that the CIA had been torturing prisoners at the base.

AL-QAEDA

Progress had been made in reducing al-Qaeda's operational capabilities, a UN Security Council expert panel said in a report. At the same time, the group was attracting large numbers of new recruits into newly reopened training camps in eastern

Afghanistan. The report cited significant disruptions to the network's infrastructure and said countries had increased efforts to identify and break up cells, arrest al-Qaeda members and associates and disrupt the group's finances or trace transactions supporting it.

ANGOLA

UN Mission in Angola head Ibrahim Gambari announced that remaining sanctions on UNITA, the former rebel group that had fought with the government for much of the last two decades until another peace agreement was signed earlier in the year, would be finally withdrawn when the Security Council took up the issue.

The UN Security Council decided to lift remaining sanctions on Angola's UNITA rebels. The measures had been in place for nearly a decade. The sanctions, at their height, included a freeze on UNITA assets, a ban on diamonds mined in UNITA-held areas, the prohibition of sales of oil, weapons, mining equipment, aircraft, aircraft parts and services to the former rebel group, the closure of all UNITA offices abroad, a freeze on contacts with UNITA officials and a travel ban.

The Council also decided to close the UN Trust Fund established to collect data on sanctions violations and disbanded the committee monitoring the sanctions.

BOSNIA AND HERZEGOVINA

The UN Mission in Bosnia and Herzegovina, which was founded in 1996 and was to be replaced 1 January 2003 by an EU police force, had "laid the foundation for postwar recovery and development" in the country following a devastating period of civil war, Kofi Annan said in a report to the Security Council.

Through UNMIBH, Mr Annan wrote, "the United Nations has demonstrated its ability to complete a complex mandate in accordance with a strategic plan and within a realistic and finite time frame."

Among the Mission's accomplishments, Mr Annan cited the return of 250,000 refugees, improved security, the accreditation of two police administrations, the creation of a national border service and the establishment of independent police commissioners in all 10 of the country's cantons and of police directors in Republika Srpska and the Federation of Bosnia and Herzegovina.

The Secretary General added, though, that key "rule-of-law" problems remained, including corruption, a need for judicial reform and the presence of indicted war criminals.

The Security Council closed the books on two of its Missions in the Balkans, leaving Kosovo as the only place in the region where the UN would continue to have a peacekeeping presence.

The UN Mission in Bosnia and Herzegovina (UNMIBH) ended. The EU was to take over law enforcement duties from UNMIBH.

BURUNDI

The Burundian government signed a cease-fire accord with the Conseil National pour la Defence de la Democratie-Forces pour la Defence de la Democratie, the main faction of the country's largest rebel group, but observers were sceptical that it would be effective.

The accord was signed after two days of negotiations at the 19th regional summit on Burundi and was the first that facilitators had secured with a significant Hutu rebel faction. The nation's other Hutu rebel group, the Parti pour la Liberation du Peuple Hutu-Force Nationale de Liberation, had not yet joined the peace process. According to a Ugandan diplomat close to the talks, the government and the CNDD-FDD would be allowed to retain their arms until a new national army composed of equal numbers and ranks of Tutsis and Hutus was formed. The accord also granted the CNDD-FDD a power-sharing role in the transitional government and made it a recognised political party. However, many of the details of the plan had not been worked out.

CHECHNIA

Following a suicide attack on the pro-Russian government headquarters in the Chechen capital of Grozny, the UN Secretary General immediately expressed his condolences to Russia and underscored the futility of violence in resolving the conflict.

The death toll from the attack, being blamed on Chechen militants seeking independence for the war-torn Russian republic, was 80, according to information from authorities in Grozny. According to the Russian television station ORT, the death toll from the explosion could go even higher, as a number of people were still in serious condition in local hospitals.

CONGO, DEMOCRATIC REPUBLIC OF

The UN Security Council decided to double the troop strength of the UN Mission in the Democratic Republic of the Congo and expand its presence in the east of the country.

Basing its decision on a report by UN Secretary General, the Council unanimously adopted Resolution 1445, raising the number of military personnel with the Mission from 4,250 to 8,700. The body also authorised the peacekeepers to shift their activity eastward, setting up two task forces to be based in Kindu and Kisangani. The new forces were to provide "point security" at disarmament and demobilisation sites and support commercial traffic along the Congo River, while the Mission as a whole continued to monitor the withdrawal of foreign troops.

All sides in the DRC's civil war signed up to the latest peace agreement, boosting hopes that the accord could end the central African country's brutal four-year conflict, which had killed over 2 million people and drawn in five other countries in the region.

The latest accord was different from previous agreements in that all sides had signed on. It envisioned a transitional administration until elections could be held in two and a half years, which would maintain President Joseph Kabila in power, but would award three of the four vice presidencies to the unarmed political opposition and the leaders of the two major rebel groups – Jean-Pierre Bemba of the Ugandan-backed Mouvement de Liberation du Congo and Adolphe Onusumba of the Rwandan-backed Rassemblement Congolais pour la Democratie.

The accord also envisioned power-sharing at other levels, including the transitional parliament, where the Senate would be headed by a civil society figure and the National Assembly headed by member of the MLC. The seats of the two bodies, meanwhile, would be apportioned out to the government, civil society, the political opposition, the pro-government Mayi-Mayi militia, the MLC and RCD and two smaller rebel groups, the RCD- National and the RCD-Mouvement de Liberation, which had, in the past, been linked with Uganda.

According to Associated Press, however, the real fight could have been over the country's rich mineral resources, which had fueled conflict in the past. Eventually, the DRC would have to assemble a united army from the different armed factions in the country, and the peace agreement required that all Congolese would benefit from the country's natural wealth. That could be difficult as the RCD and the MLC had turned the areas in the east under their control into virtual fiefdoms and they would possibly be reluctant to give up their wealth and power.

The leaders of three rebel groups involved in fighting in northeastern Democratic Republic of the Congo signed a UN-proposed cease-fire, which became effective immediately. Mouvement de Liberation du Congo leader Jean-Pierre Bemba, Rassemblement Congolawas pour la Democratie – National leader Roger Lumbala and Mbusa Nyamwwasi of the RCD-Kwasangani-Mouvement de Liberation were at the meeting.

According to the UN Organisation Mission in the DRC, the cease-fire called for the MLC, the RCD-N and the RCD-K-ML to return to positions recognised in the Lusaka peace accords. According to IRIN, the cease-fire agreement included the demilitarisation of several contested areas, the creation of buffer zones to be monitored by MONUC, an end to the recruitment of child soldiers and the creation of conditions to facilitate humanitarian access, free movement and the safety of relief workers.

COTE D'IVOIRE

The Mouvement pour la Justice et la Paix, the rebel group seeking revenge on loyalist troops for killing junta leader Robert Guei during a failed coup in September, seized western Man, a city of 135,000. Government soldiers ousted them with helicopter gun-ships and tanks. Soldiers at a roadblock near the town said that they were still hunting rebels in the city.

Heavy fighting left hundreds of people dead and caused terrified residents to flee the area. The fighting reportedly littered the town with hundreds of corpses. There was no official death toll yet, but there were "hundreds of dead." Bodies were being collected and buried. Water and electricity had been restored in the town, but telephones were still disconnected.

The western rebels had seized several other towns in the region, including Danane, 50 miles south of Man, and Toulepleu, near the Liberian border, where authorities said "large-scale operations" were underway to retake the town.

The rebels insisted they were fighting independently from the Mouvement Patriotique de Cote d'Ivoire, a rebel group from the predominantly Muslim north that says it was battling discrimination by the government in the heavily Christian south. The Mouvement Patriotique was responsible for the 19 September coup attempt and signed a cease-fire with the government in October.

Despite the fighting, peace talks between the government and the northern rebels continued.

A UN expert called for action against summary executions in Cote d'Ivoire, while France announced it would step up its military presence in the country ahead of a regional peace summit.

UN Human Rights Commission special rapporteur on extra-judicial, summary or arbitrary executions, Asma Jahangir, accused both Ivorian government and rebel forces of summarily killing civilians. Citing the recent discovery of mass graves in the country, she urged that those responsible for the extra-judicial executions be found and held accountable for their actions.

France, which had some 1,500 troops currently monitoring the faltering cease-fire in Cote d'Ivoire, said that it planned to send an additional 500 to 600 reinforcements in order to increase its involvement with the peace efforts.

Rebels captured for a second time the largest city in the country's cocoa-rich west after a day and night of fighting amid reports of mounting pressure on the UN to end the West African nation's bloody three-month conflict.

Western military officials confirmed that rebels controlled Man, with residents saying the rebels were Liberians speaking only English, making them likely members of the newest and most-feared western rebel faction.

The UN High Commissioner for Refugees said that urgent international support was needed to obtain safe passage and sanctuary for tens of thousands of refugees. UNHCR said it wanted to evacuate up to 60,000 Liberian refugees in Cote d'Ivoire's western conflict zone but that it needed safe passage agreements from all parties, sites in the south to which it could take the refugees and protection from other countries in the region.

The agency's assistant head said that UNHCR wanted "ideally" to take the refugees to a third country in the region but that a first step would be temporary relocation to southern Cote d'Ivoire.

The International Organisation for Migration and Cote d'Ivoire agreed on the establishment of an IOM office in the country.

Rebels clashed for the fourth time in just over a week with French troops. The fighting centred on the western town of Duekoue, important for access to the country's cocoa belt and two main ports.

Ivorian Prime Minwaster Pascal Affi N'Guessan met Economic Community of West African States Deputy Executive Secretary Oumar Diarra to work out what Diarra called "practical measures in light of the deployment of the ECOWAS force." ECOWAS heads of state agreed earlier in December to deploy peacekeepers in Cote d'Ivoire by 31 December 2002.

CYPRUS

Ethnic Greeks and Turks had both failed as to submit their responses to UN Secretary General Kofi Annan's peace plan for divided Cyprus.

Rauf Denktash, the head of the ethnic Turkish self-declared republic in the north of the island, said that Mr Annan's desire to "create a single nation on Cyprus" was an "incorrect formulation."

Responding to UN expectations that the parties' responses to the UN plan would be submitted imminently, Mr Denktash said, "The Greek Cypriot side has 31 pages of reservations. We had reservations, so they had to look at it with understanding. . . . Both sides should not be forced into a position which, within a few years, they will had to start throwing things at each other."

Yanniakis Cassoulides, the foreign minister of the internationally recognised ethnic Greek republic in the south of Cyprus, said his government's response to Mr Annan would come when the ethnic Turks submitted their reply.

The UN said it had passed on a revised draft of the Secretary General's settlement plan on Cyprus to the Greek and Turkish leaders of the divided island in a bid to reach a final deal acceptable to both sides.

Greek Cypriot officials believed the revised UN plan contained minimal changes to the original draft presented in November 2002. The original version reduced the Turkish area from 36% of the island to 28.5%. The resulting territorial shift would return 85,000 of Cyprus' 162,000 ethnic Greek refugees to their former homes, while 42,000 Turks and Turkish Cypriots would be displaced.

The UN was seeking a last-minute peace agreement for divided Cyprus as the EU began an expansion meeting in Copenhagen. With the Greek Cypriot state expected to be offered entry into the EU regardless of the outcome of the Cyprus peace talks, the UN Secretary General was racing to reach an accord before the end of the EU summit. The deadline for UN-brokered talks to reach agreement on plans to reunify Cyprus expired without a deal.

The UN Secretary General sent letters to leaders of the Greek and Turkish Cypriots, as well as to the leaders of Greece and Turkey, outlining what needs to be done to reach a comprehensive settlement agreement on the Cyprus problem by 28 February 2003, the date set by Mr Annan in his latest proposal for a settlement.

The Turkish Foreign Ministry announced that it did not accept the EU decision to invite Cyprus, represented by the internationally recognised Greek Cypriot administration, into the bloc.

EAST TIMOR

UN peacekeepers were mobilised to help East Timorese authorities deal with the most serious violence to hit the country since independence was declared in May. As many as five protesters were killed in the Timorese capital of Dili following clashes between students and police near key buildings in the city, while several more, including a senior parliamentarian, were wounded, some apparently showing signs of gunshot wounds. The clashes, which followed a clash involving students and police in Dili, began when shots were fired by unknown sources into a crowd of protestors demonstrating in front of police headquarters for the release of an arrested student. The protest then moved to the nearby National Parliament building, where shots were also fired. About 50 students invaded the governmental palace, but they quickly withdrew. During the violence many vehicles and buildings were burned. At least one UN vehicle was also burned.

LUSA reported that calm had begun to return to the capital, but the situation remained tense in the city's streets, which were under heavy police and military guard.

Preliminary investigations into the riots indicated some of the people behind the violence fled to the Indonesian province of West Timor and that the bullets that killed two students were not fired by police, East Timorese UN Ambassador Jose Luis Guterres said. He expressed hope that Indonesia would arrest the people in question after investigations were completed.

Some government officials feared the riots may have been the work of pro-Indonesian militias that had been blamed for the bulk of the 1999 violence that tore East Timor apart and left 1,000 people dead.

A parliamentary inquiry into the riots concluded that the demonstrations began "spontaneously" but that "third parties" then sparked mob violence for "political profit."

The report also questioned the professionalism of the UN Mission of Support in East Timor in responding so slowly to the violence, calling for new measures that would ensure that police and UN peacekeepers cooperated more closely.

GUATEMALA

Guatemalan Vice President Juan Francisco Reyes insisted that his government was on track to dissolve the Presidential General Staff, an elite intelligence unit with links to the military that has been accused by human rights groups of past involvement in serious human rights violations, by November 2003.

INDONESIA

The UN welcomed an accord signed between Indonesia and separatist rebels in the northwest province of Aceh, expressing hope it would lead to a return to peace in the region. The accord envisioned a quick end to the conflict, which had killed 12,000 people in the last decade, to be followed by demilitarisation of the province under international supervision.

The agreement also called for wider autonomy for Aceh, more local control over the region's natural resources of oil and timber, as well as local legislative elections and a withdrawal of most government forces, including paramilitary elements. Associated Press reported that the Indonesian military announced it had ceased all operations in line with the agreement.

IRAQ

On the second day of the new round of inspections, inspectors discovered that a fermenter was missing from an animal vaccine laboratory south of Baghdad that had once been involved in developing biological weapons. During that visit Iraqi officials said the missing fermenter had been moved and took inspectors to a veterinary site north of Baghdad to examine it.

UN weapons inspectors subsequently discovered that several pieces of equipment inspectors had tagged at a key ballistic missile site in 1998 were now missing. A team from the UN Monitoring, Verification and Inspections Commission discovered the discrepancy during an inspection of the Waziriyah site of the al-Karama General Co., located outside Baghdad. The Waziriyah site was believed to had been involved in Iraq's development of the al-Samoud missile, according to the IAEA. The al-Samoud, a scaled-down version of the Scud ballistic missile, was permitted under UN restrictions because it has a declared range of less than 150 kilometers. Some versions of the missile, however, were believed to had a range of almost 950 kilometers. Experts had been concerned about Iraq's intensive development of the al-Samoud, which had included several flight tests since the Waziriyah site was repaired in 1999. The missile was believed to be part of efforts to develop a multi-stage, long-range missile. The CIA said, however, that there were still flaws in the al-Samoud, including a shaky guidance system.

Iraqi officials said that US and British bombing destroyed some of the missing equipment in 1998 and some has been transferred to other sites.

UN weapons inspectors continued their investigation of various Iraqi sites, visiting a former chemical weapons factory and the al-Tuwaitha nuclear complex as part of their search for signs of renewed chemical, biological or nuclear weapons programs. Satellite photographs had reportedly indicated new construction at al-Tuwaitha, which was bombed heavily during the Gulf War.

In what was seen as a test of a new UN Security Council mandate that allowed inspectors to enter presidential compounds without restriction or notice, inspectors visited the al-Sajoud presidential palace – the first time such a palace has been searched.

The US called for a two-week postponement of the renewal of the UN oil-for-food programme for Iraq, insisting that 40 new items be added to a list of banned imports said to had potential military uses.

The UN Security Council unanimously agreed to extend its oil-for-food programme in Iraq for six months after US officials backed down from their bid to limit the extension to 14 days to review the list of banned goods to Iraq.

After Iraq submitted a seven-volume, 12,000-page declaration on its weapons of mass destruction to the UN, International Atomic Energy Agency Director General Mohamed ElBaradei said that the international community should be patient as experts examine the document as it would take 10 days for the IAEA to submit a preliminary report on Iraq's declaration. It planned to submit another report to the Security Council by 27 January 2003.

The US warned Iraqi President Saddam Hussein that it would retaliate with "overwhelming force," including a nuclear attack, if Iraq used weapons of mass destruction.

The newly reinforced UN weapons inspection team in Iraq rapidly expanded its schedule of surprise inspections, mounting the largest number yet by visiting 13 sites. Teams were sent again to several areas, including a large complex where Iraq once worked on a nuclear bomb and a remote uranium-mining site.

With the addition of 28 inspectors and the expected arrival of eight helicopters, monitors from the International Atomic Energy Agency and the UN Monitoring, Verification and Inspection Commission hoped to cover hundreds of industrial and research installations. In addition, they said new information provided in Iraq's dossier on its weapons of mass destruction could aid in planning their work in coming months.

The US, meanwhile, provided the other four permanent members of the UN Security Council – Russia, the UK, France and China – with uncensored copies of the 12,000 page report, and was criticised by some countries for omitting sensitive details on nuclear technologies in copies given to the 10 rotating Council members.

A UN diplomat said a preliminary assessment of Iraq's 12,000-page declaration of its weapons programmes was that much of the declaration "seems to be recycled," while US intelligence agencies said it failed to account for chemical and biological agents missing when inspectors left Iraq four years previously, omissions that White House press secretary Ari Fleischer said would constitute a violation of Security Council Resolution 1441.

Iraq's declaration of its nuclear programme left open a host of questions, including why Iraq would need to buy what the UK had described as "significant quantities" of uranium from Africa, as well as high-technology materials that US and UK officials had said were destined for a programme to enrich uranium.

International Atomic Energy Agency officials said that 2,100 of the pages appeared to be nearly identical to the declaration submitted in 1998, saying analysts were going through each page, line by line, to determine whether there were any changes at all. Another 300 pages were being translated from Arabic.

UN weapons inspectors searched at least six Iraqi sites, including a complex near al-Tuwaitha where Iraqi scientists once worked on a nuclear bomb, while the German Defence Ministry announced it was considering a UN request to supply the inspectors with unmanned spy aircraft.

A day after canceling a visit by UN atomic inspectors to two of its nuclear facilities, Iran said it was renewing the invitation. Foreign Minister Kamal Kharrazi said experts from the International Atomic Energy Agency would be invited to visit nuclear plants at Natanz and Arak.

UN inspectors dispersed throughout Iraq to search for banned weapons amid US and British comments signaling their readiness for war if Iraq breached the UN Security Council resolution aimed at ensuring it has no weapons of mass destruction.

Nuclear, biological and chemical experts – who had yet to report any significant findings in their inspections – set out for Mosul, nearly 250 miles north of Baghdad, and the Abu Ghuraib area, about nine miles west.

The 10 non-permanent Security Council members received abridged 3,500-page copies of Iraq's weapons declaration, less than two days before UN inspectors were expected to give their preliminary assessment of the document. Any information that could be used to promote the spread of weapons of mass destruction was purged from the copies.

The five permanent Council members – the UK, US, France, China and Russia – received uncensored copies of the 12,000-page dossier more than a week previously. According to a Council diplomat, sections of the censored declaration appeared to have been blacked out in a rush, leaving the names of some German and Swiss companies in the missile declaration discernable, while other important statements were left out, such as Iraq's statement that it did not have weapons programmes and a summary of the document.

The heads of the agencies investigating Iraq's programmes for weapons of mass destruction, Hans Blix and Mohamed ElBaradei, told the Security Council that their preliminary assessment of Iraq's declaration was that it fell short of a full disclosure of its weapons programmes. The US called the declaration "a deception" and "another material breach." Other permanent members of the Council were also critical of the declaration but stopped short of calling it a material breach – a finding that could lead to a war against Iraq.

Amid US and British claims of a "material breach" by Iraq for withholding key information in its weapons dossier to the UN Security Council, chief UN weapons inspector Hans Blix said that they were not providing enough intelligence information about sites where these alleged oversights may be uncovered.

UN weapons inspectors visited three new sites in Iraq, including a water purification facility and the country's main government health laboratory. The inspectors had now been in Iraq for more than a month.

President Saddam Hussein's chief science adviser, Amir al-Saadi, told a delegation of peace activists from Spain that Iraq had neither nuclear, biological or chemical weapons nor missiles to deliver such weapons and that a US attack should be avoidable if Iraq convinced UN inspectors. Mr Al-Saadi said that if the US respected the latest UN Security Council resolution, Iraq did not have to fear war.

US Secretary of State Colin Powell said that the weapons inspectors should be given time to find out what Iraq had before a decision was made on using military force. Powell added, though, that he had no doubt the US and its allies would defeat Iraqi forces in any war.

The UN received from Iraq a list of personnel associated with the country's chemical, biological, nuclear and ballistic missile programs, containing over 500 names.

The UN Secretary General said that he did not currently see any justification for a war against Iraq, as the Iraqi government had not violated Security Council Resolution 1441 demanding weapons inspections. He also said the US should wait for the inspectors' report to the Security Council before resorting to war.

KOSOVO

The Security Council closed the books on two of its Missions in the Balkans, leaving Kosovo as the only place in the region where the UN continued to have a peace-keeping presence.

MIDDLE EAST

Despite US and Israeli objections, the UN General Assembly overwhelmingly approved six resolutions criticising Israeli policies and demanding a speedy resumption of the Middle East peace process and a reversal of all measures taken on the ground since the current wave of violence began in September 2000.

The Assembly ended its annual three-day Middle East debate voting in favour of a key resolution that called on the parties and major international players, such as the US, the UN, the EU and Russia – the so-called Quartet – to exert greater efforts to halt the deteriorating situation and push for a peace agreement.

Israeli Prime Minister Ariel Sharon said that he would support the "road map" peace plan if a series of conditions was met, including a change in leadership of the Palestinian Authority and a restructuring of Palestinian security forces.

An Israeli raid outside Gaza City left two UN Relief and Works Agency school workers and eight other Palestinians dead, drawing sharp condemnation from the UN.

Senior Israeli officials said an Israeli report accusing UN Relief and Works Agency officials of involvement in refugee camp-based Palestinian terrorism was months old and was not, as some had speculated, prepared recently to deflect UN criticism over the death of UNRWA housing official Iain Hook. Citing confessions by arrested Palestinians, Israel's security service said in the document that UNRWA facilities had been used to hide alleged terrorists and support their activities. As a result of such reports, the Israeli military had been ordered to prevent UN vehicles from passing through roadblocks unless several international UN employees were aboard.

The UN Relief and Works Agency said that an Israeli soldier participating in an undercover operation in Tulkarem killed an UNRWA school attendant. The circumstances of the killing were unclear. The announcement brought to four the number of reported killings of UNRWA workers by Israeli troops in the previous three weeks. Iain Hook was killed on 22 November in Jenin in the West Bank, and an Israeli raid outside Gaza City left two UNRWA school workers and eight other people dead.

Various measures criticising Israel over its treatment of Palestinians were among 30 texts adopted by the UN General Assembly, 28 of which came out of the assembly's Special Political and Decolonisation Committee. The Assembly demanded that Israel cooperate with a special UN panel on Palestinians' human rights, end violations of Palestinians' rights, acknowledge the applicability of the 1949 Geneva Convention to the situation in the occupied territories, comply with UN resolutions on the Golan, stop hindering the movements of UNRWA, allow the return of people displaced after June 1967 and subsequent hostilities and halt settlement activity in the occupied territories.

The US refused a European appeal to adopt the "road map" peace plan for the Israeli-Palestinian conflict, despite a personal request by French President Chirac to US President Bush.

The UN Secretary General called for a six-month extension of the UN Disengagement Observer Force in his latest report to the Security Council on the Mission.

Recommending the extension until June 30 of UNDOF, which had, since 1974, monitored the Israeli-Syrian cease-fire in the Golan Heights, Mr Annan called the Mission "essential" and said the area it monitored had been "generally quiet" despite volatility in the surrounding region.

The UN Secretary General said that Israel had to comply with the position of the vast majority of the international community and deal with Palestinian Authority President Yasser Arafat as long as he was the only elected leader of the Palestinians.

Mr Arafat said that he wanted UN blue helmets or other international forces to be dispatched to the occupied territories as soon as possible to help prevent abuses by Israel.

NORTH KOREA
North Korean Foreign Minister Paek Nam-sun rejected the recent International Atomic Energy Agency call for the country to open alleged nuclear weapons programmes to international inspections.

In 1994 Pyongyang signed the Agreed Framework with the US. The Agreed Framework promised fuel aid in exchange for a freeze on suspected North Korean nuclear activities, but international officials suspended fuel shipments in November 2002 after the US alleged that Pyongyang was working to enrich uranium to develop nuclear weapons.

In response to the suspension in fuel aid, North Korea announced that it planned to restart a nuclear reactor that had been inactive since at least 1994.

North Korean threats to expel International Atomic Energy Agency inspectors who had been monitoring a nuclear reactor in Yongbyon prompted the IAEA to announce that it would withdraw all its inspectors immediately.

PREVLAKA
More than 10 years after their war, Croatia and Yugoslavia agreed to end a dispute over the strategically important Prevlaka peninsula, which lies between them. The UN Mission of Observers in Prevlaka, the smallest UN peacekeeping operation, had been monitoring the demilitarisation of the coastal border area since 1992. The Mission could now end its work when its latest mandate expired.

The Security Council closed the books on two of its Missions in the Balkans, leaving Kosovo as the only place in the region where the UN would continue to have a peacekeeping presence.

The UN Mission of Observers in Prevlaka ended. Prevlaka was to be controlled by a joint Croatian-Yugoslav administration.

SRI LANKA
Negotiators for the Sri Lankan government and the rebel Liberation Tigers of Tamil Eelam reached a breakthrough agreement to create a federal government with limited autonomy for their island's Tamil minority, in the hope of ending 19 years of war. A draft joint statement issued at the close of four days of peace talks said the two sides had decided "to explore a political solution founded on internal self-determination based on a federal structure within a united Sri Lanka." It added that "new concrete measures will be taken to facilitate further de-escalation."

The parties were reportedly studying Canada's political system as a model for the new federal arrangement. The future structure would also include a provision that Tamil courts and police not extend into government-held areas.

VENEZUELA
The UN Secretary General gave his full backing to attempts by Organisation of American States Secretary General Cesar Gaviria to mediate growing tensions in Venezuela between the government of President Hugo Chadz and opposition supporters calling for early elections.

Mr Annan's statement followed an OAS resolution rejecting "categorically any attempt at a coup d'etat or unconstitutional alteration of the Venezuelan constitutional regime that seriously impairs the democratic order," and calling for a "constitutional and electoral solution" but resisting an appeal for early elections.

In Venezuela's capital, Caracas, thousands of protestors marched to demand that Mr Chadz leave office. A general strike had paralysed much of the country for 17 days, including the country's oil industry, which was responsible for 80% of Venezuelan exports and 50% of government revenue.

Troops were deployed near the presidential palace to prevent anti-government protestors from clashing with Chadz supporters. The military had also been sent to try to restart oil production and exports.

Mr Chadz was resisting calls for an early election by those opposed to his rule, as tensions, already high following a failed military coup in April, continue to intensify in the country. The US and others had warned that if the situation continued to deteriorate, it could lead to violence.

January 2003

AFGHANISTAN

Lawyers for two US Air Force pilots facing courts martial for an accidental bombing of Canadian forces in Afghanistan said that they would argue the incident resulted in part from amphetamines given to their clients. The April 2002 incident, which claimed the lives of four Canadians and wounded eight, happened while the pilots were under the influence of Dexedrine, a drug provided to the pilots without warning about its effects, the lawyers said. An Air Force spokeswoman said the drug, given to fight fatigue, had never been reported to have caused an accident in the previous and that its use was "strictly voluntary."

The lawyers for the accused pilots also said they would argue that the fatal accident would not have taken place if their clients had been informed of the Canadian troop exercise.

The two pilots issued an apology to the families of the dead and wounded.

Several Pakistani Islamist groups called for the US to withdraw its troops in Afghanistan from the area near Pakistan's border, citing a recent skirmish. The alleged bombing took place after a Pakistani border guard reportedly opened fire on US soldiers on the Afghan side of the border. After the shooter holed up in a nearby building, the US commander at the scene ordered an airstrike. The US military, though, said the bombing involved an abandoned compound on the Afghan side and not a Pakistani school. Pakistani and US officials had played down the incident, saying it would not affect their countries' cooperation against terrorism.

The UN Assistance Mission in Afghanistan said that it had collected almost 200 weapons since resuming its disarmament programme in the north of the country. One hundred and forty of the weapons were received on 24 December in the Balkh province district of Khulm.

In the first coordinated attempt to disarm Afghanistan's powerful militia forces, the government of President Hamid Karzai and the UN were launching a campaign that would dispense cash, vocational training and employment assistance to militiamen who traded in their weapons. Under the programme, soldiers in the militias would have one opportunity to swap their weapons for a one-time cash payment. By taking their thumbprints, the government hoped to keep them from returning over and over to get more money. Kabul and the UN hoped to disarm 250,000 militiamen at eight critical regional locations, including Kandahar, Herat, Jalalabad and Kunduz. Coordinators expected the programme, partially funded by Japan, to be up and running by summer.

The disarmament plan was an effort to secure Afghanistan's central government, which faced a number of fractious regional commanders. The commanders were to be asked to dissolve their militias, sending some to the infant national army and demobilising the rest.

Government officials said that the powerful generals Abdul Rashid Dostum and Ismail Khan, among others, had agreed to the plan, although diplomats expressed doubt that they would follow through.

The Afghan government announced the formation of four commissions to oversee a speeding-up process of disarming and demobilising militias tied to regional warlords in the country, but insisted it would not forcibly disarm the forces that held sway over much of Afghanistan. With an estimated 300,000 armed men in the country and a government army of only 2,800 troops, the government had been unable to extend its authority beyond the region immediately surrounding the capital, Kabul. The separate commissions were to be responsible for the

1. disarmament,
2. reintegration,
3. recruitment and
4. retraining

of the factional fighters.

UN disarmament efforts in the north of Afghanistan had resulted in the collection of more than 6,000 weapons.

Following appeals from Pashtun tribal elders, Dostum released 50 former members of the Taliban who were captured by his forces a year previously, having already released hundreds of ex-Taliban prisoners, often following appeals by President Karzai. The ethnic Uzbek warlord had been accused of persecuting ethnic Pashtuns and of torturing prisoners.

Unknown attackers shot dead two guards traveling with a UN High Commissioner for Refugees convoy in the eastern province of Nangarhar. Nangarhar Governor Din Mohamed linked the incident to an exchange of gunfire between checkpoint guards and a group of unknown men fleeing after having been found carrying explosives.

US-led coalition forces in southern Kandahar province were fighting against about 80 rebels said to be allied with Pashtun warlord Gulbuddin Hekmatyar. A US military spokesman described the fighting just north of the border town of Spin Boldak as the largest in scale since US forces swept eastern Afghanistan in March 2002. At least 18 rebels had reportedly been killed since the fighting began, while the coalition forces had not taken any casualties.

The incident, which occurred on a stretch of road linking the cities of Kabul and Jalalabad and took the lives of two guards, may have been linked to local banditry and opium cultivation, according to a BBC report. The UN High Commissioner for Refugees said that it has suspended work in three districts in the eastern province of Nangahar following the attack. The suspension was temporary and covered Khogyani, Kunar and Hesarak districts.

BRAZIL

Brazil's new science and technology minister, Roberto Amaral, caused alarm in Brazil and abroad after making statements in a BBC interview calling for the country to develop the scientific "knowledge" necessary to create a nuclear bomb, while at the same time insisting that the country would uphold its international commitments and not develop such a weapon. In the interview Mr Amaral said nuclear and space research were two of his ministry's main priorities. Responding to further questions on the topic he said that the government was committed to investing in atomic energy, which he called "strategic," noting also the importance of "dominating the atomic cycle" and insisting on the utility of nuclear power.

Following several days of reaction to the unexpected announcement and attempts to clarify the issue, a spokesman for the newly elected Brazilian president put the issue to rest, asserting that Brazil "exclusively" intended to carry out nuclear research toward peaceful ends.

The minister's comments, which came at a sensitive time in international relations, reawakened debate over Brazil's own nuclear weapons programme and raised concern both within the country and abroad, especially in neighbouring Argentina.

Brazil's 1988 constitution, which was written after years of military rule, explicitly prohibits the development of nuclear weapons. According to the Carnegie Endowment for International Peace, Brazil officially renounced its secret nuclear weapons development programme in 1990 and promised in 1993 not to enrich uranium over 20%. It then signed the Nuclear Nonproliferation Treaty in 1995.

Following the publication of the interview, the International Atomic Energy Association said it was waiting for further clarification from Brazil on the issue, with one official expressing concern about the timing of the statements. According to the IAEA, Brazil has international and regional obligations, including an agreement with Argentina, that prevent it from undertaking the construction of a nuclear bomb, but is allowed to develop nuclear technology for peaceful use under Art. 4 of the NPT.

BURUNDI
Despite signing a cease-fire agreement with the government that came into force on 31 December 2002, the rebel Forces pour la Defence de la Democratie clashed north of Bujumbura, the capital, with government forces causing 10,000 civilians to flee. Fighting between the government and Forces Nationales de Liberation rebels outside of Bujumbura had displaced another 20,000 people.

The cease-fire agreement between the FDD and the transitional government called for a neutral monitoring force but, since no such force had been deployed, fighting had continued. The FNL had refused to sign the cease-fire.

South Africa, Mozambique and Ethiopia agreed to send peacekeeping forces to Burundi to help maintain peace in the country. The Executive Deputy President of the African Union said the temporary peacekeeping force would be deployed until the UN could send in peacekeepers.

CONGO, DEMOCRATIC REPUBLIC OF
More than 130,000 people had been displaced by recent fighting between rebel groups in the northeast, the UN Organisation Mission in the DRC announced.

Despite the signing of a cease-fire agreement, the Rassemblement Congolais pour la Democratie-Kisangani-Mouvement de Liberation, led by Mbusa Nyamwisi, accused the Mouvement pour la Liberation du Congo of attacking its positions in the area, and the MLC accused the RCD-K-ML of attacking its ally, the Rassemblement Congolais pour la Democratie-National. The situation around the town of Beni remained calm.

In an assault on a MONUC convoy in the same region, Mayi-Mayi gunmen attacked, beat and robbed staff of the UN mission. Although no one was killed in the incident, the militia threatened to shoot several people and accused foreign passengers of being the cause of the country's conflict before leaving with two of the convoy's three vehicles. The incident could have put at risk the planned deployment of MONUC observers to Mambasa and Komanda as stipulated in the cease-fire agreement.

The UN Organisation Mission in the Democratic Republic of the Congo announced the repatriation of 11 Rwandan ex-combatants from the DRC. The former Democratic Forces for the Liberation of Rwanda fighters were reportedly inspired to come forward by a MONUC video on resettlement and reintegration, especially statements in the video by repatriated soldiers citing favourable treatment.

France announced it would give more than $1 million to the UN Development Programme to help MONUC's efforts to demobilise former combatants.

Two rebel groups accused of cannibalism in a MONUC report, the Mouvement de Liberation du Congo and the Rassemblement Congolais pour la Democratie-National, announced support for the government's request that the UN Security Council set up an international tribunal to try suspected human rights violators. Both groups said the tribunal should look beyond recent events and should investigate several massacres committed since 1996.

Despite a cease-fire signed in December 2002, fighting involving rebel groups such as the MLC and the RCD-N intensified, forcing thousands of civilians from their homes. Relief workers estimated that more than 100,000 people had been affected in the previous few months. Ugandan authorities said 10,000 DRC refugees had crossed the border in recent weeks. UN officials, who said they were unaware of the influx, said about 5,000 refugees fled into Uganda in the last three months of 2002.

COTE D'IVOIRE

As rebels in western Ivory Coast clashed with peacekeepers in what was reportedly the most significant skirmish since French troops arrived in September 2002, the UN Secretary General said in his report on the UN Mission in Sierra Leone that Ivory Coast's civil conflict threatened security in the broader region.

With the UN reducing its troop presence in Sierra Leone, conflict continuing in Liberia and former armed elements from Liberia and Sierra Leone reportedly involved in the Ivorian conflict, Mr Annan called for the urgent pursuit of a comprehensive approach to the region's conflicts.

The French military said 30 rebels were killed and nine French soldiers wounded in fighting, which took place in Duekoue, a gateway to Ivory Coast's cocoa region. The town was controlled by the Mouvement Populaire Ivoirien du Grand Ouest, one of two western rebel groups that emerged in November 2002.

Sources in Tabou in southwestern Ivory Coast informed the UN High Commissioner for Refugees in the commercial capital, Abidjan, that fighting had led to panic among refugees and other civilians and that many people were fleeing in different directions. IRIN cited humanitarian sources who said the situation was becoming more and more desperate for refugees in Ivory Coast, especially Liberians.

One of two Ivory Coast rebel groups scheduled to sign a West Africa-supervised truce backed out at the last minute. Movement of Justice and Peace rebel leader Gaspard Deli said a cease-fire overseen by Togolese President Gnassingbe Eyadema, acting on behalf of the 15-member Economic Community of West African States, would not ensure his men total immunity from government attacks.

The UN High Commissioner for Refugees reiterated its appeal on behalf of Liberian refugees in the Ivory Coast, urging Ivorian authorities to keep them out of the conflict and calling on local and regional governments to help them move to safety. The UNHCR renewed its request to four West African countries to accept a number of Liberians on a temporary asylum basis. In a letter to the Ivorian government it also urged the authorities to stop recruiting refugees and asked them to instruct youth groups who controlled a number of checkpoints to stop preventing Liberians from fleeing the conflict.

Both of Ivory Coast's western rebel groups subsequently signed the truce ahead of peace talks.

French Foreign Minister Dominique de Villepin opened 10 days of talks on the Ivory Coast civil conflict by asking delegates from the country's government and three rebel groups to consider the question of defining Ivorian nationality and to make concessions for foreigners living in Ivory Coast. Agence France-Presse reported that compromise appeared unlikely. President Gbagbo said that he would not call early presidential elections as the rebels had been demanding, and his representative at the talks, Prime Minister Pascal Affi N'Guessan, said that the rebels were the ones causing problems.

Fighting between French peacekeepers and "unidentified elements" in western Ivory Coast left at least eight attackers dead or wounded and two French soldiers injured, according to the French military.

The Ivorian army said loyalist troops were attacked in the western town of Toulepleu by 400 to 500 Mouvement Patriotique Ivoirien du Grand Ouest and Mouvement pour la Justice et la Paix rebels, leading to a battle in which four regular troops and 25 rebels were killed.

Government, rebel and opposition negotiators from Ivory Coast reached a deal under which a new government would be formed but President Laurent Gbagbo would remain in power until the next elections planned for 2005. Under the deal, President Gbagbo would name a new prime minister, who would have to be approved by all the parties and would head what was referred to in the agreement as a "government of national reconciliation." The new prime minister would be barred from running for president and Mr Gbagbo would also be barred from running again.

RFI.fr reported that the agreement addressed the least difficult questions that were before the parties – Ivorian nationality, presidential eligibility, the composition of the government – but not difficult matters such as what to do with northern rebel troops; who would control the West; and what would become of the thousands of Liberians apparently involved in the conflict.

Violence followed the peace deal. Angry at the concessions to the opposition involved in the plan, government supporters set on the French Embassy and a French army installation in the country's commercial capital, Abidjan, as well as looting French-linked businesses. French forces in Ivory Coast responded with tear gas, stun grenades and water cannons.

Ten people were killed in fighting between ethnic groups in Agboville according to unconfirmed reports. The fighting came as the army rejected a peace deal signed end by the country's government, opposition and rebels. The army cited unconfirmed reports of provisions of the deal that would leave rebels in charge of the military and paramilitary police. Associated Press reported that the army had done little to quell violent protests that had followed the signing of the agreement.

Hundreds of French nationals began fleeing Ivory Coast amid fears of mounting anti-French violence and despite pro-US demonstrations in Ivory Coast's largest city of Abidjan, where protesters urged Washington to intervene, the US Embassy temporarily closed and issued an e-mail which "strongly urged" its own citizens to leave the country.

Members of President Gbagbo's cabinet and Ivorian army leaders called for a rejection of the peace accord, saying it demanded too many concessions from the government. Rebel official Guillaume Soro accused Mr Gbagbo of encouraging the street protests against the accord, saying the Ivorian president had never intended to fulfill the terms of the deal.

CYPRUS

The leader of Turkey's ruling Justice and Development Party Tayyip Erdogan called for a change in Turkish policy on the conflict in Cyprus, publicly criticising Turkish Cypriot leader Rauf Denktash in a move analysts called an attempt to push Denktash toward a settlement by the UN-set deadline of 28 February. Mr Erdogan also criticised Mr Denktash, particularly his lack of confidence in the Greek Cypriot side. Citing a recent demonstration by 30,000 Turkish Cypriots in the Turkish-backed breakaway area of Northern Cyprus calling for Mr Denktash's resignation and condemning his failure to reach a solution before the Greek Cypriot-dominated and internationally recognised state of Cyprus was invited to join the EU in December 2002, Mr Erdogan said the opinion of the Turkish Cypriot populace should not be ignored. Mr Erdogan's comments reflected growing differences between the ruling party and Mr Denktash, who still appeared to have the backing of the military establishment in Turkey. According to analysts, the Turkish military, which had 35,000 troops stationed in Northern Cyprus, could still block a settlement, in effect sidelining Mr Erdogan.

Mr Denktash met with senior Turkish Cypriot politicians in what he said was an attempt to build consensus before UN-mediated negotiations resumed with Greek Cypriots later in the month. He welcomed the UN Secretary General's second draft proposal for the settlement of the island's conflict, but criticised the UN for continuing to "satisfy" the Greek Cypriots. He also blasted attempts to form a linkage between accession by Cyprus to the EU and the conflict accusing the Greek Cypriots of seeking union with Greece and alleging that EU accession without Turkey contradicted 1960 agreements.

The Greek Cypriots welcomed Mr Erdogan's remarks.

According to the *Cyprus Mail*, a new poll in the north showed that nearly 60% of residents of areas that would revert to Greek Cypriot control under the UN plan were ready to resettle if it would help bring an end to the conflict. The poll also said that 91.6% of the 509 people it sampled said they would vote in favour of the UN plan.

Turkish Cypriot and Greek Cypriot delegates began working on the legal framework for a peace settlement, part of an effort to reach a deal on reuniting the island before the UN-imposed deadline of 28 February. The two technical committees were discussing 35 laws that would serve as the foundation for a post-settlement Cyprus.

Turkey's new government was pushing Rauf Denktash to embrace the UN plan, but the Turkish military, which still wielded strong influence in the country and has firmly backed Mr Denktash, could reportedly block a settlement.

Mr Erdogan reaffirmed his support for an agreement.

A Turkish Foreign Ministry spokesman reiterated to the press that Turkey was planning to modify its policies with regard to Cyprus, a move he said was needed in order to reach a peace agreement. He added that there was no disagreement on the matter between Turkey and the Turkish Cypriot republic.

UN special adviser on Cyprus Alvaro de Soto said that the divided island's leaders and people had the choice between Secretary General Kofi Annan's peace plan and no plan at all. About six weeks remained to reach a comprehensive settlement he said. Reaching agreement by the end of February 2003 would allow just enough time to hold referendums in both parts of Cyprus by 30 March. A yes vote at that time would allow two weeks of preparations for the country's scheduled 16 April accession to the EU.

Tens of thousands of Turkish Cypriots rallied in the north of the island's divided capital, Nicosia, in support of the Annan plan. Organisers said more people attended the rally than a similar rally in December 2002 that drew 30,000 and was the largest to date. Opinion polls indicated that most Turkish Cypriots support UN reunification efforts.

The head of the Turkish army criticised a UN plan to reunify Cyprus, saying it could lead to violence and instability in the eastern Mediterranean region.

Comments by Rauf Denktash dashed hopes for an early agreement. Mr Denktash claimed that he was fighting to save the Turkish Cypriot population from becoming slaves of Greek Cypriots and the maintenance of Turkey as the breakaway area's guarantor. He also said an agreement could not be reached unless a significant number of his proposed amendments were accepted.

DISARMAMENT

Five former presidents of the UN Conference on Disarmament presented a programme of work aimed at ending a five-year stalemate over such thorny issues as the prevention of an arms race in outer space and nuclear disarmament.

The "five ambassadors" were calling for ad hoc committees to be set up on four sticking issues:

1. guarantees not to use nuclear weapons against non-nuclear states,
2. nuclear disarmament,
3. a ban on production of weapons-grade fissile materials and
4. prevention of an arms race in space.

They were also proposing the appointment of three special coordinators to oversee work on the subjects of new types of weapons of mass destruction, a comprehensive disarmament programme and transparency in armaments.

Ambassador Jean Lint of Belgium introduced the plan on behalf of himself and the delegates from Algeria, Chile, Colombia and Sweden.

EAST TIMOR

UN peacekeepers were deployed to the border region of Atsabe following an attack on two local villages in which three people were killed and five wounded. Officials said it was unclear whether the gunmen, numbering around 15, were based in Indonesia or locally. Several people were reported missing following the attack. The incident, which appeared to have been a militia-style incursion and involved automatic weapons, was the first attack in the region for more than a year. A defence force official said that the military was investigating the activities of a 100-strong "paramilitary" group in the area.

East Timorese President Xanana Gusmao said that it might be necessary to extend the mandate of the 5,000-soldier UN peacekeeping force in East Timor beyond June 2004, its scheduled end, in light of continued instability on the island. Acknowledging the "difficulty" of extending the UN Mission of Support in East Timor's mandate, Mr Gusmao for the first time made a public plea for a study of the possibility.

According to East Timorese authorities, three men were killed in two villages southwest of the capital, allegedly by former members of pro-Indonesian militias. Indonesia denied involvement. According to President Gusmao, the country's own internationally trained defence force would be unable to cope with such security problems when UN troops left.

The East Timorese Foreign Minister said that UN peacekeepers in East Timor were failing to prevent border incursions by pro-Indonesian militia groups that he said could be linked to the Kopassus, or Indonesian special forces. He appealed for the deployment of the East Timorese defence force, possibly aided by UN Mission of Support in East Timor peacekeepers, to enhance communication with locals and prevent further incursions.

GEORGIA

The resumption of rail communication between Russia and the breakaway Georgian republic of Abkhazia was expected to exacerbate tensions and mistrust between Russia and Georgia. The UN Observer Mission in Georgia deputy head said UNOMIG had not been informed about the decision and immediately lodged a protest against the Russian move.

The UN Security Council unanimously approved a resolution extending until 31 July 2003 the mandate of the UN Observer Mission in Georgia, which was responsible for monitoring a cease-fire between Georgian forces and separatist Abkhaz rebels.

The Council also said it would further review the mandate of UNOMIG unless a decision was reached on the fate of the Commonwealth of Independent States peacekeeping force by 15 February. A top presidential aide to the leader of the breakaway republic of Abkhazia told Civil Georgia that the peacekeeping force, which consisted almost entirely of Russian troops, was "the only guarantee of peace and stability in the region," and reiterated Abkhaz opposition to any withdrawal.

In its resolution the Council also gave its full backing to efforts to resolve the status of Abkhazia within the state of Georgia, expressing its regret about the failure to start talks and emphasising that the proposals outlined in the *Basic Principles for the Distribution of Competences between Tbilisi and Sukhumi* aimed to foster negotiations between the two sides and were not part of an attempt to impose or dictate any specific solution to the parties.

The Council said it deeply regretted the refusal of the Abkhaz side to discuss the document, which proposed autonomy for Abkhazia within a Georgian state.

The Council also called on the Georgians to improve security for joint UNOMIG-CIS peacekeeping patrols in the tense Kodori Valley and underlined that it was up to both sides to provide security to and ensure free movement for both the CIS and UNOMIG forces.

In addition to renewing its call for more investigations by both sides to determine who was responsible for the downing of a UNOMIG helicopter in October 2001, the Council stressed the urgent need for progress on the issue of refugees and internally displaced persons who were forced from their homes because of armed conflict nearly 10 years previously.

IRAQ

With UN Monitoring, Verification and Inspection Commission chief Hans Blix set to report to the UN Security Council twice this month on Iraq weapons of mass destruction inspections, the UN inspectors in Iraq stepped up their activity by assembling a fleet of six helicopters and planning to open a branch office about 240 miles from Baghdad.

During their five weeks in Iraq, inspectors had checked out 230 sites, taking no weekend or holiday breaks. Iraq maintained the inspections had yielded no evidence of prohibited weapons, and some UN officials had anonymously agreed.

Iraq was growing annoyed with inspection teams and stepping up anti-US rhetoric as US troops were dispatched to the region despite the fact that the inspections were yielding little. News of US troop movement plans appeared to have convinced Iraq that inspections would not change US President Bush's mind about the need for war.

In Western-protected, Kurdish-dominated, northern Iraq, two Kurdish parties said that they had formed a joint committee to plan for the protection of residents against a possible chemical or biological attack. The parties criticised the UN for allegedly failing to respond to their appeals for help in preparing for the effects of a possible war.

Iraqi President Saddam Hussein accused UN arms inspectors of conducting "intelligence work" rather than searching for weapons. An International Atomic Energy Agency spokeswoman denied the allegations, saying that any information gathered was solely for the UN.

President Hussein also accused the US of pushing inspectors to be more aggressive in questioning scientists beyond the declared objectives of the UN Security Council, adding that his military would be able to defeat foreign forces in a war.

Some inspectors said they were concerned that the US administration would accuse Iraq of violating Security Council Resolution 1441, leading to a war regardless of their findings.

UN inspectors visited 16 sites, the largest number since the inspections regime resumed in November 2002. The locations included some within the National Monitoring Directorate compound, which the inspectors sealed off for several hours. Other sites visited included a graphite facility and hospitals in the cities of Basra and Mosul.

The World Food Programme, UNICEF, the World Health Organisation and seven other UN agencies issued a $37.4 million appeal to donor nations in preparation for a possible war in Iraq. The funds would go toward purchasing food, medicine and tents and for transporting the supplies to countries bordering Iraq, said an Office for the Coordination of Humanitarian Affairs spokeswoman.

Some US nongovernmental organisations said they wanted their government to provide more information about the possible war in order to plan relief operations.

The UN Secretary General was reported to have forbidden UN agencies from planning for a humanitarian crisis in Iraq as long as the Security Council was still considering the Iraq situation.

International Atomic Energy Agency Director General Mohamed ElBaradei said that UN inspectors had yet to uncover evidence that Iraq had resumed its nuclear programme but added that it was still too early to come to a conclusion on the matter.

UN inspectors took to the skies for the first time during the current round of inspections, making a return visit to the Akashat uranium mine, 260 miles from the Syrian border. Other sites visited included the al-Mutasim missile plant and the University of Mosul.

The inspection team covered six sites, including a veterinary drug factory, a pesticide plant and an Iraqi army base, where inspectors began the task of tagging all of Iraq's ground-to-ground al-Fatah rockets.

A leaked UN document predicted that up to 500,000 Iraqi civilians could suffer dire injuries if US-led forces invaded Iraq – 100,000 in combat and another 400,000 in the ensuing chaos. The confidential report, which was posted on a Cambridge University anti-war web site, forecast 10 million Iraqis in need of humanitarian assistance immediately following an attack and predicted a massive refugee crisis, with nearly a million fleeing to neighbouring countries and another 2 million people displaced within Iraq. The report, *Likely Humanitarian Scenarios*, said a humanitarian crisis would be far more grave than the one that followed the 1991 Gulf War because a decade of economic sanctions had rendered the population heavily dependent on the government for basic necessities.

UN officials scrutinising the biological weapons section of Iraq's 12,000-page arms declaration said it yielded nothing new about stocks of biological agents such as anthrax, and consisted largely of reprocessed information from earlier reports to the UN.

UN inspectors, aided by eight new helicopters, were expecting to improve the surprise element of their searches. UNMOVIC and IAEA teams continued their inspections, visiting a total of eight sites and reportedly stepped up their inspections schedule in anticipation of the 27 January Security Council briefing that could determine whether or not the US would lead a war against Iraq.

For the first time since it suspended talks with the Red Cross three years previously, Iraq was expected to discuss the fate of Kuwaiti prisoners of war with Kuwaiti officials. Six hundred Kuwaitis had been missing since Iraq invaded Kuwait in August 1990.

Iraqi Foreign Minister Naji Sabri accused Kuwait of violating UN resolutions by allowing US troops to conduct maneuvers in the demilitarised border region separating the two countries. He accused the United Sates of sending 60 tanks and other vehicles as well as an unspecified number of troops into the demilitarised zone.

The government of Iraq submitted a plan to the UN for distributing a $5 billion humanitarian budget from the proceeds of the oil-for-food programme. The UN Secretary General approved the budget, which dedicated $1.27 billion for food, more than $350 million for fixing the water supply and $272 million to address problems with the electrical power network. Another $143 million would go to the medical sector.

UN Monitoring, Verification and Inspection Commission chief Hans Blix told reporters that weapons inspectors had not found any "smoking gun" demonstrating Iraq had violated UN resolutions but that the 12,000-page weapons of mass destruction declaration Baghdad submitted in December 2002 "failed to answer a great many questions."

Weapons inspections in Iraq had yielded no hard evidence that the country was producing weapons of mass destruction, chief UN weapons inspector Hans Blix and International Atomic Energy Agency Director General Mohamed ElBaradei told the Security Council, but gaps in Iraq's weapons declaration had made it impossible to clear the nation of any wrongdoing.

But inspectors remained unwilling to declare Iraq innocent of manufacturing weapons prohibited under a 1991 disarmament agreement.

Top British officials added their voices to a growing chorus of nations urging the US to allow UN weapons inspectors sufficient time to do their work and to seek backing from the UN before leading a military campaign against Iraq. According to a poll by ITV, 58% of Britons were unconvinced that Iraq's supposed weapons of mass destruction posed a global menace. A mounting number of members of Tony Blair's Labour party opposed unilateral or bilateral war against Iraq.

Other European leaders were attempting to avert a rush to war. "Our desire and intention is that there should be no war. We don't want a war," said Greek Prime Minister Costas Simitis. French President Jacques Chirac said that "the use of force is always a statement of failure and the worst of all solutions." German Chancellor Gerhard Schroeder reiterated his position that Germany would not participate in military action, even if the Security Council approved it, without indicating how Germany would vote.

In Russia, the speaker of the lower house of Parliament denounced unilateral action against Iraq.

There were, however, 65,000 US troops in the Gulf region and 62,000 more were headed there.

A panel of British health experts warned that international aid agencies were totally unprepared to cope with a chemical or biological attack on Iraqi civilians. A paper produced by the British charity Merlin and the London School of Hygiene and Tropical Medicine suggested that relief agencies had no experience in decontamination or quarantine and have no way to protect themselves while administering aid. The situation left them with an unpalatable choice: develop, at great effort and expense, their ability to handle chemical and biological attacks, or work cooperatively with the military and thus compromise their neutrality.

UN Monitoring, Verification and Inspection Commission head Hans Blix said Iraq had to provide new evidence about its weapons of mass destruction activity or face the threat of war. Dr Blix said UN inspectors working in Iraq under Security Council Resolution 1441 needed months to finish the job but that a Council decision to end inspections or a US attack could prevent them from having the time.

Following UN complaints that the US and the UK were not providing inspectors with sufficient intelligence to back up claims that Iraq was pursuing banned weapons, UN officials said that such intelligence had started coming in and more was expected.

Following comments by the UK International Development Secretary Clare Short and other British officials stressing the need for any action on Iraq to be approved via the UN, Prime Minister Tony Blair said that Washington and London reserved the right to take action on their own if necessary. British Foreign Minister Jack Straw reiterated that London would prefer a second Security Council resolution but could participate in military action without one if necessary.

UN arms inspectors visited a presidential palace for a second time in the heart of the Iraqi capital amid warnings from London and Washington that they would not necessarily be deterred from a possible attack on Iraq if the UN Security Council failed to agree on military action.

The UN Secretary General said he saw no reason for an invasion, saying UN weapons inspectors were "just getting up to full speed."

The US was deploying about 100,000 troops to the Persian Gulf and had told a group of Iraqi exiles who had volunteered to serve with US forces to assemble at marshaling centres.

The head of the UN nuclear watchdog agency, warned Baghdad of growing international impatience over the UN-mandated inspections, urging it to cooperate more actively in demonstrating that it had no weapons of mass destruction.

With chief UN weapons inspector Hans Blix proposing more time for inspections and a second briefing to the Security Council on 27 March 2003, the Bush administration prepared to pressure the body to reject Dr Blix's plan and instead make the 27 January briefing on Iraq's suspected weapons of mass destruction the final one.

The permanent members of the Security Council were divided on the issue of the March report, with Russia and France standing by the legitimacy of the 1999 resolution (Resolution 1284 – the 1999 resolution that created UNMOVIC, required quarterly reports to the Council and paved the way for the possible suspension of UN sanctions against Iraq) and the US and the UK maintaining that the November 2002 resolution trumped the older one.

Despite the objections of other nations, the US was indicating that it might attack Iraq whether or not weapons inspectors produced hard evidence that Saddam Hussein was manufacturing weapons of mass destruction. Russian Foreign Minister Igor Ivanov condemned unilateral action against Iraq as "capable only of worsening the already difficult situation in the region," and Canadian Prime Minister Jean Chretien said the world "must speak and act through the UN Security Council."

US officials continued to make preparations for possible military action, asking NATO to help in the event of a war by defending Turkey and sending Patriot antimissile systems, along with 600 troops, to Israel.

The US offered U-2 spy planes, which provide high-altitude surveillance, to the UN weapons inspection effort. The team accepted the offer but had not flown the planes.

The UN approached Cyprus and asked it to serve as the centre for a relief operation in the event that the US led an attack against Iraq, to which Cyprus agreed.

UN weapons inspectors said they had discovered 11 empty chemical warheads at an ammunition depot south of Baghdad that were not reported in Iraq's declaration in December 2002 to the UN Security Council. The announcement sparked immediate debate over whether the discovery constituted a "material breach" – possibly leading to eventual military action – under UN Resolution 1441.

The US said that both Security Council resolutions governing the work of UN weapons inspectors remained valid and that reports on Iraq's weapons programme might continue beyond 27 January when, under Resolution 1441, UNMOVIC and the IAEA were to report to the Security Council on their findings.

Dr Blix accused Iraq of illegally importing arms-related material including missile parts.

As foreign ministers in the UN Security Council debated the wisdom of a war with Iraq, US Defence Secretary Donald Rumsfeld said a decision on whether to go to war was imminent. He also announced the appointment of a former US military official to supervise planning for postwar operations in Iraq.

The Iraqi government concluded two days of talks with UN inspectors , conceding to the inspectors' demands on a number of procedural issues, including private interviews of Iraqi scientists and the disclosure of empty chemical munitions stockpiles. Iraq also agreed to logistical arrangements for helicopter-borne inspections in US- and British-patrolled "no-fly zones." Another agreement resulting from the talks involved a promise by Iraq to investigate whether its military has any empty chemical warheads, such as those discovered and to "respond to questions" about its weapons declaration in December 2002 to the Security Council.

The Security Council, meeting at the foreign minister level, issued a declaration calling for greater international cooperation against terrorism, while the US and the UK, the two major proponents of military action against Iraq, pressed their case linking Saddam Hussein's government to international terrorism. Washington and London made the link by raising the spectre of Iraq supplying weapons of mass destruction to terrorists, rather than establishing any direct link to the attacks on the US of 11 September 2001, or other terror attacks. Most other countries warned that the international unity that existed in combating terrorism would be damaged by an invasion of Iraq.

UN weapons inspectors asked, and received support from key US allies for, more time to assess Iraq's weapons programmes. US President Bush questioned the idea of giving UN weapons inspectors more time in Iraq but resistance to an early military strike against Iraq appeared to be building in the Security Council. French Foreign Minister Dominique de Villepin objected to the Bush administration's position on Iraq. Two other veto-wielding Council members, China and Russia, said they were willing to let inspections continue for months if necessary. Among countries other than the five permanent Council members, opposition to the US stance had also been expressed.

Despite a statement by British Prime Minister Tony Blair that "some intelligence" suggested links between al-Qaeda and Iraq, the chair of the Security Council panel that monitored sanctions against al-Qaeda said he had seen no evidence of a connection between Iraq and the terrorist group.

The leaders of Germany and France said that they opposed resorting to war in the UN's effort to disarm Iraq, while US officials dismissed the comments and warned that military action was still possible.

British Prime Minister Tony Blair said that the UK would join the US in a war not sanctioned by the UN if other countries presented "unreasonable blockage" of Security Council authorisation of military action.

Not only the UK but also Poland, Spain, Italy and others supported a Security Council indictment of Iraq. According to Associated Press, among the 15 members of the Security Council, eight generally favoured military action – the US, the UK, Bulgaria, Cameroon, Guinea, Angola, Chile and Spain. In addition to France and Germany, Russia was said to oppose a military strike, while China, Mexico, Syria and Pakistan were reportedly of uncertain opinion.

Iraq stepped up its criticism of the weapons inspections, with the Information Ministry organising a press conference to air the complaints of an Iraqi farmer whose land was searched twice by the UN team. UN spokesman Hiro Ueki addressed another complaint, issued by a Muslim cleric who said five inspectors violated the sanctity of his mosque. Mr Ueki said the inspectors' visit there was a private sightseeing trip and that they received permission from the mosque's authorities.

Addressing the Security Council, Hans Blix and Mohamed ElBaradei detailed the first 60 days of their inspections as authorised by Resolution 1441. They were critical of Iraq's cooperation in providing information about its programmes for weapons of mass destruction but said they needed more time to come to any definitive conclusions. They provided ammunition both to proponents of using force against Iraq, in particular the US, by detailing cases of noncooperation, and to those seeking more time for inspections, such as France and Germany, by failing to find conclusive evidence of prohibited weapons.

KOSOVO

The UN police regional headquarters in western Kosovo was attacked by what appeared to be an anti-tank missile. The attack, the first on a UN police building in Kosovo, resulted in no casualties.

LEBANON

The UN Secretary General advised the Security Council to extend the mandate for the UN Interim Force in Lebanon until the end of July 2003, citing sporadic hostilities between Lebanon and Israel despite general stability in the area.

No further UNIFIL troop size reductions were planned.

The UN Security Council unanimously approved a resolution extending the mandate of the UN Interim Force in Lebanon until 31 July 2003 and expressed concern about repeated Israeli violations of the withdrawal line separating the two Middle Eastern countries, a development which it said risked escalating tensions in the region. The new resolution came as Israeli planes staged their biggest mock raids over Lebanon since Israeli forces withdrew from Lebanon in 2000. The air raids, which included mock dive-bombing and overflights of Lebanese cities and Palestinian refugee camps, as well as the Bekaa Valley, a Hezbollah stronghold, sparked anti-aircraft fire from Lebanese forces and panic in the populace.

MIDDLE EAST

Israeli troops raided three Palestinian refugee camps in the Gaza Strip after five Palestinians were killed in clashes between the two sides.

The latest violence brought the Palestinian death toll over the previous month to 50, including both militants and civilians. Israeli forces also demolished a home belonging to an Islamic Jihad leader named Mohamed Brewesh. Soldiers also used tear gas and stun grenades to put down a protest by inmates at a West Bank detention camp.

The al-Aqsa Martyrs Brigade, an armed group linked to Palestinian Authority President Yasser Arafat's Fatah movement, meanwhile claimed responsibility for the killing of a 70-year-old trader from northern Israel.

Israeli President Moshe Katsav said neither side in Israeli politics seemed to have a viable plan to solve the Israeli-Palestinian conflict.

Israeli human rights group B'Tselem said that 1,007 Palestinians were being held by Israel without formal charges or trials. The group called for the immediate release of the detainees. The detainees were held under renewable periods of six months under a law based on British regulations that dated from the period when the UK governed the country.

Two men identified as residents of the West Bank town of Nablus killed at least 22 people and wounded about 100 when they blew themselves up in apparently coordinated attacks near Tel Aviv's Old Central Bus Station.

Among those killed in the attack were at least five foreigners and 17 Israelis, with the rest of the dead unidentified as of this morning. The neighbourhood is home to many foreign workers. Scores of the wounded were still hospitalised.

Islamic Jihad, Hamas and the al-Aqsa Martyrs Brigades, a group affiliated with Palestinian Authority President Yasser Arafat's Fatah movement, all claimed responsibility for the attack. Fatah itself denied any connection to the bombings.

The attack was the deadliest since March 2002, when a hotel bombing left 29 dead.

In response to the attack, Israel moved to close three Palestinian universities, intensify raids against suspected militants and prevent Palestinian officials from attending key meetings, including one in London at which US-backed reforms of the Palestinian Authority were to be discussed. Israeli helicopters also fired missiles at metal workshops in the Gaza Strip that were believed to produce weapons, injuring eight people. The Palestinian Authority condemned the bombings, and Palestinian Cabinet Minister Saeb Erekat said Israel's response would add "fuel to the fire."

Israeli troops shot and killed a Syrian soldier and captured another during a rare border incursion into the Israeli-controlled Golan Heights. Three men dressed in civilian clothes apparently infiltrated Israeli-held territory and opened fire on a military post. Israeli troops returned fire, killing one. In response, Syrian soldiers across the border fired into Israeli territory, but the Israelis did not respond. Syrian authorities said the men were only seeking water from a nearby river in the disengagement zone. They accused Israel of firing first, violating a cease-fire agreement that has held since 1974. It was the first flare-up on the disputed border since September 2001, when Israeli troops discovered a bag of explosives and weapons.

The UN Secretary General in December 2002 had called for a six-month extension of the UN Disengagement Force, which he called "essential" despite the fact that the area under its mandate had been "generally quiet." The Security Council renewed the mandate until 30 June based on Mr Annan's recommendation.

A UN Relief and Works Agency spokesman strongly criticised Israeli authorities over their handling of the investigation into the death of UNRWA employee Iain Hook. In a recent intelligence report, Israeli authorities had asserted that Palestinian gunmen were inside the UNRWA compound in the West Bank town of Jenin on 22 November 2002 when they opened fire, killing Mr Hook. UNRWA complained that Israeli authorities had not shared that intelligence report despite a specific request.

Israel turned over a captured Syrian and the body of another man to the UN following the shooting incident.

Syria responded angrily to Israel's claim that the men were attempting to infiltrate the border, saying that Israeli forces fired on a civilian who had gone to the disengagement zone to draw water and on two police officers.

The last border incursion into Israel had occurred 15 years before.

An outbreak of violence left 11 people dead, including at least three civilians, two of whom were Palestinian and one of whom was Israeli. The fighting marked the bloodiest 24-hour period in the Palestinian-Israeli conflict in a week. The killings came one day after Palestinian President Yasser Arafat called for Palestinians to halt attacks against Israeli civilians. Israeli Prime Minister Ariel Sharon criticised Arafat's statement, however, saying it was a ploy to influence Israel's general election.

Palestinian officials taking part in a Middle East peace conference agreed to draft a new constitution by the end of the month, and several participants described the talks as an overall success.

British Foreign Secretary Jack Straw said the Palestinian Authority would present other reform proposals on public administration and civil service issues within the following two weeks. Mr Straw said that despite the Israeli occupation, the Palestinian side could still make progress and should continue efforts to rein in terrorist groups. He said Palestinian officials had responsibilities to improve the security situation and "because they can't do everything on account of the security situation doesn't mean they can't do anything" and that "[t]here was a clear recognition that without credible Palestinian performance on security, the reform agenda will founder."

Fighting between Israelis and Palestinians killed 14 people as Israeli troops made repeated incursions into the Gaza Strip in response to Palestinian rocket attacks. Israeli troops also destroyed several buildings, including three homes belonging to members of the militant Hamas movement.

Israeli voters overwhelmingly endorsed the hardline policies of Israeli Prime Minister Ariel Sharon's Likud party, marking the worst-ever defeat for the Labour party, which campaigned on a promise of ending the country's occupation of Palestinian territories and initiating immediate peace talks with the Palestinians.

NEPAL

After seven years of fighting that had cost nearly 8,000 lives, Maoist guerrillas and the Nepalese government agreed to suspend the conflict.

NORTH KOREA

The UN Security Council was unlikely to take up the matter of North Korea's nuclear programme in the near future, diplomatic sources cited in *Financial Times* said. The Council would wait for a report on the matter from the International Atomic Energy Agency and then would favour waiting for North Korea's response before taking up the question.

South Korean and Chinese officials said that they planned to cooperate in seeking a resolution to the crisis through dialogue. South Korean President-elect Roh Moon-hyun, planned to seek a solution involving both North Korean and US compromises.

The US rejected opening talks before North Korea unilaterally halted its nuclear programme, and the Bush administration was likely to insist on the deployment of UN inspectors to the East Asian communist state.

North Korean Ambassador to China Choe Jin-su, however, restated his country's rejection of any US preconditions for talks and demand for a nonaggression treaty before halting the nuclear programme.

The US publicly confirmed that it did not plan to suspend food aid to impoverished North Korea but added that it wanted monitors to make sure the supplies were distributed to those in need.

The International Atomic Energy Agency said North Korea was in possession of enough plutonium to create a radiological "dirty bomb" but not a nuclear bomb. The agency said North Korea probably also had access to 20 damaged fuel rods that were in storage and about 8,000 spent nuclear fuel rods, from which plutonium could be extracted. It gave North Korea one last chance to abandon efforts to build nuclear weapons, declining for the time being to refer the matter to the UN Security Council. The 35-nation board of governors decided to give North Korea a final chance to abandon its secret nuclear weapons programmes and readmit nuclear inspectors into the country before it turned over the issue to the UN Security Council. The board said in a resolution that it was taking a "zero tolerance" approach and would turn the matter over to the Security Council if North Korea failed to act.

Passing on the issue to the Council would be a last resort for the IAEA and could lead to sanctions on the isolated regime of Kim Jong-il for its decision to expel inspectors in December 2002 and reactivate an inactive nuclear complex.

The UN Command accused North Korea of violating the armistice that established the demilitarised zone between North and South Korea 50 years ago, citing an incident in December 2002 when North Korean troops took machine guns into the zone, which is prohibited by the armistice. North Korea, though, insisted the armistice did not apply to the transportation corridor, where the incident took place. The North Koreans were building road and rail links to South Korea through the zone in cooperation with the South Korean government.

North Korea accused the US of attempting to resolve the dispute through the use of force.

South Korea was trying to put together a deal for the US to give written assurances that it would not attack North Korea and would resume oil shipments to the energy-deficient country after the country renounced its nuclear ambitions. According to the South Korean newspaper *Munhwa Ilbo*, the proposal would also include international economic assistance and a multinational security guarantee for North Korea, including China and Russia.

The US insisted it would not negotiate another deal with North Korea following the country's alleged abandonment of their 1994 pact.

The World Food Programme warned that up to one-third, or 7 million of North Korea's population, would be without food unless new deliveries were received. Following Japan and South Korea's suspension of food aid, the WFP had been forced to cut 3 million recipients from its aid programme in North Korea. It also scaled down the 2003 appeal for the country by 16% to 512,000 tons of grain. Only Italy and the EU had responded to the appeal. The US, which was one of the major donors of food aid to North Korea, had been withholding aid to North Korea, but it insisted the move was only until such food aid could be adequately monitored and refuted suggestions that it intended to use food as a political weapon.

The International Atomic Energy Agency gave North Korea just weeks to allow weapons inspectors back into the country before the matter was referred to the Security Council, which could lead to "serious consequences, not unlike Iraq," according to an IAEA statement issued a day after the agency's 35-nation governing board passed a resolution to condemn the country for violating its international nonproliferation obligations.

Washington agreed to talk with Pyongyang about its obligation to end its nuclear programme despite previous opposition to direct talks, adding though that there would be no compromise, according to a statement issued after 's talks with South Korea and Japan. The trilateral talks were opened in response to North Korea's expulsion of nuclear inspectors.

The World Food Programme, meanwhile, said it was in danger of running out of supplies for North Korea within weeks, warning that mounting tensions over its nuclear programme threatened to deepen the country's long-running food crisis, which was the result of years of drought and economic mismanagement. With 33,000 metric tons of food aid in the pipeline, the UN agency said it needed another 80,000 metric tons to meet the country's needs during the following three months. For the entire year, the agency said it needed 500,000 metric tons of food, totaling $200 million. The WFP had already been forced to reduce the number of people it was helping in 2002 from 6.4 million to 3.4 million, or over 20% of the population. North Korea's refusal to provide more information on how food aid was used and allow spot checks to ensure that nothing was diverted to the armed forces had discouraged humanitarian relief organisations from providing assistance.

North Korea said it was withdrawing from the Nuclear Nonproliferation Treaty, a move that would prevent any future inspections by the International Atomic Energy Agency. It added, however, that it was not seeking to build nuclear weapons. North Korea signed the NPT in 1985. The decision grouped North Korea with India, Israel and Pakistan, all of which had nuclear weapons but were not signatories of the NPT.

Following the announcement, a North Korean envoy to China said his country would be willing to reverse the decision if the US and its allies resumed oil shipments halted in October 2002, when the North Korean government in Pyongyang admitted it was continuing to develop its nuclear programme. He said that in addition to withdrawing from the NPT, his government considered all previous treaties and accords with the US to be void and that the country's military would now resume missile testing.

US Undersecretary of State John Bolton said the US wanted the UN Security Council to take up the matter of North Korea, a move that could result in sanctions against the impoverished nation, even as he indicated that the Bush administration might consider handing Pyongyang a formal guarantee of nonaggression.

With envoys from South Korea in Pyongyang seeking a peaceable solution to the nuclear standoff between the US and North Korea, the North rejected international involvement by dismissing the IAEA as biased and demanding that it stay out of the dispute.

South Korean envoy Lim Dong-won returned from a visit to Pyongyang without having met with North Korean leader Kim Jong Il, saying officials there had reiterated the North's position that the only solution to the nuclear dispute was through direct talks with the US.

SRI LANKA

Sri Lanka and the separatist Liberation Tigers of Tamil Eelam continued peace negotiations following the resolution of a dispute that threatened to sink the talks. According to AFP, the rebels and the government agreed to put off discussion of the controversial matter of resettling thousands of displaced Sri Lankans near military bases in the north of the island.

The LTTE wanted Sri Lanka to reduce the size of high security zones near military bases to allow the displaced to return to property currently held by security forces. Scandinavians monitoring a February cease-fire agreement, though, said de-escalation that was not bilateral could undermine the peace process by changing the balance of power. The rebels had publicly accused the monitors of siding with the government and ruled out any decommissioning of their weapons before a final settlement was reached.

The two sides agreed to ask a multilateral agency to administer development funds that had already been pledged for areas in the north and east affected by the conflict. The multilateral agency would reportedly administer part of the $70 million countries pledged for such activities. The sides also agreed on the formation of a subcommittee on reconstruction and rehabilitation, which would prioritise projects prior to a donor conference.

The government side hoped to link the return of displaced ethnic Tamils to their homes in the north with the disarming of LTTE forces. LTTE negotiators, however, said they would not discuss disarmament at the present time and withdrew from a committee set up to discuss the topic. Instead, the two sides set an agreement on the return of displaced Tamils, the distribution of some $70 million in aid and the demining of the conflict zone.

THAILAND

Thailand called a meeting of its top military chiefs after Cambodian protesters attacked the Thai Embassy and ambassador's residence in Phnom Penh, seriously wounding four policemen guarding the buildings, according to a witness. Protesters torched and looted the embassy itself. The Thai Ambassador and his staff narrowly escaped through a back door. Mobs were said to have roamed the city damaging at least 10 Thai businesses. The Thai military believed at least one Thai died in an attack on the Royal Phnom Penh Hotel, which had been set on fire.

The Cambodian protesters began their rampage after alleged comments by Thai television star Suvanan Kongying that the famous Angkor Wat temple had been stolen by Cambodia. She has denied making the comments.

Hundreds of Thais were evacuated from the capital on board four Thai Air Force C-130 transport aircraft. Two more planes were on standby in case further rioting forced others to flee.

UGANDA

A 19-month-old Ugandan judicial commission set up to look into UN accusations that Ugandan officials were involved in the plunder of DRC's natural resources submitted its 211-page report over to government officials. The findings were not released, but Junior Foreign Minister Tom Butime said the government would make the report public soon and that a copy would be sent to the UN.

The last 200 soldiers of Jean-Pierre Bemba's Congolese Liberation Movement, in accordance with a 30 December 2002 cease-fire, withdrew from the DRC.

WESTERN SAHARA

The Polisario Front rejected a peace plan for disputed Western Sahara that was presented in the region by UN envoy James Baker. Mr Baker proposed "four years of self-government, at the end of which an electoral body, which would be 65% Moroccan colonists, would decide in a referendum on the definitive status of the territory." The front, backed by Algeria and seeking to rid Western Sahara of Moroccan rule, said that the plan offered nothing new.

The UN Security Council unanimously approved a resolution to extend the mandate of the UN Mission for the Referendum in Western Sahara until 31 March 2003 in order to give all concerned sides more time to consider a UN proposal for the resolution of the status of the disputed territory.

Diplomats familiar with a plan put forward by UN special envoy for Western Sahara James Baker said the proposal would make the Moroccan-occupied former Spanish colony a semi-autonomous part of Morocco for a transitional period of up to five years. After that a referendum, which was the main goal of MINURSO, would be held, allowing residents to choose between independence or remaining part of Morocco. The plan would allow people who had resided in the territory since 1975, when it was annexed by Morocco, to vote – a marked change from an earlier plan that would have allowed people with only a year of residency to vote. Regardless of the change, however, it would still give the advantage to Morocco, which moved hundreds of thousands of people into the resource-rich territory after annexing it. According to the Polisario Front there were only about 86,000 indigenous residents of Western Sahara.

February 2003

AFGHANISTAN

US forces searching caves in Afghanistan near the southeastern border town of Spin Boldak were still coming under fire from armed gunmen despite large-scale operations in the area.

According to a US forces spokesman, American troops clearing caves had had only brief engagements with armed rebels and expected more clashes in the future as the operation wound down.

Armed men robbed the main UNICEF office in Kabul during a break-in. A spokesman said the robbers took cash but that there were no casualties. A UNICEF employee, however, said that some staff were assaulted.

The International Security Assistance Force had to stay in Afghanistan's capital, Kabul, two or three more years to ensure security and stability, the commander of the force said. Hilmi Akin Zorlu said an early departure could create chaos and hamstring the government. Mr Zorlu, who was to hand over control of the 19-country force to Germany and the Netherlands, said Afghanistan's national army and police had to be fully established all over the country before the peacekeepers left.

Despite sporadic bombings and rocket attacks, Mr Zorlu said the 4,000 armed peacekeepers in Kabul had helped to make the city safer and provide a stable foundation for reconstruction.

Germany doubled its contingent in the peacekeeping force to 2,500 in December 2002 and extended its participation by a year, while the Turkish contingent, then at about 1,400, would probably be reduced to 160, according to Mr Zorlu.

German General Norbert van Heyst assumed command of the International Security Assistance Force in Kabul saying the unit would "press forward for peace, which would finally allow us to take ISAF troops home." General Van Heyst, who was to serve as the force's head for the following six months with Dutch General Robert Bertholee as his deputy, added that "although the name and face of ISAF's commanders may change, its purpose would not."

German Defence Minister Peter Struck had urged NATO to take over ISAF from the United Nations and was cited by the BBC as saying the United States also supported the idea of a NATO command. Mr Struck said he would discuss the proposal with President Karzai.

Donors pledged $50.7 million for disarmament in Afghanistan. Japan donated $35 million to support a new UN-backed programme to disarm fighters across war-torn Afghanistan. The United States, the United Kingdom and Canada rounded out the aid package. The new funds were to go towards helping fighters in Afghanistan rejoin civil society. The money was to cover the first year of a three-year demobilisation programme that the UN Development Programme estimated would cost about $134 million overall. The support would aid efforts to track, collect and store weapons around the country and provide former combatants with alternative sources of income, the UN Development Programme said. The programme would offer money and microcredit to ex-fighters to start businesses and seek to wean fighters from dependency on mid-level commanders and toward self-sufficiency.

Most of Afghanistan was still under the sway of powerful regional warlords, while the central administration led by President Hamid Karzai barely extended beyond Kabul, which was protected by the International Security Assistance Force. Attempts to disarm warlords' forces had often been slow and had stopped in some areas amid fighting between rival commanders.

The new programme was to begin in Kabul in March and be expanded later to cities such as Mazar-e Sharif, Kandahar, Jalalabad and Herat.

Afghanistan's central government needed continued funding and its own army more than it needed a fortified international military presence, and above all it needed to remain a priority for the United States, Afghan President Hamid Karzai told the US Senate Foreign Relations Committee in Washington. President Karzai asked senators for support to strengthen Afghanistan's fledgling army of 3,000. His sphere of influence was generally agreed to be restricted to the borders of the capital, Kabul, where the UN-mandated International Security Assistance Force and the small national army were seated.

Many analysts had pointed to the need to expand ISAF from its level of 4,800 troops but Mr Karzai insisted on the need for a permanent state militia, saying that although he would not turn down an ISAF expansion, neither would he seek it.

AL-QAEDA
Al-Qaeda continued to use "blood diamonds" culled from mines in Sierra Leone to fund its international operations, a senior official with the special UN court for the West African country said. Chief prosecutor David Crane noted the connection between the sale of conflict diamonds, which comprised about 4% of the $7.8 billion annual diamond trade, and the al-Qaeda terrorist organisation. He questioned the international industry's commitment to the UN plan to create a certification system that would block the sale of conflict diamonds, saying the special UN court in Sierra Leone planned to indict those who profited through the illicit trade.

The United States raised its official threat level to Code Orange, the second-highest security alert, warning of fresh threats of attacks by al-Qaeda. Officials said new intelligence warned about the possibility of attacks on synagogues, Jewish community centres, Jewish hospitals, youth groups, hotels and resorts, saying the situation was particularly alarming because of the unusually large number of reports that had come in over the previous few days.

Five Australian families related to victims of bombings in Bali in October 2002 and a sixth individual who was seriously injured were joining the relatives of about 900 victims of the 11 September 2001 terrorist attack in a US class action suit targeting financiers of al-Qaeda's terror campaigns – including wealthy Saudi individuals, banks corporations and Islamic charities implicated in the financing of al-Qaeda.

Agence France-Press reported that two suspects in the Bali bomb attack said Australians were deliberately targeted because of Australia's roles in East Timor and Afghanistan. One suspect named Australia and the United Kingdom as being close allies of the United States, which he blamed for the deaths of 200,000 innocent men, women and children in Afghanistan.

ANGOLA

The UN Security Council recommended the UN Mission in Angola be terminated when its current mandate ran out. The Council also welcomed Angola's steps to implement the Lusaka Protocol, which provided the base for the peace process between the government and the former rebel group UNITA.

In his report, Kofi Annan had pointed to progress in solidifying the country's 10-month-old peace process and to its improving but uneven human rights climate, saying much work remained in demining, reintegration of ex-UNITA fighters and electoral assistance. UN Resident Coordinator Erick de Mul was expected to take over these activities after the mission's mandate ended.

BALI *see* AL-QAEDA

COLOMBIA

Following Colombia's imposition of a curfew in the oil-rich, conflict-torn northeastern department of Arauca, the Colombian branch of the UN Office of the High Commissioner for Human Rights had said the department had witnessed a "dramatic deterioration" and called for dialogue to end clashes there between government security forces and the country's three major rebel groups. OHCHR in Colombia said that in 2001 and 2002, 247 homicides were registered in the city of Arauca, while in Tame in the first 23 days of 2003, there were as many "selected assassinations" registered as during all of 2002.

Colombian Defence Minister Martha Lucia Ramirez said the government was "not thinking about regional dialogue in Arauca" and that any such dialogue should be national and carried out through the United Nations, adding that Colombian military operations in Arauca, where US advisers were training security forces, were part of a "pilot project" to combat the three rebel groups and stem corruption and drug trafficking. Colombian Ombudsman Eduardo Cifuentes and some local officials supported dialogue, but security conditions in the department did not permit it, Governor Oscar Munoz said. Gilberto Toro, the executive secretary of the Colombian Federation of Municipalities, said, "Given the complex situation that now exists in Arauca, a regional dialogue could only lead to the dissolution of national sovereignty."

Colombian Attorney General Luis Camilo Osorio called on the UN office to show proof that security forces were involved in forced disappearances in Arauca, saying the United Nations "had the responsibility to formulate accusations based on real incidents."

AUC head Carlos Castano called on the United States to stop referring to him as a terrorist and said he was willing to face the International Criminal Court when his work was done in Colombia. Mr Castano said he had asked all elements of the AUC to maintain their cease-fire "where possible" and that all AUC factions were ready to sign a peace accord with the government and disarm "when the state pledges to protect areas it had abandoned." Inviting the FARC and ELN to join the peace process, Mr Castano blamed the country's problems on the state and said peace waspossible if the government affirms its authority in Colombia's regions.

CONGO, DEMOCRATIC REPUBLIC OF

Leaders of the DRC and Uganda amended an earlier peace deal, lengthening the stay of Ugandan troops in northeastern DRC until 20 March 2003.

The new deal, struck by DRC President Joseph Kabila and Ugandan President Yoweri Museveni, came after reports of a major Ugandan troop build-up in the Ituri region following rising tensions with a DRC rebel group, the Union of Congolese Patriots, over control of territory and resources.

Officials of the UN Organisation Mission in the DRC, international aid groups, rebels and residents all warned of unprecedented bloodshed if renewed fighting broke out.

Some 2,500 Ugandan soldiers were stationed in Bunia, the regional capital and headquarters for the rebel group. Under the original peace deal 700 Ugandan troops who remained to help stabilise the region were to withdraw by 15 December 2002.

President Museveni's defence adviser, Lieutenant General David Tinyefuza, said the increased troop presence was necessary because the UPC had "become a real menace" after arming itself "massively" to attack other tribes in the region. More than 60,000 people had died in fighting between ethnic groups in Ituri since 1998.

Ugandan defence officials also claimed the UPC had allowed anti-Ugandan government activists to train near their western border.

According to UN officials in Bunia, the troop build-up occurred after the UPC demanded Ugandan forces withdraw, accusing them of arming and training rival tribal groups. The UN officials said Uganda was reluctant to give up control of rich gold reserves, vast timber resources and regional commerce.

In response to the build-up, the UPC had increased its ranks from 4,000 fighters to 12,000 fighters, mainly through the addition of thousands of underage combatants, another unnamed aid worker said.

Under the amended peace plan, an Ituri Pacification Commission would be set up by 17 February. It was expected to complete its work by 10 March, with total Ugandan withdrawal 10 days later.

Meanwhile, in a lawsuit brought by the DRC against Uganda in 1999 for "acts of armed aggression" during Congo's civil war, the International Court of Justice in The Hague authorised the DRC to submit an additional pleading in response to Ugandan counter-claims.

All flights by the MONUC to the northeastern city of Bunia had been suspended after the helicopter of MONUC force commander Mountaga Diallo was fired on, a MONUC spokesman announced. He added that flights would resume following an inquiry into the shooting and that the mission had not severed contacts with Thomas Lubanga, the leader of the Bunia-based rebel movement Union des Patriotes Congolais.

MONUC had received reports of fighting around Bunia, but observers were unable to travel to the area to confirm the information because of lack of security.

COTE D'IVOIRE
In the biggest protest since the onset of civil war in Ivory Coast five months previously, hundreds of opposition supporters clashed with police after the discovery of a body believed to be that of key opposition figure, Kamara Yerefe, from the Muslim north. Supporters of the opposition Rassemblement des Republicain said the body was found in a rubbish bin. His family accused paramilitary police of the assassination. A Western diplomat said agents of the internal security service had picked up Mr Yerefe, although police said the body had not been identified. Opposition supporters blamed death squads for the murder, saying it was the latest in a series since the war started. A group of rebel supporters in Abidjan called for a three-day "dead city" general strike beginning to protest against the death and demand that his killers be brought to justice.

In a more peaceful rally, more than 100,000 pro-government supporters protested against the French-brokered power-sharing deal that rebels had said would give them control over the country's military. Thousands of women marched to the French Embassy in Abidjan to protest against the French-brokered peace deal.

The United States, France and West African leaders, meanwhile, urged President Gbagbo to implement the accord. The presidents of Ghana, Nigeria and Togo, representing the 15-nation Economic Community of West African States, met with Mr Gbagbo and urged him to act.

The UN High Commissioner for Refugees resumed most of its operations in the Ivory Coast after a three-day suspension due to security concerns in the country, with 158 Liberian refugees leaving the volatile southwest. Since the UNHCR's emergency repatriation started on 17 January, more than 1,250 Liberian refugees in the southwestern Ivorian town of Tabou had returned home. More than 1,700 Liberians had registered and were waiting to return with one of the daily convoys traveling into eastern Liberia, where they would receive UNHCR assistance in transit centres.

Some Liberians in Tabou, however, were desperate to leave the area, where the local community suspected the Liberians of involvement with rebel fighters. The refugees asked the UNHCR to help arrange free passage through a number of checkpoints between Tabou and Prollo then being guarded by young vigilantes.

The head of Ivory Coast's main rebel group said there "had never been any question of questioning . . . or of renegotiating" the peace deal reached in January 2003 by the country's government, rebels and opposition. The statement by Guillaume Soro, head of the northern Mouvement Patriotique de Cote d'Ivoire, followed indications from some rebels that they were considering accepting a junior defence minister post instead of the defence minister position they had been reportedly promised. West African diplomats cited by Reuters said compromise on the post was still on the table but that rebels would agree to it only if new Prime Minister Seydou Diarra became defence minister. Mr Diarra had been prevented from returning to the country's main city, Abidjan, amid sometimes violent demonstrations against the deal. French diplomats reportedly said a deal on the Defence and Interior ministries was not part of the formal agreement reached in France and could be revised. Mr Soro evoked the possibility of overthrowing President Laurent Gbagbo's government if the deal were to fall through.

The country's army had rejected the Paris accord, and the National Assembly was to discuss it. Ivory Coast's Economic and Social Council rejected the deal.

The African Union had also reiterated its support for the deal. South African President Mbeki, who was then chairman of the 52-nation Union, said, however, that "there needs to be continuing negotiations with the government and with the rebels to see what amendments might need to be made so that the . . . agreement becomes acceptable to everybody."

The UN Security Council unanimously approved a resolution giving "full support" to French and Economic Community of West African States peacekeeping forces in Ivory Coast. Passing Resolution 1464, the Council also urged implementation of the peace agreement between the government and various rebel groups, signed in France in January 2003. It condemned human rights violations connected to the conflict and provided for the council to review the situation in six months.

The new resolution came as Ivorian army spokesman Jules Yao Yao said that rebels had attacked government positions west of the cocoa-producing hub of Daloa. French peacekeepers, however, reported no fighting. The northern rebel Mouvement Patriotique de Cote d'Ivoire denied any involvement in the alleged attack, but the two main western rebel movements did not comment.

Debate over the peace accord continued, with MPCI leader Guillaume Soro saying he would not accept any renegotiation of the pact, which included a power-sharing arrangement with the rebels. Ivorian President Laurent Gbagbo had suggested that he might reject the deal. The Ivorian National Assembly held a special session to debate the accord, with Gbagbo's Ivorian Popular Front rejecting it and the opposition Democratic Party of Cote d'Ivoire-African Democratic Rally saying it would wait for further statements on the issue from the presiden. Mr Gbagbo's party had also accused France of displaying a "partisan and contemptuous attitude" in its support of the accord.

Thousands of trade union members and others staged a protest against the peace deal in the country's largest city, Abidjan. Much of the opposition to the accord had been directed against the French.

The French Catholic daily newspaper *La Croix* reported Deputy UN High Commissioner for Human Rights Bertrand Ramcharan as having said in a report that death squads responsible for recent violence in Ivory Coast were made up of government elements, including presidential guards and militias from Mr Gbagbo's Bete tribe. *La Croix* also reported that the western rebel groups had violated human rights standards by recruiting children for combat, according to UN special representative on children and armed conflict Olara Otunnu. A spokesman for President Gbagbo described the article as unfair. A spokesman for the UN Office of the High Commissioner for Human Rights, said the report did not indicate direct links between the death squads and Mr Gbagbo and other senior officials.

The United Nations moved to withdraw nonessential employees from war-torn Ivory Coast, declaring the country to be at phase four of a five-phase risk scale. Employees of about 30 of the 110 international groups operating in Ivory Coast were to withdraw, and no UN official could visit the country without the UN Secretary General's express consent.

The African Development Bank, which was headquartered in Abidjan, previously said it would relocate if and when the United Nations declared phase 4. The bank had about 1,000 employees, and 450 were expected to relocate in the first phase of the move.

Amid controversy over reported concessions made to rebel groups at in January 2003's Ivorian peace talks, Economic Community of West African States Executive Secretary Mohamed ibn Chambas told Integrated Regional Information Networks the African body was" not saying that rebel groups should be in government." He called on the United Nations to "look at UN intervention within the context of what the subregion was doing."

President Gbagbo installed opposition leader Seydou Diarra as the country's new prime minister, instituting the first part of a French-brokered plan to end nearly five months of civil war. Mr Diarra, like the MPCI leaders, was a Muslim from Ivory Coast's north. Plans for him to meet with the rebels at their stronghold in Bouake fell through, but he said he was prepared to travel there whenever necessary.

Rebel leaders threatened to return to combat unless more steps were taken to implement a coalition government.

A summit of regional leaders began in the capital Yamoussoukro to seek to cement the nation's fragile peace agreement. The largest rebel group, Mouvement

Patriotique de Cote d'Ivoire, refused to send delegates to the meeting, warning instead that they would march on the Ivorian commercial capital Abidjan unless Mr Gbagbo quickly implemented the peace agreement. The faction's leader, Guillaume Soro, said his group wanted seven government positions, including leadership of the Defence and Interior ministries. The pro-Gbagbo "Young Patriots" movement warned against including the rebels in the government.

As French President Jacques Chirac evoked the possibility of bringing Ivorian death squad members before an international court, UN Secretary General Kofi Annan said that the United Nations planned to send an investigation team to war-torn Ivory Coast as soon as possible.

According to the UN Office of the High Commissioner for Human Rights, a UN rights mission that visited the country in December 2002 concluded that some death squad members might be members of President Gbagbo's party but that killings were not necessarily being committed on the government's orders or with its knowledge.

Thirteen technical experts sent by the UN Secretary General arrived in Ivory Coast to assess the situation there and prepare recommendations to the UN Security Council about what the world body might do to support a peace deal reached in January 2003 by the country's government, opposition and rebels.

The composition of a new government remained a major point of contention, with new Prime Minister Seydou Diarra, appointed by President Gbagbo following the Paris agreement, facing army and political party opposition as he tried to form an administration that included rebel representatives as stipulated in the agreement.

An international panel led by Albert Tevoedjre, UN Secretary General Kofi Annan's special envoy for Ivory Coast, called on parties to the country's conflict to work quickly to create a new government as stipulated in a peace agreement reached near Paris in January.

The committee was responsible for overseeing the January deal, which capped months of fighting that began with a failed coup in September. Rebels said that under the agreement they were supposed to obtain the Defence and Interior ministries, and they had threatened to resume fighting if their demands were not met. President Gbagbo had reportedly drawn up a new government in which the two posts would go not to rebels but to figures he deemed neutral.

Mr Tevoedjre's committee met with President Gbagbo and met the same day with new Prime Minister Seydou Diarra. The committee said that Mr Diarra should be given greater power to form a government. The committee also stressed the importance of protecting members of the new government. It said that task would fall to thousands of French and Economic Community of West African States peace-keepers now on the ground.

Following reports by Amnesty International, the United Nations and others of human rights abuses committed by both rebels and loyalists in the conflict, lawyers for Mr Gbagbo's government asked the UN Security Council to refer the matter to the International Criminal Court.

CYPRUS

Tassos Papadopoulos trounced two-term incumbent Glafcos Clerides in presidential elections in Cyprus, a result that could have had repercussions for a UN-proposed peace deal between the island's southern ethnic Greeks and northern ethnic Turks, which Mr Papadopoulos had sharply criticised.

Mr Clerides had been regarded as more accommodating than Mr Papadopoulos to a settlement with Turkish Cypriot leader Rauf Denktash. Mr Papadopoulos had campaigned on a platform promising a better deal for Greek Cypriots, but gradually softened his stance as the elections approached.

Mr Denktash responded to the developments on the Greek side of the island with criticism for both its present and future leaders. He also took issue with Mr Papadopoulos' position on the contested territory of Karpasia and pronounced the new president partly responsible for divisiveness within Cyprus.

After meeting with UN special envoy Alvaro de Soto, Cypriot President-elect Tassos Papadopoulos agreed to resume talks on the reunification of Cyprus.

In order for a reunited Cyprus to be able to join the European Union on 16 April as planned, the United Nations had set 28 February as a deadline for agreement between the internationally recognized, ethnic Greek republic that Mr Papadopoulos would now head and Rauf Denktash's breakaway ethnic Turkish state in the north of the island, which was recognised only by Turkey.

Mr Denktash had criticised Mr Papadopoulos' call for changes to the UN reunification plan, including a proposal to give Greek Cypriot refugees the right to return to the north, as well as Papadopoulos' pledge to be "president of all Cypriots."

Meanwhile Mr Clerides said that it was not possible to reach a solution by February 28 and that was pessimism among EU diplomats, some of whom saw the defeat of Mr Clerides, who negotiated Cyprus' EU membership and accepted the UN peace plan in the main, as a rejection of EU policy on Cyprus.

The UN Secretary General arrived in Cyprus for meetings with Greek and Turkish Cypriot leaders to present his revised plan to secure a settlement of the island's division and allow a united Cyprus to sign an accession agreement with the European Union. Mr Annan said that his push was part of a last-ditch effort to secure a deal before the 28 February deadline for agreement.

According to sources quoted by Reuters, however, Mr Annan was likely to give Cypriot President-elect Tassos Papadopoulos and Turkish Cypriot leader Rauf Denktash until 7 March to consider his new plan, the third so far.

Mr Annan added that both the United Nations and the EU favoured a reunited Cyprus signing the accession agreement.

As the UN Secretary General began talks opposition to his latest plan arose immediately.

Shortly after an initial 45-minute meeting, Turkish Cypriot leader Rauf Denktash said of the latest UN proposal, "There was trickery. . . . It's all sleight of hand." The United Nations was proposing reducing Turkish Cypriot territory from 36 to 28% of the island and allowing tens of thousands of displaced Greek Cypriots to return to the Turkish-held north.

The leaders of the island's South said they needed more time to consider the plan.

Kofi Annan postponed, until 10 March 2003, the deadline for Cypriot leaders to sign on to a peace deal and called for a referendum to resolve reunification if the leaders themselves cannot by then. The new deadline further stretched a tight timetable for Mr Annan, who hoped Messrs Denktash and Papadopoulos would sign an agreement in The Hague on 10 March in time for both sides of the divided island to hold a referendum on a signed deal by 30 March. If his new timetable held, then a newly reunified Cyprus would be ready to enter the European Union on 16 April, when EU member states were set to finalise enlargement treaties in Athens.

EAST TIMOR

Militia groups opposed to East Timor's independence had launched a "terrorist" campaign in an effort to subvert the country's elected government before the United Nations wraps up its mission in the country, UN Mission of Support in East Timor deputy peacekeeping commander Justin Kelly said.

According to Mr Kelly, the killing of five former pro-independence activists in January 2003 in East Timor showed the dangers posed by renewed operations of militia forces, who were accused of ravaging the island after the Timorese over-whelmingly voted for independence in 1999. In the ensuing violence that followed, about 1,000 people lost their lives and hundreds of thousands fled across the border into Indonesia. Mr Kelly said the group, which claimed to number around 300 fighters, was sponsored by Tome Diogo, a Timorese national who wasworking for the Indonesian military in the key West Timor border town of Atambua. He also said that the militia appear to be involved in a "classical terrorist strategy of trying to separate the people from the government," comparing their actions to those of the Viet Cong in Vietnam. The same view had been echoed by East Timorese leaders.

The East Timorese government announced an emergency meeting together with UN officials following an attack by armed elements on a bus in a rural area south-east of the Timorese capital of Dili. The attack left one dead and three injured.

East Timorese defence chief Taur Matan Ruak told LUSA that the country's nascent armed forces were still waiting for promised international aid in the wake of severe logistical shortages. Citing the example of one battalion of 450 soldiers who were still living in tents left by Korean peacekeepers, Mr Ruak asked for donors to give what they could.

Timorese Foreign Minister Jose Ramos Horta appealed to UNMISET to allow 20 UN policemen to testify at an investigation into violent riots late in 2002 that shook the capital and the town of Baucau. While the government recognised the UN officials' right to immunity, Mr Ramos Horta called for understanding from UNMISET to help clear up the incidents. UNMISET deputy head Sukehiro Hadegawa told LUSA that while the officials would not testify, UNMISET remained committed to help determine the truth of what happened. According to an unnamed UN official, UNMISET's refusal only served to suggest that the mission might be trying to hide something. The official recommended that the government request the United Nations lift immunity to allow collaboration.

Following an attack in the Maliana border district of East Timor by unidentified gunmen, the UN Mission of Support in East Timor had rushed about 300 peacekeepers to the border. Two people were killed in the attack and five others were wounded.

The deployment came in the wake of repeated warnings by East Timorese and UNMISET officials that anti-independence militia groups were stepping up their activities in an effort to undermine East Timor's first post-independence government. Following an emergency meeting, Prime Minister Mari Alkatiri asserted that militias, believed to have crossed the border from the Indonesian region of West Timor, were behind the latest attacks.

Indonesia, which was accused of having links in the past with the militia groups, had dismissed any connections with the militia attacks.

EHIOPIA-ERITREA

A February 8-9 meeting of the Eritrea-Ethiopia Boundary Commission resulted in a decision to start demarcating the countries' contested border from the east rather than from the west, according to sources cited by Integrated Regional Information Networks.

Diplomatic sources reportedly said Ethiopia wanted the process, which was expected to start in May, to begin in the east. IRIN reported Ethiopia called for "comprehensive clarifications" to the Permanent Court of Arbitration's ruling last April demarcating the border, notably as pertains to the western sector, where the disputed Badme village was located. The countries' border conflict began in Badme in 1998.

The commission had ordered that both countries replace their liaison officers to the commission.

The head of UN personnel clearing land mines along the Ethiopian-Eritrean border said that new mines were still being laid along Eritrean roads.

Mine explosions in the security zone separating Ethiopia and Eritrea had killed 21 people and maimed 64 others, according to UNMEE. The mine clearance team estimated that between 250,000 and 300,000 land mines were buried on the countries' border.

IRAN

In the wake of allegations by the United States that Iran was secretly developing nuclear weapons, UN nuclear agency head Mohamed ElBaradei planned to ask Tehran to agree to an inspections regimen. Mr ElBaradei said he would like to discuss the allegations and the possibility of Iran joining the Additional Protocol, a programme created by the International Atomic Energy Agency in 1991, under which parties gave weapons inspectors access to all their facilities and, in some cases, agreed to submit to surprise visits.

Iran had one Russian-built light-water reactor and two nuclear plants under construction that it said were for peaceful purposes. The United States said they were part of a surreptitious atomic arms programme.

Russia had agreed to take the spent fuel from the Bushehr plant so it could not be used for arms manufacture.

Iranian President Mohammad Khatami announced that researchers had discovered and mined uranium reserves in central Iran and that his country was "determined to make use of advanced nuclear technology for peaceful purposes." President Khatami said processing facilities had been set up in the central cities of Isfahan and Kashan.

Iran previously invited inspectors from the International Atomic Energy Agency to verify its nuclear facilities later in January and the inspection team was scheduled to arrive in Iran on 25 February. The IAEA said that Iran's plans to mine and process uranium came as no great shock.

The United States had criticised Russia for helping Iran build a nuclear power plant in the country's southwestern port of Bushehr, which was expected to come on line in early 2004. Moscow had said that all spent fuel would be returned to Russia to ensure that it would not be diverted to a weapons programme, but President Khatami's announcement included Iran's intention to retain control of the entire fuel cycle, from mining and processing the uranium ore to reprocessing the spent fuel.

Defence Minister Ali Shamkhani was quoted as saying Iran had developed the capacity to produce composite solid fuels for its missiles.

Iran had rejected allegations by the United States and European Union that it was seeking to acquire weapons of mass destruction. The government said it needed nuclear plants to increase electricity generation by 6,000 megawatts over the following 20 years.

An Iranian opposition group said it would reveal details of a new site in Iran that housed equipment for enriching uranium for possible use in nuclear weapons. The announcement came ahead of a scheduled visit from International Atomic Energy Agency inspectors to two nuclear sites in Iran.

The National Council of Resistance of Iran also accused Iranian officials of having removed sensitive equipment from the nuclear facility at Natanz, one of the sites to be visited by IAEA inspectors. The group had provided reliable information in the past. In August 2002 it disclosed the existence of Natanz and Arak, the other site to be inspected.

Government officials claimed these sites were part of their efforts to end the country's dependence on oil and gas reserves for energy.

During a visit by International Atomic Energy Agency inspectors, Iran announced that it had rejected for the time being a request to cooperate with enhanced measures to monitor its nuclear activities. The IAEA had asked Iran to sign an additional protocol to its safeguards agreement with the nuclear watchdog that would permit the agency to conduct more intrusive inspections and environmental monitoring in Iran. Gholamreza Aghazadeh, Iran's top nuclear energy official, said Iran would not sign the protocol because few other countries had done so. It would, however, comply with its existing nuclear nonproliferation commitments as it built new nuclear reactors and fuel production facilities, he said.

IRAQ
A consensus was emerging to allow UN weapons inspections in Iraq to continue until as late as the middle of March before the UN Security Council decided whether to authorise military action, according to UN diplomats.

Under a possible timetable cited by the newspaper, International Atomic Energy Agency Director General Mohamed ElBaradei and UN Monitoring, Verification and Inspection Commission Executive Chairman Hans Blix would report to the council late in February after they delivered a report already scheduled for 14 February.

Security Council members remained divided over the use of force against Iraq, but 10 Eastern European countries were expected to issue a statement in support of US policy. The countries reportedly included new NATO members Bulgaria, Estonia, Latvia, Lithuania, Romania, Slovakia and Slovenia, as well as prospective members Albania, Croatia and Macedonia.

A declaration of support for the US position was signed by the leaders of seven other European countries. British Prime Minister Tony Blair, one of the signatories, failed to convince French President Jacques Chirac to support a new Security Council resolution authorising military force.

A British government report indicated security agents had bugged all rooms and telephones used by the weapons inspectors. The report also indicated that inspectors were outnumbered 20,000-to-108 by Iraqi intelligence officers. The report further backed US claims that Iraq had hidden documents related to weapons production in hospitals, mosques and homes.

Kurdish leaders in northern Iraq protested against a surprise visit by UN weapons inspectors, saying they said came without notice and without permission. Inspectors had carried out searches in Kurdish areas before and said that some Kurdish officials had said they would cooperate with the inspectors.

South African President Thabo Mbeki said that the effects of a war in Iraq on the oil market could seriously damage African economic progress.

The head of the Iraqi National Congress, an exile opposition group, said the United States was backing him as the transitional leader of a postwar Iraq, according to a former Iraqi diplomat. Ahmed Chalabi said the Bush administration had approved him to lead the country immediately after President Saddam Hussein was deposed.

Although the US State Department budgeted $25 million to fund Iraqi opposition groups during the current fiscal year, which was to end on 30 September, the following year's budget contained no funding for the opposition. The *Boston Globe* reported that the decision not to request money for the groups could indicate that the Bush administration felt that the future of Iraq was too uncertain.

US Secretary of State Colin Powell made a presentation at the Security Council of what he called "facts and conclusions based on solid intelligence" that Iraq was deceiving UN weapons inspectors and was hiding prohibited weapons of mass destruction. He played audiotapes, showed satellite photos and quoted intelligence reports that he said demonstrate "an active and systematic effort by the Iraqi regime to keep key materials and individuals" from inspectors. Mr Powell also accused Iraq of hiding biological weapons.

Following the US presentation, other members of the Council, most of them foreign ministers, commented on the report. It was clear that Mr Powell had not changed many minds. Those countries that favoured letting inspections continue, such as France, said the US charges were more evidence that the inspectors needed more time. Those siding with the United States, such as the United Kingdom, said time was running out for Iraq and that it was up to the United Nations to face the facts of Iraq's noncooperation.

Iraqi Ambassador Mohammed al-Douri said Mr Powell's charges "were utterly unrelated to the truth. No new information was provided."

Mr Powell also said Saddam Hussein's government was linked to terrorism and that the al-Qaeda terrorist network was operating freely in Baghdad. He said Abu Musab Zarqawi, an alleged al-Qaeda operative, was working out of northern Iraq and operated terror cells throughout the Middle East.

In an interview broadcast by the United Kingdom's Channel 4, Iraqi President Saddam Hussein said his country had no weapons of mass destruction and no links with al-Qaeda. The Iraqi president questioned whether US officials were looking for a pretext so they could justify war against Iraq.

Following the leak of a three-week-old British intelligence report indicating "no current links" between Iraq and al-Qaeda, British Prime Minister Tony Blair told members of Parliament that such links "unquestionably" existed but "how far the links go is a matter for speculation." In any case, Mr Blair said, the case for war did not depend "on links with al-Qaeda." The intelligence document reportedly indicated that Iraq and al-Qaeda had had contacts in the past but that the relationship suffered from mistrust and incompatible ideologies.

UN High Commissioner for Refugees Ruud Lubbers said that as many as 600,000 Iraqis could be expected to flee in the event of war, nearly half to Iran and "a considerable part of the remainder" to Turkey. Two hundred UNHCR employees were on standby to go to the region in a deployment that would double the agency's presence there.

Red Cross- and UN-sponsored talks in Jordan in January 2003 on the fate of 600 missing Kuwaiti prisoners detained by Iraq during the 1990-91 Gulf War accomplished nothing, according to a Kuwaiti official. Iraq had agreed for the first time in four years to meet with Kuwait on the matter, saying that more than 1,000 of its own people were also missing. The Kuwaiti official said, however, that the Iraqis provided no new information at the meeting.

US Secretary of State Colin Powell's detailed presentation of Washington's charges that Iraq was failing to disarm and was cooperating with al-Qaeda terrorists did little to change minds on the Security Council about whether to authorise the use of force against Iraq. Countries that favoured continuing weapons inspections used Mr Powell's evidence as proof that strengthened inspections, not war, was the best course.

Most Council members said they hoped the inspectors would find the new evidence presented by Mr Powell useful and asked the United States to share it with the inspectors. The suggestion that Washington had not provided the United Nations with everything it knew provoked an angry response from the United States.

The UN Secretary General said he still believed that war was not inevitable but a lot depended on President Saddam Hussein and the Iraqi leadership. He also said that, contrary to suggestions by some governments, he would not go to Baghdad to negotiate with the Iraqis.

UN Monitoring, Verification and Inspection Commission head Hans Blix told CNN that the fact that UN weapons inspectors were able to interview an Iraqi scientist in private for the first time showed Iraq was making an effort to cooperate with the inspectors.

US President Bush said that the United States would not wait to see what terrorist states could do with chemical, biological, radiological or nuclear weapons they could ostensibly obtain from Iraq. Citing "sources" who said Iraqi President Saddam Hussein had "recently" authorised the use of chemical weapons even though Iraq said it does not possess such weapons, President Bush said President Hussein's violations of Security Council resolutions were evident, and they continued. Amid talk of the possibility of another council resolution backing a US-led attack on Iraq, Mr Bush said Washington would welcome and support a new resolution but in any case was resolved to take whatever action necessary to defend the US and disarm the Iraqi regime.

British Prime Minister Tony Blair expressed sentiments similar to those of Mr Bush, saying London would still support war even if a Council resolution to authorise one were to be vetoed by a permanent Council member.

French President Jacques Chirac said Colin Powell's presentation was not sufficient to justify a war while the French Prime Minister Jean-Pierre Raffarin said that France was not "systematically pacifist" and could accept a war as a "last resort" but that inspectors should be given more time.

Russia said that there was no need for a second Council resolution.

Mexico and South Africa, acting on behalf of Nonaligned Movement countries, were seeking an open UN meeting on Iraq before a briefing by the inspection heads.

With war possibly approaching, UNESCO was working with Iraq to protect the country's wealth of historical artifacts. The UN agency said that any countries involved in an Iraq war must respect the Convention for the Protection of Cultural Property in the Event of Armed Conflict, which prohibits targeting cultural sites unless it was militarily necessary to do so. Neither London nor Washington was a party to the pact, but UNESCO said it was confident they would comply.

The United States gave the UN High Commissioner for Refugees $12.1 million to handle a possible humanitarian crisis in Iraq, bringing Washington's contribution to UNHCR for the purpose to $15 million. UNHCR had also received almost $900,000 from other countries for Iraq.

Iraq sent a letter to UN weapons inspectors approving the use of U-2 spy planes for surveillance of its weapons programmes, which the United Nations had been pushing for, and promised to pass legislation outlawing weapons of mass destruction.

Chief UN weapons inspector Hans Blix said after two days of talks in Baghdad that he had seen no new proof of weapons programmes in Iraq but that he had seen increased cooperation from Iraq in the form of new information on its weapons of mass destruction programmes. International Atomic Energy Agency Executive Director Mohamed ElBaradei echoed Dr Blix's report.

Key European allies blocked a NATO plan to fortify member state Turkey against a counterattack from neighbouring Iraq, arguing that doing so would presuppose war and increase trans-Atlantic tensions over Iraq that heightened with the emergence of a new French-German proposal for disarmament of Iraq.

France, Germany and Belgium opposed a move by NATO to send reconnaissance planes, Patriot anti-missile batteries and chemical-biological response units to Turkey, the only NATO member to border Iraq and a likely base for US strikes against Baghdad. The three countries said approving the proposal would force the crisis to a "logic of war."

Turkey responded with a rare request for emergency consultations under NATO's mutual defence treaty. Diplomats expect the three opposition nations ultimately to acquiesce to the plan, and Secretary General George Robertson said he was "confident" the allies would reach a consensus.

US Secretary of Defence Donald Rumsfeld condemned as "inexcusable" any delay to prepare Turkey for war and implied that any move to block the US-backed defence plan was a strike against NATO unity.

The Turkish Parliament had not yet voted to allow US troops to base operations on Turkish soil.

US officials leveled more criticism at France and Germany after the two nations agreed to present a beefed-up disarmament proposal to the Security Council. German Defence Minister Peter Struck said Germany was standing "shoulder to shoulder" with France on a plan to triple the number of weapons inspectors in Iraq, deploy thousands of UN soldiers there and declare all of Iraq a no-fly zone. The Russian Defence Minister said he had "no doubt" Russia would throw its support behind such a plan.

US President George W. Bush said that the United Nations was approaching a moment of reckoning and reiterated his intentions to go it alone should the Security Council fail to support the United States.

The UN Secretary General issued his strongest admonition yet to the United States that it should respect international law.

In a NATO deadlock, France, Germany and Belgium were showing no intention of acquiescing to an allied plan to outfit Turkey with defensive equipment in anticipation of a possible US-led invasion of Iraq that could originate in Turkey. The NATO plan would install Patriot missiles, chemical and biological response teams and surveillance planes in Turkey, the only NATO member that bordered Iraq. Turkish television reported that the country's civilian and military leaders had agreed to let the United States station 38,000 troops inside its borders and use three southern air bases, but parliament wasnot scheduled to take up a vote until 18 February. France, Germany and Belgium blocked the NATO proposal and did not budge from their positions through two sessions, arguing that fortifying Turkey would send a signal to the world that diplomacy had ended and war had begun. US Defence Secretary Donald Rumsfeld, however, said the United States would work directly with the other NATO members who support the plan for Turkey and declared that the three countries' opposition only isolated them from the rest of the alliance.

France, Germany and Russia announced a new proposal for enhanced weapons inspections in Iraq. The plan proposed doubling or tripling the number of weapons inspectors in Iraq and giving them more time to do their work. Veto-bearing Security Council member China added its support to the ramped-up disarmament proposal. A German official said that 11 of the council's 15 members support prolonging inspections, and named the United Kingdom, Spain and Bulgaria as the three council members aligned with the United States.

Chief UN weapons inspector Hans Blix gave the proposal a cool reception. "The principal problem is not the number of inspectors but rather the active cooperation of the Iraqi side," he said.

Iraq's UN ambassador, Mohammed al-Douri, said that Baghdad had decided to allow US, French and Russian surveillance planes to fly unmolested through Iraqi airspace in their efforts to collect evidence about Iraqi weapons programmes.

In a tape broadcast by Al-Jazeera, a man US officials had identified as Osama bin Laden called on all Muslims to support Iraq in a war against the United States and on Iraqis to carry out suicide attacks and lure US troops into urban fighting. The man said Iraqi President Saddam Hussein was an "infidel" but that Iraq should nevertheless join his fight against the Western "crusaders." The speaker also called on Muslims to "break free from the slavery of . . . tyrannic and apostate regimes" that "were enslaved by America," such as Jordan, Morocco, Nigeria, Pakistan, Saudi Arabia and Yemen.

With sharp disagreements continuing in NATO and the UN Security Council over how to proceed on Iraq, US Secretary of State Colin Powell said the Al-Jazeera tape supported US claims that Iraq harboured members of al-Qaeda, the bin Laden network that was believed responsible for the 11 September 2001 attacks on the United States.

Iraq had no immediate comment on the tape.

Germany, one of several UN Security Council members opposing a war on Iraq, said that the tape indicated no close links between Iraq and al-Qaeda.

British Prime Minister Tony Blair said that the Security Council could still issue a new resolution authorising a US-led attack on Iraq over its weapons of mass destruction programmes, even though Council members were split over the question, with the United States and the United Kingdom leading the push for war.

US National Security Adviser Condoleezza Rice met with Hans Blix at the US Mission to the United Nations to urge him to declare that Iraq had failed to disarm. The meeting underlined the Bush administration's concern that Dr Blix's next report might not convince Council members that war on Iraq was justified.

Divisions within NATO had mirrored those within the Security Council, with France, Germany and Belgium seeking to block alliance plans to bolster Turkey's defence in case of a missile attack from Iraq, saying the action would amount to giving up efforts to avoid a war. Talks yielded a compromise in which the United States reportedly agreed to drop a request that European troops replace US troops moved to the Persian Gulf from the Balkans and a request that European forces step up guard duties at US European bases. NATO officials said bilateral talks were continuing on the two items.

UN chemical weapons specialists accompanied by an Iraqi team set out for a chemical weapons facility about 40 miles northwest of Baghdad to conduct the first destruction of banned weapons under the current inspections regime. The UN team was to destroy 10 artillery shells containing mustard gas, a process that was expected to take up to five days. The site, the al-Muthanna State Establishment, was Iraq's major chemical weapons production facility in the 1980s.

Senior officials in the US administration said the US military would take the lead early on, should the United States attack and defeat Iraq, in providing security, destroying weapons of mass destruction and providing food aid to millions of Iraqis. In its first presentation of postwar plans, the administration said rebuilding Iraq could take years and many billions of dollars to complete.

Iraqi exile leaders said a US plan to install a military governor for up to a year in postwar Iraq risked leaving in place an Iraqi government dominated by the country's Sunni Muslim minority and veterans of Saddam Hussein's Baath Party.

As the UN Security Council prepared to hear again from UN Monitoring, Verification and Inspection Commission head Hans Blix on the status of weapons of mass destruction inspections in Iraq, Council diplomats said that Iraq had missiles that could travel farther than 112 miles, well in excess of UN limits.

Dr Blix asked experts from seven countries – China, France, Germany, Russia, Ukraine, the United Kingdom and the United States – to verify Iraq's assertion that the range of its al-Samoud missiles was within the Council-imposed 93-mile limit. They found the missile could travel beyond that range, meaning it could reach Iran, Jordan, Kuwait, Saudi Arabia, Syria and Turkey.

Iraqi Deputy Prime Minister Tariq Aziz refuted the accusations and Iraqi UN Ambassador Mohammed al-Douri said that Iraq would not destroy the missiles.

British Prime Minister Tony Blair said the missiles could be a "significant breach" of Security Council Resolution 1441, in which the Council promised Iraq would face "serious consequences" if it remained in violation of UN resolutions. Finding Iraq in "material breach" had been seen as the key to triggering military action under the resolution. Council diplomats said they saw no immediate moves to introduce a new resolution finding Iraq in "material breach" of Resolution 1441.

The United States already had special operations troops inside Iraq searching for weapons sites, establishing communications and seeking potential Iraqi military defectors. An undetermined number of US personnel had been in and out of Iraq for more than a month, according to two military officials with direct knowledge of their activities. They were laying the groundwork for conventional US troops that would overrun large parts of Iraq if the United States attacked the country.

The stand-off on the Iraq question continued at NATO headquarters.

Hans Blix told the Security Council that Iraqi cooperation with inspectors "had improved" and that inspectors "had not found" any banned weapons in Iraq but that "significant outstanding issues" concerning anthrax, VX gas and long-range missiles still remain, thus providing arguments both for countries advocating the forcible disarmament of Iraq and those promoting continued inspections. Dr Blix said experts had studied two missiles Iraq was building that could exceed the 150-kilometer range. He said the experts were unanimous that the al-Samoud 2 missile violated that limit and was, therefore, proscribed, but that the al-Fatah missile needed further study. He said UNMOVIC was unable to verify Iraq's claim that it destroyed stocks of anthrax and VX gas left over after the 1991 Gulf War.

Mohamed ElBaradei told the Council that the IAEA had to date found no evidence of ongoing prohibited nuclear or nuclear related activities in Iraq. Mr ElBaradei added, however, that several suspect programmes – including high-tolerance aluminum tubes, conventional explosives and magnets – that could be used for producing nuclear weapons needed further study. He said the IAEA was working to expand near-real-time monitoring of dual-use equipment and related activities. The focus of IAEA's inspections, had now moved from the "reconnaissance phase" into the "investigative phase" in which it was examining what had happened in Iraq in the four years since inspectors left. The IAEA was re-establishing monitoring systems at sites associated with critical dual-use equipment and was taking samples from around the country and analysing them for signatures of nuclear activities.

In 11 weeks of inspections, Dr Blix said UNMOVIC had conducted more than 400 inspections at 300 sites and Mr ElBaradei said the IAEA had investigated 125 locations in the course of 177 inspections.

Neither official explicitly asked for more time to continue inspections, but both spoke about their plans for further expanding their efforts.

Ten foreign ministers, including ministers from all five veto-holding permanent members, attended the Security Council session.

France maintained its position that inspections were working and need more time.

The United Kingdom was planning to start circulating a new draft resolution on Iraq soon. A British official said there was likely to be "an actual proposal on the table" after a Council meeting on Iraq at which non-Council members would make their views known.

German Foreign Minister Joschka Fischer echoed the comments of nearly all the 15 Council members in saying that Iraq had to disarm completely.

Iraq excused itself from assuming the presidency of the UN Conference on Disarmament in March. Iraq's scheduled turn at the rotating position had provoked US outrage.

The United States and United Kingdom intended to press forward with a new UN Security Council resolution authorising force against Iraq, despite massive peace demonstrations worldwide and the expected opposition of other Council members. Prospects for passage of a new Security Council resolution appeared dim with French President Jacques Chirac saying that France would not allow any resolution that explicitly authorised war against Iraq at this time.

US officials said they hoped that a carefully crafted resolution could receive council support. The resolution would restate that Iraq remained in material breach of its obligations, officials said. In addition, it would probably call for Iraq to perform specific tasks in the following two weeks to demonstrate that it was cooperating with UN inspectors. Those tasks would include allowing UN inspectors to interview scientists privately, destroying missiles determined to have ranges exceeding UN limits, and unconditionally permitting UN surveillance flights conducted by US, French and Russian aircraft. Hans Blix concurred with these benchmarks in meetings with US officials following his latest Security Council briefing.

A European Union joint statement called for Iraq to disarm and cooperate immediately and fully, but also supported giving UN inspectors the time and resources that the UN Security Council believed they needed. The statement reaffirmed the primacy of the United Nations in resolving the Iraqi crisis.

NATO officials resolved a major dispute by moving a discussion on providing defensive aid to Turkey to the NATO Defence Planning Council, a forum that does not include France. The move allowed NATO to approve a US request for NATO to provide Turkey, which borders Iraq, with Patriot missiles, sophisticated reconnaissance aircraft and chemical and biological warfwere defence teams. France, Belgium and Germany had objected to the US proposal, saying that a peaceful resolution to the Iraqi crisis was still possible. With France out of the decision, however, Germany agreed to support the decision and Belgium also dropped its longstanding demand that any decision be linked to a UN Security Council resolution authorising force.

Several million demonstrators in London, Rome, Berlin, Paris, New York, Canberra and other cities held protests against a war on Iraq.

A meeting of senior Arab officials in Cairo failed to agree to hold their own emergency summit on Iraq. Disagreements over the goal of such a summit highlighted the split in the region on what approach should be pursued with Iraq. At the meeting, foreign ministers from the 22-nation Arab League agreed to hold more consultations to set a date for summit. The substantive disagreement over the proper strategy on Iraq was apparent in two camps. One, led by Syria, believed that an Arab summit should only meet to send a strong message to the United States expressing the league's opposition to war in Iraq and to US Mideast policies. The other camp wanted a summit to urge Iraq to cooperate with UN inspectors.

UN weapons inspectors continued their activities, visiting several Iraqi sites and using a US U-2 aircraft for the first time. UNMOVIC missile teams visited al-Nida, which produces solid propellant mixers, Nissan Factory 17, where al-Samoud 2 missile components were produced, and the Salah al-Din State Company, where fuses and circuit boards were made. Biological teams went to the Saddam Center for Biotechnology Research in Baghdad, the Chemistry Department at Saddam University's College of Science, and An Bar College of Agriculture, about 150 kilometers west of Baghdad. Chemical inspectors flew by helicopter to the Southern Refinery Company in Basra.

Four teams of nuclear inspectors from the IAEA conducted inspections, including two at Tuwaitha to examine nuclear waste. One of these teams included inspectors with rock climbing experience who explored underground chambers at the Tamuz 1 reactor complex, bombed by Israel in 1981. The second prepared to remove a small amount of natural uranium slurry, as planned by the IAEA in 1998. Another IAEA team took radiation samples from a car driving near the Radwan and Yarmouk facilities 50 kilometers west of Baghdad, and a fourth inspected the Taji Engineering facility, which works on aircraft engines.

UNMOVIC biological inspectors visited two food processing centres, one at Baquba, 50 kilometers northwest of Baghdad, and the other near Diyala. Those teams also visited the Biology Department of the College of Sciences at Baquba University and the Diyala Tuberculoswasand respiratory disease centre.

Missile experts conducted investigations at al-Kindi, tagged SA-2 missile engines at Ibn al-Haytham, tagged al-Samoud 2 missiles near Taji, and visited al-Mamoun, where Iraq had rebuilt casting chambers destroyed previously by UN inspectors.

Chemical experts visited Fallujah 3, located 100 kilometers northwest of Baghdad.

Additional UNMOVIC teams inspected the Hadr Ammunition Storage Facility near Mosul.

IAEA officials interviewed an Iraqi scientist about Baghdad's past efforts to acquire aluminum tubing, possibly for uranium enrichment purposes.

Meanwhile, UNMOVIC missile teams visited al-Khadimia and al-Samoud Factories, which produce liquid-fueled missile engines; al-Assma Company, which makes al-Fateh missile components; al-Mutasim airfield, where unmanned aircraft were tested; al-Ameen Factory, involved in the static testing of Iraqi missiles; and Um al-Maarik General Establishment, where missile and rocket motor cases were produced.

Chemical teams went to al-Muthanna in connection with the mustard gas destruction process. Other inspectors went to al-Zahif al-Kabeer Center, a chemical plant 30 kilometres northwest of Baghdad.

A biological team flew to al-Fuwayjah, near Kirkuk, to examine a seed processing facility, and another team revisited the Hadr ammunition dump.

IAEA officials conducted a radiation survey in the Samarra area, inspected al-Nida, a heavy industrial manufacturing plant, visited Um al-Maarik again, and inspected Tho al-Fekar to examine flow forming equipment.

Inspectors visited the al-Qa Qaa chemical and explosives production plant south of Baghdad and the Harith Missile Maintenance Workshop, where Iraq maintained anti-aircraft missiles, and went for the first time to the Dar al-Salam chemical plant west of Baghdad.

IAEA officials conducted a radiation survey at the Mansour State Company, which makes electronic components.

The majority of delegates who spoke over the two-day Security Council debate on Iraq clearly felt the inspection regime was working and that inspectors needed more time. On the other hand, the argument by the United States and United Kingdom that inspections had run their course was gaining ground, although most countries supporting this view stopped short of calling for the use of force.

The United States and the United Kingdom had reportedly shifted their tactic on an expected new resolution on Iraq. Rather than seeking unanimity, they would try to persuade nine of the 15 Council members to back the resolution authorising the use of force against Iraq, then challenge the other of the five permanent members – France, Russia and China – to veto the will of the Council majority. US and British officials worked to hammer out the resolution's language in efforts to win over six wavering nonpermanent Council members, known informally as "the middle six" – Angola, Guinea, Cameroon, Mexico, Chile and Pakistan. The strategy would then be to pressure Russia, France and China to acquiesce by abstaining, according to White House officials.

US and British diplomats continued to disagree on whether to include an explicit deadline in the resolution for Iraq to disclose its weapons and start disarming and a reference to the resolution presenting the last chance for Iraq to avoid war.

Speakers at an open Security Council debate gave their support to continuing the UN weapons inspection regime to ensure Iraq's disarmament, but also stressed that the burden was on Iraq to fully cooperate with the inspectors. Few countries expressed support for the position of the United States and United Kingdom that there wasno point continuing the inspections and that the use of force to disarm Iraq wasnow necessary.

While there was little support for the US and UK positions, there was a sense that only Iraq's "proactive" cooperation with inspectors could prevent the use of force.

Iran, Jordan, Kuwait and Turkey, which all neighbour Iraq, warned against the regional instability a war would cause and reminded the Council that they were still feeling the effects of the first Gulf War in the form of refugees and the economic impact of sanctions.

Only Australia and Japan – and, to a lesser extent, Argentina and Peru – supported the US position that continued inspections were futile and that a second resolution was now necessary, but both stopped short of calling for the use of force.

The governments of the United States and United Kingdom were reportedly continuing work on a new UN resolution proposing military action against Iraq if it did not meet certain standards for disarmament.

Iraqi Ambassador Mohammed al-Douri told the Security Council session that his government had cooperated with inspectors.

Speaking at the Council meeting on behalf of the European Union, Ambassador Adamantios Vassilakis of Greece said war was not inevitable.

Few NATO countries or the Eastern European countries seeking NATO or EU membership chose to take part in the debate.

US President Bush said he remained committed to a military option if diplomacy failed. He added that anti-war protests that included millions of people worldwide would not affect his decision, even though he supported the demonstrators' right to voice their opinions. His comments came on the same day that the US military ordered an additional 28,000 troops to the Persian Gulf region. The US force ultimately sent to oppose Iraq was expected to total over 200,000, joined by 40,000 British troops.

US Ambassador to Turkey Robert Pearson said that the Turkish government had not yet decided whether to allow US and British troops to use its territory for staging an attack on Iraq. The Turkish parliament canceled a vote on the issue of allowing US combat troops in, saying they would wait for an agreement on the aid package. While Turkey had recently authorised US engineers to upgrade Turkish military bases, ruling party leader Recep Tayyip Erdogan said this did not necessarily mean the country would allow the United States to launch an attack from Turkey. US officials, however, said time was running out for a decision on the matter. US military planners had drafted an alternative set of war plans, which did not include the use of Turkish territory, according to the *New York Times*.

With costs for the postwar reconstruction of Iraq expected to add to the cost of conflict, a US spokesman said that the Iraqis themselves would have to pay for most of their country's rebuilding. He also defended the lack of definite plans for postwar Iraq.

The United Kingdom formally presented to the UN Security Council a new draft resolution charging that Iraq was still in violation of its disarmament obligations. The one-page document said nothing about authorising the use of force against Iraq but that was the clear implication of the paper, since the bulk of the draft detailed how Iraq had not cooperated with weapons inspectors. The draft, which was co-sponsored by the United States and Spain, would have the Council declare that Iraq had "failed to take the final opportunity afforded it in Resolution 1441." The draft did not give any deadlines, so passage of the resolution would be enough to trigger the use of force.

At the same time, France was circulating a two-page memorandum calling for reinforced inspections with timelines for Iraq's cooperation. That paper, supported by Germany and Russia, said, "Our priority should be to achieve [disarmament] peacefully through the inspection regime. The military option should only be a last resort. So far, the conditions for using force against Iraq were not fulfilled." Arguing that inspections need more time, the paper added that "they cannot continue indefinitely." The paper said the inspection regime should include more inspectors, mobile inspections units and increased aerial surveillance.

US Secretary of State Colin Powell said that the United States would push for action on a new resolution shortly after UN Monitoring, Verification and Inspection Commission head Hans Blix reported to the Council on 7 March.

Two days after the members of the Security Council received competing proposals on how to deal with Iraq, the uncommitted among the 10 elected members of the Council remained on the fence as diplomats began to search for a compromise, if not a consensus, on the Council's next steps.

In order to be adopted, a Security Council resolution needs nine affirmative votes without a veto from any of the five permanent members of the Council. Besides the three co-sponsors, Bulgaria was the only Council member to publicly back the new draft resolution. France, Russia, China, and Germany supported continuing inspections. Syria was the only country that had said it would not support the UK-US-Spanish draft. The other five elected members of the Council had also said they wanted inspections to continue but had refrained from making definitive positions on the draft resolution.

Spain, since beginning a two-year elected term on the Council in January 2003, had been the most outspoken supporter of the US-UK position.

On the eve of new UN Security Council talks on Iraq, US President George W. Bush said ousting Iraqi President Saddam Hussein could improve the situation in the broader region, including by contributing to a resolution of the Israeli-Palestinian conflict as President Hussein's removal would be followed by the creation of a democratic state, helping to transform the region. He suggested such developments would improve Israeli security, allowing Israel to better support the creation of a viable Palestinian state. President Bush said that he had listened carefully to world leaders who oppose attacking Iraq, but he added, "The threat to peace does not come from those who seek to enforce the just demands of the civilised world; the threat to peace comes from those who flout those demands." He also warned that, unless action was taken against Iraq, the United Nations would be severely weakened as a source of stability and order.

The United States rejected a plan Canada floated in a bid to give inspectors about another month in Iraq and bridge the divide between Security Council members on whether to go to war.

Turkish officials said that the United States had promised to prevent Iraqi Kurds from imposing a federation-style government that would ensure their continued autonomy and agreed to allow Turkish troops to enter northern Iraq and observe the disarmament of Kurdish militias once fighting had ended.

The Security Council resumed closed-door consultations over the draft resolution finding that Iraq had failed to comply with it disarmament obligations.

Hans Blix told Iraq that the al-Samoud 2 missile exceeded the permitted range of 150 kilometres set by the Security Council and thus had to be destroyed. He gave Baghdad a deadline of 1 March to begin complying.

UNMOVIC received a letter from Amer al-Saadi, an adviser to Iraqi President Saddam Hussein, saying that "in principle" Iraq accepted the request for the destruction of the missiles despite its belief that the decision to destroy was unjust and did not take into consideration the scientific facts regarding the issue.

Dr Blix said that if Iraq delivered on its promise to destroy its al-Samoud 2 missiles, it would be a "very significant piece of real disarmament" but he asked for clarification as to what "in principle" meant.

KOSOVO

Expressing concern that a security vacuum could result if NATO reduces troop numbers in the UN-administered Yugoslav province of Kosovo, Serbian Prime Minister Zoran Djindjic asked the military alliance for permission to send 1,000 troops to the province.

Mr Djindjic evoked the possible effects of a war in Iraq on NATO troop numbers and voiced concern that the UN leadership in the province could "hand over certain security duties to local [Kosovo Albanian] structures without consulting authorities in Serbia and Yugoslavia," a move that could "pre-empt [the] final status of the province."

A NATO spokesman said NATO troop numbers would continue to be reduced during year if the security situation remained stable but that NATO had "no requirement nor necessity for forces other than the Kosovo force to operate in Kosovo." The 30,000 troops then employed by KFOR could be reduced to as few as 15,000 by the end of the year as "a result of the improved security in Kosovo."

UN Mission in Kosovo head Michael Steiner said that there was no reason for the United Nations and NATO to change their position; that it was too early for Serbian forces to return to Kosovo.

Several ethnic Albanian leaders accused Mr Djindjic of attempting to divide Kosovo along ethnic lines.

Serbia announced it had put police and army units along its border with Kosovo on alert, citing a warning from the UN Mission in Kosovo that hostile armed elements could attempt to cross the border. An UNMIK spokesman, however, said he was not aware that any such information had been provided to Serbia and nothing suggested militants from Kosovo were planning an attack on Serbia.

Although tensions in Kosovo had dramatically declined, recent calls for independence from Kosovar Albanian legislators and a call for the return of Serbian forces to Kosovo by Serbian Prime Minister Zoran Djindjic had soured relations between Kosovo and Serbia.

KFOR commander Fabio Mini said that conditions in Kosovo did not favour the return of Serbian forces and charged Mr Djindjic's announcement with being more politically than practically motivated.

LIBERIA

Liberian rebels said they were prepared to talk with the government of President Charles Taylor to end the country's three-year civil war following a meeting with legislators from the Economic Community of West African States. Despite more fighting, the Liberians United for Reconciliation and Democracy rebel group had "agreed to commit itself to the peaceful resolution of the crisis within this year," an ECOWAS statement said.

Rebels came within 60 kilometres of the capital, Monrovia, capturing the town of Tubmanburg.

The Liberian government was willing to talk to the rebels but added that the issue of disarmament would probably have to be resolved before negotiations could begin.

Rebels rejected President Taylor's call to participate in elections in October, saying they did not believe the poll would be fair if he remained in power. Mr Taylor, who was under UN sanctions for his alleged support of former rebels in Sierra Leone, said he would not step down in the face of violence.

As a civil war pitting Liberia's armed forces against rebels of the Liberians United for Reconciliation and Democracy intensified, uprooting thousands of people from their homes, some internally displaced Liberians had told authorities that pro-government militias had harassed and attempted to forcibly recruit them.

Liberia Refugees, Repatriation and Resettlement Commission Executive Director Sam Brown told IRIN that he regretted the "illegal actions against IDPs" and was working with state security forces and an interagency working group, including UN agencies, to formulate a strategy to handle the problem. A senior defence ministry official warned government fighters to stop conscripting civilians, threatening to take disciplinary action against those who continued to do so.

Hundreds of Sierra Leonean mercenaries had joined forces with LURD rebels in Liberia. Liberian Justice Minister Lavela Koboi Johnson confirmed the reports but called it "unthinkable" that the mercenaries could be linked to the Sierra Leonean government.

MIDDLE EAST

Palestinian leader Yasser Arafat said that he planned to appoint a prime minister, following the urging of international mediators. Western diplomats said Quartet representatives had asked the Palestinian leader to provide a timetable for the appointment. Mr Arafat said he would convene a meeting of the Palestinian Authority's legislature and central council but did not specify a time for the meeting.

The Belgian Supreme Court decided to allow Belgium's judiciary to hear a war crimes case against Israeli leader Ariel Sharon. Mr Sharon had been accused of allowing Lebanese Christian militiamen allied with Israel to massacre Palestinian refugees at the Sabra and Shatilla refugee camps in 1982. The charges were backed up by an Israeli government finding that Mr Sharon could have prevented the killings, although the Lebanese government had since pardoned the militia members who took part in the slaughter. In response, Israeli Foreign Minister Benjamin Netanyahu berated Belgium's ambassador to Israel for what Netanyahu claimed was an anti-Semitic legal decision and recalled Israel's ambassador to Belgium.

Israel lifted a closure of the Palestinian territories, and Palestinian leaders were now scheduled to travel to London for meetings on the Middle East peace process. The meetings were to involve representatives of the Quartet of outside parties interested in the process: the United Nations, the United States, the European Union and Russia. The Israeli decision to lift the ban followed pressure from the United States.

Eleven Palestinians were killed in Gaza City during fighting between Palestinian gunmen and Israeli infantry, helicopter gunships and tanks.

The death toll was the highest in a single Israeli incursion since a 26 January operation left 12 Palestinians dead in another part of Gaza City. Palestinian hospitals said four of the dead were civilians.

In a separate incursion two Palestinians died in the West Bank town of Nablus as Israel reportedly occupied several buildings in the Casbah and two nearby schools.

The Gaza City raid began in the city's Shajaiyeh section, which was close to the Israeli border and which *Ha'aretz* called a Hamas and Islamic Jihad stronghold. Targets included metal workshops which Israel said produce mortars, rockets and other weapons. *Ha'aretz* reported that Palestinians said most of the workshops had nothing to do with the Palestinian-Israeli conflict.

Ha'aretz published a report alleging that the government of Prime Minister Ariel Sharon was seeking nearly 100 changes to the internationally supported road map which outlined a two-state solution to the Israeli-Palestinian conflict. The proposed changes included demands for a new and different leadership of the Palestinian Authority; an expansion of proposed reforms to the Palestinian Authority; the renouncement of any right of return for Palestinian refugees who fled or were forced out of Israel in 1948; and withdrawing a timetable for implementation of the road map. The proposed changes also put virtually all of the initial demands on the Palestinian side and call for specific security demands to be made on the Palestinians in the first stage of the plan. Other changes include limitations on Palestinian sovereignty, including the complete demilitarisation of the future Palestine; Israeli control of all entrances and exits, as well as total control of air space; and the prohibition of forming alliances with enemies of Israel.

Israeli and Palestinian negotiators lashed out at each other shortly after the conclusion of a three-day peace conference in London. The London negotiations appeared to have yielded little progress in the efforts of the Quartet of parties working on Middle East peace to push for the reform of the Palestinian Authority and for Israel to exercise restraint in its military operations in the occupied territories, the *Times* reported.

Palestinian Minister of Information Yassir Abd Rabbo, the head of the Palestinian delegation, left the talks accusing Israel of attempting to sabotage the peace negotiations and seeking to annex Palestinian land in the historic West Bank city of Bethlehem.

Israeli delegation head Yossi Gal accused the Palestinian Authority of failing to stop terrorist attacks against civilians.

The United Kingdom and other EU countries had been pushing for the road map proposal, which was agreed on in December 2002, to be published. The United States, however, had delayed release of the plan, first citing Israeli elections in January 2003, and then the lack of a coalition government in Israel. The road map proposal called for the establishment of a Palestinian state alongside Israel, but while it had been accepted in principle by all sides, it was viewed suspiciously by the Israeli right.

NORTH KOREA

With US armed forces on alert and senators from both the Republican and Democratic parties questioning the Bush administration's reasoning and tactics regarding North Korea, US Deputy Secretary of State Richard Armitage said that the United States would hold direct talks with Pyongyang, something the North Koreans had been insisting was the only way to resolve the nuclear standoff.

In their attempts to foster a peaceful solution, South Korea and Japan had been pressing for immediate talks between the United States and North Korea. An envoy for South Korean Président-elect Roh Moo-hyun met with US Secretary of State Colin Powell and was to deliver a letter to President George W. Bush. Without divulging the letter's contents, Chyung Dai-chul told reporters that his government wanted direct dialogue between Washington and Pyongyang.

Central to North Korea's demand for direct talks with Washington had been the absence of preconditions. A *New York Times* editorial said the North Koreans wanted to discuss dismantling their nuclear programme in the context of receiving security guarantees and promises of economic aid from the United States, whereas the administration wanted first to address the nuclear issue, then talk about security and aid. North Korea wanted talks to be strictly bilateral, whereas Washington wanted other nations involved.

Mr Armitage did not directly cite preconditions to dialogue, but he said the administration wanted a "multilateral umbrella, of any sort, in a bilateral discussion" and mentioned the desire for international support for handling the issue as a threat to world peace. He also said the North Koreans were demanding a Senate-ratified nonaggression pact as opposed to a written guarantee from President Bush and voiced doubts the Senate would approve such a treaty.

International Atomic Energy Agency head Mohamed ElBaradei told Reuters that the nuclear watchdog agency would most likely refer the North Korea issue to the Security Council when it met to discuss the matter on 12 February. He also said the standoff was not just a bilateral problem between North Korea and the United States, but an international issue.

US aircraft and ships went on notice for possible deployment to the western Pacific.

South Korea opened a road to North Korea across the two countries' militarised border, the first in over 50 years. The road was one of several projects launched at a 2000 summit between the two Koreas.

South Korean Prime Minister Kim Suk-soo indicated in Parliament that although Seoul did not condone Pyongyang's nuclear ambitions, it was reluctant to allow them to interfere with North-South relations.

North Korea announced that it had restarted its long-dormant Yongbyon nuclear plant, prompting criticism from the UN nuclear watchdog agency. Pyongyang's announcement said the reactivated nuclear facility would "for the present stage" be used solely for power generation. But the United States feared that once activated, the complex could produce nuclear weapons within months, and the US State Department responded by calling it a "very serious development."

US Defence Secretary Donald Rumsfeld labeled North Korea a "terrorist regime" and expressed the apprehension within the Bush administration that the North Koreans "could either make additional nuclear weapons for themselves or they can sell the nuclear materials . . . to another country – any country." The United States believed North Korea already had one or two nuclear weapons.

In spite of Pyongyang's insistence that it had refired the Yongbyon nuclear plant for peaceful purposes, US officials dismissed as negligible the amount of power it could produce. The complex housed a building that stored some 8,000 spent fuel rods and a reprocessing laboratory capable of extracting weapons-grade plutonium from the rods.

The International Atomic Energy Agency Board of Governors adopted a resolution declaring North Korea "in noncompliance" with a safeguard agreement under the Nuclear Nonproliferation Treaty that ensures nuclear material wasnot used in military programmes. By a vote of 31-0 with two abstentions (Russia and Cuba), the Board asked IAEA Director General Mohamed ElBaradei to report the decision to the UN Security Council and General Assembly.

North Korea appealed to the United Kingdom to persuade the United States to engage in direct talks with Pyongyang over the matter and threatened to retaliate if attacked.

US intelligence officials said that North Korea had a missile capable of reaching the western United States, although the weapon remained untested.

Following the International Atomic Energy Agency's decision to refer the issue of North Korea's nuclear programme to the UN Security Council, US Undersecretary of State John Bolton said the North Koreans would probably not stop their development of nuclear arms unless China intervened. Secretary of State Colin Powell said that the US government was urging China, a major provider of aid to North Korea, to do more to seek a resolution of the issue.

North Korea responded to the IAEA decision by calling for the Security Council to investigate US use of nuclear arms, adding that North Korea wanted a peaceful solution through negotiations with the United States, but that the US government was trying to solve the issue in a military way.

Japan, which was also a major provider of aid to North Korea, called on Pyongyang to take the IAEA resolution seriously and to immediately resume talks with the agency.

Official transmission of the resolution from the IAEA was expected at UN head-quarters, after which it would go to the Security Council, General Assembly and UN Secretary General Kofi Annan. Ambassador Gunter Pleuger of Germany, the president of the Security Council, said that he would decide when to put the matter on the Council agenda once he received the resolution.

North Korea said that it considered this to be a bilateral issue between itself and the United States and that any sanctions would be an act of war.

North Korea's military threatened to abandon its commitment to the armistice that ended fighting on the Korean Peninsula in 1953. The threat followed reports that the United States was preparing new sanctions to impose on North Korea.

US military planners were exploring ways to use US forces to stop North Korean missile and weapons of mass destruction exports. In December 2002, US-requested Spanish forces detained a North Korean ship carrying Scud missiles to Yemen, but US officials decided they had no legal standing to confiscate the shipment and allowed the delivery.

To prevent a recurrence of that situation, US officials said they would need UN Security Council authorisation to seize such shipments.

Nevertheless, the United States was not expected to request that authority soon, according to the *New York Times*. Instead, the United States would first urge the Council to condemn North Korea's withdrawal from the Nuclear Nonproliferation Treaty and its decision to restart a nuclear reactor at Yongbyon. In addition, Washington would continue to push Russia and China to take a more active role in pressuring North Korea to reverse its nuclear course.

North Korea intended to build four more nuclear plants, with each producing 40 times the power of the five-megawatt reactor that was the focus of international attention. Claiming that "desperate measures" were necessary, North Korean energy director Kim Jae Rok told the *Telegraph* that the new reactors would "enable us to meet the urgent need for electricity supplies in our country."

The Security Council held its first formal meeting on North Korea's nuclear programme since a crisis heightened over the issue in January 2003, when Pyongyang announced it was withdrawing from the Nuclear Nonproliferation Treaty. The Council decided to refer the issue to another group of experts. The International Atomic Energy Agency's Board of Governors found North Korea was in "noncompliance" with the IAEA safeguards agreement and referred the matter to the United Nations.

After a brief closed-door consultation, Ambassador Gunter Pleuger of Germany, (President of the Security Council) said that Council members were taking the IAEA report to their own national experts so that they might draw their substantial and legal conclusions and make their recommendations to the members of the Council. On that basis the Council would take the matter up and discuss it.

The UN Command in South Korea was investigating two possible armistice violations by North Korea.

In one incident, a North Korean MiG fighter entered South Korean airspace and was chased back to North Korea by two South Korean fighter jets. It was the first such incursion by Pyongyang into South Korean airspace in 20 years.

In the second incident one of a six-member Korean People's Army brush-clearing detail accompanied by five KPA guards allegedly crossed the Military Demarcation Line near the joint duty officer.

The command sent an investigation team to Panmunjom, a truce village on the border between North and South Korea.

Five thousand US troops began extensive military exercises near the Korean border to test their readiness to respond to attacks from the North.

US and international officials in Seoul said they were not surprised by a North Korean missile test conducted ahead of the inauguration of South Korean President Roh Moo-hyun. The officials vowed diplomacy would continue despite what some called a carefully timed reminder of Pyongyang's nuclear ambitions.

The test apparently involved North Korea firing a short-range missile as part of a training exercise. The missile reportedly landed somewhere between the Korean Peninsula and Japan.

US officials said that North Korea had restarted its nuclear reactor at Yongbyon, as it had earlier indicated it would do. The White House criticised North Korea over the development.

SERBIA *see* KOSOVO

SIERRA LEONE *see* AL-QAEDA; LIBERIA

SOLOMON ISLANDS

An unknown gunman shot and killed a prominent disarmament negotiator in the Solomon Islands who was attempting to demobilise former guerrillas involved in the country's four-year civil unrest. Fredrick Soaki, who was a member of the National Peace Council and a former police commissioner, was in the Malaita provincial capital of Auki to seek the disbanding of so-called special constables. The special constables were law enforcement officers recruited from the former Malaita Eagle Force and Guadalcanal guerilla groups as part of a peace deal following the country's 2001 elections. The Deputy Police Commissioner said police had no suspects, but "it must have something to do with the demobilisation of the special constables."

International and local mediators had increased efforts to disband the special constable units after a group of them, angry over delinquent salary payments, attacked the home of Prime Minister Allan Kemakeza in December. The UNDP was sponsoring workshops to encourage the special constables to give up their weapons.

SUDAN

The government of Sudan and the rebel Sudanese People's Liberation Army signed a power-sharing agreement, marking a major milestone in efforts to end the country's 20-year civil war. Under the agreement, the SPLA-controlled south would receive an allotment of Cabinet and diplomatic posts, as well as seats in the National Assembly. The accord also called for the drafting and adoption of an interim constitution prior to general elections.

On the economic front, the two parties agreed to work out a system to share petroleum revenues between the government and the people of southern Sudan, where the oil was drilled. The World Bank and International Monetary Fund helped the two sides make progress in the establishment of a petroleum commission and on banking and monetary matters.

Under the accord, brokered by the Intergovernmental Authority on Development, a cease-fire monitoring committee would be established with complete freedom of travel throughout the country.

The two sides plan to resume negotiations the following week and continue at a special IGAD meeting in early March 2003.

WESTERN SAHARA

As 100 Moroccan prisoners of war were repatriated from Western Sahara by the International Committee of the Red Cross, the UN Secretary General called on the Polisario Front to accelerate the release of all such prisoners. He also called on the parties to cooperate with the ICRC to resolve the fate of all those unaccounted for since the beginning of the conflict and with the UN High Commissioner for Refugees to quickly implement confidence-building measures.

According to Morocco, Polisario still held over 1,100 soldiers it captured between 1975, when Morocco took over Western Sahara upon gaining independence from Spain, and the early 1980s.

March 2003

AFGHANISTAN

Following a UN-mediated meeting of northern Afghan leaders in Mazar-e Sharif, three warlords agreed to end tensions in order to facilitate the return of hundreds of thousands of internally displaced Afghans, the UN High Commissioner for Refugees said.

The meeting, which was opened by UNHCR head Ruud Lubbers, brought together rivals Abdul Rashid Dostum of the ethnic Uzbek Jumbesh-e-Milli group,

Mohamed Attah of the ethnic Tajik Jamiat-e-Islami group and Saradar Saeedi of the ethnic Hazara Hizbe Wahdat in the first meeting ever of Afghanistan's Return Commission. Afghan Minister for Refugees and Repatriation Enayatullah Nazeri presided, and representatives of the UN Assistance Mission in Afghanistan and the Afghan Human Rights Commission attended. The meeting, marked the first time the chiefs had come together to discuss ethnic tensions that had led thousands of people to flee the north, particularly ethnic Pashtuns.

Following the meeting, the three tribal leaders agreed to rein in renegade lieutenants and to publicise their agreement.

According to UNHCR, there were nearly 700,000 internally displaced Afghans, most of them driven from their homes by a record drought. UNHCR said it planned to help 1.2 million refugees and 300,000 displaced Afghans return home in 2003 but that the plan could be jeopardised if ethnic conflict continued.

A UN convoy traveling in southeastern Afghanistan was attacked, leading the United Nations to suspend road travel between Wazakhan and Kairkot in Paktika province. No one was injured in the attack.

UN road movements had also been suspended in the northern province of Sar-i Pul owing to clashes between Messrs Dostum's and Attah's forces. According to Agence France-Presse, a pioneering UN disarmament programmeme in the north had been slowed because of renewed conflict between the two rivals.

The International Security Assistance Force was stepping up its presence outside Kabul, the Afghan capital, following a fatal bombing that the force called the first direct attack on one of its patrols since it was created in late 2001. The bombing left an Afghan translator dead and a Dutch peacekeeper slightly injured, ISAF said.

ISAF commander Norbert van Heyst said that Islamic extremists could use a war in Iraq as a "window of opportunity" to foment unrest in Afghanistan, but Loebbering said that ISAF did not see any contact between this attack and a possible war in Iraq nor expect a general deterioration of the security situation in Kabul if and when a war on Iraq should start.

Attackers hijacked a World Food Programme vehicle in Afghanistan's central Wardak province. The occupants were blindfolded and equipment was stolen, but no one was hurt. The attack was the second in March involving WFP vehicles.

Thousands of US and Afghan troops combed caves and searched houses in a second day of sweeps through the Kandahar region in search of Taliban and al-Qaeda forces.

Afghan officials said US forces had arrested 12 people, including members of the Taliban and followers of warlord Gulbuddin Hekmatyar. US military officials denied taking any enemy forces, saying search operations were ongoing.

Focused near the Pakistani border town of Spin Boldak, the latest US effort against renegade forces believed to be operating in the lawless tribal area began just before the opening of US military strikes on Iraq. US officials said the timing was coincidental, denying suggestions that the operation was a show of force meant to deter possible Taliban attacks prompted by fighting in Iraq.

Fearing reprisal attacks against international staff, the United Nations and other organisations closed offices in Afghanistan until further notice as the war in Iraq got underway.

Others in Afghanistan expressed worries that the country's long-term needs might fall by the wayside with all the attention Washington was giving Iraq.

In a report to the Security Council, UN Secretary General Kofi Annan identified security as the single greatest barrier to re-establishment of the rule of law in Afghanistan. Mr Annan's report observed that Afghans viewed some elements of the transitional government as existing to serve one constituency or another and cautioned that groups hostile to the new government and the world at large – a reference to the al-Qaeda network and the defeated Taliban regime – were resurfacing in the war-ravaged countryside. He urged donor countries to remain committed to Afghanistan.

Afghan authorities sent mediators to the northern village of Latti to quell fighting between powerful warlords. Forces loyal to Uzbek General Abdul Rashid Dostum clashed with followers of Tajik General Atta Mohammed on March 16 in the latest of a long string of skirmishes between the two commanders, who agreed to work together after the Taliban government crumbled in 2001.

The mediators were from a regional security commission in Mazar-e-Sharif set up a year previously. The spokesman for the UN mission in Afghanistan said that although fighting had stopped, tensions were running high.

Lieutenant Colonel Michael Shields said US troops in southern Afghanistan had seized the largest weapons cache in months, including hundreds of mortars, rockets and land mines. They also detained four suspects.

With the war in Iraq well underway, the commander of US forces in Afghanistan said he was frustrated by the West's failure to commit to rebuilding Afghanistan and said it could be a good lesson for Iraq.

Lieutenant General Dan McNeill, who oversaw 8,500 US troops in Afghanistan, said the search for al-Qaeda and Taliban members would have been easier if humanitarian aid had been in place immediately following the war. Since then, he said, foreign aid had helped prevent a crisis, but some countries had not delivered on their pledges of subsequent aid.

US-led forces in Afghanistan launched an offensive against bands of Taliban and al-Qaeda fighters thought to be hiding in the northeastern corner of the country. Warplanes attacked sites in the Kohe Safi Mountains, while ground troops moved in to seize two caches of arms that included rockets and mortars in a coordinated strike dubbed Operation Desert Lion. The new operation came two weeks after the start of a similar military effort in the southern part of the country, called Operation Valiant Strike.

In Kandahar, a relief worker with the International Committee of the Red Cross was killed by unidentified gunmen, prompting the organisation to suspend its operations in the country.

UN Assistant Secretary General for Peacekeeping Operations Hedi Annabi told the Security Council that the overall peace process in Afghanistan was in jeopardy because of the country's lawlessness. He said the fledgling US-backed government seated in Kabul had to begin to ensure security outside the capital in order to further development efforts.

US forces were increasingly finding themselves drawn into conflicts between rival warlords who controlled vast swaths of Afghanistan where the central government holds little sway.

A rocket exploded in the headquarters of the international peacekeeping force in Kabul, heightening already-rising tensions in Afghanistan over what one US military official called an "uptick" of Taliban rebel activity.

The rocket attack against the International Security Assistance Force compound, directly across from the US embassy, damaged the grounds but injured no one. A second rocket attack on the outskirts of Kabul failed to do any damage or cause any injuries.

In Kabul, embassies and military installations remained on high alert.

The UN Security Council voted unanimously to extend the UN Assistance Mission in Afghanistan for another 12 months.

The Council said continued and focused reconstruction efforts could contribute significantly to the implementation of the Bonn Agreement, a pact made by Afghan political leaders in 2001 to establish a representative government by 2004. It said donors should work closely with the top UN envoy to Afghanistan, Lakhdar Brahimi, and with the transitional administration headed by President Hamid Karzai.

The Council also called on Afghan parties to cooperate with the mission and to ensure the security and freedom of movement of its staff throughout the country.

Additionally, the Council welcomed a recent report submitted by UN Secretary General Kofi Annan in which he proposed the establishment of an electoral unit within UNAMA, among other recommendations.

AL-QAEDA

US officials said that the arrest of al-Qaeda operations chief Khalid Shaikh Mohammed in Rawalpindi, Pakistan, seriously undercut efforts by the terrorist group to stage attacks and hailed the capture as a breakthrough in counter-terrorism efforts. They also said that intelligence on Mohammed's activities were in part behind recent terror warnings in the United States, where Washington and New York were considered likely targets.

US authorities believed Mr Mohammed was involved in the 1993 attack on the World Trade Center, a failed effort in 1995 to bomb 11 US airliners and, most recently, the bombing of a synagogue in Tunisia that killed 21 people. And at least one other prisoner in US custody had linked Mohammed to the abduction and murder of *Wall Street Journal* correspondent Daniel Pearl, who was killed in Karachi in the early weeks of 2002.

Members of Congress who sat on intelligence committees said Mr Mohammed's capture would probably lead to further al-Qaeda arrests.

The United States obtained new evidence that al-Qaeda had learned how to produce chemical and biological weapons and might have already done so.

The documents, as well as interrogations conducted by the United States, indicate senior al-Qaeda leaders had completed plans for, and obtained the necessary materials to produce, botulinum toxin, salmonella and cyanide. The new evidence also showed that the terrorist group was close to developing a plan to produce anthrax.

Analysts believed that al-Qaeda planned to use the botulinum and salmonella toxins to poison the food supplies of US forces deployed in Afghanistan, which were accessible to locally hired civilians. Although the diseases would not be fatal to healthy people, they could be disabling.

The evidence also reportedly indicated that al-Qaeda was able to recruit a number of competent scientists, including a Pakistani microbiologist. The recovered information described timelines for producing biological and chemical weapons and inventories of equipment.

Much of the new information was gleaned from documents and computer hard drives obtained during the arrest of Khalid Shaikh Mohammed in Pakistan. One significant detail of Mohammed's arrest was that he was captured at a house owned by Abdul Quddoos Khan, a bacteriologist who has access to production materials and facilities and who had disappeared. Because Mr Mohammed was believed to be a senior al-Qaeda operative, his apparent connection to biological and chemical weapons production efforts was taken as an indication that al-Qaeda's weapons of mass destruction efforts were more than hypothetical.

US officials said the new evidence had changed minds about the significance of an abandoned laboratory found in 2002 in the southern Afghan city of Kandahar. At the time, US military leaders played down the find, saying there were only trace amounts of biological agents and some equipment found at the site. Some US analysts now believed, however, that the laboratory was fully equipped and might have even been operating before US troops arrived.

Al-Qaeda was probably able to move its equipment out of the laboratory before it was captured by US troops, an official said.

BOUGAINVILLE

UN Secretary General Kofi Annan said in his latest report on the UN Political Office in Bougainville that the peace process on the island, where a 10-year war for independence from Papua New Guinea ended in 1998, was strong but still needed nurturing.

Reporting to the UN Security Council on progress since November 2002 in Bougainville, where an autonomous government was expected to be elected in 2003, Mr Annan discussed a 2001 peace agreement that provided for autonomy for Bougainville, a referendum and a weapons disposal programme. The Secretary General also addressed an exit strategy for the UN office, whose mandate expired at the end of 2003.

CENTRAL AFRICAN REPUBLIC

Rebel commander General Francois Bozize, who led a coup in the Central African Republic while President Ange-Felix Patasse was in Niger for a meeting of African leaders, suspended the constitution and dismissed the legislature, tightening his hold on the country as thousands of refugees fled to Chad.

In a brief radio address, General Bozize said his forces ousted the government because of the mismanagement of the country and its inability to carry out its domestic responsibilities.

Declared president of the CAR on state radio, General Bozize said he would speedily take steps toward reconstruction of the country, including meeting with officials from the World Bank and International Monetary Fund.

The takeover by General Bozize's forces followed six failed coup attempts in six years in the CAR, one of the world's poorest countries. Three soldiers from the Republic of the Congo who were part of a 300-member African security force policing the capital died in the fighting and military sources said at least eight people were killed during the coup, and dozens were wounded.

President Bozize said in his radio address that the coup was only a temporary suspension of the democratic process and that he would meet as soon as possible with the nation's political parties and other active forces to draft a consensus programme for the country, including the preparation and holding of transparent elections.

He said searches would be carried out to identify looters, who ransacked the homes of government officials and foreign nationals as well as ministries and shops. In an effort to halt the looting he announced a curfew during hours of darkness.

The African Union condemned the coup and said its conflict prevention and resolution body would meet very shortly to consider the situation and the measures to be taken.

In neighbouring Chad, the UN High Commissioner for Refugees was setting up a field office in the border town of Gore, where refugees from the CAR had fled their country's unrest, which began in mid-February. UNHCR officials said that more than 4,000 people crossed into Chad in a week, bringing the total number of refugees in the area to roughly 30,000.

UNHCR officials appealed to Chadian authorities to reign in government troops, who had been accused of harassing refugees. Chadian troops allegedly tried to abduct women from a refugee camp in Gore, then reportedly went on a looting spree in Gore. The military was thereafter ordered to stay out of Gore.

The World Food Programme announced that donors had ignored its $6.1 million appeal for funds for the CAR. No contributions were received.

Looters in the Central African Republic capital of Bangui emptied a World Food Programme warehouse of 1,800 tons of food aid (enough to have fed hungry children in the country for some eight months) following the coup.

At least 50 people died in the unrest. Approximately 100 soldiers from neighbouring Chad flew to Bangui to protect Chadian citizens there, a Chadian government spokesman said, adding that they would join a regional security force of 300 at Bangui's airport. Former President Patasse had previously accused Chad of supporting Mr Bozize.

CONGO, DEMOCRATIC REPUBLIC OF

Rebel fighters inside the DRC accused government soldiers, tribal militias and Ugandan troops of attacking and killing hundreds of civilians in the northeastern corner of the country. Thomas Lubanga, leader of the small rebel faction called Union des Patriots Congolais said the village of Bogoro, near the Ugandan border, came under attack on February 24 and 25. A leader from a rival rebel group put the number of dead at 250, but said the body count was rising.

A UN official in the country confirmed reported of the attack at Bogoro and said the claims of civilian casualties "could be true." But Uganda's defence minister, Amama Mbabazi, said his country had no troops in Bogoro.

However, Mr Lubanga said his men had captured a Ugandan army officer in the same area following an attack by Ugandan troops against UPC forces in Bunia. Mediators from the UN mission to the country managed to free the Ugandan officer and vowed to investigate rebel claims about the Bunia fighting, which left Ugandan forces in control of the town airport after withdrawing from the centre of Bunia.

In recent months, 150,000 people had been forced to flee their homes because of fighting.

Delegates from the DRC adopted a draft interim constitution and agreed on a two-year transition process that would culminate in the first democratic elections in the country in more than 40 years.

All parties also demanded that a UN-authorised neutral force be deployed for a limited period to help guarantee the country's general security and allow an integrated police force to become fully operational. The elections in 2005 would be the first since the country gained independence from Belgium in 1960.

The process remained fragile with talks nearly stalling when major rebel group Rassemblement Congolais pour la Democratie staged a walkout and accused Kinshasa of involvement in fighting between Ugandan soldiers and a small RCD-backed rebel group in the northeast DRC town of Bunia. Each side accused the other of starting the violence in Bunia. UN officials said it was not clear who was responsible.

Humanitarian organisations warned of possible civilian massacres in the area, while a warehouse storing food provided by the World Food Programme and the offices of the UN Office for the Coordination of Humanitarian Affairs were among locations reported to have been looted.

MONUC announced that it would send a mission of inquiry into massacres perpetrated during fierce fighting among rebel groups in Bogoro in the Ituri district once security conditions enabled it to do so.

UN officials traveled to a northeastern corner of the DRC to try to broker a cease-fire between rebels and Ugandan soldiers fighting there. Both sides in Bunia accused each other of sparking clashes that ended with the Ugandan forces overrunning the town.

Meanwhile, the United Nations moved to authorise a new military force to guard the government in Kinshasa. More than 4,300 UN peacekeepers were already on the ground in the country, much of which was controlled by foreign-backed militias. The warring parties agreed to an interim government and to the creation of a neutral force to secure it. The new force would number between 600 and 1,000 troops, but officials offered no details as to where the troops would come from or who would pay.

The UN Security Council had approved a peacekeeping force as large as 8,700 troops but found little backing within the world body for the effort.

Fighters warring in northeastern Democratic Republic of the Congo agreed to a cease-fire aimed at ending years of fighting over the rich mineral resources of the Ituri region. Congolese militias, local chiefs and government forces signed the deal, as well as Ugandan troops, who controlled the area. A Ugandan commander in the region, said all the factions in the area had agreed to the peace deal except a rebel group called the Union des Patriots Congolais, which claimed that recent fighting had killed 45 civilians.

Twenty-two people were hacked to death in tribal clashes in northeastern DRC despite the recent cease-fire agreement meant to end fighting in the area. The victims of the attacks were people from the Hema tribe, who were attacked by a rival ethnic group.

MONUC denied Ugandan claims that it had asked Uganda to keep some of its troops in northeastern DRC.

The UN Security Council condemned violence in the DRC, including sexual violence against women and girls, in a resolution calling for an increased UN presence in the Ituri area. The Council asked UN Secretary General Kofi Annan to strengthen the human rights component of MONUC and to make recommendations to the Council on how to address the issue of impunity in the country.

COTE D'IVOIRE

The head of the Mouvement Populaire Ivoirien du Grand Ouest, one of war-torn Ivory Coast's two main western rebel groups, said that fighting had resumed in the country after government helicopters allegedly killed 20 civilians in an attack on the town of Bin-Houye, near the Liberian border. Felix Doh, who said he had combat planes at his disposal, added that the 3,000 French troops monitoring the country's January cease-fire "must let us pass so that we can march on [Ivorian President Laurent] Gbagbo's positions."

Liberian Defence Minister Daniel Chea said that President Gbagbo's government sponsored an operation in which 100 Liberian mercenaries captured Toe Town, Liberia, in a cross-border attack. Mr Chea called the attack "highly provocative" and "tantamount to a declaration of war" by Ivory Coast. Asked about the possibility of a counterattack, he said anything was possible.

UN Secretary General Kofi Annan said in a report that the rebel Liberians United for Reconciliation and Democracy were supported by military forces outside Liberia and that the continuation of such support could lead to "a generalized humanitarian and economic crisis" that "could engulf the entire West African region."

Mr Annan urged the UN Security Council to support the International Contact Group on Liberia, which he called the best avenue for a quick solution to the country's crisis. The Contact Group called on Liberia and the rebels to "enter immediately and without preconditions into negotiations on a cease-fire, as they have both committed to do," and asked the Security Council to consider authorising a mechanism to monitor such a cease-fire.

The Contact Group also called on Liberia's government to "act rapidly" to create the conditions necessary for free and fair elections and on Mr Annan to consider sending a team to assess the possibility of such a poll.

In an address President Gbagbo rejected reported of government ties to death squads said to be operating in Ivory Coast, the victims of which have allegedly included several opposition members.

In a report, a UN rights mission to Ivory Coast said the death squads might comprise "elements close to the presidential guard and to a tribal militia from the Bete ethnicity of President Laurent Gbagbo." In particular, the mission named Mr Gbagbo's wife, Simone Gbagbo, and the president's former top bodyguard. French President Jacques Chirac had said the death squads were a "reality" and that the affair could end up at the International Criminal Court.

Mr Gbagbo said, "I have not killed anyone; my wife has not killed anyone," adding that those who opposed him were determined to accuse him of something and "now, they have found the death squads." He added that his forces had arrested 38 people and convicted 23 for crimes committed in government-held zones. The assertion follows a report in which Amnesty International said Mr Gbagbo's forces had carried out summary executions but that no suspects had been arrested, despite a requirement in the January 2003 peace deal and in Security Council Resolution 1464 that justice be done in such cases. The President accused the French media of carrying out "ignominious and irresponsible campaigns" against him and threatened to take the newspapers *Le Monde* and *La Croix* to court in France.

The head of Ivory Coast's main rebel group called for UN troops to be deployed to the country in support of a peace agreement reached in January at talks near Paris.

About 3,000 French soldiers were in Ivory Coast supporting the peace deal, but Mouvement Patriotique de Cote d'Ivoire head Guillaume Soro, invoking the Iraq crisis, called for UN peacekeepers to be deployed.

Following resistance from government and opposition figures to including rebels in the new government the new Ivorian Prime Minister Seydou Diarra said that the new government would be announced imminently despite "blockages from all sides." Mr Diarra threatened to leave his new post unless an agreement was reached by the following week. He added that talks with President Gbagbo were "under way" on powers the president was expected to hand over to the prime minister.

Under a proposal floated by Mr Gbagbo, but rejected by the opposition and rebels, the president's own party would retain 11 of 46 posts in the new government and the Defence and Interior ministries would go to figures considered neutral.

The UN High Commissioner for Refugees said that more than 2,500 Ivorians and others had fled a UNHCR camp in Toe Town, Liberia, after fighting between Liberian rebel and government forces broke out in the town. Those who fled the Toe Town camp were fleeing for the second time in months, having initially fled the Ivory Coast conflict for Liberia. Liberia had accused Ivory Coast of sponsoring the Toe Town attack, a charge Ivory Coast had denied. Liberia said that it was in control of the town, but UNHCR said surrounding areas remained volatile.

Ivory Coast rebels dropped demands for key government posts in talks aimed at creating a ruling coalition to end five months of fighting. The rebels offered no immediate word on a possible deal, but they maintained that the Paris peace accord assured them leadership roles in the Ivorian defence and interior ministries.

Meanwhile, the Economic Community of West African States agreed to increase the number of its peacekeepers in Ivory Coast from 1,264 to 3,411.

Parties to Ivory Coast's civil conflict agreed to create a joint 15-member security council and set a deadline for forming both the council and a new coalition government that was agreed to at January talks near Paris. Meanwhile, fighting continued.

All 10 parties to the Paris deal – three rebel groups and seven political parties, including that of President Laurent Gbagbo – were present at the talks. They agreed to create a security council composed of President Gbagbo, Prime Minister Seydou Diarra and representatives from all 10 parties, the army, the paramilitary gendarmerie and the police. The council was to nominate candidates to head the defence and security ministries in the new government, but the final decision would be Mr Gbagbo's. Rebels apparently dropped their demands to be given the two ministries.

Reuters reported that the number of ministers in the new government was unclear but that some sources said it was 39 – seven fewer than Mr Gbagbo had sought but three more than were agreed to at the Paris talks. *Fraternite-Matin*, a Gbagbo-aligned Ivorian newspaper, reported, however, that the government would comprise 41 members and that only the defence and security posts remained unfilled.

The parties also agreed that Mr Gbagbo would delegate more authority to Mr Diarra and that Mr Diarra would lead the government until elections in 2005. Mr Gbagbo was confirmed as head of state and commander in chief, and the parties called for the immediate release of political prisoners and prisoners of war.

Fighting reportedly continued in the country. The French army, which had thousands of peacekeepers on the ground in Ivory Coast under the Paris deal, said that it found corpses and signs of violence targeting civilians in rebel-held Bangolo in western Ivory Coast.

Rebel commander Ousmane Coulibaly said that more than 200 civilians were killed in an attack on Bangolo by government-aligned Liberian mercenaries, and a senior French military source said the figure could be accurate. Rebels said they turned away the attack, but only after the attackers reached the centre of Bangolo and began killing civilians suspected of supporting the rebels. Mr Coulibaly said the victims were mostly foreigners and Ivorians from the mainly Muslim north.

UN special representative to the country Albert Tevoedjre said that fighting in the west appeared contained and would not endanger progress on the political front.

The Alliance des Jeunes Patriotes, a pro-Gbagbo youth group that led street protests in January against the Paris agreement, rejected the deal on the grounds that rebels and the political opposition received portfolios.

ECOWAS reportedly planned to increase its peacekeeping presence in Ivory Coast to 3,400 troops, about the same size as the French contingent.

The Ivory Coast's new power-sharing government opened its first session without any rebel representatives present.

With only 21 of the 41 Cabinet seats filled, President Laurent Gbagbo opened the inaugural meeting of the Council of Ministers, expressing confidence that the meeting marked the country's transition from a state of war despite the spectre of uncertainty raised by the rebels' absence.

An official with the rebel Mouvement Patriotique de la Cote d'Ivoire said the rebels wanted to negotiate on the nominations for key defence and security posts, while the main opposition Rassemblement des Republicains refused to participate because of what it said was poor security.

Prime Minister Seydou Diarra said the rebels were expected to attend the government's next meeting.

The World Food Programme warned of severe food shortages in western Ivory Coast, where it estimated that 600,000 people had been displaced by conflict. A WFP spokeswoman said that the UN agency planned to open an office in the region, which she said was becoming more and more inaccessible to aid workers.

The new power-sharing government met for the second time in as many weeks, despite the continuing and conspicuous absence of rebel nominees to Cabinet posts.

Mouvement Patriotique de Cote d'Ivoire leader Guillaume Soro met with Prime Minister Seydou Diarra in the Ivorian capital of Yamoussoukro after the meeting was over. In the first official visit by rebels to government-held territory since the civil war began, Mr Soro told Mr Diarra his group wanted guarantees of security, an end to fighting near the border with Liberia, and more powers for the premier.

Rebels rejected President Gbagbo's choices of opposition politicians Adou Assoa and Fofona Zemogo as interim defence and security ministers, respectively, in a coalition government comprising rebels, opposition groups and government members that was being formed under a January peace deal. Despite the rebel opposition, Mr Gbagbo held an official ceremony naming Assoa and Zemogo to the posts.

MPCI's spokesman in France acknowledged that MPCI forces might be guilty of atrocities.

CYPRUS

UN-sponsored talks to reunify the divided island of Cyprus collapsed after rival ethnic Greek and ethnic Turkish leaders failed to agree on UN Secretary General Kofi Annan's latest reunification plan, prompting Mr Annan to instruct his special envoy to close his office in the country.

The talks reportedly faltered over the ethnic Turks' insistence that their state win full recognition and over ethnic Greek demands for the right of refugees to return to northern Cyprus.

EAST TIMOR

UN Secretary General Kofi Annan called for a hold in planned cutbacks of UN military forces in East Timor to 2,780 in June 2003 and 1,750 in December 2003, due to a "significant deterioration" in the security environment. He said in a report to the Security Council that "the initial, successful progress that was achieved . . . may have favoured the development of unrealistic expectations."

Citing a rash of recent violence and civil disturbances, including riots in the capital city of Dili in December 2002, the killing of five pro-independence leaders in January 2003 and a bus attack that left two dead, Mr Annan suggested that the level of UN forces be maintained at 3,870 troops until the end 2003. He also said the UN forces had to be reconfigured to deter and react more effectively to civil violence. He added that the capability of the Timorese police had to improve.

UN officials blamed militias loyal to Indonesia for the attacks, which erupted after three years of relative stability. Several skirmishes had taken place on the border of East Timor and the Indonesian-held province of West Timor.

Four suspects in the bus attack appeared in court after being detained by UN peacekeepers. Following a surprise raid in which they apprehended the suspects, the UN forces found considerable military equipment that indicated a level of sophistication among the armed groups.

ETHIOPIA-ERITREA

The Eritrea-Ethiopia Boundary Commission said in its latest report to the UN Security Council that Ethiopia seemed to be intentionally creating border tensions with Eritrea, undermining a peace deal signed by the neighbours in 2000.

The report also indicated the Commission was concerned about the safety of its personnel as they worked to demarcate the border and called on UN peacekeepers to ensure their safety.

The UN Security Council extended until September 15 the mandate of the UN Mission in Ethiopia and Eritrea, which was set up after a 2000 peace deal and whose mandate was modified in August 2002 to focus on assisting the commission that demarcated the disputed border between the countries.

The Council urged the two countries to cooperate with the commission and expressed concern about incursions across the southern boundary of a temporary security zone between the countries.

The commission had recently said Ethiopia was appearing to undermine the boundary panel's decision, which both countries promised to respect as final and binding under their 2000 peace deal. Both countries claimed the commission had awarded them the border town of Badme.

IRAN

There were reports that UN weapons inspectors had found Iran's nuclear programme to be more advanced than was previously thought, with the country nearly capable of enriching uranium at its Natanz nuclear power facility. The site reportedly had hundreds of centrifuges capable of creating enriched uranium that could be used to build nuclear weapons.

US Secretary of State Colin Powell voiced concern at reported of Iranian efforts to create such materials and said the apparent nuclear progress of Iran bolstered the US case for war in Iraq, where, he said, President Saddam Hussein had not lost his intent to pursue nuclear weapons.

Iranian President Mohammed Khatami had vowed to keep the country's nuclear programme in step with the Nuclear Nonproliferation Treaty, saying Tehran would continue to work with the International Atomic Energy Agency.

US officials contended that Iran was pursuing nuclear weapons. US national security adviser Condoleezza Rice said the White House was not surprised by reports of Iranian progress in enriching uranium.

The International Atomic Energy Agency began processing detailed information on Iran's Natanz uranium enrichment facility to better understand its current capabilities and past activities.

News outlets reported that Iran's uranium enrichment capability was much more advanced than previously thought.

IAEA officials also planned to investigate allegations that Iran had another, undeclared uranium enrichment facility.

Tehran had said that it had not enriched uranium during centrifuge testing, but that assertion was most likely untrue, according to the head of the Institute for Science and International Security, a Washington nonproliferation research organisation.

US national security adviser Condoleezza Rice and Secretary of State Colin Powell criticised IAEA efforts to monitor nuclear weapons development in the region. A US State Department spokesman said that Washington had been urging Russia and Pakistan to avoid helping Iran develop its alleged nuclear weapons effort.

Iranian officials said again that Tehran was developing its nuclear facilities for civilian energy needs, but Washington challenged those claims. US officials had said that Iran's extensive gas and oil resources undermine any suggestion of a need to develop domestic nuclear energy. Iran, however, said that nuclear power would allow it to sell more oil and said Washington was souring Tehran's relationship with the IAEA.

Russia, which supported Iran's efforts to develop nuclear power, planned to deliver 80 metric tons of uranium in May 2003 to power Iran's Bushehr nuclear power reactor, which was set to begin operating in the second half of 2004, according to Assadollah Saburi, deputy head of Iran's national atomic agency.

Iranian officials asserted that Iran had the right to develop nuclear weapons to counter Israel.

The International Atomic Energy Agency was reviewing Iran's nuclear capabilities amid US concerns that Iran was using nuclear energy as a cover for development of nuclear weapons, notably at a facility in Natanz that Aghazadeh acknowledged had uranium enrichment capabilities. *Time* reported that IAEA inspectors had found Iran's nuclear programme to be more advanced than was previously thought.

Aghazadeh told *Le Monde* that since "Iran was a signatory of all the treaties forbidding these weapons," the country "does not even have the intention" of seeking nuclear weapons. "It was at the invitation of our government that the International Atomic Energy Agency inspectors came to Iran, in late February – a gesture that shows that we were acting transparently," Aghazadeh said.

Aghazadeh said Iran's planned production of enriched uranium, "under IAEA supervision," could reach five per cent, adding, "To make weapons of mass destruction, we would need more than 90% enriched uranium. That would necessitate other technologies that Iran does not have and was not seeking to obtain. And anyway, it was impossible to make nuclear weapons without anyone finding out." He rejected US suggestions that Iran was violating its IAEA commitments.

Asked why Iran did not at first reveal the existence of the Natanz site and an apparent heavy water production site in Arak, Aghazadeh said that nothing in the Nuclear Nonproliferation Treaty required Iran to do so.

An Iranian opposition group, the National Council of Resistance of Iran, revealed the existence of the Natanz nuclear facility in August 2002. In an interview published in the *Washington Post*, Iranian UN Ambassador Javad Zarif said the Iranian government did not at first disclose its activities at the facility because of concerns that US pressure could lead foreign suppliers of nuclear components to drop out of the project. He added, though, that Iran told the IAEA in June 2002 about the activities, a claim that could not be confirmed by an IAEA spokesman.

Following a visit during which the IAEA found 160 gas centrifuges for enriching uranium at the Natanz plant and amid reported that the number was set to grow rapidly, the IAEA head had urged Iran to sign the Additional Protocol to Iran's safeguards agreement with the agency, which would give inspectors greater latitude. Aghazadeh said Iran had nothing against signing the protocol, under certain conditions i.e. the lifting of sanctions.

Asked about Russian offers to provide Iran with enriched uranium, Aghazadeh said Iran needed another 6,000 megawatts of electricity.

Mr Zarif told the *Post* that Iran would seek to aggressively expand its nuclear energy programme because of fears the United States could persuade suppliers such as Russia, China and Ukraine to stop shipping nuclear components to Iran.

IRAQ

After the Turkish Parliament quashed US hopes of positioning troops in southern Turkey and a fractious Arab League meeting exposed deepening rifts between Gulf states, Iraq stepped up its destruction of al-Samoud 2 missiles and promised a detailed report on the disposal of biological and chemical weapons within a week.

An Iraqi Information Ministry official said that, after crushing 10 of the missiles, Iraq would destroy between a further seven and nine of them. The crushing work, executed with heavy equipment, met the March 1 deadline set by UN Monitoring, Verification and Inspections Commission chief Hans Blix to start eradicating more than 100 al-Samoud 2 missiles, which weapons inspectors said exceed the 93-mile limit imposed by the United Nations. Workers also destroyed two casting chambers used to make engines for a different missile, al-Fatah.

The hastened effort came as UN inspectors returned to al-Aziziya, an abandoned helicopter airfield 60 miles southeast of Baghdad where Iraq said it disposed of chemical and biological weaponry in 1991. Workers had been excavating R-400 bombs that contained anthrax, aflotoxin and botulin toxin and which Iraq said it destroyed. Iraq had promised to deliver a report to the United Nations within a week outlining a proposal for backing up its claims that it destroyed stores of anthrax and the nerve agent VX.

Iraqi President Saddam Hussein's scientific adviser, Lieutenant General Amer al-Saadi, said he hoped the missile destruction would "be to the satisfaction of UNMOVIC" but indicated that if the United States threatened to go to war anyway, Iraq might halt its cooperation. He took the opportunity to argue that disarmament was a cheaper and more sensible option for Americans than war. The White House called Iraq's latest moves "games of deception."

The latest report on Iraq's disarmament from Dr Blix made a harsher evaluation of Iraq's cooperation than had previously been reported. "The results in terms of disarmament have been very limited so far," Dr Blix wrote in the report, which was distributed to Security Council members. While this part of the report bolstered the US position that Iraq would never voluntarily disarm, the document also details areas where Iraq had been cooperating with inspectors, giving something to governments that want to give UNMOVIC more time. The report envisioned a work programmeme that extended beyond the end of March, what was generally viewed as the deadline for the beginning of military action against Iraq. The report was written before Iraq agreed to destroy the al-Samoud 2 missiles, which Dr Blix called "a very significant piece of real disarmament."

Continuing a theme from earlier reports, Dr Blix distinguished between Iraqi cooperation on process and substance. On process, such as providing access to sites, "in general, Iraq had been helpful," he wrote. But on substance, such as providing information on illegal weapons of mass destruction, the report says Iraq had been less forthcoming.

Dr Blix said on most access questions, including use of helicopters and surveillance aircraft, Iraq was cooperating. However, on giving UNMOVIC unrestricted access to scientists, "the reality was that, so far, no persons not nominated by the Iraqi side have been willing to be interviewed without a tape recorder running or an Iraqi witness present."

Another issue was the list Iraq provided of people involved in what Baghdad described as the unilateral destruction of chemical and biological weapons Iraq was known to have at the end of the Gulf War in 1991. A batch of documents Iraq had provided that was supposed to detail that destruction was still being examined.

Although the United States was sending strong signals that it would push for a decision on its draft resolution within weeks, Dr Blix laid out a programme of work in the report that would go on at least until the end of March.

The Turkish Parliament's unexpected rejection of US plans to deploy 62,000 soldiers in the south may have forced Washington to revise its blueprint for war. The United States was relying so heavily on permission to mount a strike against Iraq from neighbouring Turkey that American cargo ships laden with military equipment were waiting off the Turkish shore, and hundreds of army vehicles had already been unloaded in southern Turkey. Yet, with the Turkish populace dead-set against a war, even a $15 billion aid package could not convince a sufficient majority of lawmakers to agree to the deal. Turkish Foreign Minister Yasar Yakis said that his government would ask for another vote, but a high-level member of the governing Justice and Development Party, Eyup Fatsa, said Parliament would not be taking up the matter again in the "foreseeable future."

The president of the United Arab Emirates, Sheik Zayed bin Sultan al-Nahayan, proposed at a special meeting of the Arab League in Egypt that Iraqi President Hussein and his senior lieutenants should have immunity from prosecution if they stepped down within two weeks. Bahrain and Kuwait endorsed the idea, but the UAE's suggestion met an otherwise cool reception from the rest of the 22-member league. Arab League Secretary General Amr Moussa said it was not seriously considered by the body at large. The meeting was riven by another, more dramatic disagreement when Libyan leader Muammar Qadhafi made remarks about US troops on Arab soil that prompted Saudi Crown Prince Abdullah and the entire Saudi delegation to walk out of the meeting. Egyptian President Hosni Mubarak and Syrian leader Bashar Assad convinced the Saudis to return to the meeting, however. In the end, the league issued a broad statement emphasising its disapproval of war and calling on Baghdad to comply with UN demands that it disarm, as well as suggesting that inspectors have more time to search for weapons.

A three-day conference in northern Iraq of US-supported Iraqi opposition groups drew to a close with the delegates having achieved no consensus on who should be on a new opposition leadership committee. Many of the opposition factions were longtime rivals, and the question of leadership in a post-Hussein Iraq had inflamed old hostilities. Delegates were also divided over whether to consider forming a postwar provisional government even though the United States had said it would install a US general to govern in the immediate aftermath of a war.

The London *Observer* reported that it had obtained a memorandum from a senior official at the US National Security Agency ordering staff to monitor the home and office phones and e-mails of UN delegates, especially Security Council members who were undecided on the Iraq question: Angola, Cameroon, Chile, Mexico, Guinea and Pakistan.

According to the *Observer*, the January 31 memorandum from Frank Koza of the "Regional Targets" section of the NSA was circulated to senior agents and a friendly foreign intelligence agency. It sought information on how delegations might vote on a second Iraq resolution and on "alliances," "dependencies" and the "whole gamut of information that could give US policy-makers an edge in obtaining results favourable to US goals or to head off surprises."

After months of declaring it would turn away Iraqi refugees in the event of a war, Jordan had relented and said it would offer them relief and shelter. The United Nations had given Jordan $500,000, plus blankets, tents and other relief equipment sufficient for the needs of up to 10,000 people, but the world body had received only a tenth of the $150 million it needed to handle the 600,000 expected Iraqi refugees. Jordan was planning, but had not begun construction on, two camps near the town of Ruweished, 50 miles from the Iraqi border. One was to host up to 35,000 refugees for at least six months, and the other to serve as a three-day stopover for refugees moving on.

In a meeting with the 10 non-permanent members of the Security Council, Canada's ambassador to the United Nations laid out a graduated plan for assessing Iraq's progress on disarmament that would delay military action until the end of March, but the United States and the United Kingdom dismissed it, signaling that they would instead try to push through a resolution authorising war.

Canada's proposal was more stringent than the one supported by France, Germany and Russia, which would have inspections continue for at least four more months. Ottawa's plan would call on the Security Council to authorise force against Iraq on March 31 if weapons inspectors were still encountering resistance from Baghdad, but if by March 28 inspectors reported "substantial Iraqi compliance," then a stronger inspections system would be installed. Meanwhile, inspectors would report to the Security Council throughout March.

US ambassador to the United Nations John Negroponte said he thought a vote on the US-UK-Spanish resolution – which declared that Iraq had shirked its obligation to disarm – would follow closely after UN Monitoring, Verification and Inspection Commission chief Hans Blix's next report to the Council. US and diplomatic officials said, however, that the United States and United Kingdom were unlikely to press for a vote unless they were certain they would get the nine votes needed on the 15-member Council for the resolution to pass.

UN Secretary General Kofi Annan said that if the United States used force against Iraq, even if its draft resolution was rejected by the Security Council, then support for that action would be diminished.

The United States had called Iraq's recent display of cooperation with UN inspectors "the mother of all distractions" and declared it "insufficient." Iraqi workers destroyed six more al-Samoud 2 missiles, bringing to 16 the number of disposed missiles. Iraq possessed 100 of the banned weapons, plus another 20 in various stages of construction. Iraq announced its intention to crush two or three more al-Samoud 2 missiles, despite the Islamic New Year, a national holiday.

The United States continued its military buildup in the Persian Gulf, issuing deployment orders to another 60,000 troops. That brought the total number of soldiers bound for the region to over 250,000, with 215,000 of them already there.

Turkey's refusal to let the United States stage an attack from the south of the country had, as anticipated, complicated US plans, and could have been delaying an invasion by a week or more. About 40 American transport ships loaded with infantry equipment were idling off the coast of Turkey and might have had to make their way to staging areas in the Gulf, which would entail negotiating the bottleneck of the Suez Canal. Kuwait had said it would consider accepting the troops. The Pentagon was still hoping that the Turkish Parliament would reconsider its decision, but Prime Minister Abdullah Gul had given only lukewarm encouragement.

Iranian Foreign Minister Kamal Kharrazi announced Tehran's proposal for avoiding bloodshed in Iraq – UN-supervised elections that would reconcile the regime of Saddam Hussein with the Iraqi opposition.

A report in the London *Observer* that a top US intelligence official ordered heightened telephone and e-mail surveillance of Security Council members who were undecided about Iraq evoked varied responses, with many diplomats expressing no surprise about the matter. But Chilean Foreign Minister Soledad Alvear confirmed that she had ordered Chilean authorities to investigate the claims. According to Ms Alvear, there was no reason for any spying because Chile's foreign policies were "clear and transparent" and the government would refrain from making any more comments on the charges until they had investigated the allegations thoroughly. She later said Chile was more concerned with the Iraq crisis than with the spying allegations. She also asserted that it was important in the resolution of the crisis that multilateralism takes precedence, especially from the point of view of a small country such as Chile. The United States was refusing to comment on the report.

The UN Economic Commission for Europe warned that the prospect of war in Iraq was intensifying the climate of uncertainty surrounding the short-term economic outlook for Western Europe and North America. Real gross domestic product in the United States was expected to increase by about 2.5% in 2003. For Europe, it was expected to rise by 1.4%.

A UN team had reportedly recommended a central UN role in coordinating the administration of a postwar Iraq. Under the plan, the United Nations would step in about three months after a US-led defeat of Iraq, helping via a UN Assistance Mission in Iraq to set up a new government but avoiding the establishment of a full-blown UN administration, something the United Kingdom had reportedly sought. The authors reportedly recommended that the world body also avoid taking control of Iraqi oil, approving new Iraqi officials and staging elections under US occupation. The plan would further reportedly involve the appointment of a senior UN official – possibly Lakhdar Brahimi, who led Afghanistan's transition to a new government – to head up UN efforts as Secretary General Kofi Annan's special representative for Iraq. UN sources said the plan was likely to be implemented even if the United States attacked Iraq without a new UN Security Council resolution authorising the action.

The *Times* reported that the drafting of the Frechette plan even as the United Nations continued to deal with Iraqi President Saddam Hussein as a legitimate head of state violated a UN taboo and was a potential violation of the UN Charter.

Security Council diplomats and officials in US President George W. Bush's administration said Washington and London were drafting a Council resolution to establish a "day-after framework for UN involvement," the *Financial Times* reported. Sources said the resolution could be put to a vote after a separate vote on a US-British-Spanish resolution to authorise war.

As the Council considered the US-British-Spanish draft and a competing French-German-Russian measure that would bolster and prolong weapons inspections in Iraq, Kofi Annan said that "war was always a human catastrophe, and we should only consider it when all possibilities for peaceful settlement have been exhausted. . . . So let's give the process time." He called on the Council to "work in unity" and on its members to avoid acting outside the UN framework. Mr Annan said support, "popular and otherwise," for "action . . . taken outside Council authority" would "be diminished." The Secretary General added that there was "much more" to be done by UN weapons inspectors in Iraq despite Baghdad's "positive" moves to destroy banned al-Samoud 2 missiles and offer to disclose information about VX nerve gas and anthrax programmes.

News outlets were reporting that the Bush administration was considering dropping its plans to put a new Council resolution to a vote if the measure's defeat appeared likely. The *Philadelphia Inquirer* reported that two senior Bush administration officials had said Washington might not seek a vote on the new resolution and could be ready to attack Iraq as early as late the following week, with or without a new Security Council measure to authorise the attack. France and Russia indicated they could veto the measure.

British Prime Minister Tony Blair met with Russian Foreign Minister Igor Ivanov in a bid to persuade him that Russia should not veto any resolution authorising war. Senior US administration officials cited by the *Washington Post* said Russian officials had assured them Russia will not veto the US-British-Spanish resolution.

Russian UN Ambassador Sergei Lavrov was critical not only of the negotiating attitude of the US and UK but also the arguments they made that inspections were not working. He said the destruction of the al-Samoud 2 missiles defeated the approach that inspections should end. He said Russia's own data did not confirm the US charges against Iraq, including those made by Secretary of State Colin Powell to the Council on February 5. Mr Lavrov said the al-Samoud 2 missiles were misrepresented by the US government as being undeclared by Iraq while in fact the missiles were included in Iraq's December 7 declaration to the Council. He said the Canadian compromise proposal of giving inspectors more time to decide what disarmament tasks were still needed and setting a deadline of late March for Iraq's compliance was "something very close to our own ideas" in terms of setting benchmarks, but that "an artificial deadline was difficult for us."

CNN cited senior administration officials as saying Washington had not ruled out abandoning the new resolution but that if the United States went ahead with the measure, it would act after Dr Blix's next briefing. The United States had not secured the nine votes it would need or ensured against a veto by a permanent council member, CNN reported.

Colin Powell expressed optimism that a new resolution could be agreed to in the Council though, he added that "if necessary, the United States was prepared to lead a coalition of the willing, a coalition of willing nations, either under UN authority or without UN authority, if that turns out to be the case, in order to disarm" Saddam Hussein.

Le Canard Enchaine reported that French President Jacques Chirac had said on February 26 that a veto in the Council would not prevent a war.

Iraqi neighbour and long-time enemy Iran proposed a plan to avert war under which UN-supervised elections would be held in Iraq and the opposition would reconcile with Saddam Hussein. The Kurdistan Democratic Party, which controled a large area in northern Iraq, rejected the proposal.

Four members of the European Parliament who opposed the possible US war against Iraq said at UN headquarters that the key to resolving the crisis was continuing weapons inspections coupled with the easing of sanctions and maintaining military pressure, in addition to negotiating a settlement to the Israeli-Palestinian conflict. The parliamentarians, part of a 31-member delegation that was in Iraq in February 2003, said the United States was wrong to think its troops would be welcomed as liberators.

After meeting with the foreign ministers from Russia and Germany, French Foreign Minister Dominique de Villepin said the three countries would not allow the passage of a proposed resolution that would authorise the use of force. Tang Jiaxuan, foreign minister of permanent Council member China, expressed China's support for the three countries' declaration.

Dr Hans Blix reported that disarmament was proceeding in varying degrees. The destruction of the al-Samoud 2 missiles was "real disarmament," with "weapons that can be used in war" being "destroyed in fairly large quantities." He also welcomed an Iraqi initiative of digging up the R400 gravity bombs to prove they were not hiding the weapons.

Dr Blix said UNMOVIC had carried out seven "interviews completely on our terms," meaning without minders or tape recorders. Nevertheless, he said, inspectors have been getting "interesting results," such as the names of people involved in the alleged destruction of chemical and biological weapons in 1991.

This claim by Iraq that it poured into the ground prohibited weapons after the Gulf War had become a focus of UNMOVIC's work. Iraq admitted to having quantities of agents including anthrax and VX nerve gas, but claimed it destroyed the weapons without international supervision. Dr Blix said the destruction Iraq claimed would be "actual disarmament, if it took place." The Iraqis said it was possible to test the soil in the area to verify their claims. While welcoming these efforts, Dr

Blix said UN "experts were somewhat sceptical" about proving the destruction took place and about measuring the quantities that might have been destroyed.

All the weapons in question were known to exist when inspectors left Iraq at the end of 1998 ahead of a US-British bombing campaign. In a December 7, 2002 declaration to the Security Council, Iraq said it did not produce any biological or chemical weapons during the period inspectors were not in the country. "How do you verify that?" asked Dr Blix. He said UNMOVIC and Iraqi authorities were working on ideas, including closer examinations of facilities that could produce both civilian and military items and road checks around the country to seek mobile biological weapons laboratories the United States says exist.

UN Secretary General Kofi Annan denied reports that a UN team commissioned by Deputy Secretary General Louise Frechette had drawn up a secret postwar plan for the administration of Iraq.

The United States said two Iraqis working for the country's UN Mission in New York had to leave the country, accusing the two of being "engaged in activities out-side the scope of their official function," a usual code for allegations of spying. US officials added that they would ask 60 countries to expel 300 Iraqi diplomats the United States said were undercover agents who threatened US interests worldwide.

In the Security Council, UK Foreign Minister Jack Straw presented amendments to the US-UK-Spain draft resolution on Iraq that would set a deadline "on or before" March 17 for Iraq to disarm or face military action. The original draft, introduced on February 24, would only have the Council decide "that Iraq had failed to take the final opportunity afforded to it" to disarm, implying adoption of the resolution would immediately authorise the use of force. The amendments were immediately rejected by French Foreign Minster, the leading proponent of giving inspectors more time. He called for a heads of state meeting of the Council before a vote on the draft was taken.

The United States and United Kingdom argued that Iraq was not cooperating and thus inspections had run their course. Dr Blix helped that case by saying the cooperation had not been "immediate and unconditional," as called for in Resolution 1441, and that there were many questions regarding the fate of weapons Iraq was known to have at the end of the Gulf War, including anthrax and VX nerve gas, and that it was not known if Iraq resumed weapons programmes after inspectors left at the end of 1998. On the other hand, Dr Blix said UNMOVIC had found no evidence "so far" to back up two of the charges the United States had made against Iraq: that Iraq was developing biological weapons in mobile laboratories and that it was conducting illegal weapons production underground. Dr Blix also told the Council that UNMOVIC had completed a report that contained clusters of issues that would identify "key remaining disarmament tasks" as called for in Resolution 1284, which created UNMOVIC. This cluster list would provide "a more up-to-date review of the outstanding issues" than earlier documents, he said. Each cluster ended with a number of points indicating what Iraq could do to solve the issues. Hence Iraq's cooperation could be measured against the successful resolution of issues.

Mr ElBaradei, executive director of the International Atomic Energy Agency, told the Council, "After three months of intrusive inspections, we have to date found no evidence or plausible indication of the revival of a nuclear weapons programme in Iraq." While not able to completely close the books on Iraq's nuclear program-meme, he said there was "no indication" that Iraq had resumed nuclear activities in buildings identified by national intelligence agencies as conducting such work, or that Iraq had attempted to import uranium since 1990 or that the aluminum tubes Iraq attempted to import were, as the United States had said, useful for producing weapons-grade uranium.

US Secretary of State Colin Powell remained unconvinced that the Iraqi regime had made the fundamental strategic and political decision to comply with the United Nations Security Council resolutions and rid itself of all of its weapons of mass destruction, describing Dr Blix's cluster report as "a category of 12 years of abject failure" by Iraq to disarm.

Advocates of continuing inspections said there was no need to abandon inspections now that they were succeeding and when the alternative, the use of force, was attended by so many uncertainties. Foreign Minister Joschka Fischer of Germany said, "Given the current situation and the ongoing progress, we see no need for a second resolution. Why should we leave the path we have embarked on now that the inspections on the basis of Resolution 1441 were showing viable results?"

The French Foreign Minister told the Council that the lesson learned from the inspections was that Iraq "represents less of a danger to the world than it did in 1991" and "that we can achieve our objective of effectively disarming that country."

US President George W. Bush said, however, that the United States was prepared to go to war against Iraq, with or without UN Security Council approval.

Chinese Foreign Minister Tang Jiaxuan said that permanent Security Council member China supported a joint statement by France, Russia and Germany calling for continued weapons inspections under Resolution 1441. But he stopped short of threatening a veto.

Of the undecided states, Mexico had given the strongest indication of its position so far. Mexican President Vicente Fox was not prepared to change Mexico's determination to see Iraq disarmed peacefully. He also insisted that Mexico and Chile were united on the issue.

Guinea, described in the *New York Times* as torn between its former colonial ruler, France, and its biggest trade partner, the United States, had not taken an official position.

Pakistani Foreign Minister Khursheed Mehmood Kasuri said Islamabad was still undecided.

Iraqi bulldozers crushed another six al-Samoud 2 missiles, bringing to 34 the number of banned rockets destroyed. That represented about a third of the total number of al-Samoud 2 missiles Iraq was thought to possess.

The UN Iraq-Kuwait Observation Mission, which monitored the demilitarised zone between Kuwait and Iraq, observed several breaches of the zone by US Marines, including three cuts in the electric fence erected by Kuwait in one section of the zone. A UN official in Kuwait said the Kuwaitis had opened between 10 and 15 gaps in the fence, some up to 328 yards wide, and that marks had been made for a total of 30 breaks. Military activity was prohibited inside the demilitarised zone. A US military spokesman had no response.

The Iraqi military reported that US and British warplanes bombed targets in the southern "no-fly" zone and killed three civilians. Iraq said air strikes near the southern city of Basra killed six and injured 15. The US military denied the report.

A group of 16 legal scholars from prestigious British and French universities published a letter in the London *Guardian* saying a US- and UK-led war against Iraq without UN support would "seriously undermine the international rule of law."

Jordan was preparing settlements for Iraqi refugees. One of two sites near the town of Ruweishid, which weathered a torrent of 1.5 million refugees during the first Gulf War, would be for Iraqi refugees. The other would be for those refugees from other nations on their way home.

After frenzied diplomacy following UN weapons inspectors' latest report on Iraq to the Security Council, the Council resumed closed-door talks on an amended draft US-UK-Spanish resolution that would have the Council decide that Iraq had not fulfilled its disarmament obligations, therefore paving the way for a US-led attack on Iraq.

UN Secretary General Kofi Annan appealed for Council unity on Iraq and cautioned that military action without Council backing would lack legitimacy.

US Secretary of State Colin Powell said the United States was within "striking distance" of securing the nine votes it needed to pass the resolution. Besides the resolution's sponsors, Bulgaria backed the measure, but it faced clear opposition from France, Russia, China, Germany and Syria. Six of the council's members – Angola, Cameroon, Chile, Guinea, Mexico and Pakistan – had said they were undecided and were being intensely courted by both sides.

Lobbying by Chile reportedly resulted in a concession by the United States and the United Kingdom to lay out in detail the disarmament steps Iraqi President Saddam Hussein had to take to avert an attack.

It was reported that Angola would side with Washington and London as the French Foreign Minister arrived in Angola on the first stop of a diplomatic mission to convince the Security Council's undecided African nations to vote against the resolution and instead press for continued weapons inspections.

Associated Press reported that France was also lobbying for a summit at the Security Council to allow leaders of the 15 member nations to work through the Iraq debate. Colin Powell shot down the idea, which M. de Villepin presented, but French President Jacques Chirac continued to try to muster support for the proposal and had received a positive response, according to his office.

Iraq sent a communique to the United Nations declaring itself sufficiently disarmed to warrant an end to UN-imposed sanctions. It demanded that Israel be stripped of its weapons of mass destruction and withdraw from the Palestinian territories.

Iraq demolished six more al-Samoud 2 missiles and 11 additional warheads, bringing to 46 the number of banned missiles it had destroyed since March 1. The UN had supervised the demolition of 16 warheads, one launcher and five engines so far.

It was reported that the United States and United Kingdom were to demand that Dr Blix give details about a large undeclared, unmanned Iraqi aircraft whose existence was revealed in a document circulated by UN weapons inspectors after his briefing. The drone, which had a wingspan of 7.45 meters, would be the first undeclared weapon found by inspectors. British and US officials considered it a "smoking gun."

Sources inside UN Secretary General Kofi Annan's office confirmed that the United Nations would investigate allegations of US National Security Agency spying on UN delegates from Angola, Cameroon, Chile, Bulgaria, Guinea and Pakistan.

The United States and the United Kingdom accused Dr Blix of withholding evidence on the drones in his report and demanded that he attend a Security Council meeting. Dr Blix agreed that the drone was undeclared but that it was not necessarily a "smoking gun" because its actual capability might not exceed UN specifications.

France and Russia again threatened to use their veto power on the Council to reject the resolution. Chinese President Jiang Zemin insisted that UN inspections in Iraq continue and that the issue be resolved by peaceful means. It was not clear whether he spoke of a possible veto.

Commitments from the council's six swing votes remained elusive to both camps. French Foreign Minister Dominique de Villepin's whirlwind tour of undecided Security Council member nations Angola, Cameroon and Guinea mirrored that of British Minister for Africa Baroness Amos, but the flurry of shuttle diplomacy yielded no obvious results for either side. As beneficiaries of US aid, all three countries were viewed as eager not to offend Washington, though Guinea and Cameroon, former French colonies, had close ties to Paris, and Angola had professed its concern about the aftermath of a war on Iraq.

Chilean Foreign Minister Soledad Alvear Valenzuela signaled Chile's reluctance to sign on to the US-UK-Spanish resolution but stopped short of ruling it out altogether. Pressure from Chile reportedly contributed to the United Kingdom's consideration of a slightly amended resolution that would outline specific steps for Iraq to take to avoid war.

Pakistan, which had privately indicated its support for the new resolution but had not committed to it, gave a different signal when Prime Minister Mir Zafarullah Khan Jamali said his government could not become a party to the destruction of Iraq and did not want to see any harm done to the Iraqi people.

UN Secretary General Kofi Annan called weapons of mass destruction a "threat posed to all humanity" that must be curbed. But he also cautioned against unilateral action, not just because of its deleterious effects on the United Nations but because it did not work for the nations that practice it.

Iraqi bulldozers crushed six more al-Samoud 2 missiles, bringing to a total of 52 of the 100 missiles it was believed to possess having been destroyed.

The United Nations announced plans to evacuate 155 non-essential military staff and 155 civilian employees from the UN-monitored demilitarised zone between Iraq and Kuwait. The UNIKOM mission consisted of 775 Bangladeshi soldiers and 195 military observers and existed to observe rather than defend the zone.

UNICEF was delivering 1,000 metric tons of high-protein biscuits to over 400,000 malnourished Iraqi children who were at high risk of not surviving a conflict. The biscuits contain protein, calories and micronutrients and can be easily transported and eaten without preparation. UNICEF had also delivered 155 metric tons of therapeutic milk, which was being distributed from 63 centres throughout Iraq and administered by the government. These were the first shipments of high-protein biscuits and therapeutic milk to Iraq in two years. They should have lasted a month.

As 28 non-members of the Security Council spoke in an open Council session about the disarmament of Iraq, April 17 was floated as a possible new deadline for Iraq to disarm, a month more than the date the United Kingdom and United States had specified as a deadline for Baghdad to face military action.

Non-permanent Security Council members Angola, Cameroon, Chile, Guinea, Mexico and Pakistan had still not publicly declared their stands on the US-UK-Spanish draft resolution declaring Iraq in violation of its obligations to the United Nations on disarmament, or the idea to allow more time for inspections, as championed by France and Germany.

In an attempt to strike a compromise, Canadian Ambassador Paul Heinbecker detailed his government's compromise proposal. Although the Canadian proposal for a compromise deadline for Iraq had been in circulation for several weeks, this was the first time a Canadian official had publicly spelled out the plan. Mr Heinbecker said that while cooperation by Iraq "must be immediate and proactive, disarmament and verification cannot be instantaneous." Therefore the Council should ask Dr Blix "to bring forward the programme of work urgently, within a week" and then establish "the priorities among those tasks," especially concerning the stocks of anthrax, VX gas and chemical weapons shells. In addition, he said, the Council should set a deadline of three weeks "for Iraq to demonstrate conclusively that it was implementing these tasks." At the same time, the Council "should consider authorising members states now to eventually use all necessary means to force compliance," he said – in other words, authorise the use of force, but not immediately. If after three weeks, Iraq were complying, the Council would set a further deadline and continue the process until Iraq was disarmed and an on-going monitoring system to ensure compliance was in place.

The last time a Council debate on Iraq had been opened to non-members of the Council was February 18-19. Little had apparently changed, with the vast majority of speakers opposing any rush to war, but also criticising Iraq's failure to fully cooperate with the weapons inspectors.

Australia was once again the strongest ally of the United States and United Kingdom in the debate.

Iraqi Ambassador Mohammed al-Douri defended his government's cooperation and said the charges made by the United States and United Kingdom "could not stand up to the facts. . . . None of the allegations have proven to be true." He said the drone aircraft recently discovered by the UN Monitoring, Verification and Inspection Commission was "a small experimental primitive aircraft" which was "radio-controlled and within the sight range of the ground controller" and did not exceed eight kilometres. "Hence it was not a weapon of mass destruction," Mr al-Douri said.

Associated Press reported that the drone seemed to be made of balsa wood and duct tape, and that an Iraqi official said it could not be controlled for more than five miles – far short of the UN-mandated 150-kilometre limit. The official said the drone was used for reconnaissance and aerial photography.

British ambassador to the United Nations Jeremy Greenstock continued his quest for Security Council backing for a second resolution. Diplomats said the British delegation wanted to delay the March 17 deadline until March 21 or 24 and was pushing for inclusion of about a dozen benchmarks for disarmament compliance, including an accounting of stores of anthrax, VX, chemical weapons munitions and missile systems. At the top of the list would be interviews outside the country with Iraqi weapons scientists. Mr Greenstock shied away from trying to push the date beyond March. As British diplomats shuttled between the camps, one of the main disagreements was over whether Baghdad's failure to meet the deadline should prompt an automatic attack. War was an unpopular option in the United Kingdom, with only 19% of the public supporting war without a UN resolution and members of Prime Minister Tony Blair's party and Cabinet issuing challenges and threats in the event of war.

The United States was pressing for an early vote. Some undecided members of the Security Council were giving signs they might support a resolution if the deadline were pushed back by 10 days or so.

Senior Pakistani officials said that amid strong domestic anti-war sentiment, Islamabad had decided to abstain from a Security Council vote authorising war against Iraq, but Prime Minister Zafarullah Khan Jamali stopped short of declaring a policy of abstention.

The Pentagon said planes were dropping hundreds of thousands of leaflets over Iraq to convince Iraqi soldiers that resistance was futile.

There were now 225,000 American, British and Australian troops in the Gulf region.

In the meantime, Iraqi media reported that Saddam Hussein was sending Republican Guard officers to key locations where troop morale might be low. The eight Republican Guard divisions – 80,000 troops – had encircled Baghdad, and the 25,000-member Special Republican Guard was fortifying government buildings and presidential palaces.

Kurdish civilians fleeing the northern city of Kirkuk said the wellheads of the north's richest oilfields had been mined, apparently as part of a defensive strategy to virtually set the region on fire in the case of US attack.

A Council on Foreign Relations-convened task force issued a report, *Iraq: The Day After*, speculating that reconstruction could cost $20 billion per year for several years and require 75,000 to 200,000 troops or more to keep the peace. The panel urged American leaders to clearly outline a political and financial commitment to reconstruction, ensure that Iraqi civilians would be safe and adequately cared for, involve international organisations in the reconstruction process so as to share the cost, and make certain the Iraqi people were closely involved in reconstruction efforts. It also endorsed a geographically based federal system of government. The task force's stress on the need for a long-term financial and logistical commitment to rebuilding Iraq echoed what was said regarding Afghanistan before, during and after the US attack on that country in 2001.

In a glimpse of the most extensive blueprint for reconstruction seen to date, senior defence officials said the United States would bankroll employment for as many Iraqi civil servants and military troops as possible for a few months – until the United Nations or another international organisation could take over administration – but did not say where the money would come from or how much it would cost. The goal would be to avoid the instability that comes along with high unemployment rates. The Council on Foreign Relations report did not include this cost in its estimate of $20 billion per year, nor did it include payment for food if the UN oil-for-food pipeline broke down.

Regular Iraqi soldiers – as opposed to Republican Guard members, viewed as loyal to Hussein – would be utilised by US forces to help build roads and bridges and engage in other rebuilding projects. Bureaucrats would run ministries providing humanitarian assistance.

Additionally, the Pentagon's reconstruction office had begun recruiting about 100 Iraqi expatriates to serve as liaisons and help with the transition to a new government, the *Wall Street Journal* reported. Two retired US generals, including the new Pentagon postwar planning office chief Jay Garner and former US Ambassador Barbara Bodine, would run the immediate postwar effort, answering to General Tommy Franks, who would lead any US strike against Iraq.

Expecting at least 600,000 Iraqis to flee the country, mostly toward Iran and Turkey but with some probably heading to Jordan and Syria, the UN High Commissioner for Refugees was in talks with Saudi Arabia and Kuwait, which have said they would not accept Iraqi refugees. Both countries had said they would provide financial assistance to Iran to deal with the influx.

The agency asked governments not to send rejected Iraqi asylum seekers back home against their will. In 2002 more than 51,000 Iraqis World-wide had claimed asylum.

Washington said it would consider delaying for a week a Security Council vote on a resolution it proposed late in February 2003 with the United Kingdom and Spain, which would declare Iraq in violation of its obligations on disarmament and by implication authorise war.

A senior White House official said the president thought a few extra days might help British Prime Minister Tony Blair, who faced stiff domestic opposition to war. Mean while, British ambassadors further massaged the resolution in an attempt to reach consensus on the Security Council, and France reiterated its opposition to the measure.

The United Kingdom proposed six tests for Iraqi President Saddam Hussein to meet in order to avoid war:

1. a statement, broadcast in Arabic, declaring his intent to give up weapons of mass destruction immediately;
2. permission for at least 30 Iraqi scientists to go abroad with their families to be interviewed;
3. the surrender of all biological or chemical weapons, or an explanation of their destruction;
4. an explanation about a recently discovered unmanned aircraft and information about any others;
5. a commitment to destroy mobile laboratories; and
6. a commitment to destroy prohibited missiles.

The United States and Spain, which co-sponsored the resolution with the United Kingdom, did not co-sponsor the six tests.

In an effort to appeal to undecided Security Council members, the British delegation offered to alter the March 17 disarmament deadline if the members would accept the list of disarmament benchmarks, saying Hussein could possibly have 10 days to complete the tasks. But US ambassador to the United Nations John Negroponte said the United States would accept only a "very, very, very brief extension" of the deadline. Diplomats said Washington was considering a March 21 or March 24 deadline.

Consultations at which the United Kingdom presented what it called its proposal ended with Council members as divided as ever. Before the closed-door session began, US officials would not say if they would support the British plan.

In an obvious effort to help in finding a compromise, Kofi Annan requested one-on-one meetings with ambassadors from 13 of the 15 Council members, having met with Russia and the United Kingdom.

US and British sources made conflicting predictions about whether they had enough votes to pass a resolution. The US State Department said it had secured the support of four of the six undecided votes – Angola, Cameroon, Guinea and Pakistan. Along with yes votes from Bulgaria, Spain, the United Kingdom and the United States, that would total eight – one vote shy of the nine votes needed to pass the resolution. The State Department added that it was optimistic about securing votes from Mexico, Chile or both.

But the British Foreign Office said there was no sign of compliance from Mexico or Chile and that none of the other countries had signed on either. The Chilean newspaper *El Mercurio* reported that despite telephone calls between Chilean President Ricardo Lagos and US President George W. Bush, Chile remained undecided. The *Chicago Tribune* reported that Pakistan was keeping its options open.

Tony Blair said he thought passage of a resolution was "now probably less likely than at any time," a situation which British opposition Tory leader Iain Duncan Smith blamed on a "completely intransigent" France, which had threatened to veto "almost anything that was put forward to the UN Security Council." Mr Smith said French resistance would make military action more likely.

French Foreign Minister Dominique de Villepin said of the United Kingdom's benchmarks proposal, "It's not a question of giving Iraq a few more days before committing to the use of force. It's about making resolute progress towards peaceful disarmament, as mapped out by (UN weapons) inspections that offer a credible alternative to war."

Meanwhile, UN Monitoring, Verification and Inspections Commission chairman Hans Blix reportedly told UN officials in a closed-door meeting that "we could give a report after 10 days but certainly not in two days."

French ambassador to the United States Jean-David Levitte told reporters that although France might not support military action in Iraq, it considered participation in reconstruction to be "a moral duty" and would help foot a "huge" bill to do the job. Likewise, Boris Nemtsov of the Union of Right Forces party in the Russian parliament told the *Washington Times* that despite its reservations about war, Russia would eagerly participate in reconstruction. The European Union, however, said it might not contribute freely to a reconstruction effort following a war without UN approval.

The UN Iraq-Kuwait Observation Mission said it was pulling nonessential staff from their posts and relocating them to Kuwait City. Some of the UN military observers in remote regions on both sides of the demilitarised zone between Iraq and Kuwait had been relocated to headquarters.

UNICEF had started creating a programme to help distressed Iraqi children and adolescents who might become stranded in border camps. The programme was to offer schooling, recreation activities and psychological support.

US Secretary of State Colin Powell told Congress that the United States might abandon altogether a resolution in the UN Security Council authorising war against Iraq, even as the United States, United Kingdom and Spain agreed to hold an emergency summit aimed at salvaging the battered second resolution. Mr Powell's comments ran directly counter to US President George W. Bush's declaration that "no matter what the whip count is, we're going for a vote." After several days of dispute within the administration, the *New York Times* reported, Mr Powell argued that the political cost of going to war without a UN vote would be less than the cost of going to war in defiance of a vote against military action.

Meanwhile, with no signs of consensus emerging in the Security Council, the United States sped up war preparations in the Persian Gulf in a signal that Washington was prepared to go it alone.

A last-ditch effort by British diplomats to win support for a modified resolution that would ease the disarmament deadline by a few days and set forth six specific tasks for Iraq to fulfill or face military attack failed to win the support of any members of the Security Council. German and Russian officials reiterated their opposition to using force against Baghdad.

White House officials said President Bush was still making calls in an attempt to sway the six undecided nations on the council, but the support of the three African nations – Angola, Cameroon and Guinea – was described as weak, and Mexico and Chile still refused to commit to voting for the resolution or against it.

The US military continued its buildup in the Gulf in preparation for a massive and overwhelming first strike on Iraq meant to encourage a hasty surrender. The first wave of B-2 stealth bombers left for the Persian Gulf and the British island of Diego Garcia. About a dozen Navy cruisers, destroyers and submarines armed with satellite-guided, 1,000-mile-range Tomahawk missiles left the Mediterranean bound for the Red Sea, from where they could conceivably shoot hundreds of missiles across Saudi Arabia into Iraq. Two aircraft carriers currently in the Mediterranean will probably stay there and send warplanes over Israel and Jordan.

Iraq was scheduled to deliver a detailed report to the United Nations chronicling its destruction of 3.9 tons of the deadly nerve agent VX. A report explaining how it disposed of at least 2,245 gallons of anthrax was to follow in the following few days. Iraq said it produced 8,500 liters of anthrax and 3.9 tons of VX, but weapons inspectors estimated it could have produced almost three times that amount of anthrax.

UN weapons inspectors supervised the destruction of four banned Iraqi al-Samoud 2 missiles, bringing to 65 – more than half the estimated total – the number destroyed since the March 1 deadline set for starting the process, the United Nations announced.

A classified report by the US State Department challenged the assumption that installing a new regime in Iraq would begin a chain reaction in the Middle East that spread democracy. An intelligence official said the document's gist was "that this idea that you're going to transform the Middle East and fundamentally alter its trajectory was not credible." The report, *Iraq, the Middle East and Change: No Dominoes*, dated February 26, was distributed to top officials and appeared to highlight deep divisions within the Bush administration over the success of spreading democracy through forcible regime change. The report stated that "Liberal democracy would be difficult to achieve." It also speculated that "Electoral democracy, were it to emerge, could well be subject to exploitation by anti-American elements."

The UN Compensation Commission approved payments totaling more than $223 million for victims of Iraq's 1990 invasion of Kuwait. To date, the commission had awarded compensation of approximately $44 billion, of which $16.7 billion had been made available to governments and international organisations for distribution to claimants.

UN aid workers were to visit Larnaca, Cyprus, to make sure a humanitarian centre was sufficiently operational to serve as headquarters for Iraqi aid coordination, should officials need to relocate from Iraq.

The United States, the United Kingdom and Spain took a major step toward launching war against Iraq, saying they would no longer seek a vote on their faltering resolution at the Security Council and declaring that they reserved the right to take their own steps to secure the disarmament of Iraq.

French President Jacques Chirac said that Paris would "naturally go to the end" with its refusal to back an Iraq war. He proposed giving Iraqi President Saddam Hussein 30 more days to comply with UN disarmament resolutions, an offer US Vice President Dick Cheney dismissed as "further delaying tactics."

A couple of hours after the US-British-Spanish announcement, UN Secretary General Kofi Annan announced that he was withdrawing UN weapons inspectors and aid workers from Iraq. IAEA head Mr ElBaradei said that Washington had advised him to pull out inspectors from Baghdad. UN officials said the inspectors and support staff could be evacuated from Iraq in as little as 48 hours. The IAEA said it would wait for Security Council advice before deciding whether to pull out. UN Monitoring, Verification and Inspection Commission Executive Chairman Hans Blix said UNMOVIC inspectors would continue their work in Iraq "unless we call them back."

Most of the inspectors' helicopters had already left Iraq after their insurance was canceled.

UN Iraq-Kuwait Observer Mission employees began pulling out of the Iraqi-Kuwaiti border zone after their alert status was increased to level 4, which entails ceasing all operations.

German Ambassador Gunter Pleuger said his country, France and Russia, which had tried to block the US-British-Spanish move toward war on Iraq, shared the goal of the international community to disarm Iraq and did not see a need to halt weapons inspections that he said were showing signs of succeeding. He said the three countries were trying to make a "last-ditch effort" to avoid war.

Meanwhile, Saddam Hussein said that Iraq previously had weapons of mass destruction for defensive purposes but no longer had any.

The *Wall Street Journal* reported that a US plan to rebuild Iraq, according to confidential documents, would leave UN agencies and other multilateral bodies on the sidelines.

US administration officials and members of Congress cited in the *Washington Post* said US intelligence agencies had been unable to give legislators or the Defence Department specific information about the amounts of banned weapons Iraq might have or where the weapons might be hidden. One official cited a "lack of hard facts," while another said the administration has offered "only circumstantial evidence."

Twelve hours after abandoning efforts to usher a second resolution through a deeply divided Security Council, US President George W. Bush made good on prior threats to go it alone by issuing Iraqi President Saddam Hussein an ultimatum to leave the country with his sons within 48 hours or face war against the United States and a few allies.

Shortly thereafter, the United Nations evacuated its weapons inspectors in Iraq, and world leaders offered reactions ranging from staunchly supportive to deeply disapproving.

Mr Bush gave no date or time for an initial attack by the 250,000 troops amassed in the Persian Gulf. The *New York Times* reported that US officials had made it clear the allied forces, consisting of 225,000 US troops and 25,000 British troops, would invade Iraq whether or not Hussein leaves.

Mr Bush assured Iraqis that soldiers would be prosecuted for war crimes and civilians were not the targets of US artillery but the beneficiaries of a war of liberation.

Saddam Hussein responded with a rare appearance on state television in uniform at a meeting of his Cabinet. "The meeting stressed that Iraq and all its sons were fully ready to confront the invading aggressors and repel them," a television announcer said, reading a Cabinet statement.

World leaders who had previously opposed military action were unswayed. French President Jacques Chirac, who had borne the brunt of US anger toward the Security Council for leading an effort to continue weapons inspections, said that there was no justification for a unilateral decision in favour of war against Iraq at this time, even though France acknowledged the necessity of disarmament and the desirability of regime change.

German Chancellor Gerhard Schroeder asked, "Does the threat posed by the Iraqi dictator justify a war, which is sure to kill thousands of innocent children, women and men? My answer in this case is: No."

China's new prime minister, Wen Jiabao, said that "as long as there is one glimmer of hope, we will not give up our efforts for a peaceful settlement."

Mexican President Vicente Fox, whose government was one of six nations on the Security Council that never committed to a position on a divisive resolution sponsored by the United States, United Kingdom and Spain, said "the diplomatic means to achieving (the goal) have not been exhausted."

A spokesman for the Indian government noted that New Delhi's support had been for "the supremacy of multilateralism."

Indonesia, the world's most populous Muslim nation, expressed disappointment in Mr Bush's ultimatum and cast its support for a Security Council-backed solution as well.

Russian President Vladimir Putin condemned military action against Iraq as a potentially grave risk to international security.

An Arab League spokesman said that "the Arab League cannot accept such a final warning." He added, "We regret the US decision to act outside the UN Security Council and outside international legality."

Archbishop Renato Raffaele Martino of the Pontifical Council for Justice and Peace denounced the United States' intent to disarm Iraq by force.

In the United Kingdom, the political fallout for Prime Minister Tony Blair over his support for Washington began with the resignation of Robin Cook, a Cabinet minister and former foreign minister, and continued with the resignations of Lord Hunt, a junior health minister, and John Denham, a Home Office minister. Clare Short, the secretary for international development who threatened to quit if the United Kingdom went to war without Security Council approval, announced that she would stay on.

Domestic opposition within the United States was evident,

President Bush received some support from the international community. Japanese Prime Minister Junichiro Koizumi said, "It was a decision that had to be made. We support the US position." Australian Prime Minister John Howard committed 2,000 troops to a US-led attack, saying he believed "very strongly the position the government has taken is right." South Korea also backed the US president and offered to send 500 military engineers to aid the combat effort, although it ruled out dispatching troops.

Diplomats from Germany, the Czech Republic, India, China, Bahrain and the United Kingdom were leaving Iraq and Kuwait. The United States had already ordered nonessential staff out of Kuwait, Syria, Israel, the West Bank and the Gaza Strip, adding Lebanon to the list. Foreign journalists, including crews from ABC, NBC and China's Xinhua News Agency, were leaving Baghdad.

As Kofi Annan was ordering weapons inspectors and other UN staff to leave Iraq, UN Monitoring, Verification and Inspection Commission chief Hans Blix distributed to the Security Council his long-awaited report on Iraq's "key remaining disarmament tasks." The report, mandated by Resolution 1284, listed the tasks under 12 headings, most of them dealing with fate of chemical and biological weapons agents Iraq was known to have before inspectors first left at the end of 1998. Iraq maintained that these agents had been destroyed but UNMOVIC was demanding proof of this.

Dr Blix's proposed programme of work would require Iraq to "present any remaining quantities" of anthrax, botulinum toxin, mustard gas, VX, sarin, binary agents or "credible evidence" that these agents have destroyed or spoiled. Iraq would also be required to "present any remaining chemical and/or biological munitions, including aerial bombs, rockets or missile warheads, artillery shells, cluster munitions and fragmentation rounds."

The report sought that Iraq should account for its research into producing Scuds and other long-range missiles, its import of missile fuel and to "explain with credible evidence which missile systems, and their specifications, it intended to be tested" at a major test site. UNMOVIC also wanted Iraq to explain the purposes of various programmes for the production of unmanned drones. Echoing an earlier statement to the Council, Dr Blix wrote that the time needed to complete this programme of work was "months rather than weeks or years," assuming "a proactive Iraqi cooperation."

Germany and France had suggested the Council meet at the ministerial level to receive the new report. Foreign ministers from at least six countries, including France, Russia and Germany but not the United States, were planning to attend.

Fearing ethnic cleansing by Iraqi troops, thousands of Kurds began fleeing the northern Iraqi city of Kirkuk for the border of the Kurdish autonomous region.

Officials at the border crossing of Cham Chamal said 1,300 refugees had arrived in two days. Refugees told reporters that Iraqi security police had started arresting Kurdish men and taking them to Baath Party headquarters. They also said they feared conventional and chemical attack from Hussein's troops.

In Baghdad, the city's 4.5 million residents reportedly had little outside information about US plans to invade. Nonetheless they formed long lines at gas stations and stocked up on water, fuel and food. The 350-mile road to Jordan was said to be busier than usual.

The London *Guardian* reported that the United States planned to rebuild Iraq's infrastructure within a year of a war's end and would pay US companies $1.5 billion to do the job, while the United Nations and nongovernmental organisations would receive just $50 million for their role in reconstruction. Documents obtained by the *Wall Street Journal* outlined the plan, according to the British newspaper. Typically the UN Development Programme coordinates postwar rebuilding efforts. The UNDP had estimated that reconstruction would cost $10 billion a year for at least three years. By contrast, the US administration was reportedly going to ask Congress for a total of $1.8 billion for reconstruction in the first year and $800 million for humanitarian assistance. US administration officials said it was important to give contracts to US corporations in order to show the Iraqi people that the United States was a "liberator" bringing good things to their nation.

Just hours before the US deadline for Iraqi President Saddam Hussein to leave his country or face war, US and British forces in Kuwait loaded ammunition and gear into combat vehicles, broke camp and began moving toward the Iraqi border. More than 1,000 warplanes and 300,000 troops were reportedly poised to attack Iraq.

Spain, which had joined the United States and the United Kingdom in seeking UN Security Council authorisation for an attack on Iraq, said that it would not provide troops for the US effort. Among countries that would, the London *Guardian* named the United Kingdom, Australia, Poland, Albania and Romania.

France, a leading opponent of an Iraq war, suggested it could provide personnel for the effort if Iraq resorted to the use of weapons of mass destruction.

The Iraqi National Assembly convened in an extraordinary session, expressing support for Saddam Hussein following his rejection of US calls for him to leave Iraq. Iraqi Ambassador al-Douri also dismissed the US ultimatum.

The British House of Commons rejected a motion to oppose an Iraq war, but 135 members of Prime Minister Tony Blair's Labor Party voted for the measure. The body subsequently voted to back the use of "all means necessary" to disarm Iraq.

The United States and the United Kingdom were planning to channel tens of billions of dollars in Iraqi oil proceeds through a UN oil-for-food programme account to pay for humanitarian aid during an Iraq war. Officials from the two countries had been working for two months on plans for a new Iraqi administration and for humanitarian aid. Washington and London were said to be planning a three-stage transfer from US-British military rule to a civilian government that could involve a self-selected Iraqi council.

The UN Office for the Coordination of Humanitarian Affairs said UN aid workers would not operate behind Iraqi lines in a war, leaving most relief efforts on the Iraqi side to the International Committee of the Red Cross and to local Red Crescent workers.

Aid groups including Care, Oxfam and Christian Aid were refusing relief funds from countries involved in attacking Iraq.

US-led forces opened the war on Iraq with a hail of 40 Tomahawk missiles aimed at three sites near Baghdad, reportedly acting on intelligence about Iraqi President Saddam Hussein's whereabouts. President Hussein appeared on Iraqi television several hours later, however, and Iraq fired back on targets in Kuwait, forcing US troops into underground bunkers and protective gear. No troop casualties were reported.

The cruise missiles were fired from the destroyer *USS Donald Cook* and other cruisers and submarines in the Red Sea and Persian Gulf as "Operation Iraqi Freedom" got underway. F-117 stealth aircraft dropped 1-ton bombs over Iraqi targets, and armoured vehicles began preparing to cross the Kuwaiti border as the bombing began.

Iraq launched missiles into Kuwait, one of which struck near the US Marine base Camp Commando. Marines retreated into concrete-reinforced Scud bunkers and donned chemical-protection gear, but on inspection the weapon proved to contain no chemical or biological agents. At least one Iraqi missile was downed by a US Patriot missile.

The ground war opened as the US 3rd Infantry Division's artillery unit fired on Iraqi troops using howitzer cannons and multiple launch rocket systems as they advanced from Kuwait. US officials said a massive assault on the order of the "shock and awe" strike conceived to break the Iraqi military's resolve could begin later.

Witnesses in Kuwait were able to make out orange flames on the horizon in the direction of the southern oil-rich city of Basra.

The initial US strikes fell far short of the overwhelming show of force expected on the first day of an assault on Iraq.

The Pentagon dismissed speculation that the relative restraint of the opening salvo was a result of time-sensitive intelligence about Saddam Hussein's location.

According to Iraqi Information Minister Mohammed Saeed al-Sahaf, the raids were targeted at a customs office, some empty TV buildings west of Baghdad and two civilian suburbs of Baghdad. Armed members of the Baath party and security forces reportedly took up positions in Baghdad.

Elite Republican Guard troops were nowhere to be seen in the capital, suggesting defences might be set up in concentric rings around Baghdad. The streets of the city were quiet.

In preparation for the strikes to come, lines at gas stations stretched around the block, people rushed to buy food from emptied stories and expectant mothers were scheduled for Caesarean births as hospitals struggled to clear their wards of all but emergency cases.

In Israel, which was on the receiving end of 39 Scud missiles during the first Gulf War, the military told civilians to prepare their gas masks and have them ready at all times.

Anti-war protests flared up as the war began. A crowd of 40,000 brought Melbourne, Australia, to a standstill; 50,000 students marched in Berlin; and activists in the United Kingdom, France, Italy, Greece, Spain, Egypt, Pakistan, Indonesia and the Gaza Strip demonstrated against the war.

The Turkish Parliament approved US use of air space over Turkey. Under the proposal, allied warplanes were to be allowed to cross Turkey from Europe or the United States to launch strikes against Iraq, but not be allowed to refuel in Turkey or to use Turkish air bases.

At an open meeting at the Security Council Russian Foreign Minister Igor Ivanov said no UN resolution had authorised "the violent overthrow of the leadership of a sovereign state." Germany's Foreign Minister, Joschka Fischer, said there was no basis in the UN charter for a "regime change by military means." The United States, United Kingdom and Spain did not send top-level officials to the meeting, but had their UN ambassadors represent them instead.

World leaders denounced the strikes on Iraq, with Russian President Vladimir Putin calling the war a "big political mistake" and China's Foreign Ministry saying it was "violating the norms of international behaviour."

In Pakistan, religious-political coalitions expressed outrage and sentiments on the street ran high.

French President Jacques Chirac said, "France regrets this action initiated without United Nations backing," and asked French Prime Minister Jean-Pierre Raffarin to convene a meeting about the crisis.

Iraqi Ambassador to the United Nations Mohammed al-Douri said he would deliver a letter to Kofi Annan condemning the US-led war against his country as a violation of international law.

On the second day of fighting in Iraq, US and British troops advancing through the deserts of southern Iraq met resistance from Iraqi troops at the southern port of Umm Qasr and on the road to the southern city of Basra. Coalition forces in the area suffered their first casualties with a helicopter crash in northern Kuwait, and the city of Baghdad was pummeled by a second round of air assaults.

After a night of trading fire with Iraqi forces at the demilitarised zone between Kuwait and Iraq, US Marine tanks crossed the border with air support from Cobra helicopters in a push to secure the road to Basra, 20 miles north. Basra is southern Iraq's largest city, and controlling it would guarantee control of Iraq's access to the Persian Gulf.

Elsewhere along the border, one US Marine battalion delayed its move into Iraq after sighting a surprisingly large number of enemy tanks over the border. One US soldier was injured by friendly fire when, amid small arms and artillery fire from the Iraqi side, a Cobra helicopter fired a missile on an Abrams tank.

Farther west, about 200 Iraqi soldiers surrendered to a Marine unit an hour after it crossed the border.

British troops took the southern portion of the critical al-Faw peninsula – a small spur of land that provides Iraq's only access to the Persian Gulf – during the first hours of the ground assault, but were reportedly running into stiff resistance as they moved against the old port of Umm Qasr. A US Marine died after being wounded in the advance on the Rumeila oil field. Marines lowered the Iraqi flag and raised the US flag over Umm Qasr's new port, about one mile away.

US forces launched more Tomahawk cruise missiles on Baghdad, bringing the day's total to 72, according to Iraqi military reports The precision strikes pre-empted full-scale bombardment for the second time. The first attack was before dawn and lasted only 15 minutes but left the ministry of planning in flames.

Iraqi Information Minister Mohammed Saeed al-Sahhaf confirmed in a news conference that one of Iraqi President Saddam Hussein's houses was damaged in bombing but no one was injured.

Saddam Hussein offered a reward of $14,000 to any Iraqi who killed an enemy soldier and $28,000 to anyone who captured one alive, according to the Iraqi News Agency.

Agence France-Presse reported that Iraq fired 10 missiles at Kuwait, prompting residents to run for gas masks and chemical warfare suits. Two of the missiles landed in the desert, two fell in the sea, and the others apparently did not strike their targets.

US military commanders planned to drop land mines around weapons sites to prevent Iraqi soldiers from reaching stores of chemical or biological arms. Most of the land mines would include timers that would induce the bombs to self-destruct after a period of time. The British Parliament was asking its military planners not to use land mines, as the United Kingdom is one of 131 signatories to an international treaty banning land mine use. Neither the United States nor Iraq had signed it.

Although the Turkish Parliament had approved US overflights, Turkey was delaying opening its air space to US aircraft following disagreement over on a provision in the approval measure that would allow Turkey to move its forces into northern Iraq, which the United States did not want.

The White House and the Treasury Department announced that the Bush administration was seeking to seize $2.3 billion in official Iraqi funds from US and overseas bank accounts. It might also try to hunt down up to $12 billion in proceeds from what it said were illicit sales of Iraqi oil. Officials said the money would be used to help rebuild Iraq.

Activists flowed into the streets of cities around the world to voice their displeasure at the US-led campaign against Iraq. More than 100,000 people marched on the US Embassy in Athens and 30,000 rallied in Australia. More than 120,000 demonstrated in Berlin, and 40,000 marched in Paris. Demonstrators scuffled with police in Madrid and the United Kingdom. Thousands marched through the streets in Egypt, Syria and Libya as well. Protests in the Kashmiri city of Srinagar turned violent as demonstrators lobbed stones at passing cars and shouted anti-US slogans. Across the United States anti-war protesters took to the streets in their thousands.

As US forces continued their march toward Baghdad, Iraqi President Saddam Hussein promised "victory" over US and British troops in the intensifying war in Iraq.

US infantry forces supported by a heavy air assault were approaching Karbala just 50 miles south of Baghdad, but were slowed by an afternoon sandstorm. An Iraqi armored column was reportedly wiped out as it met the US troops, and some outer defences around Baghdad were said to have withdrawn toward the city.

British troops near the southern city of Basra, Iraq's second largest city, engaged in battle with Iraqi forces. The British troops reportedly remained outside Basra because of pockets of resistance in the area.

More than 20 US soldiers were reportedly killed or captured. Iraq said it shot down two US helicopters and captured two US pilots, and the US Defence Department confirmed that one helicopter was missing. Iraqi television broadcast footage of what appeared to be a downed US helicopter.

In footage broadcast by al-Jazeera, five apparent US soldiers were asked by their captors to identify themselves, and four bodies in uniform were identified by al-Jazeera as dead US soldiers. US defence officials said that they feared the bodies were those of soldiers captured along with eight comrades from a support corps backing airborne and infantry troops. The International Committee of the Red Cross, which enforces the Geneva Conventions in wartime, said that al-Jazeera's broadcast of footage of US soldiers in Iraqi custody constituted a violation of the treaties.

The London *Independent* cited unconfirmed reports of up to 77 civilians having been killed in the US-British advance on Basra. Al-Jazeera broadcast images of a young boy with the back of his head blown off and of people being treated in a hospital. Fleeing residents said the battle was engaged within the city.

US military officials cited in the *New York Times* said top US commanders had avoided bombing dozens of high-priority targets, mainly in Baghdad, in order to avoid harming civilians. US Defence Secretary Donald Rumsfeld criticised Iraq for using "human shields" at key targets.

The United Nations called on the parties to protect civilians.

Four journalists had reportedly been killed covering the war.

Syrian state media reported a US missile hit a passenger bus in Syria, killing five and wounding 10. US Central Command had no information on the report.

The British Defence Ministry said that Iraq was probably responsible for missiles that landed in Iran. An Iranian commander said that two missiles had landed in Iran and that US and British planes violated Iranian airspace.

The United States said that media reports over the discovery of a "huge" chemical weapons factory in central Iraq were "premature" although a US military commander said that the United States was questioning two captured Iraqi generals about chemical and biological weapons.

Protests continued Worldwide – in the US, UK, Spain, Ireland, Indonesia, Malaysia, India, New Zealand, Vietnam, Thailand, South Korea, Australia and Japan.

US-British forces claimed they took control of the southern port city of Umm Qasr and faced a heavily fortified Baghdad in what British Prime Minister Tony Blair called a "crucial moment" in the war. On the diplomatic front, international opposition to the war rallied as both Syria and Russia called for emergency Security Council meetings on Iraq. The securing of Iraq's only deep-water port opened the way for tankers in the Persian Gulf bearing much-needed humanitarian aid.

Coalition forces faced three Republican Guard divisions defending a heavily populated "red zone" encircling Baghdad.

Rain and sandstorms worked in the Iraqis' favour as combat missions from two aircraft carriers were postponed and two US Army movements halted. However, the Army's 3rd Infantry Division came within 50 miles of Baghdad and launched a heavy assault with rockets and howitzers.

The London *Guardian* reported that the coalition forces would eventually have to move into Baghdad itself and face Iraq's best troops, the Special Republican Guard. Meanwhile, the defensive strategy employed by the United States, which minimised reliance on heavy armored divisions and emphasised air power, had left supply columns moving up from the south vulnerable to attack and is worrying some US troops and commanders.

The battle for the Iraqi capital began in earnest with raids by B52 bombers and other aircraft. The bombardment was concentrated against the Medina division of the Republican Guard in the west.

Squadrons of Apache helicopters attacking Republican Guard divisions south-west of the city were repulsed by anti-aircraft fire. One helicopter crashed and the two US pilots were later shown on Iraqi television, reportedly seeming to be in good health.

In the southern city of Basra, British troops were poised to move against Iraq's Fedayeen paramilitary force, which was anchored in the city. Though it was unclear whether British forces would undertake full urban combat in the city a sense of urgency was mounting. Basra had no electricity or water.

The northern city of Kirkuk suffered non-stop air raids by allied forces.

Iraqi Information Minister Mohammed Saeed al-Sahaf said that US and British attacks had killed 16 Iraqis and wounded 95 over the previous 24 hours. US Sergeant Major Kenneth Preston estimated that 500 Iraqi fighters had been killed in two days during fighting in southern Iraq.

US Secretary of State Colin Powell said that US officials had received intelligence that Hussein had authorised the use of chemical weapons against Shiite Muslims in southern Iraq in order to blame US forces for the attacks.

The Pentagon said it was investigating a chemical plant in southern Iraq near Najaf as a "site of interest," but General Tommy Franks, who was commanding the coalition forces, said nothing conclusive had been found linking the plant to weapons of mass destruction. Since Iraq's possession of weapons of mass destruction was the premise for the war the discovery of few such weapons would call into question the reason behind the invasion.

A high-level Arab League meeting resulted in a resolution condemning the war against Iraq, but it highlighted divisions within the league. The Libyan delegate gave voice to widespread apprehensions when he opened the session warning that "if Iraq is to fall, many Arab countries will fall as well." He went on to say, "We have to raise our heads high and salute Iraqi heroism as proof that Arab individuals are capable of confronting the mighty, the coercive and the arrogant." The Foreign Minister of Qatar, home to US Central Command, walked out of the meeting to tend to "other business" and called the meeting "useless." The resolution demanded the immediate and unconditional withdrawal of US and British troops from Iraq. Kuwait did not sign, complaining that the resolution carried no condemnation of Iraq's missile strikes on Kuwait.

China said it would back any plan to end the war.

German Foreign Minister Joschka Fischer blasted the war on Iraq and said Germany would not go along with a new world order based on an all-powerful United States.

Independent of Syria's action, Moscow called for an emergency Security Council meeting and asked for a special meeting with the UN High Commissioner on Human Rights to discuss humanitarian issues and the war's legality.

These developments came amid US accusations that Russian companies had sold anti-tank missiles and jamming equipment for scrambling missile guidance systems to Iraq. Moscow rejected the claim, saying they had investigated the United States' privately aired grievances as recently as March 18 and found no evidence of wrongdoing.

Pentagon officials declared Iraqi troops to be committing "serious violations of the laws of war" by pretending to surrender and by wearing civilian clothes into combat.

Tens of thousands of Pakistani Islamists rallied in Lahore to protest against the invasion of Iraq. In Cairo, some 12,000 university students demonstrated against the war.

While British forces worked to secure the southern city of Basra, US troops fought in Nasiriya and Najaf in an abrupt change of strategy aimed at securing Iraq's southern cities before launching a full-bore campaign against Baghdad.

Halfway between Basra and Baghdad, in the city of Najaf, US forces waged a fierce battle against a mixture of fedayeen (paramilitary) and regular troops. Army Major John Altman estimated the Iraqi dead to number 650, far higher than the Pentagon's guess of 150 to 300. He reported no US casualties. Major Altman said the Iraqi forces were using Kalashnikov rifles and rocket-propelled grenades against US Abrams tanks and Bradley fighting vehicles and were outgunned. He added that US troops took 300 prisoners.

Iraqi Republican Guard troops in a 1,000-vehicle convoy reportedly headed south toward coalition forces in central Iraq, while in Baghdad, Iraqi officials said two cruise missiles hit a residential area, killing 14 people

Reuters reported that the death toll of the missile strike, which hit a poor residential neighbourhood in northern Baghdad, was at least 15.

Coalition air forces were firing missiles and dropping bombs over Baghdad reportedly with the intent of weakening the three divisions of the Republican Guard stationed in and around the capital. Coalition forces hit Iraq's state-run television headquarters with missiles and air strikes, taking the station off the air for a few hours. Near Baghdad, the US Army's 3rd Infantry Division drew to within 50 miles of the city. The 3rd Infantry was leading the armoured divisions north from Kuwait to the Iraqi capital.

In the southern city of Nasiriya, Marines seized a hospital flying a Red Crescent flag and found 3,000 chemical suits with masks, plus a tank, in the compound. They captured nearly 170 Iraqi soldiers whom officials said were dressed in a combination of military and civilian clothing.

Marines said they captured 500 Iraqi men believed to belong to a pro-Hussein militia on several buses at a checkpoint near Nasiriya.

In the southeastern corner of Iraq, British forces hovered around the outskirts of Basra, lobbing artillery at over 1,000 entrenched militiamen, who also reportedly faced an uprising by anti-Hussein citizens inside the city. British officials said their troops raided a suburb of Basra, where they captured a Baath party leader and killed 20 of his bodyguards.

British Defence Secretary Geoffrey Hoon said he had received reports that Iraqi militia were attacking citizens inside Basra, but said they were not eyewitness reports. However, a reporter for the Arabic-language television network al-Jazeera, speaking from inside the city, said he could find no popular insurrection.

US officials, citing a communications intercept, said they believed some of the seven captured Army mechanics were executed before the townspeople in the town of Nasiriya. The officials said the information came from one source, and they were seeking corroborating evidence.

Young Iraqi exiles were eager to return home to defend their country, even though many of them did not support Iraqi President Saddam Hussein. Jordan reported that 5,284 Iraqis had left Jordan for home since March 16. Iraq's consular office in Amman approved more than 3,000 temporary passports for exiled Iraqis in the first three days of the war. A religious decree ordered by Shiite leaders to fight the invasion was expected to speed the trend.

US President George Bush visited the Pentagon and Central Command headquarters in Tampa, Florida, to rally Americans behind the war.

The first bodies of US servicemen arrived in the United States.

Although US special forces had been in Kurdish-held northern Iraq for months, they were too few in number for the United States to open a northern front against

Baghdad, according to Iraqi Kurdish commander Babekir Zebari. The Kurds predicted that Iraqi frontlines would break when bombing started, but coalition air raids over the previous three days had not forced any major collapse.

Turkey's military chief of staff, General Milmi Ozkok, promised that he would coordinate with the United States if and when he dispatched troops to northern Iraq. Washington was worried about friendly fire with US troops and conflict between Turkish forces and Iraqi Kurds. General Ozkok said Turkey would not deploy more troops unless Turkey's security was at stake or a refugee crisis developed. Turkey already had several thousand troops in northern Iraq to defend against Turkish Kurds seeking independence. Turkish Foreign Minister Abdullah Gul said Turkey would occupy a 20-kilometre buffer zone in northern Iraq if there was an influx of Kurdish refugees. Turkey feared the establishment of an independent Kurdish state in northern Iraq might incite Kurdish separatists inside Turkey to seek independence.

Turkey was likely to receive less than $1 billion in US aid for its cooperation in the Iraq war. The country was poised to receive $6 billion until the Turkish Parliament rejected a US request to position 62,000 troops in Turkey.

The White House submitted a $74.7 billion war budget to Congress containing aid to several countries in the Gulf region. It suggested $1 billion in military aid and $9 billion in loan guarantees to Israel, $1.3 billion in aid to Jordan, $300 million to Egypt, $90 million to Bahrain and $61 million to Oman.

US forces opened a northern front in Kurdish-controlled Iraq and British troops continued their siege of the southern city of Basra while US ground troops slowly advanced on Baghdad. Reports of mounting civilian casualties sparked anger inside Iraq and prompted UN Secretary General Kofi Annan to urge more care.

Under cover of night, 1,000 US paratroopers dropped from low-flying C-17 transport planes into an airfield 30 miles south of the Turkish border in the first major deployment of ground troops in northern Iraq. Three groups of combat planes from the *USS Theodore Roosevelt* provided cover by striking at Iraqi ground troops during the deployment.

Special forces had been in northern Iraq working in concert with pro-US Kurdish fighters, but they were reportedly few in number.

With the weather improving after two days of severe sandstorms, US commanders said allied forces would step up attacks.

Several routes leading into Baghdad brought US troops, including a 10-mile long Army column, closer to the capital as the weather eased. Iraqi attempts to rebuff their progress were reportedly in vain. Outside Karbala, southwest of Baghdad, small groups of Iraqi armored personnel carriers heading for US positions were hit by air strikes before getting anywhere close.

In the southern city of Basra, an estimated 120 Iraqi tanks and armoured personnel carriers streamed south out of the city and sustained heavy fire from coalition jets and ground-based British artillery units. There were no reports on how many were destroyed. British forces reportedly destroyed a column of 20 vehicles leaving Basra via a northerly route.

The top British commander in the Gulf, Air Marshal Brian Burridge, said loyalist Iraqi forces were forcing regular army troops who wanted to desert to climb into tanks and face British forces. There were some 1,000 militia fighters and an unknown number of regular troops in Basra.

Iraqi civilians had been sneaking out of Basra to give coalition forces information about loyalist troops' whereabouts. However, intelligence sources were saying that earlier news stories of a popular uprising inside the city were exaggerated. Intelligence officers said the mostly Shiite population of Basra was afraid to mount an insurrection against Hussein's troops because people feared that US and British troops would not come to their aid. Instead, the fighting reported was between members of the ruling elite.

Iraqi Health Minister Umeed Madhat Mubarak told reporters that 350 civilians had died in US-led raids so far, 36 of them in a missile strike on a crowded market in Baghdad. Mr Mubarak put the total civilian casualty count at 4,000 and accused coalition forces of targeting noncombatants. US Central Command issued a statement acknowledging that a stray missile may have killed some civilians but blamed Iraqi commanders for storing military hardware near civilians.

Twenty-six US troops and 22 British troops had died in the fighting. Additionally, seven US troops had been captured and eight were missing, according to US and British military sources.

The *Gulf News* reported that a US officer had put the Iraqi military death toll at 1,000 in the previous 72 hours.

US Secretary of State Colin Powell added his voice to a growing chorus of US officers warning that the war could take longer than initially thought. Bad weather, long and poorly secured supply lines and a surprisingly resistant enemy had led to a reassessment by top generals of timelines, although Pentagon spokesmen refuted that view.

Hans Blix said he had seen no evidence that Iraq had used banned weapons, including al-Fatah missiles fired into Kuwait.

A UN official said documents the United States and United Kingdom put forth as evidence that Iraq had tried to buy uranium from Niger were so poorly forged that his "jaw dropped."

A Security Council meeting on Iraq began with the majority of speakers condemning the invasion of Iraq and calling for the withdrawal of US and UK forces. The toughest criticism of Iraq came from Kuwait. Several speakers also criticised Kofi Annan for withdrawing UN staff from Iraq ahead of the invasion, thus ending relief work, including the oil-for-food programme, inside the country.

Syrian President Bashar al-Assad said the United States and Britain would not be able to control Iraq and gave voice to worry that Syria could be next on Washington's list.

US President George W. Bush and British Prime Minister Tony Blair said the war in Iraq was going as planned and would last until President Saddam Hussein's regime was overthrown.

Tens of thousands of additional US and British forces were expected to be deployed to the region within days and 100,000 more US fighters were to be deployed in April.

As US-British forces continued to draw closer to Baghdad, Iraqi Defence Minister Sultan Hashim said in the capital that the battle for the city could last two months or longer and that loyalist paramilitaries would join regular Iraqi troops in street-to-street combat to defend the city.

US bombing of the capital increased to be the heaviest to date, according to the *New York Times*, and appeared to target presidential, military and communications sites. Explosions continued with reports of some 15 Iraqis killed.

In the north of the country, Iraqi troops unexpectedly retreated from positions in defence of the oil hub of Kirkuk following the arrival of 1,000 US paratroopers in the region, the first US troops in Kurdish territory.

Kurdish troops advanced after the Iraqis retreated, taking over the abandoned positions and moving seven miles into what had been Iraqi government-controlled territory.

Iraqi paramilitaries in the southern city of Basra fired mortars and machine guns at thousands of civilians attempting to flee the city, according to British military officials. The officials said British troops were trying to neutralise the fire, evacuate the civilians and treat casualties. The British commander in the Persian Gulf, Brian Burridge, said that reports of an uprising against Hussein's regime in Basra had been exaggerated and that militias loyal to the Iraqi president have been intimidating Basra residents into opposing US-British forces, adding that loyalist paramilitaries had carried out "exemplar executions" in the city.

US Army officials said intelligence indicated that Saddam Hussein had given chemical weapons to a Republican Guard division outside Baghdad. The officials said Saddam would use the weapons as US-British troops moved toward the city.

British military officials said that they found chemical weapons protection suits in a southern facility abandoned by Iraqi infantry.

A Security Council meeting on Iraq ended with US Ambassador John Negroponte walking out when Iraqi Ambassador Mohammed al-Douri accused the United States of lying about its motives in Iraq. Both he and British Ambassador Jeremy Greenstock called the action "both legitimate and cited Security Council Resolutions 678, 687 and 1441 as the legal justifications for using force against Iraq. Both also stressed the humanitarian aid they have in the region, ready for delivery into Iraq.

UN Monitoring, Verification and Inspection Commission Executive Chairman Hans Blix said, "My contract expires at the end of June, and I do not propose to stay beyond that."

US-led air forces pounded targets in Baghdad as US ground troops fought Republican Guard troops in the Euphrates River town of Hindiyah, less than 50 miles from Baghdad. Meanwhile, in south-central Iraq, US forces surrounded Najaf and prepared for possible urban combat, while in Basra, British troops continued their standoff with outnumbered but entrenched Iraqi loyalists.

In Hindiyah, the closest coalition forces had come to Baghdad, US troops killed at least 15 Iraqi soldiers and captured several dozen fighters who identified themselves as members of the Nebuchadnezzar Brigade of the Republican Guard, based in Iraqi President Saddam Hussein's home town of Tikrit.

In Baghdad, B-1, B-2 and B-52 bombers attacked leadership and command and control targets. Four telecommunication facilities in Baghdad reportedly sustained hits, as did a presidential palace near Saddam International Airport. Nearly 800 sorties were flown against the city, the majority of them aimed at Republican Guard divisions

In Najaf, about 100 miles south of Baghdad, soldiers with the Army's 82nd Airborne Division killed 100 "regime terror squad members," according to Central Command, which gave no details about the "terror squads." The Army also reportedly took about 50 prisoners.

US forces were surrounding the Shiite Muslim holy city of 300,000 and contemplating taking it street by street, as the Iraqi fighters inside the city could threaten the long supply lines reaching up to Baghdad from Kuwait. The forces were reluctant, however, to damage holy sites for fear of angering Shiites, who are considered potential allies inside Iraq.

Further south, in Nasiriya, US Marines took buildings that had been used by an Iraqi infantry division and discovered large stores of weapons and chemical decontamination equipment.

Fighting near Basra intensified when 600 British Royal Marines attacked the suburb of Abu al-Kacib, a city of some 30,000 people southeast of Basra, in an effort to encourage what was thought to be a large anti-Saddam majority to rise up against Saddam loyalist troops there. Royal Marines reported that they had taken at least 300 prisoners, including two senior Iraqi officers. Early reports that they had captured a Republican Guard brigadier general were retracted.

In northern Iraq, US aircraft fired on Iraqi ground forces near the town of Kalak in preparation for an advance by coalition troops working in concert with Kurdish fighters. Iraqi troops were fleeing on foot and in cars from their positions on a nearby ridge. Fewer Iraqi troops had been seen in the area in the previous few days, possibly because they were pulling back toward Mosul, the region's largest city. Several thousand US troops were expected to augment the more than 1,200 paratroopers in the area.

About 100 US Special Forces and 6,000 Patriotic Union of Kurdistan fighters started an assault against the small Kurdish Islamic group Ansar al-Islam, which

US Secretary of State Colin Powell identified as a link between the terrorist network al-Qaeda and the Iraqi government. About 700 Ansar fighters waged what PUK Prime Minister Barham Salih called a "very tough battle." The US-Kurdish forces overran the Ansar base camps,

Iraqi officials said at least 35 civilians, and possibly as many as 55, died when a bomb or missile struck a crowded market in the poor Shula district northwest of Baghdad. The incident followed a similar explosion that killed 17 people. At the scene of the crime people in the Shiite neighbourhood were unanimous in blaming coalition forces for the strike.

Iraqi President Saddam Hussein rewarded a suicide bomber who killed four US soldiers with a posthumous promotion to colonel, two medals and 100 million dinars (about $34,000). Iraqi Vice President Taha Yassin Ramadan said such attacks could become routine military policy, adding that thousands of Arab volunteers eager to martyr themselves in a fight against the United States had been pouring into Iraq since the start of the war. General Hazem al-Rawi, a spokesman for the Iraqi military, said that 4,000 volunteers from 23 Arab countries had pledged their willingness to carry out suicide attacks.

The International Committee of the Red Cross said that it had begun visiting Iraqi prisoners captured by US and UK forces. A team of 15 ICRC staff, including a doctor and six interpreters, visited a camp in southern Iraq. The ICRC has been in talks with Iraqi officials about several subjects, including prisoners of war but had not yet received permission to interview the prisoners.

US troops appeared to have killed at least eight civilians in two separate checkpoint incidents. In the first incident U.S. Army soldiers fired on a van that failed to stop at a checkpoint near Najaf, then found the van was full of women and children. US Central Command said seven passengers were killed. General Peter Pace of the US Marine Corps, said the soldiers "absolutely did the right thing" because they believed their lives were in danger. The United States was investigating the incident. Hours later, US marines shot and killed an unarmed driver and badly wounded his unarmed passenger when they fired on a pickup truck as it sped toward them near Shatra.

Iraqi Information Minister Mohammed Saeed al-Sahhaf said that US planes attacked two buses carrying US and European peace activists to Baghdad from Jordan and that the injured were being treated in an Iraqi hospital near the border between the two countries.

US-British planes and missiles hit Baghdad targets including one of President Saddam Hussein's palaces, Iraq's Olympic headquarters and a facility believed to be an air force officers' club. Associated Press reported that the explosions were among the strongest since the war began. Al-Sahhaf said 56 people were killed overnight, including 24 in Baghdad.

Iraqi Foreign Minister Naji Sabri called on Turkey to help Iraq "expel the attackers from our region."

The US State Department issued an annual report on human rights around the world, calling Iraq the world's "primary offender" where rights abuses were concerned.

Following a meeting between U.N. Secretary General Kofi Annan and representatives of Arab countries, Arab League representative Yahya Mahmassani said the Arabs "underlined the situation is a question of occupation and invasion and there is a government recognised by the UN still operating in Baghdad."

CNN reported that Arab countries were planning to seek a U.N. General Assembly resolution condemning the US-led military operation and calling for the withdrawal of foreign troops from Iraq.

By the end of March allied forces had more than 4,000 Iraqi prisoners.

KASHMIR

India and Pakistan both condemned a massacre that took place in a tiny village in the Indian-controlled portion of the disputed territory of Kashmir. Twenty-four Hindus, including 11 women and two children, were shot and killed in what BBC called the worst act of violence since a new government was elected in September in the Indian state, called Jammu and Kashmir.

India blamed Pakistan for the violence.

Pakistan rejected the charge that it arms and trains militants in Kashmir.

Many schools and businesses in Jammu and Kashmir observed a general strike yesterday to protest against the killings, and a group of Kashmiri Hindus held talks with Indian Prime Minister Atal Behari Vajpayee. The Hindus said India would soon announce rehabilitation plans and financial compensation for Hindus displaced by violence in Kashmir, which has increased in the past few weeks after months of relative calm.

KOSOVO

Two UN police officers died after an argument at their Kosovo police camp resulted in a shootout. The camp was sealed off and that the deaths were being investigated as homicides.

LIBERIA

Liberian President Charles Taylor, facing some of the fiercest fighting to topple his regime in three years, said he would resume importing arms despite a UN ban and accused the United States of indirectly assisting rebel forces.

Mr Taylor said he could crush the rebel movement in six months if he had the arms. His regime had been under a UN arms embargo and other sanctions for his alleged support of rebels in the civil war in neighboring Sierra Leone, which ended early in 2002. The President said he had ordered arms under Article 51 of the UN Charter in order to defend Liberia's national sovereignty.

Liberia's Defence Ministry said its forces repelled Liberians United for Reconciliation and Democracy rebels from a refugee camp 10 kilometres from the capital city of Monrovia. However, the group was reported to have resurfaced in the camp. Liberian officials said retreating rebels killed three people and abducted more than 1,000 displaced people, but a witness put that figure closer to 300.

There were also reports of intense fighting in the regional capital Gbarnga, a key central provincial city taken by LURD rebels. Gbarnga was President Taylor's main base during a seven-year civil war he started in the 1990s in which 200,000 people died. Military sources said nine rebels and one government soldier had been killed in the recent fighting.

Towns on the eastern border with the Ivory Coast had also been targeted, and fighting there continued.

Some 30,000 people had been displaced by recent fighting near Gbarnga with scores of people believed killed.

President Taylor sharply criticised neighbouring Guinea and the United States for alleged interference in Liberia's internal affairs. The United States had helped train 800 elite Guinean soldiers and supplied communications equipment. Guinea denied helping LURD rebels, but military sources said there were some links.

Elections in Liberia were scheduled for October and LURD rebels contended they would not be fair if President Taylor remained in power.

MIDDLE EAST

Nine Palestinians were killed and at least 40 injured during an operation in al-Bureij refugee camp in the central Gaza Strip, according to Palestinian security sources. *Ha'weretz*, citing witnesses in al-Bureij, reported eight Palestinians were killed and 25 wounded in the operation. The dead include at least two civilians.

In another attack in the southern Gaza Strip, four Palestinians were reportedly killed.

UPI reported that most of those killed in the operations were militants who fired on Israeli troops, but Palestinian Authority officials said most victims were non-combatants.

The al-Bureij attack focused on Mohammed Taha, a founder of Hamas. Mr Taha and five sons, who *Ha'aretz* reported were all senior Hamas activists, were arrested. Taha and at least one of his sons were wounded. The Israeli army said the son was an assistant to Mohammed Deif, who was allegedly Hamas' top bomb maker and was No. 1 on Israel's most wanted list.

Israeli troops also destroyed several houses Israel said to belong to Hamas and Islamic Jihad militants.

Israeli Defence Minister Shaul Mofaz said that Israel would step up military operations against Hamas in Gaza.

An apparent suicide bomber attack on an Israeli bus in Haifa killed at least 15 people and wounded more than 40 others, breaking a two-month lull in suicide attacks. The attack, the first since January 2003, came just days after Israeli Prime Minister Ariel Sharon established a new conservative government and stepped up counter-terrorism raids in the Palestinian territories.

Rising civilian death tolls among Palestinians in preceding weeks prompted US officials to voice concern over Israel's military actions.

Israeli forces killed eight people during raids against the militant group Hamas in the Gaza Strip.

Since June 2002, Israeli forces had demolished more than 150 houses belonging to Palestinians allegedly involved in terrorist activities, prompting outcry from human rights groups.

Following the suicide bombing in Haifa that left 15 Israelis dead, Israeli forces invaded a Gaza Strip refugee camp to arrest a Hamas fugitive. At least 11 Palestinians were killed in the operation, with Israelis and Palestinians disputing the cause of their deaths.

According to Palestinian witnesses, at least eight people died when Israeli soldiers fired on a crowd observing buildings that were being attacked by Israeli forces. The Israeli army, however, had denied firing on civilians, saying the victims died when a man in the crowd set off a bomb, killing the people around him. More than 100 people were injured in the operation, and three other Palestinians were killed during earlier Israeli-Palestinian clashes.

The recent escalation of violence in the region had left 176 Palestinians and 30 Israelis dead since the beginning of 2003.

Palestinian leader Yasser Arafat nominated his chief lieutenant and fellow Fatah member Mahmoud Abbas to be the first Palestinian prime minister. The US government welcomed the move. Israeli forces were to allow 210 of the 227 legislative council and Palestinian Central Council members to travel to Ramallah to vote on Mr Abbas' nomination. Mr Abbas himself was still waiting to see the power he would be granted before deciding upon acceptance of the post.

Israel continued military operations in northern Gaza as 100 tanks and other vehicles moved into the territory, marking the second time in two days that the Israelis had mounted large-scale incursions into Gaza in what they said was an effort to keep militants from firing rockets at Israeli towns adjacent to the territory. Although Palestinian gunmen and Israeli troops exchanged fire, no casualties were reported. Many Palestinians, however, were expecting more violence, especially after the attack by Israeli forces, which followed a suicide bombing in Haifa. The violence left 11 Palestinians dead and over 140 wounded.

No one had been seriously injured by the rocket attacks on Israel that had come from northern Gaza, but Israel vowed to stop the attacks.

Israel charged that the Palestinian Authority with doing too little to control local militants, while Palestinians charged Israel with repeated operations only serve to increase tensions and continue the cycle of violence.

For the second time in a week, the United States criticised the latest Israeli raid and the resulting civilian casualties. UN Secretary General Kofi Annan also criticised the raid.

The Palestinian Authority's legislature approved the creation of the new post of prime minister. Several legislators said, however, that they had voted on the position itself and not on the candidate or on the powers the post would entail.

A senior Palestinian official said Messrs Arafat and Abbas agreed that Mr Arafat would retain control of talks with Israel and of security forces, while Mr Abbas would run the government, including naming and supervising Cabinet ministers. Such an arrangement would fail to satisfy US and Israeli demands that a prime minister take over from Mr Arafat as head peace negotiator.

The *New York Times* reported that US President Bush had decided to put off implementing the "road map" peace plan, which stipulated a Palestinian state within three years, until the Iraq crisis had passed. The move infuriated Europeans involved in Middle East peace talks. US officials cited fears of an Iraqi counterattack against Israel and the potential for Arab discontent over demands for Arafat to step down as factors that could hinder implementation of the peace plan.

US President George W. Bush promised to release the long-awaited "road map" peace plan for the Middle East once the new Palestinian Authority prime minister was confirmed in office.

In a rocket attack on the Gaza Strip Israeli helicopters killed Ibrahim Makadmeh, a founder of Hamas and the militant group's reported recruitment chief, as well as three bodyguards who were riding in a car with him. Mr Makadmeh, the most senior Hamas figure Israel had killed since July 2002, masterminded many attacks against Israelis, according to Israeli intelligence. Tens of thousands of Palestinians marched through Gaza City in a funeral procession for Mr Makadmeh, calling for revenge against Israel. Hamas vowed to target Israeli political figures in retaliation for the assassination. Israel went on heightened alert following the threats from Hamas.

Israeli forces reportedly killed at least 10 Palestinian militants in raids on the Jenin refugee settlement in the West Bank and the nearby village of Tamoun. Nine Palestinians were reportedly killed in two raids on the Gaza Strip. *Ha'aretz* put the number of Palestinians killed at 13.

A US peace protester was run over and killed by a bulldozer during an Israeli demolition operation in southern Gaza. An Israeli army spokesman called the incident a "regrettable accident," adding that protesters "were acting very irresponsibly, putting everyone in danger." The International Solidarity Movement said that her death was not accidental, as Israel claimed. About 200 mourners attended a memorial service for her at the UN offices in Gaza City.

The Palestinian Authority legislature approved a measure granting a new Palestinian prime minister greater powers than those envisioned by Yasser Arafat, the authority's president. The move followed a related vote in which the parliament approved the creation of the post.

Mr Arafat, who reportedly agreed at a meeting of his Fatah faction to drop a demand for input into Cabinet choices under the new premier, was expected to formally ask his choice for the post, Mahmoud Abbas, to take office and form a Cabinet within two weeks.

Mr Abbas had refused to accept the job until he deemed it had been given enough power.

UN Special Coordinator for the Middle East Terje Roed-Larsen told the Security Council that for the first time in two-and-a-half years, there was a "small window of opportunity" to restart Israeli-Palestinian peace negotiations and escape "the abyss of terrorism, violence, economic misery and general suffering" in the Middle East. The special envoy cited three requirements for success:

1. the appointment of a credible prime minister;
2. the implementation of an internationally approved "road map" for peace; and
3. Israel's return to the negotiating table.

Mr Roed-Larsen's comments came on the heels of the fulfillment of one of those requirements: Mahmoud Abbas' acceptance of the newly created position of Palestinian prime minister. Mr Abbas would now control the appointment of cabinet ministers, including the post that oversaw security forces.

The creation of the position was favoured by Israel and the United States, who saw it as a means to circumvent Yasser Arafat in peace negotiations. Mr Arafat was to remain overall commander of the security forces and have a final say on any peace negotiations with Israel, but he would now have to deal with an independent-minded prime minister and an increasingly restive parliament that has shown its willingness to stand up to him.

Mr Abbas had said almost nothing about his intentions.

Mr Roed-Larsen called on the Palestinian Authority to follow up on a declaration to end violence and terrorism with visible efforts on the ground to prevent further attacks. He said Israel should stop all proactive security operations, including attacks on civilians and the demolition of Palestinian homes, dismantle settlement outposts erected since March 2001 and freeze all other settlement activity. Noting that the continuing conflict was contributing to serious economic insecurity, Mr Roed-Larsen also said Israel had to look at ways to ease the massive burden on the Palestinian civilian population in the West Bank and Gaza, adding that the Israeli economy was in distress, with rising unemployment and increasing social problems.

In response to the dire economic situation, the United States offered Israel $1 billion in direct military aid and $9 billion in loan guarantees. Israel was at this time the biggest recipient of US aid worldwide and already received $3 billion a year, mostly in direct military aid. As part of the deal, the United States would deduct from the loan guarantees any Israeli expenditure on settlement activities in Palestinian areas. The aid package, part of US President Bush's war budget, still needed approval of the US Congress.

Refugees International, citing recent reports from the international aid community on the humanitarian conditions in the Palestinian occupied territories, slammed Israel for failing to live up to its responsibilities as an occupying power under the Fourth Geneva Convention. The body cited statistics from the World Bank – which said real per capita incomes in the occupied Palestinian territories were now half their September 2000 levels and 53% of the workforce was unemployed – and from the UN Relief and Works Agency for Palestine Refugees in the Near East, which said it has gone from feeding 11,000 people to more than 700,000 people – a little more than half the total Palestinian population in the territories. Care International's 2002 nutrition survey found that chronic malnutrition for children under the age of 6 was 17.5% in the Gaza Strip and 7.9% in the West Bank.

Refugees International accused Israel of conducting "collective punishment" in response to Palestinian attacks, razing homes in refugee camps and denying Palestinians access to basic necessities for survival such as water and medicine. According to the group, the Fourth Geneva Convention "explicitly prohibits collective punishment." It also revokes protected persons status on those individuals who are "definitely suspected or engaged" in activities hostile to the occupying power. Refugees International had called on parties to the Convention, including the United States, to exert pressure on Israel to fulfill its obligations to the Palestinians in the territories.

A Palestinian blew himself up on a sidewalk in Netanya, Israel, wounding more than 50 bystanders and several Israeli soldiers who had blocked his path as he advanced toward a crowded cafe. Two of those wounded were listed in serious condition. Islamic Jihad claimed responsibility for the suicide attack, the first in Israel since war began in Iraq, and called it a "gift" to the Iraqi people. The militant group's spiritual leader, Ramadan Shallah, said the group has sent suicide bombers to Baghdad to attack US and British troops. Four US soldiers were killed in Iraq by an Iraqi suicide bomber. The Palestinian Authority condemned the Netanya attack, while Israel blamed the authority's head, Yasser Arafat, for failing to crack down on terrorists.

NEPAL

Nepal's government and Maoist rebels agreed to a 22-point code of conduct for talks, which was welcomed by the country's main political parties. The agreement said both sides were committed to finding a peaceful solution through dialogue and would halt violent activities.

The two sides had declared a cease-fire on January 29 after seven years of conflict left more than 7,800 dead.

Prime Minister Lokendra Bahadur Chand said that peace talks would begin in the first week of April, at the request of the Maoists, who wanted time to inform their ranks of the code of conduct.

Maoist negotiators, who had been in hiding since 1996, indicated they would resurface. The rebels had allegedly sabotaged the public infrastructure and caused other damage the government said would take many years to rebuild. In November 2001, the government sent the army to fight the rebels and declared a state of emergency.

Prospects for peace had seemed unlikely after Nepal's king dismissed the elected government and took executive powers in October 2002. Shortly thereafter, the nation's political parties disassociated themselves from the government and the peace process.

Four political parties now called on the king to either reinstate Parliament or create a new all-party government. That way it would be possible to amend the constitution to accommodate the Maoists, rather than having to create a new constitution – a key rebel demand.

UN Assistant Secretary General Kul Chandra Gautam said the peace process would move forward only through the cooperation of the country's three political forces. Mr Gautam said he had "personally offered" to assist in Nepal's post-conflict reconstruction efforts. He said UN agencies and international donors would agree to launch an urgent humanitarian action plan for the people most affected by the armed conflict. He suggested quadrupling the budget for villages and implementing a well-designed and credible reconstruction package funded by a mixture of national and increased international cooperation.

NORTH KOREA

US President George W. Bush evoked the possibility of taking military action against North Korea if diplomatic efforts failed to stop the country's nuclear activity.

North Korean leader Kim Jong Il said a conflict between the United States and North Korea could lead to nuclear war.

The exchange between Messrs Bush and Kim followed an incident in which North Korean fighter jets intercepted a US surveillance plane about 150 miles off the coast of the Korean Peninsula. US officials said that four armed North Korean MiGs shadowed an American RC-135S for about 20 minutes over international waters, with one North Korean plane using its radar to "lock on" to the surveillance plane briefly in an apparent threat to fire missiles.

CNN reported that US officials planned to protest the action, the first air confrontation between the two countries since 1969. A senior US administration official told CNN the forum for such a protest had not been decided but that communicating with North Korean diplomats at the United Nations was a possibility. US officials reportedly saw the spy plane incident as a deliberate effort by Pyongyang to ratchet up tensions that had risen steadily since October 2002, when the United States first said North Korea was attempting to revive its nuclear weapons programme.

Announcing the deployment of 24 bombers to the Western Pacific, the Pentagon said that the move was not prompted by an unfriendly encounter between North Korean and US aircraft but had long been in the works as part of a US "message" to Pyongyang not to take advantage of the US military preoccupation with Iraq.

Twelve US B-1 bombers and 12 B-52 bombers received deployment orders to Guam the day before a quartet of North Korean MiG fighters intercepted a US Air Force spy plane over the Sea of Japan.

A Pentagon statement declared that the latest reshuffling of military equipment in the region was ordered a month previously and was not aggressive in nature.

CNN.com reported that US officials intended to send a non-threatening message and that with the aircraft carrier *USS Kitty Hawk* having left its regular post in Japan for the Persian Gulf, extra warplanes were being sent to the area as part of routine procedure. North Korea responded by appealing to the United States for a congressionally approved non-aggression pact.

South Korean Unification Minister Jeong Se-hyun said that North Korean suspicions of a US attack were "without basis" and that the incident was a tactic employed by Pyongyang to secure face-to-face talks with Washington. The United States had repeatedly rebuffed the North's request for direct negotiations.

Some US analysts believed President George W. Bush's refusal to engage bilaterally with North Korea spelt an end to diplomacy.

The CIA estimated that North Korea already had two nuclear weapons. If the communist nation began reprocessing its plutonium stockpiles, as it was expected to do, it would be able to produce enough plutonium to make one nuclear weapon each month. A nuclear North Korea, the *Los Angeles Times* reported, would be deeply disruptive to Asia and the rest of the world, with Seoul striving to get along with the North despite popular pressure opposing that position, Japan trying to enhance its military capabilities to defend itself against North Korea and the United States struggling to convince the rest of the world to isolate Pyongyang.

The White House later ruled out allowing North Korea to gain nuclear capabilities amid press reports saying the administration had resigned itself to watching Pyongyang become the world's next nuclear power.

US officials said North Korea might be preparing to fire another test missile called the Rodong, which had enough range – about 800 miles – to strike Japan.

After a four-day visit to North Korea, UN envoy Maurice Strong said the United States and North Korea must begin speaking soon to prevent escalating the crisis over Pyongyang's nuclear activities, adding that North Korea was currently watching the US-led war on Iraq "with deep concern," worried that it could be a future US target.

North Korea said that a month-long joint US-South Korean military exercise was escalating tensions.

North Korea cut off its regular contact with the US-led UN Command, which was responsible for ensuring the divided Korean Peninsula's armistice. Pyongyang said US forces might be planning to attack North Korea.

The North Korean army told the UN Command that it would no longer attend meetings held almost weekly since the three-year Korean War ended without a formal peace agreement in 1953.

South Korean President Roh Moo-hyun called North Korea's claims of an imminent US attack "groundless."

UN envoy Maurice Strong said that in meetings in Pyongyang, North Korean officials told him they reserved the right to reprocess spent nuclear fuel rods. Experts believed the material could be used to produce enough plutonium for several atomic bombs in a matter of months. Returning from four days of talks in Pyongyang, he said North Korea was not in any rush to resolve the nuclear crisis.

The UN Command had no immediate comment on North Korea's latest move.

Breaking with a historically cooperative relationship, China exerted diplomatic and financial pressure on North Korea to give up its nuclear ambitions, sending diplomatic messages urging Pyongyang to abandon its nuclear programme and temporarily halting fuel deliveries to North Korea.

The United States proposed convening a multilateral summit and US officials were also reportedly working on a UN measure to urge North Korea to end its nuclear activities. China, though, was delaying the UN measure, which would come in the form of a statement and not a formal resolution.

SERBIA

Serbian Prime Minister Zoran Djindjic, a pro-Western leader who led the charge to topple former President Slobodan Milosevic, was slain by gunmen who ambushed him outside a government building in Belgrade.

Key suspects in the assassination were still at large, but a number of arrests were made. The government said a Belgrade-based criminal gang was behind the killing and listed about 20 of the gang's leaders.

Mr Djindjic had pledged to eradicate corruption and mafia-style activity in Serbia, and he was instrumental in the handover of former Yugoslav President Slobodan Milosevic to the International Criminal Tribunal for the former Yugoslavia, where Mr Milosevic was being tried for war crimes. It was said that the core of Serbian organised crime developed during Mr Milosevic's tenure as president.

Serbia declared a state of emergency under which the government allowed police to hold suspects for up to 30 days without charges and banned media reports that could hamper the investigation. Despite critics' charges that freedom of speech was being violated, authorities shut down the newspaper *Nacional* and banned distribution of another newspaper, *Dan*. Mr Zivkovic said the state of emergency was "a necessity and not a permanent choice of this government."

Montenegro's prime minister, Milo Djukanovic, said that the assassination, which he called a "heinous attack on democracy and a calculated terrorist action," threatened the stability of the new state of Serbia and Montenegro, the successor to Yugoslavia.

The *New York Times* reported that Mr Djindjic's assassination was seen as a setback at ICTY, where prosecutors reportedly saw the Serbian leader as their best chance to obtain the handover of key Serbian suspects.

Serbian police later netted more than 70 suspected mobsters and detained two of Slobodan Milosevic's senior security heads – former state security chief Jovica Stanisic and his deputy, Franko Simatovic.

The Serbian Interior Minister vowed to continue the police sweep.

Serbian police later said that they had arrested three suspects in the Djindjic assassination: Svetlana Raznatovic, the widow of paramilitary leader Zeljko Raznatovic, better known as Arkan; Zoran Vukojevic, a former policeman who was in charge of bodyguards for the Zemun criminal gang; and Dragan Ninkovic, known as the Fraudster.

Finance Minister Bozidar Djelic of Serbia and Montenegro asked European Union and other foreign officials for $424 million in aid to the country, promising that the government would maintain Djindjic's pro-Western stance and anti-crime campaign.

The Serbian legislature subsequently elected Zoran Zivkovic as prime minister to replace Mr Djindjic. Mr Zivkovic, a close Djindjic ally, promised to be decisive in carrying out the assassinated leader's programme of reform and promised Mr Djindjic's killers would be brought to justice.

Serbian police later shot and killed two leading suspects in the assassination. The Interior Ministry said Dusan Spasojevic and Milan Lukovic, alleged leaders of a crime gang accused of masterminding the March 12 assassination, were shot while resisting arrest. Although authorities did not comment on the specific role the two allegedly played in the murder, a police officer said the men were directly involved in the plot to kill Mr Djindjic: "they organised it; they financed it."

The government disbanded an elite 300-officer police unit said to be tied to former Yugoslav President Slobodan Milosevic. Police sources said about 15 members of the unit were arrested on suspicion they helped organise the Djindjic assassination. The unit's deputy commander, Zvezdan Jovanovic, a former Milosevic bodyguard, was arrested as the alleged shooter in the assassination. The unit commander, Milorad Lukovic, was wanted but remained at large.

The investigation into the assassination had involved the arrest of over 3,000 suspects, over one-third of whom remained in custody.

Police said they had uncovered the grave of former Serbian President Ivan Stambolic, a bitter foe of Milosevic who had been missing for three years. Police said Mr Stambolic was killed for political reasons by the special police unit that was disbanded. Four members of the unit were arrested in connection with the murder.

SIERRA LEONE

UN Secretary General Kofi Annan recommended that the Security Council extend by six months the mandate of the UN Mission in Sierra Leone but gradually withdraw the peacekeeping force, saying that Sierra Leone's situation had improved but that the country continued to need UN assistance to maintain security as security of Sierra Leone could not be fully ensured while the conflict in Liberia persisted.

The UN Security Council unanimously adopted a resolution to extend the mandate of the UN Mission in Sierra Leone for six months. The extension followed Kofi Annan's report that recommended the continued gradual withdrawal of UN peacekeepers from Sierra Leone because of "shortcomings" in the country's law enforcement forces.

The Council called on countries to provide resources to help fulfill the mission's police size and capacity targets, emphasising that "the development of the administrative capacities of the government of Sierra Leone, particularly an effective and sustainable police, army, penal system and independent judiciary, is essential to long-term peace and development."

SOMALIA

A panel of UN arms experts urged the Security Council to step up enforcement of the weapons embargo in Somalia, saying a lack of sanctions and interdiction efforts had fostered arms trade.

The report said the Security Council should pursue both interdiction of arms shipments and sanctions against embargo violators.

The report pointed to Ethiopia, Eritrea, Yemen and Djibouti as arms suppliers to Somalia.

UGANDA

The Lord's Resistance Army rebel group leader, Joseph Kony, declared a cease-fire after waging 16 years of war in northern Uganda and had asked to meet with Ugandan President Yoweri Museveni. Kony's willingness to declare a cease-fire brought the parties a significant step closer to the negotiating table.

Aid groups said Uganda's civil conflict had left thousands dead and driven nearly 1 million people from their homes. The LRA had reportedly abducted 14,000 children as part of its military tactics. It had also attacked refugee camps, forcing the UN High Commissioner for Refugees to resettle thousands. The LRA had sought to overthrow the government and instill rule based on the Bible's Ten Commandments.

The LRA later killed five Ugandan People's Defence Forces soldiers and five civilians in two separate attacks about 12 kilometers northeast of Gulu town, despite having declared a cease-fire. A group of rebels also attacked an internally displaced people's camp, breaking into shops, looting merchandise and abducting civilians. Two civilians and one soldier were seriously wounded when the Ugandan forces opened fire on the rebels.

A World Food Programme nutrition assessment in Uganda revealed that over 31% of children under the age of five were suffering from acute malnutrition in Anaka camp for displaced people, located in northern Uganda, while 18% of children under age five in Pabbo camp, the largest settlement for displaced people in the region with a population of 45,000, suffered from acute malnutrition. More than 180,000 tons of food were needed to feed 800,000 displaced people. Uganda contributed $550,000 and the WFP had received donations to cover only one-third of the total needs.

Rebels in northern Uganda shot and killed a government emissary sent to open peace talks. A spokesman for Uganda's army said that Captain Okech Kuru, who served as an intermediary between the Ugandan government and the rebel Lord's Resistance Army, was shot after meeting with rebels in the northern district of Pader. The LRA had no comment.

WESTERN SAHARA

UN Secretary Kofi Annan asked the Security Council to give UN negotiators two extra months to organise a referendum in Western Sahara, saying UN envoy James Baker needed the time in order to talk to all the involved parties about the latest proposal aimed at resolving the Moroccan-occupied territory's future status.

In mid-January, leaders of Morocco, Algeria and Mauritania as well as representatives from the independence-seeking POLISARIO Front began considering the latest referendum proposal. They were supposed to respond to Mr Baker by early March, but not all did.

The proposal would offer the people of Western Sahara, a former Spanish territory disputed since 1974, the choice of outright independence or joining Morocco.

The UN Security Council had, in January 2003 extended the mandate of the UN Mission for the Referendum in Western Sahara until March 31 and asked Kofi Annan to report back on progress by March 17. The Council now voted unanimously to extend the mandate of the UN Mission for the Referendum in Western Sahara by two months following a letter from UN Secretary General Kofi Annan requesting additional time for the parties in Western Sahara to submit views on Mr Baker's proposal.

Polisario's representative to the United States, Mouloud Said, said that "so far," the Baker plan was unacceptable to Polisario. "We can negotiate on technicalities . . . but there is no way we can negotiate on the sovereignty of the land," he said.

April 2003

AFGHANISTAN

Hundreds of Afghan soldiers and two dozen US Special Forces attacked Taliban fighters in a village on southern Afghanistan's border with Pakistan, eventually driving them into nearby mountains. US fighter jets and helicopters arrived on the scene from Bagram Air Force base north of Kabul about six hours after the start of battle and fired rockets into the mountain holdouts, where about 60 Taliban fighters were thought to be entrenched. About 600 soldiers loyal to regional Governor Gul Agha Shirzai, along with Special Forces, were fighting villagers who had answered a call to jihad and were joining Taliban fighters in a battle against Afghan and US troops near Spin Boldak.

Associated Press reported that evidence suggested the Taliban was regrouping and working with the regional commander Gulbuddin Hekmatyar, who had been labeled a terrorist by the United States. Days earlier an International Committee of the Red Cross worker was shot 20 times and his vehicle burned. Shortly thereafter, two US servicemen were killed in an ambush. The Taliban claimed responsibility for both incidents.

The United Nations said it would extend a travel ban for its staff in southern Afghanistan in order to give authorities time to secure the area. The ban followed the ICRC worker's murder on March 27.

Posters reportedly bearing a decree from Taliban leader Mullah Omar had begun appearing in eastern Afghanistan, a region where opposition to the United States and the US-backed government of President Hamid Karzai ran high. The posters were described as signed by 600 Islamic clerics and saying they called for a renewed holy war based on the US-led invasion of Iraq.

Afghan Interior Minister Ali Ahmad Jalali said coalition troops, working with Afghan soldiers, had launched a sweep in the area near Kandahar where the killing took place, adding that terrorist activities were picking up in the south and east of Afghanistan.

In a bid to quell interregional violence and establish crucial stability in Afghanistan, the government of President Hamid Karzai and the UN Development Programme signed an agreement on a programme to disarm and demobilise the armies of the country's powerful regional commanders.

If all went according to plan, the $127 million New Beginnings Programme would start July 10 and over the course of three years disarm 100,000 soldiers loyal to Afghan warlords. The programme would help enlist fighters with the small Afghan

National Army or equip them with the job training necessary to re-enter civilian life. The programme would be staffed primarily by Afghans working in a head-quarters in Kabul and eight regional offices.

Disarmament and demobilisation of the regional militias had long been viewed as necessary to secure a lasting peace in Afghanistan, and the central government was eager to get the process underway before the national elections in the middle of next year. Security was also crucial to rebuilding the country.

Reuters reported that prior demobilisation programmes had not been very successful. One programme in the north, undertaken in 2002, ended up with the most powerful commanders forcing less powerful leaders to surrender their weaponry to them.

UN special investigator for human rights in Afghanistan Kamal Hossain told the UN Human Rights Commission that security in Afghanistan had to improve. The 1,700-member Afghan National Army, he said, should be increased to 70,000 in order to control warlords in remote corners of Afghanistan who harass ethnic tribes and reverse hard-won rights for women and girls. Mr Hossain added that Afghanistan had to not be neglected by international donors.

Taliban activity was on the rise in Afghanistan and was concentrated in the south. Kandahar Governor Gul Agha Sherzai gave Taliban fighters 48 hours to leave the country after his soldiers killed two Taliban loyalists and captured seven more with bombs and artillery near the town of Spinboldak, on Afghanistan's border with Pakistan.

A US warplane killed 11 civilians, mostly women, in Shkin in eastern Afghanistan about 130 miles south of Kabul (an area frequently used by Taliban fighters seeking passage between Afghanistan and Pakistan) when an errant 1,000-pound laser-guided bomb struck a house. The US Marine Harrier jet was attempting to bomb a band of five to 10 rebel fighters after Afghan soldiers asked for air support following a midnight attack by "enemy forces" on a military checkpoint.

A US military spokesman said the "tragic incident" was a mistake.

The immediate claim of responsibility by the US military for civilian deaths was reportedly a first in Afghanistan where the military had in the past acknowledged such incidents only after an investigation.

Afghan authorities predicted that the mistake would spawn a new wave of terrorism.

Aid workers from the United Nations and nongovernmental organisations were evacuated from the northern town of Maimana amid fighting by rival warlords. Forces loyal to ethnic Uzbek warlord Abdul Rashid Dostum and his Tajik rival, Atta Mohammed, started battling in Maimana, eventually killing 13 people and leaving 17 wounded. Although fighting later eased tensions did not. After two senior commanders representing the warlords met and agreed to a cease-fire, some 400 residents reportedly demonstrated at the governor's office to demand immediate disarmament. Later they converged on the UN office in Maimana.

NATO was considering ways to expand its role in Afghanistan, the alliance's secretary general, George Robertson, said. A senior NATO official said the alliance's 19 members unanimously charged NATO planners with examining options to increase the presence of the alliance and that recommendations were expected "quite soon." NATO already provided logistic and other support to the International Security Assistance Force, which was now under Dutch-German command. The United States had suggested NATO should take over peacekeeping operations in Afghanistan, but France had been resistant.

A rash of violence in the northern city of Maimana, where aid workers were evacuated, ended when the United Nations helped broker a cease-fire between warring militias. Members of UNAMA's negotiating team met with General Fawzi of the Jumbesh militia and General Saboor of the Jamiat group to halt hostilities. According to the terms of the agreement, no militia members were allowed into Maimana except the two commanders, their deputies and two bodyguards each. The two groups withdrew half their troops to the outskirts of the city. UNAMA found unexploded ordnance in the streets of Maimana and asked the UN Mine Action Center for Afghanistan (UNMACA) to help clean it up.

Former Afghan President Burhanuddin Rabbani said that land mines in Afghanistan, one of the most heavily mined countries in the world, were claiming half as many victims as they did before the start of a campaign to remove them.

The United States had undergone a fundamental shift in its policy toward Afghanistan and was now engaged in nation-building, an activity once scorned by the Bush administration. It had moved beyond Band-Aid activities such as peacekeeping and delivering humanitarian aid and was now focused on bolstering the central government of President Hamid Karzai. For example, although in 2002 the United States spent the largest share of its contribution to Afghanistan on humanitarian aid, in 2003 it was to invest the largest chunk of money in Afghanistan's 3,000-member national army, which was scheduled to reach 70,000.

However, some of the United States' efforts ran counter to the goal of strengthening President Karzai's government. Examples were US support of regional warlords, who US commanders believed they needed for the war on terrorism, and the practice of capturing Afghans suspected of terrorist involvement and holding them or sending them to the US military base at Guantanamo Bay, Cuba, as happened with tribal leader Naeem Koochi.

The United States and other donors had given the central government "unprecedented" control of reconstruction funds in order to counter criticism that foreigners involved in reconstruction were living in luxury while ordinary Afghans' lives remained a struggle.

NATO agreed to take the helm of Afghanistan's peacekeeping force starting in August 2003.

The 19-member alliance voted unanimously to undertake its first mission outside the North Atlantic area since its formation in 1949. France, which initially objected to the move, reportedly because it feared the alliance was being dominated by the United States, dropped its resistance.

NATO would take over strategic command and control of the 4,500-member International Security Assistance Force, which was currently under a six-month rotating command system. Germany and the Netherlands currently shared the command.

NATO would provide a military commander, to be appointed by NATO Supreme Allied Commander James Jones, and military personnel who would run the peace-keeping operation headquarters in Kabul (BBC Online, April 16).

Reuters reported that the alliance had no plans to expand the operation beyond Kabul, despite the United Nations' desire for a peacekeeping force throughout the country.

NATO would reportedly lead the force until Afghanistan's first elections in 2004.

A grenade exploded in the UNICEF office in the eastern city of Jalalabad. A UN spokesman said there were no casualties.

Members of a regional security commission based in the northern city of Mazar-e Sharif brokered a cease-fire between two minority Shiite parties after violence erupted April 10 in the northern town of Surk Deh. Commission representatives met with envoys from Hezb-e-Wahadat and Harakat-e-Islami and brokered the deal that would lead to the withdrawal of soldiers from Surk Deh. A similar cease-fire agreement was reached between forces loyal to Uzbek warlord Abdul Rashid Dostum and his Tajik rival Mohammad Atta.

President Hamid Karzai was to travel to Islamabad to meet with Pakistani President Pervez Musharraf after alleged Pakistani incursions into southeastern Afghanistan raised tensions between the two countries. The two countries exchanged fire across the border following accusations by an Afghan military commander that Pakistani militia were occupying Afghan territory along the disputed border. Afghan officials had accused Pakistan of conducting similar incursions in recent months and giving sanctuary to remnants of the Taliban regime, who allegedly plot attacks on Afghan militias from the safety of Pakistan.

Pakistani Foreign Ministry spokesman Aziz Ahmad Khan said the dispute was settled by Afghan and Pakistani officials who met in the border town of Ghulam Khan.

Afghanistan's powerful regional commanders and militia chiefs agreed to work with the central government to rebuild a national army that was representative of all ethnicities. The 50 or so warlords and militia leaders met with Kabul's interior, foreign and defence ministers for a two-day conference. Among the attendees were three key warlords: Herat governor Ismail Khan, Kandahar governor Gul Agha and northern Tajik commander Mohammad Atta. A statement issued by the Defence Ministry – whose director, Marshal Mohammad Qasim Fahim, had been accused of trying to pack the national army with Tajik recruits – said, "Soldiers and officers should be recruited from all ethnicities, all provinces and from all walks of life so that each unit [was] representative of the nation and able to gain the confidence and trust of all people of the nation."

Afghanistan hoped to have a "central core" of 9,000 to 12,000 soldiers in its national army by the summer of 2004. The ultimate goal was 70,000.

Romanian troops found the largest cache of weapons to date in Afghanistan while conducting searches outside the village of Hazarkhel, about 220 miles southwest of Kabul. Two caves outside the village were being used to store 3,000 107-millimeter rockets, reportedly a staple in the guerrilla war waged against coalition troops by al-Qaeda and Taliban militia, as well as 150 mortar rounds, 30 anti-tank mines and 1.25 million rounds of ammunition.

President Karzai said he would give Pakistan a list of "most wanted" Taliban members thought to be hiding in Pakistani territory, along the border with Afghanistan. Two of the Taliban figures Mr Karzai wanted to see Pakistan arrest were Akhatar Mohammed Uzmani, a onetime military commander from Kandahar, and Mullah Dadullah, a one-legged commander thought to be behind the killing of International Committee of the Red Cross worker Ricardo Munguia on March 27 in southern Afghanistan. The US military said that it had killed a man believed to be the gunman in the Munguia killing.

Tensions were said to be increasing between the two countries amid a rise in attacks on international aid workers and agencies in Afghanistan.

Near the border town of Jalalabad, attackers fired on a UN mine-clearing vehicle with rockets and automatic weapons, injuring two Afghan workers. The incident came after months of "night letters" circulating in the area – notes handed out clandestinely by Taliban loyalists and al-Qaeda sympathisers warning international aid workers to leave Afghanistan.

Despite the imminent end of formal military operations, US troops continue to battle what were thought to be remnants of the Taliban and al-Qaeda. A second US soldier died from wounds sustained in a skirmish with 20 or so rebel fighters in eastern Afghanistan near the Pakistani border.

Pakistani authorities discovered a huge weapons cache about 125 miles south of Peshawar, near the border with Afghanistan. The owner of the store where 99 Russian missiles, 64 guns, mortar shells, remote-controlled mines and other weapons were found reportedly fled across the border into Afghanistan.

Afghan authorities discovered four anti-aircraft missiles in a house about 15 miles southeast of the eastern city of Jalalabad. On the same day, rebels blew up a vehicle transporting Afghan soldiers from Jalalabad to Tora Bora. Afghan officials had reportedly arrested 24 people in connection with the attack.

Another attack near Jalalabad, this one on a mine-clearance survey team from the Mine Clearance Planning Agency, prompted the UN Mine Action Campaign for Afghanistan to suspend all activities in the area for two days.

BOSNIA AND HERZEGOVINA

The chairman of Bosnia and Herzegovina's three-person coalition presidency, Mirko Sarovic, resigned after international investigators alleged he let aviation company Orao violate a UN arms embargo by exporting fighter plane engines to Iraq. Mr Sarovic was president of the country's ethnic Serb republic, Republika Srpska, at the time of the alleged violations. NATO peacekeepers first found evidence of the exports during a raid of the company's facilities in Bijeljina, Republika Srpska.

NATO said that evidence indicated Republika Srpska's military spied on citizens, NATO troops, European Union police and the office of the international high representative in Bosnia and Herzegovina. High Representative Paddy Ashdown said the alleged illegal exports and spying showed "systemic weakness in the civilian control over Bosnia's armed forces" and he amended Republika Srpska's laws to transfer military control to the national level. References to statehood, independence and sovereignty in the constitution and in defence laws were removed because, according to Ashdown, "too many" in Republika Srpska believed it was an independent state. The constitution of the Federation of Bosnia and Herzegovina, a Muslim-Croat entity that constitutes the other part of the country, had no such references.

Russia announced a decision to withdraw its Balkans' peacekeepers. A military official said Russia no longer had a strategic interest in the Balkans and that Moscow wanted to distance itself from problems in Kosovo. The official said Russian forces would need about a month to leave the Balkans after the order to withdraw.

Russia had 970 soldiers in the Balkans with the NATO-led international peacekeeping forces, with 650 in Kosovo and the rest in Bosnia.

BURUNDI

South Africa, Mozambique and Ethiopia announced plans to send 3,500 peacekeepers to monitor a cease-fire in Burundi.

South African Defence Minister Mosiuoa Lekota said the three countries, following a meeting of their defence ministers, planned to present their agreement to the African Union for approval. The ministers did not specify when the peacekeepers would be deployed, but Mr Lekota said the force was expected to stay in Burundi for up to a year and that a UN force was expected to replace them.

Some 300,000 people had been killed since 1993 in a war between Tutsi-led government forces and Hutu rebels in Burundi. Violence had continued in 2003 despite a December 2002 cease-fire. The African peacekeeping force had been repeatedly delayed after initial plans to deploy in January 2003 fell apart.

Agence Burundaise de Presse reported that UN Secretary General Kofi Annan's representative in Burundi, Berhanu Dinka, had welcomed Burundian President Pierre Buyoya's decision to cede power on May 1 to current Vice President Domitien Ndayizeye. The power-sharing deal, under which the presidency alternated between Tutsi and Hutu leaders in the transitional government, was part of a 2001 peace settlement.

The African Union began deploying its first peacekeeping contingent ever, sending 100 South African soldiers to Burundi to shore up an uncertain cease-fire in the country's decade-old civil war. Government troops continue to clash with Hutu rebels despite a cease-fire agreement signed in December 2002.

The peacekeepers flew into Bujumbura, Burundi's capital, as the initial deployment of an African Union force expected eventually to number 3,500. Other countries contributing to the Burundi mission would include Ethiopia and Mozambique. Forty-three African Union observers in the country since February would also join the peacekeeping mission.

The deployment followed years of unsuccessful efforts by the defunct Organisation of African Unity to establish peacekeeping missions in Africa's many war zones. As part of the new mission, peacekeepers would be called upon to demobilise rebel forces, who had voiced reluctance to cooperate.

Burundi President Pierre Buyoya, a Tutsi, peacefully transferred power to his Hutu deputy, Domitien Ndayizeye, marking one the few peaceful handovers the troubled country had seen in decades.

Mr Ndayizeye assumed the presidency of a country still in the grip of an ethnic civil war between minority Tutsis, who had dominated politics in Burundi since 1962, and Hutus, who accounted for about 85% of the country's population.

UN Secretary General Kofi Annan voiced concern about the situation in Burundi despite the peaceful transfer of power, saying the new government would have to establish the necessary mechanism for the return and resettlement of refugees and displaced persons.

Forces pour la Defence de la Democratie rebels, who had kept up fighting despite peace talks, called the handover "meaningless."

CENTRAL AFRICAN REPUBLIC

The UN Peacebuilding Office in the CAR (BONUCA) said that it planned to fine-tune its activities in order to work with new President Francois Bozize, with the mandate remaining the same, but the activities readjusted to reflect that it had worked with a democratically elected regime but would now be going to work with a different one.

President Bozize, who seized power in March 2003, was planning to install a transitional government to last between one and three years, followed by elections. The 28-member transitional administration reportedly included representatives of all parties.

BONUCA said it would wait for the transitional council to be formed before it knew what it could do.

CONGO, DEMOCRATIC REPUBLIC OF

Parties to the Democratic Republic of the Congo conflict signed a peace deal in Sun City, South Africa, that would establish a national unity government. The deal ended nearly five years of war in the country.

More than 350 representatives of rebel groups, opposition parties and the government approved the creation of a power-sharing administration and a new constitution. Elections to take place in two years under the deal would be the first since the country gained independence from Belgium more than 40 years previously. President Joseph Kabila was set to stay on in his post, while rebels and opposition groups were to get vice president positions in a two-year transitional administration.

UN Secretary General Kofi Annan sent a message to the parties saying the meeting marked a breakthrough that could be important for all of Africa.

The BBC reported, however, that continued fighting in the northeastern DRC had raised doubts about whether the peace would stand. Earlier talks were nearly halted by fighting around the northeastern town of Bunia. The Bunia clashes had led Uganda to hold off on withdrawing its troops from the DRC, in turn prompting Rwanda to threaten to send troops back into the DRC unless Uganda pulled out.

The UN Organisation Mission in the DRC deplored the seizure by Rwandan-backed Rassemblement Congolais pour la Democratie-Goma rebels of two towns in the east of the country.

The absence of Congolese President Joseph Kabila and rebel leader Jean-Pierre Bemba at a peace deal signing ceremony for the DRC raised doubts about whether the pact could bring lasting peace. Compounding fears of the deal's inefficacy were reports of continued fighting in eastern parts of the country.

The UN Organisation Mission in the DRC said that a gang of schoolchildren looted its offices in two towns in northern Kivu province – in Kanyabayonga and Lubero – breaking MONUC vehicles. A UN spokesman said that in both instances the children, who numbered about 200, had been sent by other parties.

Almost 1,000 people appeared to have been killed by armed militants in attacks on villages in the DRC's northeastern Ituri region, a MONUC spokesman said.

A preliminary UN investigation indicated about 20 mass graves in the region, and some of the dead appeared to had been summarily executed. It was unclear who was responsible for the attacks. Witnesses told UN investigators that some attackers wore military uniforms, while others wore civilian clothing and that the attackers included women and children.

The leader of the Union des Patriotes Congolais rebel group, Thomas Lubanga, said Ugandan troops and allied DRC tribal fighters were behind the attacks, and an aid worker and a tribal leader said Ugandan forces were in the area where civilians were killed. Uganda, which had more than 2,500 troops in Ituri, denied any involvement.

The Ituri Pacification Commission, headed by UN special representative to the DRC Behrooz Sadry, was inaugurated in Bunia, the region's principal town. The commission's 177 members were drawn from the DRC, Uganda, Angola, MONUC and civil society organisations and had the task of setting up a new administration and a structure for the imposition of law and order. The commission was to ensure the withdrawal of Ugandan troops from the area.

UN investigators were probing reports of a village massacre in a remote north-eastern corner of the DRC, where nearly 1,000 people were allegedly slaughtered in what may be the worst mass killing in the country's long-running civil war.

Quoting witnesses to an attack in a village named Drodro in Ituri province, UN officials said 966 people died in the span of three hours when a band of attackers entered Drodro and began executing residents with guns and machetes in apparent tribal violence. Drodro's residents were mainly members of the Hema tribe, which had a history of ethnic clashes with the rival Lendu tribe in the region.

UN officials who traveled to Drodro said they saw scraps of clothing and blood around some 20 mass graves in Drodro.

The United Nations moved to bring aid to Drodro as well, airlifting medicine and plastic sheeting to survivors of the attack.

The main rebel group in the country, Rassemblement Congolais pour la Democratie, called the Drodro killings "ethnic cleansing" and accused Uganda, one of half a dozen countries that had at times taken part in the DRC's civil war, of involvement.

Ugandan army officials denied the accusation, saiding their forces were miles away from the site of the killings at the time.

The attack came less than 24 hours after the DRC's warring factions agreed to create a national unity government to oversee a two-year transition toward democratic elections, the first since independence in 1960. President Joseph Kabila was sworn in as the interim head of country.

The DRC and the United Nations agreed to begin a joint investigation into the April 3 killing of nearly 1,000 people in the northeastern region of the country. The DRC, the MONUC and the UN Office of the High Commissioner for Human Rights would seek to identify and bring to justice those involved in the incident.

UN investigators said that they had found 15 mass graves holding 300 bodies, apparently those of people killed in the alleged massacre. The UN Office for the Coordination of Humanitarian Affairs said the bodies of at least 960 victims had been recovered, while MONUC said it was forced to distribute medical supplies to survivors by helicopter because of insecurity on the ground.

A UN official said investigators believed up to 350 people, rather than an initial estimate by local witnesses of nearly 1,000, were massacred by tribal militias in the DRC.

UN High Commissioner for Human Rights Sergio Vieira de Mello said those responsible for this act could be brought before the new International Criminal Court.

The Congolese government said that those responsible for the attack should be put on trial and that it had left the investigation to the United Nations.

DRC President Joseph Kabila vowed to bring to justice those responsible for the massacre.

Government and UN officials who visited a hospital where 79 survivors of the massacre were receiving treatment found that there was no food for the patients because farmers were too afraid to work their fields.

Ugandan President Yoweri Museveni agreed to withdraw his troops from the volatile country by April 24.

At a meeting of African heads of state Uganda, Rwanda and the Democratic Republic of the Congo agreed that the UN Organisation Mission in the DRC should take over positions from which troops from Uganda, the last outside power officially to have troops in the DRC, withdrew. There was also agreement that Rwandan troop movements would be investigated by a third-party mission, which was to include South African and UN officials.

The Ugandan army had said Rwandan troops had returned to the DRC and begun advancing toward Ugandan positions in Ituri province. The Rwandan army had denied the reports, saying that Uganda was trying to delay its scheduled April 24 withdrawal from the DRC. Ugandan President Yoweri Museveni said his troops would leave the DRC ahead of the April 24 deadline. Rising tensions between Uganda and Rwanda had sparked fears of an open battle between their armies in the DRC.

An international committee that was monitoring the transition in the DRC held its first meeting at MONUC headquarters in Kinshada. The panel comprised MONUC, the five permanent UN Security Council members, Belgium, Canada, South Africa, Angola, Mozambique, Zambia and the European Union. It discussed administrative matters and agreed to meet weekly.

In a deal brokered via the UN-organised Ituri Pacification Commission, rival militia and tribal groups in the northeastern Democratic Republic of the Congo agreed to set up a power-sharing local interim government in a bid to keep the peace until a new postwar national government took over.

The deal provided for a temporary administration in Ituri province, entailing a 32-member power-sharing assembly, a commission to examine the causes of the conflict, a provincial security committee and a 17-member human rights body.

The UN Organisation Mission in the DRC announced that it was increasing the number of peacekeepers in Ituri province. An initial deployment of 200 UN military observers would go to Bunia, the main town in Ituri. The observer contingent, made up of troops from Uruguay, was set to arrive in the area as 2,000 troops from Uganda began pulling out.

A tribal chief in the DRC said that ethnic strife in violence-racked Ituri province killed 120 people. According to Thomas Lubanga, head of the Hema-led rebel group Union des Patriots Congolais, a militia leader of the Hema tribe ordered an attack on the Lendu tribe that killed 60 people. The Lendu then retaliated by killing 60 Hema who were fleeing to Uganda to escape the violence, Mr Lubanga said. the MONUC could not independently confirm the reported.

It was not clear why Hema militia leader Chief Yves Kahwa Mandro ordered the attack that started the bloodshed, although Mr Lubanga said Mr Kahwa wanted to protect his turf from the rival Lendus. In the past the two neighbours' sparring had produced few casualties, as they fought with low-technology weapons, including spears and arrows. Since Ugandan and Congolese governments armed the tribes as proxies in their civil war, however, the violence had become more deadly.

The MONUC said that it was satisfied with "concrete steps taken" to end the DRC's four-year war, but said it was deeply concerned about continuing conflict in the east of the country. In Orientale, Kivu Nord and Kivu Sud provinces violence was on the rise.

Uganda withdrew 1,650 troops from the DRC by air. Uganda's remaining troops in the DRC, were walking home.

A UN military observer was killed and another injured in a land mine accident in northeastern DRC. According to MONUC, the two were driving through Komanda, southwest of Bunia, when their vehicle drove over a land mine. This was the second such incident since MONUC deployed observers in November 1999.

MONUC lauded a visit by a delegation of the rebel Rassemblement Congolais pour la Democratie to the capital, Kinshada – the first visit by an official delegation of the group since civil war broke out in 1998. The visit marked the end of nearly two weeks of intense negotiations led by MONUC chief Amos Namanga Ngongi.

COTE D'IVOIRE

The United Nations said that Secretary General Kofi Annan was proposing that the Security Council establish a UN mission to help Ivory Coast form a transitional government as conceived in a power-sharing peace accord.

In a new report on the West African country, Mr Annan said a proposed UN Mission in Cote d'Ivoire (MINUCI) would be directed by his special representative to the country, Albert Tevoedjre. Mr Tevoedjre would organise UN efforts to ease the humanitarian, refugee and human rights crises facing Ivory Coast after six months of conflict between the government and various rebel factions.

Mr Annan said a French-brokered peace deal reached in January, which laid out a plan whereby government and rebel leaders were to share power in a transitional government until elections in 2005, was the best hope for a peaceful resolution. He also expressed regret, though, that the agreement's implementation had been delayed.

Controversy over the arrangement had resulted in large and often violent civil protests. A rebel spokesman said rebels would join a cabinet meeting in the government-held capital, Yamoussoukro.

Rebels had boycotted two previous attempts to convene the power-sharing government, citing concerns for their safety in government-held regions and questions over President Laurent Gbagbo's willingness to devolve certain powers to new Prime Minister Seydou Diarra, who many said was in charge of building the new government under the January deal.

The rebel spokesman said rebels reserved the right to quit the government if their concerns were not resolved.

Global Witness said in March 2003 that the Liberian government under President Charles Taylor continued to import weapons in violation of UN sanctions and had been providing them to rebel forces in Ivory Coast and Sierra Leone. Global Witness said Liberia had used funds from its timber industry to maintain supplies of illegal arms, which it received from Eastern Europe via France, Libya and Nigeria. The group had called on the United Nations to renew existing sanctions against Liberia, which covered the sale of weapons to Monrovia and trade in its diamonds, and to extend them to include Liberian timber.

Mr Taylor was also reportedly helping rebels in Sierra Leone destabilise and disrupt the operations of a special UN court that was expected to indict him and other key figures in Liberia for war crimes allegedly committed during Sierra Leone's civil war.

Three rebel groups in Ivory Coast attended a meeting of the country's new Cabinet in the capital, Yamoussoukro, after refusing to go to previous meetings since a peace deal was reached in France in January.

According to Reuters new trouble could arise when rebel ministers went to Abidjan, the country's main city, to take up their posts. Anti-rebel sentiment was high in the city.

Ivorian rebels announced the effective suspension of their participation in Ivory Coast's new government following what they called government helicopter attacks against rebel positions in the west.

Mi-24 helicopters killed 15 civilians when they attacked positions of the Mouvement pour la Justice et la Paix and the Mouvement Populaire Ivoirien du Grand Ouest in the western town of Danane. The two rebel groups said they were planning to retaliate within days.

ECOWAS foreign ministers endorsed a proposal made by the organisation's defence ministers to increase the number of ECOWAS peacekeepers in Ivory Coast from 1,200 to 3,200. ECOWAS Deputy Executive Secretary Oumar Diarra said the organisation was obligated to increase its troops numbers in Ivory Coast because the Security Council in Resolution 1464 called on it to enforce the cease-fire and protect civilians and aid workers. Also, Prime Minister Diarra had said ECOWAS troops were responsible for disarming combatants.

The organisation added that it faced a shortage of funds that could hamper military operations in Ivory Coast. It called in particular on the United Nations, the United States, Canada, Japan and the European Union to help fund its Ivorian activities.

An Ivory Coast cease-fire monitoring committee headed by UN envoy Albert Tevoedjre flew to the western city of Danane on a fact-finding mission following rebel and military reported of a government-ordered helicopter attack on rebel positions there.

According to witnesses, Mi-24 helicopters killed 15 civilians when they fired on positions of the Mouvement pour la Justice et la Paix and the Mouvement Populaire Ivoirien du Grand Ouest.

Interim Defence Minister Assoa Adou appeared to acknowledge that government troops had carried out an operation in the west. He said the government had had to "react" to a rebel offensive.

An Ivory Coast cease-fire monitoring committee led by UN special representative Albert Tevoedjre said that a helicopter attack three days earlier on rebel positions near the western Ivorian town of Danane constituted a violation of a cease-fire signed on January 13. Rebels had said the attack could lead them to suspend participation in the country's new power-sharing government.

The UN Security Council planned to press Ivory Coast's government to halt helicopter attacks against rebels.

Ivory Coast's two main western rebel groups, the Mouvement Patriotique Ivoirien du Grand Ouest and the Mouvement pour la Justice et la Paix, had retaken the towns of Zouan-Hounien and Bin-Houye, which government troops captured. Sources said the rebel offensive also involved troops from the country's main rebel group, the northern Mouvement Patriotique de Cote d'Ivoire.

President Gbagbo told UN special envoy Albert Tevoedjre that renewed fighting, particularly in western Ivory Coast, demonstrated a "will of the rebels to resume the war and to take control of the state by military means, damaging the ongoing peace process, which I had always supported and would not stop supporting."

Ivory Coast's new power-sharing government, including nine ministers drawn from the country's rebel groups, held its first full meeting in the country's main city, Abidjan.

President Gbagbo was among those who attended the closed-door session, and security was provided by government forces – a switch from previous related meetings, which had been guarded by French and Economic Community of West African States peacekeepers deployed in Ivory Coast under a UN-backed cease-fire signed in January in Linas-Marcoussis, near Paris.

The new government's progress had been slowed by continued violence on the ground. Rebels had alleged that, over the past week, government troops had carried out five air raids on rebel-held towns, mainly in the west of the country.

Rebels said that government troops killed 10 civilians and one rebel fighter in a helicopter attack on a marketplace in Vavoua, a rebel-held town in western Ivory Coast. Aid workers said they knew about at least one death and were treating 50 people wounded in the attack.

Medecins Sans Frontieres said that it was treating nearly 50 wounded civilians who arrived in a hospital in Man, a major western town, and that more were continuing to arrive. The aid group said the patients were wounded in helicopter attacks on the towns of Danane and Maheupleu. It said eight people had died in the hospital from their wounds.

The leader of one of the three rebel groups that began fighting against Ivory Coast's government in 2002 and entered into a cease-fire in January, Mouvement Populaire Ivoirien du Grand Ouest chief Felix Doh, was killed near the Liberian border. The circumstances of his death remained unclear amid conflicting reports.

According to the country's main rebel movement, the northern Mouvement Patriotique de Cote d'Ivoire, Mr Doh was killed by warlord Sam Bockarie, who had been indicted for crimes against humanity by the UN-backed Sierra Leone war crimes tribunal. The MPCI said it was Mr Doh who recruited Mr Bockarie and his men to fight alongside the MPIGO in western Ivory Coast but that Mr Bockarie had Mr Doh killed because of the latter's bid to disarm and send home the foreigners. An MPCI member though, said MPCI rebels killed Mr Doh because they suspected he was plotting against them.

The MPCI issued a statement accusing both Ivorian government-allied Liberian fighters and Sierra Leonean armed groups of involvement in assassinating Mr Doh.

Both government and rebel forces in Ivory Coast had been supported by combatants from neighbouring countries. President Gbagbo and Liberian President Charles Taylor agreed to deploy a joint force to patrol the tumultuous border between their countries, with help from French and Economic Community of West African States peacekeepers already deployed in Ivory Coast. Each of the two countries stood accused of backing the other's rebels.

The UN Security Council was to meet at the request of ECOWAS to discuss the Ivorian conflict. The foreign ministers of Ivory Coast, Ghana, Guinea, Niger and Senegal were expected to brief the Council on peacekeeping efforts and to seek funding for the peacekeeping force.

UN Secretary General Kofi Annan called on the Security Council and international donors to provide an Economic Community of West African States peacekeeping force deployed in Ivory Coast with enough funds to sustain it for six months. Mr Annan asked for $47 million for the force.

He also urged the Council to approve the establishment of a UN operation in Ivory Coast including a military liaison and human rights, civil affairs and media components.

Mr Annan said the ECOWAS force needed more money because of an expansion of its mandate and an increase in its numbers. Foreign Minister Nana Addo Dankwa Akufo-Addo of Ghana had said it had become necessary to expand the force from 1,200 to 3,300 soldiers as the force's mandate, which at first entailed only monitoring a cease-fire reached in January between the country's government and rebels, had been expanded to include protecting a new power-sharing government, demobilising and disarming militias and helping the government gain control over Ivory Coast's territory.

The United Nations appealed for $85 million to respond to the Ivory Coast crisis, seeking funds for food security, health, water, sanitation, education, human rights and coordination. The money was to be used to help not only Ivorians but also people affected by the Ivorian war in five neighbouring countries – Burkina Faso, Ghana, Guinea, Liberia and Mali.

CYPRUS
In a report to the Security Council UN Secretary General Kofi Annan reportedly said Turkish Cypriot leader Rauf Denktash, who headed the breakaway northern republic in Cyprus, bore prime responsibility for the failure of UN-brokered talks aimed at unifying the divided island.

Turkish Cypriot Prime Minister Dervis Eroglu dismissed criticisms of Mr Denktash's stance in recent talks.

Cypriot President Tassos Papadopoulos, who headed the internationally recognised ethnic Greek republic in the south of the island, rejected Denktash's proposal, saying talks under the auspices of the United Nations represented "the best hope for us to proceed towards a comprehensive settlement."

UN Secretary General Kofi Annan said in his latest report to the Security Council on Cyprus that his plan to enable a united Cyprus to join the European Union remained on the table, but that he would not undertake any new initiatives until he saw the political will necessary for a successful outcome.

In March 2003 Mr Annan met with Turkish Cypriot leader Rauf Denktash and Greek Cypriot leader Tassos Papadopoulos in a failed last-minute bid to gain their approval for his proposals, which would had led to the holding of separate and simultaneous referenda in time for a reunited Cyprus to sign the EU Treaty of Accession on April 16.

Turkish Prime Minister Recep Tayyip Erdogan said Turkey would initiate its own bid to end the 29-year division of the disputed island, calling for talks with Greece and suggesting that they could take place outside the UN framework, with rapid negotiations being held among what he called Cyprus' three guarantor states

– Turkey, Greece and the United Kingdom – as well as the Turkish Cypriot and Greek Cypriot sides.

A source close to Greek Prime Minister Costas Simitis said, however, "It's the elected government of the Republic of Cyprus, which we support, that had to discuss with the leaders of the Turkish Cypriots, not us with Ankara." Mr Simitis had agreed to hear Mr Erdogan's proposal when they met at "an ordinary meeting on the sidelines" of a regional summit, but stood firm that any formal talks remain within a UN framework.

The UN Security Council passed Resolution 1475 commending UN Secretary General Kofi Annan's unsuccessful settlement plan for Cyprus, calling it a "unique basis" for further talks and condemning the "negative approach" of Turkish Cypriot leader Rauf Denktash to unification talks.

About 300 Turkish Cypriots and about 50 Greek Cypriots crossed the UN-monitored "green line" that separated Cyprus' breakaway, ethnic Turkish northern republic from its southern, internationally recognized ethnic Greek state. The crossings, which took place in the divided capital, Nicosia, were the first in 29 years and followed the authorisation of cross-border movements by both governments. The border was open in both directions, with checkpoints on both sides registering the crossings and UN peacekeepers observing the proceedings. The opening was meant to increase confidence following the collapse of UN-brokered reunification talks in March and to test whether the two sides could coexist, Turkish Cypriot officials said.

DISARMAMENT

The UN Disarmament Commission concluded its annual session without reaching consensus on either of the items on its agenda:

1. ways and means to achieve nuclear disarmament and
2. practical confidence-building measures in the field of conventional arms.

The commission began as it started – with two working papers drafted by the commission's chairmen that contained long lists of initiatives but did not enjoy any consensus. The rapporteur of the commission, Mehiedine al-Kadiri, said the failure to reach consensus owed more to the complexity of the issues and not to the political will of states.

The commission works only by consensus.

Both items were in their third years on the agenda. According to the commission's rules, an item is dropped after three years. Toward the end of 2003, the commission would meet to discuss which items to place on its 2004 agenda.

EAST TIMOR

UN Secretary General Kofi Annan asked the Security Council to extend for one year the mandate of the UNMISET, citing a deteriorating security environment that he called the most striking development since he last reported on the country in November 2002.

Earlier in March the Council had passed a resolution to bolster UNMISET's ability to handle civil unrest and to facilitate police response to new situations. The body also backed a quicker reduction in UNMISET numbers than had been previously planned.

Despite worsening insecurity, Mr Annan said that "much had been achieved" in the year since UNMISET took over for its predecessor, the UN Transitional Administration in East Timor. In particular, he said the "Timorese public administration and police force were assuming increasing levels of responsibility, with growing confidence."

IRAQ

Following reports that the United States was seeking to set up its own nuclear weapons inspection process in Iraq, International Atomic Energy Agency head Mohamed ElBaradei said that the IAEA alone was responsible for such inspections.

US troops continued to advance on Baghdad amid reports that the early stages of the battle for the city had already begun.

US Marines took a key bridge 100 miles from Baghdad in what a reporter traveling with the Marines called a "relatively fierce firefight" resulting in "scores of Iraqi dead" adding that the Marines felt like the battle for Baghdad had begun. The beginning of the end was at hand.

The US Defence Department said President George W. Bush had given Tommy Franks, the top US commander in the Persian Gulf, permission to initiate the battle for Baghdad when he saw fit.

US-British air raids continued over the capital's southern and central districts. Reportedly hit was an area near the Information Ministry, which had repeatedly been targeted in bombing.

Responding to Iraqi claims that US planes bombed two buses carrying US peace activists from Jordan to Baghdad, US Central Command said it had no evidence to support the claims.

In a new claim, Baghdad said that the killing by US soldiers of at least seven women and children at a checkpoint near Najaf was intentional. The United States had said the soldiers opened fire when the van failed to respond to orders to stop.

A serial number on a shrapnel shard found at the site of the bombing of a Baghdad market, in which dozens of civilians were said to had perished, indicated that it was a US missile that struck the market. The London *Independent* reported that its investigations showed Raytheon produced the missile and sold it to the US Navy. The United States and the United Kingdom had suggested an Iraqi missile could have struck the market.

Iraqi state television reported that Iraqi President Saddam Hussein presided over a meeting of his aides, but it did not show images of the meeting or specify the date on which it was held. President Saddam's offices and residences had been heavily bombed by US-British forces, and speculation was rampant about whether he was killed in the attacks.

Iraqi television also transmitted a statement that was said to be from President Saddam. According to the statement, US and British troops were failing in their efforts, an Iraqi victory was "at hand," and Iraqis should fight against US and British troops "so that Iraq, the bastion of religion and principles, would be secured and our (Islamic) nation would come out of this crisis glorious."

US defence officials made repeated reference to President Saddam's failure to appear in public since the war began.

Saudi Arabia called on Mr Saddam to step aside in order to end the war.

UN Secretary General Kofi Annan expressed hope that UN weapons inspectors would eventually return to Iraq, calling their departure from the country a mere suspension of work. The inspectors should go back to Iraq to conduct testing if weapons of mass destruction were found.

Asked about the possible consequences for the war's legitimacy if there was such a discovery, Mr Annan replied that the UN Security Council "had not endorsed this war." Asked about Iraqi threats of suicide attacks in other Arab countries, Mr Annan commented, "Most people would see it as illegal; it would be seen as terror against innocent civilians."

US planes had been conducting "very heavy bombing" between Dohuk and Mosul in northern Iraq, according to Kurdish tribal leader Farhan Sharafani.

The United States was gradually building up its troop presence in the north.

Kurdish officials in the northern Iraqi oil hub of Kirkuk said an armed, organised Kurdish underground in the city was ready to rise up against Baghdad's control but was waiting impatiently for US troops to attack from the outside, officials said they were aware of no US decision to launch a significouldt ground war in the north. The United States reportedly had fewer than 3,000 troops in the region.

Despite 13 days of British-US airstrikes and ground assaults on the southern city of Basra, Iraq's second-largest city, residents had said forces loyal to Hussein remained firmly in control.

Human Rights Watch said that the United States had used cluster munitions during the war that leave large amounts of dangerous unexploded ordnance behind. It renewed a call for banning such weapons. A US Army official said it was uncertain whether the weapons were being used.

US troops were reportedly within four miles of Baghdad's gates as US marines and infantry advanced on the Iraqi capital on roads scattered with dead bodies in Iraqi uniform, destroyed Iraqi vehicles and abandoned uniforms of loyalist forces. Thousands of US military vehicles were said to be approaching Baghdad from the south and west after defeating Iraqis who tried to hold a bridge 35 miles south of the city.

In Kut, about 100 miles to the southeast, US Marines and Iraqi fighters were said to be engaged in building-to-building combat. Residents said women and children had been sent out of the city and militias loyal to President Saddam Hussein had taken young men away and forced them to fight against US and British troops.

An Iraqi Red Crescent maternity hospital in Baghdad was seriously damaged when a trade centre across the street was bombed. Three bystanders were killed and 25 people were injured. In another apparent US bombing error a raid outside Hilla, 60 miles south of Baghdad, produced a "truly horrific" scene, according to an ICRC team on the scene. "There were dozens of bodies torn apart, limbs ripped off, 450 wounded," the spokesman said. The ICRC had said the raid killed 33 people.

The ICRC called on both sides in the war to do more to prevent civilian casualties.

US Central Command said it was looking into reported of civilian deaths in Hilla and acknowledged US use in Iraq of cluster bombs, which scatter tiny bomblets over large areas, could take years to go off and had been repeatedly condemned by human rights groups.

Human Rights Watch said that Iraq had violated international humanitarian law by keeping land mines in a mosque in the northern town of Kadir Karam and by placing them around the edifice before abandoning the area. The British Mines Advisory Group said it entered the mosque and dismantled more than 150 mines. Human Rights Watch said Iraq had been planting mines in various areas.

US Central Command accused Iraqi troops of using a mosque in Najaf for cover as they fired on US-British forces. US and British commanders said their troops had strict orders not to fire on sacred sites, while Iraq accused US-British forces of bombing mosques and seeking to destroy tombs of religious significance in Najaf and Karbala.

US Defence Secretary Donald Rumsfeld urged President George W. Bush to immediately install an interim Iraqi government made up of exiled opposition groups such as the Iraqi National Congress. He called on Mr Bush to ask the top US commander in the Persian Gulf, Tommy Franks, to announce that the expatriates were in charge of Iraq, adding that expatriates who had experienced democracy were better equipped to run the country than were opposition figures now inside Iraq.

US News reported that the timing and composition of the new Iraqi government was a matter of heated debate within the US government, in particular sparking battles between, on the one hand, the Defence Department and, on the other, the State Department and the CIA. Expatriate leaders installed to run Iraq would "be viewed as part of the Americould occupation," one intelligence official said.

The US Defence Department hoped the installation of a new government before President Saddam Hussein was overthrown could enable the United States to oust

Saddam's regime without a full-scale invasion of Baghdad. Describing a scenario in which the United States would take charge of basic government institutions and services, US Chairman of the Joint Chiefs of Staff Richard Myers said that the remaining members of Saddam's government "would not be in charge of anything except their own defence."

John Peabody, a US colonel whose engineer brigade was at Baghdad's Saddam International Airport, declared the airport "secure," adding that US "forces were continuing to clear the areas in and around it." US troops had reportedly dislodged Iraqi forces from the airport and closed off the airport entrance nearest Baghdad. The United States was trying to set up a base of operations at the airport. US Central Command said that the United States was "still encountering some resistance" at the airport but that resistance had in any case "not been overwhelming."

Two thousand five hundred Iraqi Republican Guard soldiers had surrendered to US Marines south of Baghdad, the Marines said.

At a checkpoint in the west of the country, a car exploded, killing three US-British soldiers, a pregnant woman and the car's driver, US Central Command said, adding that the incident appeared to be a suicide attack.

US troops at an industrial site south of Baghdad found thousands of boxes of white powder, nerve agent antidote and documents on chemical warfwere.

Amid continuing speculation about whether Saddam Hussein was still alive, Iraqi Foreign Minister Naji Sabri said that he was alive but would not said whether he had seen the president adding that the leadership were well and functioning as normal.

US Central Command said that it had targeted a presidential bunker and residence in Baghdad and a palace west of the Tigris River with precision munitions. An architect who said he designed the bunker, Karl Bernd Esser, had said the structure could withstand anything short of a direct hit by a nuclear weapon like the one that destroyed Hiroshima, Japan, in 1945.

US troops continued their increasingly deeper incursions into Iraq's capital, with more than 60 tanks and 40 armoured combat vehicles pushing to the banks of the Tigris River in what some military officials called the start of the "battle for Baghdad." The United States captured President Saddam Hussein's main palace in the capital and closed off most remaining routes out of the city.

Although Iraqi Information Minister Mohammed Saeed al-Sahhaf said there was "no presence of the American columns in the city at all" and that US forces were "surrounded" and "slaughtered," Sky television showed US soldiers inside the apparently deserted main presidential palace. US officials said their troops also took two other presidential compounds.

Heavy fighting was reported between US troops positioned on the west bank of the Tigris and Iraqis on the east bank, but US Central Command spokesman said the "Iraqi military was no longer an effective fighting force." He acknowledged, though, that there was "no telling when the final showdown" would take place.

US officials said that about 2,000 Iraqis had been killed in fighting in and around Baghdad. An ICRC spokeswoman estimated that during a US incursion into Baghdad, casualties were arriving at a Baghdad hospital at a rate of 100 per hour.

In northern Iraq, US planes unintentionally bombed a Kurdish military convoy, killing at least 17 and wounding 45. The injured include Wajih Barzani, brother of Kurdistan Democratic Party leader Massoud Barzani, who controled the western sector of Iraq's autonomous Kurdish enclave in the north.

US troops evacuated an Iraqi military compound after tests indicated the presence of sarin nerve gas. A number of US soldiers at the site earlier showed symptoms of exposure to the gas and underwent decontamination.

US troops reportedly found suspect chemicals at two sites: the military compound and an agricultural warehouse. They also reportedly found hundreds of gas masks and chemical suits.

British troops had reportedly gained control of large parts of Iraq's second-largest city, Basra, after two weeks of fighting against Saddam loyalists and conducting only limited incursions. The Britons' bid to occupy the city could reportedly take several days.

A major in a British parachute regiment involved in the Basra campaign, Andrew Jackson, said his superiors confirmed that British troops in the city had found the body of Ali Hadsan al-Majid, a senior Iraqi official known as Chemical Ali who allegedly ordered a 1988 poison gas attack that killed thousands of Kurds.It was reported that he was killed when his house in Basra was bombed with precision munitions.

British troops said that they found hundreds of boxes of human remains in a warehouse near Basra that appeared to be those of people who died long ago. Iran said that the bodies were those of Iranian soldiers killed during the 1980-88 Iran-Iraq war.

The United States started to airlift hundreds of Iraqi exiles into southern Iraq as the first elements of what was meant to become a new Iraqi army. The soldiers reportedly belonged to the Iraqi National Congress and were led by the congress' founder, Ahmed Chalabi, who, along with other opposition figures, had been flown to southern Iraq from the Kurdish-controlled north of the country.

Twenty-six Iraqi soldiers who deserted their units and fled into Kurdish-controlled areas in northern Iraq had told Human Rights Watch of executions, beatings, low pay and lack of food and water in the Iraqi army. One soldier said he witnessed the summary execution of 10 suspected deserters. Others spoke of 10- to 12-man execution squads drawn from Iraqi armed forces and military intelligence but said they had not witnessed executions. The Iraqis said the Kurdish troops to whom they surrendered treated them well, and most were registered with the ICRC. Human Rights Watch said the deserters appeared gaunt and that several had skin ailments. Several of the Iraqis spoke of being paid only about $2 per month and of going months without pay. They also described beatings and warnings that they would be executed if they tried to escape.

The fate of Iraqi President Saddam Hussein remained a key issue for coalition forces after a US warplane dropped four bombs on a restaurant where he was believed to be meeting with his sons. The bombs destroyed at least three buildings and blasted a crater 60 feet deep in the upscale al-Mansour section of western Baghdad in an attempt to kill Saddam. Iraqi rescuers, who recovered two bodies, said the death toll could be as high as 14.

US defence officials said they were confident that Saddam and his sons were in the building when it was bombed, but one unnamed official said US and British forces were working to confirm whether Saddam was killed. "There's lots of digging and DNA tests involved," the official said.

Iraqi Information Minister Mohammed Saeed al-Sahhaf made no mention of Saddam's fate.

Three journalists were killed in Baghdad and two injured during US attacks on the city. Ten journalists had been killed in combat situations during the war.

US troops launched an early morning attack against an eight-story former Republican Guard headquarter about half a mile from the airport, reportedly killing two Iraqis.

Iraqi forces staged a major counterattack, sending more than 20 buses and trucks with dozens of Iraqi foot soldiers across the Tigris River with assault rifles and rocket-propelled grenades in an attempt to overrun US forces holding a strategic intersection on the western side of Baghdad. At least 50 Iraqi fighters were killed and two US soldiers reported injured by snipers on rooftops.

US troops retook the intersection after US attack planes fired artillery and mortar against Iraqi troops. British Tornado fighter jets were also called in to hit the building occupied by snipers. Short exchanges of fire took place in other areas, with US troops showing no signs of pulling pack.

Fighting broke out at the presidential palace that US troops had entered with artillery fire focusing on one building in the compound.

A coalition warplane crashed near Baghdad's international airport. The pilot ejected safely and was picked up by coalition ground forces.

US troops operating alongside Kurdish fighters in northern Iraq were holding them back from seizing the city of Kirkuk, although they had progressed to within five kilometres of the oil-rich city. Washington had instructed the Kurds to stay outside the historically Kurdish city amid Turkish threats to intervene militarily if the Kurds make a move on Kirkuk or Mosul.

US Secretary of State Colin Powell pledged that the Kurds would be kept from advancing "beyond a certain line" around the two cities, but Kurdish officials said they were waiting for coalition forces to gain control of Baghdad.

A facility near Baghdad that one US officer had claimed might finally prove to be evidence of the "smoking gun" of Iraqi chemical weapons production turned out to contain pesticide, not sarin gas as originally thought.

The US Department of Defence had said Iraqi leaders accused of war crimes should be tried in US federal courts or military tribunals – effectively pre-empting any discussion of trying them in the International Criminal Court, the permanent tribunal set up for that purpose. It also said the United States was investigating and cataloguing war crimes in preparation for issuing war crimes charges. It had catalogued three so far: two involving the footage and killing of US prisoners of war and a third "perfidy" charge involving Iraqi soldiers who allegedly attacked US troops while carrying white surrender flags.

The United States wanted Iraqis to oversee prosecutions of pre-war human rights abuses, and that it was working with Iraqi judges and lawyers to set up a judicial system. Some human rights groups contended that the damaged and compromised Iraqi judiciary could not handle the task and that an international tribunal, or a tribunal that included international jurists in addition to locals, be installed instead.

The UN Compensation Commission released $863.7 million to 27 governments and two international organisations for distribution to 370 successful claimants for compensation from Iraq following the country's 1990 invasion of Kuwait and the subsequent conflict in the region.

Hizbullah Deputy Secretary General Sheikh Naim Qassem responded to recent news reported that unnamed US official were accusing Egyptian and Syrian nationals of fighting against coalition forces, saying his organisation had not sent any members to Iraq to carry out military operations there.

A US Central Command spokesman said that President Saddam Hussein's government no longer controlled Baghdad.

US-British tanks, troops and armored vehicles took up positions in central Firdos Square, encountering little resistance as they encircled a massive statue of Saddam. Television broadcasts showed the statue being toppled later by Iraqis on the scene.

CBS reported that an entire armored US column reached the center of Baghdad, with troops riding atop the vehicles and at least one soldier raising a US flag. Bystanders waved white flags.

US Marines in another part of the city heard explosions and said they were responding to heavy machine-gun fire. The International Committee of the Red Cross said fighting continued in northeastern Baghdad.

Widespread looting was reported in Baghdad amid an apparent absence of security forces to prevent it.

UN agencies expressed concern over looting in Iraq, telling US-British forces that they were required under international law to maintain law and order in territory they occupy. A UNICEF spokeswoman cited looting in schools but called the situation "manageable."

Iraqi Information Minister Mohammed Saeed al-Sahhaf, who had repeatedly denied claims of US-British advances and exhorted Iraqis to fight against the foreign troops, did not appear for his daily briefing. CNN reported that government minders who had been accompanying foreign reporters also did not show up.

A US Central Command spokesman emphasised, though, that the war was not over.

US bombing of a location where President Saddam was thought to be maybe have killed the Iraqi leader, but no final determination had been made.

US forces had been taking precautions to avoid a devastating release of suspected Iraqi chemical and biological agents during US air strikes over the past three weeks of conflict. Army Lieutenant Colonel Thomas Woloszyn, who was in charge of chemical and biological defence for the US Central Command at its Joint Operations Centre in Qatar, said US forces had sought to incorporate factors such as wind direction into bombing decisions to try to minimise the potential for casualties resulting from a chemical or biological release.

With US-British troops apparently in control of most of Baghdad , Iraqi UN Ambassador Mohammed al-Douri conceded in New York that "the game was over."

A prominent Iraqi Shiite Muslim leader was assassinated in an attack that began inside the Imam Ali Mosque in Najaf. CNN identified him during a broadcast as Saided Abdul Majid al-Khoei, a respected religious leader who was pro-Western and was being looked to for help with the transition from the Saddam regime. A motive for the killing was not known.

Kurdish and US troops took the northern Iraqi oil city of Kirkuk, prompting expressions of concern from Turkey, which had a sizeable Kurdish population of its own. A US military official said the United States was seeking to establish a presence in Kirkuk "in the interest of regional stability." Oil facilities around Kirkuk were reportedly completely intact, and wells continued to pump oil.

After taking Baghdad, US troops shifted their attention to Tikrit in north central Iraq, Saddam Hussein's hometown. Several thousand Republican Guard troops remained in Tikrit, according to Pentagon officials.

US forces fought with Iraqi military remnants at a palace and a mosque in Baghdad as thousands of people streamed into the city, looting government buildings. A US Central Command spokesman said US troops acted on intelligence indicating leaders of Saddam's regime were organising a meeting there.

European leaders who opposed going to war in Iraq welcomed the fall of Saddam Hussein.

UN sources said US forces might have put public safety at risk by breaking into the al-Tuwaitha nuclear storage facility south of Baghdad. The sources said there were reported that radiation was escaping from the facility, where tons of International Atomic Energy Agency-monitored material had been kept.

US Marines at al-Tuwaitha had discovered high radiation levels at 14 buildings, with some readings indicating nuclear residue levels too high for human occupation. An underground complex where large amounts of radioactive material were stored had also reportedly been found.

UN Secretary General Kofi Annan repeated his position that UN weapons inspectors should be allowed to resume their work in Iraq as soon as possible. Officials in US President George W. Bush's administration had been quoted in recent days as saying the UN inspectors would never be allowed back into Iraq.

As looting and chaos reigned in Baghdad UN Secretary General Kofi Annan said that there appeared to be no functioning government left in Iraq and that US-led forces there were responsible for Iraqis' welfare.

The International Committee of the Red Cross, which was responsible for monitoring compliance with the Geneva Conventions in wartime, expressing alarm at chaos and looting in Baghdad and in Iraq's second-largest city, Basra, and called on US-British forces in Iraq to ensure law and order.

US President George W. Bush said that US-British troops would help maintain law and order in Iraq, but a White House spokesman said that stabilising the security situation would take time. US forces were establishing a civil military operations centre in Baghdad and had asked those who ran the city's public services to come forward and help.

Associated Press reported that thousands of Iraqis continued to loot in Baghdad as US soldiers guarded key intersections and manned checkpoints. US troops were on high alert following a suicide bombing last night at a checkpoint in Saddam City that seriously wounded four US Marines.

Unrest was also in evidence among Iraqis elsewhere. In Najaf a mob at the Imam Ali Mosque hacked two prominent clerics to death after the clerics, Saided Abdul Majid al-Khoei and Haider al-Kadar, went to the mosque together in a US-backed bid to promote reconciliation.

Some observers blamed the development on rivalries between Shiite factions over who would control Najaf in the future, while others said elements loyal to ousted Iraqi President Saddam Hussein, viewing Mr al-Khoei as too supportive of the United States, instigated the violence.

Mr Al-Khoei, who had just returned to Iraq after 12 years in London, told the *Chicago Tribune* that he sought to help reconcile local leaders, religious figures and the US military and to promote democracy in Najaf.

In Tehran about 200 Iraqis stormed the Iraqi Embassy, destroying photographs of Saddam Hussein and shouting, "No Saddam! No US puppet regime! We want freedom!" Police said no diplomats were in the building at the time.

Iraqi UN Ambassador Mohammed al-Douri said that he was leaving his post, citing US pressure that he said would prevent him from doing his job "with full freedom."

Turkey, which had a sizeable Kurdish minority and had repeatedly expressed concern over the repercussions on its territory of Kurdish gains in northern Iraq, said that it was preparing to send observers to the northern Iraqi oil hub of Kirkuk, earlier captured by US-backed Kurdish forces. The move followed US Secretary of State Colin Powell's invitation to Turkey to confirm that US troops controlled the city. Kurdish forces had promised to move out and let the United States take over.

In another northern city, Mosul, an Iraqi army corps had surrendered and agreed to a cease-fire, US Central Command in Qatar said. Mosul fell without a fight and looting and chaos were reported there. Previous reported indicated that Saddam family members might have been hiding out in Mosul, preparing a last stand.

Saddam Hussein's hometown, Tikrit, remained the last bastion of his government.

US troops attacked a Baghdad mosque in an apparent unsuccessful bid to kill or capture top figures of the Saddam government. Army and Marine officials said Saddam Hussein himself might have been inside at the time. US defence and intelligence officials though, said most top US Defence Department officials suspected the President was dead.

Syria, accused by some US officials of providing Iraq with military aid and of harbouring Iraqi nuclear scientists and military officials, said that it was the United States' and not Syria's responsibility to ensure that Saddam Hussein and his top aides did not flee Iraq into Syria.

As armed resistance to US forces dwindled Syrian volunteers constituted most of the holdouts who were manning sandbagged positions in the al-Mansour district of western Baghdad. Syrian volunteers had also taken part in fighting against US forces in southern Iraq.

Volunteer fighters from Syria and other Arab countries continued to stream into Iraq and were heavily involved in the war. AP, though, reported that many such volunteers were returning home.

Marines reported finding an underground network of laboratories and other facilities at al-Tuwaitha. A team from the US Defence Department's Defence Threat Reduction Agency arrived at the site to begin investigating whether plutonium was present. The IAEA had said the facility contained only uranium used for research. US defence officials said that they were so far aware of no weapons-grade material at al-Tuwaitha.

The CIA released a report to Congress indicating Saddam Hussein's government had expanded work on banned long-range missiles and continued in 2002 to develop weapons of mass destruction.

US Marines were fighting with forces loyal to Saddam Hussein in his hometown, Tikrit, the last bastion of loyalist resistance in Iraq. US forces suspect that about 2,500 fighters were holed up in Tikrit and believed members of Saddam's government might be among them. The Marines were meeting only pockets of resistance as they secured Tikrit and that US troops had established checkpoints south and west of the city in hopes of corralling government leaders as they seek to flee.

After days of general insecurity in Baghdad, including rampant looting, more than 2,000 police officers reported back to work in response to an appeal from the head of police under Saddam's government, Zuhair al-Nuami. The capital normally had a police force of about 40,000.

According to AP, which reported that lawlessness was lessening in the city, the Iraqi police would participate in joint patrols with US soldiers, beginning as soon as possible. US patrols had reportedly been visible in many parts of the city and US Marines at a checkpoint outside the city had been stopping vehicles such as pickup trucks filled with goods. Iraqis had been translating for the Marines and helping them identify looters.

In another bid to stem looting, edicts had been posted instructing Iraqis that such behaviour was sinful and that they should fight looters.

In Basra local police were working with British troops to try to restore law and order.

Saddam's top nuclear weapons scientist, Jafar Jafar, surrendered outside Iraq. The news came a day after Saddam Hussein's top scientific adviser, Amir Saadi, surrendered to US forces in Baghdad. A US intelligence official described Mr Amir, who served as liaison between Saddam's government and UN weapons inspectors, as a "linchpin" of suspected Iraqi weapons of mass destruction activity.

UN officials said Mr Amir was believed to had been a crucial figure in Iraqi chemical weapons development. UN and US officials cited the whereabouts of Iraq's VX nerve gas as one subject on which he could be questioned.

International Atomic Energy Agency Director General Mohamed ElBaradei said that he had obtained a US promise to provide security at Iraq's al-Tuwaitha nuclear site, where high radiation readings had been found by US Marines. He called on Washington to ensure no materials were removed until UN inspectors resumed their verification work at the site. He said only IAEA inspectors had UN authorization for inspections and disarmament in Iraq and should be allowed to return to the country as soon as conditions permitted.

After nearly a week of lawlessness in Baghdad the Iraqi capital was showing the first signs of a return to order. Shopkeepers were reportedly returning to their businesses, and elements of Baghdad's city police reported back to work.

Leading Shiite clerics from Najaf distributed instructions to mosques throughout Iraq, calling on local clerics and people of authority to "establish local committees – to organise the affairs of the neighbourhood." In particular, the clerics sought to establish security and control looting. The mobilisation of armed Shiite groups acting on instructions from these clerics was a sign that an organised alternative power structure already existed in Iraq despite efforts by Washington to draw on exiled and internal opposition leaders in planning a postwar administration.

The International Committee of the Red Cross said that Baghdad's security situation appeared to be improving, allowing aid workers to renew efforts to restore water supplies and visit hospitals.

US forces controlled most of toppled President Saddam Hussein's hometown, Tikrit, establishing checkpoints and dispatching helicopters to conduct aerial patrols. The town's Sunni residents reportedly met the troops with neither jubilation nor rage. Shopkeepers had expressed relief that the US military presence had saved the bazaars from armed looters.

The commander of the Iraqi army's 16,000-soldier Anbar command, Mohammed Jarawi, surrendered to US forces.

The International Atomic Energy Agency said the United States had not responded to its call for UN weapons inspectors to be allowed back into Iraq after the war.

US military officials said they had 30 to 40 former UN weapons inspectors in the pipeline for Iraq and were working to recruit another 20. They said 1,000 military and civilian workers would likely participate in the search. US Defence Department officials said no date had been set to send civilian inspectors back into Iraq because of security concerns. At least two kinds of military arms hunters were already at work in the country. Troops on the front lines were using detectors to identify suspected deadly germs, chemicals and sources of radioactivity and were followed by a better-equipped unit that includes civilian experts and mobile laboratories. Some of the civilian experts, however, said bureaucratic confusion and infighting had delayed their efforts. So far, they said, the military's search efforts seemed superficial and misguided.

US special forces raided the Baghdad home of microbiologist Rahib Taha, who was reportedly in charge of a laboratory that weaponised anthrax under Saddam Hussein's regime. They recovered boxes of documents and brought out three men, but Mr Rahib's whereabouts remained unknown.

The chairman of the US Joint Chiefs of Staff, Richard Myers, said he remained worried that Iraqi chemical or biological weapons could fall into the hands of terrorists.

US officials said that Abu Abbas, the leader of a Palestinian terrorist group that hijacked the cruise liner *Achille Lauro* in 1985 had been captured by US-British forces in Baghdad. The arrest underscored a US-claimed link between Saddam's regime and terrorism. The Palestinian Authority demanded Mr Abbas' release, saying his arrest violated a 1995 agreement between Israel and the Palestinians.

A US military unit had reportedly found an abandoned terrorist training camp said to had been jointly operated by Iraqi and Palestinian groups, where recruits were allegedly taught to make bombs.

More than 2,000 Baghdad police officers who served under Saddam Hussein were reemerging as part of an Iraqi security force being set up by US and British forces. US forces had trained about 700 members of the Free Iraqi Forces in

Baghdad, with joint patrols being conducted to prevent looting and restore security. US civil affairs officers screened the Iraqi returnees, and the military was providing some weapons to the poorly equipped officers and warning them to respect citizens. The patrols provided only the illusion of a criminal justice system, according to the *Washington Post*. The officers were not paid, and there were no jails.

US-British forces were collecting large stockpiles of weapons and ammunition left behind by Iraqi forces, which had left them with a sizeable storage task. The *Los Angeles Times* reported that the recovered weapons – including rifles, mortars, grenades, pistols, rockets and land mines – and recovered Iraqi vehicles would be held until a new government and army were ready to receive them.

US and British media reported several deaths and injuries involving Iraqi civilians handling unexploded cluster bombs that were used by coalition forces during the attack on Baghdad.

Denmark said that, at the request of the United States, it had approached European countries about constituting an ad hoc peacekeeping force for postwar Iraq and that several expressed a willingness to contribute to such a force. The activity came as European Union leaders gathered in Athens to sign a treaty expanding the union from 15 to 25 countries.

According to the *Wall Street Journal*, Spain, Poland, Latvia, Estonia and Italy expressed various levels of support for the idea, and Dutch Prime Minister Jan Peter Balkenende said the Netherlands was "looking into" it. Italy had already authorised the deployment of up to 3,000 military police and relief workers to Iraq. A British diplomat said the United Kingdom was discussing the subject "with quite a wide range of people" at the EU meeting.

French President Jacques Chirac, though, observed that the United Nations was the only place where you find both the competence and the legitimacy to get out of a crisis of this nature.

NATO officials said a UN resolution would be necessary to authorise action in Iraq by NATO command or the deployment of troops from most individual NATO member countries. The *Post* reported that Washington had not asked NATO to take up a peacekeeping role in Iraq and was not likely to do so for weeks. France and Germany had reportedly indicated they would not object to a NATO role and could be willing to contribute troops to such an enterprise.

The United States sought bids from private US contractors to train a national Iraqi police force and remake Iraqi courts and prisons.

The top US commander in the war, Tommy Franks, said that law and order were returning to Iraq.

US troops working to maintain their control of a small part of the Iraqi city of Mosul had clashed with civilians, and forces loyal to toppled Iraqi President Saddam Hussein were present in much of Mosul. Hospital officials said 17 Iraqis had died in clashes with US Marines.

In Saddam Hussein's hometown, Tikrit, Marines broke up fighting between rival clans.

Kurdish television reported that in the northern Iraqi oil hub of Kirkuk, 3,000 unmarked, shallow graves had been found at a military camp. The bodies in the graves were apparently those of civilians.

US forces captured a half brother of Saddam Hussein, Barzan Ibrahim Hadan.

Despite calls by UN Monitoring, Verification and Inspection Commission Executive Chairman Hans Blix for his weapons inspectors to be allowed back into Iraq, the United States planned to send 1,000 of its own inspectors to Iraq to hunt for weapons of mass destruction. An official said the group should be fully operational within weeks.

The deployment of the US team of inspectors – consisting of military personnel, government intelligence analysts, civilian scientists and private contractors – was a bid to put more people into the country and undertake a more organised weapons search, based on intelligence leads.

Former UN weapons inspector in Iraq Charles Duelfer was already in Baghdad directing the US search for banned weapons. The United States had enlisted about 10 former UN weapons inspectors to help in the search for weapons of mass destruction.

US Secretary of Defence Donald Rumsfeld said US forces were taking steps to ensure the credibility of evidence that may be found, adding that US teams would need assistance from Iraqis with knowledge of the country's arms programmes.

UN Secretary General Kofi Annan expressed concern about reports of murder, looting and forced expulsions of Arabs in northern Iraq. Amid reported of widespread intimidation and displacement in and around the city of Kirkuk and in other areas, Mr Annan called for respect for human rights, including the right to live free from intimidation and forced expulsion.

The *Chicago Tribune* reported confusion over the leadership of the city of Baghdad, with various people declaring themselves to be in charge of the capital. Shiite dissident Mohsen al-Zubaidi, for example, had declared himself the governor of Baghdad and issued a proclamation urging tribal leaders to disarm their followers and cooperate with US forces.

In southern Iraq, British troops were criticised for reappointing officials from Saddam Hussein's party to lead reconstruction efforts in Basra. British forces cited the difficulty of finding qualified people not linked to the old ruling party.

US-led forces captured two more of the 55 most wanted Iraqis, whose likenesses had been printed up on decks of playing cards. The capture of Iraq's former minister of higher education and scientific research, Abd al-Khaliq Abd al-Gafar, and Saddam Hussein's son-in-law, Jamal Had toafa Sultan al-Tikriti, brought to six the number of "most wanted" Iraqis taken into custody.

The list of wanted Iraqis had expanded to the thousands and now encompassed low-level Baath Party officials. The United States was planning to prosecute tens of thousands of operatives who enforced Saddam's control in the country of 25 million people.

The US Marines pulled out of Baghdad, leaving the city in control of the Army's 3rd Infantry Division.

The *International Herald Tribune* reported that the 20,000-strong First Marine Division was a visible force on the ground in the city, patrolling the streets on foot, working with neighbourhoods to end looting and working to restore police, hospital, electric and water services. The Army soldiers, on the other hand, were mostly deployed in tanks or armored fighting vehicles stationed in front of banks, museums or palaces.

The situation in Baghdad remained chaotic.

Baghdad's self-proclaimed governor, Mohammed Mohsen al-Zubaidi, declared that Iraq's new constitution should be based on Islamic law and that he had formed 22 committees to oversee city functions, including foreign affairs. Mr Al-Zubaidi's authority was a source of some mystification.

Turkish Foreign Minister Abdullah Gul said Turkey would send soldiers into Iraq for postwar peacekeeping duties. Italy, Bulgaria and Denmark had already offered troops to help stabilise the country. Turkey's agreement to participate in a peacekeeping force, whether it was run by the United States, the United Nations or NATO, was considered a step toward healing the rift between Ankara and Washington after Turkish authorities refused to allow the United States to use Turkish soil to stage an assault on Iraq.

The White House dismissed proposals to bring UN weapons inspectors back to Iraq, saying the United States and its allies would manage the search for banned weapons.

The United States sent at least 5,000 troops to the northern city of Mosul and announced a cease-fire with the Iraq-based Iranian opposition group Mujahideen al-Khalq, a reportedly well-armed group with ties to Saddam Hussein's regime.

Forces from the Kurdistan Democratic Party had for the most part assumed control of the mainly Kurdish east side of the city of 1.25 million, which straddles the Tigris River. The mainly Arab west side had seen chaos and looting ensue from a power vacuum.

The KDP- and US-appointed governor of Mosul, Moshaan al-Jabouri, said about 1,100 of the city's 6,500 police officers were back at work.

An International Committee of the Red Cross representative in Basra said attacks on the city's battered infrastructure might be the work of regrouped Baath Party members.

The *Wall Street Journal* reported that US and Iraqi engineers had resumed the flow of Iraqi oil production in the south, with four wells producing crude oil. US General Robert Crear said southern wells should soon be pumping 170,000 barrels a day and were expected to ramp up to 800,000 barrels a day in six to nine weeks. The oil would be used for Iraq's own refineries and power plants. It was not yet clear when oil would be available for trade with other countries. Iraq's prewar oil production was 2.5 million barrels a day, 60% of which came from the southern oil fields near Basra.

Syria, the focus of US threats and accusations in recent weeks for alleged possession of its own weapons of mass destruction and harbouring of fleeing leaders from neighbouring Iraq, said UN sanctions on Iraq should not be lifted without a formal UN declaration that it had no weapons of mass destruction.

Following UN Security Council debate on whether and how to lift the sanctions now that President Saddam Hussein's government had been ousted, AP reported that Council members remained divided on when and how to lift the sanctions but were united on the need to continue getting humanitarian aid into Iraq.

The UN oil-for-food mandate for Iraq was due to expire on June 3, but the programme had been suspended. Council resolutions requiring that UN inspectors certify Iraq to be free of weapons of mass destruction before sanctions could be lifted outright. France was calling for the immediate lifting of sanctions that affect civilians and the phasing out of the oil-for-food programme, but the United States was opposing the return of UN inspectors and had set up its own inspection teams.

US forces in Iraq captured four more of Saddam's top aides. The highest-ranking official in the group was Muzahim Sa'b Hadsan al-Tikriti, No. 10 on a US most-wanted list of 55 Iraqi officials. Al-Tikriti was from Tikrit, Saddam's hometown, and led Iraqi air defences under Sadam Hussein, as well as allegedly leading Fedayeen forces accused of war crimes. The arrests brought to 11 the number of top Saddam government officials in US custody, and another three were believed to had been killed.

Amid increasing reported of Iraqi figures claiming to be the new mayors and governors of various places in the country, the top commander of US ground forces in Iraq, David McKiernan, issued a proclamation saying that US-British forces "alone [retained] absolute authority within Iraq" and that anyone challenging that authority would be subject to arrest.

US soldiers took $13.1 million from stashes of US cash found in a neighbourhood that was once home to top Iraqi officials, US commanders said. Investigators were said to have recovered all the money, and troops had been ordered to search for more cash at a site where they discovered $656 million. US forces found another $112 million nearby.

Along with members of the US media, US troops were also being investigated for allegedly taking art, artifacts and weapons out of Iraq, US officials said, adding that criminal charges had already been brought in one case. None of the items was among those looted from Iraqi museums, but customs and military officials said US troops and civilians would be permitted to bring no such souvenirs to the United States.

Tariq Aziz, a deputy prime minister in Saddam Hussein's government and No. 43 on a US "most wanted" list of 55 top officials in the Hussein government, surrendered to US forces.

US President George W. Bush said that the United States had already examined the 90 Iraqi sites where it thought chemical or biological weapons were most likely to be found and the United States was working to locate and destroy Iraqi weapons of mass destruction but that so far, nothing had turned up. Hundreds more sites were to be examined. The president acknowledged that questions about US credibility regarding Iraq's weapons of mass destruction might continue.

US troops arrested Mohammed Mohsen al-Zubaidi, the self-proclaimed mayor of Baghdad for conducting illegal political activity and also announced they had captured ousted Iraqi President Saddam Hussein's liaison with UN weapons inspectors, General Hussam Mohammed Amin, who appeared frequently in the media in the run-up to the war as Baghdad's liaison with UN weapons inspectors.

The lethal explosion of an open US weapons dump in a residential part of Baghdad set off protests in the battered Zafaraniyah neighborhood and in central Baghdad. According to the US military, unknown attackers fired four flares into the sprawling dump, setting off a violent chain reaction of exploding warheads, rockets and mortars that damaged homes miles away and killed at least six people. Many Iraqis believed that US forces intentionally caused the explosion.

The London *Telegraph* reported it had discovered documents linking Saddam Hussein to al-Qaeda, a connection the United States had been claiming for months. The three-page memorandum, found in the rubble of a destroyed intelligence headquarters office, reportedly shows that an al-Qaeda envoy was invited to a secret meeting in Baghdad in March 1998 to establish a relationship based on a shared hatred of the United States and Saudi Arabia. The newspaper reported that the meeting was apparently such a success that it was extended by a week and ended with discussions for a visit by al-Qaeda leader Osama bin Laden to Baghdad. The documents did not mention any actual meeting between bin Laden and Iraqi officials. Two of the three pages were reportedly printed on the letterhead of the Mukhabarat, the Iraqi secret service.

Unexploded ordnance and landmines – including some of the 1,500 controversial cluster bombs US forces dropped on Iraq – had killed or maimed more civilians since the end of the war than died during fighting. In northern Iraq, two weeks after the cessation of hostilities 80 people had died and 500 had been injured by unexploded ordnance. The northern city of Kirkuk, with 300 injured or dead, appeared to had suffered most.

Human Rights Watch said that Iraqi forces violated international humanitarian law by storing huge amounts of ammunition in homes, schools and other residential areas. On April 13, Human Rights Watch researchers found a classroom in Kirkuk stacked with boxes of rocket-propelled grenades, mortar shells and machine gun bullets. A school guard told the researchers that the military had brought the munitions to the school five or six days before the start of the war and left a sentry in the classroom. Students had attended classes under those conditions.

Human Rights Watch also said that general lawlessness, along with stores of ammunition left behind by the Iraqi army, were resulting in a higher civilian death toll in northern Iraq since the war's end than during the conflict.

Pentagon planners said as many as 125,000 US troops could be needed to stabilise Iraq until a new Iraqi government could provide security. Planners said that such a size force could occupy Iraq for at least a year. If all went well, the force could drop to 60,000 at the one-year point – or it could increase if there was political or religious unrest.

The Bush administration was tripling the number of scientists and engineers assigned to the military team hunting for banned weapons. The expanded team would include about 1,500 members.

Residents of the town of Fallujah, about 30 miles west of Baghdad, had said 15 Iraqi civilians were killed when US soldiers fired on protesters demonstrating against the US presence in the town. US Army Colonel Arnold Bray put the number of civilians hit at seven. Residents said at least 13 people were killed and about 75 wounded. A US Central Command spokeswoman said, "The Iraqis fired on them. The troops returned fire." She said she had no information on casualties. Residents said the US fire was provoked by the throwing of a rock, not by gunfire.

Human Rights Watch said the United States and the United Kingdom were failing to provide adequate information about their cluster munitions strikes on Iraq, thereby endangering civilians.

Former Iraqi Oil Minister Amer Mohammed Rashid surrendered to US forces. Known to some as the "missile man," Rashid reportedly had in-depth knowledge of toppled President Saddam Hussein's missile programmes and was Hussein's point man on weapons delivery systems. He was No. 47 on a US most-wanted list of 55 Iraqi officials.

The deputy commander of US ground troops in Iraq, Glenn Webster, said that the United States planned to deploy as many as 4,000 additional military police and infantry troops in Baghdad in the following two weeks to counter looting and lawlessness. The troops would join more than 12,000 US soldiers already in the city and mount joint patrols with Iraqi police.

Senior Iraqi prisoners were saying that Iraq under Saddam Hussein had no chemical, biological or nuclear weapons programmes.

Russian President Vladimir Putin rejected a British-US bid to lift UN sanctions on Iraq and ridiculed claims that there were weapons of mass destruction in Iraq. Mr Putin's remarks came at a meeting with British Prime Minister Tony Blair, who expressed opposition to a new bipolar world order, adding that the world faced a choice between a partnership with the United States and other major powers and a continued "diplomatic standoff." Mr Blair said it was important to give the United Nations a "vital role" in Iraq's reconstruction, a question that had been tied to the lifting of sanctions. Mr Putin said Russia and others believed that until clarity was achieved over whether weapons of mass destruction existed in Iraq, sanctions should be kept in place. He called for the return of UN weapons inspectors to Iraq to make a "professional" conclusion on the existence of the alleged weapons.

US troops fired on Iraqi protesters in the town of Fallujah, 30 miles west of Baghdad, for the second time in a week, reportedly killing one person and injuring 16 others. One thousand demonstrators were protesting against an incident in which US troops reportedly killed 13 Iraqis protesting the US presence in the town. US intelligence officer Michael Marti said soldiers in a passing convoy fired on the crowd after rocks were thrown at them and they were engaged by what they thought was automatic weapons fire. City officials who witnessed the incident said they neither saw nor heard shooting from among the protesters.

Former Basra governor Walid Hamid Tawfiq al-Tikriti surrendered to Free Iraqi Forces, according to the Iraqi National Congress. Mr Tawfiq was No. 44 on the US list of 55 most wanted officials.

Former Iraqi Information Minister Mohammed Saeed al-Sahhaf was seeking to surrender to US forces, according to *al-Sharq al-Aswat*. US forces had refused to arrest him because he did not appear on the most-wanted list.

Top military officials from 12 European countries, not including France and Germany, gathered to start building an independent Iraq peacekeeping coalition whose authority would lie outside NATO, the European Union and the United Nations.

With the United States poised to announce the end of combat operations in Iraq, the question of who and how to maintain security in the country had generated intense international debate. Many had suggested NATO as a natural choice, but representatives of the alliance said it was still too divided to take on peacekeeping duties in Iraq, although they add that NATO's assumption of peacekeeping command duties in Afghanistan could be a precedent for Iraq in the long run.

Reports of a UN plan to assemble a peacekeeping force surfaced early in March, but US diplomats could not said at the time whether Washington would accept any UN involvement. The plan, reportedly in the early stages, did not have UN Secretary General Kofi Annan's official endorsement.

Attackers threw two grenades into a former Fallujah police station occupied by US troops, wounding seven soldiers and marking the third violent exchange between Iraqis and US forces in four days.

The incident came hours after soldiers opened fire on anti-American demonstrators, killing two and wounding 18, according to local hospitals. US forces said they were responding to fire from within the crowd.

The march was a protest against previous violence, which killed 16 demonstrators and wounded 50 more when US forces fired into a crowd protesting outside a school where the troops were stationed. The soldiers said they were being shot at and returned fire.

US military officials met with local religious and tribal leaders about the situation.

KOSOVO

Russia announced a decision to withdraw its Balkans' peacekeepers. A military official said Russia no longer had a strategic interest in the Balkans and that Moscow wanted to distance itself from problems in Kosovo. The official said Russian forces would need about a month to leave the Balkans after the order to withdraw.

Russia had 970 soldiers in the Balkans with the NATO-led international peacekeeping forces, with 650 in Kosovo and the rest in Bosnia.

The Serbian government dismissed a UN plan for a handover of powers in Kosovo from UN offices to local authorities in the largely ethnic Albanian province. A government statement said a proposal by the UN administrator in Kosovo, Michael Steiner, was against "the principles and politics of the United Nations Security Council and our state, and thus, absolutely unacceptable."

An ethnic Albanian rebel group in Kosovo called the Albanian National Army was placed on the UN list of terrorist organisations following an explosion at a bridge. The group claimed responsibility for the blast, which damaged a main railway link between Kosovo and the rest of Serbia. The group said it was fighting for the unification of Albanian lands in the Balkans.

LIBERIA

West African ministers and UN officials said the conflict in Liberia would probably worsen without some sort of peacekeeping intervention to halt fighting between rebel forces and troops loyal to Liberian President Charles Taylor.

UN agencies said fighting in Liberia had kept them from delivering humanitarian aid to most of the country, and relief supplies were running low.

The UN office for the Coordination of Humanitarian Affairs said that the majority of people in Liberia could not be reached by aid workers, who had access to only about 30 percent of the country. In the areas that were open to them, aid workers face dwindling supplies and were having to dispense smaller food rations to people in need. OCHA officials also stressed that many of the aid workers who vanished on March 27 were still missing.

UN Secretary General Kofi Annan said in a report to the Security Council that security in Liberia had deteriorated badly, making it nearly impossible for humanitarian workers to reach refugees and internally displaced people, and that rebels now appeared to hold most of the country.

Annan urged the Council not to "lose sight of the urgent need to find an early solution to the conflict in Liberia, whose deleterious effect [was] fast spreading throughout an already troubled subregion."

Mr Annan cited an ECOWAS estimate that rebels now controlled 60% of Liberia, adding that, also according to ECOWAS, there was no safe haven for internally displaced people, who suffered constant attacks from both rebel and government forces. He also transmitted ECOWAS warnings that government opponents were frequently threatened and that sanctions against Liberia were being used as a pretext for a government failure to meet responsibilities to the people. He added that internally displaced people and refugees had been abducted and forcibly conscripted and had fallen victim to rights violations.

ECOWAS was recommending that an international security force be deployed in Liberia.

President Taylor and Ivorian President Laurent Gbagbo agreed to deploy a joint force to patrol the tumultuous border between their countries, with help from French and ECOWAS peacekeepers already deployed under a cease-fire in Ivory Coast's civil conflict. Each of the two countries stands accused of backing the other's rebels.

Tens of thousands of displaced people were living in the west, and nongovernmental organisations had reported that at least 50 civilians claiming to be victims of government helicopter attacks were treated at a hospital in the main western town, Man. At least eight were said to have died.

MIDDLE EAST

Israeli Foreign Minister Silvan Shalom said Israel was "serious" about working with the Palestinians on a US-supported peace plan but would seek changes to the "road map" plan. He listed conditions for resuming talks with the Palestinians, including a halt to "terror and the incitement." He added that Israel would not accept a plan that confined Israeli settlements to their existing boundaries in the West Bank and Gaza Strip. Israeli opposition leader Amram Mitzna said he suspects Israel was playing for time. "This is a recipe to said 'yes' while in reality saiding 'no,'" he said.

US national security adviser Condoleezza Rice said the plan was not open for negotiations, and US Secretary of State Colin Powell called on Israel to stop expanding settlements.

Backed by tanks and helicopter gunships, Israeli forces launched raids against suspected Islamic militants in a Gaza refugee camp, touching off a two-hour gun battle that killed four Palestinians and wounded an Israeli soldier.

Witnesses in the Nusseirat refugee camp said Israeli snipers fanned out over rooftops, while on the ground, soldiers searched houses. Israeli military officials refused to said for whom they were looking, but troops surrounded the house of Hamas member Abdel Hakim Jahjooh, who apparently was not there.

In the West Bank town of Tulkarem, Israeli forces arrested a leader of the militant group Islamic Jihad and began withdrawing after a two-day operation in the area.

Israel's strikes in Tulkarem had prompted an official complaint in New York from the UN Relief and Works Agency for Palestine Refugees, which said Israeli forces took over an UNRWA girls' school and used it as a detention centre during the raids.

Negotiators from the Quartet of outside parties involved in the Middle East – the United States, Russia, the European Union and the United Nations – agreed to publish the "road map" peace plan. Officials hoped to air the plan once a new Palestinian government was sworn in.

In Washington the plan was drawing criticism from lawmakers who were planning to press US President George W. Bush to support changes sought by Israel.

An Israeli fighter jet killed seven Palestinians, including senior Hamas leader Saad Arabid, when it fired missiles into a crowded Gaza City neighbourhood in what was reportedly the first air attack on Palestinian territory since war began in Iraq. Doctors said up to 47 Palestinians were injured.

US President George W. Bush said that the "road map" plan for Israeli-Palestinian peace would be published when new Palestinian Prime Minister Mahmoud Abbas named a Cabinet. Palestinian Authority President Yasser Arafat, though, was seeking to delay the new Cabinet's formation by blocking the ouster of Arafat loyalists from the body. Mr Abbas had chosen several tough Arafat critics as ministers and many Palestinians supported removing current Cabinet members.

Palestinian sources said Mr Abbas had told Mr Arafat he could abandon his bid to form a Cabinet because of what he saw as attempts to undermine his authority, including Mr Arafat's alleged blocking of Cabinet appointments and efforts to retain control of areas such as security and peace talks.

The Middle East peace process suffered a setback when Palestinian Authority President Yasser Arafat rejected the Cabinet picked by incoming Palestinian Prime Minister Mahmoud Abbas, a move that could delay the release of the internationally approved "road map" to Palestinian statehood.

Mr Abbas' proposed Cabinet included reformists in key posts. Mr Abbas kept one of the most closely watched appointments – that of interior minister, which had ultimate control of the security forces – for himself and selected former Gaza security chief Mohammed Dahlan, a critic of attacks on Israelis, to serve under him as minister of state for interior affairs. Mr Dahlan would oversee security but still report to Mr Abbas.

Mr Dahlan's appointment was reportedly a primary reason for Yasser Arafat's opposition. *Ha'aretz* reported that Mr Abbas' decision to install himself as interior minister was an attempt to make the choice of Mr Dahlan more palatable to Mr Arafat, but the move did not work.

Other reform-minded Abbas appointees include former Cabinet member Nabil Amr, who resigned from his post as minister for parliamentary affairs in 2002 over disagreements with Arafat, and former security official and moderate Nasser Yousef as deputy prime minister, one of two new positions Mr Abbas created for his 20-member Cabinet (the other bring minister of external affairs).

An Israeli delegation headed for Washington to outline Israel's reservations to the plan:

- security
- rate of progress – Israel wanted each step to be conditional on fulfillment of the previous one, whereas Palestinians want a strict timetable – and
- right of return. Palestinians wanted refugees who fled what was now Israel during the 1948 Middle East war to be able to return, while Israelis feared they would be outnumbered and their nation's existence jeopardised by such an influx.

Sharon hinted that he would consider giving up some Jewish settlements in the Palestinian territories and said that he viewed a Palestinian state as inevitable.

The British Foreign Office had placed a draft copy of the "road map" plan for Israeli-Palestinian peace in the House of Commons library in what *Gulf News* called an apparently deliberate attempt to pre-empt further delays in releasing the plan. The newspaper added that the draft in the Commons library was essentially the text that would be published, something *Gulf News* sources said would happen within two weeks.

The document cited by *Gulf News* indicated a need for a Palestinian renunciation of violence and terrorism and for a Palestinian leadership that was able to build an effective democracy. Israel was called on to facilitate the creation of a democratic Palestinian state, and both sides were required to unambiguously accept the goal of a negotiated settlement. The Quartet was to facilitate the plan's implementation by brokering direct talks, among other steps.

Palestinian Authority Chairman Yasser Arafat and Prime Minister-designate Mahmoud Abbas, known as Abu Mazen, formed a Cabinet, clearing the way for Abu Mazen to take up his new post and step into Middle East peace negotiations.

The Cabinet agreement between Messrs Arafat and Abu Mazen came after lengthy negotiations about the makeup of the next Palestinian government, which Middle East peace brokers including the United States and the United Nations hope would renew talks with Israel in step with a "road map" for a Palestinian state that Washington plans to air once Abu Mazen was in power.

Israel was preparing to pull back some of its forces from Palestinian areas and release prisoners in a show of support for Abu Mazen. Israeli Prime Minister Ariel Sharon had said he plans to meet Abu Mazen after he was sworn in.

At least five Palestinians died in a raid by Israeli forces on the Rafah refugee camp in the Gaza Strip, one of the biggest operations since the start of the intifada two-and-a-half years previously.

Reuters reported that 70 people were injured in the raid. More than 35 tanks, bulldozers and jeeps raided the town of 60,000 from three directions, with air support from five attack helicopters. Five died in the attack, which destroyed two tunnels the Israeli army said were used for smuggling weapons under the Gaza-Egypt border. The army also blew up the house of a Hamas leader, Mahmoud Abu Shamala.

The raid on Rafah came hours after a clash in the West Bank city of Nablus in which 17 Palestinians were wounded.

Incoming Palestinian Prime Minister Mahmoud Abbas and Palestinian Authority President Yasser Arafat locked horns over Mr Abbas' chosen Cabinet. Mr Abbas reportedly stormed out of a meeting with Mr Arafat and threatened to resign unless his Cabinet was approved. The main sticking point was former Gaza security chief Mohammed Dahlan, whom Mr Abbas wanted to serve as minister of state for internal affairs, a post that would partly oversee security. Mr Arafat disapproved of the choice. Senior Palestinians submitted a compromise deal to Messrs Abbas and Arafat that would have Mr Abbas preside over a 24-minister Cabinet, 14 of whom were members of the previous Cabinet. The list did not include Mr Dahlan, who reportedly tried to defuse the crisis by offering to give up a seat in the Cabinet.

Hours before the deadline that could had spelled the end of an internationally backed peace plan for the Middle East, Palestinian Prime Minister-designate Mahmoud Abbas and Palestine Liberation Organisation Chairman Yasser Arafat ended a weeks-long power struggle and struck a deal on a new Cabinet. Mr Abbas agreed to serve as both prime minister and interior minister and got to keep Mr Dahlan in his Cabinet. Mr Dahlan would serve in a somewhat reduced capacity as the minister overseeing the internal security portfolio.

The Cabinet still had to meet the approval of the Palestinian Legislative Council.

In the first such incident inside Israel in nearly a month, a suspected Palestinian suicide bomber blew himself up at a train station in the central Israeli town of Kfar Saba, killing one person and injuring 13. The explosion took place during morning rush hour as commuters poured through the station, which serves as a link between Tel Aviv and its suburbs. No one claimed responsibility but Palestinian militants opposed Mr Abbas and his choice of Cabinet.

Hours after Palestinian Parliament approval of the controversial Cabinet of new Prime Minister Mahmoud Abbas, a suicide bomber detonated in a crowded Tel Aviv bar, killing three and injuring at least 40 and underscoring the difficulties facing the long-awaited "road map" to peace in the Middle East as militants protested reformist Mr Abbas' policies. Later US officials met with Israeli Prime Minister Ariel Sharon to present the peace plan. The al-Aqsa Martyrs' Brigades, the militant wing of Abbas' own Fatah political party, claimed responsibility for the bombing in Tel Aviv and told Associated Press the attack was a message to the new leader that "nobody could disarm the resistance movements without a political solution."

Hamas and Islamic Jihad leaders confirmed their commitment to their chosen course of action. Hamas also reportedly claimed responsibility for the bombing.

Israeli Cabinet Minister Dan Naveh said the bombing revealed the difficulties facing Abbas as he strove to meet conditions – including disarmament of militants – required by the road map to Palestinian statehood.

Ha'aretz reported that Israeli military intelligence had told Israeli politicians that Mr Abbas felt too powerless to effect actual disarmament and plans to avoid confrontation.

The road map drawn up by the European Union, Russia, the United Nations and the United States laid out three phases of a plan to establish an independent Palestinian state by 2005:

1. the Palestinians to reorganise security cooperation, end violence and disarm extremists. In exchange, as part of the first phase Israel would end settlement activity, dismantle settlement outposts built since March 2001 and withdraw from the Palestinian areas it had occupied since the intifada began in September 2000;
2. addressing "provisional borders" of a Palestinian state and Palestinian economic recovery; and
3. tackling the most divisive issues between the two sides, including the status of Jerusalem, permanent borders and the right of return for Palestinian refugees.

NORTH KOREA

UN Secretary General Kofi Annan's envoy for North Korea, Maurice Strong, called it "entirely possible" for a war to result from US-North Korean tensions over North Korea's nuclear ambitions.

North Korea said that it would not renounce efforts to develop missiles. Responding to US sanctions imposed over North Korea's alleged transfer of missile technology to Pakistan, the state-run Korean Central News Agency said it was Pyongyang's "sovereign right to produce, deploy or export missiles to other countries."

The agency added that North Korea's missile programme was "defensive in nature and poses no threats to any country that respects our independence."

North Korea failed to confirm that talks with South Korean Cabinet officials would take place as scheduled in Pyongyang, effectively canceling talks at which South Korea hoped to coax North Korea into negotiations to end international tensions over its nuclear ambitions.

North Korea stepped up rhetoric about its renewed nuclear programme, saying it would ignore any punitive actions by the United Nations. A statement released by the official North Korean news agency indicated Pyongyang "would not recognise but consider invalid any 'resolution' or other document to be adopted by the UN Security Council" at the Council's scheduled meeting on the matter.

The Security Council meeting was to follow North Korea's expulsion of IAEA inspectors more than six weeks previously and Pyongyang's move to restart a mothballed nuclear power plant capable of producing bomb-making materials. The United

States and the IAEA had pressed the Council to act against North Korea, which had said any UN sanctions would amount to a "declaration of war."

South Korean Foreign Minister Yoon Young-kwan held out hope that the situation could be resolved with talks involving the United States and other countries, but outside the United Nations.

The five permanent UN Security Council members, hampered by Chinese opposition, could not reach agreement on a joint statement condemning North Korean nuclear efforts, according to the Associated Press.

The United States, Russia, China, France and the United Kingdom met in a prelude to a meeting of the full, 15-member Security Council. Earlier efforts to bring the five together were unsuccessful when China and Russia decided not to attend.

Russia also warned that US efforts to censure North Korea could hurt relations between Washington and Moscow.

The United States asked North Korea to take part in multilateral talks. Council diplomats did not know if North Korea had responded, but Pyongyang had long resisted anything but direct negotiations with Washington.

South Korean defence officials said multilateral talks could focus on moving US forces away from the South Korea's border with the North, and possibly reducing the number of US military personnel in the country. Seoul's delegation, including Cha Young-koo, the assistant defence minister for policy, was against a drastic reduction in frontline US troops while the nuclear crisis lasted.

The Security Council held its first meeting in almost two months on North Korea without making any progress on how to deal with the possibility of Pyongyang's development of nuclear weapons. No new Council consultations were scheduled.

Ninety days after announcing its intention to withdraw from the Nuclear Nonproliferation Treaty, North Korea officially became the first of the pact's 187 signatories to bow out.

The UN Security Council met to discuss the situation on the eve of the withdrawal, but took no action on the matter. The United States wanted the council to condemn Pyongyang's move, but the initiative was blocked by China and Russia. North Korea had warned that it would consider Security Council action a "prelude to war" and said the US-led war in Iraq demonstrated the need for a deterrent against the United States.

South Korean media outlets reported that a US spy satellite in November 2002 detected an explosion at a North Korean ballistic missile test site. The blast reportedly occurred during a missile engine test and crippled activity at the site, as well as delaying the development and testing of North Korea's Taepodong missiles.

North Korean diplomats declared that Pyongyang possessed nuclear weapons and threatened to test them, a source told CNN.

A senior Bush administration official said that the White House was still working to determine what exactly the North Koreans meant by their claim.

North Korea threatened to export nuclear weapons if the United States did not restore a former commitment to provide energy to the isolated communist country.

North Korea claimed to be close to completing the reprocessing of 8,000 spent fuel rods that were being stored at the Yongbyon nuclear complex. US intelligence analysts had not been able to confirm the claim.

North Korea presented what was described as an extensive proposal for ending the nuclear crisis, reportedly seeking to re-establish the 1994 Agreed Framework, under which it agreed to end its nuclear programme in exchange for energy aid, but said it would end its nuclear programme only if the United States fulfilled its side of the agreement.

The US said North Korea had to verifiably dismantle its nuclear programme before other US-North Korean matters could be addressed.

North Korea offered to suspend missile tests and exports and to dismantle its nuclear development programme, but only after the United States met a long list of demands, including the completion of light-water nuclear reactors in North Korea and full diplomatic relations with Washington and Tokyo. US officials said that North Korea's request had also included oil shipments, food aid, security guarantees, energy assistance and economic concessions. After the United States completed its end of the deal, North Korea would announce its willingness to abandon its nuclear programmes. It was not clear if that included both its established plutonium weapons effort and the recently revealed uranium project.

North Korea also demanded economic aid, in part through the United States permitting Pyongyang to participate in international financial institutions and to receive foreign investment.

In what could have been a significant concession, Pyongyang announced that it would consider multilateral talks with its regional neighbours.

As part of the overall deal, North Korean officials reportedly offered to allow nuclear inspectors into the country.

Both moderate and hawkish US officials rejected the North Korean proposal but both also favoured continuing talks with Pyongyang. According to the hard-line view, more talks would demonstrate North Korea's impossible negotiating position, thereby reinforcing the idea that aggressive US policies were necessary.

While the overall package was considered unworkable, some officials said it could be a start and it was significant that North Korea put its nuclear programme on the bargaining table, albeit at an exorbitant price.

Some analysts agreed that the steep price of nuclear dismantlement might be overshadowing the fact that an offer was made at all.

China did not intend to support UN Security Council action against North Korea over alleged nuclear weapons development, a Chinese military adviser said.

North Korea said it told US officials a decade previously that it had nuclear weapons. The US officials who negotiated the 1994 Agreed Framework disputed the contention.

The US rejected the North Korean proposal to give up nuclear and missile capability in return for US economic, energy and diplomatic concessions, reiterating the US policy of not granting concessions for what Washington views as belligerent behaviour.

North and South Korea completed three days of meetings in Pyongyang but reached no agreement to resolve the nuclear crisis. The Cabinet-level talks produced a joint declaration to continue to address the issue.

REPUBLIKA SRPSKA *see* BOSNIA AND HERZEGOVINA

SOMALIA

Rival warlord factions in Somalia had not transformed the country into "a haven for international terrorists" as many feared, but it was a fertile transit point for terrorists and their material, a UN expert panel on Somalia said in a report.

Focusing on violations of a 1992 UN arms embargo imposed on Somalia, the 62-page report said the country's "continuing lawlessness [. . . was] a threat not only to Somalis but also to the international community."

Yet concerns that Somalia's lack of a central government would provide terrorists an ideal base to renew operations after the September 11, 2001 attacks on the United States "at present . . . appear unfounded," the panel said.

The panel said it found few formal links between the Somali group al-Ittihas al-Islami and al-Qaeda and "a largely local agenda."

Somalia had by now been without an effective government since opposition leaders united to oust dictator Mohamed Siad Barre in 1991. Since then, opposition leaders had fought with one another for control, turning the nation into fiefdoms ruled by clan-based factions. A transitional government chosen at a peace conference in Djibouti in August 2000 had had little influence outside the capital, Mogadishu.

Following a report by UN arms experts on the flourishing illegal arms trade in Somalia, the UN Security Council unanimously agreed the panel should carry on its investigation of the country for another six months.

Resolution 1474 acknowledged that the arms embargo prohibiting the delivery of all weapons and military equipment to Somalia "had been continuously violated" since its imposition in 1992. Other nations had illegally traded arms with Somalia even since October 2002, when an important national reconciliation conference was held in Kenya and saw the signing of a cessation of hostilities agreement. The resolution said the arms trade was "severely undermining peace and security" in Somalia.

The new resolution authorised the panel, originally established for six months in September 2002 by order of Resolution 1425, to investigate violations and identify violators, make recommendations to toughen the embargo and work with regional and international players such as the African Union to install monitoring mechanisms on the trade.

The UN Security Council voiced concern about the continued flow of weapons into Somalia in violation of a UN embargo.

After a Council discussion on ways to better implement the embargo, Council President Adolfo Aguilar Zinser of Mexico said an expert panel's report submitted to the Council in March indicated the embargo continued to be violated despite peace agreements between the country's warring parties. According to the report, most factions continued to fight and to receive weapons, including from sources outside Somalia.

The Council expressed concern that foreign sources continued to supply arms to parties in Somalia and urged UN members to cooperate with the expert panel, which the Council President said was "mandated to collect independent information on violations of the arms embargo in Somalia and to provide recommendations on possible practical steps and measures for its effective implementation."

SUDAN

Sudan welcomed US President George W. Bush's decision not to impose sanctions on Khartoum because the government had shown good faith in negotiating with the rebel Sudan People's Liberation Army to end 20 years of fighting.

Sudan asked the United States to take its name off the list of countries Washington accused of sponsoring terrorism.

Sudanese Finance Minister Abda al-Mahdi appealed for US aid for reconstruction projects in Sudan.

Medecins Sans Frontieres warned of "alarming" food shortages in two counties of Sudan's southwestern Bahr al-Ghazal state and called on the World Food Programme "to continue with its general food distributions in a manner adapted to the population to ensure that the situation in the region does not deteriorate even more." MSF set up a supplementary feeding center in the area, where malnutrition was said to be increasing.

SYRIA

The United States ratcheted up pressure on Syria when President George W. Bush accused the country of manufacturing chemical weapons and providing safe harbour to fugitive officials from neighboring Iraq.

Adding to repeated charges that Damascus had been helping senior Iraqi leaders escape, US Defence Secretary Donald Rumsfeld said that Syrian nationals had been found in Iraq fighting against US forces.

Syrian Deputy Ambassador to the United States Imad Moustapha said that his country would accept international weapons inspections, but said Israel should be inspected, too. As to allegations of Syrian assistance to Baath party officials fleeing Iraq, Mr Moustapha said they were part of "a campaign of misinformation and disinformation" about Syria that had been going on since before the war began. Responsibility for securing Iraq's border with Syria, he said, rested with the United States.

Washington's allegations drew worried responses from the European Union and the United Kingdom. EU foreign policy chief Javier Solana urged the United States to soften its rhetoric against Syria.

British Foreign Secretary Jack Straw said he was unsure whether Syria possessed illegal weapons but stressed the importance of Syria's full cooperation over the weapons and fugitives questions. Mr Straw called Syrian Foreign Minister Farouk al-Shara to assure him that London did not support US allegations against Syria.

As Washington simultaneously toughened its rhetoric against Syria and issued assurances that the United States would not take military action there, UN Secretary General Kofi Annan released a statement discouraging the escalation of tensions in the region.

Spanish Prime Minister Jose Maria Aznar, one of the strongest supporters of the US-led war against Iraq, said that there would be no confrontation with Syria and announced his plans to meet with Syrian President Bashar al-Assad as soon as possible. Syria's ambassador to Spain, Mohsen Bilal, expressed his confidence that the Spanish government would "take a clear position against the threats" of the United States.

US Secretary of State Colin Powell said the United States had no war plans against Syria or any other country in the region, despite continued accusations by Washington that Syria had banned weapons and had harboured fleeing Iraqi leaders.

Syrian Foreign Minister Farouq al-Shara said Syria would support a treaty making the Middle East free of weapons of mass destruction.

At the United Nations, Arab diplomats said they would seek a Security Council resolution banning weapons of mass destruction. They pointed to Israel's arsenal, which was thought to contain as many as 200 undeclared nuclear warheads. Arab suspicions about US motives in the region following the US invasion of Iraq had deepened as relations had worsened between Washington and Damascus.

Donald Rumsfeld said US-led forces in Iraq had cut off oil flow along a pipeline from Iraq to Syria that reportedly pumped about 200,000 barrels a day in violation of UN sanctions on Iraq.

Syria would not allow international inspections of its military arsenal, Syrian Foreign Minister Farouk al-Sharaa said. The remark was an apparent shift in Syria's position as indicated in officials' previous statements.

Syrian President Bashar al-Assad said that Syria would not grant asylum to Iraqis wanted for war crimes and that it would expel any Iraqis who enter the country without a visa, in a gesture apparently meant to counter Washington's accusations that Syria was harbouring Baath party leaders. US President George W. Bush responded with praise for Syria's cooperation.

Egyptian President Hosni Mubarak visited Mr al-Assad in what diplomatic sources described as an effort to repair strained relations following the war in Iraq, which Syria strongly opposed. Egypt adopted a more lenient attitude toward the war. That meeting followed one in Riyadh in which the foreign ministers of Egypt, Saudi Arabia, Kuwait, Syria, Jordan, Turkey, Iran and Bahrain condemned US threats against Syria.

TAJIKISTAN
The International Atomic Energy Agency was concerned for the security of radioactive waste storage sites in Tajikistan, it was reported.

Tajikistan was the focus of increased concern partly because it was rich in uranium.

One issue facing all former Soviet states, including Tajikistan, was a lack of expertise in material security issues, which were mainly handled by Russian officials during the Soviet era.

May 2003

AFGHANISTAN
The UN mission in Afghanistan welcomed US Defence Secretary Donald Rumsfeld's message in Kabul that the United States was ending combat operations and redoubling efforts to rebuild, but nongovernmental organisations warned that a lack of security in the country remained a grave problem and that declarations of victory were premature.

Afghan Constitutional Commission member Shukraya Bwerekzai said Mr Rumsfeld's visit in the wake of the Iraq war was a good sign of US commitment to Afghanistan but noted that Washington had done little to combat the warlordism that threatened the country's stability.

A UN Assistance Mission in Afghanistan spokesman said the shift from combat to reconstruction was a positive development.

Mr Rumsfeld pronounced "the bulk" of Afghanistan to be "secure." He acknowledged that pockets of resistance remained, as coalition troops had clashed with suspected bands of Taliban and al-Qaeda militants several times in April 2003.

Eight Provincial Reconstruction Teams, each consisting of 40 to 60 civil affairs soldiers, diplomats and aid workers, would eventually be positioned throughout Afghanistan, the *Chicago Tribune* reported, but international aid workers reportedly cautioned that the teams would blur the lines between military and humanitarian work and put aid workers at risk.

Unidentified gunmen opened fire in Wardak province on a vehicle belonging to the Afghan Development Agency, a demining organisation, killing the driver and injuring two others. It was the second attack on deminers in less than two weeks. The United Nations ordered its staff to avoid the section of the Kabul-Kandahar highway between the towns of Maidan Shah and Ghazni until further notice.

The UN Security Council, in response to a statement made by the United Nations' top representative in Afghanistan, said that the extension of central government authority to all parts of Afghanistan and the creation of a new national army and national police were essential to promote peace in the country. The Council also said reforms in the security sector, starting with the Ministry of Defence and intelligence institutions, should take place in 2003.

Taliban gunmen in the southeastern province of Zabul fired on an ambulance belonging to an Afghan demining team, injuring two. The attack followed an ambush that killed one deminer and injured two others. Deminers suffered an earlier attack on April 22.

A crowd of 300 Afghan government employees and university students demonstrated in Kabul against growing insecurity, the slow pace of reconstruction and lagging payments of government salaries by Kabul's US-backed central government. Some protesters called for US-led coalition forces to leave the country. According to Reuters, it was the first anti-American demonstration since US-led forces had brought down the Taliban regime in 2001.

Following the attacks the UN Assistance Mission in Afghanistan announced that until security improved, it was halting road missions south of the town of Ghazni and all missions to Zabul and Oruzgan provinces and part of Helmand province. Spokesman Manoel de Almeida e Silva said UNAMA was also imposing a 6 p.m. to 6 a.m. curfew on road missions nationwide. Demining operations along the road between Kabul and Kandahar were also being suspended. UN staff in Afghanistan would begin traveling with armed escorts in parts of the country, UN officials said. A UN spokesman said the Afghan government would provide armed guards for UN vehicles in certain provinces considered dangerous because of suspected activity by bands of fighters from the ousted Taliban regime.

An Afghan policeman who served as security liaison for the UN mission in Afghanistan was killed in factional fighting in the northern city of Mazar-e Sharif. He was investigating violence between rival militias near a UNICEF warehouse when he was killed. Two suspects, police commanders from the Wahdat and Jamiat factions, were in custody and would be handed over to police. As a result of the incident, the Mazar Multiparty Security Commission agreed that all "unauthorised" armed fighters from the Jamiat, Jumbesh and Wahdat Mohaqiq factions should leave the city. A delegation made up of representatives of the groups and UNAMA would verify their departure.

Afghan President Hamid Karzai was meeting with a dozen provincial governors to demand millions of dollars of revenue owed to the central government. The 12 provincial governors were supposed to collect customs revenue and send the money to the central government in Kabul, where it would be used to pay state employees and finance social programmes. Afghanistan's Finance Ministry estimated that the governors collected more than half a billion dollars' worth of customs revenues in 2002,but forwarded only $80 million of it to Kabul.The bulk of customs were reportedly collected by Ismail Khan, governor of the western province of Herat. Khan transferred $3 million to the central government, but Reuters reported that sum was a fraction of what was owed.

Mr Karzai said that he would step down if he failed to extend his control over the rebellious provinces within the following few months, the Afghan daily *Arman-e-Millie* reported.

US soldiers guarding the US Embassy in Kabul, shot and killed four Afghan soldiers in an apparent misunderstanding. The US troops fired on a group of Afghans as they unloaded weapons from a truck that were meant to be stored at a nearby building, Afghan officials said. The International Security Assistance Force cited unconfirmed reports that the Afghan troops fired first, shooting at a passing car for unclear reasons and prompting the US soldiers to return fire.

Afghan warlords and governors signed a pledge to hand over customs revenues to the central government, obey national laws and halt factional fighting. The agreement, if kept, would extend the powers of Mr Karzai's government, which controlled virtually nothing outside Kabul. The agreement could also stave off a financial collapse of the Karzai government, which had struggled for months to pay employees. The agreement lacked any enforcement measure, however, and it remained unclear whether warlords who had sworn support for Mr Karzai would actually abide by their promises.

AL-QAEDA *see* MOROCCO, SAUDI ARABIA

CHECHNYA

The death toll from a suicide bombing attack in Russia's breakaway Chechnya republic climbed to 54 as rescue workers began to give up hope of finding survivors in the rubble of the provincial government building destroyed in a blast.

Some 200 people were injured when a truck exploded in the Chechen village of Znamenskoye. Suicide attackers had packed the truck with as much as a ton of explosives in a strike apparently aimed at local government authorities allied with Moscow. The great majority of the dead were civilians.

Separatist rebels vowed to stage attacks following a referendum in March that cemented the republic's status as a part of Russia, but leading rebel figures denied involvement in the blast.

CHEMICAL WEAPONS CONVENTION

The first review conference of the Chemical Weapons Convention concluded with unanimous approval of a political statement and a final review declaration.

In a three-page political statement, the treaty parties attending the conference in The Hague reaffirmed their support for the basic goals of the treaty, including:

- the elimination of the possibility of future chemical weapons use,
- destruction of declared stockpiles and production capacities,
- support for chemical weapons nonproliferation and confidence-building measures and
- establishment of a system for verification of compliance with the treaty's provisions.

They also offered support for complete national implementation of the treaty's requirements, and of international cooperation and assistance in the peaceful uses of chemistry, a goal emphasised by developing states.

They also emphasised continuing the consideration of scientific and technological developments, which some experts had argued should prompt treaty parties to address the issue of the legality of chemical incapacitating agents. The political declaration made no specific reference to such agents, however.

COLOMBIA

UN special envoy to Colombia James LeMoyne caused an uproar with comments he made to two Colombian newspapers, saying it was "a mistake to think that the FARC members were only drug traffickers and terrorists" and suggesting that wealthy Colombians were not making sufficient sacrifices in the civil war, which had lasted 39 years. Mr LeMoyne also said that the FARC has in its "spinal core between 1,000 and 1,500 men and women who were profoundly politically engaged."

The government was outraged, prompting Colombian Defence Minister Marta Lucia Ramirez to accuse the United Nations of "defending terrorists." Business leaders accused Mr LeMoyne of being out of touch with reality.

Mr LeMoyne subsequently released a statement saying that "the United Nations does not support terrorism" and reaffirming that the institution would never justify the violence of any armed group.

CONGO, DEMOCRATIC REPUBLIC OF

Following the demobilisation of hundreds of former rebel fighters in the Republic of the Congo, observers were urging the governing to quickly reintegrate the guerrillas – called Ninjas – into civilian life to prevent them from resuming aggression.

The Ninjas began demobilising in the Pool region surrounding Mindouli, near the capital Brazzaville, on April 22 following a peace accord signed in March 2003. Now the rebels wanted farming equipment so they could earn a living as part of the government's promised reintegration aid.

According to Integrated Regional Information Networks, at least 2,300 Ninjas had surrendered with their weapons. The government had promised them amnesty.

Ninja military chief Bernard Mikisi vowed to halt the group's raids on railways in the Pool region as part of the peace deal.

Demobilised Ninja fighters had been given temporary barracks in one of the large buildings in Mindouli, where they awaited a government assessment and reintegration assistance.

Hundreds of civilians took cover in a UN regional headquarters in the north-eastern DRC, where a pullout of Ugandan troops had been followed by a flare-up of ethnic violence. The UN headquarters in Bunia, the main city in the DRC's Ituri region, was being guarded by 40 UN peacekeepers in battle position, as fighters armed with machine guns, machetes and spears roamed the road outside.

The fighters who overran Bunia and forced thousands to flee appeared to be tribal Lendus set on attacking ethnic Hemas, their rivals.

There were fewer than 400 UN peacekeepers in Bunia, all from Uruguay. They guarded the UN compound as street violence unfolded but made no effort to intervene. The UN force's deputy commander, Daniel Vollot, said he needed more peacekeepers.

UN officials said that fighting in northeastern DRC was hampering relief efforts, leaving up to 4,000 people in need of aid. Clashes between rival ethnic militias in Bunia forced 2,000 people to take shelter at the area airport while another 2,000 sought safety in the regional UN compound.

Fighting between the Lendu and Hema tribes left at least five dead, an unknown number wounded and many Bunia buildings looted, including some UN facilities.

UN officials said peacekeepers in the area were in control of the airport and patrolling the town, which erupted into tribal violence following the withdrawal of Ugandan troops earlier, as mandated by a recent peace agreement.

The fighting sparked an influx of refugees to Uganda, which appealed for international aid to help deal with what Ugandan officials said was a mounting humanitarian crisis. Up to 120,000 Hema had fled the Bunia area for Uganda and remained in need of food, medicine and shelter.

Three babies were killed with machetes and 15 others were killed in a mortar attack during fighting between the rival Hema and Lendu tribes in and around Bunia, aggravating the crisis in the region and making more urgent the UN Security Council's scheduled review of the situation.

Bunia had been controlled by the Lendu tribe, but two rebel groups of Hema fighters seized the town after a dawn raid with rockets, mortars and other heavy weapons.

The UN Organisation Mission in the DRC had approximately 675 troops on the ground, but had been unable to stop the violence and looting. The tribes had up to

28,000 fighters in the region and the aid agency Oxfam said MONUC was unable to control the situation.

UN Secretary General Kofi Annan urged action by the Security Council to calm the situation, and called on Uganda to use its influence over militia forces in the region to stop the violence. Ugandan troops were withdrawing from northeastern DRC.

The council was briefed on the situation. Security Council President Munir Akram of Pakistan said that Council members had condemned attacks on MONUC headquarters and called on all parties to "immediately cease aggression and acts of violence, especially against the civilian population and MONUC." Council members commended MONUC personnel, particularly the Uruguayan contingent, which had been deployed to Bunia.

Aid workers were able to distribute food and water to an estimated 8,000 people who gathered at a MONUC base near Bunia airport, a few kilometers from the town. According to MONUC officials, thousands more were without shelter, hiding in the bush or heading to the border with Uganda. Ugandan President Yoweri Museveni said that the refugees would be welcomed in Uganda but also criticised MONUC's mission in Bunia, saying that the troops were practicing "dangerous tourism."

The Security Council discussed the possibility of organising an emergency peace-keeping force to intervene in the northeastern corner of the DRC, where violence recalled memories of the 1994 genocide in Rwanda.

The United States and other council members were prompting France to head up an intervention force. French diplomats said they were considering what, if any, role to play in an emergency peacekeeping mission in the country, where nearly 700 UN peacekeepers already on the ground had been unable to maintain order.

Fighting had subsided after two Hema militias gained control of Bunia from Lendu fighters.

Nearly 5,000 people had fled the area across the border to Burundi.

As rebel groups continued their assault on Bunia France promised to send peace-keeping troops to the region.

The Union des Patriots Congolais, a militia group backed by Rwanda whose members were mostly from Ituri's Hema ethnic minority, said prior to France's announcement that French peacekeeping forces would be regarded by their group as an enemy force in Ituri.

Heavy fighting broke out as Lendu troops, who had been reportedly driven out of Bunia by Hema fighters, launched a counteroffensive to try to regain control of the town. The fighting came within 500 metres of the UN headquarters compound. More than 25,000 tribal fighters were thought to be in Ituri province.

Fearing that hundreds of thousands of people were fleeing the fighting, UNICEF sent two planeloads of essential drug kits, water purification products, intravenous drips to care for the injured, tents and oral rehydration salts to Bunia.

More than 10,000 civilians had taken cover in a UN compound in Bunia as fighting continued between gun- and machete-wielding ethnic rivals and the United Nations hastened to assemble a peacekeeping force and deploy it to the area. At least 10 people died in the fighting, most reportedly hit by mortar fire as they crowded around the UN offices.

UN Organisation Mission in the DRC commander Mountaga Diallo said the withdrawing Ugandans left behind anti-aircraft weapons, antitank guns and other weapons that the ethnic militias had seized.

DRC President Joseph Kabila met with Hema and Lendu officials in a bid to curb the violence in Bunia.

France, which previous reports indicated would send about 700 soldiers to the area at the request of the United Nations, now said it had been asked to provide up to 1,000 troops. The United Kingdom said it was considering a UN request for troops, and Uganda said it was willing to send its forces back in if asked. A Western UN diplomat said France had approached other African countries, India and Pakistan about providing troops.

UN Deputy Emergency Relief Coordinator Carolyn McAskie echoed remarks by chief UN war crimes prosecutor Carla Del Ponte indicating a genocide could be brewing in the DRC. Ms McAskie spoke of "shades of Rwanda in 1994" and said entire villages in the Bunia area were participating in the violence, a development she called "Rwanda-like."

UN High Commissioner for Human Rights Sergio Vieira de Mello also voiced concern over reports that civilians were being killed because of their ethnic affiliations.

President Joseph Kabila met with representatives of armed rebel groups to negotiate a cease-fire in the DRC's northeastern Ituri region.

Thousands of civilians jammed the roads out of Bunia as sporadic fighting continued. According to Associated Press, it was not known if the decrease in fighting was due to a request from the UN Organisation Mission in the DRC commander for a 24-hour cease-fire in the region. MONUC commander, Roberto Martinelli, met with leaders of the warring factions in an attempt to secure a cease-fire long enough to allow displaced persons to reach safer areas.

Aid workers tried to restore water supplies at the UN compound, fearing outbreaks of cholera and dysentery. Suspected cases of the diseases appeared among the 8,000 displaced people who were in the compound.

Two UN military observers who had gone missing in the troubled northeastern region of the DRC were found dead. The bodies of the unidentified observers were discovered in Mongbwalu, a gold mining town about 45 miles northwest of Bunia. The murder of the two UN observers followed the death of two International Committee for the Red Cross workers, who died on May 11 while working in the same area.

Amos Namanga Ngongi, head of the UN mission in the country, said UN officials would investigate reports of cannibalism in Ituri during fighting between rival Hema and Lendu ethnic factions.

President Kabila and rival ethnic militia groups fighting in Ituri signed a cease-fire agreement.

In Bunia, UN workers reported an uneasy calm.

UN aid agencies and other humanitarian organisations working in Ituri stepped up relief efforts as the fighting subsided. UN officials said there were about 12,000 civilians in need of aid in Bunia who had sought refuge with the United Nations. About 4,000 people had gathered at the UN compound in Bunia, while another 6,000 huddled at the area airport and 2,000 camped on the airport road.

The UN Security Council urged UN Secretary General Kofi Annan to organise an emergency peacekeeping intervention force for Ituri. Mr Annan had been pressing France to lead a contingent of international troops to the region to halt the violence. French officials had so far held off, though, insisting on firm pledges from other nations to join any such mission and a limited timetable for deployment.

UN Organisation Mission in the Democratic Republic of the Congo military officials headed into Bunia where ethnic Lendu militia fighters re-entered the town following a lull in fighting there with Hema tribesmen.

The European Union was considering a UN request to send peacekeepers into the area. Chief EU foreign affairs envoy Javier Solana said EU defence ministers were "generally positive" about the UN appeal and that the request would be studied further.

The UN High Commissioner for Refugees reported finding an additional 10,000 DRC refugees from Ituri camped near Lake Albert in Uganda, bringing the total number of DRC refugees in Uganda to 20,000. UNHCR officials said more people fleeing fighting in Ituri could still be on the move.

UN Controller Jean-Pierre Halbwachs told the UN General Assembly Administrative and Budgetary Committee that MONUC was constantly evolving and needed a flexible budget. Kofi Annan initially requested $516.8 million to fund MONUC in 2003-04, but the budget was revised following the Security Council's move to expand the mission in December and was now projected at $634.7 million.

The UN Organisation Mission in the DRC said it had found 50 more bodies in Bunia, bringing the number of people killed there in May to at least 280.

According to Associated Press, some of the bodies were mutilated and might have been cannibalised. Aid workers reported evidence of atrocities in Bunia, saying that among the bodies of people killed in the streets since May 4, some had been decapitated, while others were found with hearts, livers and lungs missing. Women and children were among the dead. The reports followed allegations by church leaders and residents of Bunia that after killing fighters and civilians, armed militia members cut open their victims' chests and ate their still-warm organs. UN officials were investigating the reports of cannibalism.

Human Rights Watch and Amnesty International sent a joint letter to the Security Council calling for the speedy deployment of troops with a "clear and robust mandate to protect civilians" and arguing that "the potential for the situation to rapidly escalate into further killings of civilians demands an immediate and urgent response."

France dispatched a military reconnaissance team to Ituri in preparation for what could eventually be the deployment of a major international force. The team's nine officers were reportedly planning to stay in Bunia and had been briefed by the local MONUC commander. France had committed to sending troops to the country under the aegis of the United Nations, and the Security Council had pressed Secretary General Kofi Annan to send a peacekeeping force to the region to augment the 700 UN soldiers already there.

Representatives of African nations called for better funding for MONUC and the UN Mission in Sierra Leone. Jean Christian Obame of Gabon said MONUC, which had proven to be one of the most complex UN peacekeeping missions in the world body's history, required a troop deployment and the training of civilian police in order to protect the progress made so far.

In the capital city of Kinshasa, the commission monitoring DRC's transition to democratic rule issued a new timetable for the installment of a two-year transitional government leading to elections. According to the timetable the new transitional Cabinet would meet for the first time on May 31. An armed forces chief would be appointed on May 27, and the national assembly and Senate would be set up by June 10. President Joseph Kabila would remain president of the country. Four vice presidents representing the government, the two main rebel groups and the unarmed opposition party would serve under him.

Aid workers found a mass grave on the outskirts of Bunia. A spokeswoman for the MONUC said the bodies' advanced state of decomposition made it hard to say how many were in the grave or whether they were civilians or soldiers, but aid workers had identified at least 32. Together with seven corpses discovered in the streets of Bunia, the death toll from fighting that broke out earlier in May was 319.

MONUC was planning to send a human rights officer and child protection officer to the town, where 4,000 people were seeking shelter at the MONUC compound and another 9,000 were camped out at the airport. A UN spokesman said that militias had reportedly been trying to infiltrate the camps, prompting MONUC to mount stricter surveillance.

The Office of the UN High Commissioner for Refugees described some of the results of the withdrawal of Ugandan troops from northeastern DRC after six years – many Congolese followed them back to Uganda. Frightened by reports of massacres in the fighting between Hema and Lendu, columns of people made the trek into neighbouring Uganda, camping with the soldiers and sometimes getting food from them. Now more than 20,000 refugees, mostly Hema and Alur, were crowding villages in the western Ugandan districts of Nebbi and Bundibugyo. One village on the banks of Lake Albert, Ntoroko, had swelled from a population of 2,500 to 7,400, with predictable deteriorations in sanitary conditions.

The UN Organisation Mission in the Democratic Republic of the Congo was discussing a plan with the country's interim administration to separate rival combatants in the Ituri region, where reports indicated renewed fighting in the northern part of the district, in the area of Aru.

Civilians in Bunia pleaded with UN Undersecretary General for Peacekeeping Jean-Marie Guehenno to protect them from fierce fighting in the region.

In the capital city of Kinshasa, the main rebel group, Rassemblement Congolais pour la Democratie, said it was withdrawing from a follow-up committee on the peace process because of what it called bad faith on the part of the government. The RCD disagreed with the government of President Kabila over issues related to the army and on the appointment of an opposition member to the position of vice president.

The UN Security Council approved deployment of a French-led peacekeeping force in the DRC.

French Defence Minister Michele Alliot-Marie said that the force would total 1,400 troops, half of them French. Pledges had been received "in principle" from Belgium, Germany, Spain, Italy and the United Kingdom to provide troops, the minister said.

Diplomats warned that the biggest obstacle would be getting cooperation from Ugandan President Yoweri Museveni and Rwandan President Paul Kagame, whose countries had been involved in the DRC's five-year civil war. While Uganda and Rwanda had reportedly withdrawn their forces from the DRC, the northeastern region of the DRC remained particularly volatile.

The new force was not a UN mission, but was approved by the Council under Chapter 7 of the UN Charter, which allows authorisation for use of deadly force if deemed necessary. The force's mandate was to protect the airport at Bunia, the main town in Ituri, and nearby refugee camps, and "if the situation requires it, to contribute to the safety" of the civilian population, UN troops and staff and aid workers. The UN peacekeepers already in the area had no such authority to use force.

The force's deployment was authorised until September 1, at which time a UN multinational force of 1,500 troops led by Bangladesh would take over.

COTE D'IVOIRE
Ivory Coast's government and three major rebel groups signed a new cease-fire in a bid to halt continuing fighting that had endangered a French-brokered, UN-backed peace deal signed in January 2003.

Following a meeting of government and rebel negotiators in Ivory Coast's main city, Abidjan, Defence Minister Adou Assoa issued a statement saying the army, the "forces nouvelles" (the "new forces") – meaning the three insurgent groups taken together – and "the other parties have agreed on a total halt to hostilities and a complete cease-fire."

A source close to Ivorian President Laurent Gbagbo said the deal also stipulated an end to fighting in western Ivory Coast with forces loyal to Liberian President Charles Taylor, who had been repeatedly accused of stoking the Ivorian rebellion.

Togolese Defence Minister Assani Tidjani, who presided over the talks, said the signing would be followed by the deployment in the west of French and Economic Community of West African States peacekeepers already deployed in other parts of Ivory Coast and that new steps would be taken to step up security at the Liberian-Ivorian border. UN Secretary General Kofi Annan called on donors to provide $47 million to sustain the ECOWAS peacekeeping operation for six months.

The cease-fire followed the assassination of the leader of the rebel Mouvement Populaire Ivoirien du Grand Ouest, Felix Doh, an act variously attributed to Liberians, Sierra Leoneans and other Ivorian rebels. Kofi Annan's humanitarian envoy for Ivory Coast, Carolyn McAskie, said that the killing had shaken the security situation in the west but that Doh's rebels "were very much trying to stay in control." Ms McAskie added that no government or private services were functioning on the rebel side of western cease-fire lines and that aid workers were unable to access many parts of the west.

The African Development Bank proposed establishing a conflict prevention fund for West Africa and said it would contribute $15 million to such a fund. The proposed fund, outlined at a meeting of UN officials in Abidjan, could raise up to $60 million, an official at the meeting said. The money would be used to fund job creation for ex-combatants, microcredit for widows and other projects and would be available in all 15 ECOWAS countries.

A new cease-fire signed by rebels and the government in Ivory Coast appeared to be holding.

After the signing but before the cease-fire came into effect, the western Mouvement Populaire Ivoirien du Grand Ouest rebel group said pro-government forces had attacked in Danane in western Ivory Coast. A rebel spokesman said the offensive was a bid to retake positions for the government's side before the cease-fire came into effect. The government, however, said it was the rebels who launched the attack.

The *Financial Times* reported that a proposed $27 million UN operation in Ivory Coast had been criticised as "bloated" by US officials and that UN-US negotiations were under way on the matter.

Refugees at a camp near Guiglo said that Guiglo authorities had been coming to the camp to recruit soldiers to fight for the government in the country's civil war.

The UN Security Council agreed tentatively on a resolution authorising the deployment of up to 76 unarmed peacekeepers to war-torn Ivory Coast.

Under a draft resolution members reportedly agreed on at least 26 and as many as 76 military officers being sent to Ivory Coast, along with civilian employees. UN Secretary General Kofi Annan initially requested a 255-member force with a one-year mandate, but the United States balked at the $27 million cost, and a compromise was reached under which the Council was to authorise the smaller force for six months.

The UN Mission in Cote d'Ivoire (MINUCI), as the mission would be known, would work with thousands of French and Economic Community of West African States peace-keepers already in Ivory Coast to police a peace deal the country's government, rebels and opposition reached at talks in January 2003. The UN force would not be armed but would provide military advice, monitoring and other services.

The Council was told that up to 750,000 people had been internally displaced by the Ivorian civil war.

UN High Commissioner for Refugees Ruud Lubbers said his agency was especially concerned about an estimated 9,000 refugees in the Nicla camp, near the western town of Guiglo.

With a cease-fire signed May 1 appearing to hold, Ivory Coast's government lifted a curfew imposed when the country's conflict began in September. Also, the first train to depart from the country's main city, Abidjan, since the civil conflict began traveled to the rebel stronghold of Bouake.

The UN Security Council formally approved a resolution creating the UN Mission in Cote d'Ivoire.

The council voted unanimously in favour of sending an initial contingent of 26 unarmed UN military observers to Ivory Coast, as well as a number of nonmilitary employees. Fifty more military observers could be sent later under the resolution.

MINUCI's military officials were to:
- work with UN Secretary General Kofi Annan's Ivory Coast envoy, Albert Tevoedjre, on military affairs;
- follow the military situation in the country and monitor the security of Liberian refugees in Ivory Coast;
- cooperate with thousands of French and Economic Community of West African States peacekeepers already in Ivory Coast to police a January peace deal; and
- establish ties with government and rebel forces.

The nonmilitary MINUCI employees were to work with Mr Tevoedjre on political, legal, civil, police, electoral, media, humanitarian and human rights matters.

The Ivorian government reimposed a curfew on the western towns of Duekoue and Guiglo as rebels killed about 150 civilians there.

President Gbagbo approved deployment of French and West African troops to restore law and order on Ivory Coast's border with Liberia, where activity by armed militias has impeded efforts to end the country's civil war. His deployment orders would send about 900 French soldiers, along with West African and Ivory Coast troops and a 76-member unarmed UN contingent, to the western part of the country.

CYPRUS

The United Nations welcomed the crossing in recent weeks of thousands of Greek and Turkish Cypriots across the UN-guarded buffer zone that divided Cyprus' two sides. UN officials said, roughly 170,000 Greek Cypriots had crossed through the zone to the north, while 75,000 Turkish Cypriots had crossed in the other direction.

Cypriot President Tassos Papadopoulos said the movements were "important" but insufficient.

GUATEMALA

Citing recent human rights abuses, public insecurity and impunity, UN Verification Mission in Guatemala head Tom Koenigs said the country's eight-year-old peace process was in a crisis. The human rights situation had deteriorated in 15 months and the peace process was deadlocked. He said there has been a lack of decisive action and political will. Little had been done to address poverty, racism and impunity.

Budget allocations were cited as evidence of the government's skewed priorities. The armed forces had reportedly been receiving as much money as before the accord was signed, while social spending had been lagging.

Guatemalan Peace Secretary Catalina Soberanis cited advances but said implementing the accords in their entirety would be costly and take at least two more administrations.

INDONESIA

UN Secretary General Kofi Annan said that he was "deeply concerned" by fighting that erupted between separatists and government forces in the northwestern Indonesian province of Aceh and urged all parties to "do their utmost" to restore the peace process.

The government and the Free Aceh Movement failed to agree to adhere to a peace accord reached in December 2002. According to the government, the Free Aceh Movement refused to end its struggle for independence and accept special autonomy.

Indonesia said it had 28,000 troops in Aceh. The guerrillas number about 5,000. According to Agence France-Presse, this was Indonesia's biggest military operation since it invaded East Timor in 1975.

Later UN Secretary General Kofi Annan again expressed deep concern over reports of renewed violence against civilians in Aceh, saying he was particularly disturbed by reports of extrajudicial killings and the widespread burning of schools.

He called on Indonesia to establish conditions to allow humanitarian workers complete access to affected populations.

UNICEF and the World Health Organisation flew 15 metric tons of emergency medical supplies into the regional capital of Banda Aceh.

The Indonesian military denied it had been targeting noncombatants, but said it was making fast progress on its vow to "eliminate" all the Free Aceh Movement separatist forces. According to CNN.com, as government troops passed from village to village they were shooting suspected rebels on sight.

Under the martial law imposed on Aceh May 18, the military had broad powers to arrest suspected rebel sympathisers. It was using a 40,000-troop force to put down the estimated 5,000 separatist guerrillas.

The military reportedly said that 82 rebel fighters had been killed and 72 captured or surrendered. Only seven government soldiers and police had been killed.

Separatist sources said the death toll for both sides was much higher but the Indonesian Red Cross and other independent monitors had been unable to verify the claim.

Indonesia's semiautonomous national human rights commission said it would send a team to the special region to monitor any rights violations by government forces or the rebel group.

IRAN *see also* NUCLEAR NONPROLIFERATION TREATY

Officials in the US administration said that they were putting pressure on the International Atomic Energy Agency to take action on alleged violations by Iran of the Nuclear Nonproliferation Treaty.

Amid claims by US analysts and outside experts that Tehran could be capable of producing weapons-grade material on a regular basis by late 2005, US Assistant Secretary of State for Nonproliferation John Wolf reportedly met with IAEA Director General Mohamed ElBaradei to press the case against Iran.

An IAEA spokeswoman said that inspectors were not in a position to pass judgment on Iran's compliance.

The International Atomic Energy Agency was not yet ready to render a decision as to whether Iran's nuclear programme violated the Nuclear Nonproliferation Treaty.

The agency was still reviewing the results of a February 2003 visit to Iranian facilities. While some observers expected the agency to report conclusively on Iran's programme at a June 16 meeting of its board of governors, the diplomats doubted such a report would be ready.

There were indications that the centrifuges Iran was using at a uranium-enrichment facility in the southern city of Natanz were of Pakistani origin, according to IAEA inspectors and senior US officials.

Iran said that it would only be willing to accept more stringent nuclear oversight if economic sanctions were lifted.

An Iranian Foreign Ministry spokesman said that the Nuclear Nonproliferation Treaty obliged Washington to assist Tehran with peaceful nuclear development.

The IAEA, meanwhile, said that it was not yet clear if Iran's expanding nuclear programme was intended to develop nuclear weapons.

IRAQ

US President George W. Bush said that US-British forces had prevailed in their war in Iraq and that their focus was now on securing and reconstructing the country.

Mr Bush alleged that toppled Iraqi President Saddam Hussein's government had weapons of mass destruction and sought to tie Saddam Hussein to global terrorism but offered no evidence of such claims.

The Bush administration had in the past alleged links between the Saddam's regime and the al-Qaeda global terrorist network, which was thought to have been behind the September 11, 2001 attacks on the United States, but had not claimed to have proven any such link yet through postwar intelligence-gathering in Iraq.

Mr Bush nevertheless said that the United States had "removed an ally of al-Qaeda and cut off a source of terrorist funding," adding, "No terrorist network will gain weapons of mass destruction from the Iraqi regime, because that regime is no more."

The administration repeatedly cited Iraq's alleged weapons of mass destruction programmes in seeking to justify the war, but so far, all reported leads in US soldiers' hunt for such weapons in Iraq appeared to have turned up nothing.

Tests on the latest find deemed suspicious by US forces in Iraq, consisting of 55-gallon drums found in northern Iraq, had indicated no nerve agent was in the drums as US forces suspected. A US Army spokesman said the drums contained a component of rocket fuel. The United States had announced earlier that initial tests indicated the presence in the drums of chemicals used to make chemical weapons.

US-British forces captured three more officials from Saddam's government that were on a US most-wanted list of 55 such officials. US Central Command in Qatar announced the capture of No. 16 on the list, former military industrialisation chief Abd al-Tawab Mullah Huwaysh, and No. 42, former Vice President Taha Muhie-eldin Marouf. Hours earlier, US military officials in Baghdad said a top leader in Saddam's Baath Party, Mizban Khadr Hadi, was captured in Baghdad. Mr Hadi was No. 41 on the most-wanted list.

Amid reports of serious looting at Iraqi nuclear facilities, IAEA Director General Mohamed ElBaradei wrote to the US government to request permission for an IAEA mission to investigate the state of the sites. The mission being sought would be different from the UN weapons inspection teams that were in Iraq until shortly before the war and which the IAEA was seeking to send back to the country. The mission the IAEA requested in the letter would be an investigative mission to find out what had happened at the facilities that were reportedly looted.

In what the *Washington Post* called the second case since the war's end in which a known nuclear stock was looted to such an extent that authorities could not say for sure whether deadly materials were taken, a special US Defence Department team found the Baghdad Nuclear Research Facility to have been heavily looted and said it was impossible to know whether nuclear materials were missing. The facility contained isotopes that the *Post* reports "terrorists" had sought in an effort to produce a radiological "dirty bomb." It did not contain materials suitable for making a nuclear fission weapon. The site was less than a mile from the al-Tuwaitha research facility, which the *Post* called the most important looted Iraqi nuclear

site. The IAEA had produced extensive documentation of partially enriched and natural uranium at al-Tuwaitha and identified the facility April 11 as one of two sites
needing the most urgent protection against looting. It was not known whether nuclear
material was looted from the site, in part because of differences of opinion over
how to proceed, both between Washington and the IAEA and within US President
George W. Bush's administration. The department's "special nuclear programmes"
teams had visited seven such sites since the end of the war and none had been found
intact, according to the *Post.*

The *Los Angeles Times* reported that several of ousted Iraqi President Saddam
Hussein's top weapons scientists had placed telephone calls to former UN inspectors seeking advice on how and whether to surrender to US forces.

US Defence Secretary Donald Rumsfeld said he was confident US forces would
find weapons of mass destruction in Iraq and that lower-level officials in Saddam's
government could be more helpful in this regard than top leaders.

President Bush said that it was only "a matter of time" until weapons of mass
destruction were found.

Italy, Spain, Denmark, Bulgaria, the Netherlands and Ukraine agreed to provide
peacekeeping troops in Iraq and would assist the United States, the United Kingdom
and Poland in maintaining order in the country. Some European Union countries,
though, continued to express opposition to the deployment of an international force
without a direct UN mandate.

The Bush administration was planning to divide Iraq into three peacekeeping
sectors, with US, British and Polish forces each overseeing one sector.

The US contingent in the peacekeeping force was to be under the control of the
top US commander in the Iraq war, Tommy Franks, and would number 20,000.

The *Chicago Tribune* reported the first large-scale return of Iraqi police officers
to the streets of Baghdad. US Army Captain Corey Brunkow said his soldiers
quickly arrested some of the police for abuses such as putting friends and relatives
at the front of gasoline lines and taking money from banks. US military police
planned to train the Iraqi police in US-style law enforcement.

Records from Baghdad's 19 largest hospitals indicated that at least 1,101 civilians died in the US offensive on the capital. The total was almost certainly higher
since records identify another 1,255 of the dead as probable civilians and many others never made it to hospitals. The records also indicated more than 6,800 civilians
were wounded.

The Bush administration said it would not attempt to count Iraqi civilian or military deaths.

US officials said that no final decision had been made on whether to allow
International Atomic Energy Agency inspectors to visit Iraqi nuclear sites but
indicated that the United Nations was not likely to be given such a role over the
short term.

US arms control officials rejected an IAEA request for access to the al-Tuwaitha nuclear site.

US officials said that US-British forces in Iraq have captured the country's "Mrs. Anthrax," Huda Salih Mahdi Ammash. Also known as "Chemical Sally," Ms Ammash was believed to have been responsible for rebuilding Iraqi biological weapons programmes after the 1991 Gulf War. She was No. 53 on a US most-wanted list of 55 Iraqi officials who served under toppled President Saddam Hussein. She was the only woman on the list. The United States had now reported detaining 19 of the 55, and another was believed dead.

The *Washington Times* reported that US intelligence officials had said French officials in Syria gave passports to officials in Saddam Hussein's government who were fleeing Iraq, allowing them to escape to Europe. The newspaper reported that the move undermined the US-British search for officials who served under Mr Saddam. A French Embassy spokeswoman rejected the charges, saying French authorities had issued no visas to officials in Saddam's government since the war in Iraq began.

US officials indicated that the return of the IAEA was unlikely in the short term.

Employees of the al-Tuwaitha nuclear facility said looters at al-Tuwaitha were after not uranium, but the drums the uranium was stored in. The employees said looters emptied barrels of low-grade uranium onto the ground, then took the barrels away to use for food and water storage. The workers said they then buried the uranium.

A US State Department spokesman said that US forces in Iraq had recovered about $800 million that may have been part of $1 billion that was stolen from the Iraqi Central Bank by Saddam's son Qusay just before the bombing of Baghdad began.

No. 32 on the US most-wanted list of 55 top officials in Saddam's government, regional Baath Party leader Ghazi Hamud al-Adib, was captured, bringing to 19 the number of officials on the list who were in US custody.

US ground forces commander William Wallace said US forces had found "plenty of evidence" that an Iraqi weapons of mass destruction programme was active before the war.

US Central Command's top official in charge of weapons of mass destruction defence, Tom Woloszyn, said US military officers had "very promising" documents, including orders for chemical weapons precursors, that could allow them to compile an overall picture of Iraqi weapons of mass destruction programmes before the war.

Germany rejected Poland's proposal to send German troops from a Danish-German-Polish corps stationed in Poland to Iraq for peacekeeping duty under a US plan but did not rule out providing troops under a UN or NATO mandate. German Defence Minister Peter Struck, Polish Defence Minister Jerzy Szmajdzinski and

Danish Defence Minister Svend Aage Jensby met and agreed that Poland could send its troops from the corps to Iraq but that Germany and Denmark would not do so.

The United States, United Kingdom and Spain asked the UN Security Council to end sanctions on Iraq and give Washington and London control over Iraq's oil revenue to finance reconstruction, with international oversight.

Under the resolution, the council would endorse US-British political and financial control of Iraq for at least a year, transferring all new oil revenue, as well as $3 billion now controlled by the United Nations, to a special assistance fund to be "disbursed at the direction of" US-British authorities in consultation with interim Iraqi officials. The UN oil-for-food programme would be phased out over four months.

An advisory board to monitor the oil funds' use would be set up and would include representation from the United Nations, the International Monetary Fund and the World Bank.

The United Nations' role in Iraq's future would also involve the appointment of a UN special coordinator who would work with "the authority and the people of Iraq with respect to the restoration and establishment of national and local institutions for representative governance."

Under the US timetable for Iraq's political future, the coordinator would arrive after a transitional government was in place but before the second phase of building a new government. No explicit government-building authority would be granted to the coordinator under the US-British-Spanish resolution but that the resolution specifically envisioned that the official would coordinate UN and nongovernmental organisation reconstruction efforts.

Fifteen countries met in London for the second time to plan for an Iraq peace-keeping force. The British Defence Ministry called the meeting a work session and said no announcements would be made.

US defence officials said that US forces had released 7,000 Iraqi prisoners captured during the war, including more than 3,700 who pledged in writing not to participate in hostilities with US troops. US military police were still detaining about 2,000 Iraqi prisoners.

The United States had not found the weapons of mass destruction it expected to find in Iraq, and the main US team searching for the banned weapons were to leave in June.

The principal arm of the US weapons hunt – the 75th Exploitation Task Force, which includes biologists, chemists, treaty specialists, nuclear operators, computer experts, document specialists and special forces soldiers – had found no proof that Saddam Hussein secretly stocked banned weapons and was preparing to leave Iraq.

The leader of site assessment teams from the US Defence Threat Reduction Agency said that the task force no longer expected to "find chemical rounds sitting next to a gun."

Of 19 top weapons sites identified at the war's outset by US Central Command, 17 had been searched, to no avail. Forty-five of another 68 "non-WMD sites" that were deemed to have the potential to offer clues in the hunt had also been fruitlessly searched.

A US military official told CNN that US forces had "pretty conclusive evidence" that a trailer they discovered near the northern city of Mosul was a mobile chemical weapons laboratory. The trailer was found at a former missile factory that has been looted since the war. It was made up of refrigeration units and piping, according to CNN. The military official said an apparent spraying device was found nearby. The find, if confirmed, would be the second of its kind for the United States, which repeatedly cited Iraq's weapons of mass destruction programme in the buildup to war but so far had found little to justify such claims.

The *Financial Times* reported that US President George W. Bush's administration, concerned that it might not find a large weapons of mass destruction arsenal in Iraq, was beginning to focus on proving that Saddam Hussein had developed what a White House official called a "just-in-time delivery" system.

Iraq's "Dr. Germ," microbiologist Rihab Taha, surrendered to US forces. The United States reportedly believes that Mr Taha, who allegedly refined weapons-grade anthrax and engaged in other weapons of mass destruction work under Saddam, could help in the search for such weapons.

The International Atomic Energy Agency said that it wanted to investigate reports that some Iraqis living near the looted al-Tuwaitha nuclear site were displaying symptoms of radiation sickness. Experts cited by Reuters said Iraqis who looted uranium-tainted barrels from the site might see rising cancer rates within months.

For the third time in a little more than a month, IAEA Director General Mohamed ElBaradei called on the occupying forces in Iraq to allow IAEA experts to return to the country to investigate what Mr ElBaradei called "a potential radiological emergency." Referring to reports of "yellow cake" (uranium oxide) being emptied on the ground from containers looted and taken to people's homes, as well as radioactive sources being stolen and removed from their shielding, Mr ElBaradei said, "We have a moral responsibility to establish the facts without delay and take urgent remedial action." He said he regretted that he had not yet received a response to his previous requests for admission to Iraq by the IAEA's international teams of specialists in radiation safety, nuclear security and emergency response.

The *Washington Post* reported that US military personnel originally tasked with the search for weapons of mass destruction in Iraq were increasingly being assigned to other missions. All four of the original Site Survey Teams were now dedicating much of their time to "sensitive sites" that had no known connection to weapons of mass destruction, while three of the four "mobile exploitation teams" had shed their weapons experts and moved on to other objectives, the report said.

The US military personnel interviewed in the report cited a lack of security at potential weapons sites, widespread looting, language barriers and unresolved disputes between the Bush administration and the IAEA as hindrances to their work. They also said that at some sites, the damaged appeared to be calculated to destroy evidence.

In one example of the US military's search for weapons, a survey team on May 1 painstakingly entered a heavily secured facility, listed as priority No. 26 on the US Central Command search list, and found nothing more than a cache of vacuum cleaners.

Following IAEA Director General Mohamed ElBaradei's third call in a month on the United States to allow his nuclear inspectors to return to Iraq, US Defence Secretary Donald Rumsfeld said that his department would have "no problem" with the inspectors' return but that it could not take place until after the UN Security Council approved a new resolution on Iraq that it was then debating.

A US State Department spokesman said that the United States and the International Atomic Energy Agency would conduct "joint inspections" of a storage area at Iraq's al-Tuwaitha nuclear facility, which was the country's major nuclear site during the tenure of President Saddam Hussein and had reportedly been heavily looted since Baghdad fell to US-British troops.

In a bid to compare prewar assessments of the threat posed by Iraq to intelligence gathered in the country since the war ended, a team of retired CIA officers appointed by CIA Director George Tenet was reviewing classified intelligence reports that were circulated within the US government before the war about subjects including Hussein's government and Iraq's weapons of mass destruction programmes.

News of the review, which a senior intelligence official said was based on a prewar request by Donald Rumsfeld, came as the United States' main weapons of mass destruction hunters in Iraq wrapped up their work, having found little to support prewar US claims of a serious Iraqi threat.

Independent researchers cited in the *Christian Science Monitor* said there was growing evidence that the war in Iraq took between 5,000 and 10,000 civilian lives, which would make it, in terms of civilian deaths, the deadliest conflict with US involvement since the Vietnam War.

The 19 NATO countries decided unanimously that they would help Poland to establish a peacekeeping force in central Iraq. NATO experts would help Poland plan for a force of at least 7,000 soldiers in the sector, and the alliance will provide Poland with other assistance in areas such as establishment of headquarters, communications and intelligence. Poland asked the United States to pay about two-thirds of the cost of the peacekeeping operation, which Poland estimated at $90 million.

US Ambassador to NATO Nicholas Burns said he did "not exclude that NATO will play a bigger role in the future," adding that 's decision put the alliance "squarely in the mix in Iraq." NATO Secretary General George Robertson, though, said that "we were not talking about a NATO presence in Iraq; we were talking purely and simply about NATO help to Poland."

UN Monitoring, Verification and Inspection Commission Executive Chairman Hans Blix said that he was "beginning to suspect" the government of Saddam Hussein had no weapons of mass destruction. He said Baghdad's evasive behaviour in recent years could have stemmed from a desire not to hide weapons of mass destruction but to protect Iraqi honour and control the conditions on which outsiders could enter the country.

US Iraq administrator Paul Bremer said that Iraq's military and security services had been dissolved and that a new force would be set up that would be "representative of all Iraqis."

The town of Fallujah was the scene of yet another skirmish when Iraqi attackers reportedly fired on US soldiers, leaving four dead and nine injured. Two of the dead were armed assailants. The rest were US troops. Two other US soldiers died in accidents and two were killed when attackers fired on an eight-vehicle Army supply convoy near Hadithah, about 120 miles northwest of Baghdad.

About 100 former Iraqi soldiers demonstrated in Baghdad to protest the US-led coalition's decision to dissolve the army with no more than a month's pay. Agence France-Presse reported that officers above the rank of lieutenant colonel would receive no severance pay at all unless they could prove they were not members of the Baath Party. The soldiers threatened to take up arms against US troops.

US Secretary of Defence Donald Rumsfeld said that Iraq may have destroyed its alleged stores of chemical and biological weapons before the US-led invasion in March. He stressed that US search teams combing Iraq for evidence to support the claims had only been at work seven weeks trying to investigate hundreds of sites.

Following the rash of violence against the occupying forces, US officials said they would keep a larger force in Iraq than originally anticipated. Approximately 160,000 US and British troops were now in Iraq. The majority would probably stay until security improved.

Four US soldiers died and 15 were injured in violence in Baghdad and the city of Fallujah. Residents of the western town of Heet rioted in the streets, threw stones at US armored vehicles, stormed the police station and set police cars on fire. The unrest was reportedly due to house-to-house searches conducted by US troops.

British Prime Minister Tony Blair criticised claims that his government forced intelligence services to fabricate evidence that Saddam Hussein had weapons of mass destruction in the country as "completely absurd." Mr Blair said he had "absolutely no doubt about" the truth of evidence of weapons of mass destruction.

A US Presidential spokesman also responded to the allegations , saying the US government relied on prewar intelligence reports that Iraq had weapons of mass destruction.

US military commander David McKiernan declared that "the war has not ended," saying a new military phase to root out die-hard supporters of former president Saddam Hussein was about to start. His statement came after another US soldier was killed in an ambush on a highway north of Baghdad.

A British soldier serving in Iraq was arrested after allegations of torturing an Iraqi prisoner of war. The soldier, who had returned to the United Kingdom on leave, was arrested after his local photographic shop called the police because of developed photos of an Iraqi bound, gagged and suspended from a forklift truck and of British soldiers apparently committing sex acts close to captured Iraq soldiers.

In Basra, British and US occupation authorities said Iraq's second-largest city was not yet ready to govern itself. The statement came after the authorities dismissed, in the past week, the mayor and his council, after concluding that the interim government was composed mostly of tribal sheiks with ties to Saddam Hussein and his Baath Party.

The United States revoked the diplomatic status of the members of foreign missions in Iraq who stayed in the country after the collapse of Hussein's government after three diplomats from the Palestinian mission were arrested.

An International Atomic Energy Agency team was due to arrive in Iraq June 6 to resume inspections in nuclear sites. The agency however would be working under close supervision of the United States, which had said that the team of fewer than 10 members can only inspect the town of Tuwaitha, 30 miles southeast of Baghdad. Team members could stay in Iraq for up to two weeks and they had to stay in Tuwaitha, and not in Baghdad, where they were before the war.

KASHMIR

Following a similar move by India, Pakistani Prime Minister Zafarullah Khan Jamali said that his country would reopen air, road and rail links with India. Mr Jamali announced plans for several new measures designed to help improve relations with India, including the release of Indian fishermen who had been detained after entering Pakistani waters, the return of both countries' embassies to full staff and the resumption of cricket and field hockey matches between the two countries. Both India and Pakistan have said their gestures could help lead to talks later this year to help resolve the status of the disputed Kashmir region.

Mr Jamali said he favoured a tiered approach to negotiations with India, concluding with a bilateral summit between the countries' leaders. India, however, rejected Pakistan's offer, calling it "completely inadequate" because it did not address the issue of cross-border terrorism in Kashmir.

LIBERIA

Following the recommendation of an expert panel on Liberia, the UN Security Council announced it would renew sanctions against Liberia for allegedly fomenting conflict in West Africa, adding a ban on timber exports to existing arms and diamond embargoes.

The Council was extending for 12 more months a two-year ban on arms, diamonds and travel, while a new ban on timber exports, which were reportedly used to finance arms and enrich government officials, would begin on July 7. The council said Liberia had failed to demonstrate that revenue from its timber industry, the country's largest employer, was used for legitimate social, humanitarian and development purposes.

Human Rights Watch said Liberia was "a source of instability to its neighbours" and urged the Council to maintain sanctions against Liberia and to condemn Guinea and Ivory Coast as well. The group cited alleged human rights abuses against civilians by Liberian government and rebel groups during the previous year, including summary executions, recruitment of children, sexual violence, looting of civilian property and forced labour.

A UN-backed special war crimes court for Sierra Leone reiterated its claim that Liberia was harbouring two key fugitives. Prosecutor David Crane called for the arrest of Johnny Paul Koroma and Sam Bockarie, who had reportedly been fighting alongside rebels in Ivory Coast.

The World Food Programme called on Liberia for security guarantees to allow the resumption of food distribution to refugees and internally displaced people in camps near the capital, Monrovia. The UN agency alleged a direct link between food distribution and attacks by armed groups on refugee and transit camps. The WFP added that aid agencies had lost access to 70% of the country because of the long-running civil conflict.

Liberian officials said indicted Sierra Leonean war crimes suspect Sam Bockarie, whom the *Washington Post* called one of the most feared guerrilla fighters in West Africa during the previous decade, was killed while resisting arrest in a shootout near the border with Ivory Coast. Mr Bockarie had been indicted in March 2003 on charges that included mass murder, enslavement, mutilation and rape. He had recently been associated with an Ivorian rebel faction.

UN High Commissioner for Refugees Ruud Lubbers blamed Liberian President Charles Taylor for conflict and refugee problems plaguing West Africa and said Mr Taylor should be forced out of office.

The civil conflict between the Taylor regime and the Liberians United for Reconciliation and Democracy had displaced 1 million people inside the country and caused 300,000 to flee since it began in 1999, creating a refugee problem for neighbouring Ivory Coast.

Liberia accused the UN High Commissioner for Refugees of supporting the new Liberian rebel group Movement for Democracy in Liberia by providing it with food while neglecting government-controlled areas.

The rebel group captured the port town of Harper on May 19. MODEL and the country's main rebel group, the Liberians United for Reconciliation and Democracy, controlled as much as 60% of Liberia's territory.

A UNHCR representative said the agency had never done business with MODEL and that there were no UNHCR staff in Harper.

MIDDLE EAST

Israeli tanks and helicopters attacked a residence in Gaza City in a counterterrorism raid that left eight Palestinians dead and 25 others wounded and cast a shadow on the unveiling of a peace process "road map" aimed at restarting negotiations.

The Gaza fighting erupted when Israeli forces moved against a house belonging to the family of a senior Hamas military leader, Yusuf Abu Hin.

UN Secretary General Kofi Annan welcomed the formal introduction of the so-called peace plan road map, a blueprint for talks between Palestinians and Israelis drawn up by the United Nations, Russia, the United States and the European Union. Mr Annan said the plan gave the Israeli and Palestinian peoples "a real chance to end their long and painful conflict."

He praised Mahmoud Abbas, also known as Abu Mazen, who was sworn in as prime minister of the Palestinian Authority in a move that cleared the way for the "Quartet" that drafted the road map to begin pushing for renewed negotiations.

In Washington, US President George W. Bush called Mr Abbas "a man I can work with."

The road map called for, among other things:
* an immediate cease-fire,
* dismantling of terrorist groups,
* elections in Palestinian areas,
* Israeli withdrawal from occupied Palestinian territory and
* an end to illegal Jewish settlements on Palestinian land.

Israeli forces killed 16 Palestinians in operations in the West Bank and Gaza Strip.

Thirteen of the deaths occurred in an Israeli army raid on a Gaza City neighbourhood that was reportedly approved following a suicide bombing in Tel Aviv that was thought to be the work of Hamas. Israel said the Gaza City raid was necessary to prevent more attacks by senior Hamas military leader Yusuf Abu Hins.

Israel said at least seven of those killed in Gaza City were armed and that three were Hamas members. According to witnesses, Israeli soldiers called on Palestinians in a house to give themselves up or at least to allow women and children out of the house, but the men in the house shouted, "Everyone here will die as martyrs, including the children," and fired on the Israelis.

New Palestinian Prime Minister Mahmoud Abbas' Cabinet, approved by Palestinian legislators, said the Gaza City raid was "a message to the entire world that the Israeli government is not interested in creating an atmosphere conducive to a return to the negotiating table and a peace process."

UN Secretary General Kofi Annan was "deeply disturbed" by Israel's incursions. Mr Annan thought the operations "contradict the international community's efforts to restart the Israeli-Palestinian peace process, following presentation of the 'road map' to the parties."

US officials presented the road map to Israeli Prime Minister Ariel Sharon.

Hamas said a call by Mr Abbas for it to disarm was "a clear message to everybody – our weapons were our blood. We will cut any hand that tries to take these weapons away from us." Hamas added that "anybody who cooperates with the road map is collaborating with Israel's criminal occupation."

US Assistant Secretary of State William Burns met with Palestinian Authority Prime Minister Mahmoud Abbas to discuss the "road map" Middle East peace plan, saying the Palestinians had to stop violence and Israel had to loosen restrictive security measures in order for the plan to succeed.

Mr Abbas said the Palestinians "were already well on our way to implementing the road map, while Israel has yet to even accept the road map." The new Palestinian prime minister had vowed to disarm militants. Israeli Prime Minister Sharon had said he would not scale back security measures until he was certain Mr Abbas was committed to taming the militants.

Mr Abbas' government would reportedly try to persuade, rather than force, militants to disarm, because it feared civil unrest could result otherwise.

Egypt reportedly intended to resume its sponsorship of talks between Palestinian officials and militant groups including Hamas, Islamic Jihad and the al-Aqsa Martyrs Brigade.

Mr Sharon said that he had "taken the oath to do everything in my power to lead the country to peace, and such a chance exists this spring."

Israeli army chief Moshe Yaalon said the worst of the current conflict, which began in September 2000, was over, despite ongoing attacks. Since the uprising began, 2,420 Palestinians and 730 Israelis had been killed in the violence.

International donors to Palestinians, including the United Nations, condemned Israeli efforts to wall off parts of the West Bank, saying a barrier under construction would separate 12,000 Palestinians from their land, jobs and social services.

The commissioner general of the UN Relief and Works Agency for Palestine Refugees in the Near East called on Palestinians and Israelis to accept the "road map" Middle East peace plan but acknowledged that similar efforts in the past "never have led to anything." Peter Hansen said that the plan, which he called "more advanced and more synchronized" than past peace plans, would fail without support from both sides.

Israeli Prime Minister Ariel Sharon said that demands for Palestinian refugees to be allowed to return to Israel had to be dropped as "a condition for continuing the process" – the first time Israel had made renouncing the right of return a condition for conducting peace talks, according to the *Jerusalem Post*. Under the road map, the right of return would be negotiated in a third and final phase of peace talks.

Mr Abbas, called Sharon's demand "unacceptable and unreasonable," saying, "The right of return is one of every refugee, and I cannot abandon this right."

Israel had raised 15 objections to the peace plan.

Human Rights Watch had also criticised the plan, expressing concern over what it called insufficient safeguards of human rights in the document.

Palestinian Authority officials had reportedly been meeting secretly with armed groups to try to obtain an end to attacks on Israeli civilians and appeared to reach an agreement with Hamas on a cease-fire. Aides to two top Palestinian officials said Hamas agreed to a cease-fire, though Hamas founder Ahmed Yassin rejected any cease-fire before Israel withdrew to its 1967 borders and a Palestinian state was established with Jerusalem as its capital.

Israeli Prime Minister Ariel Sharon said that Israel would not renounce settlements in the Palestinian territories as the peace process developed. Under the terms of the "road map" peace plan such areas could have become part of an independent Palestinian state.

Mr Sharon denied that the United States has been putting heavy pressure on him to dismantle such settlements.

Speaking on a security fence Israel had been building around major West Bank cities and towns, Mr Sharon said the Jewish settlements Ariel and Emmanuel were likely to be on the Israeli side of the fence – a change from the original plan that would undoubtedly spark serious Palestinian opposition. According to the American-Israeli Cooperative Enterprise, approximately 20,000 people lived in the two settlements.

UN Secretary General Kofi Annan renewed calls on Israel and the Palestinian Authority to make peace according to the terms of the road map.

Israel arrested Islamic Movement head Raed Salah and 14 other members of the Arab political party, one of Israel's largest, over charges that the party channeled funds to the armed group Hamas.

Israeli forces shot and killed three Palestinian policemen in the Gaza Strip after receiving what the Israeli military called "a very intense warning about an attack" planned against a Jewish settlement in central Gaza. When Israeli soldiers saw armed men in civilian clothes walking toward the Netzarim settlement, they opened fire.

A top Palestinian security official in Gaza, General Abdul Razzaq Majaydah, said the Palestinian policemen were on a routine assignment to protect the settlement against Palestinian militants and accused the Israelis of trying to "break up" the UN-backed road map peace plan with the killings. Among other things, the plan called for an end to violence through Palestinian control of the militants.

Hours before the policemen were killed, an Israeli missile struck a refugee camp in southern Gaza, injuring 30 Palestinians. The strike was in retaliation for attacks from Hamas against settlements and Israeli military posts in the Gaza Strip and at Israeli towns outside the Gaza boundary. Ten Israeli soldiers and three Israeli civilians were injured in that incident. A Hamas spokesman said the attacks had been in retaliation for Israeli operations that had injured Palestinians.

The Palestinian official who had managed peace negotiations with Israel for the last 11 years, Saeb Erekat, tendered his resignation as new Palestinian Prime Minister Mahmoud Abbas prepared for a meeting with Israeli Prime Minister Ariel Sharon. Associated Press reported that the move signaled deep divisions within the Palestinian camp.

More than 60 mortars and rockets were fired by Palestinian militants at Israeli settlements in Gaza and elsewhere. A convoy of 25 Israeli tanks subsequently rolled into Beit Hanoun, demolishing four homes said to belong to militants and plowing under several acres of orange trees. The raid came hours before the start of what Palestinians call "al-Naqba" (the Catastrophe), commemorating their displacement from towns and villages in 1948, upon Israel's creation.

Armed Palestinian militants continued attacks after a series of strikes that left nine Israelis dead, casting doubt on the future of the internationally supported "road map" peace plan.

A suicide bomber blew himself up at a shopping mall in northern Israel, killing at least four people in the crowded mall and injuring at least 31. Palestinians fired rockets and mortars at Jewish settlements in the Gaza Strip and Israeli vehicles were fired on. Hamas claimed responsibility.

In the Gaza Strip, a suicide bomber on a bicycle attacked an Israeli Defence Forces patrol, injuring three soldiers in the fourth suicide bombing since evening. Nine Israelis were killed and 23 wounded in the four attacks. In one attack, a Hamas operative disguised as an observant Jew bombed an Israeli bus, killing seven and injuring 20.

Meeting to discuss how to respond to the attacks, the Israeli Cabinet decided to bar Palestinians from entering Israel except for humanitarian reasons but rejected proposals to expel Palestinian Authority President Yasser Arafat. Israeli Defence Minister Shaul Mofaz said that such an expulsion could be reconsidered if attacks on Israelis continued. The Cabinet also decided to boycott any foreign dignitary who met with Mr Arafat.

Before most of the attacks had occurred, Israeli Prime Minister Ariel Sharon met with new Palestinian Prime Minister Mahmoud Abbas in talks that Israeli government sources cited by *Ha'aretz* called a failure. According to the sources, Mr Sharon offered to hand over security responsibility for certain areas to the Palestinian Authority, but the Palestinians refused.

The internationally backed "road map" peace plan had to be implemented soon, because conditions for peace would otherwise continue to worsen in Israel and the Palestinian territories, top UN peace envoy Terje Roed-Larsen told the Security Council. Mr Roed-Larsen said Palestinian attacks on Israeli civilians and Israeli expansion of Jewish settlements in the territories were radicalising both populations, meaning that creating a Palestinian state would become more difficult with time. Creating such a state was central to the road map.

Calling Israeli roadblocks and checkpoints "the single largest impediment to the Palestinian economy," Mr Roed-Larsen said there was 60% poverty and 53% unemployment in the territories. He criticised Israel for recent restrictions on the movements of UN employees in the Gaza Strip, measures he said were severely curtailing the United Nations' ability to provide services to Palestinians.

Israeli forces withdrew from Beit Hanoun in the Gaza Strip despite the recent wave of Palestinian suicide bombings. The town is part of an area Israel had said it could hand over to Palestinian security control as a test of Palestinian Prime Minister Mahmoud Abbas' commitment to the road map and to combating armed militants.

Israeli Prime Minister Ariel Sharon announced that he was "prepared to accept" the "road map" Middle East peace plan if Washington took account of his concerns about matters such as Jewish settlements in the West Bank.

Palestinian Authority officials said that they would accept no changes to the plan, adding that the Bush administration had assured them there would be none.

Mr Abbas met with leaders of the armed Palestinian group Hamas, asking them to curb attacks against Israelis. Hamas leaders said they could accept a partial truce on the condition that Israel stopped hunting down Hamas members. Israel repeated its position that it found such a cease-fire unacceptable.

The UN Relief and Works Agency announced that it had told donors that it would continue humanitarian operations in the Gaza Strip despite a new Israeli closure imposed following the recent suicide bombing wave.

Following a stormy Cabinet meeting at which ministers approved the peace plan and in what was being hailed as a sign of political transformation, Israeli Prime Minister Ariel Sharon warned conservative Likud Party members that Israel's "occupation" was harmful for both Israelis and Palestinians – the first time Mr Sharon had publicly called Israel's presence in the Palestinian territories an "occupation." This fueled speculation that he might be responding to strong US pressure to adopt the peace plan.

The following day Mr Sharon said that the West Bank and Gaza Strip were "disputed," not "occupied" – the Palestinian people living in a situation of occupation, not the territories themselves being occupied.

Prime Minister Ariel Sharon promised to withdraw Israeli forces from Palestinian city centres and the West Bank after meeting with his Palestinian counterpart, Mahmoud Abbas, in deliberations both sides called "beneficial" and "positive."

In their second meeting in two weeks to discuss the road map peace plan, Mr Sharon said he would unilaterally end the two-week closure of the West Bank and allow some Palestinian workers into Israel as a measure of good faith. He also renewed promises to withdraw Israeli troops from West Bank city centres, ease some restrictions at roadblocks around Palestinian towns and release some Palestinian prisoners on the condition that Mr Abbas "act decisively to stop terrorism."

Mr Abbas was planning to meet with two of the main Palestinian militant groups, Hamas and Islamic Jihad, the following week and said he expected to obtain a cease-fire. But according to Hamas sources any cease-fire agreement might be temporary, lasting for only a few weeks rather than the full year Mr Abbas wanted. The prime minister and the militant group were further divided on the extent of the cease-fire as Hamas was probably prepared to stop its suicide attacks inside Israel, but it would not halt its resistance against Israeli soldiers and settlers in the occupied territories – the West Bank and Gaza Strip.

The al-Aqsa Martyrs Brigades, the militant wing of Palestinian President Yasser Arafat's Fatah faction, said they "reject the road map to hell" and would not stop attacks on Israel until "the rights of the Palestinian people were restored without condition."

The White House said the immediate goal was to begin implementation of the road map peace plan. To that end, Bush said he would call on Israel to freeze settlement activity in the occupied territories and appeal for an end to Palestinian violence.

MOROCCO

At least 42 victims and 13 perpetrators were dead following nearly simultaneous suicide bombings in Casablanca, Morocco, against a Spanish social club, a hotel, a Jewish cemetery, a Jewish community centre and the Belgian Consulate. More than 100 people were wounded in the attacks.

Morocco arrested as many as 30 people in connection with the bombings, including a man suspected of being one of the attackers who police said was arrested after being injured by another attacker's bomb. The detainees were Moroccans between 18 and 22 years old and frequent "Islamic circles," the country's Interior Ministry said.

A US counterterrorism official cited "strong suspicion" of an al-Qaeda role in the Morocco attacks, which followed by four days an attack involving nearly simultaneous car bombings in Riyadh, Saudi Arabia, for which the global terrorist network had been blamed. A man who had been identified as al-Qaeda head Osama bin Laden, speaking on a tape in February, cited Saudi Arabia and Morocco, among other countries, as being "ready for liberation" from "tyrannical and apostate regimes" that "were enslaved by America."

Moroccan Justice Minister Mohamed Bouzoubaa said some of the 14 Moroccan bombers involved in the attacks had returned to Morocco "recently from a foreign state" and that the bombers "have a link" with an Islamic fundamentalist group called Assirat al-Moustaqim.

Three of the bombers reportedly had ties with Islamist groups in Morocco that were directed by Abou Hafs, who had been accused of having ties to al-Qaeda and was sentenced this month to six months in jail for inciting violence. The newspaper cited Assirat al-Moustaqim, Salafiya Jihadia and al-Higra wa Takfir as three groups Moroccan investigators were focusing on in the wake of the attacks.

NORTH KOREA

The United States detected smoke coming from a North Korean nuclear facility that could have been a sign that Pyongyang had begun reprocessing spent nuclear fuel rods. US officials provided South Korea with a satellite photograph of the smoke plume. Intelligence officials had not detected other signs of reprocessing, such as chemical traces or heat releases.

Top White House foreign policy advisers met to discuss the next US move in the Korean nuclear crisis, and officials said the United States would probably meet with North Korean officials for another round of talks despite the reprocessing activity, the *New York Times* reported.

Officials previously did not believe North Korean reprocessing had begun, but the reassessment came after national security adviser Condoleezza Rice ordered an intelligence review, which was delivered to the White House in mid-April, according to the *Times*.

Ten years previously, Japanese officials examined the possibility of a pre-emptive air attack on a North Korean military facility to prevent a missile attack, Agence France-Presse reported. The study was conducted after Pyongyang launched a missile into the Sea of Japan, but was scuttled after Japanese officials agreed that they did not have the proper aircraft at their disposal to achieve success in the mission.

NUCLEAR NONPROLIFERATION TREATY *see also* IRAN

The parties to the Nuclear Nonproliferation Treaty concluded their annual meeting with the acknowledgement that the treaty faced challenges to the integrity of the regime under which most countries of the world renounce nuclear weapons while the nuclear powers commit to eliminate their nuclear arsenals.

In his summary report of the meeting, Ambassador Laszlo Molnar of Hungary, the chairman of the Preparatory Committee for the 2005 Review Conference, wrote that states "stressed the increasingly grave threat to the treaty and international security posed by the proliferation of weapons of mass destruction, nuclear, biological and chemical. . . . The gravity of this threat reinforces the need to strengthen the treaty."

North Korea, which withdrew from the treaty earlier in 2003, and Iran were criticised for not complying with the treaty in pursuit of nuclear weapons, while the nuclear weapons powers, in particular the United States, were criticised for not pursuing nuclear disarmament. The United States was also criticised for embracing military doctrines that envisioned more uses for nuclear weapons.

SAUDI ARABIA

Twenty-nine people were killed and 194 wounded in suicide bombing attacks on three housing compounds in the Saudi capital, Riyadh. The assailants apparently shot their way into the upmarket, gated developments before setting off car bombs.

There was no claim of responsibility. US officials suspected al-Qaeda was behind the blasts. Saudi officials, who also suspected an al-Qaeda connection, said they were seeking 19 suspects who were discovered earlier in May with a large weapons cache in the same neighbourhood where the attack took place. The suspects, including 17 Saudis, a Yemeni and an Iraqi with Kuwaiti and Canadian citizenship, were believed to have received orders directly from al-Qaeda leader Osama bin Laden.

Saudi officials seized tons of explosives and other equipment that one official described as being "of very high grade" and meant to inflict "maximum damage."

The attacks came two weeks after Washington announced it would withdraw US troops from Saudi Arabia following the defeat of President Saddam Hussein in neighbouring Iraq. Bin Laden, a Saudi national, had long protested the US military presence in Saudi Arabia.

SIERRA LEONE

The chief prosecutor in charge of the UN-backed Special Court on Sierra Leone labeled Liberian President Charles Taylor a "player" in world terrorism and accused him of harbouring international terrorists, including members of al-Qaeda.

David Crane, a former inspector general at the Pentagon and assistant general counsel for the US Defence Intelligence Agency, said his investigations of Sierra Leone's civil war had revealed evidence of al-Qaeda operations in West Africa, principally in the diamond trade.

President Taylor had denied earlier allegations promulgated in the press about his purported links to terrorism.

Mr Crane also accused President Taylor of ordering the May 6 murder of his longtime associate, Sam Bockarie, who had been indicted by the Special Court and was viewed as a potential witness against Mr Taylor.

According to UN experts, the rebel group Liberians United for Reconciliation and Democracy now occupied between 40 and 60% of national territory.

SOMALIA

UN Secretary General Kofi Annan appointed a four-person expert panel to investigate violations of the arms embargo against Somalia. The Council decided to re-establish the team after considering the panel's latest report, in which the experts said most factions in Somalia had continued to import or receive weapons in breach of the arms embargo. Some of the same leaders signed 2002's Eldoret Declaration rededicating themselves to the search for peace.

SRI LANKA

The Norwegian special envoy to the peace process in Sri Lanka, Erik Solheim, left the island with no immediate results on the attempt to resume peace talks between the government and the rebel Liberation Tigers of Tamil Eelam.

The opposition Liberation Tigers of Tamil Eelam rejected a proposal by Norwegian diplomats and the government offering them more power to rebuild the Tamil-majority northeast region in exchange for their presence at a Tokyo donor conference in June.

Despite the failure to resume peace talks, the rebel group had said that there would be no return to armed conflict.

TAJIKISTAN

UN Secretary General Kofi Annan told the Security Council he was extending the mandate of the UN Tajikistan Office of Peacebuilding until June 1, 2004 because of instability in the country.

WESTERN SAHARA

UN Secretary General Kofi Annan proposed that the UN Mission for the Referendum in Western Sahara be extended until July 31 while the Security Council considered how to proceed in the disputed territory. He called on the Council to endorse a peace plan developed by his envoy to the territory, James Baker, calling the Baker plan a "compromise" between plans favoured by Morocco, which administered Western Sahara, and Algeria, which backed the Polisario Front, a group seeking independence for the territory.

The Security Council unanimously adopted a resolution extending by two months until July 31 the mandate of the UN Mission.

June 2003

AFGHANISTAN

French President Jacques Chirac told US President George W. Bush that France would soon send special forces to take part in peacekeeping operations in Afghanistan. The French special forces would be an addition to the French troops already in Afghanistan helping to train the new Afghan military.

Clashes between Taliban guerrilla forces and Afghan fighters loyal to the provincial government of Kandahar killed 47, one of the highest single body counts in months of sporadic fighting along Afghanistan's border with Pakistan.

Afghan authorities said 40 of those killed in nine hours of firefights in villages north of Spinboldak were Taliban rebels. Seven of the dead were government troops loyal to Kandahar Governor Gul Agha Sherzai.

The fighting broke out in a village called Nimakai then spread to a neighbouring village, Populzai.

Russia's increasing involvement with NATO, which was set to take over peacekeeping operations in Afghanistan Aug. 11, would not include sending forces to Afghanistan, Russian Foreign Minister Igor Ivanov said. Moscow was, however, reportedly offering intelligence and other support.

Afghan President Hamid Karzai arrived in the United Kingdom in another of his continuing efforts to increase international aid to Afghanistan, where the central government in Kabul was struggling to shore up its finances and assert control beyond the capital. Afghan Finance Minister Ashraf Ghani said the country needed $15 billion in foreign aid over the next five years beyond the $5.2 billion already pledged. The country also needed $15 billion in private investment, Mr Ghani said.

A recent push by Karzai to convince powerful regional commanders to remit millions of dollars of customs revenue owed the government yielded some success when Ismail Khan, governor of Herat, sent $20 million to Kabul. Thousands of government salaries had reportedly gone unpaid for months due to the national treasury's crisis.

An explosives-filled taxi detonated next to a busload of German peacekeeping troops in eastern Kabul, killing four and injuring 31 in the worst attack the international force had suffered since arriving in Afghanistan 18 months previously.

No one had claimed responsibility for the explosion, but authorities suspected al-Qaeda, Taliban or supporters of rebel leader Gulbuddin Hekmatyar. The three were allies.

An ISAF spokesman said the 5,000-strong force would not shrink from its duty of making Kabul safer in the blast's aftermath.

President Hamid Karzai reiterated the need for more aid to start Afghanistan's economic engine and secure the country from attacks by former Taliban and al-Qaeda members. Mr Karzai was seeking an additional $15 billion to $20 billion for reconstruction, well beyond the $5 billion international donors had pledged since the Taliban regime fell in 2001.

Afghan police and International Security Assistance Force peacekeepers defused a remote-control bomb discovered on a busy road in Kabul.

The interior minister said suicide bombers were being trained to target foreign soldiers in the country.

The UN Assistance Mission in Afghanistan said that teams were to resume demining work along parts of the Kabul to Kandahar road, considered one of the most important routes for commerce and relief aid in the country.

Because of renewed rocket attacks against the definers, the agency suspended their work again. According to a UNAMA spokesman security measures were put in place and deminers were able to start working again. The mission did not know why the 8,000 deminers who were in Afghanistan were being targeted.

UNAMA estimated that approximately 55% of the areas that contained mines and unexploded ordnance were in grazing areas and about 29% of all the contaminated area was agricultural land.

Senior UN officials told the Security Council that Afghanistan continued to be endangered by instability, with opium production both a cause and effect of that instability.

Undersecretary General for Peacekeeping Jean-Marie Guehenno told the council that "the poor security environment," including "an apparent marked increase in Taliban infiltration," continued to threaten "the gains made so far and the tasks that lie ahead." Mr Guehenno told the council, as had every UN official who had briefed the council on Afghanistan, that limiting the current peacekeeping force to the capital, Kabul, was not sufficient. About one-third of the country was currently inaccessible to the UN, which seriously hindered the ability of the UN and others to carry out reconstruction efforts.

The Afghan government said that before it started a disarmament programme aimed at demobilising regional militias and bringing stability to the country, it would reform the Defence Ministry. The ministry was run by a group of ethnic Tajiks headed by Defence Minister Mohamed Fahim and was reportedly viewed as just another armed militia, albeit one with an official government imprimatur.

Jean Arnault, deputy to the UN special envoy to Afghanistan, said no one would surrender their weapons to the government – the principal aim of the disarmament programme – "unless they feel that they were disarming on behalf of an institution that was no longer factional."

President Hamid Karzai said he would reconstitute the ministry to better reflect Afghanistan's ethnic mix.

Former Afghan Taliban regime leader Mullah Omar had named a 10-man leadership council to spearhead a renewed drive against foreign troops in Afghanistan, Reuters reported. According to the news agency, the Pakistani daily *The News* quoted Taliban spokesman Mohammed Mukhtar Mujahid as saiding Mullah Omar sent an audiotape announcing the council from his hiding place in Afghanistan.

Former Taliban provincial governor Mullah Abdul Rauf said members of the Rahbari Shura, or council, were named after five days of talks at a secret location in Afghanistan. He said they were mostly Taliban military commanders from southwest Afghanistan.

Taliban intelligence official Mullah Abdul Samad said the council was already working.

ANGOLA *see* KIMBERLEY PROCESS

BOSNIA

The United Nations announced the closure of the UN liaison offices in Zagreb, Croatia; Sarajevo, Bosnia and Herzegovina; and Belgrade, Serbia and Montenegro. The

Sarajevo closure ends a peacekeeping presence the world body kept in Bosnia and Herzegovina for a decade.

The Belgrade liaison office would merge with the UN Mission in Kosovo's office in Belgrade to create a new UN office in the Serbian capital.

In Bosnia and Herzegovina, the United Nations would stay involved through the work of its agencies.

CENTRAL AFRICAN REPUBLIC *see also* KIMBERLEY PROCESS
The political situation in the Central African Republic was evolving and had seen positive changes since March 2003, when General Francois Bozize overthrew former President Ange-Felix Patasse, UN Assistant Secretary General for Political Affairs Tuliameni Kalomoh said at the end of a two-week mission to Africa.

President Bozize had promised a constitutional referendum followed by elections in 2004.

CONGO, DEMOCRATIC REPUBLIC OF *see also* KIMBERLEY PROCESS
The United Nations uncovered evidence of cannibalism in the DRC. The evidence included "photographs and information" collected by investigators that would be made public "in due time."

UN investigators identified the killers of two unarmed military observers whose bodies were discovered May 18. Major Sarwat Oran of Jordan and Captain Siddidn Davis Banda of Malawi were tortured by having their genitals cut off before being shot in the head.

The Hema-allied Party for the Unity and Safeguarding of the Integrity of Congo accused a rival faction of massacring more than 350 civilians in a town on the shores of Lake Albert. A spokesman said the attack on the town of Tchomia, carried out with mortars and automatic weapons, began at 5 a.m. and lasted all morning. Tchomia was about 30 miles east of Bunia, the main town in war-ravaged northeastern DRC. A Ugandan army officer placed the number of dead closer to 100.

The leader of the Hema-affiliated Union des Patriots Congolais warned that the United Nations would face violent resistance when it deployed a 1,400-strong French-led force in DRC. The emergency force was being sent to quell violence that had killed more than 400 and raised the spectre of the Rwanda genocide 10 years ago. The fighting in DRC had been particularly brutal, with some victims killed with machetes and parts of their bodies reportedly cannibalised.

The UN food agency began a large-scale food distribution operation in Bunia. A World Food Programme spokeswoman said the 9,000 people camped near the town's airport would receive 21-day rations of maize meal, beans and oil. She said the distribution was made possible by MONUC, which was providing security for a non-governmental partner, German Agro-Action, to handle the distribution and also added that WFP had registered 50,000 displaced people in Nord-Kivu province, many of whom had fled Bunia.

UN Secretary General Kofi Annan told the Security Council that the peace-keeping force soon to be deployed in northeastern DRC should be tripled and that the UN mission's mandate should be extended by one year,

In addition to calling for the one-year extension (through to June 2004) of the mandate of the MONUC, Mr Annan said the 1,400-strong French-led UN peace-keeping force to be deployed in Bunia should be replaced by a force of 3,800. He wanted MONUC's authorised military strength to be increased to 10,800 by June 2004.

DRC President Joseph Kabila was warning the United Nations that the British and French troops set to arrive in Bunia would have to remain beyond September if they were to successfully quell fighting in the country. Mr Kabila effectively called for an indefinite stay, saying violence would erupt again as soon as a peacekeeping force withdrew.

Tribal militia in Bunia began withdrawing ahead of the arrival of the French-led peacekeeping force. Some 600 troops with the Union des Patriots Congolais moved to barracks outside Bunia.

The UPC, which had an estimated 15,000 fighters in the area, said its troops would stay in barracks outside Bunia.

The withdrawal of the UPC fighters followed a cease-fire deal signed by rival Hema and Lendu tribal militias in the area and the DRC government. Under the deal, troops who had been fighting recently in Bunia would remain in temporary quarters.

Aid workers in Bunia came under attack. At least five local aid workers had been beaten in their homes or in UN-controlled refugee camps.

A contingent of French troops arrived in Bunia, marking the initial deployment of an emergency international force sent to quell recent ethnic violence. The advance party was made up of several dozen soldiers tasked with securing the Bunia airport ahead of the arrival of the rest of the international force, which was expected to number up to 1,500 troops from Canada, South Africa, Senegal, Nigeria and Pakistan. Code-named Artemis, the emergency force joined 750 UN peacekeepers already in the area guarding UN installations.

The UN High Commissioner for Refugees said it had started moving thousands of Congolese refugees who fled the fighting to camps around Uganda. Ugandan authorities estimated that up to 60,000 people had fled the Bunia area for Uganda.

At least 30 more people died in Bunia when fighting broke out between feud-ing Hema and Lendu tribesmen, the day after the advance contingent of French peacekeepers arrived at the Bunia airport. The peacekeeping force was tasked with securing the Bunia airport and protecting civilians and UN personnel in Bunia, but was not allowed to intervene in tribal fighting elsewhere in the area.

The ethnic violence around Bunia had been marked by widespread reports of sexual attacks. UNICEF, in a statement, said it was alarmed by recent reports of thousands of women and girls being raped, mutilated and murdered in Ituri.

The first French combat troops to arrive in northeastern DRC landed in the embattled city of Bunia amid a fresh burst of fighting by the tribal militias whom their presence was supposed to quell.

Hours after 100 soldiers armed with assault rifles arrived at the Bunia airport, and while they were still sorting out their provisions, the 2,000 refugees, aid workers and journalists seeking shelter at the UN compound in Bunia came under shell fire. A German correspondent reported that a "handful" of French troops arrived at the compound, presumably to reinforce the UN mission peacekeepers already there, but did not intervene in the fighting between Hema and Lendu militias.

Another 50 combat troops were expected to arrive to reinforce the first 100 but most of the advance team would leave once the entire force, which could number as many as 1,700, was deployed. More than 700 troops had arrived in recent days in Uganda, which was serving as a temporary base for operations.

The French troops would be authorised to shoot to kill if needed. They were being deployed under the European and United Nations flags, but they would not be wearing the trademark blue helmets of UN peacekeepers.

A leader of the pro-government Mai-Mai militia in the central DRC province of Maniema accused South Africa of illicitly shipping weapons to the province in containers with UN markings. He said the first of such alleged shipments, in mid-May, coincided with the arrival of some 150 South African "trainers." He called for an inquiry by the international community to find out who these men were.

French fighter jets, equipped with bombs, rockets and guns, flew over Bunia. The French troops were authorised by the Security Council to use force to protect the population in the area. The jets were supporting French ground troops that so far numbered 200.

Zambian Vice President Nevers Mumba said that Zambian troops were sent to the border of the DRC after Congolese fighters threatened to extend the conflict to the southern region of the DRC.

More European peacekeepers had arrived in the northeastern DRC following an incident near Bunia in which French troops were fired on by militia fighters and returned fire. No injuries were reported. The incident was the first confirmed instance of fighting by the European Union-approved force.

Lendu fighters killed 77 people in Nyoka, near the Ugandan border. Some reports indicated that up to 100 people might have been killed.

MONUC declared null and void the nomination by a small rebel group, Union des Patriotes Congolais, of one of its members as mayor of Bunia.

The UN Security Council extended the mandate of the UN Organisation Mission in the DRC by a month, preventing it from expiring. The mandate would now expire on July 30 if further action was not taken.

UN Secretary General Kofi Annan had recommended the mission mandate be extended through to June 2004 and its numbers increased, but MONUC forces in the northeast of the country came under siege as violence flared up again, and the council instead authorised the creation of the French-led multinational force that had since been deployed in the region.

The government of the DRC and the two main rebel groups opposing it overcame one of the biggest hurdles to a power-sharing transitional government when they agreed on the formation of a unified military. Under the agreement, the government would keep the top positions of military chief of staff and head of naval forces. The rebel groups would divide the other two top posts, with head of ground forces going to the Rassemblement Congolais pour la Democratie and chief of air forces going to the Mouvement Liberation Congolais.

Over 1,000 people had returned to Bunia since the UN-mandated, French-led peacekeeping force imposed a deadline for rebel militiamen to leave the town.

The French-led force was to remain in Bunia until September 1, 2003 when it would be replaced by a UN contingent. Following a unanimous Security Council vote to extend until July 30 the mandate of the UN Organisation Mission in the DRC, which included 750 UN peacekeepers deployed in Bunia since April, UN Secretary General Kofi Annan sent a letter to the Council asking that a brigade-sized UN force be deployed in northeastern DRC.

Aid groups report that the five-year war had caused the deaths of more than 3.3 million people, mostly from hunger and disease.

CYPRUS

Following the recommendation of UN Secretary General Kofi Annan, the Security Council unanimously extended the mandate of the UN Peacekeeping Force in Cyprus until December 15, 2003.

The Council also approved Mr Annan's recommendation to increase the mission's police component by up to 34 officers. The recommendation was made to accommodate the need for more manpower at the border separating the island's Greek and Turkish communities following the partial easing of restrictions on movement across the green line, which had seen thousands of people crossing every day to a side of the island they had not seen since Cyprus was divided in 1974.

Noting the limited steps taken by the Turkish Cypriot side to ease restrictions on the UN mission's operations, Council members nonetheless called on the Turkish Cypriot authorities to drop all remaining restrictions.

Among other duties, the UN peacekeeping mission in Cyprus monitors the cease-fire lines dividing the island, conducting surveillance through a system of observation posts as well as air, vehicle and foot patrols.

GEORGIA

Three UN observers charged with monitoring the cease-fire between Georgian government troops and Abkhazian separatists were abducted along with five other people near Georgia's border with the breakaway Abkhazia region.

Unknown assailants captured the group of eight, including four Russian peace-keepers and one interpreter, before releasing the four troops, who subsequently notified authorities. Local officials had previously said eight UN observers were captured in the Kodidri Gorge.

The monitors belong to the UN Observer Mission in Georgia, which oversees the cease-fire between Georgia and the once-autonomous Abkhazia, which regained de facto independence from Georgia after a two-year struggle ending in 1993. In January the 10-year-old UNOMIG had 114 observers patrolling the buffer zone between the two regions.

This was the fourth time UN observers had been kidnapped. They had been released each time following negotiations.

Georgian authorities said they had learned the whereabouts of four kidnapped members of the UN Observer Mission in Georgia – two Germans, a Dane and their interpreter – and that they were optimistic about their release.

The UN Security Council urged the immediate, unconditional release of the four.

The unidentified kidnappers were demanding $3 million. According to an Abkhaz government spokesman, the kidnappers telephoned the UN office in Abkhazia to issue their demand. The United Nations had said it would not pay any ransom.

The three UN observers and the interpreter were later released by their captors.

Georgia ratified a comprehensive agreement with the International Atomic Energy Agency that included an "additional protocol" allowing the UN nuclear watchdog to conduct especially rigorous searches to verify that the former Soviet republic had no illegal nuclear material. The agreement was part of the Nuclear Nonproliferation Treaty, to which Georgia was a signatory.

The additional protocol was the primary vehicle by which the IAEA was attempting to bolster its system for verifying that nations involved in nuclear activities were engaged in peaceful purposes. The agency had forged 231 agreements in 147 countries establishing safeguards against illegal nuclear activities. With Georgia's approval of the additional protocol, the IAEA was now implementing safeguards in all the former Soviet states known to have had nuclear facilities or material.

GUINEA-BISSAU

The UN Security Council called on Guinea-Bissau's leaders and on other countries to work harder to put development, humanitarian efforts and peacebuilding "quickly . . . back on track" in the country.

Guinea-Bissau was scheduled to hold legislative elections on July 6, but according to UN Peacebuilding Support Office in Guinea-Bissau head David Stephen, the UN Department of Political Affairs this month determined it was not feasible to hold the elections then and called for a postponement. Mr Stephen said Guinea-Bissau's president, Koumba Yala, had expressed support for a postponement but that the government had not announced such a measure.

IRAN

The Group of Eight industrialised countries called on Iran to address growing concerns surrounding its nuclear efforts and released an action plan on combating terrorism that included assistance to countries to help develop their capabilities to prevent international terrorism.

G-8 also pledged to "not ignore the proliferation implications of Iran's advanced nuclear programme." Group members emphasised the need for Iran to fully comply with its obligations under the Nuclear Nonproliferation Treaty and called on Tehran to sign an additional protocol to its IAEA safeguards agreement, which would give the agency the authority to conduct more intrusive inspections of Iranian nuclear facilities.

As International Atomic Energy Agency inspectors arrived in Iran to take stock of the country's nuclear activities, a spokesman for the nation's Atomic Energy Organisation said Tehran had not violated any nonproliferation agreements and was unconcerned about accusations that it had.

Iran had admitted that it secretly imported uranium from China more than a decade ago, an action that spelled its failure to comply with nuclear nonproliferation obligations, according to a recently released document from the IAEA.

Specifically, the report said Iran imported 1.8 metric tons of natural uranium, an amount that was "not insignificant in terms of a state's ability to conduct nuclear research and development activities."

Summarising, the report said, "the number of failures by Iran to report the material, facilities and activities in question in a timely manner as it was obliged to did pursuant to its safeguards agreement was a matter of concern."

Iranian officials admitted that they did not report the uranium imports but they said Iran did not violate any international nuclear agreements. The head of Iran's Atomic Energy Organisation maintained that the 1991 incident did not reflect on Iran's current compliance.

Iranian officials said that the report actually shows Tehran was cooperating with the international atomic agency.

A Western diplomat in Vienna said inspectors from the International Atomic Energy Agency had been obstructed from conducting inspections in Iran after inspectors were denied access to a Tehran electric company that they wanted to investigate. Iranian officials denied the charge.

Iran also denied that it was in violation of the NPT – a charge Washington had repeatedly made – and called on US officials to stop leveling accusations about a secret Iranian weapons programme without concrete proof of its existence.

Despite Tehran's denials, US Defence Secretary Donald Rumsfeld again claimed that Iran was developing nuclear weapons.

Iranian officials said they would not accept international inspectors to monitor nuclear facilities unless Tehran was allowed to acquire more modern technology.

Tokyo's *Sankei* newspaper reported that Iranian nuclear scientists had traveled to North Korea three times in 2003, perhaps in an effort to learn techniques to evade international inspectors. Two Iranian scientists visited North Korea in March, an Iranian nuclear official traveled there in April, and two others spent more than a week there in May.

UN nuclear inspectors left Iran after officials refused them access to a nuclear facility.

International Atomic Energy Agency inspectors visited the site in March and again in May, but this time they had intended to collect samples to check for nuclear material.

The IAEA team discussed the proposed visit with Iranian officials but was rebuffed.

A spokesman for Iran's Atomic Energy Organisation denied that the inspectors were stopped from inspecting any site.

An IAEA report, circulated to its board of governors, said Iran had been developing an experimental nuclear fuel programme, processing various forms of uranium and not reporting the activity to the IAEA. Iran also moved nuclear material around the country without notifying the agency, according to the report. Moreover, Iran processed some uranium tetrafluoride into uranium metal, displaying knowledge of skills needed for nuclear weapons production, and produced some uranium dioxide fuel pellets to test chemical production, the IAEA reported. Significantly, however, the report never said that Iran enriched uranium outside of NPT safeguards.

Western officials said that Iran had developed uranium enrichment centrifuges that would not have been possible without conducting tests using uranium, *Nucleonics Week* reported.

Iran said that the uranium movement, and earlier revelations of illicit uranium importing, were not reported to the IAEA because of differences over reporting obligations.

Despite Iran's purported failure to inform the IAEA of its activities, IAEA Director General Mohamed ElBaradei was strongly opposed to citing Iran for the alleged infractions. Instead, he would probably call for additional reports on Iran's nuclear programme in September 2003 and again in March 2004.

Iran restated that it would accept more intrusive monitoring of its nuclear activities only if it received Western nuclear technology in exchange.

Iranian officials claimed that their cooperation with the agency had exceeded their current obligations.

US officials, however, called on the IAEA board to pressure Iran and Washington rejected the prospect of sending advanced nuclear technology to Tehran in exchange for the signing of the Additional Protocol.

IRAQ

It was revealed that US and British claims that Iraq's weapons of mass destruction could be deployed within 45 minutes were based on a single source as scepticism deepened over the coalition's primary reason for going to war.

According to the *Independent*, a defector recruited by the exile group Iraqi National Congress told his story to US intelligence officers, who passed it along to London. British intelligence officers were reportedly unable to corroborate the "45 minutes" claim with any other evidence and considered the source unreliable. The claim was a salient feature of the "intelligence dossier" released in September 2002 and figured prominently in Prime Minister Tony Blair's and US President George W. Bush's public case for going to war.

Iraqi residents of the town of Madaen said their children had fallen ill after wearing clothes washed in barrels used to store processed uranium at the Iraqi Nuclear Energy Agency. US officials said they were buying back the containers from people who purchased them from looters. The looters reportedly dumped the "yellow-cake" uranium at a waste disposal site at the nuclear complex just south of Baghdad.

Few Iraqis showed up at Baghdad police stations to surrender their weapons to coalition troops in a bid to make the city's streets safer on the first day of a two-week weapons amnesty proposed by US-led forces. Under the order, only coalition forces, police officers and others in uniform would be allowed to carry most heavy weaponry. Those who did not turn in their weapons by June 14 could face a year in prison and a $1,000 fine. The reasoning, according to Associated Press, was that getting weapons off the streets would help improve security in Baghdad. Yet Iraqis quoted by the news agency said the security situation was precisely the reason they did not want to be left unarmed. US and British officials backtracked from the original amnesty plan, which banned all weapons, and announced that Iraqis would be allowed to keep AK-47 assault rifles in their homes. The coalition did not give an explanation for the change.

In his final report to the Security Council, chief UN weapons inspector Hans Blix said that his team had found no evidence of Iraq's alleged banned weapons programmes but that it also had not had sufficient time to follow up on leads before evacuating the country two days prior to the US-led invasion on March 20.

British Prime Minister Tony Blair responded to allegations that he had misled the public about Iraq's weapons of mass destruction by saying he stood "absolutely, 100% behind the evidence." US Secretary of State Colin Powell backed up Mr Blair's claims.

Seven inspectors from the International Atomic Energy Agency headed to Iraq, where they planned to inspect the country's main nuclear facility after reports of looting at the site,

The IAEA team would try to determine how much nuclear material was taken by looters from a storage site at al-Tuwaitha Nuclear Research Center following the US-led invasion of Iraq.

The United States had limited the IAEA team's mission to tallying missing containers of radioactive material and resealing any material found in the open. The inspectors would not be allowed to assess possible environmental damage in the area or check into reports of locals suffering radiation sickness.

The United States approved the IAEA visit after many warnings by IAEA Director General Mohamed ElBaradei, who said looters reportedly dumped uranium at the site from containers they later took home, which could create widespread health and environmental problems.

US forces stationed more than 1,500 troops in two central Iraqi cities in an effort to stem recent attacks on US troops in the area. The US troops arrived in Fallujah, 40 miles west of Baghdad, and in Habaniyah, five miles farther west. Both towns had a reputation for Islamic conservatism and sympathy for the ousted regime of former Iraqi President Saddam Hussein. Fallujah had been the scene of several violent confrontations between US soldiers and Iraqis.

A US soldier was killed when a patrol came under fire in northern Baghdad. Another attack occurred in Baghdad's Mansour district, when a man threw a grenade into a US Humvee. No one was seriously injured.

A team of International Atomic Energy Agency experts returned to Iraq for the first time since before the war began in March to determine the extent of looting of radioactive materials from the Tuwaitha complex, the main site in Iraq's former nuclear programme. The team's visit was a one-time event to help enforce the Nuclear Nonproliferation Treaty, Pentagon officials said, adding that the visit should not be seen as a type of weapons inspection. US military commanders said they were not equipped to sufficiently monitor the Tuwaitha complex. Pentagon officials had also said they had found more radioactive material at the Tuwaitha complex than originally expected. US officials had so far recovered more than 100 containers believed to have been taken from the complex, according to the *Washington Times*. None of the people who returned the containers, who were paid $3 per container, had shown elevated levels of radiation, officials said.

UN Security Council members called on the United States to allow experts from the UN Monitoring, Verification and Inspection Commission to return to Iraq to certify whether it possessed biological or chemical weapons. The calls for the return of UN inspectors to Iraq appeared to reflect a growing belief within the Security Council that inspectors should be allowed to test the US and British claims that Iraq possessed weapons of mass destruction prior to the war.

British intelligence officers had said that the MI6 intelligence service inadequately evaluated information on Iraqi weapons efforts that was passed on to the British government. Most of the Iraq-related intelligence given to Prime Minister Tony Blair's office was from "raw" MI6 intelligence, according to senior government sources. Other information came from US Defence Secretary Donald Rumsfeld and Deputy Defence Secretary Paul Wolfowitz, according to security sources. Officers in the British intelligence services said that MI6 wanted to please the prime minister's office regarding Iraq to the point where "short cuts" were taken. For example, MI6 officers were believed to had approached the prime minister's office directly with information, without having first passed it through the Joint Intelligence Committee, the *Independent* reported. While MI6 was allowed to do so, such actions resulted in a lack of filtering of the information, the newspaper reports. A source described by the BBC as being "close to British intelligence" had said the prime minister's office asked intelligence services at least six times to rewrite a dossier released in 2002 on Iraq's weapons efforts, according to the Press Association. Blair was personally involved at one point in the decision to have the dossier rewritten, the source said.

British claims that Iraq attempted to purchase uranium from Niger prior to the war were not based on falsified information. The United States provided the IAEA with documents purporting to illustrate the attempted sale, but those documents were later revealed to have been forgeries. The British government, however, never possessed those documents and did not base its claims about the attempted uranium purchase on them, the *Times* reported.

Pentagon officials had said that ousted Iraqi President Saddam Hussein was probably alive and behind a recent series of attacks on US troops in Iraq, according to ITAR-Tass. The attacks, which had killed nine US soldiers over the past month, might have been coordinated by former senior Iraqi officials, according to intelligence reports.

One US soldier was killed and give others wounded in an ambush in Fallujah, hours after the US Army sent reinforcements to the volatile town. Attacks on US-led forces rose from 30 in April to 85 in May 2003, purportedly initiated by remnants of Saddam's fallen government.

Donald Rumsfeld said that Ali Hassan al-Majid – known as "Chemical Ali" for ordering a 1998 chemical weapons attack on Kurdish rebels in Northern Iraq – might still be alive. US officials had previously believed that he was killed during a US airstrike on the southern Iraqi city of Basra in April.

An International Atomic Energy Agency team began inspecting parts of the Tuwaitha complex, the main site in Iraq's former nuclear programme, to determine the extent of looting of radioactive materials there.

The seven-member team surveyed a three-building storage center at the complex known as Site C, according to Reuters. The IAEA team was accompanied by US troops.

A former senior Iraqi intelligence officer said the Iraqi intelligence services established a network of small laboratories after 1996 with the goal of eventually resuming full biological and chemical weapons production. Each weapons team consisted of up to four scientists who were unknown to UN inspectors, the officer said. The teams worked on computers and conducted experiments in bunkers and safe houses around Baghdad. The small weapons laboratories did not produce any actual weapons, nor did any weapons now exist in Iraq, the officer said. The teams did, however, create plans to quickly begin producing weapons of mass destruction if UN sanctions were lifted, the officer said.

Some US and British intelligence analysts were sceptical of Bush administration claims that two trailers discovered in Iraq were mobile biological facilities. Instead, they said the White House claims were marked by a rush to judgment. The trailers lacked equipment for steam sterilisation, normally required for any type of biological agent production, analysts said. The lack of such a piece of equipment would increase the risk of contamination, thereby producing failed weapons agents, according to the *Times*. The trailers also only had the ability to produce small amounts of biological agents in liquid form, which would then have to be furthered processed at another facility, according to analysts. In addition, the trailers lacked equipment to easily remove germ fluids from the processing tanks onboard. The CIA stood by its assessment that the trailers were most likely for use to produce biological weapons agents.

A number of top Bush administration officials had recently defended the US intelligence on Iraqi weapons of mass destruction prior to the war, according to reports. US national security adviser Condoleezza Rice said the White House had made the best judgment on Iraq's suspected illegal weapons efforts as it could with the information it had, and that previous CIA directors had made the same assessments since 1996. Both Ms Rice and Secretary of State Colin Powell denied that the Bush administration had exaggerated Iraq-related intelligence in order to increase support for war. They both said more time was needed to find evidence of Iraq's weapons programmes.

Defence Secretary Donald Rumsfeld also defended US intelligence on Iraq, saying the current weapons search in Iraq would validate the presentation made by Colin Powell in February to the UN Security Council.

British intelligence officers said they had a "smoking gun" that proved that British Prime Minister Tony Blair's staff pressured them on Iraqi weapons-related intelligence. In addition, British Home Secretary David Blunkett said that a dossier on Iraq's efforts to conceal weapons of mass destruction programmes should not have been published. The dossier, which included information taken from a graduate student's thesis that had been published online, was prepared by Alastair Campbell, Tony Blair's communications director, Mr Blunkett said. Mr Campbell had previously written the chief of the Secret Intelligence Service to apologise for discrediting the service by releasing the dossier, promising that the government would take "far greater care" in using material prepared by them in the future.

An independent investigation by the Associated Press revealed that at least 3,240 civilians died in the recent US-led war in Iraq, 1,900 of them in Baghdad.

The results of the investigation, based on records from 60 out of Iraq's 124 hospitals and spanned the period from March 20, when the war started, to April 20, when fighting had died down. The news agency reported that the count was "still fragmentary" and that a final tally, if ever computed, would likely be "significantly higher." Of the civilian deaths recorded, 1,896 were in Baghdad, 293 were in Najaf, 200 were in Karbala and 145 were in Nasiriya. The tally dides not include figures for Basra, Iraq's second-largest city, where hospitals signed 413 death certificates but did not track whether the casualties were civilian or military.

The 30th soldier to die since US President George W. Bush declared the war in Iraq over on May 1 was killed when unknown assailants fired a rocket-propelled grenade at a weapons collection point in Baghdad. Another was injured in the attack. Both were US soldiers.

A military effort, dubbed Operation Peninsula Strike, to end attacks by Saddam loyalists began as US troops and Iraqi police scoured the Tigris River north of Baghdad in search of paramilitaries blamed for the deaths of 11 US soldiers in the previous two weeks. The effort, with tanks, artillery and aircraft, was reportedly the largest military undertaking since the war ended.

A US missile strike that destroyed a convoy in western Iraq might have targeted Saddam Hussein and other top officials from his ousted government. US military sources said the attack was launched after the United States intercepted a satellite telephone call involving the former president or his sons. Sources expressed what the *Observer* described as cautious optimism that Saddam was killed in the strike, adding that DNA tests were underway to determine whether such officials had been killed.

US and Iraqi officials cited in the *Washington Post* said a loose network bringing together fighters from Saddam's Baath Party and security agencies was partly behind recent attacks on US troops in Iraq. The network was dubbed *Awdah*, or the Return.

Top US Iraq administrator Paul Bremer said that the Iraqi resistance had been bolstered by foreign combatants coming into Iraq.

Mr Bremer's administration was releasing plans for creating a new Iraqi army and for paying back wages to former soldiers under Saddam's government. The US-led administration said that payments to former soldiers would begin July 14 and that "recipients must renounce Baathism and violence."

International Atomic Energy Agency Director General Mohamed ElBaradei told Reuters that IAEA inspectors had found most of the uranium that was missing from a storage facility at al-Tuwaitha, Iraq's major nuclear site, after the site was looted following the US invasion.

UN Secretary General Kofi Annan and his Iraq envoy, Sergio Vieira de Mello, met with Paul Bremer. Mr Annan said the United Nations and the United States were "working very well together" in Iraq, while Mr Bremer said the three had discussed "the many ways in which the United Nations and its specialised agencies can help us with the urgent task of reconstruction in Iraq and the efforts to create a political council which would be representative of the Iraqi people and in the efforts to move forward towards an elected democratic government in Iraq on the basis of a new constitution."

Former British Foreign Secretary Robin Cook, who resigned from his post as leader of the House of Commons because of his opposition to the war in Iraq, called portions of British intelligence dossiers on Iraq's alleged weapons of mass destruction programmes "plainly inaccurate."

Such intelligence was held up repeatedly by the United States and the United Kingdidm as justification for invading Iraq, but US-British teams had come up largely empty-handed in their postwar search for evidence of banned weapons. British Prime Minister Tony Blair's government had generally maintained that the intelligence was solid but had come under fire over two dossiers in particular, one of which the government had acknowledged had inappropriate materials such as part of a graduate student's thesis taken from the Internet.

In particular, Mr Cook cited as erroneous government claims that Saddam Hussein's government had the capability to fire chemical or biological weapons within 45 minutes.

The UN High Commissioner for Refugees asked for another $31 million for its work in 2003 with more than 110,000 mainly Iranian, Palestinian and Turkish refugees in Iraq and with displaced Iraqis who spontaneously returned home.

The chairman of the Security Council group monitoring sanctions against al-Qaeda and the Taliban said that while al-Qaeda was still able to function in many countries, the group had seen no evidence of a link between the terrorist organisation and the former Iraqi government of Saddam Hussein.

The United States had argued in justifying the invasion of Iraq that the Saddam government and al-Qaeda were working together. In particular, Secretary of State Colin Powell, addressing the Council on February 5, 2003 said al-Qaeda was "operating freely in Baghdad."

US forces launched a series of raids dubbed Operation Sidewinder in an effort to root out what the military called "various subversive elements" responsible for attacks on US soldiers in central Iraq, historically a Saddam Hussein stronghold.

In 23 raids conducted primarily in Diyala province north of Baghdad, US troops arrested 61 people and confiscated more than a dozen weapons. Unlike two previous series of raids in the same region, Operation Sidewinder consisted of targeted rather than house-to-house searches, in keeping with the military's sense that recent attacks on US troops had been part of an organised effort.

Operation Desert Scorpion, launched near Baghdad on June 15, continued to net suspected Baath party loyalists,

The remains of two US soldiers were discovered near a quarry about 20 miles northwest of Baghdad. Twelve suspects were being interrogated, and intensified checkpoint searches near the town where the soldiers were last seen backed up traffic for miles.

Another soldier was killed in the capital when attackers threw a grenade into a military vehicle. Assailants also fired a rocket-propelled grenade at a US military checkpoint. No one was injured. A US soldier was also killed in Najaf. Two soldiers were wounded when their convoy was struck by attackers on the road between Baghdad and the airport.

According to the *Washington Post*, 23 US soldiers had been killed since the war ended on May 1.

Syrian Foreign Minister Farouq al-Shara said that Israel was to blame for US failure to return five Syrian border guards captured when US troops pursued an Iraqi convoy near the Syrian-Iraqi border.

KIMBERLEY PROCESS

The UN-backed Kimberley Process, an initiative meant to curb trade in diamonds that fueled armed conflict, was about to certify nearly all the African diamond-producing countries as legitimate producers and exporters and could lose credibility as a result.

Under the initiative, countries that passed implementing legislation on stemming the flow of conflict diamonds could be certified as legitimate producers and exporters. Having passed such legislation, Sierra Leone, the Central African Republic and the Democratic Republic of the Congo were to be cleared July 31, and Angola would receive the same endorsement from the initiative if it approved legislation by then. Liberia was reportedly likely to be the only African country that did not receive the approval.

Experts and nongovernmental organisations had criticised the process, saying the passage of legislation did not ensure that diamonds would be clean.

According to some NGOs, the initiative's biggest problem was excessive respect for state sovereignty. Some activists had called for an independent monitoring group to be set in each country.

The industry estimated that diamonds produced in conflict areas accounted for four percent, or $300 million, of the world's total production and trade.

KOREA see also NORTH KOREA

US troops would pull back from the demilitarised zone separating North and South Korea, US and South Korean officials said, ending the permanent presence of US forces who had been in the zone since the Korean War ended in 1953. A joint statement by US and South Korean officials said US troops would withdraw at least 75 miles from the demilitarised zone, or DMZ, and vacate a large US military base in Seoul. The redeployment would affect about 18,000 of the 37,000 US troops in South Korea. The statement offered no specific timetable for the redeployment, but

US officials had said they might begin shifting forces in 2003. South Korea hoped to delay the redeployment until current tensions on the peninsula ease.

The prospect of US forces leaving the zone had raised concerns among some in South Korea who feared renewed clashes on the peninsula stemming from increasing tensions between the United States and North Korea.

LIBERIA *see also* KIMBERLEY PROCESS, SIERRA LEONE
The day after being indicted by the Special Court for Sierra Leone for war crimes during that country's 10-year civil war, Liberian President Charles Taylor said in an address to his nation that an attempt to oust him by coup d'etat had failed and that a foreign ambassador in the capital, Monrovia, had rallied government officials to attempt the coup. He did not mention the name or nationality of the diplomat he accused.

Mr Taylor said he had accepted the resignation of Vice President Moses Blah and that he would explain his action to the Liberian people in the next few days. Agence France-Presse reported that Mr Blah was involved in the alleged coup attempt.

President Taylor also said he would dissolve his government to allow for a transitional government that may be formed in Akosombo, a town near Ghana where working sessions of peace talks he began with rebels were to begin.

Ghanaian officials apparently made no attempt to arrest Taylor while he was in Ghana. Ghana's attorney general, Papa Owusu Ankohah, said authorities had not received the indictment and when they did, would need time to review it. The Special Court, however, said that Ghanaian authorities received an international arrest warrant for Mr Taylor before he left the country and returned home. Court spokesman Robin White said that Taylor's indictment was "electronically sent to the Ghanaian Foreign Ministry in Accra" and that a senior official at the ministry confirmed they had been received. Ghana's minister of foreign affairs said that as far as Ghana was concerned, there was no formal request from any authority to arrest Mr Taylor.

Rebels seeking to overthrow Liberian President Charles Taylor were engaged in fighting on the outskirts of Monrovia, prompting foreigners to evacuate and forcing resident to flee. Helicopters ferried Westerners from embassy compounds in the city to a ship waiting in the Atlantic.

Nearly 10,000 Monrovia residents took shelter in the city's stadium, filling concrete bunkers under the stands.

The main rebel group making gains against Taylor, the Liberians United for Reconciliation and Democracy, ordered Taylor to step down within 72 hours.

A cease-fire announced between representatives of the rebels and the government at talks in Ghana did not stop the fighting. President Taylor appealed for calm in the city during a radio address that day and warned his ranks against looting.

The peace talks in Ghana had expanded to include a secondary rebel group, the Movement for Democracy in Liberia, which had previously refused to join the negotiations, bringing the talks to a halt.

In addition to the fighting, Liberia was experiencing torrential rains, complicating the work of UN agencies trying to help civilians.

The UN High Commissioner for Refugees said fighting in Liberia had over the past two weeks displaced tens of thousands of Liberians near Monrovia and sent 23,000 into Ivory Coast seeking refuge.

The World Food Programme said the conflict had stopped it from delivering food to the 115,000 displaced persons around Monrovia, adding that security was deteriorating daily and that without an end to hostilities Liberians would continue moving within the country and outside of it in search of refuge. An estimated 70% of Liberia was now reportedly inaccessible to humanitarian groups.

After French helicopters evacuated more than 500 foreigners from the strife-ridden Liberian capital of Monrovia, US and UN officials called on rebels and the government to give peace talks in Ghana a chance to work.

As the evacuations began, artillery exploded on the city's western edge, where rebel forces battled President Taylor's troops.

The fighting had reportedly left the city's centre without water or electricity and threatens food and fuel shortages. According to Integrated Regional Information Networks, the price of rice had doubled, as had gasoline.

President Taylor and rebels attacking Monrovia had agreed in principle to a cease-fire accord, according to Ghana's foreign minister.

The UN High Commissioner for Refugees, which had pulled its last three international staff members from Monrovia, expressed concern for the agency's remaining national staff, their families and the 15,000 Sierra Leonean refugees in the area. Another 5,000 internally displaced persons had taken refuge in the national stadium, according to the UN Office for the Coordination of Humanitarian Affairs. The World Food Programme had been forced to abandon food deliveries to as many as 115,000 displaced persons in camps around Monrovia. The International Committee for the Red Cross and Medecins Sans Frontieres were the only aid organisations still working in Monrovia. The Red Cross had appealed for $1.7 million in emergency funds for humanitarian efforts in the eastern part of Liberia.

UN Secretary General Kofi Annan appointed an expert panel to assess Liberia's compliance with international sanctions and investigate any socio-economic impact the sanctions had caused.

President Taylor appeared to cast doubt on his willingness to honour a cease-fire deal calling for him to step down as reports of clashes in the east of the country raised fears of renewed fighting. He had backed away from an apparent offer to leave office in the interest a peace deal to end the country's civil war, which had pitted him against two rebel groups now controlling huge swaths of the country.

His apparent reconsideration of such a move came as troops fighting for his government reportedly attacked rebel positions in the east of the country, despite a cease-fire that was supposed to halt the fighting for talks among government, rebel factions and various political parties gathered for negotiations in Ghana.

Mediators at the peace talks had questioned Mr Taylor's intention to leave power and were said to remain concerned that any effort he made to stay in office could undercut the peace process. The plan called for a 30-day deadline for establishing a transitional government without Mr Taylor.

Liberian government officials said rebel forces broke a cease-fire by attacking troops loyal to President Charles Taylor.

In Monrovia, the Liberian capital, a Taylor spokesman said government troops took fire from the main rebel group, the Liberians United for Reconciliation and Democracy, in Klay, some 22 miles north of Monrovia. Also, Taylor's government said, a secondary rebel group, the Movement for Democracy in Liberia, fired on government troops in the southeast.

Following a call by US President George W. Bush for the resignation of embattled President Taylor, rebels attacked anew in the capital, Monrovia.

Reuters reported that the rebels had fought their way back into Monrovia after being pushed out by government troops earlier. Integrated Regional Information Networks reported that rebels had moved into the capital's eastern suburbs, where President Taylor and other top government officials lived, and appeared to want to open a second front in order to isolate government troops in Monrovia from the interior of the country.

The BBC reported that as many as 300 people had been killed in fighting over three days and up to 250,000 had fled their homes.

Aid workers in Monrovia said President Taylor's troops were looting in parts of the city after fighting off a rebel thrust, adding that government soldiers broke into a World Food Programme warehouse and stole trucks along with an unknown amount of food stocks.

In an apparent response to such reports, Mr Taylor ordered a special force to patrol Monrovia and warned government militia soldiers against breaking the peace.

The UN Security Council met to discuss the possibility of deploying an international force to Liberia, which UN Secretary General Kofi Annan said was heading toward "total disintegration."

African and other countries were pressing the United States to head up a peacekeeping force to Liberia. West African leaders were asking for 2,000 US troops. US Secretary of Defence Donald Rumsfeld suggested that African nations could handle the peacekeeping operations in Liberia, pointing to training US forces gave to Nigerian and other African troops.

A US official reportedly told the Security Council that the United States had three conditions for considering a peacekeeping force:

1. Liberian President Charles Taylor stepping down,
2. a political agreement among the warring factions and
3. international support for a peace process.

The UN High Commissioner for Refugees moved to evacuate Sierra Leonean and other refugees trapped in the Liberian capital, Monrovia, as a cease-fire held in the city for a fourth day. The agency had plans to send a ship from the Sierra Leonean capital, Freetown, to Monrovia to pick up refugees. More than 1,000 Sierra Leonean refugees and displaced Liberians had taken shelter in UN and embassy compounds in Monrovia. The refugees were among some 15,000 Sierra Leoneans previously cared for in UN-run camps around Monrovia.

The chairman of the Economic Community of West African States called on the UN-backed war crimes court for Sierra Leone to consider dropping an indictment against Taylor in a bid to facilitate peace talks in Liberia.

MAURITANIA

Mauritanian President Maaouya Ould Taya said his forces quashed a coup. Mr Taya said his troops fought off coup plotters who moved to take the capital, Nouakchott, shelling the rebel fighters and destroying "tank after tank."

The insurgents, reportedly led by a former army officer opposed to Mr Taya's ties to Israel, stormed the presidential palace in the most serious bid against Mr Taya since he came to power in his own coup in 1984. He won elections in 1992 and 1997, and had been expected to run again in 2003.

MIDDLE EAST

Arab leaders of Bahrain, Jordan, Saudi Arabia, Egypt and the Palestinian Authority meeting with US President George W. Bush backed the basic concept of an internationally approved "road map" to Palestinian statehood and pledged to fight terrorism.

A key provision of the peace plan, drawn up by the United Nations, the United States, the European Union and Russia, was the disarmament of Palestinian militias. Allegations that Israel's Arab neighbours had funded attacks on Israelis had focused attention on their role in the peace process.

The first concrete result of a meeting between Messrs Abbas and Sharon came when the Israeli military lifted a two-week travel ban on Palestinian workers imposed after a spate of suicide bombings. The army said it would allow 10,000 workers to enter Israel. Palestinian officials said about 3,500 Palestinians with work permits crossed through the Erez point in Gaza. However, those trying to cross a checkpoint in the West Bank towns of Ramallah and Bir Zeit had to leave their cars behind and walk four miles.

Israeli Prime Minister Ariel Sharon promised to dissolve illegal settlements and Palestinian Prime Minister Mahmoud Abbas vowed to end violent attacks on Israelis at a long-awaited summit on the internationally approved "road map" to Palestinian statehood.

The leaders' statements constituted crucial concessions necessary to fulfilling the steps outlined in the peace plan, which was drafted by a so-called "Quartet" of parties involved in the Middle East peace process, the United Nations, the United States the European Union and Russia. Bush praised the two leaders and pledged training and support for the Palestinian security service. He also said he would enlist US diplomat John Wolf to monitor the progress of the peace plan.

In a goodwill gesture leading up to the summit, Israel released about 100 Palestinian prisoners. Most of them had been held without charges for weeks or months.

The militant Palestinian group Hamas broke off cooperation with Palestinian Prime Minister Mahmoud Abbas on ending attacks against Israelis, saying Mr Abbas made unacceptable compromises at the summit with Israel and the United States where he had called for an end to the Palestinian armed struggle for statehood.

Hamas warned it would continue violent opposition against Israel, sentiments which were echoed by leaders of the Islamic Jihad and other militant groups.

Palestinian leader Yasser Arafat, who was excluded from the summit, criticised decisions reached there, accusing Israeli Prime Minister Ariel Sharon of offering the Palestinians nothing "on the ground." He dismissed the Israeli pledge to uproot some Jewish settlements on the West Bank. An anonymous Palestinian official told AP that Mr Arafat was also upset by Mr Abbas taking centre stage at the summit, and by his failure to mention the Israeli siege of Arafat's Ramallah headquarters. Other Palestinian officials said that Mr Arafat, who had been restricted to the West Bank for more than a year, played a large behind-the-scenes role in directing Mr Abbas at the summit. Mr Arafat was in constant phone contact with the Palestinian delegation, and he made adjustments to Mr Abbas' final speech.

Two Hamas members were shot by Israeli troops while preparing a suicide attack in the West Bank. Israeli police reported discovering the bodies of an Israeli man and a teenage girl whom they suspect were killed by Palestinian militants west of Jerusalem. The new outbreaks of violence demonstrated the obstacles in implementing the "road map" for peace in the region and Palestinian statehood.

The US administration said it would consider easing restrictions on US aid to the Palestinian Authority, which could not receive direct US aid as part of long-standing policy. The decision could help improve confidence and funding for the new Palestinian government, but a senior Bush administration official warned that it was "not something that had to be done tomorrow."

The Palestinian Ministry of Interior would be receiving European and US police equipment in an effort to rebuild the Palestinian security apparatus for implementation of the road map.

Israeli troops began dismantling an uninhabited settlement in the West Bank, marking Israel's first step in implementing the road map peace plan.

Settlers had been defiant about the Israeli policy, however, posing a challenge for an Israeli government that had agreed to the road map but was facing increasing opposition at home. After army commanders met with settler leaders and gave them a list of 14 mostly uninhabited settlements to be razed, the settlers said they would not cooperate.

Although many observers considered all 160 settlements in the West Bank and Gaza Strip illegal, Israeli Prime Minister Ariel Sharon announced that only a handful were "unauthorized." Approximately 225,000 out of about 5 million Israeli Jews were living in settlements.

Palestinian gunmen killed five Israeli soldiers in three separate attacks. The first occurred in a military post in the Gaza Strip, where four Israeli soldiers were killed and four more wounded by three Palestinian terrorists. Two other attacks took place later, killing another Israeli. Hamas, Jihad and the al-Aqsa Martyrs Brigade were responsible for the attack, clearly showing their discontent over the result of peace talks between Ariel Sharon and Palestinian Prime Minister Mahmoud Abbas.

Mr Sharon repeated his warning to Mr Abbas that he needed to take measures against hard-line militants, saying that Palestinians would not regain their rights if the violence continued. Mr Abbas defended himself, saying he would keep trying to engage the militants in dialogue and that he would not use force against the groups.

The groups, especially Hamas, said that Mr Abbas failed during the summit to claim Jerusalem as the capital of a future Palestinian state and to demand that Palestinian refugees be allowed to return to their homes in what was now Israel.

Palestinian leader Yasser Arafat appointed a new West Bank chief for preventive security services, responsible for supporting Palestinian authorities in regaining control over the situation in the territories.

Hamas leader Abdel Aziz Rantisi was wounded when Israeli helicopters fired missiles at his car in Gaza City, killing two bystanders and injuring 26 others and casting uncertainty over the recently renewed peace process. The attack happened as Hamas leaders, including Mr Rantisi, were saying they would consider talks with Palestinian Prime Minister Mahmoud Abbas about the road map peace plan, although a cease-fire against Israel, according to Mr Rantisi, was out of the question. Hamas' willingness to talk with Mr Abbas was a reversal of the group's decision to boycott the prime minister after he denounced violence at a peace summit. Palestinian authorities called the attack on the Hamas leader an action designed to destroy the peace process. Israeli officials did not comment on the accusations, AP reports.

According to AP, Israel was sending mixed messages, since the missile attack came after Israeli troops finished dismantling several small and uninhabited settlements, showing their commitment to fulfill the first road map requirement. AP reported that 10 were dismantled. Agence France-Presse reported that nine settlements were destroyed, out of 15 that were scheduled to be dismantled.

A suicide bomber on a bus in Jerusalem killed himself and 15 others and injured 70. Israel retaliated an hour later, killing two Hamas officials and at least five other people in a helicopter strike on Gaza City.

Three Palestinians were killed and 17 others were wounded after two Israeli helicopters fired missiles near Jabalya, in the northern Gaza Strip, hours after another attack that injured Hamas leader Abdel Aziz Rantisi.

Hamas responded to the attack on Mr Rantisi by firing rockets into a nearby town in Israel, which prompted the second Israeli helicopter attack.

The second Israeli attack was launched after US officials called Israeli leaders to complain about the first attack, an obvious sign that Israel did not listen to the US authorities.

Israeli settlers said they want the dismantling of outposts in the West Bank to stop. Rabbis from the settlements said in a statement to Israeli Prime Minister Ariel Sharon that the decision to remove some settlements was "a crime from a Jewish, national and moral point of view."

The scope of the settlement dismantlement also failed to satisfy Palestinians. Palestinian Cabinet Minister Yasser Abed Rabbo said that the dismantling was "a game of deception through the evacuation of some of the empty trailers in order to give legitimacy" to the settlements established during Mr Sharon's term of office. Mr Abbas had said that all settlements were illegal, not only the small ones that were being dismantled.

The UN Relief and Works Agency for Palestine Refugees handed over 19 new shelters to 20 refugee families which included 129 persons in the Gaza Strip. The project, funded by the Arab Popular Committee in Syria and other UNRWA donors, cost $455,000. According to UNRWA, 1,134 shelters had been destroyed by Israeli military forces since the beginning of the current intifada in September 2000, leaving more than 10,049 Palestinians without homes.

A seven-year-old Israeli girl was killed and a five-year-old girl was seriously wounded in a highway shooting just after a meeting between Palestinian Prime Minister Mahmoud Abbas and militant groups failed to produce a cease-fire accord. Israeli Army Radio said the gunfire came from the West Bank. Meanwhile, Israel agreed to limit strikes on militants to those who pose an immediate threat.

During a three-hour meeting with militant leaders, Mr Abbas suggested a Palestinian leadership that included Hamas and other armed groups, according to Ismail Abu Shanab of Hamas. As the parties agreed to continue talks, Hamas leader Abdel Aziz Rantisi said his group was considering halting attacks on Israeli citizens inside Israel but would still carry out strikes on troops and settlers in the Palestinian territories.

Israel had reportedly said it would accept a cease-fire of three to six weeks. According to a security source cited by Reuters, Israeli authorities would limit "track-and-kill" strikes to 'terrorists who were definitely 'ticking bombs,'" leaving political leaders alone. "When it comes to more borderline cases such as Rantisi, who was in a command position, we would hold fire as much as possible," said the source.

A suicide bomber blew himself up in a grocery in the Israeli village of Sde Trumot, near the West Bank, killing the storeowner and casting a shadow over continued negotiations for a Palestinian cease-fire.

The attack came only hours after Palestinian Prime Minister Mahmoud Abbas wrapped up meetings with leaders of militant groups in a bid to end violence against Israelis, a chief condition of the peace plan. Hamas said it was still considering halting attacks on civilians inside Israel's border, but would maintain its right to target Israeli troops and settlers inside the West Bank. In a separate meeting with Mr Abbas, Islamic Jihad leaders said they would continue targeting Israelis in the West Bank and the Gaza Strip.

Later, settlers overran roadblocks and burned fields in clashes with Israeli soldiers attempting to dismantle the first inhabited outpost since Israel started targeting settlements in compliance with the road map peace plan. Settlers from the targeted West Bank Mitzpeh Yitzhar outpost were joined by other settlers until, hundreds strong, they were able to turn back soldiers and elite police forces trying to take down the main tent. The troops were armed only with knives for removing community and family tents.

Settlers set ablaze Palestinian-owned wheat fields and olive groves and succeeded in disrupting the dismantlement for several hours.

Unlike the 10 illegal outposts Israel removed earlier, Mitzpeh Yitzahr was inhabited. Settlers had sued without success to prevent the dismantlement of inhabited outposts.

Israeli police said they arrested two Palestinians thought to be en route to stage a major attack in central Israel. Police also said they found a bag with a large amount of explosives in it. Israeli authorities destroyed the bag in a controlled explosion that blew out nearby windows and echoed for miles.

Military and police went on high alert after receiving intelligence warnings that an alleged suicide bomber and an accomplice entered Israel and were planning an attack.

The arrest of the alleged would-be bombers came as Palestinian officials waited to hear from militant groups about a plan to halt attacks on Israelis in a bid to revitalize foundering peace talks.

Israeli troops killed two Hamas militants during a gun battle in the Gaza Strip as US envoy John Wolf held talks with the Palestinian Prime Minister Mahmoud Abbas.

The new fighting opened questions about whether Hamas, the main group behind a campaign of suicide bombings against Israelis, would call off attacks in line with peace talks.

Hamas and other Islamic militant groups were expected to announce a truce following a statement from a top Hamas official appeared to show a new willingness by the group to accept Israel as a state alongside a Palestinian state, a view that represented a break from the group's long-held vow to destroy Israel.

Israeli and Palestinian security officials were expected to resume meetings to discuss details of a partial withdrawal by Israeli forces in northern Gaza Strip and the West Bank city of Bethlehem, places where Israelis planned to hand over policing duties to Palestinians. Israeli authorities planned to grant the areas a so-called grace period of no military action lasting up to four weeks but would continue to target suspected terrorists thought to be on their way to carry out attacks against Israelis.

An Israeli Air Force commander said Israel's practice of airstrikes against Palestinian militants harmed innocent civilians up to 35% of the time, despite efforts to prevent civilian casualties. Major General Dan Halutz said that up to 85% of such attacks, mainly using rockets fired from helicopter gunships, were successful.

Shortly after Palestinian militant groups agreed to stop all attacks on Israelis for three months, Israeli helicopters fired rockets on two cars in the Gaza Strip, injuring a Hamas leader and killing two people in a taxi. Associated Press reported that 17 were injured in the attack.

Israel's action could jeopardise the truce, said Palestinian Fatah party official Kadidura Fades, as the cease-fire document called for an end to assassinations of resistance leaders, incursions into Palestinian towns and release of Palestinian prisoners.

The Israeli military said it had fired on a group of militants planning to strike an Israeli target in the Gaza Strip.

There was confusion about whether the cease-fire had indeed been signed. According to the *Independent*, Mr Fades said Hamas leader Khaled Mashal and Islamic Jihad leader Ramadan Shalah, both of Syria, had signed, as had Gaza Strip-based Islamic Jihad leader Mohammed al-Hindi and imprisoned Fatah leader Marwan Barghouti. However, Hamas leader Abdul Aziz Rantisi said the deal was not final and that "Israeli terrorist actions would be taken into account when we decide" on the final version, an apparent reference to the helicopter strike.

Israel had not agreed to abide by the terms of the cease-fire agreement, which was forged by the Palestinian Authority in concert with the militant groups. Some Israeli officials had dismissed the truce as a delay tactic to allow militants to regroup.

Israeli Deputy Prime Minister Ehud Olmert said Israel would not take any chances on security.

US President George W. Bush dismissed the truce altogether.

Israeli-Palestinian talks on a potential Israeli pullback from the Gaza Strip and the West Bank town of Bethlehem made "real progress," according to a Palestinian official cited by Associated Press. The source said the sides resolved a dispute over the main north-south road in the Gaza Strip.

Agence France-Presse reported that a senior Palestinian security source said the Palestinian and Israeli negotiators at the talks, which were also attended by US representatives, agreed on an "immediate army withdrawal" from the northern Gaza Strip and Bethlehem, and that the Palestinian Authority would take over security in the areas in question. The source also cited agreement on other matters, including the controversial road, Israeli house demolitions and border crossings.

An Israeli Defence Ministry spokesman, however, said that "there was no agreement on a withdrawal," although Israeli Foreign Minister Silvan Shalom said the sides could be "very close to an agreement."

A cease-fire deal with the Palestinian armed group Hamas and other such groups, appeared to be making progress as well. A senior official from a Palestinian armed group confirmed that the groups had accepted a three-month cease-fire in talks with Palestinian Authority officials.

Amid the reports of progress on a cease-fire by militias, Israel undertook a military operation that was aimed at top Hamas bomb maker Adnan al-Ghoul. Al-Ghoul was not present, but three Palestinian gunmen and a bystander were killed. Hamas leaders had said such strikes by Israel could jeopardise the cease-fire talks, but Israeli officials had said the operations, which they view as necessary to Israeli security, would continue until a cease-fire was reached and possibly longer.

The UN Security Council renewed the mandate of the UN Disengagement Observer Force, which monitors Israeli-Syrian disengagement, for six months.

Following the announcement by the Palestinian militia groups Hamas and Islamic Jihad of a three-month moratorium on attacks against Israelis, Israeli troops began pulling back from some Palestinian areas. Two smaller groups, the Popular Front for the Liberation of Palestine and the al-Aqsa Martyrs Brigades, refused to sign on to the cease-fire. The latter group was affiliated with Palestinian Authority President Yasser Arafat's Fatah movement.

Israel had said it would continue to assassinate those who plan attacks on Israelis, and there was no plan to release prisoners. Israeli Education Minister Limor Livnat called the condition-bound truce a "trick," and Israeli Foreign Minister Silvan Shalom also criticised it.

Israeli Prime Minister Ariel Sharon, however, had ordered the Shin Bet security service to undertake a comprehensive review of the cases of all Palestinians now imprisoned by Israel in order to see which could be freed.

Israeli troops had pulled back from the Gaza Strip town Beit Hanoun after six weeks there, and their positions had been taken up by Palestinian police. AP reports that traffic was flowing freely on the main road in Gaza after Israel dismantled roadblocks.

Israeli troops were to withdraw from the West Bank town of Bethlehem according to a plan worked out by Palestinian and Israeli officials. Palestinian Authority security chief Mohammed Dahlan said the two sides agreed on the pullout, but a senior Israeli security source told Reuters the deal was "not final."

NATO

As NATO foreign ministers launched a two-day meeting in Madrid, one of the items on the agenda would be the role of the alliance in postwar Iraq. The alliance had asked military planners to help draft a plan for NATO to help Poland manage a stabilisation force in its assigned sector of Iraq.

AFP reported that NATO's transformation from a Cold War bloc to a global security force in the wake of the September 11, 2001 terrorist attacks on the United States would be the conceptual backdrop to the meeting. In August 2003, the 19-member alliance was to assume command of the International Security Assistance Force in Afghanistan, its first major military assignment outside Europe.

NORTH KOREA *see also* KOREA

The Group of Eight industrialised countries called on North Korea to address growing concerns surrounding its nuclear efforts and released an action plan on combating terrorism that included assistance to countries to help develop their capabilities to prevent international terrorism.

The G-8 – Canada, France, Germany, Italy, Japan, Russia, the United Kingdom and the United States – harshly criticised North Korea's uranium enrichment and plutonium production programmes, as well as Pyongyang's failure to abide by its International Atomic Energy Agency safeguards agreement. Such actions "undermine the nonproliferation regime and were a clear breach of North Korea's international obligations," the G-8 said.

The G-8 called on Pyongyang to "visibly, verifiably and irreversibly" end its nuclear weapons efforts as a first step to finding a peaceful solution to the crisis surrounding North Korea's re-launched nuclear programme.

UNICEF appealed for more humanitarian aid to North Korea, saying 70,000 children were suffering serious malnourishment. UNICEF offifficials said they had so far gathered only 27% of the $12 million in aid the agency hoped to raise for North Korean children in 2003.

SIERRA LEONE *see also* KIMBERLEY PROCESS

The UN Security Council announced it would not renew sanctions on "blood diamonds" from Sierra Leone when they expired. Council members believed Sierra Leone now had a system to certify the gems that could work with international support, and that the situation no longer posed a threat to international peace and security.

The Council's Liberian diamond ban would remain in place.

The UN Security Council subsequently did drop its ban on diamonds from Sierra Leone, which was imposed three years previously to try to prevent illegal trade of the precious stones, which were believed to finance armed conflicts.

According the Security Council president, Sierra Leone's efforts to control the diamond mining areas and the country's commitment to the Kimberley Process, which had established international standards for the trade of diamonds, prompted the Council to decide not to renew the embargo.

SRI LANKA

New fears emerged about the state of the peace process in Sri Lanka between rebels and government forces following the sinking by the country's navy of a Tamil rebel merchant ship carrying 12 people. The rebels and the government entered into a Norwegian-brokered truce on February 23, 2002, but the agreement did not extend fully to activities at sea.

Since the truce, the rebels had been accused of carrying out attacks against military informants and rival political activists. The LTTE had been blamed for at least 30 killings since February 2002, including the shooting of a top leader of a rival Tamil group, who became the most senior politician to have been killed during the truce.

Donors had pledged $4.5 billion to rebuild war-torn northern and eastern regions of the country, and the LTTE was to have a say in how $1 billion earmarked for the northeast would be spent. The LTTE said, though, that it would not enter into talks unless the government granted it an interim administrative council with extensive political power, rather than just the financial authority that the government had offered.

UNMOVIC

UN Secretary General Kofi Annan appointed UNMOVIC Deputy Executive Chairman Demetrius Perricos to take over as acting head of the commission on July 1, when Dr Hans Blix retired. Mr Perricos was the commission's director of planning and operations for three years prior to his appointment in January 2003 to the body's number two post.

UNITED NATIONS PEACEKEEPING: THE COSTS

The UN General Assembly's Fifth Committee, which handles budgetary and administrative matters, approved $2.17 billion to finance 11 active peacekeeping missions for the financial year beginning July 1, 2003 and ending June 30, 2004.

The amount, $430 million less than the previous year, would cover peacekeeping missions in Georgia, Kosovo, Cyprus, Syria, Lebanon, East Timor, Western Sahara, Sierra Leone, the Democratic Republic of the Congo, Ethiopia-Eritrea and Kuwait.

The UN Mission in the Democratic Republic of the Congo would receive the most funding, $608.23 million, followed by the mission in Sierra Leone with $543.49 million and Kosovo with $329.74 million. The UN Observer Mission in Georgia would receive the least amount of money at $32.1 million.

According to the assembly, the overall reduction in the budget was due to the closing of the mission in Bosnia and Herzegovina and the downsizing of operations in Kosovo, East Timor, Sierra Leone and Lebanon.

Out of the $2.17 billion, $70.29 million would be used to maintain the peace-keeping support account, which would allow the organisation to deploy peace-keeping operations more rapidly. An additional $33.25 million in excess of the Peacekeeping Reserve Fund's limit of $150 million would also be applied in the support account. Around $21.51 million would go to the UN Logistics Base in Brindisi, Italy, and up to $12 million would also be available to the UN Iraq-Kuwait Observation Mission through the end of October.

The committee also made suggestions on the disposal of assets from closed missions in Angola, Tajikistan, Liberia, Rwanda and the Central African Republic.

ZIMBABWE
Clashes between police and protesters entered their second day in Zimbabwe, during a week of national protest called by the opposition party Movement for Democratic Change against the government of President Robert Mugabe.

Police stationed throughout the capital city of Harare used tear gas to contain the crowds. One demonstrator was shot in the leg and others were beaten with rubber batons.

According to the opposition party, Mr Mugabe's government, in power for 23 years, was responsible for the country's political and economic crisis, the worst since independence in 1980. Although international food aid had alleviated starvation, the country faced 269% inflation p.a. and serious shortages of currency, gasoline and medicine. Human rights abuses by the state, a decrease in foreign aid and investments and the government's seizure of thousands of farms previously owned by white farmers had also contributed to the crisis.